World Economic and Financial Surveys

WORLD ECONOMIC OUTLOOK
May 2000

Asset Prices and the Business Cycle

International Monetary Fund

Production: IMF Graphics Section
Cover and Design: Luisa Menjivar-Macdonald
Figures: Theodore F. Peters, Jr.
Typesetting: Choon Lee and Joseph A. Kumar

World economic outlook (International Monetary Fund)
World economic outlook: a survey by the staff of the International
Monetary Fund.—1980– —Washington, D.C.: The Fund, 1980–

    v.; 28 cm.—(1981–84: Occasional paper/International Monetary Fund
ISSN 0251-6365)
    Annual.
    Has occasional updates, 1984–
    ISSN 0258-7440 = World economic and financial surveys
    ISSN 0256-6877 = World economic outlook (Washington)
    1. Economic history—1971– —Periodicals. I. International
Monetary Fund. II. Series: Occasional paper (International Monetary
Fund)

HC10.W7979   84-640155
                  338.5'443'09048--dc19
                        AACR 2 MARC-S

Library of Congress   8507

    Published biannually.
ISBN 1-55775-936-7

Price: US$42.00
(US$35.00 to full-time faculty members and
students at universities and colleges)

Please send orders to:
International Monetary Fund, Publication Services
700 19th Street, N.W., Washington, D.C. 20431, U.S.A.
Tel.: (202) 623-7430   Telefax: (202) 623-7201
E-mail: publications@imf.org
Internet: http://www.imf.org

recycled paper

CONTENTS

Figures

ASSUMPTIONS AND CONVENTIONS

A number of assumptions have been adopted for the projections presented in the *World Economic Outlook*. It has been assumed that real effective exchange rates will remain constant at their average levels during January 25–February 22, 2000 except for the currencies participating in the European exchange rate mechanism II (ERM II), which are assumed to remain constant in nominal terms relative to the euro; that established policies of national authorities will be maintained (for specific assumptions about fiscal and monetary polices in industrial countries, see Box 1.3); that the average price of oil will be $24.50 a barrel in 2000 and $19.80 a barrel in 2001, and remain unchanged in real terms over the medium term; and that the six-month London interbank offered rate (LIBOR) on U.S. dollar deposits will average 6.8 percent in 2000 and 7.1 percent in 2001. These are, of course, working hypotheses rather than forecasts, and the uncertainties surrounding them add to the margin of error that would in any event be involved in the projections. The estimates and projections are based on statistical information available in mid-March 2000.

The following conventions have been used throughout the *World Economic Outlook*:

. . .   to indicate that data are not available or not applicable;

—   to indicate that the figure is zero or negligible;

–   between years or months (for example, 1997–98 or January–June) to indicate the years or months covered, including the beginning and ending years or months;

/   between years or months (for example, 1997/98) to indicate a fiscal or financial year.

"Billion" means a thousand million; "trillion" means a thousand billion.

"Basis points" refer to hundredths of 1 percentage point (for example, 25 basis points are equivalent to ¼ of 1 percentage point).

In the main text, shaded areas of figures and tables indicate IMF staff projections. In the Statistical Appendix, projections are shown in white.

Minor discrepancies between sums of constituent figures and totals shown are due to rounding.

As used in this report, the term "country" does not in all cases refer to a territorial entity that is a state as understood by international law and practice. As used here, the term also covers some territorial entities that are not states but for which statistical data are maintained on a separate and independent basis.

FURTHER INFORMATION AND DATA

This report on the *World Economic Outlook* is available in full on the IMF's Internet site, *www.imf.org*. Accompanying it on the website is a larger compilation of data from the WEO database than in the report itself, consisting of files containing the series most frequently requested by readers. These files may be downloaded for use in a variety of software packages.

Inquiries about the content of the *World Economic Outlook* and the WEO database should be sent by mail, electronic mail, or telefax (telephone inquiries cannot be accepted) to:

World Economic Studies Division
Research Department
International Monetary Fund
700 19th Street, N.W.
Washington, D.C. 20431, U.S.A.
E-mail: weo@imf.org   Telefax: (202) 623–6343

PREFACE

The projections and analysis contained in the *World Economic Outlook* are an integral element of the IMF's ongoing surveillance of economic developments and policies in its member countries and of the global economic system. The IMF has published the *World Economic Outlook* annually from 1980 through 1983 and biannually since 1984.

The survey of prospects and policies is the product of a comprehensive interdepartmental review of world economic developments, which draws primarily on information the IMF staff gathers through its consultations with member countries. These consultations are carried out in particular by the IMF's area departments together with the Policy Development and Review Department and the Fiscal Affairs Department.

The country projections are prepared by the IMF's area departments on the basis of internationally consistent assumptions about world activity, exchange rates, and conditions in international financial and commodity markets. For approximately 50 of the largest economies—accounting for 90 percent of world output—the projections are updated for each *World Economic Outlook* exercise. For smaller countries, the projections are based on those prepared at the time of the IMF's regular Article IV consultations with those countries or in connection with the use of IMF resources.

The analysis in the *World Economic Outlook* draws extensively on the ongoing work of the IMF's area and specialized departments, and is coordinated in the Research Department under the general direction of Michael Mussa, Economic Counsellor and Director of Research. The *World Economic Outlook* project is directed by Flemming Larsen, Deputy Director of the Research Department, together with Tamim Bayoumi, Chief of the World Economic Studies Division.

Primary contributors to the current issue include Luis Catão, Mark De Broeck, John H. Green, Maitland MacFarlan, Peter Sturm, Cathy Wright, Francesco Caramazza, Barry Eichengreen, Luca Ricci, Ranil Salgado, and Torsten Sløk. Other contributors include Eduardo Borensztein, Paul Cashin, Martin Cerisola, Juan Pablo Cordoba, Paula De Masi, Luiz de Mello, Sanjeev Gupta, Benjamin Hunt, Charles Kramer, Douglas Laxton, Carles Pinerua, and Patricia Reynolds. The Fiscal Analysis Division of the Fiscal Affairs Department computed the structural budget and fiscal impulse measures. Mandy Hemmati, Bennett Sutton, Siddique Hossain, Toh Kuan, and Yutong Li provided research assistance. Gretchen Byrne, Nicholas Dopuch, Staffan Gorne, Olga Plagie, Di Rao, and Anthony G. Turner processed the data and managed the computer systems. Lisa Nugent, Patricia Medina, Jemille Tumang, and Marlene George were responsible for word processing. Jeff Hayden and Jacqueline Irving of the External Relations Department edited the manuscript and coordinated production of the publication.

The analysis has benefited from comments and suggestions by staff from other IMF departments, as well as by Executive Directors following their discussion of the *World Economic Outlook* on March 22 and March 24, 2000. However, both projections and policy considerations are those of the IMF staff and should not be attributed to Executive Directors or to their national authorities.

CHAPTER I

PROSPECTS AND POLICY CHALLENGES

Global economic and financial conditions have improved dramatically during the past year. The effects of the recent financial crises may be felt for some time, but the emerging economies in Asia have for the most part staged a strong V-shaped recovery, and the transition countries and Latin America have begun to recover from the subsequent turbulence that particularly affected Russia and Brazil. The impressive expansion in the United States is now the longest on record and the outlook has also improved for Europe. The Japanese recovery, however, remains tentative and fragile.

The main themes developed in this issue of the World Economic Outlook *include:*

- *How to achieve a better balanced pattern of growth among the major currency areas and to avoid a disruptive adjustment process.*
- *The interaction between business cycles and asset prices, particularly in equity and property markets, and the associated challenges for monetary, fiscal, and regulatory policies.*
- *The persistence of high levels of poverty across many regions in the world and the need for a broader, more determined effort in the fight against poverty.*
- *Some of the most striking aspects of economic developments in the twentieth century, the lessons to be learned, and key challenges for the new century.*

Evidence of a strong rebound in the global economy has continued to accumulate in recent months and the momentum of recovery from the 1997–98 slowdown has proven much stronger than anticipated (Table 1.1). Global growth is now estimated to have reached 3.3 percent in 1999 compared with a projection of only 2.2 percent prepared at the end of 1998, at the height of financial market turbulence and the low point in the associated confidence crisis.[1] North America and the emerging market countries of Asia account for much of the stronger growth picture but other regions also contribute. In retrospect, the global downturn in the wake of the crises in Asia and other emerging market countries since 1997 now appears to have been relatively mild and brief (Figure 1.1). The world growth projection for 2000 has been raised as well, to around 4¼ percent. Moreover, the risks for the current year now appear to be mainly on the upside, given the

continued strong forward momentum in the United States and the possibility that recovery in Europe might be more robust. Indeed, the experience from earlier global business cycle upturns is that they have often turned out to be stronger than anticipated. At the same time, however, considerable uncertainty remains about the sustainability of the expansion in some countries.

The remarkable turnaround from the weak and uncertain outlook that prevailed a year ago is testimony to the policies that have been pursued to address shocks that had the potential to lead to a global recession. The strength of the U.S. economy has played a major role, with subdued inflation allowing the Federal Reserve to maintain an accommodating monetary stance that has supported the exceptionally buoyant growth of domestic demand and promoted easy financial conditions worldwide. In Europe, the authorities have also pursued relatively easy monetary policies, while in Japan both fiscal and

[1]See *World Economic Outlook and International Capital Markets: Interim Assessment* (Washington: International Monetary Fund, December 1998).

Table 1.1. Overview of the *World Economic Outlook* Projections
(Annual percent change unless otherwise noted)

	1998	1999	Current Projections		Difference from October 1999 Projections[1]	
			2000	2001	1999	2000
World output	**2.5**	**3.3**	**4.2**	**3.9**	**0.4**	**0.8**
Advanced economies	2.4	3.1	3.6	3.0	0.3	0.9
Major industrial countries	2.5	2.8	3.3	2.7	0.2	0.9
United States	4.3	4.2	4.4	3.0	0.5	1.8
Japan	−2.5	0.3	0.9	1.8	−0.7	−0.6
Germany	2.2	1.5	2.8	3.3	0.1	0.3
France	3.4	2.7	3.5	3.1	0.2	0.5
Italy	1.5	1.4	2.7	2.8	0.2	0.3
United Kingdom	2.2	2.0	3.0	2.0	0.9	0.6
Canada	3.1	4.2	3.7	2.7	0.6	1.1
Other advanced economies	2.0	4.6	4.5	4.1	1.0	0.9
Memorandum						
Industrial countries	2.7	2.9	3.4	2.8	0.3	0.9
Euro area	2.8	2.3	3.2	3.2	0.2	0.4
Newly industrialized Asian economies	−2.3	7.7	6.6	6.1	2.5	1.5
Developing countries	3.2	3.8	5.4	5.3	0.3	0.7
Africa	3.1	2.3	4.4	4.5	−0.4	−0.4
Asia	3.8	6.0	6.2	5.9	0.7	0.8
China	7.8	7.1	7.0	6.5	0.5	1.0
India	4.7	6.8	6.3	6.1	1.1	0.8
ASEAN-4[2]	−9.5	2.5	4.0	4.4	1.1	0.4
Middle East and Europe	2.7	0.7	4.6	4.0	−1.1	1.6
Western Hemisphere	2.1	0.1	4.0	4.7	0.2	0.1
Brazil	−0.1	0.5	4.0	4.5	1.5	—
Countries in transition	−0.7	2.4	2.6	3.0	1.8	−0.1
Central and eastern Europe	1.8	1.4	3.0	4.2	0.7	−0.2
Excluding Belarus and Ukraine	2.0	1.5	3.6	4.6	—	−0.3
Russia	−4.5	3.2	1.5	1.4	3.2	−0.5
Transcaucasus and central Asia	2.3	4.4	4.9	3.7	1.6	2.1
World trade volume (goods and services)	**4.2**	**4.6**	**7.9**	**7.2**	**0.9**	**1.7**
Imports						
Advanced economies	5.5	7.4	7.8	7.1	1.5	1.9
Developing countries	0.4	−0.3	9.8	8.5	−1.4	2.7
Countries in transition	2.9	−5.4	6.1	6.9	−3.0	−2.0
Exports						
Advanced economies	3.7	4.4	7.2	6.8	1.4	1.0
Developing countries	4.5	1.7	9.7	8.3	−0.6	4.2
Countries in transition	6.3	3.9	5.9	5.6	1.2	−1.4
Commodity prices						
Oil[3]						
In SDRs	−31.2	37.6	36.5	−19.4	1.0	26.0
In U.S. dollars	−32.1	38.7	35.1	−19.2	1.0	24.0
Nonfuel (average, based on world commodity export weights)						
In SDRs	−13.5	−7.7	6.0	2.9	1.5	2.1
In U.S. dollars	−14.7	−6.9	4.9	3.2	1.6	0.5
Consumer prices						
Advanced economies	1.5	1.4	1.9	2.0	—	0.1
Developing countries	10.1	6.5	5.7	4.7	−0.9	−0.3
Countries in transition	21.8	43.7	19.5	14.2	−9.2	−2.1
Six-month London interbank offered rate (LIBOR, percent)						
On U.S. dollar deposits	5.6	5.5	6.8	7.1	0.1	0.7
On Japanese yen deposits	0.7	0.2	0.2	0.4	—	—
On euro deposits	3.7	3.0	4.1	4.9	—	0.6

Note: Real effective exchange rates are assumed to remain constant at the levels prevailing during January 25–February 22, 2000.
[1]Using updated purchasing-power-parity (PPP) weights, summarized in the Statistical Appendix, Table A.
[2]Indonesia, Malaysia, the Philippines, and Thailand.
[3]Simple average of spot prices of U.K. Brent, Dubai, and West Texas Intermediate crude oil. The average price of oil in U.S. dollars a barrel was $18.14 in 1999; the assumed price is $24.50 in 2000 and $19.80 in 2001.

monetary policies have been helping to restart the economy after a severe recession in 1998.

Among the emerging market countries the turnaround is also testimony to the resolute actions by policymakers to deepen adjustment and reform efforts in response to the sharp curtailment of capital inflows in the wake of the recent crises. In Asia, the rapid return of confidence and recovery of activity demonstrate the efficacy of the stabilization strategies that have been pursued. There is no doubt that the region's growth potential remains very strong, provided the institutional and other shortcomings that contributed to the recent crises are adequately addressed through continued reforms. In Brazil, policy reforms have also served to lessen the severity of the downturn and to prepare the ground for recovery in the period ahead. Economic policies have helped to mitigate the effects of the crisis in Russia as well, although much more remains to be done to secure a lasting recovery.

The recovery in global activity has been accompanied by a more than doubling of oil prices since early 1999, mainly due to production curbs by the Organization of the Petroleum Exporting Countries (OPEC) and several other oil producers. To a large extent, the rise in oil prices represents a recovery from exceptionally weak prices in early 1999, and this recovery has brought prices back closer to a long-term equilibrium. With oil having become a less important factor in the world economy since the 1970s, the consequences of the recent price increase for oil importing countries are smaller than they would have been in the past. In addition, the price rise is contributing to significant improvements in external balances and fiscal positions of oil exporters, including Russia, many countries in the Middle East, and some African countries (as discussed later in this chapter), although net global demand will still fall somewhat as oil importers reduce demand more than oil exporters raise it. The production increases agreed by OPEC in March 2000 will probably stabilize oil prices. However, in the relatively unlikely case that prices continue to increase, the benign effects

Figure 1.1. Global Indicators[1]
(Annual percent change unless otherwise noted)

The world economy has continued to strengthen following the relatively mild slowdown in the wake of the emerging market crises.

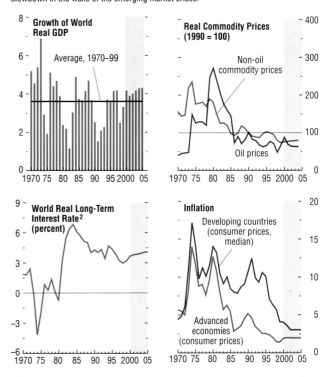

[1]Shaded areas indicate IMF staff projections. Aggregates are computed on the basis of purchasing-power-parity weights unless otherwise indicated.

[2]GDP-weighted average of 10-year (or nearest maturity) government bond yields less inflation rates for the United States, Japan, Germany, France, Italy, the United Kingdom, and Canada. Excluding Italy prior to 1972.

on global activity to date could turn more worrisome.

The main concern about the outlook stems from a series of economic and financial imbalances that have been building for several years, including:

- The lopsided pattern of growth among the principal currency areas and the resulting increase in external imbalances, with the U.S. current account in record deficit and persistently large surpluses in Japan and, to a lesser extent, in the euro area (Table 1.2). These imbalances appear unlikely to be sustainable, based on recent and past experience. On a smaller absolute scale, large external deficits also persist in Australia, New Zealand, most of Latin America, and among some countries in transition.

- The seemingly significant misalignments of several key currencies relative to what would be consistent with medium-term fundamentals, notably the strength of the dollar relative to the euro. Such deviations can be explained in part by large capital inflows into rapidly growing economies, and therefore appear justified on cyclical grounds. Nevertheless, combined with the large external imbalances mentioned earlier, there remains a risk of sudden changes in market sentiment, associated shifts in capital flows, and potentially disruptive realignments of exchange rates.

- The very high stock market valuations around the world. These may be justified in part by investors' favorable assessments of the impact of new technologies, but they may also reflect unrealistic expectations of future earnings growth that have been nourished by the now record-long expansion in the United States. Moreover, there are reasons to suspect that the relatively ample growth in global liquidity in recent years—warranted by the need to overcome the effects of financial crises in Asia, Russia, and Latin America, and more recently by concerns related to potential Y2K computer problems—has helped fuel demand for fi-

Table 1.2. Selected Economies: Current Account Positions
(Percent of GDP)

	1998	1999	2000	2001
Advanced economies				
United States	−2.5	−3.7	−4.3	−4.4
Japan	3.2	2.5	2.2	2.3
Germany	−0.2	−0.8	0.2	0.7
France	2.7	2.8	2.6	3.1
Italy	1.8	0.9	0.9	1.1
United Kingdom	−0.1	−1.4	−1.5	−2.0
Canada	−1.8	−0.5	−0.4	0.1
Australia	−5.0	−5.7	−5.1	−4.9
Austria	−2.2	−2.3	−1.9	−1.0
Finland	5.7	5.0	5.4	5.7
Greece	−1.9	−1.3	−1.6	−1.8
Hong Kong SAR[1]	0.8	4.8	4.1	4.2
Ireland	0.9	0.6	−0.4	−0.9
Israel	−0.9	−1.6	−1.2	−1.8
Korea	12.7	6.1	3.0	2.2
New Zealand	−5.1	−7.3	−6.2	−5.2
Norway	−1.5	4.2	7.0	7.5
Singapore	25.4	25.3	23.4	22.0
Spain	−0.2	−2.1	−2.0	−1.7
Sweden	2.9	2.6	2.4	2.2
Switzerland	9.1	12.9	10.0	9.9
Taiwan Province of China	1.3	2.5	2.1	2.3
Memorandum				
Euro area	1.3	0.7	1.0	1.4
Developing countries				
Algeria	−1.9	0.0	10.8	5.6
Argentina	−4.9	−4.3	−4.5	−4.7
Brazil	−4.3	−4.1	−3.5	−2.5
Cameroon	−2.7	−4.3	−2.8	−2.1
Chile	−5.7	−0.1	−2.2	−3.2
China	3.4	1.6	1.6	1.5
Côte d'Ivoire	−4.5	−5.0	−5.9	−4.5
Egypt	−3.4	−3.2	−3.1	−2.9
India	−1.7	−1.2	−1.3	−1.4
Indonesia	4.2	3.6	1.9	0.5
Malaysia	12.9	18.4	13.3	10.4
Mexico	−3.7	−2.9	−3.1	−3.2
Nigeria	−9.1	−10.8	−1.9	−6.7
Pakistan	−2.7	−2.6	−2.5	−2.3
Philippines	2.0	9.1	8.2	8.1
Saudi Arabia	−10.2	−2.8	5.5	−2.4
South Africa	−1.6	−0.4	−1.3	−1.5
Thailand	12.7	9.1	5.8	5.3
Turkey	0.9	−0.5	−1.9	−1.7
Uganda	−2.2	−4.1	−3.1	−2.8
Countries in transition				
Czech Republic	−1.9	−1.0	−1.5	−1.8
Estonia	−9.2	−4.1	−5.5	−6.0
Hungary	−4.9	−4.4	−4.5	−4.3
Latvia	−9.5	−8.7	−7.7	−7.4
Lithuania	−12.1	−10.9	−9.2	−8.4
Poland	−4.4	−7.6	−6.9	−6.6
Russia	0.9	10.8	9.1	4.7
Slovak Republic	−10.4	−4.9	−3.0	−2.8
Ukraine	−3.1	−1.1	−2.9	−2.6

[1]Data include only goods and nonfactor services.

nancial assets in many countries. Property prices have also been rising sharply in some economies. Experience shows that such asset price inflation can be particularly destabilizing because it may encourage households and businesses to over-consume and over-invest, and because of the danger that the financial system may become vulnerable to an eventual downward correction in asset prices.

These imbalances have been present for some time, and concerns about how they might unwind have been discussed repeatedly in recent issues of the *World Economic Outlook*. These assessments have cautioned that the continued strength of domestic demand in the United States, while playing a critical role in alleviating the adverse effects of the recent crises in emerging markets, did not seem sustainable. It might be tempting to conclude that since the perceived imbalances have not given rise to any obvious difficulties so far, they may not be a problem after all. Such a view has more than a few adherants, and could be correct, but if it is wrong such complacency could have severe consequences. The potentially disruptive effects could become much more serious if the imbalances were allowed to increase further while, at the same time, the chances of a benign outcome would probably diminish. As the alternative "harder" landing scenario reported in Box 1.1 illustrates, continued strong growth in the United States in 2000 could lead to higher inflationary expectations and interest rates, lower earnings expectations, and severe corrections in the stock market and the exchange rate. The attendant fall in domestic demand could well lead to a mild recession in 2001 in the United States and more limited output losses in the rest of the world.

It is therefore becoming a matter of urgency to secure a smooth transition to a more sustainable pattern of global growth, as in the current forecast. The priorities in this regard are to contain excess demand pressures in the United States, including the avoidance of a significant relaxation in the fiscal stance, and to promote robust and durable economic expansions in Japan and Europe. Part of the policy challenge needs to be met through asymmetric adjustments of monetary stances. Global financial conditions will naturally tend to tighten with the pickup in growth, and in the short term the bulk of the monetary firming should probably occur in the United States. In contrast, the euro area has more room to maintain relatively easy monetary policies until the recovery is on a sufficiently strong footing. Such a policy stance would foster the absorption of existing slack and help to offset any slowdown in the United States and the effects of the potential realignment of exchange rates that may accompany a slowdown. Similar arguments apply to Japan; indeed, the fragile nature of the recovery and recurrent upward pressure on the yen underscore the need to explore the scope for further monetary easing. Greater progress on structural reforms also remains critical to sustaining and strengthening growth over the medium term in Japan and Europe.

Two data-related issues may have an important bearing on assessments of global economic conditions and prospects. First, the widening global current account discrepancy (see Table 27 in the Statistical Appendix) raises the possibility that export growth may be underestimated, implying a further upside risk to the near-term projections for world growth. Second, recent revisions in national accounts methodologies in the United States, Europe, and elsewhere have had an important impact on the estimated level and growth of GDP, on reported personal saving rates in the United States, and on other economic aggregates (Box 1.2). Particular care is needed with the interpretation and use of national accounts data while the full range of revisions is being phased in.

How Much Longer Will the Expansion in North America Continue?

The U.S. economy continues to expand rapidly. After a brief slowing in the second quarter of 1999, annualized real GDP growth bounced

Box 1.1. An Alternative Scenario

The baseline projections in the *World Economic Outlook* represent a relatively benign scenario with a moderation of growth in the United States to sustainable rates (i.e., a "soft landing") and sustained recoveries in Japan, Europe, and the emerging market countries. This is an entirely plausible projection, especially in view of the subdued rates of inflation in most economies, but judging the likelihood of this scenario is difficult. Indeed, the margin of error, even for a forecast horizon as short as one year, is very large—typically plus or minus 1 percentage point for individual country forecasts and almost as large for the aggregate of the industrial countries.[1] Experience also shows that growth is much more cyclical in reality than forecasters usually are prepared to project, with upturns often surprising on the upside and downturns on the downside. And finally, it is the shared experience of all forecasters that turning points are notoriously difficult to anticipate. For example, many forecasters, including IMF staff, expected 1999 to mark the trough in the global slowdown of the late 1990s; in reality, 1999 became the first year of recovery.

In considering the risks to the outlook for the next several years, there is a distinct possibility that the global upturn now under way may turn out to be stronger than expected. Moreover, a stronger upturn in 2000 might well give rise to sufficient additional pressures on actual and expected inflation that monetary authorities will need (or be expected) to raise interest rates. Higher actual or expected inflation, tighter monetary policy, and the attendant reconsideration of future prospects for growth and earnings could significantly change currently buoyant investor sentiment regarding equities and the dollar. If investors' expectations of future returns

on equities are revised down while the returns on available substitutes rise, the resulting exodus of funds could trigger a notable correction of equity markets and realignment of exchange rates, leading to a more general erosion of confidence. This would be felt mostly in the United States, where the stock market has helped to sustain exceptionally rapid growth in domestic demand in recent years. However, other countries would probably experience at least a partial correction in their stock prices (this is suggested by the correlations between stock markets analyzed in Chapter III) as well as spillovers through trade and confidence.

The scenario results shown in the table assume that world growth in 2000 would be somewhat stronger than expected in the baseline. This would eventually (some time in the second half of 2000) generate an increase in inflation expectations, a downscaling of earnings expectations, a marked (25 percent) correction in U.S. equity prices, and a depreciation of the U.S. dollar (assumed at almost 20 percent) in response to a reversal of capital inflows. The large negative impact on U.S. domestic demand implied by these assumptions would be partially offset by an improvement in the foreign balance but would still bring U.S. growth almost to a halt in 2001. Because the U.S. financial system remains well capitalized and unlikely to be seriously impaired by a cyclical correction of the magnitude assumed here, the slowdown would be likely to be of relatively short duration (the scenario does not assume any specific countercyclical fiscal action, although automatic stabilizers and normal monetary rules are assumed to operate).

Other countries would be less affected, mainly because the stock market correction in Europe and Japan would be likely to be smaller and have much less impact on domestic demand. Easier monetary conditions would provide support for domestic output, and lead to relatively buoyant domestic demand. Nevertheless, in view of the fragility of the recovery under way in Japan and the limited room for further macroeconomic stimulus, this country would be particularly vul-

---

[1]Forecast errors of this magnitude are also typical among private sector forecasters. See Michael Artis, "How Accurate Are the IMF's Short-Term Forecasts? Another Examination of the World Economic Outlook," *Staff Studies for the World Economic Outlook* (Washington: International Monetary Fund, December 1997).

"Harder Landing" Scenario
(Percent deviation from baseline levels unless otherwise noted)

	2000	2001	2002	2003	2004
World					
Real GDP	0.7	−0.9	−0.7	−0.5	−0.2
United States					
Real GDP	0.5	−2.0	−1.9	−1.3	−0.6
Domestic demand	0.6	−3.7	−4.2	−3.8	−3.0
Net private saving (percent of GDP)	−0.3	1.6	2.2	2.1	1.8
Current account (billions of U.S. dollars)	−5.7	33.9	111.6	160.4	201.9
CPI inflation	0.3	0.8	−0.7	−0.6	−0.2
Short-term interest rate	1.0	0.9	0.1	−0.9	−1.7
Nominal effective exchange rate	1.1	−17.5	−15.3	−13.0	−10.0
Euro area					
Real GDP	0.8	−0.7	−0.3	−0.3	−0.1
Domestic demand	0.7	1.0	1.3	1.3	1.3
Net private saving (percent of GDP)	−0.3	−0.1	−0.6	−1.0	−1.3
Current account (billions of U.S. dollars)	1.1	23.7	3.8	−23.2	−50.9
CPI inflation	0.2	−0.7	−0.5	−0.6	−0.6
Short-term interest rate	0.2	−0.6	−1.1	−1.4	−1.5
Nominal effective exchange rate	−0.3	12.0	10.4	8.5	6.6
Japan					
Real GDP	0.6	−0.6	−0.6	−0.4	0.0
Domestic demand	0.4	0.5	1.0	1.4	1.6
Net private saving (percent of GDP)	−0.1	−0.1	−0.7	−1.3	−1.8
Current account (billions of U.S. dollars)	4.6	23.3	−19.3	−51.2	−73.6
CPI inflation	0.1	−1.1	−0.5	−0.5	−0.5
Short-term interest rate	0.1	−0.3	−0.6	−1.2	−1.3
Nominal effective exchange rate	−0.9	18.9	16.0	12.8	9.6
Developing countries					
Real GDP	0.8	−0.4	−0.4	−0.4	−0.3
Memorandum: Baseline Growth in Real GDP					
World	4.2	3.9	4.0	4.2	4.3
United States	4.4	3.0	3.0	3.0	3.0
Euro area	3.2	3.2	3.0	2.7	2.5
Japan	0.9	1.8	2.4	2.5	2.4
Developing countries	5.4	5.3	5.4	5.9	6.2

nerable to a marked slowdown in the United States and to a further appreciation of the yen.

The emerging market countries would also be adversely affected, but only temporarily. Latin America would appear to be the most vulnerable to a possible firming of global financial conditions and a significant slowdown in the United States, although a depreciation of the U.S. dollar would provide some relief for those countries that peg their exchange rate to the dollar.

back to a remarkable 5¾ percent in the third quarter and over 7 percent in the fourth. While some of this represented Y2K-related stock building, monthly indicators point to continued buoyancy in the opening quarter of 2000. Private domestic demand continues to drive growth, with consumer confidence remaining strong and business investment still increasing rapidly. The growth in housing activity has leveled off somewhat, partly in response to higher interest rates, but remains at a very high level. In 1999 as a whole, real GDP rose by 4.2 percent and real do-

Box 1.2. Revisions in National Accounts Methodologies

Statistical agencies in most Organization for Economic Cooperation and Development (OECD) countries and elsewhere are in the process of introducing comprehensive revisions to their national accounts, based on a number of significant changes in definitions, classifications, data sources, and statistical procedures as suggested in the 1993 System of National Accounts (SNA93).[1] In the European Union (EU), GDP data prepared under the new European System of Accounts (ESA95) have been available for most countries since around mid-1999; in the United States, initial results of the latest benchmark revision of the National Income and Product Accounts (NIPA) were released in October 1999.[2] National accounts data prepared under SNA93 guidelines have also been available in Canada and Australia since the end of 1998, and are expected to become available in Japan later in 2000. The new methodologies, which have a substantial impact on some economic variables, will improve the quality and international comparability of national accounts data. As discussed below, however, particular care will be needed with the interpretation and use of these data while the revisions are being phased in.

Principal Changes

The main methodological changes are the following:
- *A broader concept of capital formation.* In particular, business and government purchases of computer software are now included as fixed capital formation, rather than production inputs or government consumption expenditures. Under ESA95, some military purchases that used to be classified as current expenditures are now included under capital formation, along with literary and artistic works and also mineral exploration (the last-mentioned was already included as investment in the NIPAs). Correspondingly, capital consumption allowances (depreciation) now reflect use of computer software and other new investments.
- *An improved treatment of services.* This includes more detailed coverage of the financial sector. In the United States, for example, there are better measures of bank services, including ATM transactions and electronic fund transfers; and the ESA95 revisions reflect the increasing role in the economy of insurance and pension funds.
- *Reclassification of some social expenditures.* The ESA95 revisions reclassify reimbursable health expenditures, and some other areas of social spending, from private to government consumption.
- *Reclassification of U.S. government employee retirement plans.* Under the NIPA revisions, government contributions to these plans (covering federal, state, and local government employees) are now recorded under personal income rather than as government receipts (of contributions) and expenditures (of compensation). Similarly, interest and dividends paid to plans are included under personal income, while plan benefits are treated as transactions within the personal sector rather than as

[1]The guidelines of SNA93 were developed under a working group consisting of representatives of the OECD, IMF, the United Nations Statistical Division, the World Bank, and the Commission of the European Communities. The changes introduced under the 1995 European System of National Accounts are broadly consistent with SNA93, with more specific interpretation in some areas, and many of the SNA93 guidelines are also incorporated in the latest revisions to the National Income and Product Accounts in the United States.

[2]The European Central Bank's Monthly Bulletins of June, August, and December 1999 (available at: *www.ecb.int*), and the EU Commission's *European Economy,* Supplement A, Economic trends, *No.10/11 October/November 1999* (available at: *http://www.europa.eu.int/comm/economy_finance*), provide detailed reviews on the implications of the switchover to ESA95. In the United States, detailed information and data are available on the website of the Bureau of Economic Analysis (*www.bea.doc.gov*) and in the August, October, and December 1999 editions of the *Survey of Current Business* (Washington: Commerce Department). See also the OECD *Economic Outlook* 65/66, June/December (Paris: Organization for Economic Cooperation and Development, 1999).

transfer payments from government to recipients.

- *More widespread use of accruals principles.* Under ESA95, transactions involving interest payments, taxes, and other items are now recorded on an accruals basis rather than at the time of payment. For example, interest expenses are recorded as accruing continuously over time to the creditor, not when actual cash payments are made.
- *Wider use of chain-linked volume measures.* This allows the impact of relative price changes on volume growth to be reflected more quickly and accurately.

Impact on GDP and Saving Estimates

The new accounting methodologies have tended to raise the reported level of nominal GDP, but with varying effects on real growth. In the European Union as a whole, the transition to ESA95 increased the level of nominal GDP by around 2 percent in the base year (1995), but with quite wide variation from country to country.[3] Of the overall increase, 1½ percentage points came from the wider definition of fixed capital formation. The level of final consumption in the European Union increased by 1 percent, comprising a 7 percent decrease in private consumption and 32 percent rise in government consumption, and this explained slightly more than ½ of a percentage point of the rise in GDP. The revisions to real GDP lowered annual growth rates in the EU by 0.1 to 0.3 percentage points over the 1996–98 period (e.g., from 2.9 to 2.6 percent in 1998), without broadly changing the overall cyclical profile.

The revisions in the United States increased the level of nominal GDP by 2¼ percent on average over 1995–98, mainly because of the inclusion of computer software purchases as investment. The revisions have generally increased

through time—for example, nominal GDP was revised up by 2.9 percent (amounting to a rise of almost $250 billion) in 1998. Reflecting this, together with adjustments in price deflators, real GDP growth has also been revised up in most years—by just over 0.4 percentage points on average in 1995–1998, including from 3.9 percent to 4.3 percent in 1998. As in Europe, however, the timing of cyclical peaks and troughs over the revision period (starting in 1959 in the United States) is unchanged. A striking result of the U.S. revisions has been the sizable increase in reported personal saving rates, due particularly to the reclassification of government employee retirement plans. While the long-standing downward trend in personal saving is maintained, the revisions have increased personal saving rates by 2 to 3 percentage points each year since the early 1980s, and from 0.5 percent to 3.7 percent in 1998. The national saving rate has been revised up a smaller amount—by 0.5 to 1.5 percentage points in most years since 1982, the largest increase (from 17.3 to 18.8 percent) coming in 1998.

Words of Caution

As noted, the national accounts revisions will significantly improve the quality of these data in terms of their measurement of key economic concepts and for purposes of international comparison. However, the many revisions to the various components of the national accounts are being phased in at different rates both within and across countries. During this interim period, therefore, more than the usual degree of caution will be required in interpreting data, deriving related concepts, and applying these results to policy development. For example, revised data for the main national aggregates contained in expenditure, household, and government accounts are now available for the United States and most euro area economies, but these revisions are not yet available for Japan and a number of smaller OECD countries. Even among the larger economies, revised capital stock data are not yet widely available, complicating the estimation of potential output and other derived se-

---

[3]This variation reflects not just the switch to ESA95, but also differences in the rate at which EU members have introduced other changes in sources and methods in recent years—with some introducing many of these changes at the same time as switching to ESA95.

Box 1.2 *(concluded)*

ries, and the program for the full set of revisions—including sectoral and regional breakdowns—stretches several years ahead. A further complication comes from the varying extent of revisions to historical data within and across countries, with many revised series available for only short time spans. For example, ESA95 data for several EU members (including Austria, Greece, the Netherlands, and Spain) are avail-

able only for 1995–1998, and for most other countries in the EU the revised series begin in the late 1980s or early 1990s. While data-splicing and other methods can be used to compile longer series, the results should be viewed as rough approximations. Hence, intertemporal comparisons and estimations requiring long runs of data must necessarily be carried out with caution.

mestic demand by 5.1 percent, continuing the pattern seen since 1996 of the growth of demand outstripping that of supply.

To date, the discrepancy between the growth of demand and supply has been mostly reflected in a sharp widening of the external deficit, rather than in inflationary pressures. Rapid growth in demand resulted in a record current account deficit of nearly $400 billion at an annualized rate in the last quarter of 1999, up over $150 billion from the equivalent figure in 1998. At 3.7 percent of GDP, the current account deficit for 1999 as a whole exceeded the previous record of 3.4 percent set in 1985 and 1986. The labor market has tightened further, with the rate of unemployment at about 4 percent, a level last seen in the 1960s, although exceptionally strong productivity gains and moderate wage growth have thus far contained upward pressures on unit labor costs. Rising energy prices have affected CPI inflation, which reached 3.2 percent in February 2000 compared with the year before, but the equivalent increase in the core rate of inflation (which excludes energy and fresh food) was 2.1 percent. It is unlikely, however, that inflationary pressures will continue to be contained in the face of growth above potential, higher oil prices, and strong signs of global recovery.

Even though inflationary pressures have remained quiescent thus far, the falling household saving ratio points to other internal imbalances. Buoyed by rising asset prices, the household saving rate has fallen by about 5 percent of dispos-

able income since the early 1990s, the private investment ratio has increased by over 3 percent of GDP in this period, and private debt is at record levels. In spite of rising profits, private borrowing (defined as the difference between private investment and private saving as a ratio to GDP) is at a postwar record and is of a magnitude that has proved unsustainable in several other advanced countries over recent decades, where such borrowing was also accompanied by buoyant growth, relatively subdued inflation, and strong government finances (Figure 1.2). Private sector balance sheets have remained relatively robust, in a large part because they have been buttressed by rapid increases in asset price valuations, particularly in the stock market. However, a significant vulnerability for the economy is that a rapid reversal in asset prices could leave many borrowers in financial difficulties if asset values fall relative to debt servicing commitments.

The process by which this widening of internal and external imbalances will ultimately be reversed is one of the major uncertainties facing the world economy. Every effort needs to be made to ensure that this occurs in an orderly manner (the so-called "soft landing") rather than in an abrupt and discordant one (a "hard landing"). The forecast assumes that the economy slows fairly early in 2000, still producing year-on-year growth of 4.4 percent before settling at a relatively steady rate of growth of 3 percent subsequently (Table 1.3); that the current account stabilizes at close to its current value; and that there is no rapid stock market correction. Such an outcome would allow the necessary slowing of U.S. activity without seriously disrupting the recovery of world output.

Prudent macroeconomic policies are an important element in ensuring the needed slowdown in activity. With the near-term balance of risks facing the U.S. economy still very much on the upside, the Federal Reserve's decision to raise rates by a further ¼ percentage point in February and again in mid-March was clearly warranted, even after three increases since June 1999 that fully reversed the easing that occurred in the wake of the Russian default and problems at Long-Term Capital Management, a highly leveraged hedge fund. Although the full effects on demand of the 1¼ percentage point rise in short-term interest rates and the rapid increase in oil prices since the summer have yet to be fully seen, there is little evidence of U.S. growth slowing of its own accord or of existing imbalances reversing. Even with considerable short-term volatility, continued high equity valuations and the large share of household wealth held directly or indirectly in equities may complicate the task of achieving the needed slowdown, as they work against the needed recovery in the household saving rate. Very high valuations, particularly in the technology and bio-tech sectors, continue to pose the risk of a large market correction and a sharper economic slowdown later.

The Federal Reserve probably needs to continue to move progressively but prudently to a tighter monetary stance. The money markets anticipate a rise in short-term interest rates of ½–¾ of a percentage point over the next six months, although the eventual extent of any tightening will depend upon changing economic considerations and is difficult to project. A more significant tightening of monetary conditions might well be needed to slow U.S. demand growth to a sustainable pace, avoid a rise in inflationary pressures, and minimize the risk of an abrupt market correction at a later stage and an associated rapid deceleration in growth.

On the fiscal side, it is important to resist proposals to substantially raise spending or cut taxes. Sustained robust growth and prudent fis-

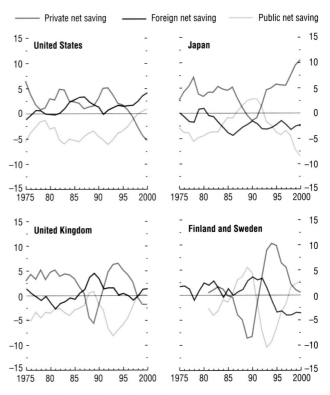

Figure 1.2. Selected Countries: Net Financial Balances[1]
(Percent of GDP)

Private net saving in the United States has fallen to levels that have not been sustainable in other advanced economies in recent years.

[1]Data for 2000 are IMF staff projections. Public net saving is the general government current balance less government net investment, as defined in the national accounts. Foreign net saving is the current account balance, shown with opposite sign. Net private saving is the sum of public and foreign net saving, with opposite sign; it represents household disposable income less expenditure, plus after-tax corporate profits, less investment. The net saving of a sector is also known as its financial balance.

Table 1.3. Advanced Economies: Real GDP, Consumer Prices, and Unemployment
(Annual percent change and percent of labor force)

	Real GDP				Consumer Prices				Unemployment			
	1998	1999	2000	2001	1998	1999	2000	2001	1998	1999	2000	2001
Advanced economies	**2.4**	**3.1**	**3.6**	**3.0**	**1.5**	**1.4**	**1.9**	**2.0**	**6.7**	**6.4**	**6.0**	**5.8**
Major industrial countries	2.5	2.8	3.3	2.7	1.3	1.5	1.8	1.9	6.2	6.1	5.9	5.7
United States	4.3	4.2	4.4	3.0	1.6	2.2	2.5	2.5	4.5	4.2	4.2	4.2
Japan	−2.5	0.3	0.9	1.8	0.6	−0.3	0.1	0.9	4.1	4.7	4.7	4.6
Germany	2.2	1.5	2.8	3.3	0.6	0.7	1.2	1.3	9.4	9.0	8.6	8.1
France	3.4	2.7	3.5	3.1	0.7	0.6	1.3	1.1	11.7	11.0	10.2	9.8
Italy	1.5	1.4	2.7	2.8	1.7	1.7	2.2	1.6	11.8	11.4	11.0	10.4
United Kingdom[1]	2.2	2.0	3.0	2.0	2.7	2.3	2.0	2.4	4.7	4.4	4.3	4.5
Canada	3.1	4.2	3.7	2.7	1.0	1.7	2.1	2.0	8.3	7.6	6.7	6.6
Other advanced economies	2.0	4.6	4.5	4.1	2.4	1.3	2.3	2.4	8.1	7.3	6.3	6.0
Spain	4.0	3.7	3.7	3.4	1.8	2.2	2.3	2.2	18.8	15.9	14.4	13.2
Netherlands	3.7	3.5	3.8	3.4	2.0	2.0	2.3	3.5	4.1	3.2	2.3	2.0
Belgium	2.7	2.3	3.3	2.9	0.9	1.1	1.7	1.4	9.5	9.0	8.5	8.1
Sweden	3.0	3.8	3.9	3.2	−0.1	0.4	1.4	1.8	6.5	5.6	4.8	4.2
Austria	2.9	2.0	3.1	3.3	0.8	0.5	1.2	1.0	4.7	4.3	4.0	3.9
Denmark	2.7	1.3	1.7	2.1	1.8	2.5	2.3	2.0	6.4	5.6	5.8	6.1
Finland	5.0	3.6	4.1	3.5	1.3	1.3	2.4	2.5	11.4	10.3	9.0	8.2
Greece	3.7	3.5	3.6	3.1	4.5	2.3	2.4	2.7	10.9	10.5	10.2	10.1
Portugal	3.9	3.0	3.4	3.1	2.8	2.2	2.1	1.9	5.0	4.4	4.3	4.3
Ireland	8.9	8.4	7.4	7.2	2.4	1.6	3.5	3.0	7.4	5.6	4.8	4.8
Luxembourg	5.0	5.2	5.1	5.0	1.0	1.0	1.6	1.4	3.3	2.9	2.7	2.3
Switzerland	2.1	1.7	2.1	2.1	0.1	0.8	1.3	1.5	3.9	2.7	2.2	2.0
Norway	2.1	0.8	3.3	2.3	2.3	2.3	2.3	2.0	2.4	3.2	3.5	3.8
Israel	2.0	2.2	3.8	3.5	5.4	5.2	2.9	2.7	8.6	9.3	8.8	8.0
Iceland	5.1	5.6	4.7	3.5	1.7	3.5	3.2	3.0	3.0	1.7	1.7	1.5
Korea	−6.7	10.7	7.0	6.5	7.5	0.8	3.0	3.0	6.8	6.3	4.3	4.2
Australia[2]	5.1	4.4	3.9	3.5	0.9	1.5	4.4	3.2	8.0	7.2	6.7	6.6
Taiwan Province of China	4.7	5.5	6.2	6.0	1.7	0.2	1.8	2.1	2.7	2.9	2.6	2.3
Hong Kong SAR	−5.1	2.9	6.0	4.7	2.8	−4.0	−2.0	4.7	6.1	4.7	3.8	
Singapore	0.4	5.4	5.9	6.0	−0.3	0.4	1.3	1.7	3.2	3.5	2.9	2.5
New Zealand[2]	−0.3	3.0	3.9	3.4	1.6	1.3	2.3	2.0	7.5	6.9	6.6	6.4
Memorandum												
European Union	2.7	2.3	3.2	3.0	1.4	1.4	1.8	1.8	9.7	8.9	8.4	8.0
Euro area	2.8	2.3	3.2	3.2	1.2	1.2	1.7	1.6	10.9	10.1	9.4	8.9

[1]Consumer prices are based on the retail price index excluding mortgage interest.
[2]Consumer prices excluding interest rate components; for Australia, also excluding other volatile items.

cal management have contributed to the emergence of a small general government budget surplus in 1999 (Table 1.4). The administration's recent budget proposal for FY 2001 preserves a significant budget surplus for the near-term (Box 1.3). Maintaining such surpluses is necessary to avoid exacerbating existing risks of overheating and to assist monetary policy in achieving the needed slowing of activity in a smooth fashion—indeed, somewhat larger surpluses would in principle be helpful in both respects. There is also a structural reason for running significant budget surpluses at this point in time, since such surpluses are needed to help prepare

the government's accounts for the rising tide of unfunded liabilities associated with the aging population. In the event of a sharper slowdown in activity than is currently anticipated, there would then be scope for a temporary fiscal expansion for countercyclical purposes.

In *Canada*, the long period of expansion that began in 1992 has also continued and activity picked up further strength in 1999. Real GDP growth accelerated to a 4.7 percent annual rate in the second half of 1999, and averaged 4.2 percent for the year as a whole. Output growth is projected to remain strong, at around 3.7 percent, in 2000. The recent strengthening in activ-

Table 1.4. Major Industrial Countries: General Government Fiscal Balances and Debt[1]
(Percent of GDP)

	1983–93	1994	1995	1996	1997	1998	1999	2000	2001	2005
Major industrial countries										
Actual balance	–3.8	–4.2	–4.1	–3.4	–1.9	–1.3	–1.2	–1.1	–0.6	0.6
Output gap	–0.9	–2.2	–2.3	–1.8	–1.4	–1.5	–1.3	–0.5	–0.3	—
Structural balance	–3.3	–3.1	–3.1	–2.6	–1.3	–0.6	–0.6	–0.8	–0.5	0.5
United States										
Actual balance	–4.9	–3.8	–3.3	–2.4	–1.2	–0.1	0.5	1.0	1.2	1.9
Output gap	–1.6	–2.7	–3.2	–2.8	–1.8	–0.7	0.3	1.3	1.0	–0.1
Structural balance	–4.3	–2.8	–2.2	–1.5	–0.6	0.1	0.3	0.5	0.8	1.8
Net debt	46.0	60.1	59.6	59.2	57.3	54.0	50.6	46.6	43.1	29.8
Gross debt	60.1	72.8	72.9	72.8	70.6	67.2	62.4	57.4	53.1	36.8
Japan										
Actual balance	0.1	–2.3	–3.6	–4.2	–3.4	–4.3	–7.1	–8.4	–6.7	–2.0
Output gap	0.3	–1.6	–1.7	1.3	0.9	–3.4	–4.5	–4.6	–4.0	–0.1
Structural balance	0.3	–1.8	–3.1	–4.7	–3.7	–3.1	–5.4	–6.6	–5.2	–2.0
Net debt	18.2	7.7	13.0	16.4	17.9	30.4	37.7	46.1	51.6	60.7
Gross debt	69.0	82.2	89.7	94.4	99.2	114.0	125.1	136.1	141.5	147.6
Memorandum										
Actual balance excluding social security	–3.0	–5.1	–6.5	–6.8	–5.9	–6.4	–9.0	–9.6	–7.6	–3.2
Structural balance excluding social security	–3.1	–4.8	–6.1	–7.2	–6.1	–5.6	–7.8	–8.4	–6.7	–3.2
Germany[2]										
Actual balance	–2.0	–2.5	–3.2	–3.4	–2.6	–1.7	–1.1	–0.7	–1.0	–0.4
Output gap	–1.3	—	–0.3	–1.6	–2.2	–2.2	–2.8	–2.1	–1.0	—
Structural balance	–1.6	–2.3	–2.9	–2.3	–1.1	–0.3	0.6	0.5	–0.4	–0.4
Net debt	22.0	40.6	49.4	51.1	52.2	52.0	52.4	49.9	48.1	41.5
Gross debt	41.8	50.2	58.3	59.8	60.9	60.7	61.1	58.6	56.8	50.2
France										
Actual balance	–2.0	–5.5	–5.5	–4.2	–3.0	–2.7	–1.8	–1.5	–1.0	—
Output gap	0.3	–3.0	–2.7	–3.3	–3.1	–1.9	–1.6	–0.5	0.1	—
Structural balance	–2.0	–3.5	–3.7	–2.0	–1.0	–1.5	–0.8	–1.2	–1.0	—
Net debt	21.6	40.5	45.9	48.1	49.4	49.6	49.0	48.4	48.3	42.9
Gross debt	32.7	48.5	54.6	57.1	59.0	59.3	58.6	58.1	57.4	52.6
Italy										
Actual balance	–10.9	–9.1	–7.6	–7.1	–2.7	–2.8	–1.9	–1.5	–1.1	—
Output gap	0.1	–2.5	–1.1	–2.0	–2.3	–2.7	–3.3	–2.6	–1.9	–0.1
Structural balance	–10.9	–7.9	–7.0	–6.2	–1.6	–1.6	–0.5	–0.4	–0.3	0.1
Net debt	79.8	117.2	116.6	115.7	113.4	110.1	108.8	104.9	101.5	88.9
Gross debt	87.1	123.8	123.2	122.2	119.8	116.3	114.9	110.7	107.2	93.9
United Kingdom										
Actual balance	–2.4	–6.8	–5.8	–4.4	–2.0	0.2	0.3	0.2	0.2	–0.5
Output gap	–0.9	–1.9	–1.2	–0.8	0.4	0.5	0.1	0.7	0.5	—
Structural balance	–1.8	–4.7	–4.7	–3.7	–1.8	–0.1	0.1	—	–0.2	–0.5
Net debt	33.0	33.0	39.1	41.6	43.3	44.6	41.1	39.8	37.6	33.8
Gross debt	49.4	51.4	54.9	56.2	54.8	51.0	47.1	45.6	43.2	38.5
Canada										
Actual balance	–5.7	–5.6	–4.3	–1.8	0.8	0.9	2.8	2.3	2.0	1.7
Output gap	–1.9	–4.3	–4.0	–4.7	–3.2	–2.6	–0.9	0.4	0.6	0.4
Structural balance	–4.6	–2.9	–2.0	0.8	2.5	2.3	3.3	2.1	1.7	1.5
Net debt	38.2	68.7	70.2	69.8	65.5	62.3	56.7	51.3	47.0	32.8
Gross debt	70.4	99.4	102.2	101.8	97.7	95.8	88.1	80.9	75.4	56.7

Note: The budget projections are based on information available through March 2000. The specific assumptions for each country are set out in Box 1.3.

[1]The output gap is actual less potential output, as a percent of potential output. Structural balances are expressed as a percent of potential output. The structural budget balance is the budgetary position that would be observed if the level of actual output coincided with potential output. Changes in the structural budget balance consequently include effects of temporary fiscal measures, the impact of fluctuations in interest rates and debt-service costs, and other noncyclical fluctuations in the budget balance. The computations of structural budget balance are based on IMF staff estimates of potential GDP and revenue and expenditure elasticities (see the October 1993 *World Economic Outlook*, Annex I). Net debt is defined as gross debt less financial assets of the general government, which include assets held by the social security insurance system. Debt data refer to end of year; for the United Kingdom they refer to end of March. Estimates of the output gap and of the structural budget balance are subject to significant margins of uncertainty.

[2]Data before 1990 refer to west Germany. For net debt, the first column refers to 1987–93. Beginning in 1995, the debt and debt-service obligations of the Treuhandanstalt (and of various other agencies) were taken over by general government. This debt is equivalent to 8 percent of GDP, and the associated debt service to ½ to 1 percent of GDP.

Box 1.3. Economic Policy Assumptions Underlying the Projections for Selected Advanced Countries

The short-term fiscal policy assumptions used in the *World Economic Outlook* are based on officially announced budgets, adjusted for differences between national authorities and IMF staff regarding macroeconomic assumptions and projected fiscal outturns. The medium-term fiscal projections incorporate policy measures that are judged likely to be implemented. These projections and policy assumptions are generally based on information available through February 2000. In cases where the IMF staff have insufficient information to assess the authorities' budget intentions and prospects for policy implementation, an unchanged structural primary balance is assumed, unless otherwise indicated. Specific assumptions used in some of the advanced economies follow (see also Tables 14–16 in the Statistical Appendix for data on fiscal and structural balances).

United States. The fiscal projections are based on the Administration's FY 2001 Budget released in February 2000. The projections are adjusted for differences between the IMF staff's and the Administration's macroeconomic assumptions. State and local government fiscal balances are assumed to remain constant as a percent of GDP.

Japan. The projections take account of the FY 1999 supplementary budgets and the FY 2000 initial budget. The ¥18 trillion stimulus package announced in November 1999 includes additional public investment of ¥6.8 trillion (headline figure) through FY 2000, most of which would take place in the first two quarters of CY 2000. Local governments are projected to largely offset their share in the stimulus package with cuts in own-account expenditures elsewhere. A typical supplementary budget of ¥1 trillion, to cover routine budgetary overruns, is included in the calculations for FY 2000. The use of public funds to resolve problems in the banking sector is assumed to decline sharply in 2001, which is the main factor behind the improvement in the fiscal balance in that year.

Germany. The projections assume implementation of the government's fiscal consolidation and tax reform measures for the year 2000 and beyond, which were announced in June 1999 and approved by parliament in December 1999. The projections further incorporate the effects of the recently proposed income tax reform package for 2001–2005. The relevant draft legislation was approved by Cabinet in February 2000.

France. The staff's projections for France are in line with the authorities' official fiscal targets. For 2000, the projections incorporate tax cuts that will be included in the 2000 supplementary budget. For the medium term, the projections are broadly consistent with the government's Stability Program, adjusted for the better-than-expected 1999 outturn.

Italy. The fiscal projections are based on the authorities' estimates for 1999, on the 2000 budget approved in December by parliament, and on the medium-term fiscal plan covering the period 2000–2003 released in May 1999 and updated in September 1999. Official projections are adjusted for differences between the staff's and the authorities' macroeconomic assumptions. The fiscal measures included in the 2000 budget are assumed to be implemented fully, and to have the impact as indicated in the government's fiscal plan (the government's medium-term plan does not envisage, at this stage, additional measures for 2001 and beyond). However, the staff's revenue projections are somewhat more pessimistic than the authorities', as recent estimates on the 1999 outturn seem to indicate lower collection than anticipated at the time the official projections were developed; and the staff's expenditure projections include primary expenditure slippages that have emerged in 1999 but have not been accounted for in the official projections.

United Kingdom. The budget projections are based on the pre-budget report announced by the Chancellor in November 1999, adjusted for a slightly different assessment of potential output. The staff's estimates also include ongoing expenditure savings that the pre-budget report did not take into account for reasons of budgetary prudence. For revenues, the medium-term projections incorporate the effect of tax changes introduced in the current and previous budgets.

Canada. The fiscal outlook prepared by the staff assumes tax and expenditure policies in line with those outlined in the February 2000 budget, adjusted for the staff's economic projections. It is expected that the federal government will continue to target a balanced budget on an ex ante basis, with any unspent portion of the contingency reserve allocated to reducing federal government debt. On this basis, the staff assumes that the federal government budget will be in surplus by Can$3 billion a year (the full amount of the contingency reserve) over the medium-term. The consolidated fiscal position for the provinces is assumed to evolve in line with their stated medium-term targets.

Australia. The fiscal projections through FY 2003 are based on the *Mid-year Economic and Financial Outlook*, which was published by the Australian Treasury in November 1999. For the remainder of the projection period, the staff's projections incorporate announced future policy measures that are judged likely to be implemented.

Netherlands. In line with the authorities' fiscal framework, the staff's projections assume annual real expenditure growth of less than 1 percent for the period 2000–2002. For subsequent years, for which no framework has been established, annual real growth of 1.2 percent is assumed. Nominal expenditure is derived using the staff's projected deflator. The projections for revenues are based on the authorities' framework, including the effects of planned tax cuts in conjunction with a major tax reform package planned for 2001 but reflect the staff's real GDP growth projection, which is significantly higher than was assumed by the authorities. Beyond 2002, the projections assume a further gradual reduction of the revenue ratio of about 0.3 percent of GDP annually.

Portugal. The fiscal projections for 2000 are based on the staff's projections for the forth-

coming budget. The exact components of the budget (revenues, expenditures, etc.) were not known at the time these projections were prepared, but the deficit target of 1.5 percent of GDP had been released. For 2001–2005, a constant structural primary balance is assumed.

Spain. The projections are in line with the authorities' official targets as expressed in their Stability Program. Projections for the outer years are consistent with the trends established in the Stability Program.

Sweden. The fiscal projections are based on the authorities' policies as presented in the 1999 fall budget bill. The authorities have the objective of achieving a fiscal surplus of 2 percent of GDP on average over the cycle. Since this objective has already been achieved, the staff assumes that the surplus will remain at about 2 percent of GDP through 2002, when the economy is projected to reach full employment.

Switzerland. The projections for 2000 are based on official budget plans adjusted for different macroeconomic assumptions. For 2001–2003, projections are in line with the official financial plan that incorporates announced fiscal measures to balance the Confederation's budget by 2001. Beyond 2003, the general government's structural balance is assumed to remain unchanged.

Monetary policy assumptions are based on the established framework for monetary policy in each country. In most cases this implies a nonaccommodative stance over the business cycle, so that official interest rates will firm when economic indicators suggest that inflation will rise above its acceptable rate or range, and ease when indicators suggest that prospective inflation will not exceed the acceptable rate or range, that prospective output growth is below its potential rate, and that the margin of slack in the economy is significant. On this basis, the London interbank offered rate (LIBOR) on six-month U.S. dollar deposits is assumed to average 6.8 percent in 2000 (70 basis points more than projected in the October 1999 *World Economic Outlook*) and 7.1 percent in 2001. The projected path for U.S. dollar short-term interest rates reflects the assumption that the Federal Reserve will raise the target federal funds rate by around 60 basis points over the next six months, which is consistent with market expectations in early April. The rate on six-month Japanese yen deposits is assumed to average 0.2 percent in 2000, with the current accommodative policy stance being maintained, and 0.4 per-

cent in 2001. The rate on six-month euro deposits is assumed to average 4.1 percent in 2000 and 4.9 percent in 2001. The projection for 2000 reflects a further 75 basis point rise in short-term rates by the end of the year, in line with market expectations. Changes in interest rate assumptions compared with the October 1999 *World Economic Outlook* are summarized in Table 1.1.

ity has been driven both by strong external demand—particularly from the United States and from the global pickup in demand for commodities—and by robust domestic sales.

Underpinning the economy's strong performance have been the sound macroeconomic and structural policies pursued through most of the past decade. The general government budget has been in surplus since 1997 and is projected to remain so, contributing to a rapid fall in the debt-to-GDP ratio; inflation is very low, expected to remain well within its target range of 1–3 percent; interest rates are currently below those in the United States; and unemployment has fallen to an 18-year low. Nevertheless, given the current and projected strength of activity, and uncertainty about how much slack remains in the economy and about the outlook for the United States, Canada may need to gradually introduce a moderately tighter monetary stance to contain inflation pressures. Ongoing fiscal restraint is also important, with surpluses used primarily for further debt reduction and for income tax reforms.

Reenergizing the Japanese Recovery

The recovery of the Japanese economy from recession remains halting. After falling through much of 1997 and 1998, real GDP rebounded in the first half of 1999, with private sector demand being buoyed by government spending. In the second half of the year this process went into re-

verse, however, with a decline in government investment being associated with a fall in private domestic spending. The economy contracted in the second half of the year at an annualized rate of almost 4 percent, as private consumption remained depressed by falling real earnings and uncertainty about employment prospects, although private business investment rebounded strongly in the fourth quarter. Recent indicators provide some positive signs, including improvements in corporate profitability and a pickup in industrial production and business confidence (Figure 1.3). Deflationary pressures have eased but have not completely dissipated, as shown by the sharp drop in the GDP deflator in the fourth quarter. Real growth was 0.3 percent in 1999 and is projected at 0.9 percent in 2000, partly reflecting the base effects of the sharp decline in output in the second half of 1999.

The chief macroeconomic goal remains a self-sustaining recovery, which in turn will provide a supportive environment for restructuring. The recent setback in activity underlines the continuing dependence of domestic demand on fiscal stimulus. Despite its depreciation since the beginning of the year, the yen has risen by over 10 percent in nominal effective terms between July 1999 and mid-March 2000, and this rise will tend to reduce external demand. In these circumstances, monetary and fiscal policies need to continue to be directed toward encouraging a lasting recovery in domestic demand. The FY 2000 budget, together with the November 1999 stimulus package, implies an almost unchanged fiscal stance on both a calendar and fiscal year basis although, to avoid a sharp drop in public investment beyond mid-year, a further supplementary budget is likely to be necessary. At the same time, with the government debt ratio continuing to spiral upwards, fiscal policy is rapidly reaching its limits. While current circumstances warrant an expansionary fiscal stance, the authorities need to begin designing reforms that will facilitate medium-term fiscal consolidation as economic conditions improve. High levels of government and private sector debt also underline the potential costs of significant price deflation.

Growing concerns about the fiscal situation, the need to prevent deflation, and the continued strength of the yen despite its recent fall (and its effect on overall monetary conditions) underline the need to keep monetary policy as accommodative as possible. The Bank of Japan is continuing to follow the "zero interest rate" policy, which has been in place since early 1999. With the recovery looking fragile, however, additional steps to ease liquidity seem appropriate to provide further support to activity.

The key to a lasting recovery remains structural reform. Without thorough financial and corporate restructuring, the dismal growth record of the 1990s is likely to continue into the new century. Bank restructuring, continues under the framework established in late 1998, and recently announced bank mergers, together with "Big Bang" reforms, may help catalyze a needed further reduction in capacity and improvement in core profitability. But more needs to be done to address remaining weaknesses, particularly with regard to smaller banks and the life insurance sector, and to avoid delays in the reform process—such as the recent decision to delay by a year the return to partial deposit insurance that had been planned for early 2001. Similarly, while corporate restructuring has begun in earnest, it still has a long way to go to address sizable excess capacity and excess debt burdens. It is particularly important for the authorities to provide a supportive environment for financial and corporate restructuring and to encourage

Figure 1.3. Selected European Countries, Japan, and the United States: Indicators of Consumer and Business Confidence[1]

Consumer confidence strengthened further in the latter part of 1999; business confidence remains strong in the United States, but it appears hesitant in other major industrial countries.

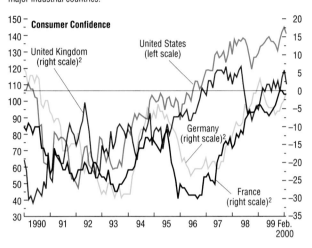

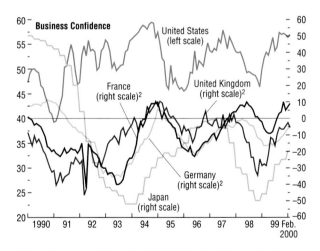

Sources: Consumer confidence—for the United States, the Conference Board; for European countries, the European Commission. Business confidence—for the United States, the U.S. Department of Commerce, Purchasing Managers Composite Diffusion Index; for European countries, the European Commission; for Japan, Bank of Japan.

[1]Indicators are not comparable across countries.

[2]Percent of respondents expecting an improvement in their situation minus percent expecting a deterioration.

labor mobility. Priorities include the early intro-duction of plans for consolidated corporate taxa-tion and easily portable defined contribution pension schemes, and comprehensive reform of the social security system and the Fiscal Investment and Loan Program. Wide-ranging regulatory reform is also needed to increase competition and reduce market distortions, and little progress has been made recently in other important areas such as land use reform, partic-ularly with regard to agricultural land.

Recovery and Divergence in Europe

Recent data suggest that the projected recov-ery in the euro area is on track. Real GDP growth accelerated to 4 percent (annual rate) in the second half of 1999, and the forward mo-mentum seems to have been maintained into 2000. Moreover, buoyant business confidence and survey data point to further gains ahead. Consumer confidence has returned to its earlier peaks, boosted in part by a fall in the area-wide unemployment rate to below 10 percent and ris-ing stock and property prices. The euro contin-ues to be extremely weak—below parity with the U.S. dollar—apparently due in large part to the continuing differences in cyclical conditions be-tween the euro area and the United States and to the attendant capital flows from the former to the latter. Much of this effect could be rapidly reversed if market participants revise their assess-ment of the medium-term prospects for the euro area. Although rising oil prices and a depreci-ated currency have resulted in an increase in an-nual headline inflation to 2.0 percent in February 2000, the core inflation rate remains at a subdued 1.2 percent over the same period. Growth is now forecast to pick up from 2.3 per-cent in 1999 to 3.2 percent in 2000; supportive macroeconomic policies, a highly competitive exchange rate, and buoyant global activity may well produce an even stronger upswing.

Monetary policy appropriately remains accom-modating, particularly taking into account the weak exchange rate. The European Central Bank (ECB) cut short-term interest rates by ½ of a percentage point in April 1999, amid concerns about deflation and hesitant activity in the euro area coming from weak import demand in Asia and international financial tensions. With these concerns having dissipated, in part thanks to this more accommodative stance, the ECB moved on November 4 to fully reverse the earlier cut in rates, and recently nudged short-term rates a ¼ point higher in early February and again in mid-March on fears over inflation. Recently, markets have been factoring in a further rise of ½ of a percentage point over the next six months. Higher energy prices will temporarily affect headline inflation in the short term, but infla-tionary pressures should remain subdued due to the large output gap (projected at about 1¼ per-cent in 2000) and increased competitive pres-sures caused by the deregulation and restructur-ing across the area. While the ECB needs to maintain a strong anti-inflationary stance, and a gradual shift to a less accommodative stance is to be expected as slack is absorbed, inflation prospects remain benign and it is important cur-rently to avoid holding back the ongoing recov-ery through a rapid tightening of policy. Any as-sessment of the need for further interest rate adjustments also needs to take into account the likelihood of a stronger euro as the relative cycli-cal situation improves.

This overall picture continues to mask signifi-cant differences in the momentum of activity across the euro area. Among the three largest economies, growth remains quite strong in France, and recovery is also now under way in Italy and Germany. However, it is not yet clear that the cyclical positions of this group of coun-tries have begun to converge. Moreover, the mo-mentum of activity seen in the larger economies continues to differ markedly from the much more rapid expansion in the smaller euro area countries, mostly in the periphery, in particular Ireland, Spain, Portugal, and Finland. Growth in the periphery has been generally associated with rapid increases in asset prices, particularly for property, raising questions about whether cur-rent price levels are sustainable (see Chapter III). Some increases in asset prices are probably justified by fundamentals, including the lower interest rate premia resulting both from the disappearance of exchange rate risks and from stronger growth prospects associated with the single market and structural reforms. But a significant speculative element may well also be present.

The substantial fiscal retrenchment associated with the Maastricht treaty criteria for entry into the Economic and Monetary Union (EMU) and the low growth experienced by many entrants over the past few years have inevitably led to adjustment fatigue and pent up pressures for further government spending. Available indications are that the relatively unambitious fiscal objectives for 1999 were met, while targets for 2000 imply little change in the structural budget position of the area as a whole despite more ambitious fiscal targets and spending reductions adopted in Germany, Belgium, and Finland. It is particularly unfortunate that fiscal policies are not being more restrained in the dynamic economies on the European periphery as, with monetary policy being made on a euro-wide basis, fiscal policy is the remaining macroeconomic tool to address overheating concerns in individual countries. More generally, while most of the adjustments required to achieve structural balance have been achieved, more ambitious medium-term goals still need to be set. Current plans imply that a small structural deficit will endure through 2003, while macroeconomic prudence would point to a target of structural balance or surplus by that point.

The biggest challenge for fiscal policy, however, is to lower high levels of taxation by reducing excess levels of government expenditures. Compared with the dynamism of the U.S. economy, many economies of the euro area seem hamstrung by their very high tax rates, which are likely to have negative effects on incentives and thereby impede growth. Medium-term fiscal programs would therefore benefit from more ambitious spending restraint to allow tax levels to be reduced significantly from current levels while maintaining fiscal prudence. Policymakers in France, Germany, and Italy have recently an-

nounced plans to cut tax rates, and the German government's recent decision to bring forward to 2001 a personal income tax cut equivalent to ½ percent of GDP and to implement further cuts during 2003–2005 is encouraging. However, additional spending restraint will be needed to avoid generating a pro-cyclical fiscal impulse.

Structural reform of labor and product markets also remains central to enhancing medium-term growth and employment prospects. While progress has been made in some countries, particularly the Netherlands and Ireland (and Denmark, which could join the euro zone in 2002, pending a new referendum to be held on September 28), poor labor market performance continues to impose a heavy burden on the region as a whole. Decisive measures are needed, even in some of the faster reformers, to remove obstacles to job creation, labor mobility, and disincentives for those not employed to enter the workforce, as incremental reforms appear to have had generally little impact. Striking a better balance between the legitimate objective of strong safety nets and the desire to avoid creating poverty traps or disincentives to work is particularly important. On the product and service market side, existing progress with privatization, liberalization, and deregulation needs to be continued through promoting market access in still-sheltered sectors and further reducing government involvement in commercial activities. Given the complementarities between reform efforts, a comprehensive approach to product and labor market reforms is needed. Actions to address existing high profile and difficult issues could boost investor confidence and enhance recovery prospects. Conversely, actions perceived as inconsistent with a move toward more flexible, market-oriented policies have the potential to undermine confidence.

Economic activity in the *United Kingdom* has picked up substantially following the slowdown in late 1998. As in the United States, the expansion that began in 1992 is now the longest on record. GDP increased by 2 percent in 1999, with buoyant private consumption supported by rising asset prices and robust employment growth—on a claimant count basis, the unemployment rate fell to 4 percent in February 2000, the lowest level in 20 years. Economic momentum is expected to increase further in 2000, taking GDP growth up to around 3 percent. The low inflation rate achieved during a period of high resource utilization is testimony to the successful management of monetary policy since the Bank of England gained operational independence in May 1997. The risks to inflation are mainly on the upside, however, given the ongoing strength of private demand and some signs of tightening in the labor market. As a result, some additional firming of macroeconomic policy settings may become necessary. The Bank of England reversed policy direction in September 1999 and by February 2000 had increased the policy rate by 100 basis points to 6 percent as the economy strengthened. Further upward adjustments may be needed to contain inflationary pressures. It is important for fiscal policy not to add to these pressures. In this regard, the recently announced budget for 2000/2001 appears to be regrettably pro-cyclical.

Sweden also grew more rapidly than expected in 1999, with GDP increasing by around 3¾ percent. Growth is projected to pick up further, to about 4 percent in 2000, supported by robust expansion in private domestic demand and exports. Inflation remained subdued in 1999—well below the 2 percent midpoint of the central bank's target zone—and in 2000 is projected to remain comfortably within the zone. However, with excess capacity being rapidly absorbed, monetary policy will need to become less expansionary. The Riksbank raised its policy interest rate by 50 basis points in February and further adjustment may well be needed.

Economic growth in *Denmark* and *Switzerland* slowed to around 1½ percent in 1999 and to under 1 percent in *Norway*, among the lowest rates in western Europe. The slowdowns in Denmark and Norway were in part the intended outcome of policy measures designed to reduce macroeconomic imbalances. In Denmark, declines in both cyclical and structural unemployment and fiscal reforms introduced in 1998 have pro-

duced a budget surplus and assisted in further lowering gross public debt to around 50 percent of GDP at the end of 1999 compared with more than 80 percent at the end of 1993. In Norway, a sharp drop in investment in the energy sector was a major factor behind slower growth while, in Switzerland, lower export growth and a broad-based weakening in domestic demand produced the slowdown. In 2000, growth in Denmark and Switzerland is projected to pick up slowly, reaching 1¾ to 2 percent, supported by stronger exports, firmer household spending in Denmark, and a pickup in investment in Switzerland. A stronger rebound to more than 3 percent growth is projected for Norway, underpinned by a recovery in oil revenues. As the projected strengthening in growth takes hold over the next few years, all three countries will need to maintain firm fiscal policies. This stance would help to contain potential upward pressures on interest rates and the exchange rate over the medium term and, in Norway, would support more rapid growth in non-energy sectors of the economy.

Recovery in Latin America: Emerging But Still Vulnerable

Following a difficult year for many Latin American countries in 1999, a broadening recovery is expected to emerge in the region in 2000 (Figure 1.4). The recovery is generally being led by stronger domestic demand, including a turnaround in investment after a sharp contraction in 1999, and by a pickup in exports supported by earlier exchange rate depreciations in most countries and the general strengthening in the regional and global economy. The contribution of rising export volumes to growth is not expected to be as strong as in the Asian recovery, given the less open character of most Latin American economies and the commodity concentration of exports. Nevertheless, increases in commodity prices—including rebounds over the past year in the prices of oil and metals, and projected improvements in food and beverage prices—are playing an important role in the recovery, both in supporting domestic demand and in easing external financing conditions.

Access to international finance remains the principal vulnerability of the region (see Chapter II). As a result, the costs and volume of global capital flows—including the extent of further adjustment required in U.S. interest rates—could have an important bearing on the strength and resilience of the regional recovery. The combined current account deficit of the four largest countries in Latin America (Brazil, Mexico, Argentina, and Colombia) is projected to be $55 billion in 2000, compared with a combined surplus of $36 billion in the four Asian economies most directly affected by the 1997 crisis.[2] When debt repayment and amortization are also considered, the gross external financing requirement of these Latin American countries is projected to be around $160 billion in 2000; in several countries, including Argentina and Brazil, the financing requirement is equivalent to over 90 percent of merchandise exports.

Most governments in Latin America have appropriately focused on reducing their fiscal deficits as the key measure needed to build investor confidence and contain the risks associated with the high external financing requirements. Budget plans for 2000 suggest that substantial further progress will be made in this regard in most countries, including the largest four. In addition to tight expenditure controls and revenue measures designed to achieve rapid deficit reductions, governments are taking important steps to ensure durable improvements in public finances through reforms to the structure of spending and taxes and through the strengthening of public sector governance. Firm monetary policies have been maintained in most

Figure 1.4. Selected Latin American and Asian Economies: Real GDP Growth[1]
(Annual percent change)

The crisis-hit Asian economies have made strong V-shaped recoveries from the recessions of 1998, and ongoing recoveries are also projected for Latin America after milder-than-expected downturns.

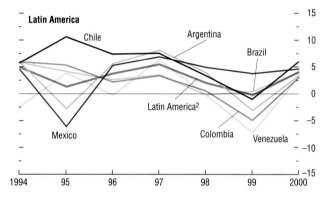

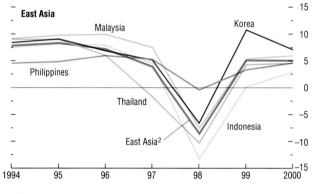

[1]Data for 2000 reflect IMF staff projections.
[2]Weighted average of the countries shown in the figure.

[2]The four Latin American countries are ordered according to GDP-purchasing power parity weights. The Asian economies included in this comparison are Indonesia, Korea, Malaysia, and Thailand. For all emerging market economies in the Western Hemisphere, the current account deficit in 2000 is projected to be $57 billion, while the overall current account surplus is projected to be over $80 billion in the newly industrialized and developing countries in Asia.

countries in the region, another significant departure from the past. Reflecting this, exchange rates have stabilized in several economies following sharp depreciations in early 1999, with some currencies again appreciating, and inflation is generally projected to decline in 2000. The maintenance of cautious macroeconomic policies, together with the improvements projected in external earnings, should contribute to a steady improvement in investor sentiment toward Latin America, helping to lower interest rates and promoting further recovery in domestic economic confidence.

At the same time, economic developments and prospects are quite diverse across individual countries and appear particularly fragile in several cases. Of most concern, *Colombia, Ecuador,* and *Venezuela* experienced particularly severe output contractions in 1999—from 5 to more than 7 percent (Table 1.5). The downturn in Colombia appears to have bottomed out in the second half of the year, with tentative signs of recovery emerging. A broader-based increase in output of 3 percent is projected for 2000 but, to be sustained, growth will need to be supported by measures to strengthen the fragile banking system, combined with further fiscal restraint and progress with privatization. In Venezuela, hard-hit by devastating floods and mudslides in December 1999, the rebound in international oil prices has been particularly significant in boosting export earnings and funding a projected increase in public spending (largely because of reconstruction costs). GDP is expected to rise by 3 percent this year, supported by rising domestic demand, and the fiscal deficit is projected to decline. However, while inflation is coming down, it remains one of the highest rates in the region. Overall, the sustainability of recent economic trends and Venezuela's vulnerability to a sharp decline in energy prices are of concern. The economic situation in Ecuador deteriorated further in early 2000, and little or no growth is now projected for this year. A collapse in the exchange rate and rapid monetary growth have fueled a rapid increase in inflation, while severe difficulties in the financial sector and with

foreign debt servicing have also contributed to uncertainties about the future course of economic policies. Priority needs to be given to restoring monetary and fiscal discipline, so that the deep-seated financial and structural problems in the economy can be tackled under more stable economic conditions. For the policy of official dollarization of the economy (announced in January 2000) to succeed, it will need to be accompanied by substantial fiscal and structural adjustment in the economy (Box 1.4).

Brazil has recovered more rapidly than expected from the economic crisis of early 1999. Its economy is estimated to have grown by ½ of a percent in 1999, despite projections at the onset of the crisis of a significant output decline, and is projected to grow by 4 percent in 2000. Leading this recovery have been increases in agricultural output, industrial production (including higher import substitution), and exports—the latter two areas being supported by the lower exchange rate and improving regional prospects. Also contributing to improved macroeconomic stability and confidence has been the modest impact of the exchange rate depreciation on inflation, with consumer price inflation under 9 percent at the end of 1999 and projected to fall again in 2000. The terms of trade are expected to rise in 2000 following their deterioration in 1999. This, along with higher export volumes, is projected to lead to a trade surplus and a lower current account deficit, which should be fully covered by foreign direct investment inflows. As discussed in Chapter II, significant progress has been made in tackling the fiscal problems that were at the root of the crisis, with the authorities pursuing a range of measures directed at putting the medium-term fiscal position on a sound footing. These measures include reforms to public administration and to the public sector pension scheme, and a wide-ranging privatization program. Effective implementation of these and other reforms, together with successful application of the new inflation targeting framework, should improve Brazil's access to international finance and hence support the recovery through lower interest rates.

Table 1.5. Selected Developing Countries: Real GDP and Consumer Prices
(Annual percent change)

	Real GDP				Consumer Prices[1]			
	1998	1999	2000	2001	1998	1999	2000	2001
Developing countries	**3.2**	**3.8**	**5.4**	**5.3**	**10.1**	**6.5**	**5.7**	**4.7**
Median	3.6	3.5	4.3	4.5	5.7	4.0	4.0	3.6
Africa	**3.1**	**2.3**	**4.4**	**4.5**	**9.2**	**11.0**	**9.6**	**6.1**
Algeria	5.1	3.4	4.2	4.2	5.8	2.6	4.0	3.0
Cameroon	5.0	4.4	4.2	5.3	2.8	0.0	2.0	2.0
Côte d'Ivoire	4.5	4.3	4.8	5.0	4.5	0.7	2.5	2.5
Ghana	4.6	5.5	6.0	6.0	19.3	12.4	11.4	5.7
Kenya	2.1	1.8	2.3	3.3	6.6	3.5	5.0	4.5
Morocco	6.3	0.2	5.2	3.3	2.9	0.8	3.0	2.5
Nigeria	1.9	1.1	3.9	4.5	10.0	6.6	5.8	7.3
South Africa	0.6	1.2	3.8	4.0	6.9	5.2	4.7	5.9
Sudan	5.0	6.0	6.5	5.5	17.1	16.0	12.0	7.5
Tanzania	3.3	5.3	5.2	5.6	12.6	7.9	5.7	4.5
Tunisia	5.0	6.5	6.0	6.0	3.1	3.1	3.0	3.0
Uganda	5.4	7.8	7.0	7.0	5.8	−0.2	5.0	5.0
PRGF countries[2]	5.0	5.2	5.4	5.7	7.4	4.0	4.8	3.7
CFA countries	4.7	3.3	4.6	4.9	3.0	0.2	2.3	2.4
Asia	**3.8**	**6.0**	**6.2**	**5.9**	**7.6**	**2.5**	**2.6**	**3.0**
Bangladesh	4.7	4.3	4.5	4.5	8.0	7.2	5.8	6.3
China	7.8	7.1	7.0	6.5	−0.8	−1.4	1.0	1.4
India	4.7	6.8	6.3	6.1	13.2	5.0	4.6	5.3
Indonesia	−13.2	0.2	3.0	3.5	58.4	20.5	3.5	4.8
Malaysia	−7.5	5.4	6.0	5.8	5.3	2.7	2.5	3.2
Pakistan	3.3	3.1	4.0	4.5	7.8	5.7	4.0	5.0
Philippines	−0.5	3.2	4.5	4.5	9.7	6.7	5.5	5.0
Thailand	−10.4	4.2	4.5	5.0	8.1	0.3	3.0	3.0
Vietnam	3.5	3.5	4.5	5.5	7.7	7.6	6.0	4.5
Middle East and Europe	**2.7**	**0.7**	**4.6**	**4.0**	**26.0**	**20.3**	**16.2**	**9.4**
Egypt	5.3	6.0	5.6	5.0	4.7	3.8	4.0	4.0
Iran, Islamic Republic of	1.9	2.6	5.0	5.0	22.0	15.0	10.0	8.0
Jordan	2.2	2.0	2.5	3.5	4.5	1.9	2.8	2.4
Kuwait	2.0	−2.4	0.8	2.0	0.5	1.9	1.5	1.8
Saudi Arabia	1.6	−2.3	2.2	2.0	−0.2	−1.2	1.1	1.9
Turkey	3.1	−4.3	4.5	4.8	84.6	64.9	46.5	17.0
Western Hemisphere	**2.1**	**0.1**	**4.0**	**4.7**	**9.8**	**8.8**	**7.7**	**6.4**
Argentina	3.9	−3.1	3.4	3.7	0.9	−1.2	0.6	0.8
Brazil	−0.1	0.5	4.0	4.5	3.2	4.9	7.0	5.0
Chile	3.4	−1.0	6.0	6.5	5.1	3.3	2.9	3.2
Colombia	0.4	−5.0	3.0	4.8	18.7	10.9	9.0	8.7
Dominican Republic	7.3	8.3	6.5	6.0	4.8	6.5	4.2	3.5
Ecuador	0.4	−7.0	1.5	4.0	36.1	55.1	36.2	17.6
Guatemala	5.2	3.3	3.0	3.0	6.6	5.3	9.3	9.2
Mexico	4.8	3.7	4.5	5.3	15.9	16.6	10.1	9.0
Peru	0.3	3.5	4.0	6.0	7.3	3.5	3.9	3.5
Uruguay	4.5	−2.5	2.0	4.0	10.8	5.7	4.4	3.0
Venezuela	−0.1	−7.2	3.2	3.1	35.8	23.6	18.6	16.3

[1]In accordance with standard practice in the *World Economic Outlook*, movements in consumer prices are indicated as annual averages rather than as December/December changes as is the practice in some countries.

[2]African countries that had arrangements, as of the end of 1999, under the International Monetary Fund's Poverty Reduction and Growth Facility (formerly the Enhanced Structural Adjustment Facility, or ESAF).

Economic activity in *Mexico* has held up relatively well throughout the regional economic slowdown, with real GDP increasing by an estimated 3½ percent in 1999 and projected to rise by 4½ percent in 2000. Supported by the ongoing strength of the U.S. economy, export volumes have grown rapidly—especially non-oil exports. With the terms of trade also improving,

Box 1.4. The Pros and Cons of Dollarization

Dollarization—the adoption of the U.S. dollar (or other foreign currency) as the domestic legal tender—is the latest alternative to emerge in the search for stable and credible monetary and exchange rate regimes. In January 2000, Ecuador announced the intention to adopt the U.S. dollar as the domestic legal currency, maintaining only a minor role for the sucre which will circulate in denominations smaller than one U.S. dollar, and this policy is now being implemented. A year before, dollarization was being discussed in Argentina, where a currency board already has tied the peso to the U.S. dollar on a one-to-one exchange rate since 1991. One spur for this recent interest in dollarization has been the wave of speculative attacks against even the hardest pegs, such as Argentina's currency board. Another is the adoption of a common currency by 11 countries in the European Economic and Monetary Union. Moreover, there is some empirical work suggesting that the use of a common currency by itself has a large effect in stimulating trade and economic integration, especially by reducing transaction costs and exchange rate uncertainty.

The economic arguments presented for adopting a common currency have shifted over time. The traditional analysis found benefits of using a common currency for countries that, by virtue of sharing similar economic structures, formed an "optimal currency area" (OCA). Most of the current analysis, in contrast, focuses on financial stability and external creditworthiness. Especially for emerging economies, benefits in these areas may dwarf any disadvantages resulting from not fulfilling the OCA conditions.

What are the pros and cons of dollarization? It is useful to compare the merits of dollarization to those of its nearest "competitor"—the currency board. This permits an analysis of the implications of giving up the domestic currency, as opposed to the more general implications of the choice of floating versus fixing the exchange rate.[1]

---

[1]See Andrew Berg and Eduardo Borensztein, "The Pros and Cons of Full Dollarization," IMF Working Paper 00/50 (Washington: International Monetary Fund, 2000).

Risk premiums. An immediate benefit from the elimination of the risk of devaluation would be a reduction of country risk premiums and thus lower interest rates, which would result in a lower cost of servicing the public debt and also in higher investment and economic growth. While the part of the interest premiums attributable to devaluation risk would disappear with dollarization (as devaluations are no longer possible), the part attributable to sovereign risk would not. The key question, then, is what effect dollarization would have on the overall cost of dollar-denominated borrowing.

The presence of devaluation risk might increase default risk for several reasons. First, governments attempting to avoid a currency crisis may impose currency controls that force a suspension of payments on foreign debt. Second, default risks could rise with a devaluation owing to the higher cost of servicing dollar-denominated debt. And third, a devaluation could cause heavy losses in the financial sector, and governments may end up bearing most of the cost. Not all default risks arise from the risk of currency crises, however. Sovereign defaults may result from an unsustainable fiscal position or political turmoil, and dollarization cannot prevent this sort of crisis. Although data show that sovereign risk and devaluation risk move together, this does not establish a causal link from devaluation risk to sovereign risk (or vice versa). For example, a general "flight to quality" (unrelated to fears of devaluation) would raise both the measured risk of default and the risk of devaluation. Evidence from Panama, a dollarized economy since 1904, suggests that, indeed, the observed comovements in sovereign risk and devaluation risk reflect common factors. That is, the absence of currency risk in Panama does not isolate that country's sovereign spread from swings in international market sentiment (see figure).

Stability and integration. Speculative attacks and currency crises are costly not only because their possible emergence widens risk premiums but also because they have dire consequences for the domestic economy when they occur. Of

course, dollarization would not completely eliminate the risk of external crises; indeed, Panama
has had several crises in recent decades.
Nevertheless, dollarization holds the promise of
at least reducing the frequency and scale of
crises and the extent of contagion. And, in addition to promoting financial integration, dollarization may contribute to trade integration with
the United States to an extent that would not be
likely otherwise.

Seigniorage. A country adopting a foreign currency as the legal tender would lose the income
from seigniorage. First, the country would have
to purchase the stock of domestic currency held
by the public (and banks) and pay them with
dollars from its international reserves or borrowed funds. Second, the country would give up
future seigniorage earnings stemming from the
flow of new currency printed every year to sat-
isfy the increase in the demand for money.
These increases are likely to become smaller
over time, however, as financial development results in a reduced need for currency to effect
transactions.

The costs of losing seigniorage can be significant. In Argentina, for example, domestic currency in circulation is equivalent to roughly $15
billion (5 percent of GDP), and the annual increase in currency demand has averaged
roughly $1 billion (0.3 percent of GDP) in re-
cent years. The lost seigniorage would accrue to
the United States. For this reason, it has been
suggested that the United States share this
seigniorage with dollarizing countries according
to some agreed-upon formula (seigniorage-shar-
ing arrangements exist in the euro and the
South African rand areas).

Exit option. Countries with flexible exchange
rate regimes can adjust to severe overvaluation
by allowing the currency to depreciate. With
dollarization or fixed rates, the real devaluation
must be achieved through a *fall* in nominal
wages and prices (or at least slower increases in
these compared with their trading partners).
Experience has shown that these declines are often achieved only at the cost of economic recessions, because resistance to nominal wage and

Sovereign Bond Spread[1]
(Percentage points)

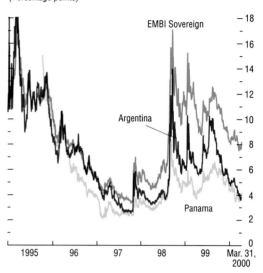

Sources: Bloomberg Financial Markets, LP; and IMF staff calculations.
[1]J.P. Morgan's Emerging Market Bond Index (EMBI) spread relative to U.S.
zero-coupon yield curve, and secondary market yield spreads on U.S. dollar-
denominated Eurobonds.

price reductions can be strong. Countries with
currency boards have already eliminated much
of their choice with regard to the exchange rate.
But what distinguishes such countries from dollarized economies is that, in extreme cases, the
former could in principle devalue. In fact, dollarization's key distinguishing feature is that it
would be permanent, or nearly so. It would presumably be much more difficult to reverse dollarization than to modify or abandon a currency
board arrangement. Reversing dollarization implies introducing a new national currency to dis-
place a strong and convertible foreign currency,
and acceptance of the new currency would likely
not be immediate.

Departures from the gold standard in the interwar years and the devaluation of the CFA
franc in 1994 suggest that an exit option may indeed be valuable in the presence of extreme
shocks. During the Great Depression, countries
abandoned the fixed exchange regime of the

Box 1.4 *(concluded)*

time—the gold standard. Argentina suspended convertibility in 1929 and followed an active policy to sterilize the monetary impact of capital outflows, which contributed to the relatively minor impact of the Depression on Argentina. More recently, when countries of the CFA franc zone in west and central Africa faced a prolonged worsening of their terms of trade and a steep rise in their labor costs, combined with a nominal appreciation of the French franc against the U.S. dollar, they decided to depart from their firm-peg regime, which had lasted since 1948, and devalue the CFA franc in 1994. This exchange rate realignment led to a significant economic turnaround during 1994–97 and little inflation pass-through.

Despite those experiences, many countries might not benefit from an exit option even when the currency is overvalued. Where policymakers have little credibility, or where the dollar is in practice already the unit of account, a nominal devaluation may rapidly lead to an inflation that would undo the devaluation's positive effects. As observed in a variety of recent currency crises, large depreciations in a context of weak banking systems and large foreign exchange exposure in the private sector damage the financial health of banks and businesses, sharply disrupting economic activity. This implies that devaluation may be so costly a policy option in some cases that moving to full dollarization would not entail the loss of an important policy tool.

Lender of last resort and dollarization. As lenders of last resort, central banks stand ready to provide liquidity to the banking system in the event of a systemic bank run. The central bank does this essentially by using its ability to create liquidity—something that it would not have in a dollarized system. Currency boards face a similar constraint, because they can create base money only to the extent that they accumulate reserves. Currency board arrangements can, however, retain some flexibility to create money that is not fully backed by reserves, so as to be able to address banking crises. During the 1995 "tequila" crisis, the central bank of Argentina was able to partially accommodate the run on domestic deposits by temporarily reducing the reserve coverage of the monetary base. Following some episodes of liquidity crunch in 1997, the Hong Kong Monetary Authority also introduced a discount window to provide short-term liquidity to banks.

In any case, the importance of a curtailment of the lender-of-last-resort function should not be exaggerated because the cost of a financial crisis is ultimately a fiscal problem that can be addressed by other means. Dollarization may, moreover, make a bank run less likely. Indeed, without significant currency mismatches in the banks' positions, depositors may have more confidence in the domestic banking system. If large foreign banks play a dominant role in the banking system, which presumably would be encouraged by dollarization, this would also reduce the danger of a weakened lender of last resort.

It is impossible to make a blanket generalization about the net benefits of full dollarization. But the analysis can at least shed some light on which countries are likely to benefit most. A traditional group of candidates is formed by countries that are highly integrated with the United States (or the European Union for "euroization") in trade and financial relations (and are candidates to form what the economics literature calls an optimal currency area). Yet most countries in Latin America are quite different from the United States in their economic structure and would probably not benefit greatly from dollarization from this perspective, unless it took place in the context of deep market integration (in European Union style). The most relevant case deserving consideration is that of a different group: emerging market economies exposed to volatile capital flows but not necessarily close, in an economic sense, to the United States. For this group, the more the U.S. dollar is already used in their domestic goods and financial markets, the smaller the advantage of keeping a national currency. For an economy that is already extremely "dollarized" in this sense, seigniorage revenues would be small (and the cost of purchasing the remaining stock of domestic currency also would be small), the exposures of banks and businesses would make devaluation financially risky, and the exchange rate would not serve as a policy instrument because prices would be "sticky" in dollar terms. In such cases, dollarization might offer more benefits than costs.

The balance of costs and benefits also depends on how far along a country is in "supportive" structural reforms. In principle, it would be desirable to adopt dollarization as the result of a well-planned process and after having achieved fiscal consolidation, more flexible labor markets, and a stronger financial sector. In practice, countries may adopt dollarization as a response to crisis, as with Ecuador, without time to prepare or fulfill prerequisites. In such cases, dollarization may "raise the stakes" and thus force the political system to undertake necessary reforms, but it may also make failure to enact those reforms even more painful.

the current account deficit declined to under 3 percent of GDP in 1999, largely financed by inflows of foreign direct investment. Private investment also grew strongly in 1999, and later in the year there were signs of a broader-based pickup in domestic spending. Indeed, a range of indicators point to a general improvement in financing conditions and economic confidence. For example, domestic interest rates have declined significantly; equity prices almost doubled in U.S. dollar terms in the year to December; and the currency has appreciated by 6 percent against the dollar. These improvements have been underpinned by, and need to receive continued support from, firm macroeconomic policies (see Chapter II). There is also scope for additional reforms to improve the medium-term fiscal outlook, such as measures to broaden the tax base and improve the targeting of social spending. With the banking system still fragile, policy emphasis should be on implementing a tighter regulatory and legal framework and providing sufficient incentives to strengthen the system's financial fundamentals and foster conservative banking practices.

Prospects for economic recovery in *Argentina* have improved, with several of the influences that led to the 3 percent contraction in GDP in 1999 weakening or turning around. The stronger outlook projected for Brazil should support a pickup in export growth; reductions in regional financial market tensions should also contribute to lower interest rates and sup-port investment (which fell by 9 percent in 1999); and the terms of trade are expected to begin to recover as a result of higher international food and oil prices. Overall, GDP is projected to increase by 3½ percent in 2000, with inflation remaining very low and unemployment declining modestly. Progress is needed in two key policy areas to support these improving economic prospects. First, following a larger than expected expansion in the public sector deficit in 1999, rapid progress is needed with fiscal consolidation. Tax and spending reforms introduced by the new government have been an important step forward in this regard. Second, implementation of a range of labor market reforms is also needed, directed in particular at lowering non-wage costs, increasing the flexibility of bargaining and contracting arrangements, and improving external competitiveness.

Another encouraging development is that *Chile* and *Peru* appear poised to attain relatively healthy growth of 6 and 4 percent, respectively, in 2000, supported by last year's exchange rate depreciations, lower interest rates, and a pickup in commodity prices (e.g., copper prices in the case of Chile). Underpinning the improved outlook for both countries are their relatively strong fiscal positions, moderate public debt, and low inflation. Holding on to these strengths would provide key support for a resumption of sustained growth and, in Peru, for the required strengthening of the banking sector.

Recovery in Asia-Pacific: The Momentum Increases

The momentum of economic recovery in Asia increased significantly in 1999, with growth exceeding—by a wide margin in some countries—earlier expectations. Among the crisis-hit countries, the pickup has been strongest in *Korea*, where GDP increased by a remarkable 10½ percent in 1999, and in *Malaysia* where growth was 5½ percent. *Thailand* also grew solidly by 4¼ percent in 1999, and even in *Indonesia*—the hardest hit economy in the region—real activity was broadly stable for the year as a whole, a notable turnaround from the 13 percent contraction in 1998 and the Consensus Forecast at the beginning of 1999 of a further 3 to 4 percent decline in output. This recovery is projected to continue in 2000 and to become more evenly balanced across most of the advanced and developing countries of the region. Growth in Korea is expected to moderate somewhat to around 7 percent, roughly the same as in *Hong Kong SAR*, Malaysia, *Singapore*, and *Taiwan Province of China*, while the economies of Indonesia, the *Philippines*, and Thailand are projected to strengthen by 3 to 5 percent.

The driving forces of recovery have been generally similar among the crisis-affected economies. With initial support provided by fiscal stimulus and a rebuilding of inventories, the upturn has been driven more recently by a faster-than-expected improvement in the volume and value of exports. This has been supported by real devaluations compared with pre-crisis values and export market growth, the latter reflecting continued strength in the United States along with recoveries in Europe and, to a lesser degree, in Japan. A significant sectoral trend has been the rebound in the electronics industry—an important sector for the Philippines, Singapore, and Taiwan Province of China, and also of growing significance in Malaysia and Thailand. In response to this stronger external performance, the severe import compression and destocking that followed the financial crisis came to an end in 1999. For example, import

volumes last year surged upwards by around 30 percent in Korea and over 25 percent in Thailand; similarly, a strong pickup in import growth is projected for Indonesia in 2000 as the economy gathers strength.

As reflected in the import surge, final domestic demand has also played an important role in the recovery. Public consumption and investment continued to support economic activity in all the crisis-affected economies in 1999, and this is projected to continue in 2000. Private consumption has also increased, particularly in the countries more advanced in recovery, as incomes and wealth pick up and household confidence returns. The contribution from private fixed investment to recent and projected growth has been less buoyant, as might be expected given the over-investment that preceded the recent economic crisis and subsequent excess capacity. Nevertheless, investment has picked up more rapidly than expected in Korea as business activity increases and profitability improves. Influenced by the same trends, a steady increase in investment is also expected in other countries in the region.

Fiscal policy has, as noted, provided important support for the recovery in Asia, and should continue to do so where necessary until growth is firmly established. As recoveries strengthen, however, some tightening of fiscal and monetary policies will clearly be required to reduce risks of overheating. These pressures may be apparent relatively soon in Korea, where the process of fiscal consolidation has begun in 2000, but may be some distance away in Thailand and other regional economies where output gaps still appear to be large. When firmer policies do become necessary, relatively rapid progress with fiscal consolidation would help to reverse unfavorable public debt dynamics and reduce the extent of adjustment required in interest rates. Low rates of consumer inflation—under 3 percent in most of the crisis-hit economies in 1999—have helped to hold down interest rates, and hence have lowered debt servicing costs arising from the extensive bank recapitalization and corporate debt rescheduling. But, with inflation expected to pick up over the medium term as spare capacity is absorbed, interest rate pressures may raise substantially the financial costs of restructuring, especially in Indonesia and Thailand, where short-term or floating-rate debt has been widely used for this purpose.

The strong export-led expansions and resulting current account surpluses in Asia have allowed the crisis-hit countries to rebuild official foreign exchange reserves that were depleted during the crisis period. In Korea, for example, usable gross reserves have increased from $9 billion at the end of 1997 to $83 billion at the end of March 2000. With economic recovery now well under way, there is scope for further appreciation of some regional currencies—a trend that would help to moderate risks of overheating and consequent inflation pressures.

While major steps have been taken regarding financial and corporate sector restructuring, progress remains mixed and much remains to be done (see Chapter II). In Korea, for example, the restructuring of Daewoo has provided an important signal of the authorities' resolve to pursue far-reaching changes in traditional business arrangements, and the other large *chaebol* (industrial conglomerates) have made substantial progress in reducing their debt–equity ratios. However, further efforts are needed to strengthen management and operations among all the *chaebol*. More rapid progress with bank and corporate restructuring is needed in Thailand, supported by improved bankruptcy and foreclosure procedures. Indonesia faces the most severe challenges regarding economic restructuring, and full implementation of the new government's ambitious and wide-ranging program of reforms is needed. Policy priorities are to complete the bank recapitalization program and to step up the recovery and restructuring of corporate debt, including strengthening the state institutions involved in the reform process.

Turning to the largest economy in developing Asia, *China* grew by 7 percent in 1999. Economic activity has been supported by a sharp pickup in exports, reflecting in part the rebound in the regional economy, and by an additional fiscal stim-

ulus package that took effect late in the year. These influences helped to offset continued weakness in private domestic demand during 1999 and, together with some recovery of private investment spending, are expected to underpin growth of around 7 percent again in 2000. While consumer prices fell by a further 1½ percent in 1999 as a whole, deflation pressures appeared to be abating in the second half of the year and prices may increase marginally in 2000. The authorities' emphasis on interest rate liberalization and broader financial market reforms is appropriate, given that there is limited scope for further interest rate reductions to support activity.

Recent developments suggest a decline in the external vulnerability of China during 1999. The real effective exchange rate has continued to depreciate from its peak reached in early 1998 as a result of domestic price deflation and recoveries in other regional currencies, reducing short-term pressures for a nominal depreciation and supporting export growth. And net capital inflows have resumed (mainly reflecting a reduction in outflows), offsetting a decline in the current account surplus and contributing to a further increase in official reserves to almost $160 billion.

China's prospective membership in the World Trade Organization is likely to add momentum to the structural reform process. Anti-smuggling efforts in 1999 produced a notable rise in recorded imports, as well as a welcome boost to customs revenues. Nevertheless, given China's emerging medium-term fiscal sustainability problems, growth cannot be sustained through fiscal stimulus indefinitely. Rather, continued financial and operational restructuring of state-owned enterprises needs to be pursued vigorously through, among other moves, active participation of the new asset management companies in the reorganization of businesses in which they have become owners or creditors. Closely related to this and the associated financial market reforms, the scope for private sector initiative and enterprise needs to expand, and the authorities' reiteration in January 2000 of their intention to strengthen the role of the private sector is encouraging.

Growth in *India* accelerated to an estimated 6¾ percent in 1999, as a pickup in industrial production that began during 1999 helped offset the slowdown of agricultural output in mid-year, and growth is projected to continue at over 6 percent in 2000. Wholesale price inflation has fallen sharply with easier agricultural supply conditions, but is projected to rebound to around 5½ percent in 2000. Exports also have strengthened, and continued robust export growth over the medium term is expected to help contain the current account deficit to under 2 percent of GDP.

However, even stronger economic growth is needed over the longer run for meaningful progress to be made in addressing India's poverty problem, and sustaining current growth rates may be difficult without significant policy action (see Chapter IV, Box 4.2). The foremost challenge is to make prompt and credible progress in reducing the fiscal deficit. With budgetary slippages having occurred at both central and state government levels, the consolidated public sector deficit is now expected to have risen to around 11 percent of GDP in the 1999/2000 fiscal year, over 2 percentage points higher than initially budgeted. India's large fiscal imbalances have pushed public debt up to 80 percent of GDP, are crowding out private investment, and are constraining the scope for the monetary authorities to ease interest rates—which are high in real terms—without jeopardizing recent gains on the inflation front. Although the central government budget for 2000/2001 contains some commendable structural measures, it envisages disappointingly modest fiscal adjustment in the coming year, and fiscal sustainability remains a serious concern. Moreover, while the new government has signaled its intention to reestablish the momentum of structural reforms, important challenges still need to be addressed, including further deregulation and privatization, measures to increase labor market flexibility, and reform of the agricultural sector.

Despite political instability, economic growth in *Pakistan* reached over 3 percent in 1999, supported by good cotton and wheat crops and a pickup in manufacturing output. Also contributing to recent improvements in macroeconomic performance and confidence have been a fall in inflation, a rebound of exports to east Asia, a much greater degree of exchange rate stability following the rapid depreciation in previous years, and the substantial progress made in restructuring Pakistan's foreign debt. Implementation of a range of reforms would consolidate and extend recent gains. These include fiscal measures designed to broaden the tax base and improve the targeting of social expenditures on poverty alleviation; increased private sector participation in the energy sector, along with financial restructuring and privatization among other public enterprises and banks; and further price deregulation in the energy and agricultural sectors. A similar reform agenda needs to be pursued vigorously in *Bangladesh* to sustain higher growth than the 4 to 6 percent achieved during most of the 1990s. As in India and Pakistan, a stronger performance is necessary if substantial inroads are to be made on poverty.

Growth in *Australia* is projected to slow slightly to just under 4 percent in 2000, and *New Zealand*, gaining further strength after the brief downturn in 1998, is also expected to grow at around this rate. An important contribution to recent and projected growth is coming from a continuing recovery of export volumes and some commodity prices as markets strengthen following the economic crisis in east Asia. The rather strong pickup expected in the "headline" inflation rate in Australia, to over 4 percent, is associated in part with the introduction of the new goods and services tax (GST); excluding GST, inflation is projected to rise to around 2½ percent, as in New Zealand, compared with 1½ percent in each case in 1999. Both countries continue to experience high current account deficits that, while projected to decline from their 1999 levels, are expected to be 5 percent of GDP in Australia and 6¼ percent in New Zealand in 2000 as a whole. As discussed in the October 1999 *World Economic Outlook*, the risks surrounding these imbalances are mitigated by the sources and structure of capital inflows and

Table 1.6. Countries in Transition: Real GDP and Consumer Prices
(Annual percent change)

	Real GDP				Consumer Prices			
	1998	1999	2000	2001	1998	1999	2000	2001
Countries in transition	**–0.7**	**2.4**	**2.6**	**3.0**	**22**	**44**	**20**	**14**
Median	3.7	2.7	4.0	4.2	10	8	8	5
Central and eastern Europe	**1.8**	**1.4**	**3.0**	**4.2**	**19**	**21**	**19**	**12**
Excluding Belarus and Ukraine	2.0	1.5	3.6	4.6	17	11	11	7
Albania	8.0	8.0	8.0	8.0	21	—	3	2
Belarus	8.3	3.0	—	2.0	73	294	250	148
Bosnia and Herzegovina	18.0	8.0	14.0	14.0	10	5	3	3
Bulgaria	3.5	2.5	4.0	4.5	22	—	7	3
Croatia	2.3	–2.0	2.5	3.5	6	4	3	3
Czech Republic	–2.3	–0.5	1.6	2.7	11	2	4	5
Estonia	4.0	–1.3	4.0	6.0	8	3	5	3
Hungary	4.9	4.1	4.5	4.6	14	10	8	5
Latvia	3.6	0.8	4.0	6.0	5	3	3	3
Lithuania	5.1	–3.3	2.1	4.0	5	1	2	2
Macedonia, former Yugoslav Rep. of	2.9	2.5	6.0	5.0	–1	—	3	2
Moldova	–8.6	–5.0	2.0	4.0	8	39	29	10
Poland	4.8	4.1	5.2	5.5	12	7	8	6
Romania	–5.4	–3.9	1.3	4.0	59	46	39	20
Slovak Republic	4.4	1.0	2.0	3.9	7	11	10	6
Slovenia	3.9	3.8	4.0	4.6	8	6	6	4
Ukraine	–1.7	–0.4	0.5	3.0	11	23	23	10
Russia	**–4.5**	**3.2**	**1.5**	**1.4**	**28**	**86**	**20**	**16**
Transcaucasus and central Asia	**2.3**	**4.4**	**4.9**	**3.7**	**13**	**15**	**16**	**18**
Armenia	7.2	4.0	6.0	6.0	9	1	3	3
Azerbaijan	10.0	7.4	4.6	7.9	–1	–9	2	3
Georgia	2.9	3.0	4.0	5.0	4	19	8	5
Kazakhstan	–2.5	1.7	3.0	3.5	7	8	12	9
Kyrgyz Republic	2.3	2.2	2.4	3.2	12	37	28	12
Mongolia	3.5	3.5	4.2	4.5	9	8	6	4
Tajikistan	5.3	3.7	5.0	6.5	43	28	15	7
Turkmenistan	5.0	16.0	18.9	2.2	17	23	24	55
Uzbekistan	4.4	4.1	3.0	2.0	29	29	30	39

by each country's highly credible macroeconomic policies. Nevertheless, to reduce longer-term vulnerabilities, policies need to be directed at maintaining public sector surpluses and fostering higher levels of private saving.

Russia and the Commonwealth of Independent States (CIS): Growth, But Uncertain Prospects for Sustained Recovery

Following widespread weakening in the wake of the Russian crisis, growth in the transition economies generally improved in 1999 and is expected to strengthen further in 2000 (Table 1.6).

But economic performance and prospects vary widely among these countries, depending crucially on the extent of stabilization and restructuring. Overall, reform efforts in Russia and most other countries of the former Soviet Union continue to lag significantly behind those in the better-performing transition economies that have been accepted for the European Union (EU) accession process. The divergence in outcomes between these two groups appears likely to widen in the period ahead.

Russia's macroeconomic performance in 1999 was, in many dimensions, substantially better than had been anticipated. Compared with projections in the previous *World Economic Outlook,* for example, GDP picked up more rapidly—increasing by over 3 percent rather than remaining flat; and the fiscal position was stronger, inflation lower, and the current account surplus larger than expected. These improvements, however, have been built on a narrow and not necessarily sustainable base including higher prices of energy exports, ongoing import compression, and, associated with this, increases in industrial production driven mainly by import substitution. Unlike in Asia and Latin America, export volumes have yet to show a sustained increase in response to the fall in the real exchange rate since 1998, and export values even declined in 1999. Furthermore, the current account surplus of $18 billion was largely offset by continuing high outflows of private capital, reflecting an ongoing lack of confidence in economic policies and prospects. Hence, gross reserves increased by only $1.6 billion in 1999. The effects of military operations in Chechnya and of the eventual reconstruction efforts on the fiscal position and outlook are unclear.

Looking ahead, the scope for further economic expansion through import compression and substitution is declining, and prospects for a broader-based pickup in private sector activity depend on a recovery of domestic demand. While there are some signs of a revival in consumption and investment, accompanied by continued vigorous growth in industrial output, prospects remain uncertain as to whether growth can be sustained at the same level as in 1999.

For a durable recovery to emerge, significant progress would need to be made in tackling the fiscal and structural difficulties that have undermined growth prospects since the start of transition. Some improvements have been apparent over the past year—for example, public revenues have increased as a share of GDP, partly because of better tax compliance, and a higher proportion of taxes is being paid in cash. Further reforms in the tax structure and administration are now needed to consolidate and extend these gains. Robust fiscal progress would also reduce pressures for central bank financing of the

deficit and would thereby contribute to further disinflation and stronger confidence in the ruble. Determined progress is also needed with banking sector reforms, supported by the implementation of a stronger legal framework to facilitate public intervention in troubled banks and, if necessary, their closure. Particular attention needs to be given to determining the future role and structure of state-owned banks. More generally, much remains to be done to develop the institutional and legal underpinnings of a market economy and hence to provide a reliable framework for improving governance, strengthening the rule of law, reducing corruption, and attracting the long-term capital needed for deep restructuring and sustained growth.

In other countries of the CIS, there are mixed prospects for durable recoveries. In *Ukraine*, despite the slowdown in the contraction of GDP in 1999 and growth in early 2000, the economic situation remains difficult, although prospects for restructuring a substantial portion of the heavy debt service payments due in 2000 and 2001 appear to be good. Further adjustment efforts and progress in structural reforms in the area of privatization, public administration, and restructuring the key agriculture and energy sectors are needed to ensure a sustainable output recovery. In *Belarus*, economic conditions remained difficult in 1999, undermined by a rapid rate of monetary growth and, correspondingly, by accelerating inflation and rapid depreciation of the exchange rate in all segments of the foreign exchange market. Firm commitment to significant monetary and fiscal tightening, together with extensive liberalization and restructuring, would be needed to turn economic prospects around. In contrast, the outlook has strengthened in *Kazakhstan*, with growth of 3 percent projected for 2000. While higher agricultural output and oil prices are contributing to this recovery, growth prospects are underpinned by what appears to be a clear commitment of the authorities to ongoing stabilization and adjustment measures. These include a medium-term strategy of fiscal consolidation; monetary policy clearly focused on lowering inflation; and further structural reforms directed at promoting private-sector-led growth, strengthening the social safety net, and securing macroeconomic objectives (e.g., through improvements in tax policy and administration).

Countries on the European Union Accession Track

The decision at the European Union's Helsinki summit in December 1999 to widen the accession process to 13 applicant countries provided a significant incentive and challenge for the countries concerned to push ahead with the economic, legislative, and other adjustments required to prepare them for full European Union membership. For example, progress in many areas of structural reform, including financial sector development, business restructuring, and privatization, is still quite mixed among these economies. Even the countries most advanced in the reform process have a legacy of problematic sectors and regions that so far have been largely left behind in the adjustment to modern market-based economies. Specific policy attention in this regard needs to be given to improving the climate for the creation and growth of small- and medium-sized enterprises, allowing support for nonviable businesses to be steadily withdrawn; and assisting labor market adjustment both through housing and infrastructure development and through well-targeted social support and training programs.

Economic activity in the more advanced transition economies of central Europe and the Baltics is generally expected to strengthen in 2000. In *Hungary* and *Poland*, GDP growth is projected to pick up to 4½ to 5 percent in 2000 following mild slowdowns in 1999. Hungary's fiscal and current account deficits declined in 1999, despite signs of weakening early in the year. Supported by continued firm macroeconomic policies, a further decline in the fiscal deficit is projected for 2000. In Poland, a particular source of concern has been the significant increase in the current account deficit, which reached over 7½ percent of GDP in 1999 and

contributed to a period of downward pressure on the currency. A modest decline in the external deficit, to around 7 percent of GDP, is expected in 2000, together with a fall in the fiscal deficit. A long-awaited recovery is expected in the *Czech Republic* after three years of very weak economic performance, and stronger growth of around 2 percent is also projected for the *Slovak Republic*. The economic vulnerability of these two countries appears to have declined as a result of substantial reductions in their current account deficits and renewed, but overdue, efforts to restructure the bank and enterprise sectors, although a great deal of structural adjustment still lies ahead. Activity in the Baltic countries is also picking up again following sharper-than-expected slowdowns in the wake of the Russian crisis, which led to a significant deterioration in their fiscal positions and higher unemployment. *Estonia* and *Latvia* appear to be recovering quite rapidly while a more muted pickup is projected for *Lithuania*, which experienced particularly severe economic and fiscal difficulties in 1999.

A key contribution to the stronger outlook for these countries is coming from an upswing in exports to western Europe as growth in this area also strengthens. But also important is a recovery in the investment climate and in overall confidence following the uncertainties brought on by the financial crisis in Russia. Sustaining these improvements will require prudent policy management on a number of fronts. In almost all of the advanced transition economies, some rebalancing of the macroeconomic policy mix would be desirable, and this is already under way in some countries (notably the Baltics). This rebalancing would generally involve a faster rate of fiscal consolidation to contain pressures on inflation and interest rates that could arise from the projected pickup in economic activity. Such an approach would help to hold down the costs of bank and enterprise restructuring, encourage investment, and lower the risk that strong capital inflows could resume and put pressure on exchange rates and competitiveness. In most countries, fiscal restraint over the medium-term needs to be supported by measures to improve the efficiency of the tax regime, including broadening the tax base, lowering direct tax rates, and placing relatively more emphasis on indirect taxes. And further support would come from reforms to the funding and delivery of health care, pensions, and other social services to improve the quality and sustainability of these programs, where public spending pressures have tended to be the greatest. Wage moderation, in both public and private sectors, would also contribute to improving fiscal positions, lowering inflation and interest rates, enhancing competitiveness, and raising employment.

Growth in *Bulgaria* slowed to 2½ percent in 1999 under the impact of poorer external trading conditions and rapid domestic restructuring but, with activity already picking up, the economy is expected to grow by 4 percent in 2000. Bulgaria's relatively robust performance since its financial crisis in 1997 is attributable to a prudent fiscal stance and low inflation, underpinned by the currency board and complemented by widespread structural reforms—including further privatization, enterprise restructuring, and firm wage restraint imposed on poorly performing state enterprises and monopolies. These reform efforts need to be maintained to consolidate recent economic progress. In *Romania*, large corrections in the fiscal accounts and the exchange rate brought about massive external adjustment in 1999, but at the cost of a further decline in output and higher inflation. The current account deficit more than halved and official reserves were replenished following large debt repayments at midyear, while real GDP contracted by an estimated 4 percent in 1999 (implying a decline of about 15 percent since 1996). A modest turnaround to around 1½ percent growth, together with lower inflation, is projected for 2000, but the outlook is fragile and ongoing international financial support will be required. Sustained recovery will need to be supported by a lasting commitment to fiscal reforms and lower deficits, underpinned by wage restraint, rapid progress with bank restructuring, and much

stronger financial discipline in public and private enterprises.

Following the 4½ percent contraction in GDP in 1999, *Turkey* is projected to rebound in 2000. Contributing to this turnaround are an expected recovery in exports and tourism receipts, post-earthquake reconstruction, lower real interest rates, and a general improvement in confidence. But underpinning the strong medium-term outlook is an ambitious IMF-supported program of reforms that should lead to sustainable improvements in the fiscal position, a more credible exchange rate regime, and a rapid reduction in inflation to rates not seen since the 1970s (see Chapter II, Box 2.1). Fiscal measures, most of which have already been enacted, include a significant strengthening in the pension system, reforms to contain the cost of agricultural support programs, and privatization of public utilities and other state enterprises. Anchoring the expected reduction in wage and price inflation is a firm, pre-announced crawling peg for the exchange rate, backed by strict rules regarding domestic base money creation. With Turkey now accepted for the EU accession process, full implementation and consolidation of the reform agenda is now required to secure the improvements in economic strength and stability that such membership would demand.

Middle East and Africa: Stronger But Narrowly Based Growth

The economic prospects of most countries in the Middle East, and several of the larger countries in Africa, have improved significantly over the past year, particularly as a result of higher international oil prices. Although OPEC production quotas have restrained growth in oil output and export volumes, the rapid increase in prices has made a major contribution toward reducing fiscal and current account imbalances in oil-producing countries and has supported a general strengthening of domestic confidence, asset prices, and demand.[3] At the same time, the fluctuations in economic conditions over recent years have again highlighted the need to push ahead with reforms for economic diversification and liberalization in order to promote private-sector-led growth in non-oil areas of their economies. The same reforms are required in non-oil producing countries, many of which are being hit not just by higher prices of oil imports but also by continued weaknesses in export prices of primary goods and other non-fuel commodities.

In the Middle East, relatively strong growth is expected in *Egypt*, underpinned by an environment of low inflation. The external accounts have, however, been under pressure over the past year, reflecting, in part, rapid growth of domestic credit. A tightening of macroeconomic policies, combined with an expected further strengthening of tourism receipts, would help ease these pressures. For Egypt's high rate of growth to be sustained over the medium term, the structural reform effort needs to be reinvigorated. Key reforms should include wide-ranging privatization, trade liberalization (partly under the impetus of the EU partnership agreement and World Trade Organization commitments), tax reform, and a range of measures to improve the business and investment climate. The government of the *Islamic Republic of Iran* has announced a further five-year program of structural reforms, including measures to diversify the economy, support private sector activity, and strengthen the social safety net. Though politically difficult, such reforms are required to reduce macroeconomic imbalances and increase growth to the much higher rates needed to substantially boost living standards and reduce unemployment. *Saudi Arabia* and *Kuwait* are expected to grow by 1–2 percent in 2000, as the recent fiscal and external pressures brought on by low oil prices dissipate. In these countries also, stronger and more robust growth over the medium term would need to be underpinned by measures to boost the non-oil sectors of the econ-

omy, especially by expanding the scope for private initiative and investment. Implementation of privatization plans in each country would be an important step in this regard.

Economic growth in Africa is projected to recover to over 4 percent in 2000 after slowing to under 2½ percent in 1999. A rebound of activity in three of the largest economies, *Algeria, Nigeria,* and *South Africa,* is expected to lead this recovery, but also significant is the continuing strong performance projected for many of the smaller countries (including *Ghana, Tanzania, Tunisia,* and *Uganda*). Although past experience points to the risk of policy slippages, several positive factors account for the improved regional prospects. The stronger growth projected for Europe—the major market for many African countries—and for the global economy more broadly is expected to support growth in the volume and prices of African exports. Oil-producing states such as Algeria and Nigeria are benefiting from higher oil prices, while rising non-fuel commodity prices are also helping to reduce imbalances and support activity in a number of countries. Higher metals prices, for example, are contributing to stronger growth in South Africa. However, not all commodity prices are increasing. For example, prices of coffee, tea, and cotton are expected to remain relatively weak, limiting export earnings and growth in many countries, including *Kenya* and Uganda. Agricultural activity in these two countries and others in sub-Saharan Africa was also affected by poor rainfall in 1999, and the torrential rains and flooding that hit *Mozambique* in early 2000 appear likely to lead to slower growth after several years of very strong economic performance.

Underpinning the improved economic prospects for many African economies is the progress that has been made with macroeconomic stabilization, structural adjustment, and political reforms. In South Africa, for example, the fiscal deficit has declined more rapidly than

---

[3]See Chapter II of this *World Economic Outlook* and Box 1.4 of the October 1999 *World Economic Outlook* for estimates of the impact of higher oil prices on activity, trade, and government revenues of selected oil exporting countries, as well as the effect on growth and inflation among oil importers.

expected, monetary risks have been reduced, and interest rates have fallen, providing a favorable context for the introduction of the planned inflation targeting framework. More broadly, many African countries—with the exception of the conflict-affected regions in the sub-Sahara—have had notable success over recent years in lowering inflation and improving public sector finances. For example, inflation in 2000 is projected to be around 6 percent or less in many countries in the region (see Table 1.5), and only 2 to 3 percent in *Cameroon, Côte d'Ivoire, Morocco,* and *Tunisia.* Most of the countries listed in Table 1.5 have also adopted wide-ranging structural adjustment programs, with support from the IMF, World Bank, and regional institutions. These programs typically include the privatization of public enterprises; reductions in subsidies and price liberalization more generally; and the opening up of international trade, including reforms introduced under a range of recent bilateral and multilateral trade agreements (see the October 1999 *World Economic Outlook*). Encouraging political developments include the restoration of a democratically elected government in Nigeria, the consolidation of democratic reforms in South Africa, and the government's efforts in restoring stability in Algeria.

However, with many African economies still facing significant institutional and structural impediments to growth, and continuing to be heavily dependent on agriculture and/or single-commodity exports, reform efforts need to be sustained and expanded in order to broaden the base of economic development and promote private sector initiative and investment. Continued conflicts in the Democratic Republic of the Congo, Angola, and other countries in sub-Saharan Africa, and political uncertainty elsewhere, add to the difficulties of these countries—and probably of the region as a whole—in attracting capital and laying the groundwork for stronger growth. The economic and political challenges facing Africa, particularly to reduce persistently high levels of unemployment and poverty, are discussed further in the following section on Poverty and Globalization, and in Chapter IV on "How Can the Poor Catch Up?" Illustrating these challenges, in South Africa—the largest and arguably the strongest economy—unemployment is currently close to 40 percent (including "discouraged" workers, who have given up looking for work); in Algeria, the second largest economy, it is nearly 30 percent.

Poverty and Globalization

The arrival of the year 2000 is an appropriate time to reflect both on the successes and failures of the past century and on the main challenges lying ahead. Somewhat unusually for a *World Economic Outlook,* Chapter V provides such a long-term view of past and prospective economic developments. A core issue in this regard—and perhaps the most striking exception to the otherwise remarkable economic achievements of the twentieth century—has been the persistent failure to break the cycle of stagnation and poverty in the poorest countries. The global income distribution across countries is somewhat less skewed today than 25 years ago when weighted by population, largely on account of rapid growth in China, as well as in India. But this is no consolation for the large number of very poor (living on a dollar or less per day) that has remained stubbornly high in the range of 1.2 to 1.3 billion—about one-fifth of the world's population. Moreover, per capita incomes have been regressing in absolute terms in a large number of countries during the past 25–30 years. As a result, the world is entering the twenty-first century with the largest divergence ever recorded between rich and poor. The widening income gaps within many countries and the gulf between the most affluent and most impoverished nations are, in the words of the then Managing Director of the IMF, morally outrageous, economically wasteful, and potentially socially explosive.[4]

---

[4]See Michel Camdessus, "Development and Poverty Reduction: A Multilateral Approach," Address at the Tenth United Nations Conference on Trade and Development, Bangkok, February 13, 2000.

The reasons for poverty are complex and differ from country to country. However, common and often mutually reinforcing causes found in many cases include misguided economic policies, weak institutions, political instability, and recurrent civil unrest and armed conflicts. External factors often contribute to the problem through frequent negative terms-of-trade shocks in commodity exporting countries and a shortage of foreign capital. Also important has been the legacy of support provided during the Cold War era to nonreformist, unaccountable, and often corrupt political leaders. The applications of medical advances, including vaccinations and improvements in water supplies and hygiene, made possible partly through foreign assistance, have played key roles in raising life expectancy in even the poorest countries, although the AIDS pandemic is rapidly reversing these gains in some. In too many cases, however, even generous levels of foreign aid have been unable to put the recipients on a sustainable growth path. Indeed, in some cases aid may even have been counterproductive, to the extent that it may have reduced the incentives for the recipient countries to deal with their problems effectively and allowed governments to divert scarce resources into unproductive areas.

At the same time, experience has shown that flows of foreign aid (including concessional lending) into countries with weak supportive policies often fail to produce positive results. This may be due to a lack of complementary reforms to help make investment projects viable, a propensity of donor countries to favor projects that benefited their own exporters of goods and services more than they met the needs of the recipients, or a propensity of recipient countries to spend on prestigious "white elephant" projects. As a result of the large scale of unprofitable investments as well as loans for unproductive purposes—for example, to finance military purchases—many of the poorest countries have accumulated large debt burdens to official creditors, which they are unable to service. Even with recurrent debt restructurings, these countries have therefore been caught in an unsustainable

debt spiral, which has become an obstacle to reform and a barrier to private capital inflows.

On the other hand, where the policy environment is strong, reforms are consistently implemented, and there is a sense of domestic ownership of the reform process, foreign assistance does often play a key supporting role in enhancing growth and reducing poverty and human misery.

The virtual absence of foreign direct investment and other private capital flows into the poorest countries and their apparent inability to compete in increasingly contested world export markets might be interpreted as indications that these countries are casualties of the process of globalization that has marked the final quarter of the twentieth century. The globalized economy has the potential to penalize policy shortcomings very strongly, and this aspect of globalization increases the risk that a poor country becomes (or feels) excluded from the global economic system. As a result, a country's leaders might stop trying to create the domestic preconditions for economic takeoff, ensnaring the country in a spiral of decline or stagnation. The growing income gap has probably also contributed to cultural and nationalistic backlashes against globalization and the "western" values that are often perceived to be the ideology behind it. Countries that choose to turn their back on the outside world may also consider that they are victims of globalization.

Such rejections of globalization principles are quite rare at a national level, however. These views are not shared, for example, by the many emerging market countries in east Asia and elsewhere that have successfully integrated their economies into the global trading system. Even among countries that are less well integrated, the overall trend in most cases is toward a greater rather than lesser degree of trade and financial liberalization. Rather, the most vocal critics of globalization are often found among advocates of developing countries who come from the advanced countries.

Retreats from globalization are very costly and are especially harmful for the poor. This is clearly suggested by the experience of the twentieth century. When world trade and cross-border investments spiraled downward in the 1930s, all regions, including those comprising developing countries, suffered badly. Similarly, in the 1970s and 1980s, much of Latin America and Africa paid a high price through resource misallocation, hyperinflation, financial instability, and mediocre growth as a result of inward-oriented, protectionist economic policies. In contrast, during the past 40 years, outward-oriented, growth-oriented policies have transformed much of east Asia from one of the poorest areas in the world to the most dynamic. This success would have been unthinkable without access to, and progressive integration with, world markets. The recent financial crises in no way change this conclusion; they have only underscored that globalization both increases a country's economic opportunities and adds to demands on its economic policies and institutions to contain the risk and impact of external shocks.

Rather than being a problem, globalization—through the opportunities it offers—is an indispensable part of the solution. Indeed, when poor countries do begin to seriously tackle their institutional and policy deficiencies they, too, have the potential to benefit from foreign direct investment, higher export growth, and from an easing of financing constraints that will allow them to grow at higher and more robust rates. Recent examples of poor countries that bucked the trend, at least for a period, include Botswana, Côte d'Ivoire, Mauritius, Mozambique, Senegal, Uganda, and Vietnam.

Sustained progress has, however, eluded many countries, and much stronger efforts are required by the poorest countries themselves and also by the international community. The policy priorities among the poorest countries include the mutually reinforcing objectives of:

- Fostering macroeconomic stability through prudent fiscal and monetary policies and the adoption of sustainable exchange rate regimes;
- Harnessing market forces for development by liberalizing external trade and payments; removing price controls, subsidies, and other distortions in domestic markets; subjecting public enterprises to market discipline; strengthening financial and legal systems; and combating corruption;
- Improving the quality of government by reducing wasteful public sector outlays; raising expenditures on basic education, health care, and essential infrastructure; putting in place tax and transfer systems that are efficient and equitable; and promoting transparency and accountability in government operations; and
- Promoting domestic ownership of the reform agenda through closer involvement of unions, employers' organizations, and other representatives of civil society in the design of reforms.

For the international community, a priority task is to address the debilitating debt problem with greater resolve. Moreover it is essential to quickly reverse the downward trend in some advanced countries' official development assistance and to ensure that development aid is used more effectively—for example, by strengthening incentives for reform in the recipient countries.

The advanced countries also need to reform their trade policies in areas that discriminate against the poorest countries. This particularly concerns import restrictions on agricultural products and textiles, and agricultural subsidies in various forms that lead to recurrent problems of overproduction. These production distortions have added to the downward pressure on world food prices, eroded the competitiveness of many farmers in the poorest countries, reduced the scope of these countries for exporting food, and made many of them excessively dependent on food imports. A solution to these distortions is long overdue, with the advanced countries needing to introduce new ways to support agricultural incomes at home that do not jeopardize the global fight against poverty. Similar considerations apply to trade in textiles and other products in which poor countries often have a comparative advantage but where trade liberalization remains incomplete and market access limited.

As part of its contribution to the global anti-poverty effort, the IMF has replaced its concessional facility, the ESAF, with a broader focused Poverty Reduction and Growth Facility (PRGF). The new facility seeks to strengthen the mutually reinforcing relationship between macroeconomic stability and structural reform on the one hand, and growth and reduction of poverty and inequality on the other. It emphasizes the need for the poorest countries to assume ownership of their poverty reduction strategies. At the same time, the enhanced initiative for the Heavily Indebted Poor Countries (HIPCs) will provide large-scale debt relief to eligible countries that adopt the needed reforms. The new approach is based on the closest possible collaboration between the IMF and the World Bank.

It is encouraging that eliminating the excess debt burden of the poorest countries is now widely acknowledged to be a necessary condition to strengthen prospects for robust growth and to alleviate poverty. However, it would be a serious mistake to believe that this would be a cure-all for these countries' problems. And it would be particularly dangerous to think that simply removing the debt burden would automatically ensure that social needs, such as improving health care, education, and social safety nets, will be much better met. Rather, if these improvements are to be realized, comprehensive reforms still need to be adopted, as emphasized above, com-bined with adequate flows of well-targeted foreign aid. The crucial difference is that with meaningful debt reduction, undertaken in a strong policy framework with the support of civil society, these reforms and higher levels of foreign aid stand a better chance of success.

Moreover, many elements of the reform strategy that needs to be pursued in the poorest countries are also relevant for other emerging economies—for example, in south Asia and Latin America—where per capita incomes are higher on average, but where a sizable proportion of the population is still enmeshed in poverty. While these countries may not be eligible for the latest debt reduction initiative, they would nevertheless benefit substantially from other forms of support from advanced countries, notably reductions in trade protection and increased development assistance. But, as in the poorest countries, the key conditions that are needed to make significant and sustainable inroads on poverty lie within the ambit of *domestic* policies. These include macroeconomic stability, trade liberalization, removal of distortions in domestic markets, improvements in the quality of government, and measures directly aiming at improving income distribution. In strengthening the economic foundations needed for sustained growth, such measures would also provide these countries with greater scope for meeting social needs and alleviating extreme poverty.

CHAPTER II

THE ONGOING RECOVERY IN EMERGING MARKET ECONOMIES

Financial and macroeconomic conditions in the emerging market economies have continued to improve since the middle of 1999. Equity prices have rallied, exchange rates have stabilized, and yield spreads in external debt markets have begun to ease. In Latin America, the recessions have been generally short-lived and, in Brazil, unexpectedly shallow. Growth in east Asia has picked up strongly in the course of 1999, especially in Korea. This overall improvement notwithstanding, conditions among emerging market regions and countries continue to differ, reflecting divergences in cyclical positions and in budgetary and external balances and the need for structural reform. In view of persistently high current account deficits and continued subdued net private capital flows, Latin American emerging market economies remain vulnerable to reversals in market sentiment and financing flows. In east Asia, however, the rapid pace of the recovery will require some moderation in stimulative fiscal and monetary policies, and additional progress in banking and corporate sector restructuring is needed to transform the recovery into robust and sustained growth.

The improvement in the economic and financial outlook for Latin America and east Asia owes much to the policy responses to the recent crises. In addition to sound macroeconomic policies, many countries have adopted strong structural reform measures, including actions to strengthen financial systems, improve fiscal and monetary policy frameworks, and, in particular in east Asia, promote corporate restructuring. The welcome focus on structural reform stands in contrast with earlier crisis episodes in emerging markets, when the emphasis was much more on macroeconomic policies to achieve short-term external adjustment. The current structural agenda is far from finished, however, and the pace of reform needs to be maintained, es-

pecially as ongoing rapid recoveries heighten the risk of complacency. Priorities include initiatives to assist further financial sector and corporate restructuring, as well as broader institutional, legal, and regulatory reforms aimed at strengthening the environment for market-based activities. Provided the reform momentum can be maintained, the east Asian and Latin American countries will be well placed to achieve sustained robust growth and to reduce the risk of new crises.

In addition to sound macroeconomic policies and structural reform measures, other factors are also expected to help lower the risk of renewed crises in the emerging market economies. International investors have generally become more cautious toward these economies, and are differentiating among countries based on credit quality. In spite of an easing in secondary market spreads and some pickup in flows since early 1999, conditions overall remain less generous and market access more limited than during 1996 and most of 1997, in the run-up to the east Asian crisis. The easing in spreads has generally been more pronounced for the east Asian emerging markets than for their Latin American counterparts, reflecting credit fundamentals. External positions in east Asia have improved considerably in the wake of the 1997–98 crisis and financing patterns in the region are shifting from debt to equity. In contrast, current account deficits and refinancing needs remain sizable in Latin America, although for a number of countries increases in oil and nonfuel commodity prices have helped ease the external vulnerabilities somewhat. Latin America would also be more affected by a sharper-than-expected slowdown in the United States. Nevertheless, ongoing reforms and more realistic assessments of risk have reduced the immediate probability of a sudden and generalized reversal in flows followed by extensive contagion of the type seen in the east Asian crisis of 1997–98 and the more recent crises in Brazil and Russia.

The chapter first discusses the substantial improvement in financial market conditions facing the emerging market countries and the diverging forces likely to influence these economies in the period ahead. It then assesses developments in global commodity markets, emphasizing both the impact of the pickup in world growth on commodity prices and the effects of the recent sharp increase in oil prices on the global economy. The last two sections analyze the improving economic outlook for Latin America and east Asia, comparing remaining vulnerabilities and identifying key policy challenges. Russia and other countries in transition have also been in crisis, but the economic situation in Russia remains complex and its recovery is tentative, as a wide range of financial and structural issues still need to be addressed. The performance of the countries of central and eastern Europe remains quite mixed, although most seem to be recovering from the effects of the Russian crisis. Many of these countries are also benefiting from their ongoing reorientation toward western Europe (see Chapter I). These and other developments in the transition countries will receive special attention in the forthcoming October 2000 *World Economic Outlook*.

Financial Conditions Facing Emerging Market Economies

Reflecting a further recovery in economic activity and rising investor confidence, domestic financial conditions in the emerging market economies generally continued to improve in the second half of 1999 and early 2000. This was, in particular, the case for *emerging equity markets*, which staged a sharp rally in the final months of 1999, as fears of higher U.S. interest rates and Y2K-related problems eased, information technology-related stocks surged in the United States, and economic prospects for both east Asia and Latin America continued to improve (Figure 2.1). Building on a strong performance in the first half of 1999, the rally resulted in eq-

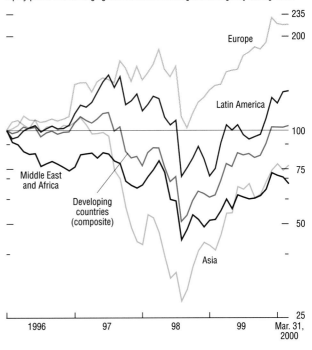

Figure 2.1. Emerging Market Economies: Equity Prices
(U.S. dollar terms; logarithmic scale; January 1996 = 100)

Equity prices in all emerging market economies staged a strong rally during 1999.

Source: Standard and Poor's Emerging Markets Database.

uity price increases in U.S. dollar terms of more than 60 percent on average in 1999 as measured by the Standard & Poor's/International Finance Corporation (IFC) investable price index. This overall strengthening, however, masks a variety of country experiences in economic performance and policies.

In Asia, equity prices more than doubled in China and Korea last year and almost doubled in Indonesia. But markets in Thailand and, especially, the Philippines lagged behind the regional average because of concerns about the pace of bank restructuring (Thailand) and the overall course of economic policy (the Philippines). Indian equities finished the year with an 81 percent increase, in part driven by gains in the country's fast growing information technology sector. In Latin America, Brazil and Mexico recorded the strongest gains in 1999, in line with favorable economic developments. In Brazil, where the stock market soared in the last month of the year on the improving economic outlook, equity prices by year-end had strengthened by 67 percent since the beginning of the year, while the Mexican market rose even more. But markets in Colombia and Venezuela closed 1999 with losses, which were attributable mainly to deep recessions in the two countries.

Among other emerging market economies, stock exchanges in Russia and Turkey posted exceptionally strong rebounds in 1999, in part on the back of sharp year-end rallies. Improving economic prospects and a successful political transition lifted Russian equity prices by 65 percent in December, while the announcement of a macroeconomic stabilization program and positive news on European Union accession sent Turkish prices sharply up in the same month. The South African market also gained momentum in late 1999, amid falling interest rates, rising commodity prices, and a recovering economy.

The Czech, Hungarian, and Polish markets, which had lagged other markets in late 1999, registered strong gains in the first quarter of 2000 on the back of an improving growth and external outlook, capital inflows, and rallies in technology-related assets, while Russian equity

prices strengthened further, reflecting higher oil prices and reduced political uncertainty. In Asia, equity markets in Indonesia, the Philippines, and Thailand weakened significantly during this period, in part because these markets offer fewer technology-related investments than competing regional exchanges. However, China reported price gains, as did Malaysia, where portfolio inflows picked up. In Latin America, the main markets other than those in Colombia and Venezuela posted moderate price increases. Overall, the composite S&P/IFC investable price index (measured in U.S. dollars) rose by 1 percent in the first quarter of 2000, in contrast to declines in many advanced economy equity markets during this period.

In *foreign exchange markets*, the currencies of the emerging market economies regained a measure of stability in the early fall of 1999 when mid-summer pressures related to uncertainties about U.S. interest rate movements abated (Figure 2.2). In emerging east Asia, the Indonesian and Thai currencies broadly returned to their June–July 1999 highs against the U.S. dollar in the fall of 1999, and the Korean won appreciated further to a post-crisis high of less than 1120 per U.S. dollar in March 2000. The Philippine peso came under some downward pressure in late February–March, reflecting concerns about policy slippages, in particular in the fiscal area. In Latin America, the Brazilian *real* strengthened to below 1.75 per U.S. dollar in March 2000, following some weakening in the early fall of 1999, as concerns of a pickup in inflation eased and capital inflows rose. Elsewhere on the continent, the Chilean and Colombian pesos, supported by strengthening recoveries and rising commodity export revenues, appreciated against the U.S. dollar in late 1999 and, in the case of the Chilean peso, early 2000. The Mexican peso also strengthened against the U.S. dollar in February–March 2000 on the back of higher oil prices and rising capital inflows. By contrast, Ecuador's currency lost more than half of its value against the U.S. dollar between September 1999 and early January 2000, reflecting the country's deepening economic and financial crisis, but appeared to be stabilizing following the announcement of the government's intention to move toward dollarization.

In central and eastern Europe, the Polish zloty weakened significantly in early November 1999 amid inflation fears and political uncertainty, but then rebounded following a tightening of the monetary policy stance and an easing of political uncertainties. In part reflecting the weakness of the euro, the zloty strengthened by around 15 percent against the euro between early November 1999 and the end of March 2000, as foreign inflows associated with privatization receipts and with portfolio investments in high yielding zloty assets surged. Several of the other currencies in the region, in particular the Czech and Slovak korunas, also faced upward pressure against the euro, and the Czech and Slovak authorities responded by intervening in the foreign exchange market. By contrast, the Russian ruble came under renewed downward pressure against the U.S. dollar in late 1999–early 2000, mainly because of a temporary easing of monetary conditions. The South African rand broadly stabilized at around 6.1 per U.S. dollar in the fall of 1999, but then weakened somewhat in early 2000.

With exchange rates stabilizing and inflation generally remaining under control, the monetary policy stances in most emerging market economies were eased considerably in the course of 1999, as reflected in *short-term interest rates* (Figure 2.3). In a number of cases, however, monetary policy has been put on hold since the early fall of 1999, either because of concerns about potential currency pressures or because further easing would have been inappropriate in view of strengthening recoveries and risks of overheating. The Bank of Korea held the overnight call rate steady at around 4¾ percent until early February 2000, when the rate was raised to 5 percent to narrow the spread between long- and short-term interest rates. Money market rates have stabilized in the 2 to 3 percent range in Malaysia and Thailand and at around 9 percent in the Philippines. In mid-November 1999, China reduced the required reserve ratio

Figure 2.2. Selected Emerging Market Economies: Bilateral U.S. Dollar Exchange Rates
(U.S. dollars per currency unit; January 5, 1996 = 100)

The currencies of most emerging market economies have been broadly stable against the U.S. dollar since the fall of 1999.

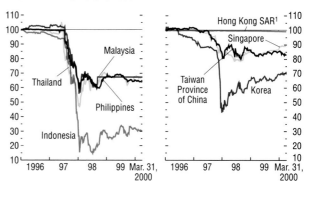

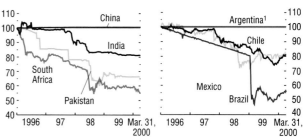

Sources: Bloomberg Financial Markets, LP; and WEFA, Inc.
[1]Pegged to U.S. dollar.

**Figure 2.3. Selected Emerging Market Economies:
Short-Term Interest Rates**
(Percent)

Short-term interest rates in emerging markets have generally eased in the wake of Brazil's currency crisis.

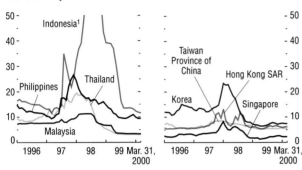

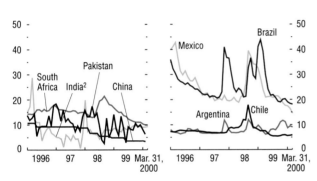

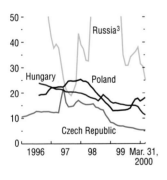

Sources: Bloomberg Financial Markets, LP; and IMF, *International Financial Statistics.* Three-month interbank rate or, if unavailable, comparable market-determined short-term rate.

[1]The Indonesian short-term rate in the first half of September 1998 averaged 70.6 percent.

[2]The mid-rate in the overnight call money market.

[3]Three-month interbank transactions were suspended on August 17, 1998, when interest rates reached 127.6 percent, and transactions resumed on February 26, 1999 with an interest rate of 55.1 percent.

from 8 percent to 6 percent to boost liquidity and encourage bank lending.

In Latin America, after having lowered the benchmark SELIC rate to 19 percent at the end of September 1999, from a high of 45 percent in late March, the Brazilian central bank abstained from further interest rate reductions during a six-month period to keep inflation under control. At the end of March 2000, the SELIC rate was cut to 18½ percent in view of the *real's* tendency toward appreciation and reduced concerns of the inflationary effects of higher oil prices. Also reflecting inflation-related considerations, the Mexican central bank reduced its daily lending to commercial banks so as to increase money market rates in mid-January 2000. By contrast, the Colombian central bank used a move to a free-floating exchange rate in the early fall of 1999 to ease monetary policy in support of the recovery, lowering its repo rate gradually from 17 percent in mid-August 1999 to 12 percent in mid-January 2000. Monetary policy was tightened again somewhat in February 2000 as the Colombian peso tended to weaken.

Elsewhere among the emerging market economies, the South African Reserve Bank continued to bring its repurchase rate down gradually during the second half of 1999, until it reached 12 percent by the late fall. At that time, the Reserve Bank fixed the rate to help reduce Y2K-related concerns. In mid-January 2000, when the float of the repurchase rate was resumed, the repurchase rate dropped by an additional 25 basis points. In Turkey, the introduction of a new crawling peg exchange rate regime supported by stronger adjustment policies in early January 2000, allowed the central bank to substantially cut its overnight bid and offer rates (Box 2.1). In central and eastern Europe, interest rate hikes in Poland and reductions in the Czech Republic and, in particular, Hungary, reflected differences not only in the growth, inflation, and current account outlook, but also in exchange rate regimes and monetary policy frameworks.

The improved prospects for the emerging market economies have also led to a further narrowing of *spreads on emerging market external debt* (Figure 2.4). Average spreads, as measured by the JP Morgan EMBI+ index, fell from around 1100 basis points at the end of September 1999 to a year-low of 824 basis points at the end of December, which was still well above levels observed before the Russian crisis, including those at the peak of the east Asian crisis in late 1997. During the first quarter of 2000, average spreads fluctuated in the 750 to 900 basis points range, broadly in line with movements in U.S. bond and equity markets. The overall narrowing in spreads during the fall of 1999 masks considerable regional differences, however, evidence of increasing investor differentiation among emerging markets. Spreads on bond issues by east Asian entities (except from Indonesia) were broadly stable at low levels during this period, after having eased in the first half of the year on the back of improvements in credit fundamentals. Spreads for Latin American countries, however, rose in mid-1999, reflecting concerns about U.S. interest rate movements and domestic fiscal policies, before easing again to year-lows by the end of 1999. They remain above spreads for the major east Asian borrowers, in line with Latin America's relatively high external vulnerability and uncertainties about the prospects for fiscal consolidation.

The improvement in secondary market conditions in emerging debt markets reflects a number of factors. In the early fall of 1999, investors grew more confident that the emerging market economies would avoid major Y2K-related problems and they began to anticipate a rally in emerging debt markets in early 2000. Investor pre-positioning for this expected rally brought it forward to November–December 1999. The rally was also supported by relatively small inflows of new money into the market and by some country-specific developments, in particular a sharp fall in spreads on Russia's external debt owing to the country's improved economic outlook and expectations of a restructuring agreement on Soviet-era debt held by London Club (commercial bank) creditors.

Average secondary market spreads do not appear to have been affected strongly by the fail-

Figure 2.4. Selected Emerging Market Economies: Eurobond Yield Spreads and Brady Bond Spreads
(Basis points)

External debt spreads for Latin American countries generally remain above those for their east Asian counterparts.

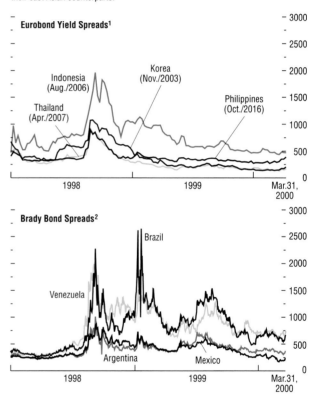

Sources: Bloomberg Financial Markets, LP; Reuters; and Salomon Brothers.
[1]Spreads are calculated relative to a U.S. treasury bond of comparable maturity.
[2]Stripped yields are adjusted to exclude both the value of collateral held as security against repayment of the bond and the value of coupon payments. Spreads are calculated relative to a U.S. treasury bond of comparable maturity.

Box 2.1. Turkey's IMF-Supported Disinflation Program

Macroeconomic instability—characterized by chronic inflation, wide swings in output, volatile interest rates, and persistent fiscal imbalances—has been the norm for the Turkish economy during the last two decades. The country launched at least five disinflation programs during the 1990s, but these were ineffective in lowering the inflation rate, which averaged over 80 percent over the period (see the first table). As a result, Turkey has been a striking exception to the disinflation trends observed worldwide since the 1970s.

The ultimate cause of chronic high inflation in Turkey has been the existence of deep structural weaknesses in public sector finances. Opaque indirect agricultural support policies, other nontransparent fiscal and nonfiscal activities by budgetary and nonbudgetary funds and state enterprises, and credit subsidies through state banks have contributed to substantial primary deficits.[1] These deficits have persisted

[1]For a more detailed analysis, see Rakia Moalla-Fetini, "Inflation as a Fiscal Problem," IMF Staff Country Report No. 00/14 (Washington: International Monetary Fund, February 2000), pp. 7–27. (This document is also available online at *www.imf.org*).

since the 1970s and have been consistently monetized to alleviate the government's budget constraint (see the second table). As the inflation tax base eroded, however, the same level of money creation extracted lower amounts of seigniorage and provided further upward pressure on prices. Inflation was also sustained by a strong expectational component, which impeded the success of the disinflation programs of the 1990s. In particular, in the programs implemented in 1994–95 and 1998, the fiscal primary position strengthened significantly, and inflation performance also improved, but nominal interest rates failed to come down as envisaged. This was partly because financial markets remained worried about the sustainability of the situation, especially in the light of the crises in Asia and many other emerging market countries in 1997–98. The end result was sizable increases in real interest rates from already very high levels, thus undermining the authorities' resolve to continue disinflation.

The new disinflation program supported by the Stand-By Arrangement approved by the IMF Board on December 22, 1999 was designed to address upfront the issue of the credibility of

Disinflation Attempts
(percent change)

Disinflation Program (starting date)	Monetary Framework	Inflation Before the Beginning of the Program[1]	Inflation Target for the First Year of the Program[1]	CPI Inflation after Six Months[2]	T-Bill Rates Six Months After the Beginning of the Program	
					In nominal terms	In real terms[3]
Jan. 1990	Base money targeting	66.8	54.0	61.3	50.4	–2.3
Jan. 1992	Base money targeting	70.9	42.0	56.1	97.7	39.2
May 1994	Nonbinding crawling exchange rate floor	115.9	45.4[4]	71.9	113.2	47.0
Jan. 1995	"Enhanced" crawling floor[5]	125.1	40.0	100.4	103.2	44.5
Jan. 1998	Inflation targeting	90.4	50.0	46.8	92.2	28.0

[1]GDP deflator (annual average) for 1990; CPI (Dec./Dec.) for 1992; CPI (June/June) for 1994; CPI (Dec./Dec.) for 1995; WPI (Dec./Dec.) for 1998.
[2]CPI inflation in the first six months of the program, seasonally adjusted and annualized.
[3]Deflated with the inflation target.
[4]Inflation target for the period May 1994–April 1995, derived from the annual targets for 1994 and 1995 under the Stand-By Arrangement program.
[5]In addition to the announcement of quarterly exchange rate floors, the authorities were committed, in case of slack under the floor, to avoid a rate of depreciation significantly different from the targeted inflation rate. This commitment, however, was expected to guide interest rate policy, with no specific commitment on intervention policy.

Selected Macroeconomic Indicators

	1990	1991	1992	1993	1994	1995	1996	1997	1998	1999
Real sector (percent change)										
Real GDP	9.2	0.8	5.0	7.7	−4.7	8.1	6.9	7.6	3.1	−4.3
CPI (period average)	60.3	66.0	70.1	66.1	106.3	93.7	82.3	85.7	84.6	64.9
WPI (period average)	52.3	55.3	62.1	58.4	120.7	88.5	77.9	81.8	71.8	53.1
Monetary and exchange rate sector (percent change)										
Broad money	52.2	81.7	77.4	63.4	144.7	103.4	117.1	87.9	96.4	85.7
Bank claims on central government	36.5	74.9	60.2	78.8	123.6	83.9	240.2	105.7	186.7	124.1
Interbank money market rate (percent)	51.9	72.8	65.4	62.8	137.2	72.5	76.4	70.4	74.8	73.4
Exchange rate	23.0	59.9	64.7	59.9	170.1	54.0	77.4	86.6	72.0	60.6
Public sector (percent of GDP)										
Public sector balance	−7.6	−11.3	−12.4	−13.1	−10.2	−6.4	−13.2	−13.1	−15.9	−24.2
of which:										
Primary balance	−3.6	−6.2	−7.0	−5.6	−0.2	2.7	−1.2	−2.1	0.5	−2.7
Net debt of the public sector	28.8	35.2	35.7	35.1	44.7	41.3	46.5	42.9	44.5	58.0
External sector (percent of GDP)										
Current account deficit	−1.7	0.2	−0.6	−3.5	2.8	−0.5	−1.4	−1.4	0.9	−0.5
External debt	32.6	33.0	34.8	36.9	50.1	42.4	45.3	47.0	51.2	56.2

the disinflation effort. To this end, the program rests on three pillars: a large front-loaded fiscal adjustment; a strong exchange rate commitment underwritten by a no sterilization monetary policy rule and income policies; and a wide range of upfront structural reform measures. This is expected both to stabilize the fiscal situation and to bring CPI inflation down from 65 percent at the end of 1999 to 25 percent by the end of 2000, and to single digits by the end of 2002.

The front-loaded fiscal adjustment is necessary as fiscal weakness is at the root of the inflationary process. A shift in the primary position of the fiscal sector to long-term fiscal sustainability is to be undertaken in the first year of the program. In particular, the primary balance of the public sector is expected to improve from a deficit of 2.7 percent of GNP in 1999 to a surplus of 2.2 percent of GNP in 2000. The achievement of these fiscal goals will be facilitated by the tax package that was approved by Parliament in late November 1999 (the package includes important adjustments in a wide range of both indirect and direct taxes), as well as by additional revenue-boosting and expenditure-cutting measures that were included in the 2000 budget prior to its approval in late 1999. As the disinfla-

tion will bring about a temporary rise in the burden of interest payments relative to GDP, reflecting high ex post real interest rates while inflation falls, the improvement in the overall balance of the public sector will be more limited. Sizable privatization receipts will be used to keep the public debt-to-GDP ratio at its 1999 level this year.

The nominal anchor—absent in earlier programs—will be provided by a forward-looking commitment on the exchange rate. A nominal exchange rate anchor was chosen because of the high visibility and strong effect on prices that the exchange rate has in Turkey, the difficulty in finding suitable alternatives (money demand appears unstable), and the need to facilitate a rapid decline in interest rates. The exchange rate commitment (a preannounced exchange rate path with a devaluation rate of 20 percent) is supported by strong fiscal adjustment and consistent income policies in the government sector (civil servant and minimum wages will rise only in line with targeted inflation). In addition, the conduct of monetary policy will be guided by a rule, whereby base money will only be created by changes in the net foreign assets of the central bank (apart from short-term fluc-

Box 2.1 *(concluded)*

tuations). Finally, to avoid being locked in this rigid monetary framework beyond the disinflation stage, a preannounced exit strategy has also been incorporated. A gradual shift into a more flexible exchange rate regime (with widening symmetric bands around the preannounced exchange path) will be introduced in mid-2001.

A comprehensive and front-loaded structural reform agenda, which is expected to be supported by the World Bank, will underpin the program. The agenda includes privatization, a restructuring and strengthening of the banking sector, an overhaul of financial support to agriculture, and pension reform. In addition, fiscal management and transparency will be strengthened, and tax policy and administration improved. The structural reform effort is also expected to generate efficiency gains; limit contingent claims on the government; and, through increased privatization receipts, stabilize the level of public debt.

A breakthrough pension reform was implemented in mid-summer 1999, which will allow for a gradual but significant strengthening of the pension system. Additional changes in administration, coverage, compliance, and the legal framework (including legislative changes allowing for the creation of private pension funds) are expected to deepen these reforms in the coming years. In the agricultural area, the long-term goal is to replace existing indirect support policies with a direct income support system. In the interim, the government has taken several steps to contain the cost of the existing system, most notably by phasing out credit subsidies and support to industrial crops. As regards fiscal management and transparency, changes will be implemented to strengthen budget preparation, execution, and control, most notably through the implementation of an integrated financial system based on a single account and a general ledger. Fiscal transparency will be enhanced by broadening the effective coverage of the budget and by limiting the operations of quasi-fiscal entities. The tax system will be improved to provide for a broad revenue base with low and predictable tax rates.

Far-reaching reforms are also envisaged to address long-standing weaknesses of the banking sector. Legislation increasing the independence of supervisors and streamlining bank resolution procedures has already been passed, and a fully independent Banking Regulation and Supervision Agency has been established. Further changes in the regulatory framework—including the implementation of internationally accepted prudential regulations—are due to be implemented early in 2000. The program also includes measures to deal with the problems of the operations of state banks by increasing transparency and hardening the budget constraints facing their management. Finally, some commercial banks were taken over for restructuring by the deposit insurance fund at the inception of the program.

The privatization effort is another key area of reform. The government intends to sell large stakes in the telecommunications operator Turk Telecom and major state enterprises and to transfer operating rights for electricity distribution and power plants. This privatization program is expected to lead to significant efficiency gains in key sectors of the economy, and to also generate sizable budgetary proceeds, which will help achieve the program's fiscal goals. Total receipts from these operations are expected to reach about $7½ billion (about 3½ percent of GNP) during the course of 2000. The attainment of this target has been facilitated by major revisions in the legislation regarding privatization, including a constitutional amendment to allow for international arbitration, a law changing the role of the State Council, a new energy law, and a new telecommunications law.

Initial indications of the positive impact of the program are encouraging, including favorable developments in the fiscal area. Interest rates have fallen from over 90 percent in November 1999 to about 40 percent in January 2000, and sentiment on the part of foreign and domestic investors has been bullish, as reflected in strong gains in equity prices and successful international bond issues.

ures of certain emerging market economies to fully meet external payment obligations. In October 1999, Ecuador became the first country to default on Brady bonds after a swap offer had been rejected by investors. The country subsequently also defaulted on its other external debt, including a Eurobond loan. In mid-November 1999, Pakistan's government announced an offer to exchange three outstanding Eurobonds for a new six-year instrument with a three-year grace period, which was accepted by an overwhelming majority of the bondholders. In early February 2000, Ukraine announced an offer to exchange its outstanding external debt for new seven-year euro- and U.S. dollar-denominated Eurobonds so as to relieve its heavy debt burden in 2000 and 2001; the offer was accepted by bondholders owning more than 95 percent of the outstanding debt. Finally, in mid-February 2000, Russia reached an agreement with its London Club creditors on the rescheduling of Soviet-era debt. The agreement, which involves an exchange of outstanding debt for Eurobonds, reduces significantly the net present value of the debt and lengthens its maturity profile. The lack of contagion from these events to the other markets was a result of investors largely anticipating these difficulties and increasingly differentiating between countries.

The overall improvement in secondary market conditions since the fall of 1999 has not translated into a commensurate narrowing in average spreads for new issues at launch. The improvement was driven in part by lower secondary market spreads for some countries, including Russia, that still have to regain access to the primary market. In early 2000, major U.S. dollar-denominated issues by Argentina, Brazil, and Turkey were priced in the range of 500 to 600 basis points above Treasuries, and a Eurobond from Mexico carried a premium of 315 basis points; these terms showed only a moderate improvement when compared with primary market conditions prevailing in early 1999. Conditions improved, however, in February–March and these four countries—as well as South Africa and Venezuela—issued bonds at yield spreads that

were significantly tighter than those they had faced in the late 1990s. Conditions were also more favorable for issues by a range of central and eastern European sovereigns, as they benefited from improved prospects for integration with the European Union.

Gross private financing flows (not including foreign direct investment flows) to emerging market economies remained subdued in the second half of 1999, as broader investor interest in instruments issued by these economies continued to be rather weak (Table 2.1). Bond issues rose in the final quarter of the year, but this pickup mainly reflected exchanges of Brady bonds for Eurobonds that generated only small amounts of net inflows. At around $173 billion for 1999 as a whole, gross private financing flows were only moderately above the low level recorded in 1998 and significantly below the 1996–97 average. The share of syndicated loan commitments continued to decline in 1999, largely because of ongoing changes in risk management practices at major banks. Equity issues, however, gained in importance, with activity by east Asian entities well above pre-crisis levels, as companies in the region reduced their traditional dependence on bank credit. Bond issues were broadly stable at 1998 levels in 1999 as a whole, with, however, a shift in regional composition toward east Asia. Bond issues, however, picked up considerably in the first quarter of 2000 as a number of major sovereigns came to the market, while activity in the syndicated loan and equity markets declined from end-1999 levels.

As a result of continued subdued levels of gross flows and substantial net repayments to banks, in particular in Asia but also in the Western Hemisphere, *net private capital flows* to emerging market economies in 1999 rose modestly to $80½ billion from a decade low of $75 billion in 1998 (Table 2.2). This small increase is accounted for by a decline in net outflows from Asia that more than offset a reduction in net inflows to the Western Hemisphere, where net repayments to foreign creditors rose and portfolio investment fell around the time of the Brazilian crisis. Net flows are projected to again decline to

Table 2.1. Gross Private Financing to Emerging Market Economies
(Billions of U.S. dollars)

	1997	1998	1999	1999				2000			
				Q1	Q2	Q3	Q4	Q1	Jan.	Feb.	Mar.
Total	292.5	149.8	173.1	32.6	52.0	34.7	52.8	52.7	17.8	19.4	15.5
Asia	128.6	35.0	62.7	11.9	17.1	17.4	16.4	20.5	2.6	12.5	5.4
Europe	37.7	35.9	26.0	3.2	7.9	5.1	9.8	7.6	2.7	1.7	3.2
Middle East and Africa	30.9	13.1	20.0	4.4	6.0	2.4	7.2	7.1	4.8	0.6	1.7
Western Hemisphere	95.3	66.1	64.4	13.2	22.0	9.8	19.4	17.5	7.6	4.6	5.3
Bond issues	133.2	80.2	87.0	21.8	27.5	15.9	21.8	29.5	10.3	7.1	12.1
Asia	45.5	12.4	24.1	7.0	6.3	6.2	4.7	6.8	1.5	1.4	3.9
Western Hemisphere	59.0	40.2	42.2	10.8	14.1	6.9	10.5	14.7	6.1	4.3	4.4
Other regions	28.7	27.6	20.6	4.1	7.1	2.9	6.5	8.0	2.7	1.4	3.9
Other fixed income	10.0	0.5	0.0	0.0	0.0	0.0	0.0	0.0	0.0	0.0	0.0
Asia	9.8	0.5	0.0	0.0	0.0	0.0	0.0	0.0	0.0	0.0	0.0
Western Hemisphere	0.0	0.0	0.0	0.0	0.0	0.0	0.0	0.0	0.0	0.0	0.0
Other regions	0.0	0.0	0.0	0.0	0.0	0.0	0.0	0.0	0.0	0.0	0.0
Loan commitments	123.2	60.0	63.0	8.4	18.9	12.6	23.0	18.1	5.3	11.1	1.7
Asia	58.9	17.7	20.3	3.5	5.1	5.9	5.8	10.8	0.3	10.2	0.3
Western Hemisphere	30.9	25.7	21.4	2.2	7.9	2.7	8.5	1.4	0.2	0.3	0.9
Other regions	33.4	16.6	21.2	2.7	5.9	4.0	8.6	5.9	4.8	0.6	0.5
Equity issues	26.2	9.4	23.2	2.4	6.6	6.1	8.0	5.1	2.2	1.2	1.6
Asia	14.4	4.5	18.3	1.4	5.7	5.3	5.8	2.9	0.9	0.9	1.2
Western Hemisphere	5.4	0.2	0.8	0.2	0.0	0.3	0.3	1.3	1.3	0.0	0.0
Other regions	6.4	4.8	4.1	0.8	0.9	0.5	1.9	0.8	0.0	0.3	0.5

Source: Capital Data Loanware and Bondware.

$71 billion in 2000, but to pick up considerably next year. With net direct investment expected to be broadly stable, the recovery will probably stem mainly from higher bond issuance and, in particular, from lower net reimbursement of bank loans. On a regional basis, the Western Hemisphere is projected to remain the main destination for funds, in line with the region's sizable current account deficits, which, as discussed later, increase its vulnerability to external financial shocks. The five east Asian economies most affected by the 1997–98 crisis are expected to see further, and increasing, net outflows in the form of reimbursement of bank loans and reserve accumulation in 2000, but positive net flows are projected to increase in the other emerging market economies of Asia this year. Flows to Africa are projected to remain modest this year and next.

Pronounced adjustments in the external accounts of the emerging market economies of the Western Hemisphere and Russia and continued sizable external surpluses in emerging Asia swung the combined current account balance

position of the emerging markets economies into a $14 billion surplus in 1999, compared with a $51 billion deficit in 1998. The surplus is projected to widen moderately this year, as more robust growth and associated stronger import demand in the emerging market economies will be more than offset by the net beneficial impact of higher commodity prices elsewhere. The surplus of the east Asian countries is expected to narrow further and the deficits of the emerging market economies of the Western Hemisphere are projected to begin to widen again. But the combined current account positions of the countries in the Africa, Middle East, and Europe regions are projected to improve significantly in 2000, reflecting the net impact of higher commodity prices. Mainly owing to a further narrowing of east Asia's surplus and a widening of the deficit in the Western Hemisphere, and also to a renewed weakening of the current account position of the oil exporting countries, the overall current account position of the emerging market economies as a group is expected to swing into deficit again in 2001. The projected imbal-

Table 2.2. Emerging Market Economies: Net Capital Flows[1]
(Billions of U.S. dollars)

	1992	1993	1994	1995	1996	1997	1998	1999	2000	2001
Total										
Net private capital flows[2]	112.6	172.1	136.3	226.9	215.9	147.6	75.1	80.5	70.9	127.8
Net direct investment	35.4	59.4	84.0	92.6	113.2	138.6	143.3	149.8	153.0	144.6
Net portfolio investment	56.1	84.4	109.6	36.9	77.8	52.9	8.5	23.3	30.4	33.5
Other net investment	21.0	28.3	−57.3	97.4	24.9	−43.9	−76.7	−92.5	−112.5	−50.3
Net official flows	21.2	17.2	3.4	11.7	0.4	23.5	44.7	3.0	14.4	6.6
Change in reserves[3]	−56.9	−63.7	−63.6	−117.9	−114.2	−73.1	−37.8	−78.5	−102.2	−100.7
Memorandum										
Current account[4]	−78.5	−118.9	−75.8	−107.0	−94.4	−72.1	−50.9	14.0	22.8	−25.5
Africa										
Net private capital flows[2]	−4.0	−1.8	2.9	10.9	7.5	16.7	11.5	14.8	16.1	15.9
Net direct investment	0.6	1.9	2.3	2.2	4.8	7.4	5.2	9.5	9.2	8.3
Net portfolio investment	1.8	1.0	2.0	1.4	1.3	3.7	4.3	4.4	2.6	2.3
Other net investment	−6.4	−4.7	−1.4	7.3	1.4	5.6	2.0	0.9	4.4	5.3
Net official flows	10.4	6.3	7.7	7.3	4.6	−1.4	2.5	1.6	−4.5	0.7
Change in reserves[3]	0.7	3.2	−6.0	−3.3	−9.2	−11.2	1.2	−3.0	−11.7	−7.4
Memorandum										
Current account[4]	−10.0	−11.2	−11.5	−16.5	−7.0	−7.4	−20.0	−16.8	−7.7	−13.8
Asia[5]										
Crisis countries[6]										
Net private capital flows[2]	29.0	31.8	36.1	74.2	65.8	−20.4	−25.6	−24.6	−40.6	−18.1
Net direct investment	7.3	7.6	8.8	7.5	8.4	10.3	8.6	10.2	12.0	7.2
Net portfolio investment	6.4	17.2	9.9	17.4	20.3	12.9	−6.0	6.3	6.6	3.0
Other net investment	15.3	7.0	17.4	49.2	37.1	−43.6	−28.2	−41.1	−59.2	−28.3
Net official flows	2.0	0.6	0.3	0.7	−0.4	17.9	19.7	−4.7	5.0	−1.9
Change in reserves[3]	−18.1	−20.6	−6.1	−18.5	−5.4	30.5	−52.1	−44.5	−17.2	−20.3
Memorandum										
Current account[4]	−16.1	−13.5	−23.2	−40.4	−53.0	−25.0	69.1	62.9	43.1	36.7
Other Asian emerging markets										
Net private capital flows[2]	−8.3	25.6	27.5	30.8	38.3	19.0	−17.0	−2.5	10.6	10.3
Net direct investment	8.4	26.3	38.3	39.1	44.6	45.1	49.7	39.6	41.3	39.3
Net portfolio investment	2.6	4.6	1.8	−3.2	−7.4	−9.4	−11.9	−11.9	−0.4	−3.5
Other net investment	−19.3	−5.3	−12.7	−5.1	1.1	−16.7	−54.7	−30.2	−30.4	−25.6
Net official flows	8.3	7.9	10.4	5.8	4.1	3.7	7.9	3.8	5.1	8.6
Change in reserves[3]	−6.6	−16.6	−47.3	−27.6	−44.8	−46.7	−18.2	−15.9	−32.9	−40.2
Memorandum										
Current account[4]	14.0	−8.2	16.8	−4.5	16.2	48.2	44.5	32.9	31.7	33.7

(continued on next page)

ance of $25½ billion would still be considerably below levels seen prior to the east Asian crisis.

The current account outlook for the emerging market economies remains subject to considerable uncertainty and could be affected by opposing forces. Stronger-than-expected recoveries led by domestic demand in east Asia and Latin America could result in wider-than-projected current account deficits, in part because sustaining the higher growth would require additional imports of capital goods. These higher deficits would probably be fully financed, to the extent that increased investor confidence associated with the improved growth prospects would tend

to reduce spreads and boost inflows. Alternatively, unfavorable developments in the advanced economies, in particular higher-than-projected interest rate hikes or a sharper slowdown in the United States, could harm the prospects for emerging market economies for attracting inflows or boosting exports, and affect in particular economies with current account deficits. These economies would then need to adjust in order to reduce the deficits below those projected in the baseline scenario. This adjustment would require a combination of import compression and lower growth and could also lead to downward pressure on exchange rates.

Table 2.2 *(concluded)*

	1992	1993	1994	1995	1996	1997	1998	1999	2000	2001
Middle East and Europe[7]										
Net private capital flows[2]	38.0	28.7	16.0	13.9	15.2	24.0	21.9	27.1	−0.0	18.6
Net direct investment	1.1	4.3	6.1	5.5	2.1	2.9	2.7	3.3	8.7	9.5
Net portfolio investment	14.9	8.8	9.0	5.0	3.5	5.0	0.2	10.2	−0.1	7.9
Other net investment	22.0	15.7	0.8	3.3	9.6	16.0	19.1	13.5	−8.5	1.2
Net official flows	−1.3	2.3	−1.1	−1.2	−1.1	−0.7	−0.5	−1.8	0.6	−0.7
Change in reserves[3]	−8.7	1.6	−3.0	−9.2	−21.5	−20.7	14.7	−12.0	−13.7	−10.1
Memorandum										
Current account[4]	−26.7	−31.8	−7.9	−7.0	4.5	2.2	−31.1	−5.5	19.7	−4.7
Western Hemisphere										
Net private capital flows[2]	55.6	66.8	49.4	53.1	72.1	85.5	70.0	54.1	69.8	74.9
Net direct investment	13.9	13.4	23.1	24.7	39.5	53.1	56.1	63.6	57.0	55.4
Net portfolio investment	30.3	44.0	66.7	3.0	41.0	19.2	14.7	10.6	12.9	16.6
Other net investment	11.4	9.4	−40.4	25.5	−8.4	13.2	−0.8	−20.1	−0.2	2.9
Net official flows	−1.8	0.5	−3.6	8.1	−4.7	−3.6	6.1	3.6	6.8	−1.1
Change in reserves[3]	−22.6	−20.1	4.6	−21.9	−30.8	−15.3	17.4	5.1	−17.5	−12.0
Memorandum										
Current account[4]	−34.5	−46.0	−52.2	−36.8	−38.3	−64.1	−88.6	−54.2	−56.5	−60.8
Countries in transition										
Net private capital flows[2]	2.3	21.0	4.5	44.0	17.0	22.8	14.2	11.6	15.1	26.1
Net direct investment	4.2	6.0	5.4	13.6	13.7	19.7	21.0	23.5	24.8	24.8
Net portfolio investment	0.1	8.7	20.0	13.3	19.2	21.5	7.2	3.7	8.9	7.1
Other net investment	−2.0	6.3	−21.0	17.1	−15.8	−18.4	−14.0	−15.6	−18.6	−5.8
Net official flows	3.6	−0.4	−10.3	−9.0	−2.1	7.6	9.0	0.6	1.4	1.0
Change in reserves[3]	−1.7	−11.2	−5.7	−37.4	−2.4	−9.6	−0.8	−8.2	−9.2	−10.7
Memorandum										
Current account[4]	−5.1	−8.2	2.1	−1.8	−16.9	−26.1	−24.8	−5.3	−7.5	−16.7

[1]Net capital flows comprise net direct investment, net portfolio investment, and other long- and short-term new investment flows, including official and private borrowing. Emerging markets includes developing countries, countries in transition, Korea, Singapore, Taiwan Province of China, and Israel. No data for Hong Kong SAR are available.

[2]Because of data limitations, other net investment may include some official flows.

[3]A minus sign indicates an increase.

[4]The sum of a current account balance, net private capital flows, net official flows, and the change in reserves equals, with the opposite sign, the sum of the capital account and errors and omissions.

[5]Includes Korea, Singapore, and Taiwan Province of China. No data for Hong Kong SAR are available.

[6]Indonesia, Korea, Malaysia, the Philippines, and Thailand.

[7]Includes Israel.

Commodity Market Developments

World commodity prices have strengthened considerably since the middle of 1999, as reflected in an increase in the IMF's overall index of primary commodity prices by more than 25 percent in U.S. dollar terms between June 1999 and March 2000. While a large part of this has been due to the continued increases in oil prices, the index of nonfuel commodity prices has also begun to pick up, rising 5 percent during this period (Figure 2.5). This increase in nonfuel commodity prices has, however, not been uniform. There are significant differences in the behavior of prices across commodity groups, and these prices overall have yet to recover from their late 1990s slump (see Box 2.2).

In the oil market, the sharp rally in prices seen in the first half of 1999 gathered pace in the second half of the year, and in early March 2000 prices reached a nine-year high. The tightness of the world oil market has been mainly a consequence of the relatively high compliance to production cuts agreed to by major oil producing countries in March 1999. The one-year agreement stipulated that the Organization of Petroleum Exporting Countries (OPEC) members and four non-member countries (Mexico, Oman, Norway, and Russia) would cut supply by

4.7 million barrels a day, or about 6 percent of world output. The rate of compliance—the ratio of actual to agreed production cuts—declined from more than 90 percent in the late summer of 1999 to 75 percent in early 2000, but this decline did not put significant downward pressure on prices.

In late 1999 and early 2000, supply side constraints interacted with a sharp increase in demand partly due to the cold weather in North America and partly reflecting the strengthening of global activity. The result was a marked drawdown in commercial inventories, which fell to their lowest level since the 1970s. Oil prices peaked in early March 2000, but then eased on expectations that the OPEC meeting at the end of the month would agree to raise production. At the meeting, nine OPEC members indeed agreed to raise official production ceilings from April 1 by 1.45 million barrels a day or 7½ percent. Iran and non-members Mexico and Norway announced additional production and export increases to the tune of 0.5 million barrels a day. Following the end-March agreement, oil prices stabilized at around $25 per barrel, down by about 20 percent from the early-March high but still up by more than two-thirds from levels one year before.

Prospects for oil prices remain subject to considerable uncertainty stemming from both demand and supply factors. On the demand side, prospects are highly dependent on the strength of the rebound in global economic activity. The evolution of supply will reflect compliance by OPEC with the announced new production ceilings, Iraq's future output levels (Iraq is an OPEC member but operates outside OPEC agreements because of international sanctions), and the supply response to higher prices from non-constrained market sources. The latter could result from either the reactivation of oil fields closed during the 1998 oil price slump or, over a longer period, the introduction of new capacity. As discussed in Box 2.3, price reversals in the oil market can be abrupt and severe, and their timing cannot be predicted by referring to the pattern of past price cycles.

Figure 2.5. Prices of Crude Petroleum and Nonfuel Commodities[1]
(1990 = 100)

Oil prices have increased sharply since early 1999, while the recovery in nonfuel commodity prices has been more modest.

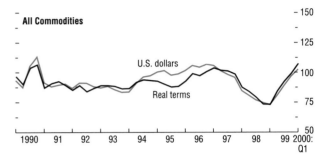

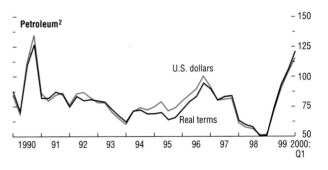

[1]Indices in real terms are obtained by deflating the nominal U.S. dollar price series by the unit value of manufactures exported by 20 industrial countries.
[2]Average Petroleum Spot index of UK Brent, Dubai, and West Texas.

Box 2.2. Cycles in Nonfuel Commodity Prices

Cycles are a dominant feature of movements in world commodity prices. Indeed, dealing with the economic consequences of rapid (and often unexpected) transitions from periods of rising prices to falling prices is among the most challenging issues facing policymakers from the many developing countries that rely on exports of primary commodities. It is therefore important to understand the properties of commodity-price cycles, and to put recent price movements in a longer-run perspective.[1]

In this Box, commodity-price cycles are identified with reference to turning points of the underlying price series, and are demarcated by price peaks and troughs that are determined using a cycle-dating procedure. Periods from troughs to peaks—that is, periods of generally rising commodity prices—can be described as booms, and periods from peaks to troughs as slumps.[2]

Cycles in the real index of prices of nonfuel commodities from 1957 to 1999 are depicted in the first figure, with booms denoted by no shading and slumps by dark shading. The cycles are demarcated by peaks (solid line) and troughs (dashed line). The first trough in nonfuel prices is in late 1960 and the first peak in early 1966, while the second trough is in late 1971. The first half of the 1960s is therefore the first boom phase for nonfuel prices, and the period of the

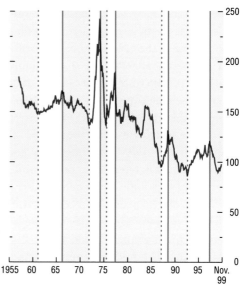

Cycles in Real Prices of Nonfuel Commodities, January 1957–November 1999[1]
(1990 = 100)

Sources: IMF, *International Financial Statistics;* and IMF staff estimates.

[1]Cycles are demarcated by peaks (solid line) and troughs (dashed line), with periods from peaks to troughs being slumps (shaded areas), and periods from troughs to peaks being booms (no shading).

[1]For analyses of the time series properties of commodity prices, see Angus Deaton and Guy Laroque, "On the Behaviour of Commodity Prices," *Review of Economic Studies*, Vol. 59 (1992), pp. 1–25; Angus Deaton, "Commodity Prices and Growth in Africa," *Journal of Economic Perspectives*, Vol. 13 (1999), pp. 23–40; and Paul Cashin, Hong Liang, and C. John McDermott, "How Persistent Are Shocks to World Commodity Prices?" *IMF Staff Papers*, forthcoming.

[2]This is done through a pattern-recognition procedure that determines the location of peaks and troughs using rules restricting the minimum length of booms, slumps, and complete cycles. A more detailed description of the procedure, and its application to dating booms and slumps in commodity prices, can be found in Paul Cashin, C. John McDermott, and Alasdair Scott, "Booms and Slumps in World Commodity Prices," IMF Working Paper 99/155 (Washington: International Monetary Fund, 1999).

late 1960s and early 1970s the first (completed) slump phase.

There have been four completed cycles in the nonfuel index, and about 64 percent of the sample has been spent in a slump phase, indicating that there is quite a large difference in the duration of booms and slumps. The period during which the greatest slump in the nonfuel index occurred was from early 1977 to early 1987—almost an entire decade—when the index fell by close to 50 percent; the biggest boom occurred from late 1971 to early 1974, when the index rose by about 44 percent in just over two years, with almost all of the price rise occurring in the last few months of this period.

Imbalances between world consumption and production of commodities, related to develop-

World Industrial Production and Commodity Prices
(Percent change from a year earlier)

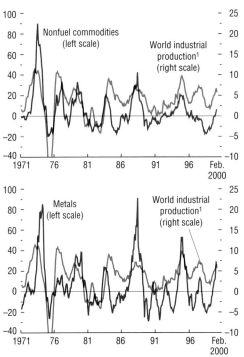

Sources: WEFA, Inc.; OECD; and IMF, *International Financial Statistics.*

[1]Three-month centered moving average, based on data for 32 advanced and emerging market economies representing about 75 percent of world output. Data through 1994 exclude one or more countries.

ments in world industrial production, underpin the timing and duration of many of these booms and slumps (see the second figure). The long slump in nonfuel commodity prices during the period of the late 1970s to mid-1980s (which included some temporary upward price movements) was associated with a deceleration in real economic growth in industrial countries, as well as a number of supply factors: record production of food, beverages, and agricultural raw materials that created large carryover stocks, and high capacity and production of metals. The recovery in commodity prices over the next year-and-a-half followed the pickup in economic ac-

tivity in industrial countries. The recovery was particularly pronounced for industrial inputs, after years of production cutbacks, but less so for food and beverages, as production of these goods had not been curtailed to the same extent during the preceding price slump.

The subsequent short-lived recovery was followed by another slump in commodity prices from mid-1988 to mid-1992. The decline in prices in the second half of 1989 was mainly due to large decreases in the prices of metals caused by a weakening demand from durable goods manufacturers, particularly in Japan and the United States. From mid-1992 to mid-1997 there was a recovery in prices (punctuated by some sharp price declines), following the strong economic performance by some major industrialized countries and many emerging market economies. From 1997 onwards the prices of nonfuel commodities entered another slump, from which they have yet to emerge, as the Asian crisis followed by the Brazilian and Russian crises contributed to a sharp downturn in commodities prices.

Several striking facts about these periods of boom and slump can be identified. There is an asymmetry in commodity-price cycles, as the average duration of slumps (63 months) is almost double the average duration of booms (37 months). The magnitude of price falls in a typical slump is slightly larger than the magnitude of price rebounds in a subsequent boom (falls of 37 percent and rises of 28 percent, respectively). This differing relative magnitude of price changes has resulted in an overall downward movement in real nonfuel commodity prices over the past 34 years. Third, large shocks to the nonfuel index occur quite frequently. Finally, there is no apparent relationship between the severity of price slumps and booms and their duration, nor does the probability of a boom or slump ending depend on the length of time already spent in the boom or slump.

There is a common perception that the prices of individual primary commodities move together. This proposition is broadly supported using correlations of prices for a set of unrelated commodities (cocoa, copper, cotton, crude oil,

Box 2.2 *(concluded)*

gold, lumber, and wheat)—unrelated in that they are not coproduced, are not obvious substitutes or complements, and are not inputs to the production of another.[3] When co-movement is defined in terms the proportion of time that the prices of pairs of commodities are both in a boom or slump period, however, there is much less evidence that prices for these six commodities move together over the last 34 years, except for gold and oil prices, which may be linked by inflation expectations. Consequently, there is some doubt as to the validity of the notion that prices of unrelated commodities move together.[4] This reflects the importance of supply factors in the behavior of individual commodity prices. Movements in world demand can affect many commodity prices in a similar manner, but the supply side of markets for individual commodities differs considerably, limiting comovement in prices across individual commodities.

These results suggest that caution is warranted when drawing policy implications for developing countries from analyses of movements in aggregate commodity price indices, such as the IMF's index of nonoil commodity prices. For industrial countries, which import a wide range of commodities, aggregate commodity price indices may be useful indicators of general movements in commodity prices. But developing countries often export only a limited range of such goods. In such cases, market conditions faced by a particular commodity-exporting country will not be well-represented by an aggregate index formed from indices of individual commodities, whose prices do not move synchronously. Accordingly, it is important to examine developments in the prices of individual commodities.

Given the limited co-movement in the prices of individual commodities, an analysis of the key features of cycles in the prices of six important

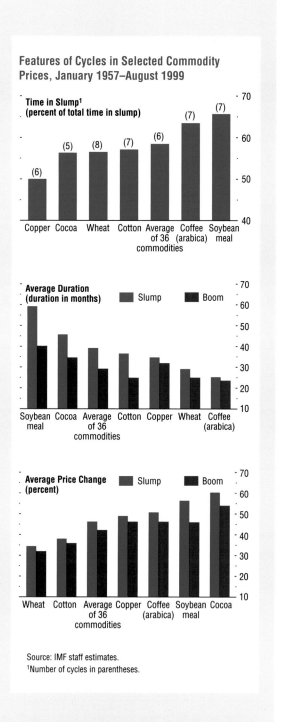

Features of Cycles in Selected Commodity Prices, January 1957–August 1999

Source: IMF staff estimates.
[1]Number of cycles in parentheses.

[3]See Robert Pindyck and Julio Rotemberg, "The Excess Co-Movement of Commodity Prices," *Economic Journal,* Vol. 100 (1990), pp. 1173–89.

[4]See Paul Cashin, C. John McDermott, and Alasdair Scott, "The Myth of Comoving Commodity Prices," IMF Working Paper 99/169 (Washington: International Monetary Fund, 1999).

nonfuel commodities—cocoa, coffee (arabica), copper, cotton, soybean meal, and wheat—can be informative. These commodities are also representative of the range of outcomes observed for the 36 individual commodities that comprise the IMF's index of nonfuel commodities.[5]

For the six selected commodities, complete cycles range from a low of five for cocoa to a high of eight for wheat (see the third figure). The length of booms and slumps appears to be nearly symmetric for copper, yet the price of soybean meal has spent a clear majority of its time in a slump. Apart from the beverages (cocoa and arabica coffee), the biggest booms in prices coincide with the first oil shock of the early 1970s and largest slumps in prices (apart from cocoa and cotton) in the years immediately following this oil shock. For three of the six individual commodities (cocoa, arabica coffee, and wheat), there is some evidence that there is a relationship between the severity of commodity price slumps and their duration, yet for no commodity is there evidence of a relationship between the severity of price booms and their duration.[6]

[5]Monthly data on the real price of these commodities is taken from the International Monetary Fund's *International Financial Statistics*.

[6]These results are consistent with earlier findings in the literature, in particular of commodity prices

The asymmetry in duration of slumps and booms observed in the aggregate index can also be seen for the six selected commodities in the third figure, which orders the commodities by the (decreasing) duration of slumps. The duration of the phases varies quite dramatically across the six commodities, ranging from an average slump of about 59 months for soybean meal to an average slump of 25 months for the price of arabica coffee. The average price decline during commodity price slumps is in most cases slightly larger than average price rise during commodity price booms. Indeed, for each of the six commodities analyzed, the differing relative magnitude of price movements in booms and slumps results in a downward trend in real prices.

These findings suggest that there is relatively little consistent pattern to cycles in the prices of individual nonfuel commodities, and emphasize the importance of examining developments in individual commodity markets, in addition to movements in aggregate commodity price indices.

declining at a steady rate, interspersed with sharp booms (see Angus Deaton and Guy Laroque, "On the Behaviour of Commodity Prices").

Indications are that OPEC members intend to keep oil prices at relatively moderate levels and want to avoid the large price swings observed between the end of 1998 and early 2000. They have announced more frequent meetings to review market developments and output adjustments if prices were to move outside the $22 to $28 per barrel range. As a result, the sharp price fluctuations seen in the first quarter of 2000 may be dampened and the "backwardation" (a situation whereby futures prices for the nearest months are higher than those for delivery in later months) in the oil futures markets reduced. The baseline assumption is for oil prices this year to average $24½ per barrel compared with $18¼ in 1999, an increase by 35 percent.

The higher level of world oil prices in 2000 is expected to raise significantly the export re-

ceipts of the oil exporting countries, with a corresponding increase in costs to oil importers. The direct (first round) effect on oil exports and imports of a $5 per barrel increase in world oil prices from their 1999 average levels is estimated to be around $60 billion, assuming the volume of oil trade was unchanged at 1999 levels. On a regional basis, the bulk of the higher oil export revenues would accrue to the Middle Eastern exporters, to the tune of almost $30 billion. Outside of the Middle East, oil trade is largely balanced across the main emerging market economy regions, so that oil importing advanced economies would absorb most of the higher oil import costs. Taking into account second round effects, however, the impact on current account positions would be significantly more limited. Oil exporting countries are likely

Box 2.3. Booms and Slumps in the World Oil Market

Movements in world petroleum prices have traditionally played an important part in world economic activity and inflation. Following the high-price period of the mid-1970s to mid-1980s, real petroleum prices have remained relatively flat. However, petroleum prices rose strongly during 1999 and early 2000, due largely to supply constraints, after having sharply declined during 1998. This Box presents a discussion of some stylized facts of cycles in oil prices.

Monthly data on the real price of oil, taken from the IMF's *International Financial Statistics* for the period 1957 to 1999, are shown in the figure. Also depicted are the results of the application of the cycle-dating procedure described in Box 2.2. The cycles are demarcated by peaks (solid line) and troughs (dashed line), with periods from peaks to troughs being slumps (dark shading), and periods from troughs to peaks being booms (no shading).[1]

The first completed boom and slump phases, in the early 1960s and from the middle of 1962 to early 1971, are likely to be artifacts of the structure of world oil markets. During this period, oil prices were largely unchanged in nominal terms as a result of price-setting by the Seven Sisters oil oligopoly, but eroded in real terms in line with world inflation, with cyclical movements in real oil prices reflecting fluctuations in the relative price of manufactures. Oil prices rose sharply following the first and second Organization of Petroleum Exporting Countries (OPEC) oil shocks, and these shocks were the main factors underpinning the boom periods of the early and late 1970s. Following the short-lived 1978–79 boom, there was a long slump in prices from the end of 1979 until mid-1986, interspersed by some short-term ups and downs, particularly at the beginning of the period. The 1979–86 slump was largely attributable to the breakdown of OPEC's constraints on production, with almost all of the price decline occurring in the last few months of this period. During the rest of the 1980s, there were consecutive booms and slumps as OPEC's effectiveness in constraining supply waxed and waned, and demand for oil remained relatively flat. Following the sharp jump in oil prices caused by the 1990–91 Gulf crisis, the slump in the early 1990s was largely caused by the industrial country recession during that period. Oil prices boomed again between the end of 1993 and early 1997, due to rising demand for oil, but then entered another slump phase (distinguished by a rather sharp fall in prices of 2.8 percent a month), largely due to weak Asian demand for oil and excess supply. At present oil prices are in another boom phase, having

**Cycles in Real Petroleum Prices,
January 1957–November 1999[1]**
(1990 = 100)

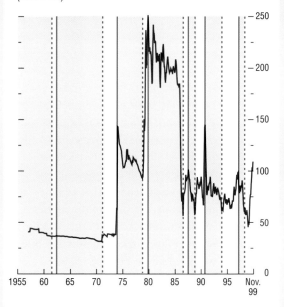

Sources: IMF, *International Financial Statistics;* and IMF staff estimates.
[1]Cycles are demarcated by peaks (solid line) and troughs (dashed line), with periods from peaks to troughs being slumps (shaded areas), and periods from troughs to peaks being booms (no shading).

[1]For further details see Paul Cashin, C. John McDermott, and Alasdair Scott, "Booms and Slumps in World Commodity Prices," IMF Working Paper 99/155 (Washington: International Monetary Fund, 1999).

reached their lowpoint in December 1998, with price rises largely driven by high compliance with the latest OPEC agreement to curtail production.

The oil market has had six completed cycles over the sample period, spending 71 percent of the time in a slump phase. This indicates that oil price changes are not symmetric in duration. On average, the duration of slumps (51 months) is more than double the duration of booms (22 months). When they occur, price slumps and booms can sometimes be severe—the maximum change in oil prices during slumps is a fall of 79 percent and during booms a rise of 78 percent. Not surprisingly, the biggest boom period for oil occurred between early 1971 and early 1974 (at the time of the first oil shock), while the greatest slump occurred between late 1979 and mid-1986. On average, the magnitude of price falls in a slump is slightly smaller than the magnitude of price rebounds in a subsequent boom (falls of 45 percent and rebounds of 48 percent, respectively).

These features of past cycles, however, do not allow us to make inferences about the duration and shape of future cycles. There is little evidence of a consistent "pattern" to oil price cy-cles, as there is no relationship between the severity of oil price slumps and booms and their duration. There is also no indication that the probability of ending a slump or boom in oil prices is dependent on the time already spent in that slump or boom.

Consistent with earlier work, these empirical findings support the view that oil price shocks tend to be long-lived, with prices steadily declining in slumps, interspersed by sharp booms.[2] These booms and slumps are typically associated with institutional changes in the world oil market, such as the implementation and collapse of supply-constraining agreements among major oil producers. Following sharp and virtually uninterrupted increases since the beginning of 1999, oil prices in February 2000 were two-and-a-half times as high as one year earlier. Despite their pronounced character, these recent price movements are not informative for determining when the current boom in oil prices might end, which appears to depend much more on supply conditions and, in particular, the behavior of OPEC.

[2]The behavior of real oil prices exhibits a substantial asymmetry, as there are few large downward spikes to balance the many large upward spikes in prices.

to use some of the additional export revenue to ease spending restraints adopted during the 1997–98 price slump, and increase non-oil imports. A MULTIMOD simulation suggests that the overall deterioration in the current account positions of the oil importing main industrial countries could be about $20 billion. Financially constrained oil importing developing countries, however, would cut other imports to the extent the higher oil import bill could not be covered through additional external financing.

The projected higher level of oil prices will have an impact on other macroeconomic variables as well. As discussed in Box 1.4 of the October 1999 *World Economic Outlook*, the overall effect on inflation and growth in both the major industrial countries and the oil importing emerging market economies should remain relatively modest, in contrast to the early 1970s, due to the reduced importance of oil in world production and consumption. The scenario would become more unfavorable if the increase in oil prices were large enough to trigger a significant increase in inflationary pressures, which would necessitate preemptive monetary tightening in the industrial countries. However, the impact effect on inflation so far has been limited to the energy components of general price indices, without second round effects on wages and other costs. According to MULTIMOD, the overall inflationary effect of a $5 per barrel price increase is not expected to exceed ½ of 1 percent in the United States and the euro area and ¼ of 1 percent in Japan in the first year. The impact on real GDP is also expected to be relatively small in both oil importers and exporters because rising oil prices have only limited effects on incentives to produce. The more important impact is on real incomes and domestic demand through the terms of trade. The simulation indicates that in response to a $5 per barrel oil price increase, domestic demand could decline by around ½ of 1 percent in the euro zone and by somewhat more than ¼ of 1 percent in Japan and the United States—about double the impact on real GDP in all three cases. The oil importing emerging market economies are expected to experience significant terms-of-trade losses, although these will be moderated in a number of cases, most notably Brazil and South Africa, by the impact of higher nonfuel commodity prices. The oil exporting countries will benefit from considerable terms-of-trade and real income gains. Outside the Middle East region, Indonesia, Mexico, Russia, and Venezuela will be the main beneficiaries.

With regard to nonfuel commodity prices, all the main aggregate price indices appear to have bottomed out since the summer of 1999. This has brought to an end a cyclical decline in nonfuel commodity prices by over 30 percent from their peak in May 1996 (Box 2.2). This decline had been longer and deeper than the two previous cyclical declines in the early and late 1980s. Part of the reason for the severity of the declines this cycle was a stronger than usual confluence of significant supply and demand shocks, with a deceleration in the rate of growth of world consumption that coincided with sustained production increases. The slowdown in consumption was associated particularly with the economic difficulties in east Asia: several of the Asian crisis countries had exhibited rapid growth in the consumption of primary commodities prior to the 1997–98 crisis. At the same time, production of many commodities had continued to increase rapidly, owing to technological innovations that lowered production costs, and, in the case of agricultural commodities, lengthy periods of favorable weather that resulted in exceptionally good harvests.

The recent pickup in nonfuel commodity prices is due to a reversal of these supply/demand factors. The story is somewhat different for specific commodities. For most agricultural products, tighter supply conditions due to bad weather and a pickup in demand growth have led to some limited price increases. The increase in prices for agricultural raw materials reflects mainly timber prices, which strengthened throughout 1999 due to strong demand in the U.S. housing sector and tight supplies of tropical timber in Asian markets. For industrial metals, prices tend to be driven by the cycle in world industrial production, and the upturn in the production cycle since the summer of 1999 has continued to push metals prices up. This has been aided by cuts in production, as in the case of copper, and supply disruptions, as in the case of nickel.

The prospects for the nonfuel commodity prices this year are mixed. The high level of stocks for most agricultural commodities are likely to preclude a significant rise in prices. In the case of metals, although stocks generally also remain at high levels, the synchronized increase in world growth is increasing demand rapidly. Metals prices are expected to continue to increase over the near term.

For exporters of nonfuel commodities, the net effects of this year's projected 5 percent average price increase depend on the specific commodities that they export (in addition to quantity effects related to weather and other supply disturbances) and on the extent of their dependence on imported oil. On balance, growth prospects this year for nonfuel commodity exporters appear to be marginally worse than had been projected in the October 1999 *World Economic Outlook*, but these countries' external imbalances would be reduced.

Policy Responses and Vulnerabilities in Latin America

The Latin American economies experienced recessions in varying degrees in 1998–99 as they adjusted to contagion from the east Asian crisis and from Brazil's currency devaluation in January 1999.[1] However, they generally avoided the sharp economic downturns observed in east Asia during the regional crisis. With a few notable exceptions, the recessions were mostly short-lived, and recoveries were already under way by the third quarter of 1999 as demand for the region's exports rose and conditions in international financial markets improved. Inflation continued to decline in most cases and, in spite of sizable currency depreciations, increased only moderately in Brazil and Colombia, held back by significant output gaps and, in Brazil, tight fiscal and monetary policies.

Compared with the generally similar output and inflation patterns among countries in east Asia during the 1997–98 crisis, developments during Latin America's region-wide recessions of 1999 were considerably more heterogeneous (Figure 2.6). In Mexico, year-on-year growth, while remaining positive, slowed in late 1998 and further in early 1999, but picked up to above 4 percent in the second half of the year. In Brazil, where growth had already turned negative in the latter part of 1998, the additional adverse output effects from the January 1999 financial crisis were shallow and short-lived, and output growth rebounded to 3 percent in the last quarter of the year compared with one year before. By contrast, Argentina, Chile, Colombia, and Venezuela continued to be confronted with rather sharp recessions in the first half of 1999, followed by recoveries in the fourth quarter (although year-on-year growth remained negative in Colombia and Venezuela in late 1999). Ecuador has yet to recover from its deep recession. The inflation picture was equally diverse, with consumer price inflation at the end of 1999 ranging from below zero in Argentina to 61 percent in Ecuador.

The recessions generally did not lead the authorities to relax macroeconomic policies, in marked contrast to episodes in earlier decades. Reflecting the heterogeneity in cyclical patterns, however, policy responses, while aimed overall at

maintaining macroeconomic stability, were quite diverse. Moreover, underlying fiscal deficits in Latin America remain rather large, contributing to the region's relatively low national saving rates and sizable external financing needs, as discussed below. In a number of countries, the financial crises and ensuing weakness of activity also prompted the authorities to abandon fixed exchange rate regimes. Brazil, Chile, and Colombia adopted flexible exchange rate arrangements, while Ecuador moved toward dollarization.

Brazil and Mexico generally pursued stability-oriented policies. Brazil's monetary policy was partially supportive of the recovery from April until late September 1999, but then turned more restrictive as concerns over a pickup in consumer price inflation and continuing pressure on the exchange rate prompted the central bank to refrain from further interest rate reductions. The fiscal authorities sustained their adjustment efforts in 1999 through a combination of tight expenditure controls and revenue enhancing measures, and the primary balance of the consolidated public sector swung into a surplus of just over 3 percent of GDP from a deficit of 1 percent in 1998; further consolidation and a surplus of 3¼ percent of GDP are targeted for 2000. In Mexico, monetary policy continued to focus on bringing down inflation to single digits, with progress toward this objective providing scope for further interest rate reductions. Sustained fiscal consolidation, facilitated by solid growth, helped Mexico achieve an overall fiscal deficit target of 1¼ percent of GDP for 1999 (Table 2.3). Chile, by contrast, was able to pursue counter-cyclical monetary and fiscal policies in response to the sharp downturn in early 1999. Real interest rates were brought down sharply and a fiscal stimulus package involving additional spending was introduced. Monetary policy was tightened in January 2000 and further in March to prevent inflation from picking up as the recovery gained momentum.

---

[1]For the purpose of this section, the Latin American economies comprise the Western Hemisphere developing countries for which private flows are the main source of external financing.

Figure 2.6. Selected Emerging Market Economies: Quarterly Real GDP
(Percent change from four quarters earlier)

The emerging market economies of Latin America experienced recessions of varying degrees in 1999. The east Asian countries have rebounded strongly from deep recessions.

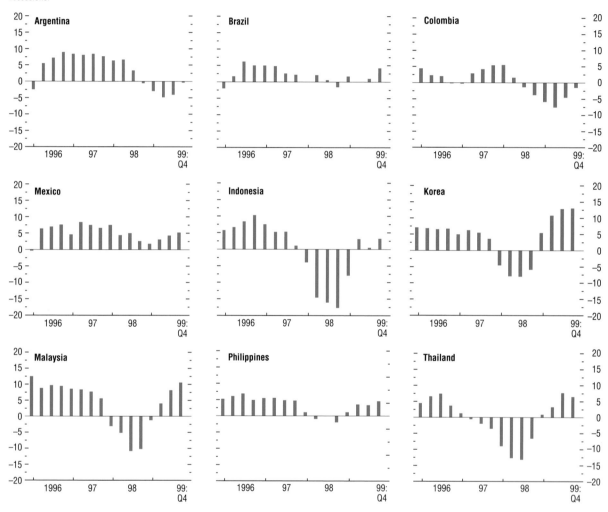

Sources: Country authorities; and IMF staff estimates.

Table 2.3. General Government Balance
(Percent of GDP)

Country	1994	1995	1996	1997	1998	1999
Argentina	−1.8	−2.3	−3.2	−2.0	−2.1	−3.8
Brazil	−3.3	−7.0	−5.9	−6.3	−8.1	−10.0
Chile	2.5	3.9	3.1	2.5	0.1	−2.0
Colombia	−0.8	−0.8	−2.5	−3.0	−3.6	−6.4
Mexico	−0.1	−0.9	−0.3	−1.4	−1.2	−1.6
Indonesia	0.0	0.8	1.2	−0.7	−1.9	−2.3
Korea	1.0	1.3	1.0	−0.9	−4.0	−2.9
Malaysia	3.3	2.2	2.1	4.0	−1.0	−4.1
Philippines	−1.8	−1.4	−0.4	−0.8	−2.7	−4.4
Thailand	1.9	3.0	2.5	−0.9	−2.5	−3.0
Of which: central government						
Argentina	−0.5	−1.5	−2.2	−1.1	−1.3	−2.5
Brazil	0.1	−2.3	−2.6	−2.6	−5.5	−7.4
Chile	2.5	3.9	3.1	2.5	0.1	−2.0
Colombia	−1.4	−2.8	−4.5	−3.5	−5.2	−7.1
Mexico	−0.4	−1.6	−1.0	−1.6	−1.6	−1.1
Venezuela	−7.3	−4.3	0.6	1.6	−2.6	−3.0
Indonesia	0.0	0.8	1.2	−0.7	−1.9	−2.3
Korea	0.1	0.3	0.0	−1.7	−4.4	−3.5
Malaysia	1.4	1.3	1.1	2.4	−1.5	−3.5
Philippines	−1.8	−1.4	−0.6	−0.8	−2.7	−4.4
Thailand	2.0	2.5	1.0	−1.7	−2.9	−3.7

The macroeconomic policy mix has been somewhat less balanced in Argentina, Colombia, and Venezuela. In Argentina, the fiscal deficit widened considerably toward the end of 1999, despite the incipient recovery, largely as a consequence of an election-related weakening in tax compliance and spending overruns at both the federal and provincial levels of government. Faced with the risk of a further deterioration of the public sector finances in 2000, the federal government at the beginning of the year introduced selective cutbacks in spending and enacted a package of tax measures so as to reduce the federal budget deficit to 1½ percent of GDP, down from 2½ percent in 1999. In Colombia, the fiscal position deteriorated markedly during the first half of 1999, as the economy contracted. A widening deficit was not so much the result of deliberate counter-cyclical measures but rather the consequence of unintended additional spending, in part because of an adjustment in nominal salaries and pensions based on inflation projections that exceeded the outturn. Subsequently, the authorities sought to tighten

the fiscal stance and also introduced measures to address structural imbalances in the fiscal accounts, but loosened monetary policy. In Venezuela, monetary policy has continued to support an exchange rate crawl aimed at bringing down inflation. The use of a crawl as a disinflationary tool without the full backing of macroeconomic policies has proven costly in terms of losses in external competitiveness. The authorities adopted a moderately expansionary fiscal policy stance in late 1999 to provide a boost to activity, as the economy was slow to emerge from recession.

In Ecuador, assistance to troubled banks has both undermined monetary policy and severely weakened the fiscal position. Massive liquidity assistance to the banking sector led to a sharp acceleration in money growth. Substantial losses on central bank operations and higher costs of servicing U.S. dollar-denominated debt also offset the improvements in the fiscal accounts stemming from higher oil-related revenues and expenditure restraint.

In contrast with east Asia during its 1997–98 crisis, Latin America avoided generalized financial distress in the banking and corporate sectors, although severe problems emerged in some cases—particularly in Ecuador. Policy efforts to strengthen financial systems were maintained or intensified. In most countries, however, bank lending to the private sector stagnated or even declined during the recession (Figure 2.7). As bank loans are still the dominant outside financing source for the region's corporate sector, continuation of this weakness could slow the pace of the recovery.

Financial sectors in Brazil and Mexico were little affected by the less favorable economic developments between late 1998 and early 1999. In Brazil, the corporate and financial sectors had largely hedged the risk of a devaluation, while in Mexico the growth slowdown was too short and shallow to have a significant impact on the quality of loan portfolios. Both countries made further progress in strengthening prudential regulations and supervision. In Brazil, authorities are auditing and evaluating the (publicly owned)

Figure 2.7. Selected Emerging Market Economies: Claims on Private Sector
(Real terms; January 1996 = 100)

Bank lending to Latin America's private sector stagnated or declined during the 1999 recession. Except in Korea, east Asia's recovery has not led to a pickup in bank credit to the private sector.

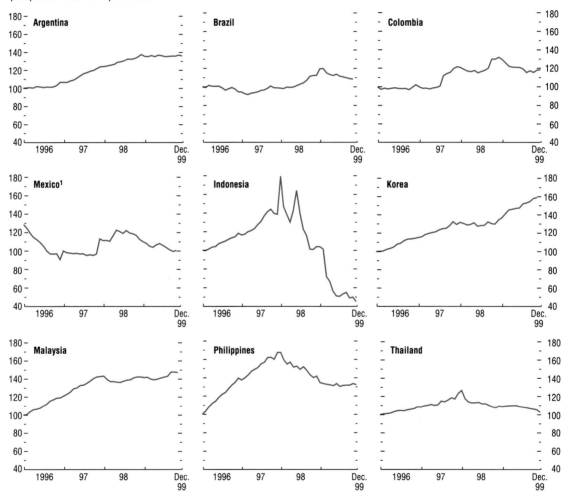

Source: IMF, *International Financial Statistics.*
[1]For Mexico, January 1997 = 100.

federal banks and preparing the privatization of 9 of the remaining 16 state banks. In Mexico, new legislation on bankruptcy and credit guarantees is expected to improve financial discipline. But the country also continues to deal with the consequences of the 1994–95 banking crisis, including a rising fiscal burden from the associated recapitalization measures and depressed bank lending activity.

The banking system in Argentina in 1999 remained generally sound, as in previous years, despite a relatively sharp fall in activity. Bank deposits grew and restructuring continued with increasing participation of foreign capital, although the recession and a related increase in nonperforming loans led to greater caution in bank lending. In Colombia, by contrast, the banking system was more affected by falling output, and pressures on the system already apparent in late 1998 intensified in 1999. The ratio of nonperforming to total loans continued to rise during most of the year, and solvency and liquidity indicators deteriorated further, particularly among public banks. The Colombian authorities responded by strengthening banking supervision and regulation. They also began to liquidate the largest public bank and introduced a recapitalization plan for viable private institutions.

In Ecuador, the banking sector entered a full-blown crisis as the country's recession deepened in early 1999. In the wake of the declaration of an early-March bank holiday, bank balance sheets continued to deteriorate as a result of a reduction in external credit lines, an increase in nonperforming loans—to more than 40 percent of total loans by the end of 1999—and capital flight. Following successive interventions by the country's deposit guarantee agency, the share of total banking system assets that remains privately owned has fallen to less than one-third. In the context of the country's dollarization, which was formally approved in early March 2000, the Ecuadorian authorities have taken steps to address major liquidity problems in the banking system and have designed a strategy for a more comprehensive restructuring of the banking system.

In addition to focusing attention on reducing financial sector vulnerabilities, the Latin American countries also remained generally committed to structural reform in other areas.[2] Fiscal reforms were introduced in a range of countries, and in some cases advanced significantly. Argentina and Brazil strengthened their overall fiscal policy framework by approving laws that establish limits on the deficit and public debt and improve the management and transparency of the public finances. In Mexico, the authorities have improved the efficiency of the tax system, and they are preparing a comprehensive tax reform aimed at broadening the tax base. In addition, Brazil and Colombia took steps to put their social security systems on a sounder financial footing. Also in Brazil, the authorities have initiated public debt management reforms to reduce the costs and interest rate sensitivity of debt service. To strengthen monetary policy credibility, Brazil adopted an inflation targeting framework in July 1999. In Chile, where such a framework is also in place, the authorities in the fall of 1999 announced their intention to target an inflation range (rather than a level) in 2001. Colombia and Mexico have been moving toward the introduction of an inflation targeting framework. In Argentina, the authorities took steps toward further deregulation of the labor market so as to increase the economy's resilience to shocks—an important direction of reform given that the exchange rate cannot be adjusted under the currency board arrangement.

Latin America avoided a sharp region-wide contraction during 1999, and maintained its commitment to prudent macroeconomic policies and structural reform. The region remains vulnerable, however, in view of sizable net external financing requirements stemming from rather large and persistent current account deficits. These deficits partly reflect the region's significant external interest burden, and have as domestic counterpart relatively low national sav-

[2]See Box 2.3 of the October 1999 *World Economic Outlook* for a more detailed description.

Figure 2.8. Selected Latin American and East Asian Economies: Balance of Trade
(Billions of U.S. dollars; three-month centered moving average of annualized monthly data)

The trade balances of the Latin American economies generally improved in 1999. The east Asian crisis countries have consolidated the trade balance gains achieved in 1998.

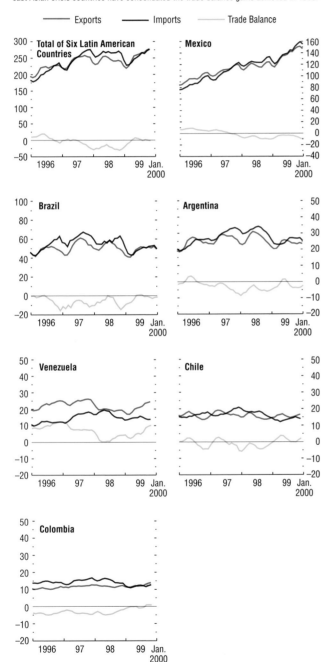

ing rates that fail to fully match investment needs. Moreover, Latin America each year needs to refinance a significant fraction of its outstanding external debt owing to a relatively unfavorable debt maturity profile.

The current account deficit of the Latin American countries narrowed to around $55 billion in 1999 from a decade high of almost $90 billion in 1998 as trade balances improved on the back of contractions in domestic demand (Figure 2.8). For Brazil and Colombia real effective exchange rate depreciations and, for Mexico, robust import demand in the United States also helped improve trade balances (Figure 2.9). Despite this improvement, the regional current account deficit remained relatively high by the standards of the early 1990s. Moreover, it is expected to widen again in 2000 and 2001 owing to a robust recovery in imports that will only partially be offset by an increase in export revenues in line with stronger world demand and higher commodity prices.

Latin America's current account deficits are large compared with the pool of external financing projected to be available for the emerging markets. In view of the relatively closed nature of the region's economies and sizable net external interest payments, the deficits are also large relative to underlying export and import levels. Current account adjustment prompted by reduced availability of external financing would therefore require significant exchange rate depreciation or domestic demand contraction to generate the needed expansion in exports and reduction in imports. In addition, in view of unfavorable conditions in local capital markets, domestic borrowers, including the public sector, have turned to international markets to cover a substantial portion of their financing requirements. This lack of domestic intermediation, which mainly reflects financial market imperfections and the consequences of high inflation in the past, has increased even more the region's foreign currency debt exposure (Table 2.4).

In view of these financial vulnerabilities, the most significant risk to Latin America's near-

Table 2.4. External Debt

(Percent of GDP)

Country	1994	1995	1996	1997	1998	1999
Argentina	33.3	38.2	40.3	42.5	46.9	52.1
Brazil	18.2	22.6	23.2	24.9	31.4	39.7
Chile[1]	42.2	33.3	33.5	35.3	43.5	49.5
Colombia	27.4	27.9	31.6	31.5	35.8	41.7
Mexico	33.7	58.7	49.5	38.1	38.1	33.0
Venezuela	68.7	49.3	53.1	41.1	39.3	36.7
Indonesia[1]	57.0	56.3	53.4	63.9	149.4	95.5
Korea	24.1	26.0	31.6	33.4	46.9	33.0
Malaysia	38.6	37.6	38.4	44.0	58.8	55.3
Philippines	60.4	53.1	50.5	55.3	73.3	68.0
Thailand	44.9	49.1	49.8	62.0	76.8	61.5
Of which: short-term debt						
Argentina	3.5	4.8	5.0	6.5	7.2	6.8
Brazil	3.5	4.3	4.9	4.6	3.0	4.1
Chile[1]	10.7	7.9	6.5	4.8	5.4	5.7
Colombia	5.4	5.8	5.1	4.4	4.6	4.3
Mexico	7.5	9.1	7.7	5.6	6.6	5.5
Venezuela	4.3	1.9	2.6	2.7	2.2	1.5
Indonesia[1]	6.5	8.7	7.5	27.5	76.4	45.1
Korea	13.3	14.6	17.9	13.4	9.6	10.9
Malaysia	7.5	7.2	9.9	11.1	11.7	9.4
Philippines	8.1	7.1	8.7	10.3	11.0	3.6
Thailand	20.2	24.5	25.1	24.6	27.0	21.1

[1]The data for Chile and Indonesia exclude trade credits.

term outlook stems from potential unfavorable developments in the advanced economies, in particular higher-than-expected interest rate hikes in the United States and associated reductions in private capital flows. A considerable external adjustment effort would be required in this case, mostly in countries such as Argentina and Brazil that combine sizable current account deficits with large refinancing requirements on maturing external debt.

In addition, the move toward a more balanced growth pattern among the major advanced economies may involve a sharper-than-expected growth slowdown in the United States or strong movements among the three major exchange rates. Such developments would also have an impact on the emerging market economies of Latin America, but on a differentiated basis. A sharp slowdown and fall in import demand in the United States would mostly affect countries with strong trade links to the United States, especially Mexico, while a weakening of the U.S. dollar could benefit

Figure 2.8 (*concluded*)

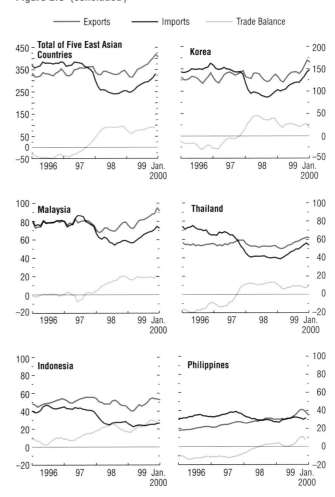

Sources: Country authorities; and IMF staff estimates.

Figure 2.9. Selected Emerging Market Economies: Real Effective Exchange Rates[1]
(June 1997 = 100)

Real effective exchange rates have depreciated in Brazil and Colombia since early 1999, but have strengthened in Mexico. They remain significantly below pre-crisis levels in east Asia.

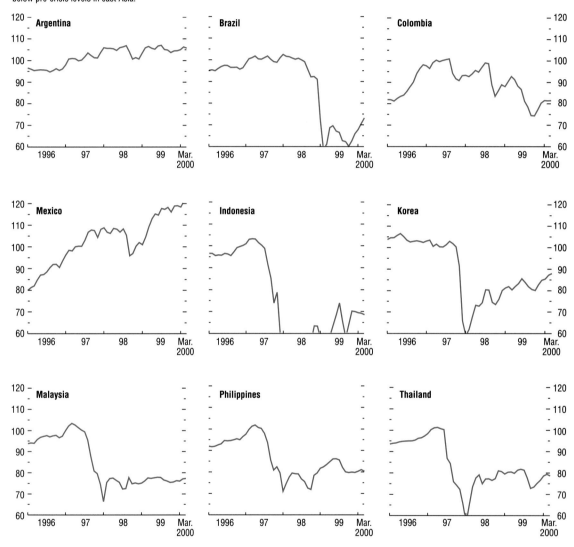

Source: IMF staff estimates.
[1]Defined in terms of relative consumer prices based on 1988–90 trade weights.

Argentina and possibly also Brazil and Chile, reflecting these countries' trade orientation and exchange rate regimes. Some of the Latin American countries are also major commodity exporters and hence are also exposed to risks stemming from fluctuations in commodity prices. Overall, however, the external position of these commodity exporters has improved as a result of the recent increases in oil and non-fuel commodity prices.

Improved Outlook in East Asia, But Policy Challenges Remain

The adjustment efforts in the emerging market economies of east Asia in the wake of the 1997–98 crisis have reduced the region's external vulnerabilities substantially. Foreign currency liabilities, especially those with short maturities, have fallen; current account balances have swung strongly into surplus; and exchange rate misalignments have been corrected. The strength of the recovery that is now under way in part mirrors the depth of the recession earlier, however, and the region now faces the challenge of transforming the recovery into high and sustained growth. This will require rebalancing macroeconomic policies toward a more neutral stance and stepping up structural reform efforts.

The external adjustment process following the onset of the east Asian crisis has resulted in a sharp turnaround in the current account balances of the crisis countries (Figure 2.10). Reflecting a deep import contraction, the countries' combined trade balances improved by almost $100 billion in 1998, or an average of more than 10 percent of GDP. Imports fell by more than 25 percent in U.S. dollars in Indonesia, Korea, Thailand, and Malaysia. Exports in U.S. dollar terms also declined in 1998, by an average of around 5 percent. The value of exports failed to pick up due to a number of factors, including lower worldwide commodity and electronics prices, currency adjustments and demand contraction in other crisis countries, and a pass-through to export prices of depreciations vis-à-

Figure 2.10. Selected East Asian and Latin American Economies: Current Account Balance[1]
(Percent of GDP)

The current account positions of the east Asian economies have improved considerably since the crisis, but those of the Latin American countries remain relatively weak.

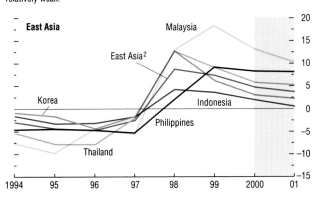

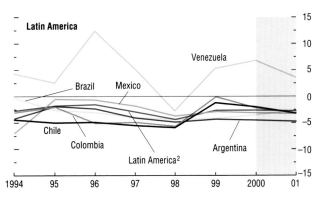

[1]Shaded areas indicate IMF staff projections.
[2]Weighted average.

vis the U.S. dollar.[3] In addition, export volumes responded with a considerable lag to improvements in overall competitiveness in the wake of substantial currency depreciations.

The current account gains achieved in 1998 were largely consolidated in 1999, as more robust export growth for the most part offset a sharp rebound in imports. Exports were boosted by the competitiveness gains from currency realignments, the effects of which began to be felt in late 1998. A surge in worldwide sales of electronics, robust import demand in the United States, and, in the second half of 1999, further currency depreciations relative to the Japanese yen had additional positive effects. The export recovery was outpaced, however, by an even faster rebound in imports, which surged in U.S. dollar terms by more than 40 percent in Korea, more than 30 percent in Thailand, and more than 20 percent in Malaysia in the fourth quarter of 1999 compared with corresponding levels one year before. In most of the east Asian countries, this import surge has been underpinned by the very strong revival in domestic demand associated with the arrival of the more advanced stages of the recovery, and has been accompanied by a self-sustaining rebound in intraregional trade.

Despite narrowing current account surpluses and also significant repayments on external loans, the overall balance of payments positions of the emerging market economies of east Asia continued to improve in 1999, as net portfolio and foreign direct investment inflows picked up, in particular in Korea. These inflows reflected improved market sentiment, with expectations of further currency appreciation and more equity price gains. In Korea, an increase in foreign equity participation in the financial sector has been an additional source of inflows. Balance of payments surpluses have allowed the crisis countries to accumulate additional international reserves and let currencies gradually appreciate (Figure 2.11). Unlike the early 1990s, the recent

capital inflows in Korea have been mostly non-debt creating, and so the country has been able to reduce further its total external liabilities. With short-term liabilities in particular being redeemed, the maturity profile of the external debt has improved significantly.

Robust current account surpluses and renewed non-debt-creating capital flows have reduced east Asia's external vulnerabilities considerably, but they also confront authorities with new policy challenges. This is particularly the case for Korea, where the recovery has been very robust and the rebound in inflows strong and where the exchange rate has been under upward pressure. On a more prospective basis, other countries in the region, including Malaysia and Thailand, face similar challenges. To meet these challenges, exchange rate policies need to find the right balance between additional reserve accumulation through intervention and further gradual currency appreciations. A case can be made for acquiring some additional international reserves in view of still relatively high ratios of short-term external debt obligations to international reserves. At the same time, the sizable current account surpluses and other indicators of relatively strong external competitiveness, including real effective exchange rates that are still significantly below pre-crisis levels, suggest that there is still scope for further currency strengthening before possible overvaluation becomes an issue.

In this regard, the implications for monetary policy also need to be considered. As interest rates have to be kept at relatively low levels to facilitate corporate and financial restructuring, further exchange rate appreciation could provide the tightening in monetary conditions that is required to keep inflationary pressures in check. In view of its potentially strong impact on banking sector soundness, the composition of the new capital inflows also requires careful monitoring. In particular, a shift toward short-term debt-creating inflows could increase the

---

[3]For a discussion of these factors, see Rupa Duttagupta and Antonio Spilimbergo, "What Happened to Asian Trade During the Crisis?" IMF Working Paper (Washington: International Monetary Fund, forthcoming).

Figure 2.11. Selected Emerging Market Economies: Total Reserves Excluding Gold
(Billions of U.S. dollars)

Brazil's international reserve position has stabilized in the wake of the currency crisis in early 1999. The east Asian countries, in particular Korea, have strengthened their international reserve positions since 1998.

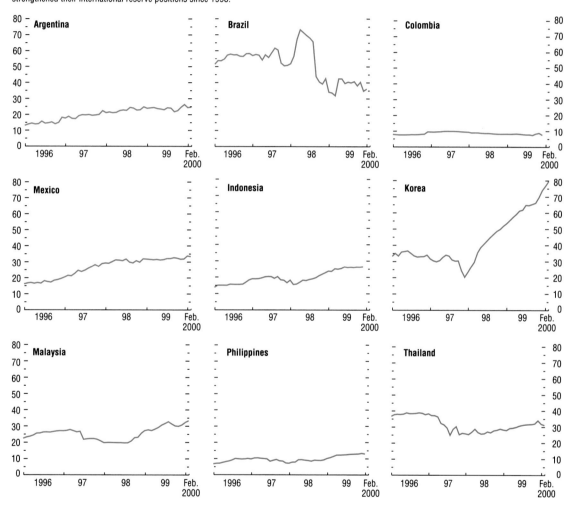

Source: IMF, *International Financial Statistics.*

Table 2.5. Indonesia, Korea, and Thailand: Sources of Changes in the Fiscal Balance
(Percent of GDP as of October 1999; a negative number indicates a fiscal deterioration)

	Indonesia[1]			Korea			Thailand[2]		
	1997/98	1998/99	1999/00	1997	1998	1999	1996/97	1997/98	1998/99
Fiscal balance (level)[3]	–0.9	–2.2	–6.8	0.0	–3.2	–5.6	–1.6	–5.1	–5.3
Changes in fiscal balance	–2.2	–1.0	–4.7	–0.3	–3.4	–2.5	–4.0	–3.0	–0.2
Changes due to economic environment[4]	–4.2	–3.7	2.2	. . .	–1.6	–0.4	–0.3	–2.8	0.6
Policy changes	2.7	2.6	–7.4	. . .	–2.1	–1.4	–2.6	–0.2	–0.9
Expenditures	2.7	2.2	–6.7	. . .	–3.6	–1.7	–2.6	0.3	–0.3
Bank restructuring	0.0	–0.4	–6.9	. . .	–0.3	–0.8	–0.7	–1.9	0.5
Other[5]	2.7	2.6	0.2	. . .	–3.3	–0.9	–1.9	2.2	–0.8
Statutory revenue change	0.0	0.4	–0.7	. . .	1.4	0.4	0.0	–0.4	–0.6
Residual (unexplained)	–0.7	0.1	0.5	. . .	0.3	–0.7	–1.1	0.0	0.0

Source: Jack Boorman and others, "Managing Financial Crises: The Experience in East Asia," *Carnegie–Rochester Public Policy Conference Series*, forthcoming; and IMF staff estimates.
    [1]For Indonesia, the fiscal year runs from April 1 to March 31.
    [2]For Thailand, the fiscal year runs from October 1 to September 30.
    [3]According to data as of March 2000, the fiscal balance for Indonesia was estimated at –3.8 percent of GDP in 1999/00 and for Korea at –2.9 percent of GDP in 1999.
    [4]Comprises changes in fiscal position attributable to economic activity, the exchange rate, interest rates, and (in the case of Indonesia) oil prices.
    [5]Includes outlays for social safety nets and other expenditures.

vulnerability of the financial system if the associated risks are not well managed. To avoid difficulties in this area, authorities need to ensure that prudential regulation and supervision are effectively enforced.

A key feature of the east Asian recovery process has been the supportive role of monetary and fiscal policy.[4] Monetary policies remained accommodative in the second half of 1999 and early 2000. In Korea, Malaysia, and Thailand, money market interest rates have been broadly unchanged since the middle of 1999 at levels significantly below those observed before the crisis in 1997. In Indonesia, a market-led decline in short-term interest rates resumed in the late fall of 1999 as political uncertainty eased, but interest rate levels continue to exceed those elsewhere in the region. Lower interest rates have helped reduce the pressure on heavily indebted corporates and contain the nonperforming loans problem. With the exception of Korea, however, the transmission of lower money market rates to bank lending rates has been slow, and credit to the private sector has stagnated or fallen in real terms.

Fiscal policies generally have provided further support for the recovery (Table 2.5). In Korea, a supplementary budget adopted in August 1999 was aimed at providing additional stimulus, while targeting a consolidated central government deficit of 5 percent of GDP for 1999. Even higher deficit targets for the financial years covering the bulk of calendar year 1999 were adopted in Indonesia and Thailand, with the Thai budget also including measures to stimulate specific components of domestic demand. In all three cases, however, actual deficits have fallen short of the budget targets. In Indonesia, this was due to spending delays, while in Korea, the shortfall stemmed primarily from the operation of automatic stabilizers, as the robust recovery boosted tax revenues and reduced unemployment-related outlays. In the Philippines, however, the 1999 deficit overshot the budget target, mainly owing to weaknesses in the country's revenue management.

While stimulative fiscal policies generally have been appropriate, such support has to be balanced against the objective of reducing the public debt burden. Rising deficits in combination

---

[4]For an in-depth analysis, see Jack Boorman and others, "Managing Financial Crises: The Experience in East Asia," *Carnegie-Rochester Public Policy Conference Series*, forthcoming.

Table 2.6. Gross Public Debt in the East Asian Countries
(Percent of GDP)

Country	1996	1997	1998	1999
Indonesia[1]	24.5	106.4	103.4	96.0
of which financial sector restructuring	. . .	39.9	55.3	60.1
Korea	8.8	12.7	24.4	29.6
of which financial sector restructuring	. . .	1.5	8.5	12.9
Malaysia	47.7	49.0	53.5	56.4
Philippines	68.2	66.4	72.9	74.4
Thailand	14.5	31.1	49.5	56.3
of which financial sector restructuring	1.2	13.8	28.9	31.0

Source: IMF staff estimates.
[1]Financial years running through the end of March.

with very substantial financial sector restructuring costs have contributed to a rapid increase in public sector debt since the onset of the crisis. Relative to GDP, Indonesia and Thailand have experienced the largest debt buildup since 1996, much of which is the result of financial sector restructuring, and they now face very considerable debt burdens (Table 2.6).[5] Despite a rapid debt buildup for similar reasons, Korea's debt-to-GDP ratio remains relatively low, reflecting the country's favorable debt position before the crisis. Public debt accumulation during the crisis was less rapid in Malaysia and the Philippines, but these countries started with higher pre-crisis public debt burdens. While a resumption of output growth and, for foreign currency denominated debt, real exchange rate appreciations are expected to help bring down public debt-to-GDP ratios from their current peak levels, deficit reduction and asset recovery from nonperforming loans taken over from the financial sector will also be required.

The case for a gradual shift in fiscal policies toward a more neutral stance is reinforced by the need for macroeconomic restraint as output gaps narrow and inflationary pressures may reemerge. Since interest rates need to be kept at low levels

to facilitate corporate and financial sector restructuring, the bulk of the adjustment in the macroeconomic policy stance should be borne by fiscal policy. The more than usual uncertainty regarding the sustainability of the ongoing sharp output recovery, which could be interpreted either as a cyclical rebound from the steep output falls during the initial crisis stages or as an indicator of incipient overheating risks, strengthens the argument for fiscal caution. This argument holds in particular for Korea, where the output gap could close as early as 2001 and where there is also considerable uncertainty about the outlook for cost-price behavior as the gap closes. Appropriately, Korea intends to bring down the budget deficit target from 5 percent of GDP in 1999 to 3½ percent in 2000 and to eliminate the deficit in the next few years. In Thailand, the public sector deficit in 2000 is projected to remain relatively large, at more than 5 percent of GDP, and additional tax revenue from faster-than-expected growth should be used to bring down the fiscal deficit below this target.

A particularly acute fiscal challenge faces Indonesia's authorities, as they have to weigh carefully the balance between supporting the recovery and beginning fiscal consolidation. A target for the fiscal deficit of 5 percent of GDP in 2000 is appropriate given the depth of the economic downturn during the crisis and the lagged recovery compared with the other east Asian economies. But public debt is now above 90 percent of GDP, and further rounds of bank recapitalization are still required, with interest payments on outstanding bank restructuring bonds expected to already reach 4¾ percent of GDP in 2000. The deficit could be even higher if authorities fail to properly sequence and implement a far-reaching fiscal decentralization program. Moreover, authorities will have to meet the financing needs stemming from the budget deficit. Financing for around half the deficit is expected to come from privatization proceeds and asset sales from state controlled banks,

---

[5]These numbers should be interpreted with caution as the coverage of the public sector and the costs of financial sector restructuring is not uniform across the east Asian countries.

where results to date have been generally below target. As room for noninflationary domestic financing is still limited, in the absence of a developed bond market, the remainder of the deficit is expected to be financed from external public sources, including a rescheduling of external debt held by Paris Club creditors.

A distinguishing characteristic of east Asia's financial crisis has been the extent of corporate and financial sector distress it has caused. The distress resulted from a combination of heavy dependence on bank financing and associated high debt-equity ratios in the corporate sector and lax risk management practices, as manifested in considerable external exposures. Nonperforming loans have risen to levels far in excess of those observed in other crises in emerging markets, including the 1994–95 tequila crisis. This is particularly the case in Indonesia and Thailand. In view of the scope of the financial crisis, authorities in the east Asian countries have given high priority to financial and corporate sector restructuring.[6] Both the restructuring strategies and progress toward corresponding reform objectives continue to vary from country to country, and the reform agenda is far from completed.[7]

Korea and Malaysia have achieved the most progress in restructuring and strengthening the financial sector. In Korea, the government asset management company set up to take over nonperforming loans from the financial sector has been relatively successful in terms of both the overall transfer rate and the subsequent liquidation of claims. Nonperforming loans of the financial system in the fall of 1999 stabilized at around 10 percent of total loans in the financial system (equivalent to 12 percent of GDP), and Korean banks have strengthened further their capital bases with both public and private money, including significant foreign investment. The reform agenda is far from finished, how-

ever, and weaknesses remain, in particular in the nonbank financial sector. These weaknesses were exposed in the early fall of 1999, when the investment trust industry faced considerable redemption pressure in the wake of debt servicing problems by the major *chaebol* Daewoo, which prompted financial institutions to establish a bond market stabilization fund to stabilize markets. Malaysia has also adopted the asset management company approach, and this company has been relatively successful in taking over nonperforming loans, with a view to rehabilitating them. By the end of 1999, recapitalization requirements for the financial sector had been largely met, and the ratio of nonperforming to total loans in the financial system (including those held by the asset management company Danaharta) had fallen to around 25 percent. Malaysia has also made progress in its plans to streamline the financial sector through extensive mergers between problem institutions and profitable banks.

In Thailand, which has opted for a strategy of virtually closing the nonbank financial sector but letting banks deal with problem loans on a decentralized basis, the major commercial banks have met Bank for International Settlements (BIS) capital adequacy ratios through raising additional capital, including from foreign investors. While private banks formally meet regulatory requirements, concerns exist that their underlying value is less than that derived from the application of prudential regulations. The public banks continue to be in a weak financial position. Despite a significant reduction in the second half of 1999, the nonperforming loans ratio remains relatively high, at around 39 percent at the end of the year (equivalent to 45 percent of GDP).

Financial sector restructuring is less advanced in Indonesia, in part because the financial distress induced by the crisis has been deeper and

---

[6]For a more detailed analysis, see Carl-Johan Lindgren and others, *Financial Sector Crisis and Restructuring; Lessons from Asia,* Occasional Paper No. 188 (Washington: International Monetary Fund, 2000.)

[7]The Philippines largely avoided the systemic banking sector problems that afflicted other emerging market economies in east Asia. This can be attributed in part to the beneficial effects of reforms implemented in the mid-1990s.

more widespread. The ratio of nonperforming loans to total loans remains above 60 percent (equivalent to more than 40 percent of GDP). The Indonesian Bank Recovery Agency has taken over the bulk of nonperforming loans, but the agency's asset recovery efforts have only been partially successful. Most of the financial sector is still in a precarious financial position, and less than 30 percent of the banking system remains privately held. Financial sector restructuring in Indonesia needs to remain focused on operational restructuring of the state banks and on moving ahead with loan recovery efforts.

Authorities in the east Asian economies most affected by the crisis have also been confronted with large-scale financial distress in the corporate sector, the counterpart to the nonperforming loan problem. In response, they have established out-of-court procedures to settle claims, and also introduced institutional and legal reforms, where needed, to strengthen bankruptcy systems and improve financial transparency and corporate governance. This corporate reform process has advanced the most in Korea and Malaysia, which have made the best use of out-of-court arrangements, in part because of stronger legal enforceability, and in part because of the relatively small number of cases. To streamline the process, and recognizing that the country's top five *chaebol* were too large and complex to be involved in an out-of-court work process, Korean authorities let these companies develop their own restructuring plans. In the wake of Daewoo's debt servicing problems in mid-1999, however, the authorities strengthened the restructuring framework for the other *chaebol* in the top five groups. Reform efforts now need to be extended into broader operational restructuring among the smaller *chaebol* as well.

Voluntary debt restructuring has met with less success in Thailand, however, in part because of more widespread balance sheet problems—by the end of 1999, almost 2,000 debtor firms were involved in voluntary arrangements—and in part because of a bankruptcy legislation that failed to provide strong incentives to comply with such arrangements. The bankruptcy law was reformed in March 1999, but shortcomings in the bankruptcy procedures remain. Indications are that corporate debt restructuring arrangements have mainly involved rescheduling debt to longer maturities at temporarily low interest rates, but with little debt relief in net present value terms.

Corporate sector restructuring is less advanced in Indonesia, where authorities have been unable to sustain the implementation of the corporate restructuring program. Continued weakness in the procedural capacities of key institutions established for this purpose, including the bank recovery agency and the Jakarta Initiative Task Force, and of the court system has been an important factor. Improvements in accountability and transparency in corporate governance have also fallen short of expectations.

The strength of the recoveries that are under way has not changed the need to make further progress toward financial and corporate sector restructuring in the east Asian crisis countries. As capital markets in the region are developing only slowly, bank credit will remain the main outside funding source for the corporate sector. Absent further reductions in nonperforming loans and improvements in corporate sector balance sheets, the lending capacity of the banking sector and corporate incentives to invest will remain impaired, and investment efforts, much curtailed during the crisis, will fail to return to levels required for robust and sustained growth. In view of the deep corporate sector weaknesses brought to the fore by the crisis, the transformation of the current recoveries into long-term growth will also require stepped-up efforts toward corporate restructuring, supported by higher rates of capital accumulation. The need to limit the risks stemming from renewed private inflows commonly associated with an improving growth outlook provides an additional rationale for further corporate and financial sector reform, including a strengthening of risk management practices. Ultimately, such reforms provide the best safeguards against a repetition of the 1997–98 financial turmoil and social hardship.

The tentative conclusions that emerge from this chapter suggest that the likelihood of an early repetition of the turmoil in emerging markets seen in recent years has declined considerably as a result of a variety of factors. These include notably the macroeconomic adjustment and structural reform efforts by many emerging market economies; the recoveries in commodity prices, in particular oil prices, which have helped improve the external position of many countries; and greater risk awareness on the part of international investors. Some Latin American economies nevertheless remain vulnerable to potential changes in investor sentiment and to developments that would adversely affect their external positions and the cost and availability of external financing. These vulnerabilities underscore the need for continued efforts to safeguard macroeconomic stability, increase national saving, and attain sustained growth through increases in efficiency and productivity. The emerging market economies more generally, including the east Asian countries that have achieved current account surpluses, still need to persevere with structural reforms to reduce the risk of a repetition of the recent crises.

CHAPTER III

ASSET PRICES AND THE BUSINESS CYCLE

Following widespread financial deregulation and increased globalization of capital markets since the early 1980s, industrial economies have witnessed a clear upward trend in asset prices. Alongside this trend, stock, property, and land prices have undergone—in both real and nominal terms—swings around typical business cycle frequencies ranging from three to ten years. Such swings have been quite pronounced. In some cases, such as in Japan and Scandinavia during the late 1980s and early 1990s, these swings turned out to have far-reaching disruptive effects on domestic financial systems and contributed to prolonged recessions. In other cases, such as in the United Kingdom during 1990–92, the financial system withstood the asset price collapse well but the ensuing recession was nevertheless quite severe.

While large asset price fluctuations are by no means a new phenomenon, a distinctive feature of the last two decades is that prolonged build-ups and sharp collapses in asset markets have taken place amidst a decline in consumer price inflation and a more stable macroeconomic environment in most of the industrialized world. Reflecting the primacy of low and stable inflation as a central goal of macroeconomic policy and the design of new monetary arrangements to help achieve this goal,[1] goods and services price inflation not only has declined to levels well below its post-war mean but its variability has also been significantly

reduced.[2] Greater monetary discipline has been supported by fiscal consolidation. Public sector deficits have been significantly reduced in most of the European Union (EU). In Australia, Canada, New Zealand, the Scandinavian countries, and the United States fiscal balances have posted surpluses for the first time in a generation.

Notwithstanding the remarkable progress on these fronts, asset price fluctuations have remained substantial and highly correlated with business cycles in the industrialized world (Figure 3.1). This juxtaposition of low and stable consumer price inflation with asset price volatility, which in turn is correlated with output fluctuations, has motivated an intense debate in academic and policy circles about the complex interrelationships between asset prices, output growth, and inflation, and the challenges they pose to the broader task of macroeconomic stabilization. Key questions that have been raised in this connection include:

- What drives asset prices?
- What are the channels through which asset prices affect economic activity?
- Do asset prices contain valuable information about the future evolution of economic activity?
- When do large swings in asset price pose a threat to macroeconomic stability and how should policymakers respond to them?
- Do the answers to these questions depend on the different classes of assets considered?

---

[1]These include greater central bank independence, more accountability and enhanced transparency in the conduct of monetary policy in most countries. The introduction of inflation targeting or an unequivocal commitment to money and exchange rate targeting (including through the establishment of "hard" pegs such as currency boards and monetary unions) have also been instrumental. For an overview of recent experiences with different monetary regimes, see Frederic Mishkin, "International Experiences with Different Monetary Policy Regimes," NBER Working Paper 6965 (Cambridge, Massachusetts: National Bureau of Economic Research, 1999).

[2]In the second half of the 1990s, consumer price inflation in industrial countries has fluctuated within the range of 1 to 2 percent a year, down from some 10 percent in 1980–82. Meanwhile, its standard deviation has declined fivefold, to around 1 percent in 1998.

Bearing these questions in mind, this chapter examines the determinants of asset price fluctuations in industrialized countries, their information content, as well as their impact on economic activity and financial fragility. In light of their overwhelming role in the composition of private sector portfolios, the focus of the analysis will be on equity and property prices.[3] The chapter also discusses the circumstances under which policymakers need to respond to large swings in the price of these assets, and concludes with a brief discussion of current policy challenges in the European Union and the United States arising from the high levels of asset prices seen recently.

What Drives Stock Prices?

Since asset ownership constitutes a claim on goods and services, modern asset pricing models build upon the assumption that people engage in asset transactions with the objective of optimally distributing consumption over time. In doing so, people seek to equate the marginal benefit of consuming one more real dollar today to the marginal benefit from investing the dollar in some asset and eventually selling it in order to consume the proceeds in the future. This gives rise to an arbitrage condition between the risk-adjusted *expected* rate of return on the asset and the risk-free interest rate, so that the market value of a given asset will be determined by the present risk-adjusted discounted value of its expected income stream. This relationship can be simplified and the price of an asset at time t can be expressed as the ratio of its dividend at time $t + 1$ over the sum of the nominal risk-free interest rate, an interest risk premium for holding securities, and the negative of the nominal growth rate of dividends or

Figure 3.1. Industrial Countries: Output Gap, Real Property Price Change, and Real Equity Price Change[1]
(Percent)

Asset price swings have been closely correlated with, and tended to lead, output cycles.

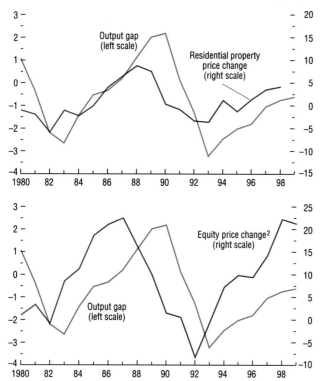

Sources: IMF, *International Financial Statistics*; IMF staff estimates; and BIS, *69th Annual Report*.

[1]Arithmetic averages of the respective variables in 16 industrial countries, excluding Portugal prior to 1989 owing to lack of availability of data.

[2]Three-year moving average.

---

[3]The relationship between the business cycle and the exchange rate—another important asset price that affects economic activity through various channels—was analyzed in depth in "The Business Cycle, International Linkages, and Exchange Rates," *World Economic Outlook* (May 1998), Chapter III.

earnings.[4] This simple but widely used formula indicates that equity prices should rise (fall) as the risk-free interest rate or investors' risk premium falls (rises), and/or the growth of earnings increases (decreases).[5]

One problem with practical applications of this (or any other) stock valuation formula is that it is based on future values of earnings and interest rates, both of which are unobserved. Thus, its practical implementation must rely on present expectations about the future path of these variables, which can be influenced by over-optimistic or unduly pessimistic assessments by the investor. The fact that over the past century or so there have been several episodes in which stock prices appeared to "overreact" to swings in earnings and dividends does provide some initial evidence that investors' sentiment plays a key role in driving asset prices.[6] And, if investors' sentiment can at times play a prominent role in asset price formation, actual valuations can then deviate con-

siderably from levels consistent with the "fundamental" determinants discussed above, which possibly helps explain why real stock prices have been subject to large swings in the various countries (Figure 3.2).[7] This begs the question of how to gauge the "fair" or "equilibrium" stock value in practice. A simple and widely used yardstick is the historical evolution of price-earnings (P/E) ratios. In the United States, for instance, the inverse of the P/E ratio (the so-called earnings yield) for broad stock indices has closely tracked the average real rate of return on stocks over fairly long time spans. A P/E ratio of 15, which corresponds to the average for the S&P 500 stock index for 1950–99, entails an earnings yield of close to 7 percent a year, which happens to be the average annual real rate of return on U.S. stocks since the end of World War II.[8] Judged by this yardstick, the 1999 price-earnings ratio of 32 would imply a real annual rate of return of stocks of 3.1 percent, which is less than half of that his-

[4]This formula is usually known as the "Gordon equation," after Myron J. Gordon, *The Investment, Financing, and Valuation of the Corporation* (Homewood, Illinois: Irwin, 1962). Algebraically, it can simply be written as,

$$P_t = \frac{D_t(1+g)}{i + \rho - g},$$

where P, D, g, i and ρ stand for the price of the asset, the dividends it pays, the growth rate of dividends, the risk-free interest rate, and the equity risk premium, respectively. With dividends being generally paid as a stable percentage share δ of earnings (i.e., $D = \delta E$), E can be shifted to the left-hand side of the equation to derive the "equilibrium" price-earnings ratio,

$$\frac{P_t}{E_t} = \frac{\delta(1+g)}{i + \rho - g},$$

where g stands for the growth rate of earnings. As will be discussed later, the P/E ratio is a commonly used benchmark indicator for stock valuations.

[5]It is important to note that while the derivation of this formula makes no assumption about equity repurchases by firms, the growing importance of equity repurchases relative to dividend payouts in recent years does not affect its validity. Equity repurchases affect only the time pattern of expected future dividends per share but not the respective totals. See John Campbell, A. Lo, and A. MacKinlay, *The Econometrics of Financial Markets* (Princeton, N.J.: Princeton University Press, 1997), Chapter 7.

[6]Using time series data from 1880, it has been found that a 1 percent increase in the level of dividends is typically associated with a 1.5 percent increase in equity values, implying that faster (slower) dividend growth increases (depresses) stock prices more than proportionately. See Robert Barsky and J. Bradford De Long, "Why Does the Stock Market Fluctuate?" *Quarterly Journal of Economics*, Vol. 108 (May 1993), pp. 291–311. Indications that investors tend to overestimate the persistence of variations in dividend growth—or, equivalently, to underprice risk—have motivated studies on stock valuations in which the rational expectations assumption that investors use optimally current information to forecast future dividend growth is relaxed. See N. Barberis, A. Shleifer, and R.W. Vishny, "A Model of Investor Sentiment," NBER Working Paper No. 5926 (Cambridge, Massachusetts: National Bureau of Economic Research, 1997). A comprehensive review of the literature on investors' herding behavior as a driving force behind stock valuations is provided in Sushil Bikhchandani and Sunil Sharma, "Herd Behavior in Financial Markets: A Review," IMF Working Paper (forthcoming).

[7]The consumer price index (CPI) is used here to deflate stock prices. This is consistent with the underpinnings of standard asset pricing theory, which regard asset ownership as a claim on consumer goods. Deflating asset prices by the GDP deflator would not, however, change the basic picture.

[8]U.S. data over the past 200 years indicate that the average real return on equity has in fact been remarkably stable in the range of 6½–7½ percent a year over different long sub-periods. See Jeremy J. Siegel, *Stocks for the Long-Run* (New York: McGraw Hill, 1998).

Figure 3.2. Industrial Countries: Real Stock Prices and Real GDP
(Logarithmic scale; 1985 = 100)

Stock prices have risen markedly in most industrial countries in recent years, often outpacing real GDP growth.

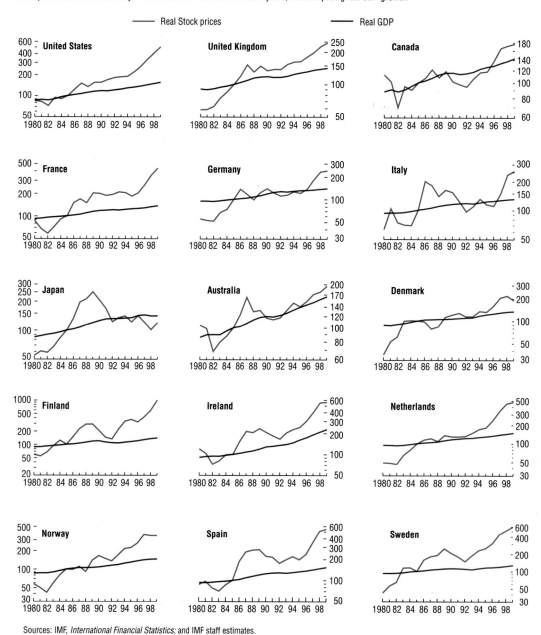

Sources: IMF, *International Financial Statistics;* and IMF staff estimates.

torically demanded by investors. At face value, this seems to indicate that U.S. stocks are currently overvalued. Following the same reasoning, a look at the historical evolution of P/E ratios in other countries points to the possibility of some stock price overvaluation across much of the industrialized world (Figure 3.3).

As discussed above, however, P/E ratios are a function of the risk-free interest rate, the risk premium, and expectations on earnings growth, and these can vary over time with changes in macroeconomic fundamentals and in the financial sector structure.[9] Sound macroeconomic policies leading to lower interest rates and faster earnings growth, together with financial innovations that help reduce transaction costs and allow greater opportunities for portfolio diversification (thus lowering investors' demanded risk premium), may well justify a higher P/E ratio than warranted by historical trends. Substantial productivity growth brought about by major innovations such as those in information technology (IT) in recent years may likewise justify historically high stock valuations in some industries. To the extent that the participation of such sectors in broad stock market indices are significant, this may end up pushing aggregate stock prices to new highs, despite more subdued valuations in other sectors. This has been clearly observed in the United States (Box 3.1).[10]

---

[9]Average levels of P/E ratios also vary widely across countries reflecting a host of institutional factors, such as the tax treatment of corporate profits and the degree of stock cross ownership in the business sector.

[10]As discussed in Box 3.1, it remains unclear, however, the extent to which recent productivity gains and the associated earnings growth in those industries (and in the non-farm sector as a whole) are sustainable. It is also noteworthy in this connection that the recent rise in corporate earnings and stock prices has been especially strong relative to the historical record. Previous technological revolutions, such as the dissemination of electricity-based industries in the 1920s (which brought about substantial and long-lasting productivity gains), did *not* produce the sharp rise in stock valuations and in corporate earnings similar to that observed in recent years for the IT sector. See Nicholas Crafts, "Globalization and Growth in the Twentieth Century," IMF Working Paper 00/44 (Washington: International Monetary Fund, 2000).

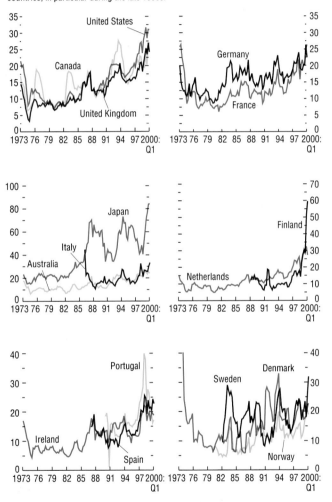

Figure 3.3. Industrial Countries: Price-Earnings Ratios
(Percent; end of period)

Stock prices have also risen faster than corporate earnings in most industrial countries, in particular during the late 1990s.

Source: Primark Datastream.

Table 3.1. Estimates of Potential Stock Market Overvaluation[1]
(Percent, except for price-earnings ratios)

Historical[2]	Price-Earnings Ratio	Dividend Yield	Real GDP Growth	Real Interest[3] Rate	Inflation Rate	Implicit Equity[4] Premium
Canada	15.8	3.1	2.5	4.9	4.3	0.8
France	12.5	3.8	2.0	4.2	4.6	1.7
Germany	16.5	2.3	2.0	4.1	2.6	0.3
Italy	18.8	2.3	1.9	3.4	7.6	0.8
Japan	44.8	1.0	2.7	2.4	1.9	1.4
United Kingdom	13.7	4.4	2.1	3.6	5.6	3.2
United States	15.6	3.4	3.0	3.9	4.2	2.8
Norway	10.5	2.4	3.0	3.8	5.3	1.8
Sweden	18.0	2.5	2.7	4.5	5.6	0.8
Spain	14.2	3.5	3.0	3.6	7.2	3.2
Netherlands	13.0	4.1	3.1	4.6	2.6	2.8
Portugal	18.0	3.0	2.9	1.3	11.6	5.3
Finland	12.8	2.2	2.7	2.7	4.7	2.4
Ireland	12.1	4.4	5.8	4.2	5.7	6.6

Current[5]	Price-Earnings Ratio	Dividend Yield	Potential GDP[6] Growth	Real Interest Rate	Inflation Rate	Implicit Equity[7] Premium
Canada	21.3	1.6	2.4	3.5	2.2	0.6
France	20.6	2.2	2.5	3.6	1.0	1.1
Germany	20.1	1.5	2.1	3.6	0.7	0.0
Italy	25.0	2.1	1.8	3.2	2.1	0.7
Japan	67.7	0.7	1.5	1.2	0.0	1.0
United Kingdom	23.7	2.6	2.4	3.3	1.2	1.7
United States	29.5	1.2	3.2	3.4	2.6	1.0
Norway	16.1	2.0	2.5	3.2	2.7	1.5
Sweden	20.5	1.8	2.3	3.9	0.7	0.3
Spain	21.8	1.9	3.4	2.3	2.7	3.2
Netherlands	27.9	2.0	2.6	2.9	2.3	1.9
Portugal	22.7	2.3	3.1	3.1	2.0	2.4
Finland	29.6	1.3	2.8	4.0	1.1	0.2
Ireland	19.0	2.0	6.4	2.3	1.4	6.3

Potential Overvaluation	Implied Equity[8] Premium Reduction	Implied Excess[9] Real Dividend Growth
Canada	0.2	0.2
France	0.6	0.6
Germany	0.3	0.3
Italy	0.2	0.2
Japan	0.3	0.3
United Kingdom	1.5	1.4
United States	1.8	1.8
Norway	0.4	0.4
Sweden	0.5	0.5
Spain	0.0	0.1
Netherlands	1.0	1.0
Portugal	2.9	2.9
Finland	2.2	2.2
Ireland	0.3	0.3

Sources: IMF staff estimates based on Datastream global stock indices and IMF, World Economic Outlook (WEO) database.

[1]Calculations based on the Gordon equation which incorporates the simplified assumptions discussed in the text. P/E and D/P ratios are measured using end-of-period stock prices and trailing earnings and dividends, respectively.

[2]Averages for 1980–99 (through third quarter 1999 or most recent data available).

[3]Nominal 10-year or longer government bond deflated using the CPI.

[4]Calculated using the historical averages of the dividend yield, real interest rate, inflation rate, and real GDP growth. Algebraically, $\rho = (1 + g)(1 + \pi)D/P - (r + \pi) + (g + \pi)$, where D/P stands for the trailing dividend yield, g for the growth rate of GDP, and r for the risk-free nominal interest rate (here proxied by the 10-year government bond yield on the assumption that ten years is, in most cases, a representative investment horizon in stocks) deflated by the current consumer price inflation π.

[5]1999 average for the price-earnings ratio and the dividend yield; latest quarter 1999 for inflation and real interest rates.

[6]IMF staff estimates.

[7]Calculated as in footnote 4.

[8]Historical implicit equity premium less current implied equity premium.

[9]Implied real dividend growth less potential GDP growth.

Box 3.1. Productivity and Stock Prices in the United States: Are Recent Trends Sustainable?

The sharp rise in U.S. equity prices over the past five years has raised concerns about the current levels of market valuation. Based on traditional indicators, such as the dividend-yield or the price-earnings (P/E) ratio, U.S. equity prices appear to have moved significantly out of line with historical values. A breakdown of S&P500 stocks by sectors (industrial, financial, transportation, and utilities) reveals that P/E ratios have varied considerably across sectors, and that the high valuation of S&P500 stocks reflects primarily high equity prices in the industrial sector—which is the overwhelming weight in the index (see the first table). The P/E ratio for S&P500 industrial stocks suggests that the growth in real earnings would be expected to accelerate in the period ahead, exceeding by 25 to 50 percent its growth performance since 1995, depending on the assumed equity risk premium.[1] Alternatively, to justify the current P/E ratios would require the equity premium for industrial sector stocks to be virtually eliminated.

The acceleration in future real earnings growth implied by current stock valuations in the indus-

trial sector would be plausible if the pickup in U.S. labor productivity growth in the non-farm business sector since the mid-1990s continues. Gains have been mainly concentrated in the manufacturing sector, and in particular in the durable goods sub-sector where the recent average growth rate has reached about 8 percent a year (see the second table). The recent acceleration in productivity has increased corporate profits as a share of national income to levels that have not been seen since the 1960s (see the figure).

It is possible that improvements in management practices and strong investment in information technologies have contributed to this higher growth rate during the 1990s. However, evidence on whether this increase in productivity growth and profits is permanent remains inconclusive, with recent studies yielding conflicting results. These range from a pessimistic view that sees the recent increase as largely transitory, to a highly optimistic view that emphasizes a permanent rise in productivity growth.[2]

[1]As discussed elsewhere in this chapter, equity risk premia estimates tend to vary with the choice of the sample period and statistical method. Thus, calculations in the first table use a range of commonly found estimates.

[2]Data measurement issues further complicate how to interpret the recent performance of productivity over the past several years. Measures of productivity in some sectors, particularly services, tend to be biased downward because output is unobservable and expenditures on inputs are used as a proxy. For a more detailed discussion of the issue, see L. Slifman and

Price-Earning Ratios and Scenarios for Real Earnings and Risk Premium

	S&P 500 Index				
	Overall	Industrial	Financial	Transportation	Utilities
	I. Price-Earnings Ratio				
Price-earnings ratio					
1954–94[1]	16.7	17.4	10.2	26.9	15.8
1999	32.0	38.2	19.0	17.0	18.1
	II. Expected Real Earnings Growth				
Equity risk premium					
at 3 percent	5.7	6.0	5.2	5.2	3.3
at 4.5 percent	7.3	7.6	6.8	6.8	4.8
at 6 percent	9.2	9.3	8.8	9.3	6.5
	III. Implied Equity Risk Premium				
Real earnings growth at					
1954–94 average	0.3	0.2	3.5	6.5	0.6

Source: IMF staff estimates.
[1]Average over 1954–94, excluding the higher-inflation subperiod of 1970–84.

Box 3.1 *(concluded)*

Growth in Labor Productivity[1]
(Percent, average annual rate)

	1960–69	1970–79	1980–89	1990–99	1990–92	1992–95	1996–99	1996	1997	1998	1999
Business Sector	3.3	1.9	1.7	2.1	2.9	0.7	2.7	2.9	2.2	2.8	3.1
Nonfarm business sector	2.9	1.8	1.5	2.0	2.8	0.8	2.5	2.7	1.9	2.8	2.9
Manufacturing	2.6	2.6	2.8	4.0	3.7	3.0	5.3	4.0	5.1	4.8	5.9
Durable manufacturing	2.8	3.0	3.2	5.7	3.7	4.7	8.0	5.8	7.1	7.9	9.1
Nondurable manufacturing	2.6	2.2	2.1	2.2	3.3	1.6	2.1	2.5	3.1	1.1	2.0

Source: U.S. Bureau of Labor Statistics.
[1]Labor productivity is output per hour of all persons; data for 1999 are IMF staff estimates.

According to the pessimistic view, no significant trend increase in productivity has occurred.[3] Improvements in measuring price deflators beginning in the early 1990s have resulted in downward revisions to measured inflation, which implies upward revisions to real GDP and productivity. In addition, productivity follows a procyclical pattern so that with the recent growth rate of real GDP rising above trend, productivity growth has increased as well, reflecting the lags with which labor adjusts to a rise in output. Finally, the sharp decline in the price of computers has meant that real output per hour in the computer sector has risen at a rapid pace. In contrast, productivity growth elsewhere in the manufacturing sector has not recovered from its slowdown in the 1970s, and for some industries has slowed even further. Although computer manufacturing represents just 1.2 percent of the economy's output, the rapid rate of growth was sufficient to boost nonfarm business productivity. Overall, according to the pessimistic view, roughly half of the pickup in productivity growth since 1995 reflects price measurement and cyclical effects, and the remaining half reflects productivity gains emanating from the computer sector alone.

International evidence also casts doubt on the sustainability of stronger productivity growth. If a technological revolution were under way, improvements in productivity would also be observed outside of the United States. Based on international measures of labor productivity, among the Group of Seven countries, only the United States and Germany have experienced a pickup in productivity relative to the weak performance of the 1980s.[4] One explanation for why evidence of a pickup in productivity has yet to occur in other industrial countries, particularly in Europe, is that new technologies have been adopted elsewhere at a slower pace, perhaps reflecting the higher cost of labor market adjustment in these countries compared to the United States. New technologies often require the reorganization of labor and displacement of workers, which could entail costs that would reduce the return to new investment.[5] Finally, historical analysis of the impact of past technological revolutions on productivity indicates that these effects are quite small.[6]

C. Corrado, "Decomposition of Productivity and Unit Costs" (unpublished; Washington: Board of Governors of the Federal Reserve System, November 1996).

[3]This view is largely based on Robert J. Gordon, "Has the 'New Economy' Rendered the Productivity Slowdown Obsolete?" Northwestern University Working Paper (June 1999).

[4]See Charles Plosser, "Has the Productivity Boom Finally Arrived?" University of Rochester, Bradley Policy Research Center, Policy Statement and Position Papers 99–02 (September 1999).

[5]See Remarks by Chairman Alan Greenspan, "Technology and the Economy," Speech before the Economic Club of New York, January 13, 2000.

[6]Nicholas Crafts, "Globalization and Growth in the Twentieth Century," IMF Working Paper 00/44 (Washington: International Monetary Fund, 2000).

Other studies, however, are more optimistic about future productivity growth, emphasizing the remarkable growth in investment in new technologies, but concluding that it is still too soon to draw solid conclusions.[7] Real investment in computers and equipment increased at an annual rate of 41.8 percent over the period 1996–98, compared to 20.5 percent during 1990–95, and roughly 30 percent in the 1970s and 1980s. In turn, the real net capital stock of computers grew at an annual rate of about 37 percent in the recent period. This explosive growth in investment has resulted in an increase in the contribution of computers to output growth to about 0.35 percentage point per year during 1996–98, roughly double the contribution in the early part of the 1990s, and well above that in the 1970s and 1980s. Despite these impressive growth rates, new technologies are also known to contribute to improved productivity with a considerable lag.[8] This is because new technology can render established skills obsolete, and require that new skills be acquired, or in some cases that production processes be reorganized. This suggests that further gains in productivity growth may lie in the future.

Further support for the optimistic view about future productivity growth stems from the finding that none of the growth in productivity over the past year is explained by the cyclical position of the economy, or by temporary accelerations in output and employment; rather, the pickup in productivity is primarily attributable to an increase in the rate of technical advance, capital deepening, and an unexplained residual.[9]

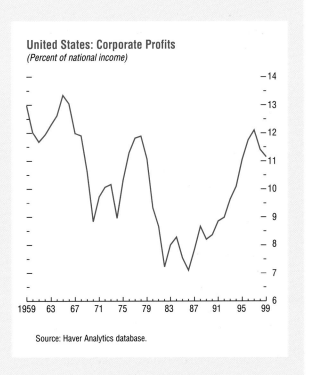

United States: Corporate Profits
(Percent of national income)

Source: Haver Analytics database.

Technical advance reflects the new methods for measuring consumer and producer prices and also the gains in the productivity of workers who *make* computers as evidenced by the accelerating decline in the quality-adjusted price of computers. Combining the effects on productivity of those who *use* computers (capital deepening) with those who *make* computers (technical advance), the computer industry accounts for about 40 percent of growth in potential productivity. Continued growth in the capital stock, and particularly in computer equipment, together with further declines in computer prices would thus be expected to make ongoing contributions to stronger future growth in productivity. Should this scenario materialize, the strong gains on U.S. equity prices in recent years could then be validated.

[7]See Daniel Sichel, "Computers and Aggregate Economic Growth: An Update," *Business Economics* (April 1999), pp. 18–24.

[8]Jeremy Greenwood and Boyan Jovanovic, "Accounting for Growth," NBER Working Paper 6647 (Cambridge, Massachusetts: National Bureau of Economic Research, 1998).

[9]This result is based on estimates of potential productivity growth for the entire economy—that is, the level of productivity consistent with sustainable utilization of capital and labor. For further discussion on this, see Macroeconomic Advisers, "Productivity and Potential GDP in the 'New' U.S. Economy," Special Analysis (St. Louis, Missouri: Macroeconomic Advisers, LLC, 1998).

Table 3.1 uses the Gordon valuation formula to gauge quantitatively the different factors behind the recent rise in P/E ratios in selected industrial countries. The first four columns of the first panel provide averages of the P/E ratio, the dividend yield (D/P), real GDP growth (which can be thought of as a proxy measure of the expected growth of real earnings),[11] the risk-free interest rate, and the inflation rate for each country over the 1980–99 period.[12] These are used to derive the respective equity risk premia, reported in the last column of the table's upper panel.[13] In contrast, the second panel provides current (1999) information on each of the variables and, using potential GDP growth as a proxy for investors' expectations of future earnings growth, derives the current implicit equity risk premium. The first column of the Table's bottom panel then compares the estimated risk premium for 1999 with that for the 1980–99 period as a whole. The results indicate that, under current P/E and D/P ratios, investors in Finland, the Netherlands, Portugal, the United Kingdom, and the United States appear to be willing to accept a substantial reduction in the risk premium. Alternatively, Table 3.1 also presents calculations assuming that the equity risk

premium has not declined.[14] In this case, the figures provided in the last column of the table's bottom panel indicate that current P/E and D/P ratios can only be validated if earnings grow faster than current estimates of potential output in the long run (in other words, if there is excess dividend growth in these countries), or estimates of potential output are too low. If none of these alternatives is plausible, it follows that current stock prices are overvalued, and an eventual stock market "correction" can be expected.

This raises the question of whether it is plausible to have either excess dividend growth or a significant reduction in the equity risk premia (or even a combination of both) on a long-lasting basis. One problem with justifying current levels of P/E ratios by assuming that earnings and dividends can grow faster than output is that, while the share of profits and dividends in national income can rise in the short to medium run—as witnessed by recent developments in the United States (Box 3.1)—it cannot do so indefinitely. In fact, historical evidence points to the relative long-term stability of the share of profits and dividends in national income, a phenomenon that has been widely accepted as a "stylized

[11]The underlying assumption is that, unless there are significant shifts in the share of profits and dividends in national income, real earnings (and hence real dividends) should be expected to grow approximately in line with the output growth trend. This assumption is discussed further below.

[12]This sample period was chosen on the basis of data availability for all countries. While there are good reasons to exclude the macroeconomically turbulent 1970s, it would be desirable to extend the sample to the early post-World War II years. However, data availability and consistency then become a problem for many countries.

[13]There are alternative ways of measuring the equity risk premium. One approach is to subtract the average *actual* rate of return on stocks over several decades from the actual yield to maturity on long-term government bonds (a proxy for the risk-free asset in industrial countries) averaged over the same period. However, several analysts have noted that this ex post measure can diverge considerably from the more technically accurate ex ante definition of equity risk premia demanded by the investor. Accordingly, some studies have applied different techniques to long time series to estimate the expected or ex ante difference between the rate of return on stocks and on government bonds. In the case of the United States (for which long time series are readily available), the results yielded by these distinct methods are similar to that obtained using the approach of Table 3.1, which points to an equity risk premium of around 4½ percent for the period between the mid-1950s and the late 1990s. See Sushil B. Wadhwani, "The U.S. Stock Market and the Global Economic Crisis," *National Institute Economic Review* (January 1999), pp. 86–105, and Olivier J. Blanchard, "Movements in the Equity Premium," *Brookings Papers on Economic Activity: 2,* Brookings Institution (1993), pp. 75–138. As will be discussed below, higher estimates of the equity risk premium when computed over a longer time span suggest that the risk premium may have declined in recent years.

[14]Econometric evidence that the equity risk premium has not significantly trended down between 1983 and 1997 in France, Germany, the United Kingdom, and the United States is provided by Simon Hayes, Chris Salmon and Sanjay Yadav, "Equities: What Can They Tell Us About the Real Economy?" in *The Role of Asset Prices in the Formulation of Monetary Policy,* BIS Conference Papers Vol. No. 5 (Basel: Bank for International Settlements, 1998), pp. 178–195.

fact" in economic growth theory.[15] So, either potential GDP growth is bound to catch up with earnings growth or the latter will fall short of expectations at some point in the future.

Evidence of a decline in the equity risk premium is more controversial. Using rolling regression analysis and other statistical techniques, some studies have found that the risk premium in the United States has about halved over the 1980–99 period relative to the post-World War II average, to values in the neighborhood of 2 to 3 percent, consistent with the estimate of Table 3.1.[16] A significant decline also appears to have taken place in a few (but not all) other countries.[17] This is consistent with the fact that opportunities for portfolio diversification have increased, and that the cost of stock transactions has been lowered with the proliferation of mutual and pension funds.[18]

Several recent studies have also indicated that demographic factors may have induced a long-lasting decline in equity risk premia. To the extent that "baby boomers" increase their savings for retirement and the purchase of stocks for retirement purposes receives a more favorable tax treatment, then the demand for stocks increases. This, in turn, lowers earnings and dividend yields in equilibrium, thus pulling down the implicit risk premium demanded by investors.[19] Although there is widespread consensus that these different factors help lower the equity risk premium in equilibrium, there is scant agreement as to whether these effects are large enough to bring about a substantial reduction in equity risk premia needed to justify current stock valuations in some countries.

The other consideration to bear in mind when judging whether the risk premium implicit in current stock valuations is sustainable is that the equity risk premium appears to have been very cyclical historically. There is evidence that periods of high economic growth tend to be associated with an underpricing of risk and vice-versa.[20] This implies that adverse shocks to aggregate productivity or other macroeconomic variables in countries that are currently experiencing faster output growth may raise the equity risk premia to levels closer to their historical averages, thus tending to produce a stock market correction. The fact that the *current* estimated risk premia in some fast-growing industrial countries are not only somewhat below 1980–99 averages but also far below longer-term historical levels, suggests that some rebound in the equity risk premia in these countries may well lie ahead.

---

[15]See Robert M. Solow, *Growth Theory* (Oxford: Oxford University Press, 1987); also Robert J. Barro and Xavier Sala-i-Martin, *Economic Growth* (New York: McGraw-Hill, 1995), Chapter 1. While recent studies have documented a significant increase in the share of profits in national income in a few OECD countries since the 1980s, this has been viewed as a medium-run phenomenon, rather than a sustainable long-term trend. See Olivier J. Blanchard, "The Medium Run," *Brookings Papers on Economic Activity: 2,* Brookings Institution (1997), pp. 89–141.

[16]See Sushil B. Wadhwani, "The U.S. Stock Market," and also Olivier J. Blanchard, "Movements in the Equity Premium."

[17]Estimates of the equity premium risk premia for a number of industrial countries going back at least to 1970 are provided in John Y. Campbell, "Asset Prices, Consumption and the Business Cycle," National Bureau of Economic Research Working Paper 6485 (Cambridge, Massachusetts: National Bureau of Economic Research, 1998).

[18]Empirical evidence relating inflows into mutual and pension funds points to a lowering of the risk premium and a decline in equity earnings and dividend yields; see Sushil B. Wadhwani and M. Shah, *The Equity-Bond Debate in the UK* (London: Goldman Sachs, 1993), and Charles Kramer, "Stock-Market Equilibrium and the Dividend Yield," IMF Working Paper 96/90 (Washington: International Monetary Fund, 1996). For a theoretical analysis of the relationship between increased household participation in equity markets, portfolio diversification, and the risk premium, see John Heaton and Deborah Lucas, "Stock Prices and Fundamentals," presented at the 1999 National Bureau of Economic Research Macroeconomic Annual Conference, (unpublished; June 1999).

[19]See, for instance, Gurdip Bakshi and Zhiwu Chen, "Baby Boom, Population Aging, and Capital Markets," *Journal of Business*, Vol. 67 (April 1994), pp. 165–202, and Robin Brooks, "What Will Happen to Financial Markets When the Baby Boomers Retire?" IMF Working Paper 00/18 (Washington: International Monetary Fund, 2000).

[20]See Barsky and De Long, "Why Does the Stock Market Fluctuate?" For a broader discussion of the time-varying nature of the equity risk premia and extensive bibliographic references on the issue, see Campbell, "Asset Prices, Consumption and the Business Cycle."

Table 3.2. Correlations between Deviations of Actual from Predicted Stock Prices for a Selected Group of Countries, 1985–1999

	United States	United Kingdom	Japan	Germany	France	Ireland	Netherlands	Canada	Sweden
United States	1								
United Kingdom	0.65	1							
Japan	0.08	0.25	1						
Germany	0.44	0.59	0.18	1					
France	0.44	0.48	0.20	0.49	1				
Ireland	0.45	0.51	0.29	0.47	0.34	1			
Netherlands	0.67	0.57	0.30	0.46	0.55	0.33	1		
Canada	0.58	0.55	0.31	0.43	0.26	0.48	0.48	1	
Sweden	0.13	0.20	0.31	0.19	0.14	0.19	0.26	0.26	1

A distinct approach to gauging the extent to which broad stock indices are over- or under-valued at a given point in time consists of estimating econometrically the relationship between (the log of) the P/E or the D/P ratio and a set of macroeconomic and financial variables believed to determine the "fundamental" or "equilibrium" stock price.[21] These include the risk-free real interest rate, the difference between short- and long-run bond yield (i.e., the slope of the yield curve, which is often considered a good business cycle indicator), actual inflation, measures of the economy's growth potential, as well as some rough proxies for the effect of greater household participation and risk diversification in asset markets. Staff estimates using a variety of alternative econometric specifications combining these variables (or empirical proxies for some of them) have found the econometric results for the different countries to be broadly consistent with the findings reported in Table 3.1. That is, stock markets in Finland, the Netherlands, the United Kingdom, the United States—and also in France and Spain—seem to be above what can be justified by movements in the explanatory variables. The size of the deviations around the estimated fundamental values varies widely across countries and should be interpreted with caution, as they prove to be quite sensitive to the period considered and choice of proxy variables. Yet, the devia-

tions between model-estimated and actual values of price-earnings ratios for Finland, the Netherlands, the United Kingdom, and the United States over the past two years are consistently positive across different specifications and sample periods, indicating that at least some degree of stock market overvaluation is likely.

In addition to marked cycles in P/E ratios along their equilibrium trends estimated by regression analyses, this econometric approach to stock valuations also provides interesting evidence of significant cross-country correlations in these deviations over time. This indicates that, besides the domestic factors explaining P/E ratios in the various countries, there are factors that seem to be common to "clusters" of countries. Such common links between stock markets can be gleaned from the matrix of correlation coefficients reported in Table 3.2.

The latter shows that correlations between Canada, the United Kingdom, and the United States are especially high. Likewise, some intra-European correlations—notably that between France and Germany, and France and the Netherlands—are also quite large. The existence of such cross-country correlations is, on the one hand, consistent with greater capital mobility across industrial economies since the mid-1980s, which has increased the scope for global liquidity conditions to affect national asset markets (Box 3.2).

---

[21]See, for instance, Charles Kramer, "Stock-Market Equilibrium and the Dividend Yield," IMF Working Paper 96/90 (Washington: International Monetary Fund, 1996), and Vincent R. Reinhart, "Equity Prices and Monetary Policy in the United States," in *The Role of Asset Prices in the Formulation of Monetary Policy*, BIS Conference Papers, Vol. 5 (Basle: Bank of International Settlements, 1998).

Box 3.2. Global Liquidity and Asset Prices

Recent commentary suggests that global liquidity has importantly influenced financial conditions in the major international markets, and that excess liquidity in one financial center can influence conditions elsewhere. For example, it has been suggested that ample global liquidity compressed risk premia during the run-up to the 1997–98 turbulence, which started with the devaluation of the Thai baht, and that "carry trades" are increasingly used to shift liquidity among financial centers.[1] The relationship of liquidity to asset prices has been extensively studied in a domestic context, but it has been little studied in an international context. In a world where capital is increasingly mobile and can be readily deployed internationally, it is important to consider the extent to which changes in liquidity conditions in one major country may be associated with changes in financial conditions elsewhere. This box reviews some recent research on the international dimension of the relationship between liquidity and asset prices.

Previous work identifies two concepts of liquidity. *Market liquidity* is the capacity of financial markets to absorb temporary fluctuations in demand and supply without undue dislocations in prices. It is most often used to describe secondary markets, such as stock exchanges, although it is sometimes applied to primary markets as well; for example, market participants often describe large issues of new equity as "liquid." *Monetary liquidity* describes conditions in short-term credit markets and is often measured by short-term interest rates or the aggregate quantity of money. When a quantity measure of monetary liquidity is used, it is often measured as a growth rate, or relative to a base such as GDP. For example, some studies focus on excess money growth (money growth less nominal GDP growth). Most studies of the liquidity effect have focused on monetary liquidity, rather than market liquidity, since market liquidity is more difficult to measure. The two are undoubtedly related.

[1]See Chapters 3 and 4 in *International Capital Markets: Developments, Prospects, and Policy Issues* (Washington: International Monetary Fund, September 1999) and the October 1999 *World Economic Outlook*, pp. 3–9 and Box 4.4.

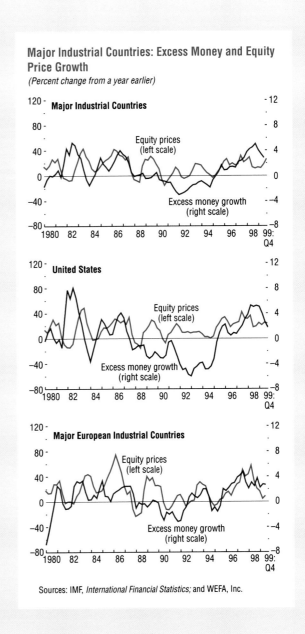

Major Industrial Countries: Excess Money and Equity Price Growth
(Percent change from a year earlier)

Sources: IMF, *International Financial Statistics;* and WEFA, Inc.

Past studies suggest several possible relationships between monetary liquidity and asset prices, consistent with the existence of a positive correlation between the two variables (see the figure). First, an increase in liquidity tends to boost the demand for a fixed supply of assets and lead to inflation in asset prices. In a context where inflation in goods and services prices is kept low due to competition, rapid productivity

Box 3.2 *(concluded)*

growth, or nominal rigidities, asset prices will then increase in real terms. Second, an increase in liquidity might simply be correlated with, rather than cause, a rise in asset prices in an environment of improving economic prospects. For example, a cyclical upturn might give rise to an increase in money demand, an improved outlook for corporate earnings, and a rise in stock prices. Third, an increase in liquidity might raise the value of assets by reducing interest rates, thereby lowering the discount rate on future cash flows from assets (the decline in interest rates might also stimulate demand and reduce corporate borrowing costs, leading to higher future dividends, and further boosting stock prices.)

These mechanisms point to at least two possible channels for the international transmission of liquidity effects. One could be characterized as a "push" channel. If excess money growth in (say) Europe gives rise to capital flows from Europe to foreign asset markets (a "push" of money overseas), upward pressure on foreign stock and bond prices (and downward pressure on foreign interest rates) would be expected. This would result in a positive correlation between European money growth and foreign stock prices, and a negative correlation between European money growth and foreign interest rates. Such correlations could also be consistent with economic spillovers, or "a rising tide that lifts all boats." For example, rapid money growth in Europe (owing either to stimulative policy or an accommodated rise in money demand) might coincide with improved economic prospects in Europe, which would suggest improved prospects for other major countries, raising asset prices in those countries.

Alternatively, spillovers could occur through a "pull" channel. Suppose that excess money growth in Europe gave rise to asset price inflation in Europe. If foreign investors viewed the asset price inflation as real and sustainable, it could attract a reallocation of capital to Europe from abroad and depress foreign asset prices (a "pull" of capital from overseas into Europe). Such capital inflows could also contribute to a deepening of European capital markets. In that case, one would expect a negative correlation between European

money growth and foreign stock prices, and a positive correlation between European money growth and foreign interest rates.

Recent work by IMF staff provides evidence on the relationship between liquidity (money growth) and asset returns at an international level.[2] Several measures of excess money growth are calculated for Group of Seven (G-7) countries separately, as well as for them as a group. A variety of econometric relationships between liquidity and real asset returns are estimated, from simple correlations to regressions and tests of Granger causality. The main results are twofold. First, excess money growth at the aggregate G-7 level is consistently related to higher real stock returns and lower real interest rates. Second, there is evidence of significant liquidity spillovers across G-7 countries. An increase in excess money growth in one G-7 country is consistent with higher real stock returns and lower real interest rates in other G-7 countries, providing support for the existence of the "push" channel described above. There is also evidence of a relationship between excess money growth in the United States and excess money growth in Japan, and some evidence (albeit limited) that volatility in money growth in one country spills over to volatility in real asset returns in other countries.

The same study also highlights some measurement issues that may be important for other analyses of liquidity in the international context. For instance, narrow money appears to have a stronger relationship to asset prices than broad money, perhaps indicating that demand deposits are more readily used to purchase assets than time deposits. This points to several pathways for future research. These include the use of different measures of liquidity, including non-monetary and off-balance sheet instruments; a full exploration of the possible transmission channels that might underlie the results; and consideration of the interaction between monetary liquidity in large industrial countries and financial conditions in emerging markets.

[2]Klaas Baks and Charles Kramer, "Global Liquidity and Asset Prices: Measurement, Implications, and Spillovers," IMF Working Paper 99/168 (Washington: International Monetary Fund, 1999).

On the other hand, notwithstanding the forces of globalization, the tighter correlation between deviations in P/E across certain groups of countries is consistent with empirical evidence that geographic proximity and other institutional factors remain important determinants of the degree of financial integration among countries.[22] It is therefore possible that assessments of asset market conditions in different countries, which focus exclusively on domestic factors and neglect these international linkages, may be missing an important factor behind the currently high stock prices across certain groups of countries.

Property Prices

While real property prices have been closely related to the business cycle in the industrialized world as a whole (as seen in Figure 3.1), in some countries the association is especially striking (Figure 3.4). Recessions in Japan and European Union countries since the early 1980s have been accompanied by falling property prices in real terms. Conversely, the strong upswings in economic activity in Australia and smaller EU countries since the mid-1990s have been associated with robust growth in property prices.

Studies on the determinants of property prices in different countries generally find them to be driven by current and lagged income growth and real interest rates (or some other proxy for mortgage costs). The fact that property prices appear to be partly determined by current and past income growth is hardly surprising. As the supply of land is fixed and that of residential dwellings and offices can only increase slowly in the short run, property prices tend to be largely demand determined over the business cycle. Financing conditions have also played a major role. Financial liberalization and stiffer competition among financial intermediaries since the 1980s have helped reduce interest

Table 3.3. Outstanding Residential Mortgage Debt as a Share of GDP in European Countries
(Percent)

	1990[1]	1998[2]
Denmark	63	69
Netherlands	40	65
United Kingdom	55	57
Germany	43	53
Norway	48	45
Sweden	47	50
Finland	32	30
Ireland	19	27
Luxembourg	24	26
Portugal	11	26
Belgium	20	25
Spain	14	24
France	24	21
Italy	5	8
Greece	5	7
Austria	4	5

Source: European Mortgage Foundation, *Hypostat* 1988–98.
[1]For Denmark 1992 is used; for Luxembourg 1994 is used.
[2]For Luxembourg 1997 is used.

margins on mortgages, while also allowing banks to finance a higher share of the assessed property value. Moreover, the combination of very high marginal tax rates with widespread tax provisions granting households partial deductibility on mortgage interest payments in many countries and the ability of households to use the higher collateral value of their houses to increase their mortgages have provided incentives to take on more mortgage debt as house prices have increased.[23]

Reflecting these developments, outstanding mortgages as a share of GDP have risen dramatically, particularly among smaller European countries (Table 3.3). In quite a few EU countries, the (negative) correlation between real housing prices and real interest rates has been especially high (Figure 3.5). Following the decline in real interest rates in the second half of the 1990s and the elimination of the exchange rate risk premium with the introduction of the euro, property prices have risen sharply in Finland, Ireland,

---

[22]See Richard Portes and Hélene Rey, "The Determinants of Cross-Border Equity Flows" (unpublished; London School of Economics, August 1999).

[23]In some cases—notably, in Denmark and the United Kingdom—tax deductions on mortgage interest payments have been rolled back recently, effectively raising the cost of new mortgages and thus helping dampen the growth of mortgage debt.

Figure 3.4. Industrial Countries: Real Property Prices and Output Gap
(Percent)

Real property prices have been highly cyclical and closely correlated with the output gap, particularly among European Union countries.

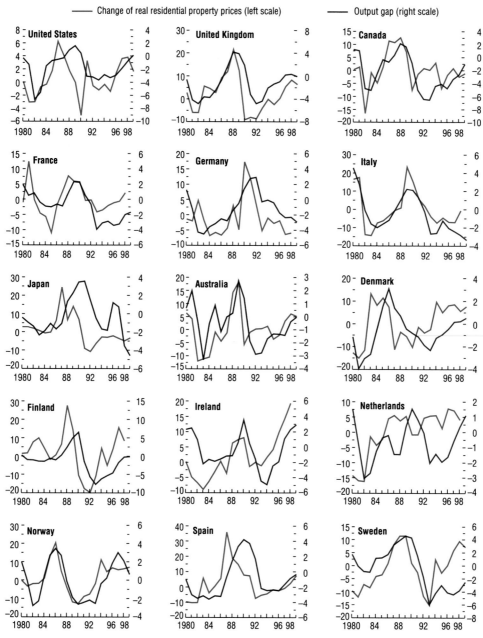

——— Change of real residential property prices (left scale)   ——— Output gap (right scale)

Sources: IMF, *International Financial Statistics;* IMF staff estimates; and BIS, *69th Annual Report.*

Figure 3.5. Industrial Countries: Real Property Prices and Real Interest Rates
(Percent)

Real property prices have tended to be inversely correlated with real interest rates across the industrial world.

——— Change of real residential property prices (left scale)　　　——— Real interest rates (right scale)

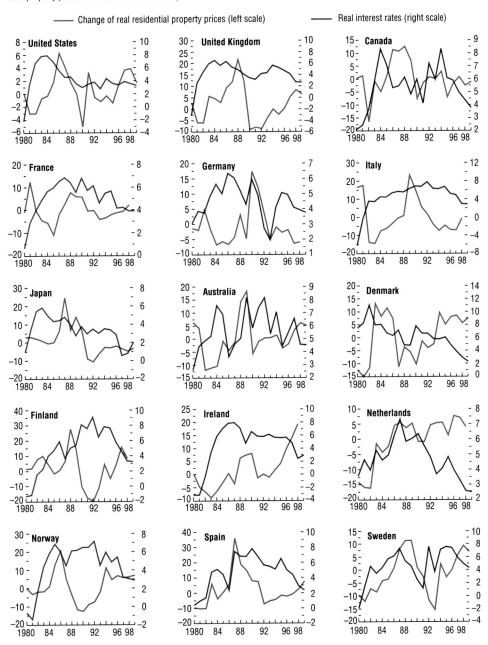

Sources: IMF, *International Financial Statistics;* IMF staff estimates; and BIS, *69th Annual Report.*

the Netherlands, Portugal, Spain, and the Scandinavian countries. In some of these countries, the growth of real property prices has far exceeded that of real GDP and has approached or even surpassed the level of previous cyclical peaks (Figure 3.6). In the United Kingdom and Australia, there is also evidence that lower real interest rates have boosted property prices in recent years; although property prices have grown rapidly in recent months, they remain below previous historical peaks. In Japan, property prices have historically been quite responsive to interest rates, but the banking solvency problem and debt overhang of the household sector following the collapse of asset prices in the early 1990s kept real property prices depressed through much of the 1990s in spite of low real interest rates.

Compared with Japan and the European Union, the correlation between property prices, real interest rates, and real GDP growth has been less pronounced in Canada and the United States. This possibly reflects less binding land constraints and a more prompt response of residential investment to imbalances between supply and demand. Property prices have been rising rapidly since the mid-1990s but have yet to reach historical highs; despite some localized pressures, they remain low for the country as a whole relative to both the level of stock prices and the pace of real GDP growth over the past decade (see Figure 3.6).

Following a similar procedure as that for stocks, the "fair" value of property prices can be estimated as a function of key fundamental variables, such as real long-term interest rate, inflation, and GDP growth.[24] The unexplained component of this relation for each country can be interpreted as an indication of an apparent misalignment. Econometric estimation using panel data for industrial countries suggests that property markets in Ireland, the Netherlands, Portugal, and Spain may be currently overvalued. At the same time, the residuals of the respective regressions also reveal that changes in property prices have been much less correlated across countries than changes in stock prices. While there are a number of factors contributing to equalization of property prices across countries, such as interest rate parity conditions and the international business cycle, these forces appear to be less strong than those observed in stock markets, reflecting the fact that property markets generally are less liquid and that there are obvious physical constraints to international arbitrage in property. This suggests that national monetary and tax policies have greater scope for affecting domestic property prices than is the case with stock prices.

Transmission Channels from Asset Prices to Economic Activity

There is extensive empirical evidence that asset price changes tend to lead output growth in industrial countries.[25] However, the leading indicator property of asset price changes appears to be limited to certain classes of assets and dependent on the depth of asset markets in the dif-

---

[24]These are the most common explanatory variables used in econometric studies of the determinants of housing prices. See, for instance, Matthew Higgins and Carol Osler, "Asset Market Hangovers and Economic Growth: U.S. Housing Markets," in *The Role of Asset Prices in the Formulation of Monetary Policy*, BIS Conference Papers, Vol. 5 (Basel: Bank for International Settlements, 1998), pp. 220–38, and Sanjay Kalra, Dubravko Mihaljek, and Christoph Duenwald, "Property Price and Speculative Bubbles: Evidence from Hong Kong SAR," IMF Working Paper 00/02 (Washington: International Monetary Fund, 2000). Some of these studies also contemplate a role for demographic and construction costs, but the significance of these factors appears to be relatively country-dependent.

[25]See Eugene F. Fama, "Stock Returns, Expected Returns, and Real Activity," *The Journal of Finance*, Vol. 45, No. 4 (1990), pp. 1089–1108, for the case of the United States. Evidence on Group of Seven and non-G-7 European countries can be found in Jongmoo J. Choi, Shmuel Hauser, and Kenneth J. Kopecky, "Does the Stock Market Predict Real Activity? Time Series Evidence from the G-7 Countries," *Journal of Banking and Finance*, Vol. 23 (December 1999), pp. 1771–92; and Mads Asprem, "Stock Prices, Asset Portfolios, and Macroeconomic Variables in Ten European Countries," *Journal of Banking and Finance*, Vol. 13 (September 1989), pp. 589–612. Stock returns also led output growth in several emerging economies. See Paolo Mauro, "Stock Returns and Output Growth in Emerging and Advanced Economies," IMF Working Paper, International Monetary Fund, forthcoming.

Figure 3.6. Industrial Countries: Real Property Prices and Real GDP
(Logarithmic scale; 1985 =100)

Real property prices have risen considerably faster than real GDP in a few countries since the mid-1990s and have exhibited a somewhat diverse cyclical pattern across the industrial world.

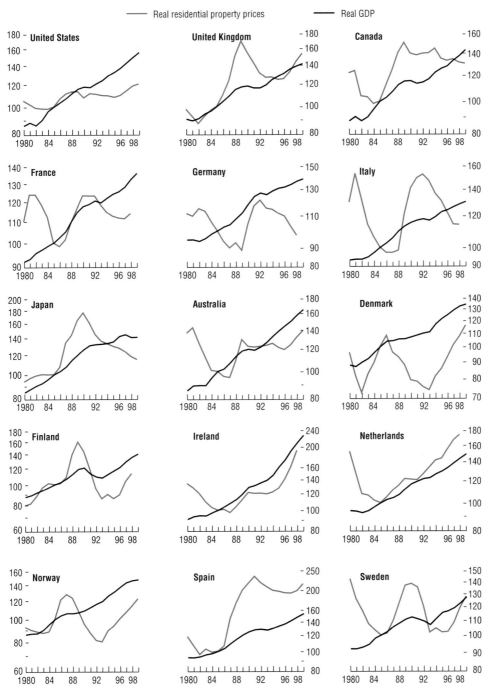

Sources: IMF, *International Financial Statistics;* IMF staff estimates; and BIS, *69th Annual Report.*

Table 3.4. Asset Prices as a Leading Indicator of Real GDP and Output Gap

	Stock Prices Leading Indicator of:		Property Prices Leading Indicator of:	
	Real GDP Growth	Output Gap	Real GDP Growth	Output Gap
Australia	•		•	
Canada				•
Denmark				•
Finland	•			•
France				•
Germany				•
Ireland	•	•		•
Italy				
Japan	•		•	•
Netherlands				•
Norway				
Sweden				
Spain	•			•
United Kingdom	•			•
United States	•			•

Note: Estimated equations are (1) GDP growth = constant + α*lagged real asset price growth, and (2) Output gap = constant + β*lagged real asset price growth. The α and β coefficients in these relations are significant for the countries marked in the table. The relations are estimated on annual data over the period 1970–1999. Including the lagged endogenous variable does not change the results significantly. Portugal is omitted because its property price series is too short.

ferent countries.[26] In general, stock prices are found to have a significant predictive power on output growth in many countries.[27] In contrast, property prices tend, for the reasons discussed above (fixed supply in the short-run and traded in less liquid markets), to be less forward-looking and more contemporaneously correlated with output growth. Yet, it appears that the leading indicator properties of property prices are considerably stronger regarding the output gap, which is a closer indicator of business cycle conditions (Table 3.4).

Despite this evidence, *causal* relationships between price changes in either of these assets and output growth are complex and empirically difficult to identify. It is therefore not surprising that views on the topic differ widely. At one end of the spectrum, it has been argued that the correlation between asset prices and economic activity is solely due to the fact that asset prices incorporate information about future output growth (i.e., asset prices affect current spending only to the extent that they are "leading indicators" of future changes in economic activity). The leading indicator properties of asset prices follow the main assumptions of the valuation model discussed above—namely, that current prices represent the discounted value of the expected dividend growth and that, to the extent that such assets are traded in deep and well-informed auction markets, expectations about future dividend growth tend to be rational. From this viewpoint, no behavioral causal relationship running from asset prices to economic activity exists; the only causal connection is between current and future output growth, with stock markets thus merely being a "side-show."[28]

At the other end of the spectrum lies the more traditional view that the impact of asset prices on output is through wealth effects and changes in the cost of capital.[29] From this perspective, the causality runs in the opposite direction to the "side-show" view of stock markets. Instead of acting merely as a leading indicator of households' labor income and business profits, higher asset prices actually raise agents' lifetime wealth which, in turn, enhances consumer and business confidence and leads to higher spending.

[26]Evidence on whether stock market capitalization to GDP has a bearing on the predictive power of stock prices is provided in Mauro, "Stock Returns and Output Growth in Emerging and Advanced Economies."

[27]The other asset price found to generally have a significant predictive power on economic activity—in some cases to a greater extent than stock prices—is the government bond yield spread (the difference between returns on short- and long-term government bonds).

[28]See Randall Morck, Andrei Schleifer, and Robert W. Vishny, "The Stock Market and Investment: Is the Market a Sideshow?" *Brookings Papers on Economic Activity;* 2 Blookings Institution (1990), pp. 157–202.

[29]Lurking behind this view is the perception that asset prices often reflect financial market excesses that detract from their information content. As expressed in an oft-cited quotation attributed to Paul Samuelson: "The stock market has predicted nine of the last five recessions." For a skeptical note on the information content of asset prices, see Mark Gertler, Marvin Goodfriend, Otmar Issing, and Luigi Spaventa, *Asset Prices and Monetary Policy: Four Views* (London: Centre for Economic Policy Research, 1998).

In practice, the two transmission channels are hard to disentangle, entailing postulated relationships between asset prices and output growth that are very similar. Notwithstanding this difficulty, it is still possible to shed light on two key aspects of the relationship between asset prices and economic activity that are important to both market participants and policymakers. The first key aspect concerns the question of whether asset price movements have some information content on the evolution of economic activity and inflationary pressures that are not detected in any other variable. On the basis of the results reported above, as well as on the findings of various studies, asset prices do seem to provide useful information about the pace of future economic activity and, in particular, about variations in the output gap. The second aspect pertains to the magnitude of the impact of asset price changes on spending and its possible side effects on financial system fragility. A key question in this connection is whether the elasticity of aggregate spending to asset prices is significant enough to bring about large fluctuations in domestic demand, private-sector indebtedness, and credit risk. Since these elasticities can be very different for consumption and investment, it is useful to assess the impact of asset prices on each of these GDP components separately.

Asset Prices and Consumption

Equity and property prices can affect private consumption via three main channels. First, since consumption spending is a function of households' lifetime financial resources—as predicated by life cycle/permanent income models—and financial assets and property wealth are an important part of those resources, changes in the price of these assets can be ex-

pected to influence consumption. [30] Accordingly, this effect can be expected to be stronger in countries where property and stock ownership are more prevalent among households—that is, where stock market capitalization and the ratio of housing wealth to income are higher. Second, consumption in any given period will be a function of peoples' expectations about their wage income. To the extent that real asset prices affect such expectations by signaling faster or slower growth of real incomes in the future, they will influence current consumption.[31] Third, the classical life cycle model of consumption assumes that capital markets are perfect, allowing households to distribute optimally their consumption spending over time according to their net wealth and permanent income. In practice, however, information asymmetries and other imperfections in credit markets often prevent households from borrowing solely on the basis of their income prospects, entailing an "excess sensitivity" of current consumption to disposable income and the availability of external finance. Since the availability and cost of external finance provided by banks and other financial intermediaries depend on their assessment of a household's net worth, loan rates on consumer loans will be a function of the market value of assets owned by the household. To the extent that the market value of these assets affect the household's borrowing capacity to finance current consumption, asset price fluctuations have a further impact on aggregate consumption.

There is evidence that changes in real property and stock prices have significant effects on private consumption in most of the industrialized world. Estimates of the magnitude of this effect vary considerably across countries, however, and are highly dependent on the type of asset in question. The effects of stock prices on consump-

[30]A concise exposition of life cycle and permanent income models of consumption can be found in Angus Deaton, *Understanding Consumption* (Oxford: Clarendon Press, 1992).

[31]Empirical support for the hypothesis that stock prices affect consumption via its leading indicator properties about the growth of labor incomes is provided in Maria Ward Otoo, "Consumer Sentiment and the Stock Market," Board of Governors of the Federal Reserve System (November 1999); see also James M. Poterba and Andrew A. Samwick, "Stock Ownership Patterns, Stock Market Fluctuations, and Consumption," *Brookings Papers on Economic Activity: 2,* Brookings Institution (1995), pp. 295–357.

Table 3.5. Household Equity Holdings as a Percent of Net Wealth

	1980–84	1985–89	1990–94	1995	1996	1997
United States	10.6	11.0	15.1	19.5	20.9	24.4
Japan	4.5	7.6	5.8	5.4	4.9	3.7
France	1.3	3.1	2.9	2.6	2.9	3.2
Italy	0.8	2.1	3.6	3.8	3.6	4.7
United Kingdom	5.5	6.3	9.4	11.3	11.3	12.4
Canada	13.7	13.9	14.2	15.6	16.5	18.3

Source: Laurence Boone, Claude Giorno, and Pete Richardson, *Stock Market Fluctuations and Consumption Behavior,* OECD Working Paper (98)21 (Paris: OECD, 1998).

tion appear to be strongest in the United States, where most estimates point to an elasticity of consumption spending relative to net stock market wealth in the range of 0.03 to 0.07. Taking the mid-point, this implies that about five cents on the dollar of an increase in stock market wealth is spent on consumer goods, with the effect taking one to three years to materialize.[32] In contrast, studies for other countries have not found any significant effect of stock prices on private consumption in France and Italy,[33] whereas for Canada, Germany, Japan, the Netherlands, and the United Kingdom the effects are significant but smaller than in the United States.[34] This appears to reflect the smaller share of stock ownership relative to other financial assets in these

countries, as well as the more concentrated distribution of stock ownership across households in continental Europe when compared with the United States (Table 3.5).

The effect of changes in real property prices on consumption, on the other hand, appears to be much stronger in European Union countries. Rising real property prices can affect consumption not only through higher realized home values but also through the household's ability to refinance a mortgage or take out (or expand) home equity loans of credit based on higher property values. The two latter channels, in particular, have become increasingly important in European Union countries in recent years, thus bolstering the sensitivity of consumption to property price cycles. In the United Kingdom, for instance, the elasticity has been recently estimated to be 10 percent within the year, and in the Netherlands to be 7 percent over two years (so that a 20 percent drop in housing prices would lead to a 1½ percent contraction in consumer spending over two years, all else held constant).[35] There is evidence that changes in housing prices have also been a main determinant of consumption growth—being far more important than stock prices—in Australia as well as in some other European countries operating through the "credit channel."[36] This evidence ac-

---

[32]See Martha Starr-McCluer, "Stock Market Wealth and Consumer Spending" (unpublished; Federal Reserve Board of Governors, April 1998), and Laurence Boone, Claude Giorno, and Pete Richardson, "Stock Market Fluctuations and Consumption Behavior: Some Recent Evidence," OECD Working Paper (98)21 (Paris: Organization for Economic Cooperation and Development, 1998). These estimates are based on U.S. national income account figures prior to recent revisions based on SNA93 guidelines, and limited to stock market wealth. Using a broader definition of wealth (including both corporate equity and other forms of wealth) the wealth effect in the United States has been estimated at around 3½ cents on the dollar.

[33]A systematic analysis of the French experience is provided in Pierre Jaillet and Pierre Sicsic, "Asset Prices: Relationships with Demand Factors and Credit and Implications for Monetary Policy," in *The Role of Asset Prices in the Formulation of Monetary Policy,* BIS Conference Papers, Vol. 5 (Basel: Bank for International Settlements, 1998), pp. 210–219. Estimates for Italy are provided in Boone, Giorno, and Richardson, "Stock Market Fluctuations and Consumption Behavior."

[34]For Canada and the Netherlands, see, respectively, Gilles Bérubé and Denise Côté, "Long-Term Determinants of the Personal Savings Rate" (unpublished; Bank of Canada, February 1999) and Jeannette Capel and Aerdt Houben, "Asset Inflation in the Netherlands: Assessment, Economic Risks, and Monetary Policy Implications," *The Role of Asset Prices in the Formulation of Monetary Policy,* BIS Conference Papers, Vol. 5 (Basel: Bank for International Settlements, 1998), pp. 264–279. Estimates for Germany, Japan, and the UK are provided in Boone, Giorno, and Richardson, "Stock Market Fluctuations and Consumption Behavior."

[35]De Nederlandsche Bank, "The Dutch Housing and Mortgage Markets: A Risk Analysis," *Quarterly Bulletin* (Amsterdam: DNB, September 1999), pp. 23–33. Estimates for the United Kingdom are from Laurence Boone, Claude Giorno, and Pete Richardson, "Stock Market Fluctuations and Consumption Behavior."

[36]On Australia, see Christopher Kent and Philip Lowe, "Property Price-Cycles and Monetary Policy" in *The Role of Asset Prices in the Formulation of Monetary Policy,* BIS Conference Papers, Vol. 5 (Basel: Bank for International Settlements, 1998), pp. 239–263. For Europe, see De Bondt, "Credit Channels and Consumption, European Evidence," De Nederlandsche Bank, Staff Report No. 39 (1999).

cords well with the close correlation between changes in property prices, consumption, and credit cycles in most countries (Figure 3.7).

Asset Prices and Investment

Equity and property prices can affect investment via three channels. First, an increase (decrease) in asset prices lowers (raises) the cost of new capital relative to existing capital. If the ratio of market valuation of capital to the cost of acquiring new capital (also referred to as Tobin's q) rises (drops), so will investment. Second, several empirical studies find that private fixed investment is well explained by expected future output growth, as predicated by the so-called "flexible accelerator" model.[37] To the extent that changes in stock prices predict future GDP growth, they will thus impact current investment. Third, over and above the simple cost of capital there is the credit channel, through which changes in the net worth of the firm will have an additional impact on the financing premium and hence the cost of capital. Rising asset prices, for instance, will improve firms' and banks' balance sheets, inducing banks to charge a lower finance premium on loans, hence lowering the cost of capital.[38]

Changes in asset prices are found to have significant effects on private investment through these distinct channels in most of the industrial-

[37]See Dale Jorgensen, "Capital Theory and Investment Behavior," *American Economic Review*, Vol. 53, No. 2 (May 1963), pp. 247–259. For empirical evidence on the explanatory power of accelerator-type models, see Mark Mullins and Sushil Wadhwani, "The Effect of the Stock Market on Investment," *European Economic Review*, Vol. 33 (May 1989), pp. 939–961.

[38]There is evidence that this balance sheet effect is often reinforced by the so-called "financial accelerator" mechanism. This postulates that firms and households at the peak of the business cycle tend to be financially overextended and an adverse shock may therefore worsen financial conditions significantly, impairing firms' and households' access to credit at the same time that the need for external funds may be rising. See Ben Bernanke, Mark Gertler, and Simon Gilchrist, "The Financial Accelerator and the Flight to Quality," *The Review of Economics and Statistics*, Vol. 78 (February 1996), pp. 1–15.

Figure 3.7. Industrial Countries: Bank Credit, Real Property Prices, and Net Private Savings

Property price cycles have been closely related to swings in domestic bank credit and negatively associated with changes in net private sector savings.

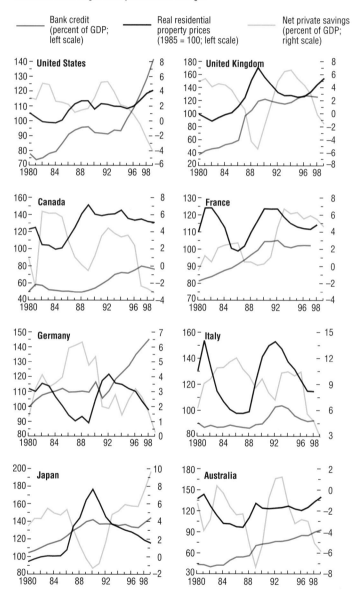

Figure 3.7 (concluded)

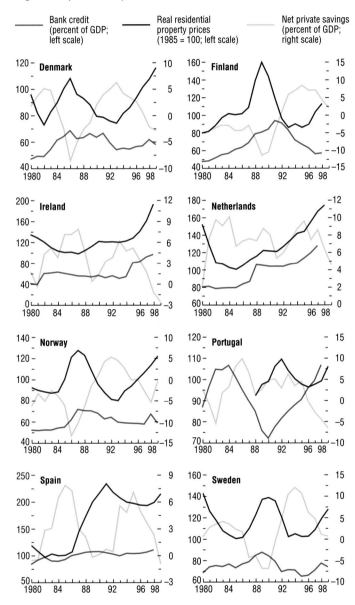

Sources: IMF, *International Financial Statistics;* IMF staff estimates; and BIS, *69th Annual Report.*

ized world. In the United States the impact of changes in stock prices on investment appears to have been particularly strong in the current expansion, with the Tobin's q having risen by 75 percent between 1992 and 1998 to reach its highest level since World War II.[39] Rapid investment growth has played a key role in raising productivity and sustaining the current U.S. expansion (see Box 3.1). Studies for other countries also yield a strong relationship between stock prices and investment for Australia, the United Kingdom, and Japan.[40] In France, Germany, and the Netherlands, however, the link between asset prices and investment seems less pronounced (Figure 3.8).[41] One possible explanation for the historically smaller role for stock prices in continental Europe is the difference in corporate laws and traditions, as witnessed by less frequent takeovers, the greater importance accorded to employees in decision making, and the higher gearing ratios. These features imply that managers tend to be less responsive to the stock mar-

[39]For evidence on the impact of stock prices and Tobin's q on investment in the United States and Canada, see Robert Barro, "The Stock Market and Investment," *Review of Financial Studies,* Vol. 3, No. 1 (1990), pp. 115–131. While the predictive performance of q-type investment models has been traditionally weak (relative to accelerator-type models, for instance), there is little dispute that the market drop in the price of capital associated with the recent boom in equity markets has contributed importantly to rapid investment growth in the United States. Empirical studies have also highlighted, however, the important role of other factors, such as the higher rates of capital depreciation in the 1990s and the permanent nature of shocks to computer prices. See, for instance, Stacey Terlin and Karl Whelan, "Explaining the Investment Boom of the 1990s," FED Working Paper 2000-11 (Washington: Federal Reserve Board, 2000).

[40]See Michael Andersen and Robert Subbaraman, "Share Prices and Investment," Reserve Bank of Australia, Research Discussion Paper 9610 (1996), Bank of England "Small, Inventory investment and cash flow," (unpublished, 1997), and Tamim Bayoumi, "The Morning After: Explaining the Slowdown in Japanese Growth in the 1990s," NBER Working Paper 7350 (Cambridge, Massachusetts: National Bureau of Economic Research, 1999).

[41]Jeannette Capel and Aerdt Houben, "Asset Price Inflation in the Netherlands: Assessment, Economic Risks, and Monetary Implications," in *The Role of Asset Prices in the Formulation of Monetary Policy,* BIS Conference Papers, Vol. 5 (Basel: Bank for International Settlements, 1998), pp. 264–279.

ket relative to their counterparts in the Anglo-Saxon countries. Studies show that investment in Germany has indeed been less sensitive to changes in stock prices relative to the United States and the United Kingdom,[42] although there are indications that this sensitivity may increase in coming years, in response to the pressure for firms to restructure to raise productivity and take full benefit of the single-currency European capital market. On the other hand, there is evidence that property prices—rather than stock prices—have a more significant effect on investment in continental Europe and Japan, consistent with the more widespread use of property collateral against loans and the greater role of bank credit in firms' financing. In these countries, cycles in property prices in fact have been closely linked to cycles in credit and investment, although the direction of the causality between these three variables is hard to pin down empirically (see Figures 3.7 and 3.8).[43]

Asset Prices and Financial Fragility

Reflecting the rapid expansion of the financial industry over the past two decades, the share of the financial sector in GDP has risen significantly in all industrial countries. As financial sector linkages within national economies strengthened, widespread deregulation and stiffening competition induced banks to become increasingly engaged in non-traditional lines of business; among these, asset trading and mortgage financing to highly leveraged households and corporations stand out.[44] In particular, banks' exposure to the property market increased markedly during the 1980s and, in some coun-

[42]Mullins and Wadhwani, "The Effect of the Stock Market."

[43]Kent and Lowe, "Property Price-Cycles and Monetary Policy."

[44]The share of lending to the private sector relative to the public sector also increased markedly during the period, partly reflecting fiscal consolidation in most industrial countries. To the extent that loans to the private sector are riskier, this contributed to the increase in the overall risk exposure of national financial systems.

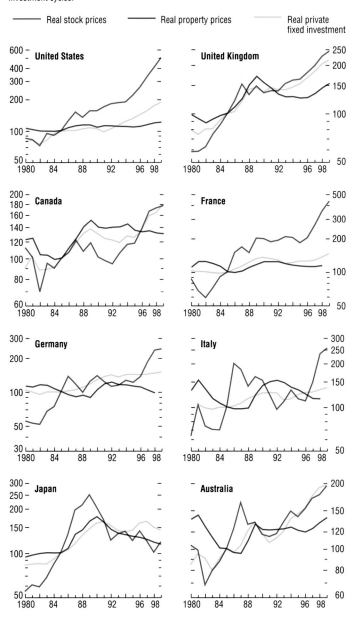

Figure 3.8. Industrial Countries: Real Stock Prices, Real Property Prices, and Real Private Fixed Investment
(Logarithmic scale; 1985 = 100)

The recent increase in real stock prices in the United States, Canada, and the United Kingdom appears to have played a key role in driving aggregate investment, whereas in continental European countries and Japan property prices have been more closely associated with investment cycles.

Table 3.6. Bank Real Estate Lending in Selected Countries[1]
(Percent of loans to private sector)

	1982	1985	1990	1992
Canada	30	33	46	51
France	28	29	31	30
Germany	44	46	42	40
Japan	12	14	24	19
Norway	51	48	50	46
Portugal	23	28	34	33
Spain	19	19	27	30
Switzerland	51	52	54	54
United Kingdom	16	19	31	32
United States	29	31	41	43

Source: Bank for International Settlements, *Annual Reports*, various years.
[1]Post-1992 data not published on a consistent basis.

Figure 3.8 (*concluded*)

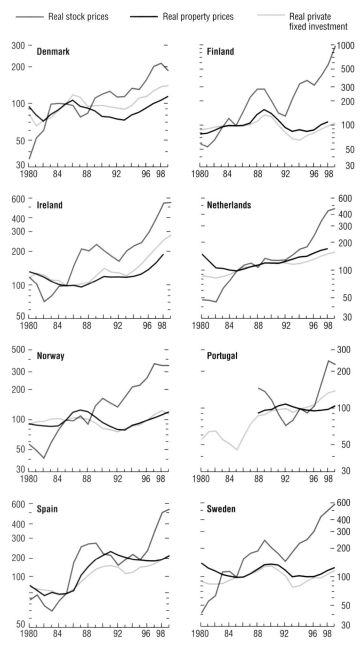

Sources: IMF, *International Financial Statistics;* IMF staff estimates; and BIS, *69th Annual Report.*

tries, this trend continued through the early 1990s (Table 3.6).

Greater exposure to asset market developments implies that sharp swings in stock and property prices, such as those observed over the last two decades, tend to have a major impact on the balance sheets of financial institutions. One direct channel is through revaluations of non-loan assets and changes in earnings accruing from brokerage fees on the value of asset transactions. A less direct but key channel is through changes in the net worth of the household and corporate sectors. To the extent that falling stock and property prices affect the solvency of household and corporate borrowers, they tend to raise the share of nonperforming loans in the portfolios of financial institutions, thereby undermining banks' capital position and lending capacity. Under generalized asset price deflation, these effects are reinforced by the falling value of loan collateral, which banks can usually recover in the case of outright defaults. As financial institutions try to sell those assets at fire sale prices, the negative impact on asset markets and banks' balance sheets can become self-reinforcing. The combination of these effects can create a "credit crunch," worsening the contractionary effects triggered by the original drop in asset prices.

Conversely, a similar mechanism tends to magnify the impact of rising asset prices during cyclical upswings. As the net worth of households and corporations increases, so do banks' balance sheet positions and lending capacity, fostering a credit boom. This transmission channel has proven to be particularly strong in countries where the financial system is bank-dominated, such as in continental Europe and Japan (where cross shareholding between the banking and corporate sector is extensive), as opposed to a financial system where stock and bond markets play a more central role, such as in the United Kingdom and the United States.[45] The potentially disruptive impact of asset price fluctuations on the balance sheets of financial institutions underscores the need for a highly capitalized and well-supervised financial system. Fragile financial systems have a reduced capacity for channeling funds from savers to borrowers, raising the cost of capital and restricting the access of innovative entrepreneurs to liquid funds, which, in turn, hampers investment and economic growth.[46] The experiences of several industrial and emerging economies over the past two decades also suggest that government-sponsored bank rescue operations following asset price collapses can be very costly. Moreover, structurally fragile financial systems can also undermine price stability in the longer term by inducing monetary policy "forebearance"; that is, to avoid the potentially high costs of financial system disruptions and fiscal rescue operations, monetary authorities may be tempted to maintain a looser policy stance than that warranted by current macroeconomic and asset market indicators, which may allow an incipient asset price bubble to inflate further. Conversely, governments may be tempted into "regulatory forebearance" following an asset price collapse, setting regulation standards too loosely. This may hinder faster progress toward needed financial system restructuring. The considerable effort spent on reforming capital adequacy standards and updating regulations on credit and market risk measurement across countries partly reflects such concerns about the higher exposure of financial institutions to asset market fluctuations and their potential impact on financial system soundness.[47]

Even if financial systems are well-capitalized and properly supervised, financial fragility can still arise in circumstances of excessive corporate and household debt. As the stock adjustment following a long boom usually takes time to unwind, this can also lead to protracted recessions even if the solvency of the financial sector is unaffected initially. Protracted stock adjustment can be particularly severe in the case of business and residential investment. This is because, as discussed above, periods of stock and property price booms often lower the real cost of capital below its fundamental-based levels, which, via expectational and Tobin's q effects, leads to overinvestment. The overshooting reduces corporate profitability while enhancing financial fragility, which, as witnessed by the experience of Japan in the 1990s, may take very long to unwind.[48] But even in milder cases where no financial crises ensued, such as in Spain and the United Kingdom in the early 1990s, the share of private investment in GDP dropped significantly following the asset price deflation and took quite long to recover (Figure 3.9).

Policy Issues

Monetary and fiscal policies have succeeded in lowering inflation in industrial countries but the broader challenge of macroeconomic stabi-

---

[45]For a discussion on the Scandinavian experience of the 1980s and early 1990s, see Buckhard Drees and Ceyla Pazarbaşıoğlu, *"The Nordic Banking Crisis: Pitfalls in Financial Liberalization?"* IMF Occasional Paper No. 161 (Washington: International Monetary Fund, 1998). For econometric evidence on the central role of financial intermediaries in magnifying the impact of asset price fluctuations on output in Japan, see Bayoumi, "The Morning After."

[46]A comprehensive discussion of the links between financial system soundness and economic growth is provided in Ross Levine, "Financial Development and Economic Growth: Views and Agenda," *Journal of Economic Literature*, Vol. 35 (June 1997) pp. 688–726.

[47]See Basel Committee on Banking Supervision, *A New Capital Adequacy Framework* (Basel, June 1999).

[48]See Ramana Ramaswamy, "The Slump in Business Investment in Japan in the 1990s" in *Post-Bubble Blues: How Japan Responded to Asset Price Collapse,* ed. by Tamim Bayoumi and Charles Collyns (Washington: International Monetary Fund, 2000).

Figure 3.9. Industrial Countries: Private Investment
(Percent of GDP)

Private investment took relatively long to recover following large asset price collapses in the late 1980s and early 1990s.

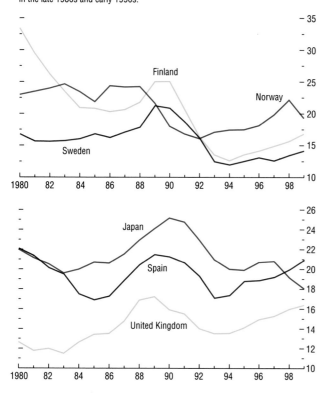

lization remains in two important respects. One is minimizing boom and bust cycles in economic activity and their disruptive effects on the financial system. The other is to keep at bay inflationary pressures while also preventing the emergence of its converse—namely, generalized price deflation. Given evidence that large asset price swings tend to have significant effects on current and future output growth as well as on financial system stability, a main challenge for macroeconomic policy in industrial countries in the current low-inflation environment is twofold: to prevent financial market excesses from spilling over to goods and services markets, thus threatening macroeconomic stability; and to minimize the risk that sustained periods of asset price inflation or deflation—even if they appear to be broadly justified by "fundamentals"—will undermine financial sector soundness.

These considerations do not imply, however, that targeting a certain level of asset prices should become a macroeconomic policy goal similar to inflation or monetary targeting. First, as discussed earlier, asset price models are based on unobserved variables and so their empirical predictions are subject to wide margins of error. This makes it very unlikely that the "right" price can be identified in all—or even in most—circumstances. Second, since an adequately designed monetary policy of targeting goods and services price inflation should take asset price developments into account (given their leading indicator properties and implications for financial fragility discussed above), it would be redundant to have an extra explicit goal of targeting an asset market index; indeed, setting a fixed policy target for goods and services price inflation and another one for, say, stock price inflation could prevent relative price movements that might well be justified by changes in fundamentals.[49] Third,

---

[49]The alternative of targeting stock or property prices indirectly by including them in an expanded monetary conditions index (MCI) is also problematic. Changes in such asset prices have varying impacts on economic activity depending on the type of asset in question and the underlying causes of its movements, so policy responses to changes in this broader index of monetary conditions could be destabilizing.

because asset markets place greater reliance on information and are generally acknowledged to be more competitive than some goods and labor markets, macroeconomic policy authorities ought to be especially cautious when pitting their judgment against those of the market.

There are, nevertheless, sound conceptual reasons and ample historical evidence in support of policies that do not always accommodate asset price movements. Conceptually speaking, given that monetary policy operates with relatively long lags, inflation targeting requires monetary policy to act in anticipation of changes in the output gap and/or inflation. Under strong assumptions about rational expectations and policy credibility, agents would fully anticipate future policy reaction to changes in the output gap and inflation, making it redundant for monetary policy to react to any forward-looking indicator other than the *current* output gap and inflation.[50] However, in a more realistic setting, where information is costly and not fully available to all agents, and learning about the "true" macroeconomic parameters is gradual, information provided by asset prices about expected changes in inflation and the output gap has a role to play; to the extent that this information is not contained in any other variable, it is clear that macroeconomic policy should take asset price movements into account. In this context, the case for macroeconomic policies to "lean against the wind" during cyclical upswings arises when asset prices rise too fast because of excessive optimism about future productivity or earnings growth. To the extent that this boosts aggregate demand in the short run but not the economy's supply potential (since actual productivity growth will lag behind expectations), inflationary pressures or other macroeconomic imbalances are likely to result. Given that the welfare costs of a belated adjustment between supply and demand tend to be very high, it is important for policy to react at a relatively early stage to the emergence of such imbalances. Conversely, the case for a looser policy stance can be made during a cyclical downswing when asset prices decline sharply to levels below those warranted by historical trends and sound valuation analyses. Insofar as this may lead to a deflationary spiral and exacerbate financial fragility, policy should be loosened.

In light of these considerations, it appears that the main error of macroeconomic policies in several industrialized countries in the 1980s and early 1990s was not that of targeting the wrong indicator (goods and services price inflation), but rather the failure of making full and more prompt use of the information content of asset prices and overlooking their impact on private-sector balance sheets. As abundantly documented elsewhere, this led to accommodative monetary policy that fueled excess demand and inflationary pressures in goods and services markets, requiring a substantial policy tightening at a later stage of the cyclical upswing.[51] This arguably ended up having more traumatic effects on the macroeconomy and the financial system than an earlier pre-emptive policy action. Another historical episode that illustrates well the inadequacy of a late policy reaction to destabilizing asset market developments is the response of the U.S. monetary authorities to the asset price collapse that triggered the Great Depression of the 1930s: by keeping a tight monetary policy stance as industrial production declined sharply and the economy spanned into a deflationary spiral, monetary policy contributed to the severity of the associated

---

[50]For a model along these lines, see, for instance, Ben Bernanke and Mark Gertler, "Monetary Policy and Asset Price Volatility" (unpublished; Princeton University, September 1999). One channel through which forward-looking private agents anticipate the policy response to future changes in the output gap or deviation in inflation from target is the long-term interest rate. For instance, if a shock to asset prices is expected to lower future output below potential, a rational bond market would anticipate the policy response to the shock by lowering the long-term interest rate. This, in turn, would help stabilize demand, obviating the need for a pre-emptive policy response to such an asset price change. As noted above, however, the efficiency of this mechanism relies on strong assumptions about the process of expectations formation.

[51]See *World Economic Outlook*, May 1992 and May 1993 issues.

recession.[52] In contrast, the prompt response of monetary policy in the U.S. to the stock market crash of October 1987 stands out as a good example of how effective early policy actions can be in mitigating the impact of asset market excesses on the macroeconomy and financial system.[53]

These distinct episodes not only indicate the need for a pre-emptive policy action in some infrequent occasions, but also that such a policy reaction has to be *symmetric*. On the one hand, the policy stance should be relaxed whenever a sharp collapse in asset prices undermines the solvency of the financial system and can trigger a severe recession.[54] On the other hand, policy should equally offer some resistance to an apparently unsustainable buildup of asset prices that—even when gradual and not immediately accompanied by inflationary pressures—carries a high risk of crashing, spilling over into the macroeconomy to produce substantial output and employment losses. In particular, the historical evidence reviewed above suggests that the need for a pre-emptive policy response to either a sustained buildup or a sharp collapse in asset prices may be warranted in the following situations. First, in cases where signs of overvaluation (undervaluation) are generalized across the different assets and, in particular, when both stock prices and property prices rise (drop) well above (below) historical or estimated equilibrium trends. Second, in light of the potentially disruptive effects that asset price swings can have on financial sector soundness and private sector solvency (even in financial systems that appear to be well-regulated ex ante), the case for some policy tightening is strengthened whenever high asset price inflation is accompanied by rapid credit and money growth, and vice versa.[55] Third, all asset bubble episodes of the 1980s and 1990s were associated with a marked drop in private savings ratios, rapidly rising investment ratios, sharp deterioration in private sector balance sheets, and large external current account deficits (usually in excess of 4 percent of GDP). When significant imbalances in these distinct macroeconomic and financial indicators begin to emerge, some policy tightening seems well warranted.

This leads to the question of which policy instruments are most effective to deal with these particular situations. The previous discussion makes clear that macroeconomic and regulatory policies can affect aggregate demand and real asset prices via four distinct channels: (1) through changes in interest rates and/or rediscount facilities controlled by the central bank; (2) through regulatory policies such as reserve and capital requirements, and loan provisioning regulations on financial institutions, which help contain the impact of large variations in market liquidity on credit supply; (3) through counter-cyclical fiscal policies aimed at dampening excessive expansion or contraction of private-sector spending, thereby affecting output and earnings growth; and (4) through selective tax changes which raise or lower the real post-tax return on asset transactions.[56]

---

[52]For a review of stock market and macroeconomic developments leading to the Great Depression of the 1930s, and the conduct of macroeconomic policy during the period, see Christina Romer, "The Nation in Depression," *Journal of Economic Perspectives*, Vol.7 (Spring 1993), pp. 19–39.

[53]See Gertler, Goodfriend, Issing, and Spaventa, *Asset Prices and Monetary Policy: Four Views*. On the other hand, while policy reaction in the wake of the 1987 asset price collapse was instrumental in preventing a repeat of the 1930s depression, it could be argued that policy should have been used to prevent such excesses from building up in the first place, given their likely adverse effects on the macroeconomy.

[54]As discussed earlier, a well-regulated and supervised financial system should in principle be able to withstand large shocks to asset prices. In practice, however, even financial systems that appear to be well-regulated and supervised ex ante are unlikely to be immune to the effects of a sharp recession triggered by a collapse in asset prices, especially when the non-financial private sector debt is high, as is usually the case in the advanced stages of a strong cyclical expansion.

[55]See Garry Schinasi and Monica Hargraves, "'Boom and Bust' in Asset Markets in the 1980s: Causes and Consequences," in *Staff Studies for the World Economic Outlook* (Washington: IMF, December 1993).

[56]One example is through higher tax rebates on mortgage interest payments. By effectively lowering the discount rate used to determine the present value of property, such tax cuts will tend to raise its price.

The combination of instruments that should be preferred will depend on a number of considerations. In general, monetary policy tends to be a more agile instrument than fiscal policy insofar as it can affect interest rates and bank credit more directly and does not require the longer lags usually associated with budget approval and implementation. Moreover, there is a strong case for fiscal policy to follow stable and transparent rules that may constrain their counter-cyclical role beyond built-in automatic stabilizers. Similarly, there is a case for regulatory policies to be stable over the business cycle, although the built-in automatic stabilizers in those rules may be a desirable feature in some contexts, as will be discussed below.

There are cases, however, where monetary policy may be either ineffective or an effective but blunt instrument to defuse macroeconomic imbalances stemming from asset market excesses.[57] One case is when the economy falls into a liquidity trap following an asset price collapse. Since the monetary authorities cannot make interest rates negative, whenever inflation in goods and services is close to zero or negative, then monetary policy loses much of its effectiveness as a counter-cyclical instrument. In such circumstances, fiscal policy may need to play a role. Limits to monetary policy are also obvious in the case of monetary unions or large currency areas in which asset price bubbles (or their converse) are not generalized, affecting only some regions, and are restricted within those regions to a specific class of assets such as commercial and residential property. In such cases, fiscal and regulatory policies may, again, have an important role to play.

Current Challenges in the Euro Area and in the United States

Despite the marked divergences across European countries, stock prices in the euro area as a whole have evolved broadly in line with those in the United States. But the increase—at least until very recently—has been less marked (Figure 3.10) and, as in the United States, the largest gains have been in the high productivity technology sector.

From a policy standpoint, a main concern about recent stock price trends is the magnitude of the observed regional divergences. Given that large stock price swings in euro countries tend to have a much less significant effect on domestic demand than in the United States due to factors already discussed, the much more rapid rise in prices in Finland, Ireland, the Netherlands, Portugal, and Spain—as well as in Sweden (which is not yet a member of the euro area)—than elsewhere in the area is a matter of greater policy concern than is the rise in stock prices for the euro area as whole. At the same time, these are countries where—with the apparent exception of Finland—signs of overvaluation have also emerged in the property market, which can have a greater impact on aggregate demand and credit conditions.

While these divergences can be, at least in part, justified by the process of regional convergence associated with economic integration, the potentially significant impact of large asset price corrections on credit growth and bank soundness in such countries (where the financial system tends to be bank dominated) poses a particular challenge for the conduct of monetary policy.[58] In some countries, nominal and real interest rates declined steeply in the run-up to the introduction of the euro in January 1999. Short-term nominal interest rates are now equal across the member countries, but real short-term interest rates are lower in the faster growing economies owing to higher inflation rates. The difficulties are not unlike those posed by regional asset price booms in other large currency unions, but may be more problematic because of the lower degree of labor mobility across regions, greater structural rigidities, and the absence of fiscal federalism. In setting monetary policy, the European

---

[57]See the October 1999 *World Economic Outlook* for a detailed discussion of these cases.
[58]On convergence in Europe, see the discussion in Chapter III of the October 1999 issue of the *World Economic Outlook*.

Figure 3.10. Industrial Countries: Equity Prices
(January 1994 = 100)

Stock prices in the United States have risen faster than in the European Union and Japan since the mid-1990s.

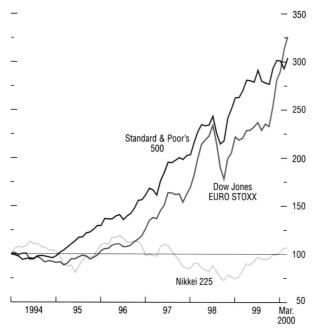

Source: European Central Bank, *Monthly Bulletin.*

Central Bank has focused, appropriately, on the medium-term inflation prospects as well as monetary developments in the euro area as a whole. This has resulted in monetary conditions that appear to be too loose for some countries and too tight for others. Asset price inflation is taken into account in the ECB's monetary policy framework in two ways: first, to the extent that the rise in asset prices, especially property prices, is sustained by strong credit growth, this will be reflected in rapid growth of the broad monetary aggregate M3 (the first pillar of the monetary policy framework); second, through their indirect effect on consumer prices, and hence on the ECB's inflation target (the second pillar of the framework).[59] The difficulty is that the risks of asset price inflation in the smaller euro-area countries may be downplayed because these countries have a relatively small weight in the euro area's aggregate harmonized index of consumer prices (HCPI) and M3. However, because of the link of asset prices to bank soundness, developments in asset prices in the smaller euro-area countries are more important than their weight in the aggregate HCPI or M3 suggests, as financial-sector difficulties in a small euro area country associated with a collapse in asset prices might affect financial sectors of other euro area countries.

Monetary policy is not well equipped alone to deal with regional asset price booms. Fiscal and regulatory policies thus have a potentially important role to play. On the fiscal front, reforms to remove distortions in the tax regime for housing, such as the elimination or reduction of the tax deductibility on mortgage interest payments, would be helpful in some countries.[60] In addition, fiscal policy could be tightened further in the

[59]The euro area harmonized index of consumer prices (HCPI) does not yet include housing and therefore underestimates the effect of asset price inflation on consumer prices.

[60]The recent Danish experience, for instance, suggests that such a policy can be effective. Private consumption growth has slowed following cuts in the tax deductibility of mortgage interest payments (which helped lower the growth of disposable income of a substantial part of the household sector), while property prices have been affected only slightly.

Table 3.7. Change in Fiscal Balances and Output Growth in the Euro Area

	Change in Actual Balance (in percent of GDP)			Change in Structural Balance (in percent of GDP)			Output Gap (in percent)			Real GDP (percent change)		
	1998	1999	2000[1]	1998	1999	2000[1]	1998	1999	2000[1]	1998	1999	2000[1]
Germany	0.9	0.5	0.4	0.8	0.8	0.0	−2.2	−2.9	−2.3	2.2	1.4	2.8
France	−0.3	0.7	0.6	−1.1	0.4	0.0	−1.9	−1.5	−0.6	3.4	2.8	3.4
Italy	0.0	0.7	0.3	0.2	0.9	0.0	−2.8	−3.3	−2.6	1.3	1.3	2.6
Spain	0.8	0.4	0.5	0.2	−0.2	0.3	−0.7	−0.3	0.2	4.0	3.7	3.7
Netherlands	0.4	1.0	0.2	−0.1	0.7	−0.1	0.7	1.3	1.9	3.7	3.4	3.3
Belgium	0.8	0.2	0.4	0.5	0.1	−0.3	−1.5	−1.5	−0.3	2.7	2.0	3.3
Austria	−0.6	0.1	0.6	−0.6	0.5	0.3	−1.2	−2.0	−1.8	2.9	2.0	3.1
Finland	3.0	1.7	1.5	2.1	1.6	1.2	0.0	0.1	0.6	5.0	3.6	4.1
Portugal	0.4	0.4	0.3	0.0	0.3	0.1	0.0	−0.1	0.2	3.9	3.0	3.4
Ireland	1.5	1.1	0.1	1.0	0.8	0.2	2.4	3.0	2.7	8.9	8.4	7.4

[1]IMF staff projections.

countries with strong domestic demand. Although, on balance, discretionary fiscal policy (measured using the structural budget deficit) was moderately restrictive in 1998 and 1999 and is expected to be so again this year, it has tended to be looser (relative to the level of economic activity) in the faster growing economies and tighter in the slower growing ones. The restrictive influence of fiscal policy on aggregate euro-area economic activity has come largely from the tightening of fiscal positions in Germany and Italy, the two slowest growing economies in the euro area; in the faster growing economies, fiscal policy has been expansionary or only mildly restrictive. At the individual country level, fiscal policy has thus tended to be pro-cyclical, in part owing to the Growth and Stability Pact's focus on actual rather than structural budget deficits (Table 3.7).

The result has been a regional policy mix in which both monetary and fiscal policies have tended to be excessively accommodating in the faster growing economies and not quite as supportive as might seem warranted in the slower growing ones. Since monetary policy cannot be differentiated by country but fiscal policy can (as it continues to be determined nationally), fiscal policy thus needs to play a much greater role in helping reduce regional cyclical divergences than was the case prior to European Economic and Monetary Union (EMU).[61] The role of fiscal policy in managing unsustainable asset price inflation should of course be symmetrical: that is to say, in the event of a sharp correction in asset prices, fiscal expansion should help to stabilize economic activity. The usefulness of fiscal policy in alleviating deflationary pressure—as well as its limitations—has been demonstrated most recently by the experience of Japan.[62]

Financial sector supervision and regulation also can contribute to avoiding regional asset price booms and busts. Prudential measures such as raising provisioning requirements for consumer and real estate loans, margin requirements, and enhanced monitoring of lending standards, along with moral suasion, may all have a role to play. To avoid potential credit problems, sufficient account must be taken of business cycle effects in lending. Indeed, banking problems have often arisen from the tendency in periods of booming asset prices and generally favorable economic conditions for credit assessments to be based on overly optimistic assumptions. Stress testing, which takes account of business cycle effects and feasible

[61]One difficulty with putting this in practice is that the fastest growing economies in Europe are already posting fiscal surpluses, making it politically more difficult to demand further improvements in their fiscal balances.

[62]See Adam Posen, *Restoring Japan's Economic Growth* (Washington: Institute for International Economics, 1998), for a discussion of this point.

Figure 3.11. United States: Economic Indicators
(Percent of GDP)

Rapid economic growth in the United States has been associated with strong increases in private investment and bank credit and a marked decline in personal savings and in the current account balance.

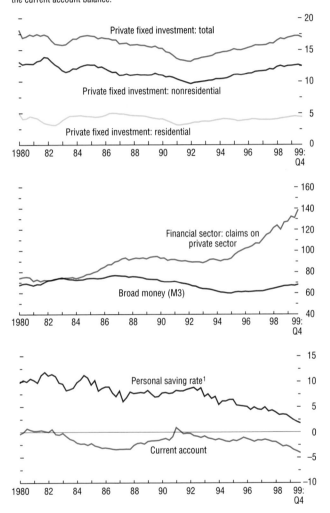

Sources: IMF, *International Financial Statistics;* IMF staff estimates; and Haver Analytics database.
[1]In percent of disposable personal income.

downside scenarios with respect to asset prices, is one way of incorporating a broader view of credit risk into credit decisions. Collateral values need to be monitored closely by banks, and in some cases it may even be desirable for collateralized lending, especially for real estate, to adopt countercyclical features. For instance, larger down payments could be required for real estate loans in periods of booming property prices. In addition, greater disclosure requirements for banks concerning their loan risk management and internal control policies and practices would increase transparency and strengthen market discipline, thereby helping to avoid some of the weak credit risk management practices and poor credit quality problems that typically underlie financial-sector fragility.[63]

In comparison with other industrialized countries, U.S. stock prices have risen more rapidly since 1994.[64] Despite the concomitant rise in productivity growth and indications that at least some of the stock price rises may be sustained (see Box 3.1), both the valuation analysis discussed earlier and evidence from other studies point to some degree of overvaluation in broad stock indices such as the S&P 500 and the overall Dow Jones. While the sharp bifurcation in the different stock sub-indices associated with the pricing of technology stocks adds further complication to the valuation assessment of broad indices, triple-digit P/E ratios for the average technology stock point to exceptionally high market expectations of future earnings growth.[65] Given

[63]See Bank for International Settlements, *Best Practices for Credit Risk Disclosure* (Basel: BIS, July 1999).

[64]Between January 1994 and December 1999, average U.S. stock prices (as measured by main stock indices such as the Standard and Poor's 500) also rose considerably faster than the Euro Dow Jones index when both are expressed in the same currency (rather than in the respective national currencies as in Figure 3.10), but the gap has narrowed considerably since.

[65]For instance, a P/E ratio of 186—such as that of the NASDAQ stock index in early March 2000—entails earnings expectations in excess of 25 percent a year for the next five years, even assuming that at the end of 2005 the index's P/E ratio will remain well above historical values, in the 75 to 100 range. See Greg Jensen and Tyler Shubert, "What Is the Nasdaq Telling Us?" *Bridgewater Daily Observations,* Bridgewater Associates (March 13, 2000), pp. 1–3.

the significant predictive power of stock prices on investment and output growth in the United States and, in particular, the higher elasticity of private consumption to stock market wealth in the United States compared with other industrial countries, a continuation of the recent trend in stock prices points to faster growth of domestic demand and real GDP relative to potential—even after estimates of the latter are revised upward in line with the recent revisions in U.S. national income accounts. Combined with a positive output gap and an unemployment rate at a 30-year low, recent stock market trends seem to be signaling further demand pressures ahead, despite the (so far) quiescent price inflation in goods and services.

In addition to indications of stock price overshooting, there are clear signs of macroeconomic imbalances in the United States. These include rapid credit growth, a sharply rising investment ratio, record low household savings, and a widening current account deficit (Figure 3.11). Although the fiscal stance (as measured by the general government structural balance) has been broadly contractionary, *real* interest rate indicators remain below their average levels in the 1980s despite the recent step increases in the Federal Reserve Funds rate (Figure 3.12).[66] International shifts in portfolio and other capital inflows to the United States fostered by the emerging market crises of 1997 and 1998 as well as by recession in Japan and slow growth in Europe have also helped fuel domestic liquidity. Although economic recoveries under way in these regions should take some pressure off domestic demand and help reduce the U.S. current account deficit gradually, symptoms of financial fragility may emerge in the wake of a significant drop in asset prices or of a sharp growth slowdown, as the U.S. private sector is highly leveraged and the personal saving ratio has reached historical lows in early 2000. Even

[66]An overview of recent trends in fiscal balances and the output gap in the United States is provided in the October 1999 issue of the *World Economic Outlook,* Chapter III.

Figure 3.12. United States: Interest Rates
(Percent)

Rapid economic growth in the United States has been associated with lower and less volatile real interest rates in the 1990s.

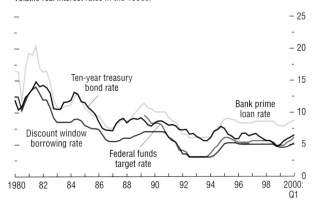

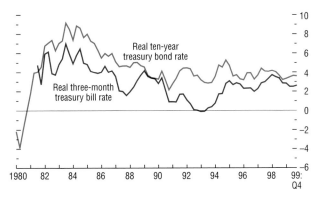

Sources: Haver Analytics database; and IMF staff estimates.

though the financial system in the United States is widely acknowledged to be well-regulated and capitalized, such concerns are heightened by evidence that periods of rapid credit growth have been historically associated with a decline in the quality of the loan portfolio of financial institutions.[67] In light of these considerations, it seems that monetary policy will have to strike a fine balance in the near future between the need to bring output growth in line with potential to keep inflationary pressures at bay, and that of preventing an abrupt correction in asset markets that could likewise be macroeconomically destabilizing.

[67]Evidence on the relationship between rapid credit growth and the easing of credit standards in the United States is provided in William R. Keeton, "Does Faster Loan Growth Lead to Higher Loan Losses?" *Federal Reserve Bank of Kansas City Economic Review*, Vol. 84, No. 2 (1999), pp. 57–75.

CHAPTER IV

HOW CAN THE POOREST COUNTRIES CATCH UP?

Progress in raising real incomes and alleviating poverty has been disappointingly slow in many developing countries, and the relative gap between the richest and poorest countries has continued to widen. In Africa, the level of real per capita income today is lower than it was 30 years ago. In developing countries in the Middle East and the Western Hemisphere, real incomes have risen, but at a slower pace than in industrial countries (Figure 4.1). Sustained and rapid improvements in relative income positions—convergence—have only occurred among the developing countries of east Asia (including China), the newly industrialized economies, and a few smaller countries in other regions. Average per capita incomes in regions with the largest populations (as represented by the thickness of the bars in Figure 4.1) remain well below those in the industrial and newly industrialized economies. Overall, the number of very poor (those living on less than $1 per day) has remained roughly unchanged over the past decade, and only limited progress has been made in reducing the share of the world population living in poverty. This represents both huge amounts of unnecessary human suffering and an enormous squandering of human potential.

Recognizing these divergences in income levels and rates of growth, and in particular the unacceptably high levels of poverty that persist in many countries, the Interim and Development Committees of the IMF and World Bank placed renewed emphasis in September 1999 on poverty reduction and on strengthening the links between debt relief and poverty reduction. Subsequently, the Executive Board of the IMF refocused the objective of the IMF's concessional lending to put greater explicit emphasis on poverty reduction (Box 4.1).

The new approach to poverty reduction, now in the initial implementation stages, builds on the traditional emphasis on macroeconomic and

Figure 4.1. Advanced and Developing Economies: Per Capita Income¹
(Thousands of U.S. dollars at 1996 prices)

East Asia, which includes China and has the largest population, and the newly industrialized economies are the only country groups that are rapidly converging with the industrial countries. The thickness of the bars reflects the population in each region.

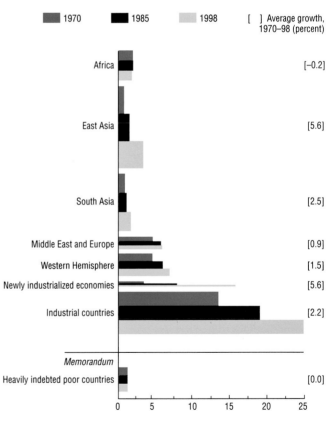

¹Converted into U.S. dollars using purchasing-power-parity (PPP) conversion rates.

Box 4.1. Poverty Reduction Strategy Papers

In September 1999, the IMF and the World Bank endorsed a new approach to enhance the focus on poverty reduction in programs supported by concessional assistance, and to strengthen the link between debt relief and poverty reduction. Underpinning the new approach, each eligible country will prepare a Poverty Reduction Strategy Paper (PRSP).

A PRSP will outline a country's anti-poverty strategy over the medium and long term. To foster ownership, the PRSP will be drawn up by the government after broad-based consultations with stakeholders, including representatives of civil society and development partners, and with assistance from World Bank and IMF staff. Long-term poverty reduction goals will be translated into annual targets for intermediate indicators (i.e., primary school enrollment, immunization rates, etc.) to facilitate shorter-term program monitoring. The PRSP is expected to become a key instrument for a country's relations with the donor community and civil society and will provide the basis for debt relief under the HIPC Initiative and all World Bank/IMF concessional lending operations. Reflecting the new policies and the central focus on poverty reduction, the IMF has replaced its concessional lending facility—formerly the Enhanced Structural Adjustment Facility—with the Poverty Reduction and Growth Facility.

It is envisaged that countries will prepare PRSPs on a three-year cycle, with progress reports in intervening years. The PRSP will diagnose poverty in the country and describe the poor and their main characteristics. The PRSP will also quantify the resources needed for various poverty reduction programs and incorporate them in a sustainable fiscal and macroeconomic framework, taking account of the availability of non-inflationary financing. Work toward the preparation of PRSPs has begun in a number of countries (e.g., Bolivia, Mozambique, and Uganda).

Since the design of robust poverty reduction strategies can take time, a phased introduction of a full-fledged PRSP is foreseen. Some governments will thus prepare an interim PRSP, stating their commitment to poverty reduction and laying out the principal elements of their strategy, the timetable to complete the PRSP, and a description of the consultative process through which the PRSP will be formulated. The three-year macroeconomic program supported by IMF and World Bank lending could then be revised to reflect the PRSP when one is completed.

structural soundness by also stressing the importance of country ownership of the poverty reduction strategy. The growing concern for country ownership, including through the involvement of civil society, is intended to reduce the risk of slippages in implementation as the countries themselves take greater responsibility for the design and success of their economic plans. The enhanced amount of debt relief under the Heavily Indebted Poor Countries (HIPC) Initiative is intended to release resources for poverty reduction, increase incentives for reforms, and remove a deterrent for both domestic and foreign investors. Of course, a successful development strategy requires progress on many fronts, as emphasized in the World Bank's Comprehensive Development Framework.[1]

Previous issues of the *World Economic Outlook* have discussed the experiences of the successfully converging countries extensively. This chapter, in contrast, investigates the main impediments to growth in the developing countries that have failed to prosper and where poverty rates remain high. The large number of countries in this group seems to suggest either that the conventional growth strategy is not being implemented forcefully enough or that the strategy has been overlooking critical obstacles to development. However, the bulk of development research reveals neither a unique set of preconditions that

---

[1]See *Entering the 21st Century: World Development Report, 1999–2000* (Washington: World Bank, 1999), p. 21.

are always present during economic takeoff nor an easily identified set of impediments that have prevented poor countries from achieving sustained growth. There is no single formula for kick-starting growth, and it is more likely that the explanation for the unsatisfactory performance of many developing countries lies in the interplay of economic and political factors that vary by country. Nevertheless, experience in the successful developing countries clearly points to macroeconomic stability, sound institutional arrangements, and openness to trade as factors that are conducive to, or at least associated with, high sustainable growth.[2] Experience in the poorest countries highlights poor education and health, ineffective governance, weak rule of law, and war as frequent impediments to prosperity.

A theme of the chapter is the plight of poor, low-growth countries and within this group the heavily indebted countries, about which there is growing consensus that unsustainable debt has become a critical barrier to future growth and poverty reduction. External debt levels, despite years of rescheduling often at concessionary terms, have become unsustainable in many cases. Without the efforts of the international community to reduce this burden substantially, there is little hope for significant improvement in living conditions, as debt overhang saps economic incentives to reform and grow. To be effective, however, debt relief must be accompanied by domestic policy reforms to address the root causes of much of the initial debt buildup.

The chapter deals less with poverty problems in middle-income countries and low-income countries that are growing rapidly. Nevertheless, it is important to remember that in countries such as China and India, which have been growing quickly and seen poverty rates fall, the number of poor remains high. Some middle-income countries, for example in Latin America, not only have pockets of absolute poverty, but also significant relative poverty.[3] In all of these cases, poverty alleviation remains important, and most of the policy considerations discussed in this chapter also apply.

Income Growth and Poverty Reduction: The Recent History

Human living conditions have improved greatly over the past 100 years, brought on by unprecedented technological and economic transformations. Global output almost tripled in the first half of the twentieth century and increased ninefold in the second half, greatly outpacing population growth. Life expectancy, education, and other indicators of well-being also improved, particularly in poor countries.[4] This chapter looks at trends over 1970–98, the longest period for which more comprehensive data are available for most developing countries. (Long-run perspectives are discussed further in Chapter V.)

Rising global prosperity, however, has not benefited all countries and regions, and the global distribution of income—measured by average incomes across countries—remains very skewed. This failure to converge can be seen in longer-term growth rates: 75 percent of developing countries recorded slower per capita income growth than in the industrial countries over the past three decades (Figure 4.2, upper panel).[5]

[2]See, for example, the May 1997 *World Economic Outlook*. For a discussion of complementarities across policies, see Robert F. Wescott and Jahangir Aziz, "Policy Complementarities and the Washington Consensus," IMF Working Paper 97/118 (Washington: International Monetary Fund, 1997), and Craig Burnside and David Dollar, "Aid, Policies, and Growth," Policy Research Working Paper 1777 (Washington: World Bank, 1997).

[3]Absolute poverty refers to the number of individuals living in poverty conditions, often defined in terms of internationally comparable monetary measures, while relative poverty refers to income differences within a country.

[4]D. Gale Johnson, "Population, Food, and Knowledge," *American Economic Review*, Vol. 90 (March 2000), pp. 1–14.

[5]Developing countries in this chapter are those classified as low income (1998 GNP per capita of $760 or less, calculated using the World Bank *Atlas* method) or middle income ($761 to $9,860) by the World Bank in *Entering the 21st Century: World Development Report, 1999–2000*. Countries heavily dependent on oil exports (Equatorial Guinea, Gabon, Oman, and Saudi Arabia), countries with populations less than 400,000, and countries in transition are excluded from the analysis. Korea, which is an advanced country in the *World Economic Outlook* classification, is considered a middle-income country in the World Bank classification and is included as a developing country in the analysis below.

Figure 4.2. Developing Countries: Grouped by Per Capita Income Growth, 1970–98[1]

The number of developing countries with slower per capita income growth than that of the industrial countries (negative growth and slow growth) is large (over 75 percent of all developing countries), although this group of developing countries comprises about 30 percent of the total in terms of population.

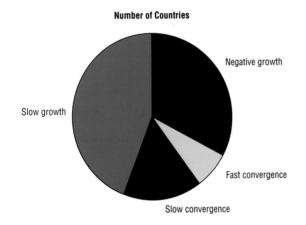

Number of Countries

Negative growth

Slow growth

Fast convergence

Slow convergence

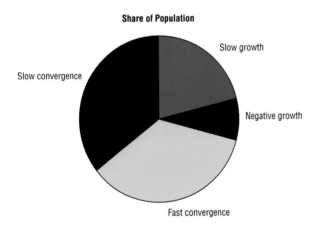

Share of Population

Slow growth

Slow convergence

Negative growth

Fast convergence

[1]Slow-growth countries have annual per capita income growth rates between 0 and 2 percent; slow-convergence countries, between 2 and 3¾ percent; and fast-convergence countries, over 3¾ percent.

Per capita income fell in 32 countries in the sample, while only seven developing countries grew fast enough to reduce substantially the income gap with—and rapidly converge toward—the industrial countries as a group.[6]

The picture is more encouraging when progress is assessed based on both per capita income growth and the size of a country's population (Figure 4.2, lower panel). Less than 10 percent of the developing world's population live in countries where average income declined, while 70 percent live in countries where per capita income growth exceeded that in the industrial countries. This more positive outcome mainly reflects strong economic growth in China in particular and also in India, which together account for about 50 percent of the population in developing countries and which had per capita growth rates of 7 percent and 2¾ percent, respectively, over the 1970–98 period (Box 4.2).[7]

A more positive picture also emerges when examining the growth performance over a shorter time frame. During 1993–98, 14 developing countries converged rapidly toward the industrial countries—double the number between 1970 and 1998—despite the problems encountered by many countries because of financial crises in Asia, Russia, and Latin America. Conversely, per capita income fell in 23 countries (compared to 32 during the longer period).[8] The improved performance in these countries partly reflects stronger domestic poli-

[6]Fast-growing or rapidly converging countries are defined for this analysis as those countries with annual per capita income growth of more than 3¾ percent. This cutoff was chosen for tractability and is similar to the cutoff chosen in Lant Prichett, "Divergence, Big Time," *Journal of Economic Perspectives*, Vol. 11 (Summer 1997), pp. 3–17. Prichett finds 11 countries (both developing and advanced) in which growth exceeded 4.2 percent over the 1960–90 period. The relatively larger number of fast-growing countries in that study mainly reflects the inclusion of advanced economies.

[7]It is important to note, however, that regional growth rates have varied considerably within China and India.

[8]Interestingly, of the 14 rapidly converging countries, only one (China) also converged rapidly during the 1970–98 period, while two others had negative growth during the longer period, five had slow growth, and six converged slowly.

Box 4.2. India: Reinvigorating the Reform Process

India has been among the fastest-growing economies in the world over the last two decades, and has achieved trend improvements in growth, literacy, mortality, and poverty rates (see the figure, upper panels). In recent years, deft handling of monetary policy has helped India to successfully weather the Asian crisis, while maintaining low inflation and a comfortable external position. Yet despite these gains, poverty rates remain high, with more than a third of the population still living below the official poverty line.[1] This uneven progress raises questions about the impact of the economic and structural reforms implemented since the mid-1980s on growth in India, and what more can be done to make greater inroads into poverty reduction.

In the three decades following independence in 1947, growth in India was stifled by a high degree of government planning and regulation, with per capita GDP rising by only 1½ percent per annum (see the first table). Industrial controls were pervasive, and restrictions on private credit, the role of the public enterprise sector, and subsidy programs increased throughout the period. Strict controls on foreign direct investment, an import licensing system, and—from the 1970s—high tariff rates further limited the economy's growth potential.

The liberalization of import and industrial controls in 1985 and improved agricultural performance spurred an acceleration of real per capita GDP growth to an average rate of 3¾ percent in the 1980s. However, this expansion also reflected other developments—increased fiscal stimulus and a debt-financed consumption and investment boom—which became unsustainable toward the end of the decade.

A balance of payments crisis ensued in 1991, reflecting the deteriorating fiscal position, rising external debt (especially short-term), a surge in world oil prices, and a sharp decline in remittances from Indian workers in the Middle East. As capital flight accelerated and official reserves were rapidly depleted, the Indian government entered into a Stand-By Arrangement with the IMF and embarked on a program of fiscal and structural reforms.

Corrective policy measures were successful in restoring macroeconomic stability. The central government deficit was brought down from 8 percent of GDP before the crisis to 4¾ percent in 1996/97,[2] through tax reforms, cuts in subsidies, and reductions in defense and other expenditures (see the figure, lower panels). The lower deficit, in turn, reduced financing that had to be provided by the central bank, and wholesale price inflation declined from a precrisis level of almost 14 percent to nearly 6 percent by 1996/97.

In addition, important structural reforms were introduced. Industrial licensing and investment approval procedures were liberalized, and the number of industries reserved for the public sector was reduced. External sector reforms included a reduction in the import-weighted tariff rate from 87 percent in 1990/91 to 25 percent by 1996/97, easing of import licensing requirements, relaxation of controls on foreign direct and portfolio investment, and greater exchange rate flexibility. Financial sector measures included interest rate liberalization, strengthened prudential norms and supervision, the introduction of greater competition into the banking system, and improvements to the operation of capital markets.

In response to the government's policy package, the recovery from the 1991 crisis was rapid. Private investment rates rose sharply, and real per capita GDP growth increased to more than 6 percent by 1995/96. Significant improvements in productivity were also achieved—as evidenced by increased total factor productivity growth at both the aggregate and firm lev-

[1]The World Bank's *World Development Report 1999/2000* suggests an even more severe poverty problem, with almost half of the population in 1994 living on less than $1 per day (on a purchasing power parity adjusted basis) and seven-eighths of the population living on less than $2 per day.

[2]The fiscal year runs from April through March.

Box 4.2 *(continued)*

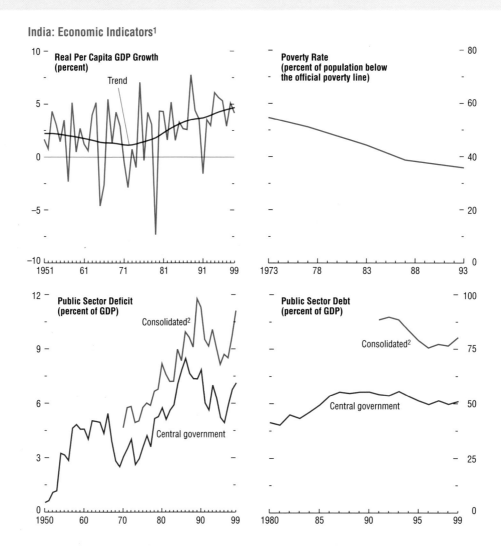

India: Economic Indicators[1]

Sources: Central Statistical Organization; Government of India Planning Commission; Union Budget documents; Reserve Bank of India; *Public Enterprises Survey; Government Finance Statistics;* and IMF staff estimates and projections.
[1]Data shown are for fiscal years, which begin in April.
[2]Consolidated public sector comprises the central and state governments, central public enterprises, and the accounts of the Oil Coordinating Committee.

els[3] and by declining incremental capital-output ratios, particularly in the services sector (see the first table).

[3]See World Bank, *India: Policies to Reduce Poverty and Accelerate Sustainable Development,* Report No. 19471-IN (2000); and P. Krishna and D. Mitra, "Trade Liberalization, Market Discipline and Productivity

However, per capita growth has slowed more recently, averaging closer to 4 percent between 1997/98 and 1999/00 compared with 4¾ percent between 1992/93 and

Growth: New Evidence from India," *Journal of Development Economics,* Vol. 56 (1998), pp. 447–62.

1996/97.[4] To some extent, this reflected the completion of cyclical catch-up following the 1991 balance of payments crisis, as well as the adverse impact of the 1997 regional crisis and agricultural supply shocks. In addition, though, economic performance appears to have been adversely affected by a reversal of fiscal adjustment, infrastructure bottlenecks, and delays in implementing structural reforms. Increases in civil service wages and subsidies, as well as rising debt service, pushed up the fiscal deficit and resulted in higher real interest rates. These higher rates, combined with banks' efforts to improve their balance sheets, slowed credit growth. Infrastructure constraints also continued to bind, as the earlier fiscal consolidation had relied too heavily on reductions in public investment. Consequently, the contribution of private investment to growth fell by half from earlier in the decade, and measured productivity growth, particularly in the industrial sector, deteriorated (see the first table).

Moreover, the poverty rate remains very high, and the impressive rate of decline from the mid-1970s through the 1980s may have slowed.[5] This outcome partly reflects the relatively poor performance of the agricultural sector during the 1990s, since some 70 percent of the labor force still relies on the land for its livelihood.[6] While adverse supply shocks played a role, the lack of agricultural reform also contributed to low investment rates and productivity in this sector. In addition, the scope for mobility of low-skilled labor out of the agricultural sector has likely been limited by the absence of robust and sustained

---

[4]The projection for growth in 1999/00 is based on Central Statistical Organization Advance Estimates.

[5]Unfortunately, the most recent official poverty statistics are for 1993/94, and do not fully capture the impact of the rapid growth in the post-crisis period. However, unofficial figures suggest that the poverty rate may not have declined appreciably during the last decade.

[6]See S. Tendulkar, "Indian Economic Policy Reforms and Poverty: An Assessment," in *India's Economic Reforms and Development: Essays for Manmohan Singh*, ed. by I.J. Ahluwalia and I.M.D. Little (Delhi: Oxford University Press, 1998).

Expenditure and Sectoral Components of Growth[1]
(Average annual percent, unless otherwise noted)

	1951–79	1980–90	1992–96	1997–99[2]
Real per capita GDP growth[3]	1.5	3.8	4.7	4.1
Real GDP growth[3]	3.7	5.9	6.7	5.8
Contribution to growth, by expenditure item:				
Private consumption	2.4	3.8	3.9	2.5
Public consumption	0.4	0.8	0.5	1.4
Gross fixed investment	0.8	1.5	1.9	1.2
Private investment	. . .	0.8	1.8	0.9
Public investment	. . .	0.6	0.1	0.3
Net exports[4]	. . .	0.1	0.1	0.6
Contribution to growth, by sector:				
Public	1.1	1.7	2.8	5.2
Private	2.2	4.2	3.8	0.7
Contribution to growth, by sector:				
Agriculture	1.1	1.6	1.4	0.5
Industry	1.0	1.7	2.0	1.5
Services	1.4	2.5	3.2	3.8
ICORs, by sector:[5]				
Overall	. . .	4.2	4.1	4.8
Agriculture	. . .	2.0	1.5	2.6
Industry	. . .	5.7	6.8	10.7
Services	. . .	4.0	2.9	2.1

Sources: Central Statistical Organisation (CSO), National Accounts Statistics.
[1]Averages computed over fiscal years beginning in April.
[2]1999 figures on GDP and sectoral production are CSO Advance Estimates; annual population growth assumed constant at 1.7 percent; average contribution of expenditure categories and private and public production computed over 1997–1998.
[3]Measured at market prices; base year is 1980 for data until 1993, and 1993 thereafter.
[4]Includes statistical discrepancy.
[5]The incremental capital output ratio (ICOR) is the ratio of the investment rate to the GDP growth rate; a falling ICOR over time therefore indicates improved capital productivity.

---

growth in the industrial sector and by the relatively larger contribution of the higher-skilled service sector to GDP growth.

What measures need to be implemented to sustain high growth rates in all sectors and achieve more substantial progress toward poverty alleviation?[7] As discussed in the text—and quan-

---

[7]Most analysts believe that a significant reduction in the poverty rate would require an annual real GDP growth rate of at least 7 percent (5 percent in per

Box 4.2 *(concluded)*

Explaining India's Relative Growth Performance

	Average Value (percent)		Estimated Difference in Contribution to Growth Rates[1] (percentage points)
	India	East Asia	
Factors contributing to growth during 1970–95			
Investment/GDP	21.9	29.6	−1.2
Net FDI/GDP	0.1	2.5	−0.8
Trade/GDP	4.5	113.5	−1.1
Government consumption/GDP	10.3	10.4	0.0
Secondary school enrollment rate	35.2	50.5	−0.3
CPI inflation rate	8.8	8.4	0.0
Convergence effect and other factors	. . .	. . .	0.2
Real per capita GDP growth (1970–95 average)	2.4	5.7	−3.3

Source: P. Kongsamut and A. Vamvakidis, "Economic Growth," Chapter 2 in *Philippines: Toward Sustainable and Rapid Growth*, IMF Occasional Paper No. 187 (Washington: International Monetary Fund, 2000).

[1]Calculated as the estimated coefficient times the difference in the independent variable value (India less East Asia). Reported differences in growth rates of real per capita GDP are actuals.

tified in the Indian context in the second table —faster growth would require durable fiscal consolidation to raise national saving and crowd-in private investment spending; further liberalization of foreign trade and investment flows; and additional reforms to labor markets and in the agricultural, industrial, and financial sectors to promote greater efficiency and export competitiveness. These reforms need to include removal of domestic pricing distortions, improvements to bankruptcy procedures, and an easing of restrictions on firm and farm size and regulations that make it difficult to shed labor (and therefore impede job creation). Fiscal priorities also need to be redirected toward investment in human and physical capital.

There is broad agreement in India that further reforms are needed—the experience of the early 1990s has demonstrated the potential benefits of reform, and consistent views on many of these key issues emerged from the major parties during the October 1999 election. Several factors argue for translating this consensus into swift action. First, the establishment of a bold agenda would be facilitated by the relatively fa-

vorable current economic situation and the significant majority enjoyed by the ruling coalition. Second, with the consolidated public sector deficit rising again and the public sector debt stock close to 80 percent of GDP, fiscal sustainability is a serious concern.[8] Third, India is committed to trade liberalization measures under the World Trade Organization, including the removal of all quantitative restrictions by 2001. For India to achieve the maximum benefits from a more liberal trade system, the structural impediments affecting domestic producers must be addressed in the interim.

Encouragingly, the new government has taken a number of initiatives that suggest a strengthened commitment to structural reform, including liberalization of the insurance sector, automatic clearance for foreign direct investment in many sectors, and a landmark agreement on state sales tax rationalization. At the same time, however, the budget introduced in February 2000 targets only modest deficit reduction in the coming fiscal year, and a clearly defined agenda for reform has yet to be established. Hence, critical and difficult challenges remain to be addressed.

capita terms) on a sustained basis. The government's Ninth Five-Year Plan (1997–2002), which targeted an average real GDP growth rate of 7 percent, projected that the official poverty rate would be reduced by 11 percentage points by the end of the plan period.

[8]See P. Reynolds, "Fiscal Adjustment and Growth Prospects in India," in *India: Selected Issues*, IMF Staff Country Reports (Washington: International Monetary Fund, forthcoming).

cies and for some of these countries, a more supportive external environment (for example, through concessional lending programs or more open trade). The better performance, however, in some instances also reflects cyclical factors, such as improved harvests or recoveries from wars or recessions. The larger number of countries in the rapidly converging category and the smaller number of countries in which per capita income fell (which in part reflects a pickup in growth performance in Africa over this period) is encouraging. But progress in alleviating poverty remains fragile and inadequate.

The percentage of the population in developing countries living under the $1 per day line has declined from 30 percent to 24 percent during the past decade (largely reflecting poverty reduction in east Asia and to a lesser extent in south Asia), but the incidence of poverty remains unacceptably high (Figure 4.3).[9] The number of people living on incomes below $1 per day has stayed roughly constant at 1.2–1.3 billion because declines in poverty rates have been broadly offset by population growth (1.9 percent a year in developing countries). Moreover, progress in poverty reduction has been uneven across geographic regions. There has been no progress in reducing poverty rates in Africa and in the Western Hemisphere, and poverty rates actually increased in the transition countries.

It should be noted that poverty is a multidimensional phenomenon, reflecting not only material deprivation but also, for example, lack of security and access to basic services including health, education, and sanitation. Health measures (for example, life expectancies) have converged more rapidly across countries than average incomes, in part because of the diffusion of medical technology. This aspect of globalization has unambiguously helped the poorest countries. Health and other dimensions of poverty are not captured in the monetary measures of poverty discussed in this chapter. See Box 5.1 for an alternative measure of economic progress

[9]The pattern of poverty rates is similar when the poverty line is defined as $2 per day.

Figure 4.3. Developing Countries: Population Living Below $1 per Day
(Percent of total population)

Poverty rates worldwide fell slightly during the past decade. Progress across regions, however, was uneven with, poverty rates decreasing substantially only in east Asia and, to a lesser extent, in south Asia. The thickness of the bars reflects the total population in each region (except for the total).

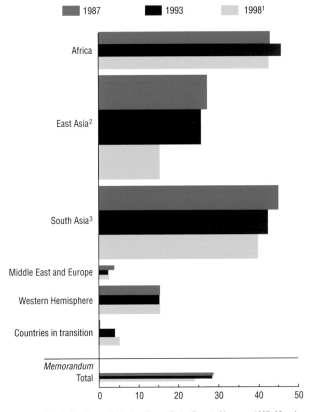

Source: Martin Ravallion and Shaohua Chen, "Global Poverty Measures 1987–98 and Projections for the Future," forthcoming.
[1]Estimated.
[2]East Asia comprises the developing countries in Asia except those in south Asia, as defined in footnote 3.
[3]South Asia comprises Bangladesh, Bhutan, India, Maldives, Nepal, Pakistan, and Sri Lanka.

that combines income, health, and education into a single summary index.

Finally, it is important to recognize the benefits of policy reforms and other accomplishments in the countries that have grown rapidly both over the full 30-year period under review and more recently. However, it is equally important to recognize the risks of slippage in the reform process or other setbacks in these very successful countries, especially the larger ones. Further, the 1997–98 financial crises demonstrated that severe recessions in a small number of countries can reverse some of the past progress in poverty reduction, while producing significant, adverse spillover effects on poverty levels in trading partners. Moreover, some have argued that over the short run economic cycles have an asymmetric effect on poverty—that is, poverty increases more in an economic contraction than it decreases in an equivalent expansion.[10]

Explanations for Diverging Performance: Analytical Complications

In the main, the empirical literature on growth and development attempts to explain the observed differences in growth and prosperity across countries by "conditional convergence." That is, each country's economic growth rate depends on a number of underlying conditions, including national endowments, preferences, macroeconomic and domestic stability, institutional and social structures, outward orientation, and the state of financial market development.

The primary thrust of these studies is to identify the conditions—some of which are policy related—that catalyze growth by promoting investment in physical and human capital, improving the efficiency of production (including the allocation of resources), and encouraging technological progress.

Unfortunately, the empirical studies generally provide only limited guidance and do not identify a single set of variables that strongly promote or inhibit growth.[11] For many of the concepts tested, the correlation with growth is often not robust to small changes in the variables being studied (that is, the *conditioning set* of other factors that may help explain differences in growth).[12] In general, factors that are considered robustly and positively correlated to growth include the share of investment in GDP, school enrollment, health indicators, openness to trade (which can be considered a proxy for outward orientation), and the share of nonprimary goods in total exports. Factors that are robustly related to poor or negative growth include weak institutional structures, measures of political instability (such as the absence of civil liberties), weak rule of law, wars, and market distortions.

The relevance and proper interpretation of these cross-sectional results have been called into question by a number of economists:

- First, the observation that a variable is correlated with growth does not mean that it helps cause growth, and therefore, an observed relationship might provide only limited insight for policymakers.[13] For exam-

---

[10]See "External Shocks, Financial Crises, and Poverty in Developing Countries," *Global Economic Prospects 2000* (Washington: The World Bank, 2000).

[11]Robert J. Barro and Xavier Sala-i-Martin, *Economic Growth* (New York: McGraw-Hill, 1995), provide a review of the theoretical and empirical literature.

[12]Ross Levine and David Renelt, "A Sensitivity Analysis of Cross-Country Growth Regressions," *The American Economic Review*, Vol. 82 (September 1992), pp. 942–63, using extreme-bounds analysis, find that only one variable, the share of investment in GDP, is robust to changes in specification (although the trade-to-GDP ratio is also robust if investment is excluded in the conditioning information set). Xavier Sala-i-Martin, "I Just Ran Two Million Regressions," *The American Economic Association Papers and Proceedings*, Vol. 86 (May 1997), pp. 178–83, and Xavier Sala-i-Martin, "I Just Ran Four Million Regressions," NBER Working Paper 6252 (Cambridge, Massachusetts: National Bureau of Economic Research, 1997), however, argue that extreme-bounds analysis is too strong a test and find about two dozen robust variables (including regional and religion variables) by examining the cumulative distributions of coefficient estimates from a large number of regressions.

[13]Instrumental variables are used in some of these cross-sectional studies to control for endogeneity. However, it is possible to find plausible reasons why these instruments are not truly exogenous because explanations for growth are so broad. Granger-causality tests, which assume only weak exogeneity, generally also provide mixed results.

ple, while a higher investment share is correlated with (and is often thought necessary for) faster growth, this correlation may result because faster growth induces more investment (reverse causation) or because some other (omitted) factor induces both faster growth and more investment. Determining the causal relationship matters for policy advice. Simply increasing investment (without concern for the efficiency of that investment) may not be sufficient to promote growth.

- Second, these results do not fully explain the growth performance of many individual economies (including many of the poor countries with negative per capita real growth over long time periods) or regions of the world, and indeed may explain well only the growth performance of industrial countries and a small set of developing countries. For example, empirical studies have found that regional dummy variables are needed to explain the growth performance of countries in sub-Saharan Africa, Latin America, and east Asia.[14]

- Third, most cross-sectional analyses assume linear relationships between growth and the explanatory factors and miss important interactions among factors. There are compelling reasons to believe that some relationships are nonlinear and that interactions between growth and other variables are significant—that good policies tend to be mutually reinforcing and that policy complementarities are important.[15]

- Fourth, cross-sectional studies generally assume that the growth process is the same in rich and poor countries. However, it has been argued that growth involves at least two dimensions: technological progress and catch-up.[16] Factors that may best promote technological progress (most relevant for advanced economies) may not necessarily be the most optimal for low-income developing countries where takeoff and catch-up are most important.

Obstacles to Growth

Overall, factors related to growth can be grouped in six areas that, broadly speaking, influence capital and the labor force, and the efficient use of their services in production. Each of these six areas is reviewed below, tying together theory and evidence from the literature and data analysis tailored to the question of uncovering impediments to growth in the poorest countries.

In order to avoid some of the pitfalls of cross-sectional studies, particularly the assumption of the homogeneity of countries at different stages of the growth process, the analysis in the rest of this section examines countries grouped by in-

---

[14]See Sala-i-Martin, "I Just Ran Four Million Regressions," which finds that regional dummies for sub-Saharan Africa and Latin America are negatively correlated with growth. The study also notes that the fraction of the population that is Buddhist or follows Confucianism, which the author interprets to be similar to a dummy variable for the east Asian countries, is positively correlated with growth. It should be noted, however, that cross-country studies based on African countries alone find results similar to the more comprehensive studies. See, for example, Dhaneshwar Gupta and Michael T. Hadjimichael, "Growth in sub-Saharan Africa," *IMF Staff Papers*, Vol. 43 (September 1996), pp. 605–34, and Dani Rodrik, "Trade Policy and Economic Performance in sub-Saharan Africa," NBER Working Paper 6562 (Cambridge, Massachusetts: National Bureau of Economic Research, 1998). For an analysis focused on sub-Saharan Africa, see Chapter VI, "Growth in sub-Saharan Africa: Performance, Impediments, and Policy Requirements," in the October 1999 *World Economic Outlook*.

[15]Chapter IV, "Globalization and the Opportunities for Developing Countries," in the May 1997 *World Economic Outlook* argues that macroeconomic stability, openness to trade, and limited government intervention in economic activity are all necessary conditions for growth and together these conditions substantially increase the probability of achieving fast growth. Burnside and Dollar, "Aid, Policies, and Growth," conclude that aid has a positive impact on growth only in countries with good fiscal, monetary, and trade policies.

[16]See Danny T. Quah, "Twin Peaks: Growth and Convergence in Models of Distribution Dynamics," *The Economic Journal*, Vol. 106 (July 1996), pp. 1045–55. Steven N. Durlauf and Danny T. Quah, "The New Empirics of Economic Growth," NBER Working Paper 6422 (Cambridge, Massachusetts: National Bureau of Economic Research, 1998) review recent studies using panel-data and distribution-dynamics econometric techniques that relax some of the assumptions about the homogeneity of countries and the growth process.

Table 4.1. Low- and Middle-Income Countries: Average Per Capita Income Growth, 1970–98

Low-Income Countries				Middle-Income Countries			
Negative Per Capita Growth (Growth rates below 0 percent)							
Angola	−1.9	Madagascar	−2.0	Algeria	−0.2	Namibia	−0.6
Burkina Faso	−0.5	Mali	−0.5	Djibouti	−4.3	South Africa	−0.1
Burundi	−0.3	Nicaragua	−2.4	Lebanon	−2.8	Trinidad and Tobago	−0.3
Central African Rep.	−0.3	Niger	−0.9	Libya	−1.3	Venezuela	−0.3
Comoros	−0.2	Rwanda	−1.3				
Congo, Dem. Rep. of	−4.3	São Tomé and Príncipe	−0.4				
Côte d'Ivoire	0.0	Senegal	−0.4				
Ethiopia	−0.1	Sierra Leone	−2.5				
Ghana	−0.6	Solomon Islands	−0.4				
Guinea-Bissau	−0.1	Somalia	−0.9				
Haiti	−0.7	Togo	−1.1				
Liberia	−2.0	Zambia	−2.2				
Slow Per Capita Growth (Growth rates of 0–2 percent)							
Bangladesh	1.1	Malawi	0.7	Argentina	0.7	Jamaica	0.1
Benin	0.1	Mauritania	1.3	Bahrain	0.5	Jordan	0.4
Cameroon	0.2	Mozambique	0.9	Bolivia	0.5	Mexico	1.6
Chad	0.1	Myanmar	1.9	Cape Verde	0.5	Morocco	1.9
Congo, Rep. of	1.2	Nepal	0.9	Colombia	2.0	Panama	1.5
Gambia, The	1.5	Nigeria	0.1	Costa Rica	1.5	Papua New Guinea	0.5
Guinea	1.2	Sudan	1.1	Ecuador	2.0	Peru	0.1
Honduras	0.5	Tanzania	0.1	El Salvador	0.7	Philippines	1.0
Kenya	1.0	Uganda	0.1	Fiji	1.5	Suriname	1.5
Lesotho	0.8	Zimbabwe	0.3	Guatemala	0.9	Swaziland	1.4
				Guyana	0.6	Uruguay	1.9
				Iran, I.R. of	0.3		
Slow Per Capita Convergence (Growth rates of 2–3¾ percent)							
Bhutan	3.3	Pakistan	2.2	Brazil	2.3	Sri Lanka	3.2
Cambodia	2.7	Vietnam	3.4	Chile	2.5	Syrian Arab Rep.	2.5
India	2.7	Yemen, Republic of	2.1	Dominican Republic	2.5	Tunisia	3.0
Lao P.D.R.	2.8			Egypt	2.6	Turkey	2.7
				Paraguay	2.1		
Fast Per Capita Convergence (Growth rates above 3¾ percent)							
China	6.9	Indonesia	3.9	Botswana	7.3	Mauritius	4.6
				Korea	6.0	Thailand	4.5
				Malaysia	4.3		

come level and growth performance. Countries are divided by income level according to the current World Bank classification of low-, middle-, and high-income countries. Developing countries in the low- and middle-income categories are then separated into eight groups (four for each income level) depending on their per capita growth rates over the period 1970–98

(Table 4.1).[17] These subgroups comprise countries where per capita income is declining or regressing in absolute terms, those with slow (less than 2 percent) per capita growth that are regressing relative to the industrial countries, those that are slowly converging with the industrial countries (up to 3¾ percent growth), and those that are rapidly converging.

[17]As mentioned above, countries heavily dependent on oil exports (Equatorial Guinea, Gabon, Oman, and Saudi Arabia), countries with populations less than 400,000, and countries in transition are excluded from the analysis, and Korea, which is an advanced country in the *World Economic Outlook* classification, is included as a developing country in this analysis because it is a middle-income country in the World Bank classification.

The classification is intended for analytic purposes only and will be used to identify average characteristics of low-income countries and contrast these with higher-income and faster-growing economies. Clearly, the makeup of the growth subgroups could change somewhat, for example, if average growth rates were calculated over a different time period. The relatively long 1970–98 period was chosen to reduce the potential impact of business cycle effects, with the risk that some countries that have experienced higher growth rates more recently would be incorrectly placed in one of the lower-growth groups.[18] It also needs to be recognized that in sorting countries by current income, the low-income group will naturally tend to have more countries with disappointing growth over the past than will the middle-income group. In other words, the two dimensions of the classification are not independent.

The Role of Investment, Saving, Human Capital, and Productivity

It is well established that the accumulation of physical and human capital and advances in production efficiencies and technology lead to higher per capita income. Studies have typically found that approximately 60–70 percent of per capita growth in developing countries reflects increases in physical capital and another 10–20 percent is due to increases in education and human capital with the remaining 10–30

percent attributed to improved (total factor) productivity.[19]

Not surprisingly, the low- and middle-income countries with declining or slowly rising per capita income had on average lower investment and saving rates than their faster-growing counterparts in recent years, confirming the importance of capital accumulation in the growth process (Figure 4.4). Causality is difficult to infer, however, because investment and saving rates were not substantially different, on average, across groups during the early 1970s except for perhaps the fastest-growing economies. Even in this latter group of countries, investment rates rose only after the growth takeoff.[20] In other words, it is far from obvious that high initial investment and saving rates are preconditions for growth. It may indeed be that higher investment and saving rates result because of higher growth or that other factors cause both growth and investment.

Low levels of schooling or investment in human capital may be impediments to growth and also delay takeoff. Secondary school enrollment rates in the 1970s were substantially lower on average in nonrapidly converging, low-income countries than in the middle-income countries (Table 4.2).[21] Moreover, the fastest-growing, low- and middle-income countries also experienced larger improvements in enrollments rates than the other developing countries did between 1975 and 1995. Although it is possible that growth induces more education as demand in-

---

[18]For example, if growth subgroups are calculated based on average annual growth rates during 1985–98, 35 countries (or approximately a third of the total) would change groups, but the number of countries in each group would remain largely the same and average characteristics (and hence conclusions) would not change substantially. It is worth noting, however, that the number of rapidly converging countries would increase by three compared to the classification based on 1970–98. The rapidly converging, low-income countries would include India, Mozambique, and Vietnam (but exclude Indonesia) in addition to China. The rapidly converging, middle-income countries would include Chile in addition to Botswana, Korea, Malaysia, Mauritius, and Thailand.

[19]See, for example, Barry P. Bosworth and Susan M. Collins, "Economic Growth in East Asia: Accumulation Versus Assimilation," *Brookings Papers on Economic Activity: 2*, Brookings Institution (1996), pp. 135–203.

[20]Christopher D. Carroll and David N. Weil, "Saving and Growth: A Reinterpretation," NBER Working Paper 4470 (Cambridge, Massachusetts: National Bureau of Economic Research, 1993) and Patricia Reynolds, "Does Growth Cause Saving and Investment?" (unpublished; Washington: International Monetary Fund, January 2000) examine the causal relationship between growth and investment or saving. The authors find that they cannot reject the possibility that causation runs from growth to investment or to saving or that some other (omitted) factor causes both growth and investment or saving—in other words, investment and saving rates are endogenous.

[21]Literacy rates and primary school enrollment rates show a similar pattern.

Figure 4.4. Developing Countries: Investment and Saving[1]
(Percent of GDP)

Investment and saving rates were higher on average in countries with faster per capita income growth, although causality is hard to infer.

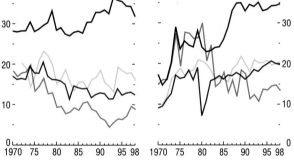

[1]Unweighted cross-country averages. For definitions of country groups, see Table 4.1.

creases with income, it is noteworthy that among the low-income countries enrollment levels in the 1970s were highest (and similar to the levels in the middle-income countries) in the countries that subsequently grew the fastest.

Basic education, including training, can contribute directly to a country's potential for growth by raising the skill level of the workforce. In addition, because physical and human capital are often complementary, education can also raise growth indirectly by inducing greater investment.[22] While increased schooling and training alone may not be sufficient to boost growth, particularly when economic opportunities to use the acquired skills are missing, improving education will be an important part of a sustainable growth and poverty reduction strategy for developing countries. It therefore makes sense for countries to shift resources toward basic education and for the donor community to emphasize education as a high priority.

Another obstacle to a productive workforce (and society) is inadequate health care. As with school enrollment rates, life expectancy rates at birth were substantially lower on average in nonrapidly-converging, low-income countries than in the middle-income countries in the 1970s (see Table 4.2), and other health indicators show a similar pattern. Even though these health indicators have improved over time in most developing countries, they remain relatively bad in many low-income countries—for example, average life expectancy is still below 55 years for the negative- and slow-growth, low-income countries—representing an enormous loss in potential human capital. In addition, progress in improving life expectancy rates has slowed in some countries mainly because of the devastating effects of the AIDS epidemic. The repercussions from the epidemic (as well as from other infectious diseases) will have long-term effects on the economic performance of

[22]See Per Krussell, Lee E. Ohanian, Jose-Victor Rios-Rull, and Giovanni L. Violante, "Capital-Skill Complementarity and Inequality," Federal Reserve Bank of Minneapolis Staff Report 239 (Minneapolis, Minnesota: Federal Reserve Bank of Minneapolis 1997).

Table 4.2. Developing and Advanced Economies: Education and Health Indicators[1]

Country Groups	Secondary School Enrollment Rate[2]			Life Expectancy at Birth[3]		
	1975	1995	Increase	1970	1997	Increase
Low-income countries						
Negative growth	11	19	8	43	50	7
Slow growth	11	21	10	44	53	8
Slow convergence	17	41	24	46	59	13
Fast convergence	34	67	34	55	67	13
Middle-income countries						
Negative growth	37	60	23	55	66	11
Slow growth	40	60	20	59	69	10
Slow convergence	35	61	26	59	70	11
Fast convergence	36	68	32	59	66	8
Memorandum						
Industrial countries	80	115	35	72	77	6
Other high-income, non-oil countries[4]	56	86	30	70	77	7
Middle- and high-income oil countries[5]	29	67	38	53	67	14

Source: World Bank, *World Development Indicators.*
[1]Unweighted cross-country averages. For definitions of country groups, see Table 4.1.
[2]Gross rates, in percent.
[3]Years.
[4]Cyprus, Hong Kong SAR, Israel, Singapore, and Taiwan Province of China
[5]Equatorial Guinea, Gabon, Kuwait, Oman, Qatar, Saudi Arabia, and United Arab Emirates.

some poor countries, particularly in sub-Saharan Africa.[23]

Inefficient investment has also been a hindrance for many countries, although, again, causality is difficult to infer. Not surprisingly, in the developing countries with declining per capita growth during the last three decades, the incremental output-capital ratio (the inverse of the incremental capital-output ratio), which is a very rough proxy for the productivity of investment, was lower on average than in the countries that were growing (Figure 4.5). Estimates of total factor productivity growth, which are available for only a subset of the countries under review, also confirm that resources were not used as efficiently in many of the negative-growth countries as in other developing countries.[24] Although a difficult task that needs to be addressed through a variety of reforms depending on country-specific circumstances, increasing productivity and allocative efficiency will allow

these countries to better use their limited resources. To the extent that this and other resource reallocations can be accomplished relatively quickly, countries could begin to grow without immediate increases in saving and investment.

The challenge then is to fashion the appropriate mix of policies and conditions for poor countries that removes impediments to the accumulation and efficient allocation of saving and investment (including in human capital) and allows growth to take off. Once growth has accelerated, there are many indications that a virtuous and mutually reinforcing cycle is possible as growth may further increase saving, investment, and productivity. The next sections will review some of the main obstacles to increasing saving, investment, and efficiency. These are generally considered to include macroeconomic instability, unsupportive institutions, inward-oriented and protectionist policies, poverty, income in-

---

[23]It is estimated that 33½ million people worldwide were infected with AIDS or the HIV virus by the end of 1999. About 32 million of these people were in developing countries—over 23 million in sub-Saharan Africa alone. This represents about 1 percent of the developing country workforce (adults aged 15 to 49 years), but 8 percent in sub-Saharan Africa. See UNAIDS and World Health Organization, "AIDS Epidemic Update" (Geneva: 1999).
[24]See Bosworth and Collins, "Economic Growth in East Asia."

Figure 4.5. Developing Countries: Per Capita GDP Growth and Incremental Output-Capital Ratio[1]

Productivity, as proxied by the incremental output-capital ratio, was substantially lower on average in developing countries with negative growth than in other countries during the past three decades.

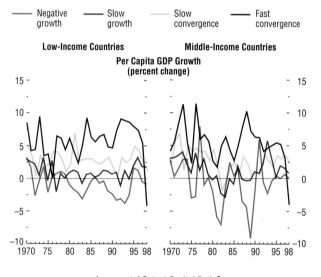

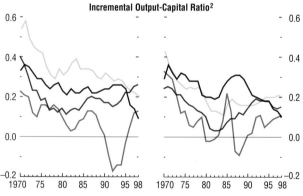

[1]Unweighted cross-country averages. For definitions of country groups, see Table 4.1.
[2]Inverse of five-year moving average of incremental capital-output ratio.

equality, and (particularly in recent years) unsustainable external debt.

Macroeconomic Instability

Uncertainty caused by macroeconomic instability—such as high inflation, volatile and overvalued exchange rates, or excessive fiscal deficits—can significantly distort economic decisions and thereby reduce capital accumulation, hamper the efficient allocation of resources, and slow growth. Empirical studies have found, for example, that high inflation rates, which are often also accompanied by more variable inflation and relative price changes, have a negative impact on growth.[25] Because the effect appears to be nonlinear, though, there is some disagreement over the precise threshold above which higher inflation becomes a detriment. Nevertheless, recent evidence indicates that inflation rates above the single digits have adverse implications for growth.

Inappropriate exchange rate regimes, generally in conjunction with high and variable inflation rates, often lead to overvalued exchange rates. These can impede the proper allocation of resources between the production of tradable and nontradable goods and may also deter inward foreign capital while encouraging capital flight. Persistently large fiscal deficits also inhibit growth through several mechanisms. As discussed in previous issues of the *World Economic Outlook*, fiscal deficits tend to crowd out private investment (or lead to higher inflation if the deficits are monetized) and inhibit financial market development.[26] In addition, they may be indicative of excessive government intervention in the economy, although this is difficult to

[25]See, for example, Michael Sarel, "Nonlinear Effects of Inflation on Economic Growth," IMF Working Paper 95/56 (Washington: International Monetary Fund, 1995), and Atish Ghosh and Steven Phillips, "Warning: Inflation May Be Harmful to Your Growth," *IMF Staff Papers*, Vol. 45 (December 1998), pp. 672–710.

[26]See, for example, Chapter IV, "Fiscal Policy Issues in Developing Countries," in the May 1996 *World Economic Outlook*.

Table 4.3. Developing and Advanced Economies: Macroeconomic Stability[1]

(Percent during 1970–98, unless otherwise noted)

Country Groups	Inflation Average	Inflation Standard Deviation	Fiscal Deficit[2]	Current Account Deficit[2]	Black Market Premium[3]
Low-income countries					
Negative growth	26.4	26.3	6.2	6.5	386.4
Slow growth	16.1	12.4	4.2	8.6	214.9
Slow convergence	20.5	19.0	6.9	3.1	112.2
Fast convergence	9.4	7.7	0.7	0.7	23.6
Middle-income countries					
Negative growth	15.1	10.6	4.6	3.1	49.1
Slow growth	25.4	21.6	4.9	4.5	59.3
Slow convergence	32.3	23.6	4.7	3.5	45.0
Fast convergence	8.4	5.3	2.3	1.7	7.2
Memorandum					
Industrial countries	6.5	3.9	3.2	1.0	0.8
Other high-income, non-oil countries[4]	13.0	11.7	1.8	0.4	4.1
Middle- and high-income oil countries[5]	7.1	7.9	1.7	−2.3	0.5

[1]Unweighted cross-country averages. For definitions of country groups, see Table 4.1.
[2]Percent of GDP.
[3]From World Bank, *World Development Indicators.* Percent difference between the official and market exchange rate.
[4]Cyprus, Hong Kong SAR, Israel, Singapore, and Taiwan Province of China.
[5]Equatorial Guinea, Gabon, Kuwait, Oman, Qatar, Saudi Arabia, and United Arab Emirates.

quantify when analyzing large groups of countries. Expectations about the financing needs associated with large fiscal deficits also create uncertainty about future taxes and future inflation and deter planning for investment.

Empirical studies have shown that fiscal deficits and overvalued exchange rates often have a negative impact on growth. Among low- and middle-income countries, other than the rapidly converging countries, there is little or no apparent relationship between growth or income and average inflation, its variance, average fiscal deficits, or average current account deficits (Table 4.3). Nevertheless, the fastest-growing, low- and middle-income countries on average generally had much lower and less variable inflation and lower fiscal and current account deficits than other developing countries (although this may partly be an outcome of stronger growth). This finding highlights that beyond a certain threshold high inflation and fiscal and current account deficits may be obstacles to growth. Moreover, large fiscal deficits and high and variable inflation can lead to mis-

aligned exchange rates. It should be noted that the black market premium, the difference between the official and market exchange rates and an indicator of the extent of exchange rate overvaluation, was higher on average for developing countries that grew more slowly—particularly among the low-income countries. The strong correlation between this premium and growth underscores the problems caused by inappropriate exchange rate regimes, including excessively high costs for investment goods and consequently lower investment.

Institutions and the Role of Government

Economic uncertainty increases when wars, military coups, political instability, and corruption are widespread or when basic institutional structures such as property rights, the rule of law, and those underpinning sound financial institutions are inadequate.[27] In most countries plagued by these problems, firms and people face constraints on saving, investing, efficiently allocating resources, and profiting from legal

[27]The negative economic consequences of war are well recognized. Thucydides, a historian in ancient Greece, commented on this link in regard to the Peloponnesian war.

Table 4.4. Developing and Advanced Economies: Political Stability and Institutions[1]
(Average 1984–98)

Country Groups	Political and Social Stability[2]	Government Stability[3]	Law and Order[4]	Contract Security[5]
Low-income countries				
Negative growth	5.0	4.2	3.9	4.1
Slow growth	5.3	4.9	4.6	5.0
Slow convergence	6.0	5.0	4.6	5.7
Fast convergence	7.0	5.9	5.6	6.8
Middle-income countries				
Negative growth	5.7	5.5	5.4	6.0
Slow growth	5.8	5.0	4.5	6.0
Slow convergence	5.5	5.4	5.3	6.3
Fast convergence	7.8	6.0	7.0	7.8
Memorandum				
Industrial countries	8.9	6.6	9.4	9.2
Other high-income, non-oil countries[6]	8.0	6.5	7.6	8.6
Middle- and high-income oil countries[7]	7.0	5.8	6.1	6.4

Source: *International Country Risk Guide* (published by the Political Risk Services Group).
[1]Unweighted cross-country averages. Data are normalized from 0 to 10: higher is better quality. For definitions of country groups, see Table 4.1.
[2]Political stability, as measured by the lack of political violence and its actual or potential impact on governance ("Internal Conflict" in the source).
[3]Government's ability to carry out declared programs, and to stay in office ("Government Stability" in the source).
[4]Strength and impartiality of the legal system and general observance of the law ("Law and Order" in the source).
[5]Absence of risk of contract repudiation ("Contract Viability" in the source. Data through 1997).
[6]Cyprus, Hong Kong SAR, Israel, Singapore, and Taiwan Province of China.
[7]Equatorial Guinea, Gabon, Kuwait, Oman, Qatar, Saudi Arabia, and United Arab Emirates.

economic activities. While there are exceptions to every rule, these economies will regress.[28]

It is hardly surprising that armed conflicts and civil wars—as well as the turmoil associated with political instability—sharply increase uncertainty and diminish the expected profitability of investments. Political instability also discourages long-term investment projects because of the risk of policy reversals. Studies have found that political, social, and government instability raised investment risk in the poor-growth countries of Africa and therefore was a major disincentive for foreign investors.[29] For the broader group of developing countries, these factors are also negatively correlated with growth performance, particularly for the low-income countries (Table 4.4).[30]

Corruption also hinders growth by distorting incentives, as government officials and favored private individuals receive a larger share of public benefits or bear a lower share of the cost of public goods. Empirical studies have found that corruption lowers private investment, distorts the composition of public expenditures toward areas where collecting bribes are easier (for example, toward excessive and inefficient physical public investments and away from education), and tends to reduce government revenue because it contributes to tax evasion, improper tax exemptions, or weak tax administration, thereby limiting the ability of the government to provide critical services.[31] There is evidence as well that corruption increases income inequality and

[28]Empirical studies generally confirm that economic growth is hampered under these conditions. See, for example, Robert J. Barro, "Determinants of Economic Growth: A Cross-Country Empirical Study," NBER Working Paper 5698 (Cambridge, Massachusetts: National Bureau of Economic Research, 1996).
[29]See Paul Collier and Catherine Pattillo, *Investment and Risk in Africa* (London: MacMillan Press, 1999), Chapter 1.
[30]Similar results are found for indices of civil war.
[31]See Paulo Mauro, "Corruption and Growth," *Quarterly Journal of Economics*, Vol. 110, (August 1995), pp. 681–712; Paulo Mauro, "The Effects of Corruption on Growth, Investment, and Government Expenditure: A Cross-Country Analysis," in *Corruption and the Global Economy*, ed. by Kimberly Ann Elliott (Washington: Institute for International Economics, 1997); and Vito Tanzi and Hamid Davoodi, "Corruption, Public Investment, and Growth," IMF Working Paper 97/139 (Washington: International Monetary Fund, 1997).

poverty by reducing the progressivity of the tax system, the level and effectiveness of social spending, and the formation of human capital, and by perpetuating an unequal distribution of asset ownership and unequal access to education.[32]

The lack of a strong and impartial judicial system, including the inadequate observance of laws and the inability to enforce laws, also significantly increases economic and social uncertainty. In particular, inadequate property rights, such as the risk of contract repudiation or of expropriation without adequate compensation, substantially increase the risks to entrepreneurship. Indicators of these risks appear largely related to growth both for low- and middle-income countries (see the last two columns in Table 4.4).

Beyond maintaining peace and providing adequate institutional structures such as a sound judicial system, the government needs to provide social or public goods, including some basic services, education, health care, and when resources are available, social safety nets. Better education, family planning, and health care—especially for women—can not only improve living conditions, but can also enhance the productivity of the labor force and reduce population growth. This, in turn, may promote per capita income growth particularly when government and household resources are being strained by a rapidly growing population. The government may also need to make direct public investments to provide infrastructure, when this is lacking or inadequate. In general, though, the government's role in the economy needs to be limited, particularly in areas of the economy where the private sector can efficiently provide goods and services and where markets are not distorted. Excessive intervention tends to foster corruption, can strain government budgets, and is prone to distort price signals and the efficient allocation of resources.[33]

Table 4.5. Developing and Advanced Economies: Financial Maturity and Deepening[1]
(Percent of GDP)

	Broad Money		
	1970	1998	Increase
Low-income countries			
Negative growth	20.5	22.4	1.9
Slow growth	29.5	23.5	−6.0
Slow convergence	22.9	35.9	12.9
Fast convergence	17.9	94.6	76.7
Middle-income countries			
Negative growth	31.8	60.8	29.1
Slow growth	29.9	48.6	18.7
Slow convergence	23.9	46.8	22.9
Fast convergence	30.4	75.8	45.4
Memorandum			
Industrial countries	58.2	74.6	16.4
Other high-income, non-oil countries[2]	51.0	125.2	74.2
Middle- and high-income oil countries[3]	11.9	49.1	37.3

[1]Unweighted cross-country averages. For definitions of country groups, see Table 4.1.
[2]Cyprus, Hong Kong SAR, Israel, Singapore, and Taiwan Province of China.
[3]Equatorial Guinea, Gabon, Kuwait, Oman, Qatar, Saudi Arabia, and United Arab Emirates.

Liberalization, along with proper supervision and regulation, is probably most important in the financial sector. The financial sector plays a primary role in intermediating saving and efficiently allocating investment. The financial system also plays a crucial role in smoothing the effect of shocks both on consumption and on investment. On average, low-income countries had a low level of financial sophistication, as proxied by the ratio of broad money to GDP, and slower-growing countries had lower rates of financial deepening, as proxied by the change in ratio of broad money to GDP, although for the latter causality is difficult to infer (Table 4.5). Cross-country empirical studies also confirm that slow growth is related to financial sector immaturity.[34] Governments, therefore, need to foster a competitive and effi-

---

[32]Sanjeev Gupta, Hamid Davoodi, and Rosa Alonso-Terme, "Does Corruption Affect Income Inequality and Poverty?" IMF Working Paper 98/76 (Washington: International Monetary Fund, 1998).
[33]See Tanzi and Davoodi, "Corruption, Public Investment, and Growth."
[34]See Ross Levine, "Financial Development and Economic Growth: Views and Agenda," *Journal of Economic Literature*, Vol. 35 (June 1997), pp. 688–726.

Table 4.6. Developing and Advanced Economies: Globalization and Trade Openness[1]
(Percent of Purchasing Power Parity Adjusted GDP)

Country Groups	Exports			Openness (Imports and Exports)		
	1970–74	1994–98	Increase	1970–74	1994–98	Increase
Low-income countries						
Negative growth	10.6	7.4	–3.2	22.9	18.0	–5.0
Slow growth	10.5	8.4	–2.1	23.9	20.6	–3.4
Slow convergence	4.8	8.1	3.3	16.4	19.5	3.0
Fast convergence	4.3	6.8	2.5	8.2	13.4	5.2
Middle-income countries						
Negative growth	16.4	15.2	–1.2	31.4	33.2	1.8
Slow growth	17.8	18.1	0.3	36.4	38.5	2.1
Slow convergence	8.4	10.9	2.5	18.4	23.4	5.1
Fast convergence	18.2	28.1	9.9	38.5	55.5	16.9
Memorandum						
Industrial countries	20.5	36.9	16.4	44.2	74.5	30.3
Other high-income, non-oil countries[2]	50.7	81.0	30.3	106.5	160.7	54.2
Middle- and high-income oil countries[3]	32.4	40.5	8.1	48.2	76.9	28.7

[1]Unweighted cross-country averages. For definitions of country groups, see Table 4.1. To account for the relative differences in prices, GDP is measured in U.S. dollars based on purchasing power parity adjusted exchange rates. Differences across groups when GDP is measured with the bilateral exchange rate are similar, although not as strong.

[2]Cyprus, Hong Kong SAR, Israel, Singapore, and Taiwan Province of China.

[3]Equatorial Guinea, Gabon, Kuwait, Oman, Qatar, Saudi Arabia, and United Arab Emirates.

cient financial sector, including a thorough supervisory and regulatory system.[35]

Inward-Oriented Policies

Developing countries with inward-oriented, protectionist economic policies (such as in much of Africa and Latin America during the 1970s and 1980s) have suffered from poor growth rates, while those with outward-oriented policies (such as in east Asia) have prospered. A closed economy hinders growth through a variety of channels. First and foremost, countries that have not adopted an orientation toward open trade cannot exploit their comparative advantages in production. This may hurt the poor because import-competing industries tend to be capital intensive and thus, without outward orientation, production moves away from labor-intensive industries, which provide employment for the poor. When economies of scale are present, inward-oriented countries also cannot benefit from larger markets and the opportunities for greater specialization provided by trade. In addition, domestic prices are less likely to reflect world prices when a country maintains trade barriers, thereby leading to a worse allocation of resources. The lack of exposure to competition from foreign sources can shield production in the short run but at the cost of reducing incentives and opportunities for domestic producers to innovate and improve productivity.

Many empirical studies have found a robust and positive impact of increasing trade on growth and income (even while attempting to control for reverse causation).[36] For the groups of countries under review, the poorer and slower-growing countries were on average less

[35]See Manuel Guitián, "Banking Soundness: The Other Dimension of Monetary Policy," in *Banking Soundness and Monetary Policy*, ed. by Charles Enoch and John H. Green (Washington: International Monetary Fund, 1997), pp. 41–62.

[36]See, for example, Levine and Renelt, "A Sensitivity Analysis of Cross-Country Growth Regressions," and Ann Harrison, "Openness and Growth: A Time-series, Cross-Country Analysis of Developing Countries," *Journal of Development Economics*, Vol. 48 (March 1996), pp. 419–47. Using instrumental variables (to control for endogeneity), Jeffrey A. Frankel and David Romer, "Does Trade Cause Growth?" *The American Economic Review*, Vol. 89 (June 1999), pp. 379–99, find that trade has a quantitatively large and robust positive effect on income.

Table 4.7. Developing and Advanced Economies: Globalization and Trade Volumes and Prices[1]
(Annual Percent Change 1970–98, unless noted otherwise)

Country Groups	Volumes			Prices	
	Partner country output growth	Real export growth	Gain in market share[2]	Goods terms of trade	Real nonfuel commodities
Low-income countries					
Negative growth	3.3	2.2	−2.8	−1.0	−1.7
Slow growth	3.4	4.3	−0.8	−1.0	−1.6
Slow convergence	4.4	6.2	−0.4	0.4	−2.2
Fast convergence	4.5	11.1	4.2	1.9	−1.7
Middle-income countries					
Negative growth	3.2	0.7	−4.1	0.9	−1.6
Slow growth	3.5	3.0	−2.2	0.1	−1.9
Slow convergence	3.2	6.9	2.2	−0.2	−2.0
Fast convergence	4.1	10.3	4.1	0.4	−1.7
Memorandum					
Industrial countries	3.2	5.6	0.9	−0.6	−1.4
Other high-income, non-oil countries[3]	4.2	9.4	3.1	−0.8	−5.0
Middle- and high-income oil countries[4]	4.5	3.1	−3.7	2.8	−0.6

[1]Unweighted cross-country averages. For definitions of country groups, see Table 4.1.
[2]Difference between real export growth and partner-country import growth, which is proxied assuming an income elasticity for imports of 1.5, consistent with world income and trading volume growth during 1970–98.
[3]Cyprus, Hong Kong SAR, Israel, Singapore, and Taiwan Province of China.
[4]Equatorial Guinea, Gabon, Kuwait, Oman, Qatar, Saudi Arabia, and United Arab Emirates.

open compared to the faster-growing, middle-income countries, and generally faster growth accompanied increasing openness (Table 4.6).[37] In addition, faster-growing, low- and middle-income countries benefited from rapid growth in their trading partners (Table 4.7). This can be explained by groups of countries or regions, such as east Asia, growing together and expanding intraregional trade. An alternative explanation is that faster-growing countries were better able to take advantage of the opportunities provided by increasing trade and globalization and to gain market share because of policies and conditions that were more supportive of export expansion. The evidence supports the latter explanation (see Table 4.7).

Many developing countries are already advanced in their efforts to open their economies to trade.[38] Unilateral liberalization began in the 1980s and early 1990s as many countries shifted away from inward-looking policies. Most progress in recent years was made in Latin America (in conjunction with structural reforms following the debt crisis) and eastern and central Europe, followed by southeast Asia, which was already relatively open to trade. Trade reforms began somewhat late in Africa, and many of these were in conjunction with IMF-supported structural adjustment programs.

Few industrial countries have allowed developing countries substantially unimpaired or unlimited access to their markets on a unilateral basis. Since the Uruguay Round, progress in expanding market access has been largely confined to regional and bilateral trade arrangements, such as those negotiated between the European Union and various developing country groups, including its neighbors and former colonies. These relatively recent agreements, though welcome, have tended to benefit selected developing countries and not necessarily the poorest ones. The present system of trade preferences excludes

[37]It is difficult to find an adequate measure for the openness to trade—which should ideally measure how open markets are to foreign competition. Proxies for openness that have been used include tariffs, nontariff barriers, effective rates of protection, trade liberalization, relative prices, import penetration, export intensity, and deviations of actual from predicted trade flows or volumes. See Harrison, "Openness and Growth."
[38]See Chapter V, "Trends and Issues in the Global Trading System," in the October 1999 *World Economic Outlook.*

a number of "sensitive products" in precisely those sectors—primarily agriculture, textiles, and footwear—where many poor countries have the greatest potential to expand and diversify their exports. Moreover, the complexity, impermanence, and lack of transparency in these arrangements have discouraged the desired response in investment and trade. A bolder and more coherent approach to liberalization by the industrial countries would be needed to spur development and promote their integration into the world trading system. Such an approach would ideally combine the provision of duty-free and quota-free market access for products originating in developing countries with a reduction in agricultural subsidies in the advanced economies.

Although trade can create opportunities, it can also create difficulties for developing countries as they are exposed to externally generated shocks. Terms-of-trade shocks may have been a particularly important hindrance in the low-income countries with negative or low growth where terms of trade have fallen by 1 percent annually on average since 1970 (see Table 4.7). Most other developing countries, however, saw flat or even rising terms of trade. A key reason why some low-income countries had falling terms of trade is that primary products are a larger share of their exports and nonfuel commodity prices fell in real terms.[39] The impact of future commodity price declines on these economies is likely to diminish automatically as they grow and become less dependent on primary products for export revenue. This process, however, can be expected to be slow.

Openness to capital flows holds risks for developing countries, but at the same time it allows countries to meet their financing needs when investment requirements exceed domestic saving. Moreover, private capital flows, particularly in the form of foreign direct investment, also pro-

vide access to new technologies and production processes through imported capital goods and management (or human capital).

During the last three decades, many developing countries (particularly the fast-growing, middle-income countries) have benefited from significant private capital flows and foreign direct investment. Exposure to capital flows, however, also makes countries vulnerable to externall generated financial shocks and increases the need for strong domestic and external macroeconomic and financial fundamentals (including adequate foreign reserves).[40] For many low- and some middle-income countries, therefore, full liberalization of their capital account may need to wait until these countries are better able to manage external risks. This includes the ability to pursue monetary and exchange rate policies that are consistent with a liberalized environment. When liberalization does occur, measures need to be carefully sequenced.

It is important to dispel the notion that it is no longer possible for poor countries to benefit from globalization. Some have argued that globalization now offers few opportunities, stemming from the belief that an outward-oriented strategy based on exporting labor-intensive goods (and taking advantage of relatively lower labor costs) has become much more difficult because large countries such as China already dominate export markets in these goods. Essentially, the argument is that it is too late for those who have not yet started. However, the same argument was made in east Asia when first Japan and then Hong Kong SAR, Korea, Singapore, and Taiwan Province of China exported labor-intensive goods. This did not prevent China, Indonesia, Malaysia, and Thailand from following suit later when the other east Asian countries shifted to less labor-intensive exports as relative wages rose. Moreover, as incomes increased in the region,

---

[39]Jeffrey Sachs and Andrew Warner, "Natural Resource Abundance and Economic Growth," NBER Working Paper 5398 (Cambridge, Massachusetts: National Bureau of Economic Research, 1995) find a negative relationship between growth and a high ratio of natural resource exports to GDP.

[40]For a more extensive discussion see Chapter IV, "Financial Crises: Characteristics and Indicators of Vulnerability," in the May 1998 *World Economic Outlook*, and Chapter III, "International Financial Contagion," in the May 1999 *World Economic Outlook*.

Table 4.8. Developing Countries: Poverty and Poverty Reduction[1]
(Percent of population)

Country Groups	Below $1 per Day			Below $2 per Day		
	1987	1998[2]	Reduction	1987	1998[2]	Reduction
Low-income countries						
Negative growth	40.7	41.6	−0.9	77.7	77.3	0.4
Slow growth	44.4	43.6	0.8	88.6	86.9	1.7
Slow convergence	47.7	42.3	5.4	85.2	70.9	14.3
Fast convergence	28.2	16.4	11.8	69.2	50.9	18.3
Middle-income countries						
Negative growth	7.0	8.6	−1.6	32.1	34.4	−2.3
Slow growth	12.9	13.8	−0.9	36.8	36.3	0.5
Slow convergence	12.0	9.0	3.0	34.4	22.3	12.1
Fast convergence	10.7	2.7	8.0	37.0	20.3	16.7

Source: Martin Ravallion and Shaohua Chen, "Global Poverty Measures."
[1]Based on survey data. It is important to note that income growth measures that underly the survey poverty data differ from national accounts income growth measures, which are used to determine the country groups.
[2]Estimated.

intraregional trade expanded rapidly, creating new markets for exports.

Poverty and Income Inequality

Monetary measures of poverty reduction, not very surprisingly, appear to be correlated with income growth (Table 4.8). One recent study confirms this relationship and finds that a 10 percent rise in per capita income is correlated with a 10 percent increase in income among the poorest quintile.[41] Other studies correlate changes in aggregate income and poverty rates directly and generally suggest that a 1 percent increase in average per capita income or consumption is associated with a reduction in poverty rates by up to 3½ percent and also find that poverty rates fall, almost always, with growth in average living standards and rise with contraction.[42]

Although poverty reduction and economic growth are correlated, the causal relationship between poverty or income inequality and growth is unclear. In a subsistence economy, it is unlikely that saving and investment (including in human capital) will be sufficient to promote growth since income is required to provide basic necessities. High poverty rates can, therefore, be impediments to growth. The observation that income is more equitably distributed in the high-growth, countries of east Asia compared to some lower- growth Western Hemisphere countries also has led to speculation that income inequality hampers growth. However, both the theoretical relationship between growth and income inequality and the empirical evidence are ambiguous.[43] If individual saving rates rise with the level of income, a less-even income distribution may actually result in a higher aggregate saving rate. However, significant income inequality also implies that low-income groups may be unable to acquire the skills necessary to benefit from economic opportunities, resulting in a potential loss of human capital.

Irrespective of the direct economic links between income inequality and growth, there are

[41]Michael Roemer and Mary Kay Gugerty, "Does Economic Growth Reduce Poverty?" HIID Technical Paper (Cambridge, Massachusetts: Harvard Institute for International Development, March 1997).
[42]Martin Ravallion and Shaohua Chen, "What Can New Survey Data Tell Us about Recent Changes in Income Distribution and Poverty," *The World Bank Economic Review*, Vol. 11 (1997), pp. 357–82.
[43]Some studies have found a statistically significant negative relationship between income inequality and growth while others have found a positive one. Overall, the relationship is not robust for a broad panel of countries. See, for example, Robert J. Barro, "Inequality, Growth, and Investment," NBER Working Paper 7038 (Cambridge, Massachusetts: National Bureau of Economic Research, 1999). In part, the lack of a robust result may reflect limited data availability and cross-country differences in the measurement of income inequality.

many other reasons to believe that the persistence of large income divergences and high poverty rates, even among many middle-income countries, can be a powerful obstacle to stronger economic growth. In addition to the waste of human potential, widespread poverty and large differences in income and wealth can be a source of social unrest and political instability. This in turn can prevent the establishment and maintenance of adequate institutional structures and policies, and eventually lead to an unstable economic environment that will adversely affect private saving and investment decisions and deter foreign investors.

In some cases, policies that promote growth may not promote immediate poverty reduction. Some studies have found evidence that policies such as fiscal stabilization and trade liberalization, which are both essential for sustained growth, may raise poverty rates in the short term.[44] This may call for complementary reforms to strengthen social safety nets. In contrast, reducing high inflation rates is almost always beneficial for the poor. In any case, the short-run negative impact, if any, of necessary adjustment measures is typically modest compared with the long-run gains to the poor from the additional growth that results from these policies.

The Role of Debt

As discussed above, access to external finance is vital for many developing countries because domestic saving is usually insufficient to meet investment needs. In low-income countries, domestic saving is limited by factors such as poverty and underdeveloped financial markets. These countries typically do not have access to private finance and must rely on official lending (and aid). Many middle-income countries, by contrast, have access to private markets so that foreign capital flows, in the form of both debt and equity, can fill the financing gap and provide the resources to spur growth. Equity is an important component of financing from the perspective of recipient countries, not only because risk is shared by foreign stakeholders, but also because it often comes in the form of foreign direct investment that tends to bring in new technology and physical and human capital, including management expertise. However, because international capital markets may be imperfect and the acquisition of timely information on investment projects by perspective investors costly, countries often rely more heavily on borrowing than equity finance. There is no evidence that moderate external indebtedness hurts growth, but when indebtedness rises to the point that debt service becomes onerous, growth prospects are substantially damaged.

External debt can become an impediment to growth for a developing country when funds are not used for productive investments that allow the country to service its debt on time. One sign of an excessive debt burden is the regular need for comprehensive rescheduling or the protracted buildup of external arrears, as has been observed in many low-income countries. Excessive levels of external debt are likely to reduce incentives for a government to undertake appropriate reforms and businesses to invest because of the real possibility that a significant share of the returns from these activities will need to be transferred to foreign creditors to repay the outstanding debt.[45] Moreover, high debt levels create moral hazard: a government may delay reforms needed to reduce the debt burden because it expects debt relief in the future.

* * *

[44]For example, see Michael Bruno, Martin Ravallion, and Lyn Squire, "Equity and Growth in Developing Countries: Old and New Perspectives on the Policy Issues," in *Income Distribution and High-Quality Growth*, ed. by Vito Tanzi and Ke-young Chu (Cambridge, Massachusetts: MIT Press, 1998).

[45]See Michael P. Dooley, "A Note on Debt Reduction and Economic Efficiency," IMF Working Paper 90/36 (Washington: International Monetary Fund, 1990). See also Ibrahim A. Elbadawi, Benno J. Ndulu, and Njuguna Ndung'u, "Debt Overhang and Economic Growth in sub-Saharan Africa," ed. by Zubair Iqbal and Ravi Kanbur, *External Finance for Low-Income Countries*, (Washington: IMF Institute, 1997).

Clearly, there are many possible explanations for the failure of the poorest countries to catch up. Many of these reasons are interrelated and contribute to a vicious circle. While it may be difficult to identify unambiguously the most critical factors, there are many shortcomings that appear to be contributing to, or at least be associated with, persistently inadequate growth. This calls for a broad-based, sustained effort if greater progress is to be achieved. This effort, first and foremost, will need to be undertaken by the poorest countries themselves: without the strongest commitment on the part of their leaders and elected bodies, supported by society at large, success will be elusive. But the poorest countries cannot succeed without support from the international community. The advanced economies, in particular, will need to increase levels of foreign aid and assistance to countries that have strengthened their own efforts to alleviate poverty. The international community also needs to liberalize fully trade in products in which the poorest countries have a comparative advantage, and the debt burden also needs to be addressed.

Debt Burden and Debt Relief

Over the past 30 years, the total external debt of developing countries has risen sharply from $90 billion in 1970 (or 15 percent of GDP) to almost $2,000 billion in 1998 (37 percent of GDP; Appendix Table 38). Debt burdens vary across countries, and although the debt profile for some countries has improved substantially since the debt crisis in the 1980s, for many low-income countries the picture is bleak. At the turn of the millennium, up to about 40 of the poorest developing countries, the Heavily Indebted Poor Countries (HIPCs), still have unsustainable debt burdens even after large-scale and persistent financial assistance provided by official donors.

Almost all of them (38 countries) are low-income countries, and about half of them (21 countries) experienced negative per capita income growth over the past 30 years.

Worldwide events in the 1970s and at the beginning of the 1980s were major contributors to the debt buildup in both the HIPCs and some middle-income countries.[46] Oil price shocks and the rise in industrial country interest rates generated balance of payment pressures for many developing countries. These factors were exacerbated by stagnant or contracting export revenues, caused mainly by the subsequent world recession and declining commodity prices, and by the appreciation of the U.S. dollar, which inflated the domestic value of dollar-denominated debt and service payments and depressed dollar commodity prices.

Domestic factors also played a large role in the debt buildup. (Compare the performance of both the high-debt countries and "successful adjusters" to the low-debt countries in Figure 4.6. See figure footnotes 1–3 for group definitions.) Countries with low saving and large current account deficits were unable to withstand the impact of these external shocks and continued to borrow heavily as their reliance on external financing grew. Because low export and fiscal revenue shares of GDP made it difficult for both the private and the public sectors to set aside the resources required to service old and new debt, external debt quickly rose to unsustainable levels. The drag on domestic resources, coupled with already low private and public investment, further constrained the potential for growth and exports, in some cases inducing a vicious cycle of unsustainable indebtedness and low growth.

International private investors, increasingly alarmed by the financial conditions of debtor countries, became more resistant to granting new lending or debt rollovers, further exacerbating the difficulties of these countries. In order to

---

[46]For a more detailed discussion, see, for example, Chapter VI in the April 1986 *World Economic Outlook*, and Chapter IV in the April 1989 *World Economic Outlook*. For specific examples, see Ray Brooks and others, "External Debt Histories of Ten Low-Income Developing Countries: Lessons from their Experiences," IMF Working Paper 98/72 (Washington: International Monetary Fund, 1998).

alleviate such difficulties, official creditors initially provided nonconcessional rescheduling of debt-service payments through the Paris Club, under the presumption that the debt crisis was temporary and liquidity related. This nonconcessional rescheduling, although granting temporary cash-flow relief, contributed to increasing the outstanding stock of debt.[47]

In the 1980s, it became apparent that the debt crisis involved more than temporary liquidity problems and actions beyond cash-flow rescheduling would be needed. The international financial community therefore launched what would become a series of assistance initiatives aimed at reducing the value of future obligations and repayments. In association with adjustment programs supported by multilateral institutions, middle-income countries with excessive debt arranged market-related debt reduction deals with their creditors under the Brady Plan, while poor countries received concessional rescheduling from official creditors and new lending on increasingly concessional terms. The assistance schemes were often complemented by, if not conditional on, macroeconomic and structural reforms undertaken by the recipient countries.

These concerted efforts, by both the international community and recipient countries, proved to be effective in helping many developing countries adjust their resource balances, reduce outstanding debt ratios to sustainable levels, and resume steady output growth. The "successful adjusters" in Figure 4.6 were mostly in the middle-income group and had access to international financial markets. As a group, they drastically reduced the public sector deficit, which helped to increase aggregate savings and reduce the trade deficit. At the same time, countries initiated macroeconomic stabilization, privatization, and market liberalization programs, which all contributed to the resumption of

Figure 4.6. Developing Countries: Economic Indicators
(Percent of GDP unless otherwise noted)

High-debt countries rank below low-debt countries in all macroeconomic and structural indicators. The successfully adjusting countries reduced fiscal deficits and increased saving and exports.

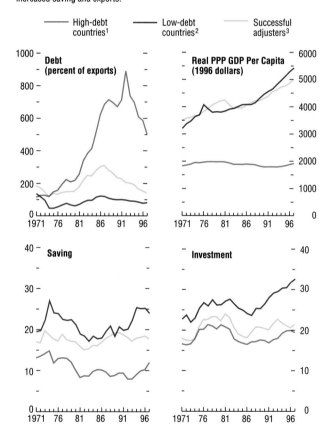

[47]See Christina Daseking and Robert Powell, "From Toronto Terms to the HIPC Initiative: A Brief History of Debt Relief for the Low-Income Countries," IMF Working Paper 99/142 (Washington: International Monetary Fund, 1999). See also the IMF's HIPC website at *www.imf.org/external/np/HIPC.*

steady growth, although in many cases the adjustment process lasted longer than anticipated. As a result, and with the global recovery, exports began to rise and debt ratios started decreasing.

However, for many low-income countries that did not have access to external private financing, it became evident by the mid-1990s that traditional debt-relief mechanisms, official assistance, and adjustment policies and their implementation were insufficient to reduce excessive indebtedness. Their economic performance has lagged and debt ratios have remained high, despite a series of Paris Club Initiatives (concessional reschedulings known as Toronto, London, and Naples terms), and additional action by a number of non-Paris Club bilateral and commercial creditors, aimed both at providing immediate cash-flow relief on the payments falling due and slowing the growth of the debt stock itself. The costs of these early debt-relief initiatives for low-income countries have been estimated to be at least $30 billion, and possibly much more.[48]

Many of these poor countries had limited success in improving their debt-burden indicators and rekindling output growth because they were unable to provide a stable macroeconomic environment, as demonstrated by persistently high fiscal deficits and increasing inflation. (See the group of high-debt countries in Figure 4.6.) Accordingly, aggregate saving fell further, and profitable investment opportunities were not exploited. High debt-service payments continued to exacerbate already wide current account deficits or forced countries to run arrears. By the mid-1990s outstanding debt of these countries remained high at around 600 percent of exports on average (compared to about 150 percent for the successfully-adjusting countries), despite large flows of official assistance.

Inappropriate choice or implementation of adjustment policies was not the only reason why some countries were unsuccessful in reducing

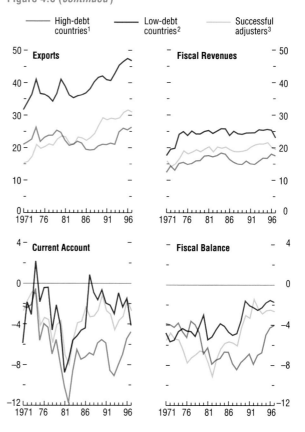

Figure 4.6 (*continued*)

____ High-debt   ____ Low-debt   ____ Successful
countries[1]   countries[2]   adjusters[3]

[48]Daseking and Powell, "From Toronto Terms to the HIPC Initiative," review debt assistance provided to low-income countries and provide estimates of the associated costs.

external indebtedness. Conditions and policies prior to the debt crisis may have played an important role. "Successful adjusters" had larger fiscal deficits on average during the initial phase of the debt buildup than high-debt countries had, suggesting that low public saving was a larger factor in the rapid accumulation of debt for the former group while low private saving may have been a larger factor for the latter. To the extent that government policies can more easily address public saving (by reducing the fiscal deficit) than private saving, adjustment may have been easier for the countries that started with higher public sector deficits. Also, low private saving in the unsuccessful countries may be partly a reflection of much lower average per capita income in this group.

The Enhanced HIPC Initiative: The Road to Sustainability?

In September 1996, the IMF and the World Bank jointly launched the Initiative for Heavily Indebted Poor Countries, or HIPC Initiative. It was based on concerted financial assistance from the international community (in addition to traditional debt-rescheduling mechanisms) and was available to countries that demonstrated a record of successful macroeconomic and structural adjustment and met other eligibility criteria. By 1999, seven countries had qualified for assistance under the Initiative.[49]

A central objective of the HIPC Initiative is to reduce external debt of the qualifying countries to sustainable levels. In theory, a debt burden is sustainable if the debtor country can be expected to meet its current and future debt-service obligations without recourse to debt relief or similar assistance. In practice, however, identifying a maximum or target level of debt that can be ex-

Figure 4.6 (*concluded*)

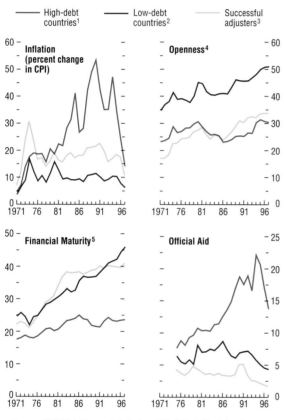

Sources: IMF, *World Economic Outlook;* and World Bank, *World Development Indicators.*

[1]HIPC countries plus countries whose debt-to-export ratio was above 200 percent in 1996–97.

[2]Countries whose debt-to-export ratio was always below 200 percent in the 1971–97 period (based on three-year averages).

[3]Countries whose debt-to-export ratio went temporarily above 200 percent during the 1971–97 period.

[4]Average of imports and exports of goods and services as a percentage of GDP.

[5]Ratio of M2 to GDP (in percent).

[49]See David Andrews and others, "Debt Relief for Low-Income Countries: The Enhanced HIPC Initiative," Pamphlet Series No. 51 (Washington: International Monetary Fund, 1999). An evaluation of the effects of the initial Initiative is provided by Stijn Claessen and others, "HIPC Debt: A Review of the Issues," *Journal of African Economies,* Vol. 2 (1997). See also *www.imf.org/external/np/HIPC.*

Table 4.9. Heavily Indebted Poor Countries (HIPCs): Selected Debt Indicators[1]
(Billions of dollars, at the year prior to the decision point, unless otherwise indicated)

		Debt in Net Present Value						
	Nominal debt Level	Level	Average ratio to exports (percent)	Average ratio to revenue (percent)	Target (at 150 percent of exports)	Target (at 250 percent of revenue)	Estimated HIPC assistance at decision point[2]	Estimated HIPC assistance in end-1999 terms[3]
Group 1[4]	**41.1**	**22.5**	**242**	**323**	...	...	**7.7**	**7.7**
Qualifying under exports criteria	21.8	11.1	288	297	5.9	...	5.2	5.2
Qualifying under fiscal criteria	19.4	11.3	150	375	...	8.9	2.4	2.4
Group 2[5]	**66.1**	**31.6**	**349**	**521**	...	...	**14.7**	**13.9**
Qualifying under exports criteria	53.4	22.4	365	509	12.4	...	10.0	9.4
Qualifying under fiscal criteria	12.7	9.3	283	566	...	4.5	4.8	4.5
Other HIPCs[6]	**81.8**	**35.9**	**275**	**426**	...	...	**8.0**	**6.6**
Qualifying under exports criteria	34.6	12.7	415	615	6.7	...	6.0	4.8
Qualifying under fiscal criteria	6.0	4.2	205	421	...	2.2	2.0	1.8
Deemed sustainable	41.3	19.0	99	145	...	...	...	...
Total	**189.1**	**90.0**	**297**	**440**	...	...	**30.4**	**28.2**

[1]For details on the HIPC Initiative and the net present value (NPV) debt ratios, see *http://www.imf.org/external/np/hipc/modify/hipc.htm*. For details on groupings and costing, see *http://www.imf.org/external/np/hipc/cost/4/index.htm*.
[2]Difference between NPV debt level and NPV debt targets.
[3]Data may differ from previous column due to base year employed in NPV calculation.
[4]Countries that are being reassessed under the enhanced HIPC Initiative: Benin, Bolivia, Burkina Faso, Côte d'Ivoire, Guyana, Mali, Mozambique, Senegal, and Uganda. The assumed decision point of each country is 1999.
[5]Countries that are expected to qualify for assistance by the end of 2000 under the enhanced framework of the HIPC Initiative: Cameroon, Chad, Ethiopia, Guinea, Guinea-Bissau, Honduras, Lao PDR, Malawi, Mauritania, Nicaragua, Niger, Rwanda, Sierra Leone, Tanzania, and Zambia. The assumed decision point of each country is 2000.
[6]Angola, Burundi, Central African Republic, Republic of Congo, Kenya, Madagascar, Myanmar, Saõ Tomé and Príncipe, Togo, Vietnam, and Yemen. The assumed decision point of each country ranges from 1999 to 2003.

pected to be sustained is far more difficult because it involves the uncertainties of projecting future earnings that would be used to service the debt. For a nation, exports are typically the appropriate measure of earnings as these provide the necessary foreign currency for external debt service, but for some countries, government revenue may be appropriate (for example, when the debt is mostly public and when tax revenue is a small proportion of output). Estimating future export earnings (or output and tax revenue) is always difficult due to unforeseen factors such as shocks; these estimates are especially uncertain for heavily indebted countries because the debt level itself can affect output through disincentives for policymakers and investors.

Sustainable debt levels are typically expressed in terms of net present value, a concept that is estimated as the stream of future scheduled debt-service flows discounted to today's value at market interest rates. The net present value of debt can differ from contract amounts (or nominal face value) when loans are made at concessional, below market, interest rates or when debt has been rescheduled at concessional rates. Thus, the difference between contract amounts (Table 4.9, first column) and the estimated net present value (second column) provides a rough indication of the concessional component of lending and of debt relief associated with traditional rescheduling techniques.[50] For all HIPCs, this difference amounts to about $100 billion. It

[50]Fluctuations in market interest rates complicate the measurement exercise and introduce an element of uncertainty in the estimated net present value of the debt. If the true level of sustainable debt were known with certainty, creditors could provide debt relief to this point without economic loss because debt above the sustainable level could not be repaid and therefore would have no value. Therefore, although debt relief can have a budgetary cost to the creditor of its full amount, it entails an economic cost only to the extent that it goes beyond the sustainable level.

does not reflect the impact of debt forgiveness, which lowers debt both in nominal and in net present value terms.

The HIPC Initiative targets the net present value of debt expressed as a percentage of exports or, in some cases, government revenue. These targets were established based on past experience of countries that have successfully avoided debt servicing problems.[51] On the basis of these targets, debt relief was already extended or committed to seven qualifying countries, while the debt burden of two other countries was deemed sustainable after traditional debt-relief mechanisms. For all of these nine countries, the debt in net present value terms was reduced to $22½ billion, or 240 percent of exports in 1998 (see Table 4.9, Group 1), and compares to a total nominal debt level of about $41 billion. The difference reflects the impact of past concessional lending and debt restructuring.

In September 1999, after a review of the initial implementation phase, it was decided to enhance the HIPC Initiative to provide deeper, faster, and broader debt relief, and to accelerate poverty reduction (Box 4.3). The enhanced Initiative specifies lower sustainability targets, more flexible eligibility criteria, front-loaded debt relief, and a specific link between debt relief and poverty reduction. Debt relief under the enhanced HIPC Initiative would be tied to the recipient country's adoption and implementation of a poverty reduction strategy (see Box 4.1).

In particular, debt-sustainability targets were lowered as a direct way of providing deeper debt relief for qualifying countries and to broaden the list of countries that could potentially qualify for assistance. Thus, debt relief will now be aimed at reducing the net present value of debt to 150 percent of exports or, for those eligible under the fiscal window, 250 percent of government revenue, whichever provides greater debt relief to the recipient country. Deeper debt relief is likely to have several advantages. First, it is hoped that additional debt reduction will free resources for poverty reduction and other important objectives set in the country's Poverty Reduction Strategy Paper. Second, the more ambitious targets of the enhanced HIPC Initiative will provide a greater safety margin for the achievement of debt sustainability and increase the chances of a permanent exit from the need for debt rescheduling. This in turn will improve the chances of future economic success by strengthening incentives for economic reform and private investment and reducing moral hazard.

Under the enhanced HIPC Initiative, all the countries in Group 1 may be reassessed for further assistance in light of the new sustainability targets. Five countries are expected to qualify under the export criteria and three under the fiscal criteria. These countries are expected to receive debt relief of approximately $8 billion (in net present value terms in 1999). Countries that are expected to qualify for assistance by the end of 2000 (Group 2 in Table 4.9) have higher average debt in net present value terms than the countries that received assistance under the original HIPC Initiative (Group 1). For the Group 2 countries, past concessional arrangements and the full use of traditional debt-relief mechanisms would lower the total debt burden from a nominal value of $66 billion to a net present value measure of about $32 billion (in 1999 terms), but before HIPC relief. Under current plans, and assuming all countries in the group can proceed with debt relief as expected, debt in present value terms would be halved, to about $17 billion.[52]

---

[51]The targets in the initial framework were net present value of the debt-to-export ratio of 200–250 percent, of the debt service-to-export ratio of 20–25 percent, and of the debt-to-fiscal revenues ratio of 280 percent. The specific sustainability targets for each country were to be based on an assessment of country-specific "vulnerability factors" (such as the concentration and variability of exports, the ratio of debt to GDP, the resource gap, the level of international reserves, and the burden of private sector debt). The empirical relevance of the various debt ratios in the assessment of debt sustainability is investigated by Daniel Cohen, "Growth and External Debt: A New Perspective on the African and Latin American Tragedies," CEPR Discussion Paper No. 1753 (London: Center for Economic Policy Research, 1997).

[52]See Andrews and others, "Debt Relief for Low-Income Countries: The Enhanced HIPC Initiative" and *www.imf.org/external/np/HIPC/cost4/index.htm.*

Box 4.3. Social Spending, Poverty Reduction, and Debt Relief in Heavily Indebted Poor Countries

Heavily Indebted Poor Countries (HIPCs) are characterized by low income, high ratios of debt to exports, a heavy debt-service burden, and poor social indicators. On average, public spending on education and health care is lower in HIPCs than in other countries eligible for concessional assistance under the Poverty Reduction and Growth Facility (PRGF), both in relation to GDP and total government expenditures (Table B4.3).[1] The increase in education and health care spending and improvements in key health and education indicators during

[1]Currently, there are 40 HIPC-eligible countries, of which 8 countries have reached the decision point—i.e., the point when a country's qualification for HIPC assistance is determined (Bolivia, Burkina Faso, Côte d'Ivoire, Guyana, Mali, Mauritania, Mozambique, and Uganda), and 4 countries have reached the completion point—i.e, the point when additional measures are taken to assist a country to reach a sustainable debt level (Bolivia, Guyana, Mozambique, and Uganda). In addition, Bolivia and Uganda have reached their second decision points. Benin and Senegal reached decision points, were determined under the Initiative to face sustainable debt burdens after traditional debt relief, and therefore did not receive assistance. There are 40 other PRGF-eligible countries in addition to HIPCs.

1985–98 have been generally lower in HIPCs than in other PRGF-eligible countries (see the first figure). Poverty is a multidimensional phenomenon, reflecting not only material deprivation but also, for example, lack of access to basic services. For targeted spending to have a broad impact on poverty, the benefits from improved basic social services have to be accompanied by greater income-earning opportunities for the poor, of the type generally produced by robust economic growth.

Debt Relief and Poverty Reduction

Debt relief for HIPCs could provide additional resources for anti-poverty programs. In the HIPCs for which data are available, debt service paid and the stock of debt as a share of GDP are higher than in other poor countries eligible for concessional lending under the PRGF. Although country experiences vary considerably, on average, HIPCs allocate slightly more budgetary resources to debt service than to education and health-care taken together, both in terms of GDP as well as total government expenditures (about 5 percent of GDP and 20 percent of total government expenditures, respectively). Total debt relief under the Heavily

Social Spending and Indebtedness: HIPC and Non-HIPC PRGF-Eligible Countries
(In units as indicated; latest year for which data are available)[1]

	Education Spending[2]		Health Spending[2]		Debt Service[3]			
	In percent of GDP	In percent of total government expenditures	In percent of GDP	In percent of total government expenditures	In percent of GDP	In percent of total government expenditures	Debt Stock In Percent of GDP	Number of Countries[4]
HIPCs[5]	3.3	13.2	1.6	6.3	5.1	19.8	117.1	30
of which program countries	3.4	13.5	1.7	6.5	5.1	20.4	130.5	28
Non-HIPC PRGF-eligible countries[6]	4.6	15.3	2.5	8.0	2.9	11.2	56.6	20
of which program countries	3.9	15.4	1.8	7.3	3.0	11.6	58.6	13

Sources: World Bank; national authorities; and IMF staff estimates.
[1]For most countries, the latest year for which data are available is 1997 for debt service and 1998 for health and education spending.
[2]In general, data on local government spending and in-kind donor contributions are not available, thereby understating total public spending.
[3]World Bank Global Development Finance (GDF) estimates of debt service paid, which may be lower than debt service due. However, caution should be exercised in interpreting these ratios due to the misclassification of debt service between cash and accrual.
[4]Sample size may vary across categories.
[5]Excludes Nigeria.
[6]Excludes transition economies (Albania, Armenia, Azerbaijan, Bosnia and Herzegovina, Georgia, the Kyrgyz Republic, the former Yugoslav Republic of Macedonia, Moldova, Mongolia, and Tajikistan) and includes Nigeria.

Box 4.3 *(concluded)*

Social Spending and Social Indicators, 1985–98[1]
(Annual percent change)

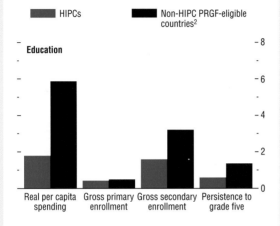

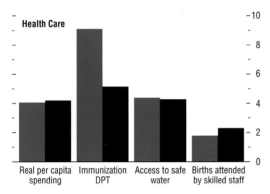

Sources: IMF staff estimates; national authorities; and World Bank, *World Development Indicators.*

[1]Average annual change between first year since 1985 and the most recent year for which data are available.

[2]Excludes transition economies: Albania, Armenia, Azerbaijan, Bosnia and Herzegovina, Georgia, the Kyrgyz Republic, the former Yugoslav Republic of Macedonia, Moldova, Mongolia, and Tajikistan.

Indebted Poor Country (HIPC) Initiative is estimated at $28.2 billion (in end-1999 present value terms), including debt forgiveness and concessional debt service.[2] However, comparing data on debt service paid and public

[2]Information is available via the Internet at *www.imf.org/external/np/vc/1999/122899.htm.*

spending on education and health care alone provides only a partial view of the relationship between international official resource flows and spending on poverty reduction programs, because public spending on poverty reduction is not confined to education and health care programs. Public spending on, for instance, rural roads, sanitation, and access to safe water could contribute as much, or more, to poverty reduction. Gross external financing flows (new loans and grants, for instance) are not necessarily independent of debt-service payments, and these flows are typically higher than either social spending or debt-service payments in HIPCs. For countries to reap full benefits from debt relief, efforts are needed to improve the efficiency of existing, as well as additional, public outlays made possible by debt relief. This will require action on at least three fronts.

In HIPCs, the allocation of budgetary resources within the social sectors (e.g., between primary and tertiary education) is typically skewed toward services that are less demanded by the poor, such as tertiary education and curative, rather than preventive, health care. For instance, data for selected HIPCs show that 14 percent of total spending on public education and 13 percent of health care outlays, on average, accrue to the poorest fifth of the population (lowest quintile), compared with 30 percent for the richest quintile for both spending categories (see the second figure).[3] Furthermore, public spending on primary and secondary education has disproportionately favored the more prosperous urban population over the rural poor.[4] In addition, corruption, poor targeting of social spending, and a high

[3]Hamid Davoodi and Sawitree Sachjapinan, "How Useful Are Benefit Incidence Studies?" IMF Working Paper (Washington: International Monetary Fund, forthcoming).

[4]In a smaller sample of HIPCs for which information is available, public spending on health favors the rural population over the more prosperous urban population.

share of wages and salaries in social sector allocations have weakened the link between public expenditures and improvements in social indicators.[5]

The capacity to formulate and execute the budget in a transparent manner is critical for anti-poverty programs. In this context, the use of poverty funds for channeling debt relief to the poor has been widely advocated. Such funds should be subject to the same level of scrutiny and oversight as other government spending, including transparency and accountability both to parliament and the executive. Anti-poverty programs should be integrated into the budget to prevent leakages, duplication, and implementation of relatively low-priority projects.

Effective monitoring of debt relief for poverty reduction requires timely and adequate data.[6] To this end, coordinated technical assistance from international organizations and donors, as well as increased efforts by HIPCs themselves, will be crucial.[7] At present, coverage of public spending data is not comprehensive in many countries, and typically excludes spending by local governments and in-kind donor contributions. Public spending data become available with a lag, which for some countries can be as long as two to three years. Moreover, virtually no HIPC-eligible country has consistent annual series for public expenditure allocations within the education and health sectors (e.g., distinguishing between outlays on primary and tertiary education, preven-

[5]Vito Tanzi, "Corruption Around the World: Causes, Consequences, Scope, and Cures," *IMF Staff Papers,* Vol. 45 (December 1998), pp. 559–94.

[6]Sanjeev Gupta and others, *Social Issues in IMF-Supported Programs,* IMF Occasional Paper No. 191 (Washington: International Monetary Fund, 2000).

[7]Currently, the IMF, the Organization for Economic Cooperation and Development, the United Nations, and the World Bank are collaborating in the Partnership in Statistics for Development in the Twenty-First Century Consortium (PARIS21) to support statistical capacity building in countries preparing poverty reduction programs.

Benefit Incidence of Public Spending on Education and Health Care in Heavily Indebted Poor Countries, Early 1990s[1]
(Percent of total spending)

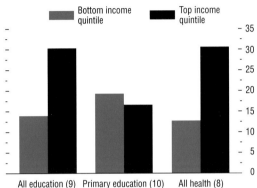

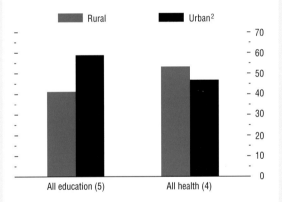

Source: Davoodi and Sachjapinan, "How Useful are Benefit Incidence Studies?"

[1]Numbers of countries are in parentheses; the latest year for which data are available.

[2]The share of the population living in urban areas averages one-third for the countries in the education and health care samples.

tive and curative health care, and wage and non-wage items). Social indicators are produced infrequently, and typically become available only every five years. Also, data for many important indicators are derived from models rather than from actual observations. Up-to-date information on poverty indicators, including the nature and locus of poverty, is often lacking.

Table 4.10. Heavily Indebted Poor Countries (HIPCs): Economic Indicators
(Percent of GDP unless otherwise indicated)

	Group 1[1]			Group 2[2]			Developing Countries excluding HIPCs		
	1990–94	1995–97	1998–99	1990–94	1995–97	1998–99	1990–94	1995–97	1998–99
Real per capita GDP[3]	0.4	3.4	2.5	−2.1	1.6	−1.1	1.6	1.7	0.2
Saving	7.4	13.2	14.8	9.0	8.5	9.2	19.7	21.8	20.4
Total investment	18.6	21.1	22.7	16.4	15.5	17.8	24.2	26.3	24.9
Private investment	10.2	12.1	14.0	8.5	7.2	8.0	...	16.7	16.8
Fiscal deficit[4]	−5.3	−2.1	−2.3	−6.8	−3.2	−4.0	−4.1	−3.1	−3.7
Current account	−9.3	−8.5	−8.8	−9.6	−8.7	−10.2	−4.6	−3.5	−4.0
Exports of goods and services	28.4	31.4	31.0	20.2	23.2	23.8	39.8	41.0	40.9
Fiscal revenues[4]	21.6	22.1	21.9	17.2	18.8	18.4	28.5	27.7	27.1
CPI Inflation[3]	15.1	9.1	3.7	31.0	15.7	11.8	19.7	10.2	7.5
Openness[5]	33.5	36.0	35.9	26.1	29.3	30.6	42.7	43.0	43.0
Broad money	26.6	28.2	28.8	19.1	18.8	18.9	49.1	49.4	...
Net private capital flows	1.6	3.7	3.7	−2.8	1.1	1.3	4.1	3.2	3.0
Official assistance[6]	12.5	2.1	5.3	14.8	12.0	11.7	...	3.6	3.4

Sources: World Bank, *World Development Indicators;* and IMF staff estimates.
[1]Countries for which assistance has been extended (Uganda, Bolivia, Guyana, Mozambique), committed (Burkina Faso, Côte d'Ivoire, Mali), or deemed not required (Benin, Senegal) under the initial framework of the HIPC Initiative.
[2]Countries that are expected to qualify for assistance by the end of 2000 under the enhanced framework of the HIPC Initiative: Cameroon, Chad, Ethiopia, Guinea, Guinea-Bissau, Honduras, Lao PDR, Malawi, Mauritania, Nicaragua, Niger, Rwanda, Sierra Leone, Tanzania, and Zambia.
[3]Percent change.
[4]Including grants.
[5]Exports plus imports.
[6]Official lending and transfers.

Debt-relief estimates for other HIPCs in Table 4.9 are very preliminary.

To qualify for HIPC assistance, countries need to implement a program of macroeconomic and structural reform and demonstrate a track record of good performance because experience suggests that progress in these areas is a necessary precondition for successful debt reduction.[53] An improved track record from 1995 onward is evident in the countries that received relief under the original HIPC Initiative (Group 1 in Table 4.10). While it is difficult to determine causality, better policies and implementation are evident in lower fiscal deficits and inflation. These and other policy improvements have contributed to a stronger resource balance and ability to service debt (a rise in domestic savings and an improving trade deficit, associated with larger export and fiscal revenues), higher levels

of private and public investment, and stronger private capital inflows. The Group 2 countries that are expected to qualify for HIPC assistance in the course of 2000 also recorded improvements in these economic variables, but their situations today remain substantially worse than those in Group 1 in 1995–97. This lack of sufficient progress indicates that many countries now anticipating HIPC debt relief will need firm implementation of policy reforms to qualify for assistance.

The New Approach to Poverty Reduction

Poverty reduction has been and will need to be for a long time among the highest priorities for domestic policymakers, the donor community, and international institutions. The development strategies followed until now have worked

[53]William Easterly, "How Did Highly Indebted Poor Countries Become Highly Indebted? Reviewing Two Decades of Debt Relief" (unpublished; Washington: World Bank, 1997) argues that when countries do not pursue macroeconomic and structural reform policies, they will tend to respond to debt relief by borrowing more or decreasing domestic assets, so as to leave practically unaltered the sustainability of their external liabilities. See also Burnside and Dollar, "Aid, Policies, and Growth."

for some countries, but for far too many, poverty remains prevalent and a stronger approach is needed.

There are, nevertheless, grounds for optimism. First, the industrial economies have demonstrated that long periods of sustained growth are possible and that living standards can improve dramatically over a few decades. Second, the newly industrialized economies, although small in number, have shown that rapid catch-up is possible with growth rates even higher than those observed during the periods of the strongest growth in the industrial countries, especially when the familiar pillars of sustainable growth—macroeconomic stability, sound institutions, and free trade—are pursued. Third, a few low-income countries—in particular China and to a lesser extent India with their large populations—have also achieved long periods of sustained growth at a rapid pace. Taken together, the successes of these groups of countries show that countries with different characteristics can achieve significant increases in per capita income. Finally, and more recently, successful implementation of growth-oriented adjustment policies and reform is clearly paying off in some low- and middle-income developing countries that have witnessed falling inflation and stronger rates of economic growth in the 1990s. More needs to be done, of course, to ensure that these improvements endure.

Still, while the fundamentals of economic growth are reasonably clear, there is no unique formula to achieve it in all countries. Solutions will vary and depend on country-specific institutions, customs, and economic conditions. Experience identifies a few key conditions that, if lacking or absent, can be an impediment to takeoff and sustained growth. Among these are an incentive structure, the rule of law, and a level of governance that allow individuals to save, invest, and ultimately benefit from these endeavors. The enhancement of public health and education standards are also important for sustainable growth, as they not only directly contribute to human well-being but also allow for an efficient accumulation of productive human cap-

ital. Each country will need to decide on how best to provide these fundamentals within its development strategy.

The enhanced development strategy framework stresses three elements. First, each country will formulate a poverty reduction strategy to elaborate its plans for development and poverty reduction in a multi-year framework. These strategies will be prepared by the country itself, with the participation of civil society, in order to increase the level of national awareness of the issues and strategy, and with it the shared commitment to implementing the agreed reforms. Greater ownership by the domestic authorities and civil society is expected to lead to stronger policy implementation. Development partners, the World Bank, and the IMF will provide a broad range of assistance. The poverty reduction strategy, when broadly endorsed by the Executive Boards of the IMF and the World Bank, will form the basis for concessional lending from both institutions. It is hoped that other development partners will also link their financial and technical support to these poverty reduction strategies.

Second, poverty reduction is now placed at the center of programs supported by the IMF's facility for concessional lending. This follows from the recognition that poverty reduction itself is a primary objective, but also the belief that by jump-starting poverty reduction, countries can begin a virtuous circle of domestic saving and investment leading to growth and further poverty reduction. Consistent with the change in objectives and practices, the IMF's facility for concessional lending—formerly the Enhanced Structural Adjustment Facility—has been renamed the Poverty Reduction and Growth Facility.

The third element of the strategy is to bring enhanced debt relief to poor countries where debt levels are unsustainable. Without debt reduction through traditional means and the HIPC Initiative, the incentive problems associated with unsustainable debt burdens will not be overcome, and policy reforms and private investment increases may not be forthcoming. The cost to debtor countries of any resulting delay would come in forgone output. The experience over the past 30 years during which per capita income growth stagnated in many of these countries demonstrates the magnitude of the potential loss. For the donor countries, the cost of inadequate debt reduction at this stage is the possibility of more debt problems and further rescheduling down the road that could come at an even greater cost to taxpayers.

* * *

The deepening of debt relief in the enhanced HIPC Initiative clearly moves in the right direction and adds an extra margin of safety that debt burdens will be brought to sustainable levels. The enhanced HIPC Initiative is an opportunity that none can afford to miss. The HIPC Initiative is no panacea for all poverty and economic problems in these countries, however, and its goals can only be achieved with continued hard work by domestic and international participants. The international community needs to increase levels of foreign aid and ensure that aid promotes reforms and poverty alleviation. Major efforts also are needed to reform trade policies that adversely affect the poorest countries. The poorest countries themselves will need to persevere with macroeconomic and structural reform, with emphasis on providing an environment conducive to private saving and investment decisions, including better governance, public sector reform, and market liberalization. Their responsibility to stay the course is a sine qua non part of the strategy.

CHAPTER V

THE WORLD ECONOMY IN THE TWENTIETH CENTURY: STRIKING DEVELOPMENTS AND POLICY LESSONS

The transformation of the world economy in the course of the twentieth century would have been impossible for even the most acute observer living in 1900 to forecast or perhaps even to imagine. Output per capita, the structure of production, and the domestic and international financial systems that sustained the growth of economic activity over this period have been altered almost beyond recognition. This chapter provides an overview of some of these changes, the connections between them, and the major policy implications. Any account of these profound changes is, by necessity, selective. The discussion focuses on three broad interrelated areas.

First, technological change has driven an enormous increase in the production of goods and services, sufficient to support both vastly higher living standards and vastly larger populations than ever before in history. The increase in productivity has been accompanied by greatly increased specialization in production, leading to the rising importance of markets that have facilitated the exchange of goods and the diffusion of technology, both within and between national economies. By greatly reducing transportation costs, technical progress has contributed to the geographical expansion of markets. The fruits of economic growth have been distributed unevenly among countries, but the extent to which this is true depends on the indicators chosen. Inequality between the world's rich and poor regions, measured by output per capita, has increased dramatically over time. However, alternative measures of development—de-emphasizing output per capita beyond a certain threshold but including non-pecuniary aspects, such as life expectancy and levels of education—actually show some convergence in the course of the twentieth century, although large differences between nations remain for these measures as well. The first part

of this chapter documents these developments and divergencies.

Second, the nature of the international monetary system has changed significantly and repeatedly in the course of the twentieth century. The second part of the chapter traces these developments, describing how the international financial system has interacted with trends and developments in the real economy, and particularly how it has affected international trade and capital movements. This includes a discussion of the forces underlying changes in institutions and policies, and how these, in turn, have influenced countries' ability to capitalize on the opportunities afforded by globalization.

Third, the role of the public sector has expanded significantly in the course of the twentieth century, both in industrial and developing countries. This is clearly reflected in the increase in the ratio of public expenditures and revenues to GDP, but regulation and various off-balance activities have also increased. At the same time, views on the appropriate role of government versus the reliance on market forces have changed considerably and are continuing to evolve. After reviewing the changing role of the public sector, the third part of the chapter summarizes some of the major lessons for public policy to be learned from twentieth century experience. The final section points to three major global policy challenges facing the international community at the beginning of the twenty-first century.

The issues discussed in this chapter, and the lessons highlighted, are not necessarily those that other analysts or observers would emphasize. These topics reflect the developments that the authors of the *World Economic Outlook*, seen from their particular vantage point, regard as particularly striking. One important issue that will be addressed only in passing is the development of demand management policies. Although this is clearly a major change—the

Figure 5.1. World GDP and Population Since 1750

During the twentieth century both output and population growth increased. However, as a result of accelerating technical progress, output growth increasingly exceeded population growth.

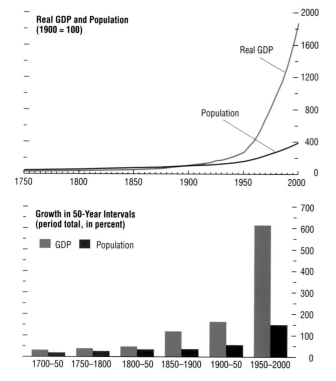

Source: Bradford J. DeLong, "Estimating World GDP, One Million B.C.–Present." Available via the internet at: http://econ161.berkeley.edu.

very concepts of macroeconomics and (cyclical) stabilization policy are essentially twentieth-century creations—this topic has been dealt with extensively in earlier *World Economic Outlooks*.

This chapter incorporates some of the many insights contained in two supporting studies commissioned for the *World Economic Outlook*.[1] "Globalization and Growth in the Twentieth Century" (IMF Working Paper 00/44), by Professor Nicholas Crafts of the London School of Economics, discusses real developments during the twentieth century and was particularly important for the discussion of growth and divergence. "The International Monetary System in the (Very) Long Run" (IMF Working Paper 00/43), by Professors Barry Eichengreen and Nathan Sussman of the University of California Berkeley and Hebrew University Jerusalem, respectively, provides an overview of the international monetary system over the last thousand years, and was particularly important for the discussion of the changing nature of international monetary relations in the twentieth century.

Global Economic Growth and Income Distribution

The two most striking characteristics of twentieth-century economic growth are its staggering size and acceleration when compared with developments in previous centuries, and its uneven distribution among different countries and regions of the world.

Growth of Output and Population

Using conventional GDP estimates over a long historical period, the total amount of goods and services produced in the twentieth century is estimated to have exceeded the cumulative total output over the preceding recorded human his-

[1]In addition to being issued as IMF Working Papers, both studies are being published in *World Economic Outlook: Supporting Studies 2000* (Washington: IMF, forthcoming).

tory (Figure 5.1, upper panel).[2] Between the years 1900 and 2000 world GDP at constant prices has increased about 19-fold, corresponding to an average annual rate of growth of 3 percent.[3] Population growth also increased significantly in the twentieth century, catapulting the world population from 1.6 billion inhabitants at the beginning to over 6.3 billion persons at the end of the century. This near quadrupling of world population over the 100 years since 1900—following a more than doubling between the start of the industrial revolution around 1750 and 1900—implies an average annual rate of increase of 1.4 percent, an order of magnitude higher than the estimated average annual increase of 0.1 percent over the thousand-year period preceding the industrial revolution. The acceleration of output and population growth in the twentieth century has frequently caused serious concerns about its sustainability in the light of finite global resources, an issue we will return to below.

The rise in population growth, which peaked in the second half of the twentieth century, was not the result of increasing birth or fertility rates, but rather due to the decline in mortality, especially infant mortality (Figure 5.2). A significant rise in average life expectancy at all ages also contributed. Both of these developments were largely a consequence of rapid progress in the medical sciences and improvements in nutrition and basic hygiene, such as the provision of safe drinking water and sewage systems. Toward the end of the century fertility rates, which, together with life expectancy, determine population levels and growth in the long run, were falling rapidly in the large majority of countries. In virtually all countries in western Europe as well as the United

Figure 5.2. Stylized Population Dynamics

As the economy develops, the fall in death rates precedes the fall in birth rates, leading to rapid population growth in the transition.

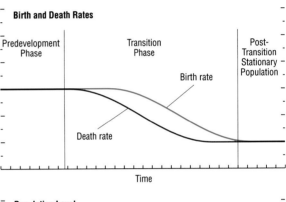

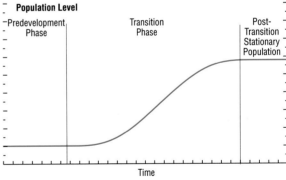

[2]Bradford DeLong, "Estimating World GDP, One Million B.C.—Present," available via the Internet at *http://econ161.berkeley.edu*. Cumulative output is measured by the area under the output curve in Figure 5.1, upper panel.

[3]Imputing output gains on account of new products and quality improvements has been estimated to add some 0.7 percentage points to the annual growth rate, implying a 38-fold increase in aggregate output over the century. See Bradford DeLong, "Estimating World GDP."

Figure 5.3. Factors Underlying Population Growth[1]
(GDP per capita in 1995 purchasing-power-parity international dollars)

Fertility, birth, and death rates tend to fall with rising income levels. In many countries fertility rates are now below replacement rates.

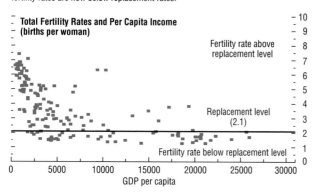

Total Fertility Rates and Per Capita Income
(births per woman)

Fertility rate above replacement level

Replacement level (2.1)

Fertility rate below replacement level

GDP per capita

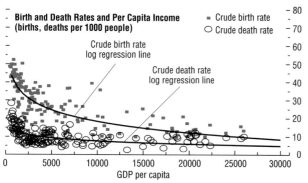

Birth and Death Rates and Per Capita Income
(births, deaths per 1000 people)

■ Crude birth rate
○ Crude death rate

Crude birth rate log regression line

Crude death rate log regression line

GDP per capita

Source: World Bank, *World Development Indicators.*
[1]Fertility, birth, death rates, and GDP per capita are averages for the period 1990 to 1997.

States and Japan the fertility rate had declined well below the replacement level (i.e., the rate required to prevent population from declining in the long run). Today, the fertility rate exceeds the replacement rate in only three of the 23 richest countries in the world (Figure 5.3).[4]

Part of the observed growth of world output is a result of the increase in the number of workers entailed by population growth. However, as the preceding figures demonstrate, total output growth greatly exceeded population growth, leading to an almost fivefold increase in GDP per capita during the twentieth century (Figure 5.1, upper panel).[5] Indeed, the record is even more impressive when the fall in average hours worked is also taken into account.[6] On the other hand, part of the measured output growth surely represents the transformation of previous home production into market production.

The enormous increase in per capita output points to the pivotal role that technical progress has played in twentieth-century growth. Twentieth-century technology built, and greatly expanded, on the significant foundations laid since the beginning of the industrial revolution in 1750, and many nineteenth-century inventions reached widespread use and commercialization only in the twentieth century.[7] This is

[4]The fertility rate is defined as the number of children each woman has on average during her lifetime. The "replacement rate," which stabilizes the level of population in the long run (if life expectancy remains constant, and abstracting from migration), is 2.1.

[5]From a historical perspective the experience of output growth permanently outstripping population growth is remarkable. This phenomenon has been increasingly pronounced and significant since the start of the industrial revolution in eighteenth-century England. The result is that for the last 250 years the world economy has escaped the "Malthusian poverty trap" in which rising population catches up with rising output, keeping per capita incomes at subsistence level.

[6]Since 1870, hours worked per capita have almost halved in western Europe and fallen by 40 percent in Japan and by 15 percent in the United States.

[7]The reasons for the lags between technological breakthroughs and their impact on measured productivity and GDP are explored in Paul A. David, "Dynamo and the Computer: An Historical Perspective on the Modern Productivity Paradox," *American Economic Review,* Vol. 80 (May 1990), pp. 355–61.

true for the automobile, electric power applications of all sorts, reinforced concrete, radio broadcasting, and cinematography, all of which contributed significantly to economic growth in the first half of the century. But the twentieth century also added entirely new areas of research and development—particularly in chemistry, aeronautics, synthetic materials, nuclear energy, electronics (including computers and television) and biochemistry. As a result, the pace of technological development accelerated to unprecedented speed, generating a significant increase in measured productivity growth. Technical progress has been manifest in the form of both new and more efficient production processes, as well as the development of entirely new products and services.

The cause of such an acceleration in technical progress remains largely a mystery. This is particularly true for the major inventions (such as the steam engine, the internal combustion engine, etc.), in contrast to incremental innovations that raise the efficiency of existing technologies at the margin. However, both types are important for the steady increase in measured total factor productivity.[8] Despite intensive research, there is as yet no commonly accepted theory of what causes a major technological breakthrough (or "macro-invention"). Nevertheless, institutions that make it easier for innovators to appropriate the quasi-rents from inventions (whether big or small), like property rights (including patent rights), as well as large and well-functioning markets, which increase the potential gain from a given invention, clearly tend to favor innovative activity.[9] The level of education and the communication infrastructure also seem to play a role, both for new inventions as well as for the ability to adopt technologies already used elsewhere

(technology diffusion). As economies become more advanced, they typically attempt to institutionalize the process of innovation by establishing research facilities (both in the public and private sectors) and raising R&D expenditure. Although this seems indeed to increase the number of micro-inventions, its effects on producing "macro-inventions" remain uncertain.[10]

Historically, the advance in total factor productivity—the conventional measure of technical progress—has coincided with an increasing division of labor and specialization in production. This, in turn, has led to an increasing importance of markets, facilitating the exchange of goods and services among specialized production units. Conversely, technical progress in communications and transportation, and the resulting reduction in transaction costs, encouraged the division of labor and the expansion of markets. By facilitating the exchange of goods that embody technical progress, markets also play an important role in technology diffusion from leading economies to those trying to catch up.

Expanding international trade is a specific manifestation of this general phenomenon of increasing division of labor and specialization in production, singled out because of the existence of national borders. It is the underlying division of labor, spread over increasingly wider territory thanks to technical progress in transportation and communications, that is the handmaiden of economic growth. Rising international trade indicates that national territories have become small relative to the regional spread of efficient specialization. However, since national borders can be (mis)used to erect formidable barriers to such optimal division of labor, a nation's trade policies can severely curtail its growth potential.

---

[8]Criticizing the distinction between "inventions" and "innovations" introduced by Schumpeter, Mokyr labels the major inventions "macro-inventions" and the incremental innovations "micro-inventions," in analogy to the concepts of macro- and micro-mutations in evolutionary biology. See Joel Mokyr, *Twenty-Five Centuries of Technological Change—A Historical Survey* (Chur: Harwood Academic Publishers, 1990).

[9]Charles I. Jones, "Was the Industrial Revolution Inevitable?—Economic Growth over the Very Long Run," NBER Working Paper No. 7375 (Cambridge, Massachusetts: National Bureau of Economic Research, 1999).

[10]See the discussion of empirical results of cross-section analysis of factors determining output growth in Robert J. Barro and Xavier Sala-i-Martin, *Economic Growth* (Cambridge, Massachusetts: MIT Press, 1999).

Figure 5.4. Differential Income Growth

In the twentieth century, per capita income has risen faster in the rich than in the poor countries and at different speeds in different subperiods.

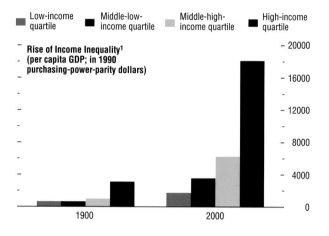

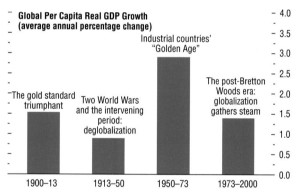

Sources: Angus Maddison, *Monitoring the World Economy 1820–1992* (Paris: Organization for Economic Cooperation and Development, 1995); and IMF staff estimates.
[1]Countries' populations have been assigned to income quartiles according to GDP per capita in each country; each quartile contains 25 percent of world population.

Similar considerations apply to the international flow of capital, which as a manifestation of the rapid growth (both national and international) of financial markets, is itself greatly facilitated by technical progress in information and communications technology. Modern financial markets promote the mutually beneficial exchange between net savers and users of capital for productive purposes over increasing numbers of economic agents and ever larger territories, thus contributing to the optimal use of capital and the maximization of world output. In addition to the international transfer of capital, international financial markets also facilitate the transfer of technology in the form of foreign direct investment and provide various insurance functions. These themes will be explored further in the following sections of this chapter.

The rising specialization in production, while raising productive efficiency, has also increased the economic interdependence (mutual dependence) of individuals, firms, and national economies. This implies, on the one hand, that economic activity in one area will be indirectly affected by shocks and disturbances originating elsewhere in the economy—a process known as "contagion" when occurring in response to a negative shock elsewhere. On the other hand, this interdependence offers the opportunity for individuals, firms, and nations to reduce hardship in cases of real shocks affecting them directly, by temporarily relying on resources from less affected producers.

Income Differentiation Over Space and Time[11]

Aggregate figures for global output and population conceal remarkable differences across individual economies, as well as uneven growth rates during major defining sub-periods of the

[11]The following analysis is based on output and population data up to 1992 presented in Angus Maddison, *Monitoring the World Economy 1820–1992* (Paris: Organization for Economic Cooperation and Development, 1995). Data after 1992 have been computed by applying growth rates of real per capita GDP from IMF staff estimates to the 1990 Maddison data.

twentieth century. Figure 5.4 summarizes the differential regional income growth, grouping countries' populations into income quartiles according to countries' GDP per capita (upper panel), and the differences of aggregate world GDP growth rates over time (lower panel). Although the richest quarter of the world population has seen its per capita GDP increase close to sixfold over the century, per capita income for the poorest quarter of the world population has increased less than threefold, although—from a long-term historical perspective—this is still a notable acceleration of income growth.

The rise in world income inequality was exacerbated by a change in the geographic pattern of output and population growth. At the start of the industrial revolution and up to 1913, population growth was strongest in countries with the most rapid output growth. In contrast, the tendency in the twentieth century was increasingly for population growth to be concentrated in the poorer countries. In the dynamic industrial (high-income) countries, population growth slowed dramatically starting in the mid-1960s, and the fertility rate in any of these countries is now well below the replacement level. In contrast, in many of the poorest countries, particularly in sub-Saharan Africa, output growth has barely kept pace with population growth, causing stagnating or even falling per capita incomes. This is one reason why income discrepancies are larger at the close than at the beginning of the twentieth century. Increasing global inequality is illustrated by the change in the world "Lorenz Curve" between the years 1900 and 2000 (based upon average income per capita in 42 countries) depicted in Figure 5.5. The Gini coefficient—a measure of inequality, ranging from 0 (perfect equality) to 1 (complete inequality)—has risen from 0.40 to 0.48 between these two benchmark years.

A closer inspection of trends in estimated GDP per capita reveals a number of interesting additional facts about the nature of income divergence in the twentieth century. The levels of real GDP per person toward the end of the century in many poor countries were still well below

Figure 5.5. World Lorenz Curve, 1900 and 2000

World income inequality has increased in the twentieth century, mainly due to a large decline in the relative per capita income in poor countries.

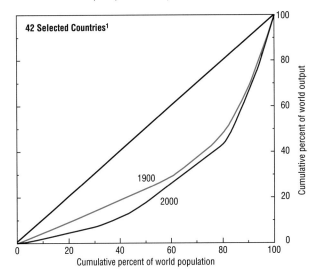

Sources: Angus Maddison, *Monitoring the World Economy 1820–1992* (Paris: Organization for Economic Cooperation and Development, 1995); and IMF staff estimates.

[1]The Maddison data set used comprises 42 countries, covering 78.2 and 89.1 percent of world population and GDP in 1990, respectively. The Lorenz curve is constructed by ordering countries' populations and total output in ascending order of countries' GDP per capita.

those already attained by the leading countries (in terms of output per capita) in 1900. Thus, the 2000 average of $1,290 for Africa is well below the 1900 averages of $3,092 and $4,022 for the countries of western Europe and the areas of recent European settlement (Australia, Canada, New Zealand, and the United States), respectively. The level of real GDP per person of $500 in Africa in 1900 was about one-ninth of that of the leading country at the time. In 2000, however, the African level was only about one-twentieth of the leading country. The gap between rich and poor measured in these terms has widened enormously or, as one author recently put it, the central feature of twentieth-century growth as measured by GDP per capita is "divergence, big time."[12]

The position of countries in terms of relative per capita output has remained remarkably stable at the upper and lower tails of the distribution, with a few notable exceptions. The 42 economies in the data set can be classified into four income groups (low, center-low, center-high, and high), each comprising one-fourth of the aggregate sample population, for both the beginning and the end of the twentieth century (Table 5.1). The bottom right corner of the resulting "transition matrix" shows a high persistence among the rich countries: only Russia, which in 1900 straddled the border line between the two higher-income quartiles, fell back to the second ("center-low") quartile. All other initial members remained in the top quartile throughout the century. High persistence can also be seen in the lowest quartile, as shown by the countries in the upper left corner of the matrix. Filling the entire second lowest quartile and straddling both the quartile's upper and lower border in 1900, China has moved to straddle the border between the two high-income quartiles in 2000—the most notable move in the entire matrix. Indeed, most changes occurred in the two

middle quartiles: with China moving up from the center-low quartile to largely occupy the center-high quartile, the countries located in this latter quartile in 1900 moved either up (three Asian countries and Venezuela) or down (most Latin American countries and some Asian countries).

Concerning the variation in income growth over time, the lower panel in Figure 5.4 shows considerable variation over four subperiods of the twentieth century, which coincide with distinctly different international monetary regimes. The pre-World War I period corresponds to the mature gold standard, with relatively free (and rapidly rising) trade and capital movements. Average annual growth in output per capita exceeded 1.5 percent during this period, a significant acceleration compared with the preceding century.[13] World output growth per capita almost halved in the subsequent period (1913 to 1950), marked by two devastating world wars and a crippling world recession in the inter-war period. Attempts to restore the pre-World War I gold standard during this period ultimately failed under the strains of a deepening world depression, entailing a severe contraction in world trade and capital movements (Figure 5.6). The post-World War II period to 1973 was characterized by exceptionally rapid output per capita growth (2.9 percent on average) and the recovery of world trade under the Bretton Woods system of fixed exchange rates and widespread capital controls. The period following the collapse of the Bretton Woods system (1973–2000) saw a slowdown in income growth, which nevertheless remained high when judged from a long-term historical perspective (and similar to the 1870–1913 classical gold standard period). Exchange rates among major currencies fluctuated, and as capital controls were increasingly dismantled, capital flows increased spectacularly (Figure 5.7).

---

[12]The term was coined in a paper by L. Pritchett, "Divergence, Big Time," *Journal of Economic Perspectives*, Vol. 11 (Summer 1997), pp. 3–17.

[13]Average global per capita output growth was 0.8 and 1.2 percent over the periods from 1820 and 1870 to the year 1900, respectively; see Maddison, *Monitoring the World Economy*.

Table 5.1. Changes in Nations' Relative Income Position: 1900–2000[1]

1900 GDP Per Capita Group	1900 listing	2000 GDP Per Capita Group			
		Lowest Quartile	Center Low Quartile	Center High Quartile	Highest Quartile
Lowest Quartile	Ghana ($462) Egypt ($509) Bangladesh ($581) India ($625) China[2] ($652)	Ghana ($1,111) Bangladesh ($932) India[3] ($1,880)	Egypt ($2,279)		
Center Low Quartile	China[2] ($652)			China[2] ($6,283)	
Center High Quartile	China[2] ($652) Myanmar ($667) Pakistan ($687) Brazil ($704) Indonesia ($745) Taiwan Province of China ($759) Thailand ($812) Peru ($817) Venezuela ($821) South Korea ($850) Columbia ($973) Philippines ($1,033) Japan ($1,135) Mexico ($1,157) former USSR[4] ($1,218)	Myanmar ($1,079) Pakistan ($1,773)	Brazil ($5,355) Indonesia ($3,136) Thailand ($5,720) Peru ($3,797) Columbia ($5,514) Philippines ($2,442) former USSR ($3,686)	Mexico[5] ($5,721)	Taiwan Province of China ($16,854) Venezuela ($7,643) South Korea ($14,293) Japan ($20,616)
Highest Quartile	former USSR[4] ($1,218) Portugal ($1,408) Finland ($1,621) Hungary ($1,682) Italy ($1,717) Czechoslovakia[6] ($1,729) Norway ($1,762) Chile ($1,950) Spain ($2,040) Ireland ($2,495) Sweden ($2,561) Argentina ($2,756) Canada ($2,758) France ($2,849) Austria ($2,901) Denmark ($2,902) Germany ($3,134) Switzerland ($3,531) Netherlands ($3,533) Belgium ($3,652) United States ($4,096) Australia ($4,299) New Zealand ($4,320) United Kingdom ($4,593)				Portugal ($14,565) Finland ($19,655) Hungary ($7,053) Italy ($18,416) Czechoslovakia[6] ($8,398) Norway ($22,297) Chile ($10,275) Spain ($15,266) Ireland ($19,511) Sweden ($19,968) Argentina ($9,122) Canada ($22,401) France ($20,377) Austria ($19,716) Denmark ($22,057) Germany ($19,119) Switzerland ($21,601) Netherlands ($20,546) Belgium ($19,958) United States ($27,272) Australia ($20,609) New Zealand ($16,072) United Kingdom ($19,704)

Source: Maddison, *Monitoring the World Economy* 1820–1992 (Paris: Organization for Economic Cooperation and Development, 1995); and IMF staff estimates.

[1]To partition the population of the 42 sample countries into income quartiles, the populations of China, India, Russia, and Mexico were split and partially allocated to different income quartiles; see specific footnotes 2 to 5. GDP per capita in constant 1990 dollars at purchasing power parities for each country and period is given in parentheses.

[2]In 1900 China's population actually filled the entire center-low-income quartile, spilling over into both neighboring quartiles. In 2000 it straddled the borderline between the two upper-income quartiles.

[3]India's population straddled the borderline between the two lowest per capita income quartiles in 2000.

[4]The population of the former USSR straddled the borderline between the two upper income quartiles in 1900.

[5]Mexico's population straddled the borderline between the two center income quartiles in 2000.

[6]Territory of the Czech and Slovak Republics.

The forces underlying these major transformations in the international monetary regime are explored in more detail in the next section. The current section looks at the relative output growth rates of major world regions during the four sub-periods of the century in order to see whether there is any systematic relationship between relative income convergence and divergence with the leading nation and the global monetary order. The relevant information, summarized in Table 5.2, provides the following stylized facts:

- During the pre-World War I classical gold standard period, the independent nations of Latin America and (especially) the territories of new European settlement were able to improve their per capita income position relative to the leading nation.[14] Africa and Asia (excluding Japan), which were largely under the control of colonial regimes and locked into unequal bilateral trade and financial relationships, lost ground in terms of relative per capita output.

- During the two world wars and the inter-war period, when international trade and capital flows collapsed, all major global regions saw per capita output decline relative to that of the United States.[15] Although this setback is clearly linked to the ravages of war for most European and Asian countries, this explanation is not applicable to Latin America, where relative incomes also declined.

- Following World War II and up to 1973, per capita output in western and southern Europe and especially Japan rose spectacularly, rapidly narrowing the gap with the United States. Eastern Europe and the Soviet Union also improved their relative positions, but by much less than the mem-

Figure 5.6. Contraction of World Trade, 1929–33
(Millions of U.S. gold dollars)

Between January 1929 and February 1933, total imports of 75 countries contracted by 69 percent. Since world prices declined during this period, the fall in volume terms, while still large, was slightly less pronounced.

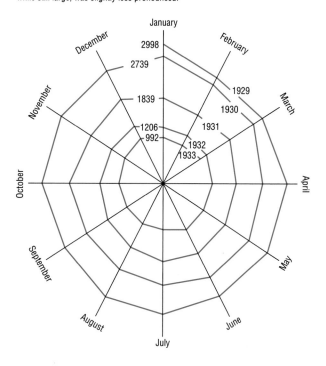

Source: Charles P. Kindleberger, *The World in Depression 1929–1933* (revised edition; Berkeley: University of California Press, 1986).

[14]The leading nation was Great Britain in 1870 and 1900, and the United States subsequently.

[15]The only exception is the Soviet Union, whose economy was already effectively cut off from the world economy before the inter-war collapse of world trade and thus was not significantly affected by it.

ber countries of the Organization for Economic Cooperation and Development (OECD). Latin America and Asia (excluding Japan and China) basically held their own, while Africa continued its relative decline.

- Following 1973, several Asian countries, including China, entered a period of very rapid growth. In contrast, Latin America and Africa lost some ground, while western Europe's catch-up came to a halt, reflecting the significant growth differential in favor of the United States in the last decade of the century. Much more ground was lost by the countries of the former Soviet Union and eastern Europe, where the contraction following the collapse of central planning in the area had not yet been fully recovered by the year 2000.

While a systematic and detailed analysis of the (inter-) relation between regional income convergence and the operation of the international monetary system has not been undertaken, the stylized facts presented above permit a number of interesting conjectures. Although periods of increasing free trade and international capital mobility ("globalization") do not guarantee convergence, they do seem to increase the convergence opportunities of those countries that are able to establish fundamental conditions favorable to economic growth and are willing to benefit from the international division of labor.[16] Conversely, administrative barriers to international trade and capital movements seem detrimental to both rapid growth in the leading economies as well as to rapid catch-up of the poorer countries. Furthermore, even star per-

[16]For example, while in the second half of the century catch-up started running into mounting difficulties in Latin America, where it was largely based on an inward-looking import substitution strategy, several Asian countries, which had adopted an outward-looking (export-oriented) development strategy, were proving increasingly successful. In most countries in sub-Saharan Africa, however, which achieved political independence only in the 1960s, economic development never took off, as the political situation remained unstable in many countries due to civil wars and military coups.

Figure 5.7. Net Flow of Foreign Investment to Developing Countries[1]
(Billions of U.S. dollars)

Net inflows of foreign investment to developing countries have grown rapidly since 1980, and flows of direct investment have been less volatile than flows of portfolio investment.

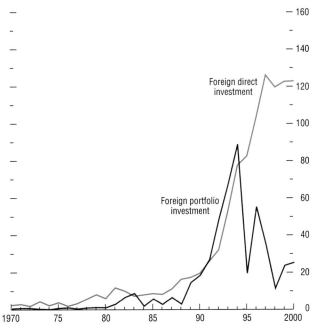

[1]Data for 2000 are IMF staff projections.

Table 5.2. Regional GDP per Capita as a Percent of Leading Nation[1]

	1870	1900	1913	1950	1973	2000
Western Europe	64.7	67.3	69.8	53.5	74.0	74.1
Areas of recent European Settlement [2]	74.8	87.6	98.7	96.7	96.8	96.5
Southern Europe (including Turkey)	34.0	34.2	33.0	21.1	36.2	36.1
Eastern Europe	33.3	29.9	31.9	27.5	34.6	15.5
Eastern Europe (excluding USSR)	35.9	35.1	38.2	23.9	30.9	13.3
USSR	31.4	26.5	28.0	29.6	36.5	16.6
Latin America	23.3	23.4	27.1	26.0	26.4	20.1
Asia	17.8	14.8	14.0	8.0	10.8	15.9
Asia (excluding Japan and China)	19.0	14.4	13.7	7.8	8.6	8.3
Japan	22.7	24.7	25.1	19.6	66.3	75.6
China	16.0	14.2	13.0	6.4	7.1	23.0
Africa	14.7	10.9	10.8	8.7	7.9	4.8
World	27.4	27.5	29.0	22.3	24.8	21.9
Memorandum: GDP Per Capita (in 1990 purchasing-power-parity dollars)						
United Kingdom	3,263	4,593	5,032	6,847	11,992	19,704
United States	2,457	4,096	5,307	9,573	16,607	27,272

Sources: Angus Maddison, *Monitoring the World Economy 1820–1992* (Paris: Organization for Economic Cooperation and Development, 1995); and IMF staff estimates.

[1]Great Britain in 1870 and 1900; the United States in 1913 and after.

[2]Australia, Canada, New Zealand, and the United States.

Note: All data up to and including 1973 are from Maddison, *Monitoring the World Economy*. The figures for the year 2000 were computed by applying growth rates of real per capita GDP at *World Economic Outlook* purchasing power parities to the Maddison GDP per capita data for 1990 (also measured in purchasing power parities).

formers over a long period can run into extended periods of stagnation or slump, either because of bad policies (the United States in the 1930s) or because they fail to adapt their institutions (Japan in the 1990s). The latter condition seems to apply even more strongly in the case of centrally planned economies. The experience of the Soviet Union suggests that while central planning allowed rapid progress at an early stage of the development process, it was unable to cope at higher levels of income, when resource allocation decisions became more complicated. Recognizing this shortcoming, China, which had adopted central planning in 1949, implemented sweeping reforms starting in the late 1970s, leading to a remarkable acceleration of output.

GDP has long dominated the discussion of economic growth and development, but it has been frequently challenged as the appropriate and most meaningful measure of economic progress. Alternative measures of development can lead to a significantly different appraisal of

convergence or divergence among national economies. For example, a comparison based on the Human Development Index (HDI), an alternative measure of progress developed by the United Nations Developmental Programme (Box 5.1), leads to different results than those based on GDP per capita (Table 5.3). One reason underlying the difference is that the HDI is more akin to an absolute indicator of poverty

Table 5.3. Dispersion of Alternative Measures of Development

Measure of Development/ Dispersion	1913	1995
GDP per capita (PPP)		
Standard deviation	1,382	6,420
Coefficient of variation	0.455	0.451
Human Development Index		
Standard deviation	0.197	0.100
Coefficient of variation	0.388	0.112

Source: Nicholas Crafts, "Globalization and Growth in the Twentieth Century," IMF Working Paper 00/44 (Washington: IMF, 2000), computed from Table 1.1.

Box 5.1. Trends in the Human Development Index

For many years, economists have used per capita real GDP as a summary measure of economic well-being, despite the many well-known caveats to using it in this way. The Human Development Index (HDI) is an alternative measure of a country's economic well-being, which has been developed under the United Nations Development Programme (UNDP).[1] It is constructed as an aggregate index of three components: education, income, and life expectancy at birth (a proxy measure for health standards), and scaled to lie within a 0 to 1 interval. The focus of the HDI is on the escape from poverty, which is defined as an HDI below 0.5. Human development is regarded as a process of expanding people's choices; income is assumed to impact on this primarily at low levels of material well-being and, above a threshold level, is considered to make a sharply diminishing contribution, the increments eventually approaching zero. Life expectancy and education are taken to be central to the enhancement of human capabilities, but are not generally dependent on private income, given the important role the public sector usually plays in their provision.

Although there are various index number problems associated with the HDI, it offers an interesting alternative perspective on development, to be considered together with the evidence on growth in real GDP per person. Long-run HDI estimates provide a comparative context in which to place recent Third World development and offer a different angle on divergence between high- and low-income countries from that which emerges from GDP per capita data.

The most striking feature is that in contrast to real GDP per capita, the 1997 HDI scores for poor developing countries are well above the 1870 scores for the leading countries at that time. Australia's score of 0.539 in 1870 would rank 134th in the world in 1997. Conversely, Mozambique's 1997 score of 0.341 (169th in the world) is distinctly above the levels achieved in some parts of Europe in 1870, for example Italy and Spain. Assuming that the HDI score of 0.055 for India in 1913 represents the lowest level at the time, the absolute HDI gap of 0.650 in 1997 between the highest and lowest HDI country scores in the world is smaller than in 1913. And since 1950 there has been a substantial reduction in the gap between the average HDI in Africa and in the advanced countries of Western Europe, North America, and Australia/New Zealand from over 0.6 to less than 0.4.[2]

Concerning the components of the HDI, the low level of life expectancy at birth in leading countries in 1870 is striking, with the highest figure at only 49.3 years, a level which has now been exceeded by the large majority of countries. Research in historical demography has concluded that, during the twentieth century, improvements in life expectancy resulting from advances in medical science and public health measures have been largely independent of changes in real income outside the leading economies.[3] The levels of life expectancy (and HDI) now enjoyed by countries like Algeria and Tunisia were simply not attainable in 1870 for any country given the state of medical technology at the time. By contrast, levels of literacy, which in 1950 were still very low in much of Africa and India, continue to compare unfavorably in many cases with those of the leading countries of 1870.

---

[1]The HDI has been described and refined in successive issues of the *Human Development Report*, published periodically by the United Nations Development Programme. For a detailed definition of the HDI, see Nicolas Crafts, "Globalization and Growth in the Twentieth Century," IMF Working Paper 00/44 (Washington: International Monetary Fund, 2000). The HDI has been quite controversial, and a useful review of various criticisms is provided in a technical note in the 1993 *Human Development Report*.

[2]The numbers quoted in this paragraph are from Crafts, "Globalization and Growth," Table 1.1 and from the UNDP, *Human Development Report*, 1999.

[3]S. H. Preston, "The Changing Relation between Mortality and Level of Economic Development," *Population Studies*, Vol. 29 (1975), pp. 231–48.

Box 5.1 *(concluded)*

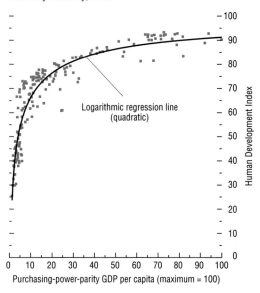

Relative Output Per Capita and Human Development Index by Country, 1997

Logarithmic regression line (quadratic)

Human Development Index

Purchasing-power-parity GDP per capita (maximum = 100)

Source: United Nations Development Program, *Human Development Report* (1999).

Regional HDI Averages[1]

	1870	1913	1950	1995
Australia/New Zealand	**0.539**	**0.784**	**0.856**	**0.933**
North America	0.462	0.729	0.864	0.945
Western Europe	0.374	0.606	0.789	0.932
Eastern Europe		0.278	0.634	0.786
Latin America		0.236	0.442	0.802
East Asia			0.306	0.746
China			0.159	0.650
South Asia		0.055	0.166	0.449
Africa			0.181	0.435
Standard deviation			0.302	0.196

Source: Crafts, "Globalization and Growth," Table 1.4.
[1]Weighted by population of countries pertaining to each region.

In contrast to the GDP per capita estimates discussed in the main text, the HDI measure shows convergence between countries (see Table 5.3). This is partly because of its heavy discounting of higher incomes and partly because it takes into account life expectancy. The diminishing contribution to the HDI from income is evident in the figure . Clearly, any index of living standards that gives a substantial weight to life expectancy will make present day developing countries look much better relative to either past or present high-income (industrial) countries than do comparisons based only on real GDP per person. This shows how important it may be not to judge progress in development by GDP alone.

The table shows the long-run HDI convergence at the level of large regional blocs—a striking contrast with developments in GDP per capita. All regions, including South Asia and Africa, exhibit significant HDI catch up with the leading countries after 1950. The averages for both South Asia and Africa in 1997 are quite near to the North American level in 1870. Indeed, all developing countries for which an estimate of HDI is possible for 1950 reduced the gap with the leading country both proportionately and absolutely between 1950 and 1997. In the period 1913 to 1950 there is catch up in HDI for both Eastern Europe (markedly) and Latin America.

Taking the change in HDI as a measure of the speed of this transition, there is an interesting contrast between the late nineteenth and twentieth centuries. The 16 countries in a state of low human development in 1870 (i.e. less than 0.5) posted an average HDI gain of 0.212 by 1913. In contrast, a more comprehensive sample comprising 48 countries with an HDI below 0.500 in 1950 had achieved an average HDI gain of 0.350 by 1995. The pace of human development has been markedly higher in the more recent period, as has been the growth of output per capita.

than to a measure of relative income.[17] The near tripling of GDP per capita in the lowest income quartile during the twentieth century implies that absolute incomes and living conditions have improved at the lower end of the income distribution as well—even if the group as a whole has seen less improvement than its counterparts in the higher income quartiles have.

Nevertheless, poverty still exists on a massive scale, not only in relative but also in absolute terms, as is documented in Chapter IV. This is because income growth within the lowest quartile has been uneven: the quartile includes countries in which per capita income has declined over long periods. Furthermore, income distribution within countries is uneven, implying that even in countries falling into the upper income quartiles, with average per capita incomes well above conventional poverty levels, a substantial number of citizens have income levels below the poverty level. Thus, using per capita GDP as an indicator clearly underestimates the problem of world poverty.[18] Finally, even though the share of poor people in the world may have declined somewhat, their absolute number has remained at a staggering level, in part because rapid population growth has been increasingly concentrated in the poorer countries.

The Role and Development of the International Monetary System

Like other major institutions, the international monetary system has undergone several radical changes in the course of the twentieth century. Some interesting parallels with a (much) earlier period or European Economic History are presented in Box 5.2. Twentieth-century development was shaped by both market forces and policy design, as policymakers repeatedly changed their priorities in trying to reconcile exchange rate stability and domestic policy objectives in an environment of variable international capital mobility. Moreover, changing perceptions concerning the role and desirability of international capital movements influenced the policies brought to bear on the system.

The classical gold standard prevailing at the start of the twentieth century is a case in point. Its resiliency has been widely commented upon. The leading industrial and commercial powers remained on gold continuously for a third of a century up to World War I. Notably, the system was uninterrupted by currency crises, even though currency crises were not uncommon at the system's periphery.[19] But those crises were less persistent, and their effects less severe, than those of the twentieth century.[20] Almost without exception, gold convertibility was restored following each crisis, generally at the previously prevailing gold price and rate of exchange.[21]

In the light of the repeated financial crises suffered in the final quarter of the twentieth century, a pertinent question is what explains the widespread political acceptance of the gold standard and its success in reconciling capital mobility with exchange rate stability. An important factor is undoubtedly the willingness and

---

[17]The marginal increases in the HDI in response to a rise in GDP per capita above a certain threshold ($5,120 in constant 1990 prices at purchasing power parties) is heavily discounted, implying that rising income levels in poor (rich) countries tend to add a lot (very little) to the HDI. This makes HDI-convergence almost inevitable as long as the poor countries' income grows in absolute terms, even if this growth is slower than that in the rich countries.

[18]Obviously, GDP per person is not the only relevant criterion for economic well-being, and a more comprehensive analysis would have to take into account additional factors like health and education (as does the HDI), as well as the preservation of the environment, hours worked, unemployment, human rights, and other factors affecting the quality of life.

[19]The gold standard had been strengthened when the United States abandoned bi-metalism in 1879, and had become all but universal with the accession of Russia and Japan toward the end of the nineteenth century. A few countries in Central and South America and Asia (notably China) did not adopt the gold standard, but they became an increasingly small minority as the period progressed.

[20]This is the finding in recent work by Michael Bordo, Barry Eichengreen, and Douglas Irwin, "Is Globalization Today Really Different Than Globalization a Hundred Years Ago?" NBER Working Paper No. 7195 (Cambridge, Massachusetts: National Bureau and Economic Research, 1999).

[21]This "resumption rule" played a major role in anchoring expectations and rendering speculative capital flows stabilizing.

Box 5.2. The Monetary System and Growth During the Commercial Revolution

There are some interesting parallels between the monetary system, globalization and growth in the twentieth century and over the period from 1100 to 1300, called the "commercial revolution" by some economic historians. These similarities serve as a reminder that underlying economic forces have operated and contributed to shaping history long before economics was recognized as a (social) science.

The commercial revolution was a period of rapid output growth, urbanization, population growth and technological innovation that transformed key parts of western Europe from an autarkic and feudal economy to a vibrant commercial one. The progress made during that period led to European economic and political hegemony of subsequent centuries. The seeds of many legal and economic institutions that prevail today were also sown back then.

One striking resemblance between the commercial revolution and the period of rapid economic growth during the gold standard era and since World War II is the performance of the monetary and financial systems. During the commercial revolution, the emerging nation states took control over issuance of coins and provided the infrastructure for the accelerating pace of interregional and international trade. The state regained monetary control by competing with private coin producers that proliferated during the eleventh century. The state prevailed because it was able to circulate a stable, reputable and therefore universally accepted medium of exchange that catered to the merchant community's demand. By 1250, gold coins were being issued and a truly international currency (the Florentine Florin) emerged. A process of regional monetary integration and an era of price stability were inaugurated.

The stability of the monetary system and rates of exchange allowed the development of banks and, in particular, bills of exchange that facilitated international transactions and contributed to the rise in trade volumes which facilitated the process of division of labor and specialization. There was also a substantial amount of foreign lending to governments. The result of these developments enabled the European periphery, most notably England, to reap the fruits of economic growth. While hard data are lacking, one can speak of a process of convergence within Europe and convergence between Europe and the more advanced regions of the world at that time—China and the Orient.

By the late of thirteenth century, growth rates started to decline and many regions descended into economic crisis.[1] Much like the reaction of states in the inter-war period and during the Great Depression, many states abandoned and others were forced to abandon stable monetary policies. Parallel to the increase in warfare, many states took recourse to inflationary finance, and monetary wars raged for almost two centuries. Foreign lending also collapsed, as did international trade credit, and the most prominent Italian banks were forced into bankruptcy. As in the 1930s, monetary disintegration and exchange rate volatility exacerbated the decline in output and delayed recovery.

[1]Historians do not agree on the reasons for this decline. Some suspect that climatic change had a significant impact, while others argue that the fall of the Crusader state and the decline in trade access to the Orient are to blame. And some think that the rapid increase in population, not matched by sustained productivity growth, sent Europe into a Malthusian trap.

---

ability of governments under the gold standard to subordinate other—mainly domestic—economic, political, and social objectives to the maintenance of gold convertibility.[22] In the late nineteenth and early twentieth centuries, pressure to direct monetary policy to other objec-

[22]This, of course, is the same factor that enables countries like Argentina and political jurisdictions like Hong Kong SAR to fix their currencies to the U.S. dollar today: they are able and willing to subordinate other objectives to the maintenance of "convertibility."

tives was minimal. There was no widely accepted theory linking monetary policy to the state of the economy. Competing policy targets were few, and central banks came under little pressure to minimize unemployment when the very concept of unemployment was unfamiliar and unionization rates were low.[23] Working class voters could not vote out of office governments that supported defending the exchange rate over and above other goals so long as the franchise remained limited to a priviledged minority, as it was until well into the twentieth century.

Another factor contributing to the positive performance of the gold standard was its smooth interaction with private markets. Investors regarded adherence to the gold standard as a "Good Housekeeping Seal of Approval."[24] Adopting it allowed countries to gain access to foreign capital more freely and on more favorable terms. And the capital flows that resulted took place in an environment of expanding trade and export-led development. The dominant use of these funds, especially in the overseas regions of recent European settlement, was for investment in infrastructure, specifically railways and port facilities, which augmented the recipient's capacity to export commodities, earn foreign exchange, and service and repay the borrowed funds.[25] Because trade was relatively free, countries seeking to export in order to earn foreign exchange and service their debts had the requisite market access.[26] And when

economic activity in Britain, the principal export market, turned down, investment was redeployed from British to foreign markets, sustaining growth in the latter. Capital flows were stabilizing because they were counter-cyclical.

Other factors contributed to this stability. The flexibility of wages and prices allowed economies to adjust without changing their exchange rates in response to internal and external shocks. The absence of major macroeconomic disturbances like those that destabilized the world economy in the 1930s limited dislocations and adjustment costs.[27] The stability of the gold standard (and of economic activity generally) in Great Britain, the nation at the center of the international monetary and financial system, buttressed stability in other countries to which Britain's finances and economy were linked. International loans in times of crisis, and in response to temporary shocks—organized by governments, central banks, or private financiers—enabled the countries at the core of this system to maintain convertibility, and protect their reputations.

This early "golden age" of world capitalism ended abruptly and irreversibly in August 1914 with the outbreak of World War I, ringing in a 35-year period of political turmoil and great economic instability and disruption. The first World War led to the suspension of the gold standard and rising price levels around the world.[28] In the case of previous major wars, the gold standard eventually had been restored after hostilities had

[23]The word "unemployment" only appeared in 1888, and the compilation of official unemployment statistics came much later.

[24]This term is borrowed from Michael Bordo, Michael Edelstein, and Hugh Rockoff, "Was Adherence to the Gold Standard a 'Good Housekeeping Seal of Approval' during the Interwar period?" NBER Working Paper No. 7186 (Cambridge, Mass.: National Bureau of Economic Research, 1999).

[25]The importance of this pattern, known as "development finance" (rather than using funds to finance government deficit spending), has been emphasized by Fishlow in his accounts of the pre-1913 world economy. See Albert Fishlow, "Lessons from the Past Capital Markets During the 19th Century and the Interwar Period," *International Organization*, Vol. 39 (Summer 1985), pp. 383–439.

[26]Britain's role as importer of last resort—the provider of an open market in distress goods for foreign debtors—has been emphasized as key to the stability of prewar capital markets by Charles P. Kindleberger, *The World in Depression 1929–1933* (revised edition; Berkeley: University of California Press, 1986).

[27]Evidence supporting this point is provided in Tamim Bayoumi and Barry Eichengreen, "The Stability of the Gold Standard and Evolution of the International Monetary System," in *Modern Perspectives on the Gold Standard,* ed. by Tamim Bayoumi, Barry Eichengreen, and Mark P. Taylor (Cambridge: Cambridge University Press, 1996).

[28]Unlike other belligerent nations, the United States never suspended internal convertibility during World War I and its immediate aftermath, but it, too, suspended gold exports (external convertibility) in 1917. It took the world depression and the concomitant financial market turbulence to finally force the United States into suspending domestic convertibility in 1933.

ceased, and this was generally expected to happen again. However, the war and its aftermath had caused enormous economic as well as political upheavals in Europe, which greatly complicated the task of restoring the gold standard to its prewar dominance. When—in the guise of the "gold exchange standard"—the system was eventually restored in the second half of the 1920s, it proved to be much less robust than it had been during the prewar period, and was unable to withstand the strains of the severe recession that commenced in 1929 in the United States and rapidly spread around the world, accelerating the reversal in the globalization process that World War I had initiated.

There are several reasons why the inter-war gold standard was more fragile than its prewar predecessor. Competing domestic policy objectives in the leading world economies diminished the credibility of their commitment to exchange rate stability, and increased reliance on foreign exchange reserves magnified the deflationary consequences of a shock to confidence. In addition, the new constellation of exchange rates established in Europe was not ideal: the British pound was overvalued, the French franc was undervalued, and a variety of other currencies were stabilized at inappropriate levels. War debt and reparation transfers strained the balances of payments of the European economies, heightening the dependence of the international system on the continued willingness of the United States to recycle its surpluses. Wages and prices adjusted less flexibly than before, reflecting the rising public provision of unemployment insurance and other relief. Finally, central bank cooperation was more difficult to arrange so long as the sour aftertaste of World War I lingered.

In addition, capital flows were less closely linked to productive investment. Two-thirds of new capital issues in London during the 1920–31 period were for governments, while the compa-

rable figure for U.S. issues was nearly 80 percent. The 1920s was a decade of budget deficits, with governments borrowing to finance public consumption and public investment of dubious value. This fiscal spending did not translate into an increase in export capacity to generate the foreign exchange needed to service and repay foreign debts. The postwar political settlement only aggravated this situation. It created new nation states, which in turn created thousands of kilometers of new national borders. These new states, forced to create tax administrations from scratch, relied on import duties for public sector revenues.

The recession that commenced in the United States in 1929, even in its early stage, was exceptionally severe. There is reason to wonder whether any system of fixed exchange rates could have survived such a pronounced downturn in the world's largest economy, its principal capital exporter, and the country at the center of the international monetary system. Although monetary policy mistakes undoubtedly contributed to the depression, it is questionable whether they can fully account for its unusual depth and duration, and its eventual spread around the world.[29] A more comprehensive explanation must include the absence of international leadership, provided earlier by the United Kingdom under the prewar gold standard. While the United Kingdom—weakened by the war—was not able to provide this leadership, the United States—which had emerged from the war as the leading world economy—was not yet willing to assume it.[30]

In 1931, the various pressures combined with the diminished credibility of the inter-war gold-exchange standard to bring the international system crashing down. Capital flows collapsed as financial market conditions grew turbulent. Different countries responded in different ways but ultimately with similar effects. Some deval-

---

[29]The argument that monetary policy errors are the major (if not only) cause for the unusually deep and protracted recession are presented in Milton Friedman and Anna J. Schwartz, *A Monetary History of the United States, 1867–1960* (Princeton, N. J.: Princeton University Press, 1963).

[30]This argument is developed in more detail in Kindleberger, *The World in Depression.*

ued quickly, while others clung to gold for as long as possible. Some slapped on capital and exchange controls, while others defaulted on their external debts. Many jacked up tariffs, while others imposed quantitative restrictions on imported goods. The result was the disintegration of the world economy, and the international monetary system was one of the casualties.

The second World War caused even more destruction than the first. But in contrast to the period in the aftermath of World War I, the dominant economic power—the United States—was willing to accept the leadership role, which no other country was in a position to assume in World War II's aftermath. Remembering the chaos and vacillation that followed the first World War, the allies began preparing for the restoration of a viable economic world order before the conflict had actually ended. These preparations culminated in the Bretton Woods agreements of 1944. Subsequently the United States confirmed its leadership role by supporting the creation of the General Agreement on Tariffs and Trade (GATT) and by jump-starting European reconstruction with a bold aid program (the Marshall Plan).

Under the Bretton Woods agreement, the U.S. dollar was to remain convertible into gold at $35 an ounce, the rate that had prevailed since 1934. Stable exchange rates were to be restored, since currency stability was considered essential to the restoration of world trade, which U.S. officials viewed as an economic and political imperative. In contrast to the classical gold standard, however, the new system involved three key innovations:

- Exchange rates, although pegged, could now be adjusted in the event of fundamental disequilibrium.

- Capital movements could be controlled by governments that wished to gain room for maneuver to address domestic problems and to avoid a replay of the inter-war experience with "destabilizing speculation."
- The International Monetary Fund was created as a way of placing international monetary cooperation at some distance from domestic politics.

Although exchange rates could be adjusted under the Bretton Woods system, realignments were relatively infrequent, entailing not much of an increase in exchange-rate flexibility compared to the "fixed" exchange rate systems that had preceded it.[31] The 1920s and 1930s had not enamored officials and others (aside from a few academic dissenters) of the merits of flexible rates. Floating in the 1930s was associated with the collapse of trade and output, although the direction of causality has not been established beyond doubt. After World War II, governments did not develop alternative monetary anchors like monetary targeting or inflation targeting. By a process of elimination, exchange-rate policy became the cornerstone of governments' entire economic strategy—the symbol of their commitment to sound and stable policies. To devalue cast doubt on that strategy and on the competence of the people in charge. And to revalue, as Germany and the Netherlands came under pressure to do, threatened the postwar social compact (which rested on an implicit agreement to pursue export-led growth) and generated strong opposition from an influential export lobby (often supported by trade unions).[32]

During the Bretton Woods period, the stability of the real economy and of exchange rates reinforced each other. The world economy was growing rapidly—by 5 percent per annum, more than

[31]There was a general realignment of European currencies in 1949 (accompanied by devaluations by the members of the sterling area and some of Britain's long-standing trading partners), designed to launch the Bretton Woods system successfully. Other realignments included the French franc devaluations of 1957, 1958, and 1969, the sterling devaluation of 1967, and the deutsche mark revaluations of 1961 and 1969. There were 69 major stepwise devaluations by (politically independent) developing countries between 1949 and 1971.

[32]The United States was not able to devalue unilaterally, as the U.S. dollar was the common reference currency. If the U.S. government raised the dollar price of gold, which was the only instrument it controlled, other governments would also raise the domestic-currency price of gold, leaving their dollar exchange rates and U.S. international competitiveness unchanged.

Figure 5.8. Capital Account Restrictions, 1950–98
(Percent of all countries)

Restrictions on capital accounts remained in effect for the majority of countries throughout the Bretton Woods period.

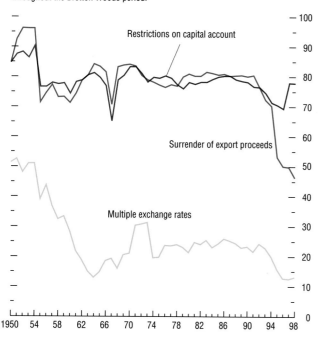

Restrictions on capital account

Surrender of export proceeds

Multiple exchange rates

1950 54 58 62 66 70 74 78 82 86 90 94 98

Source: Eichengreen and Sussman, "The International Monetary System in the (Very) Long Run," IMF Working Paper No. 00/43 (Washington: International Monetary Fund, 2000).

twice as fast as the annual rate between 1870 and 1913. This alleviated the pressure to devalue as a way of boosting growth. Commodity markets were not disturbed by large price movements, either upward as in the 1970s or downward as in the 1920s and 1930s. Wage pressures were moderate, reflecting the impact on labor markets of memories of high unemployment in the 1930s and rapid non-inflationary real wage growth, made possible by unexpectedly high productivity growth. Cyclical stability was enhanced by this combination of rapid growth and stable prices: between 1950 and 1971 there was no year in which the output growth of western Europe as a whole turned negative.

Finally, capital controls remained in place, limiting the instability from disruptive international financial flows (Figure 5.8). It was possible for a government to contemplate a change in the par value because massive amounts of capital would not immediately hemorrhage out of the country in anticipation of official action. And change in the speed with which controls were relaxed became one of the mechanisms through which governments regulated the balance of payments.[33]

However, the recovery of capital mobility in the decades following World War II ultimately proved to be one of the principal threats to the viability of this system. The progressive relaxation of the controls that had been imposed on domestic financial institutions in the 1930s and 1940s made it harder to stop capital flows at the border.[34] Financial institutions found new ways

[33]In the 1950s, members of the European Payments Union accelerated or slowed the rates at which they relaxed controls on current-account transactions in response to the development of the balance of payments. Changes in the stringency of controls substituted for exchange-rate changes as an instrument of adjustment. See the national case studies provided in Charles Wyplosz, "Financial Restraints and Liberalization in Postwar Europe" (unpublished manuscript; Graduate Institute of International Studies, University of Geneva, 1999).

[34]Financial systems in many countries emerged from World War II tightly regulated and controlled. Those controls weakened over the course of the 1950s and 1960s as memories of market instability in the 1930s faded, and postwar normalization allowed the market economy to be rebuilt.

around the remaining controls; the development of the Eurodollar market in response to the U.S. Interest Equalization Tax is a case in point. As controls became less effective, containing and adjusting to payments pressures became more difficult, since capital flows now could force the issue more quickly than before.[35] Even contemplating a change in par values was problematic, for mere rumor that devaluation was in the offing could precipitate massive capital flight. This rendered the adjustable peg less adjustable, but the countries at the center of the system were not prepared to sacrifice domestic objectives such as the pursuit of full employment in order to adjust and eliminate payments imbalances. As a result, the Bretton Woods System grew increasingly rigid and brittle.

Compounding these difficulties was the inadequacy of international reserves. The 1960s was a decade of rapid expansion in Europe, Japan, and much of the developing world. Countries needed additional international liquidity to buffer their economies from trade-related shocks and therefore sought—generally with only limited success—to run current account surpluses against the United States. Although integral to the operation of Bretton Woods, this pattern also heightened the fragility of the system, since foreign holders of dollars could "run on" U.S. gold reserves at any time. Unfortunately, the policymakers' solution to the shortage of international reserves, the creation of Special Drawing Rights, came too late to salvage the Bretton Woods System.[36]

The combination of factors that brought the Bretton Woods system ultimately to an end—despite the remarkable growth performance it had facilitated in the post-war period—was the rising international capital mobility, inadequate reserves, and diverging views on domestic policy priorities (inflation in particular) among the ma-

jor countries. Technical progress in communications technology had greatly increased the speed of transborder information and capital mobility. In these circumstances, the fixed exchange rate system implied that participating countries had to give up their independent monetary policy—and thus their control over domestic inflation. When inflation started to accelerate in the United States in the wake of easy monetary policy, effectively helping to finance the Vietnam war, countries trying to resist the spread of inflation (like Germany, Switzerland, and Japan) were experiencing destabilizing speculative capital inflows. Following various unsuccessful attempts to patch up the system, it finally collapsed in 1973 when the major economies abandoned their fixed exchange rate to the U.S. dollar and allowed their currencies to float.

The transition to flexible exchange rates was not based on a carefully prepared strategy but on decisions made under duress. Moreover, the circumstances accompanying it were not particularly conducive to a smooth transition. Shortly after the final breakdown of the Bretton Woods system, the world economy was jolted by a spectacular increase in oil prices, abruptly ending the preceding long downward trend in the real price of oil. Less conspicuous—but probably more influential in the long run—was a significant slowdown in the extraordinary rate of productivity growth experienced during the preceding "golden age." The combination of these two supply shocks initiated the hitherto unfamiliar phenomenon of "stagflation," involving a simultaneous acceleration in prices and a rise in unemployment.

Stagflation was a result of the policy response to the oil shock. Cut free from the fixed-exchange rate anchor, policymakers stepped hard on the accelerator. Monetary aggregates rose rapidly and budget deficits widened significantly

---

[35]As the British appreciated when they compared the 1967 sterling crisis with its predecessors in 1947 and 1949; see Alec Cairncross and Barry Eichengreen, *Sterling in Decline: The Devaluations of 1931,1949 and 1967* (Oxford: Blackwell, 1983).

[36]In any case, it is questionable whether the major players in the world economy were willing at the time to concede to a supranational authority the right to issue sufficient international reserves (in the form of SDRs) to overcome the rising scarcity of international reserves resulting from the rapid expansion of world trade and the basic design of the Bretton Woods system.

in the 1970s and early 1980s. Several factors help to explain why the response differed from the last time an international system of fixed rates had collapsed in the 1930s. Keynesian ideas, that fiscal and monetary policies should (and could) be used to counter unemployment, had gained considerable currency. In many countries, policies to maintain full employment were an explicit element of the postwar social compact of equity and shared growth, leaving governments little choice but to respond aggressively to the rise in unemployment.[37] Moreover, after two decades of relative stability, the fear that aggressive counter-cyclical action would excite inflation and capital flight was subdued. Finally, the widespread retention of capital controls also meant that market discipline on inflationary pressures was more limited, initially at least, than it had been four decades before.

Given that they were entering uncharted territory, it is not surprising that policymakers did not anticipate the markets' reaction. As governments responded more aggressively to rising unemployment, the markets responded more aggressively to policy. Under the fixed exchange rate system, demand stimulus was normally regarded as temporary (otherwise it would come into conflict with the exchange-rate commitment) and therefore it did not provoke sharp increases in wage demands.[38] But once that anchor was lifted, expansionary policies today simply excited fears of additional inflationary pressure tomorrow, with corresponding repercussions on wage behavior. Demand stimulus produced mainly inflation rather than additional output and employment as wages and prices responded more quickly to policy. Consequently, as governments pushed harder on their policy levers, those levers grew increasingly ineffectual.

It took the majority of industrial countries almost ten years to recognize this vicious circle

and reverse their policy approach, and close to another decade to bring the inflation and budget deficits unleashed in response to the oil crises under satisfactory control. The accelerated push toward a single market and a unified currency among member countries of what is now known as the euro area constituted a major innovation in the international monetary framework. It also provided strong incentives for—and secured ultimate success in—the restoration of monetary stability and fiscal sustainability in many European Union member countries with traditionally "weak" policies. But similar progress in the fight against high European unemployment did not (so far) materialize for reasons explored elsewhere in more detail.[39]

Given the lack of a credible anchor for the price level, exchange rates between major currencies proved much more volatile than had been anticipated when the Bretton Woods system was abandoned. And, starting in the 1980s controls on international capital movements were dismantled in many countries in pursuit of efficiency gains from deregulation. The resulting large increase in internationally mobile capital combined with domestic policy imbalances and volatile exchange rate expectations to generate repeated international financial crises.[40] Establishing a new monetary policy operating framework to replace the earlier exchange rate-centered policy regime, and designing and implementing efficient banking regulation, has occupied the international community for the better part of the last quarter century, but progress has so far been very gradual, with no universally applicable optimal solution to the problem being developed.

Lessons concerning the international monetary system are probably best understood in the context of the important insight that a pegged exchange rate, independent national monetary policy, and unrestricted international capital mo-

---

[37]*The European Economy: Growth and Crisis,* ed. by Andrea Boltho (New York: Oxford University Press, 1982).

[38]In other words, occasional recourse to demand stimulus, like temporary suspensions of convertibility under the gold standard, was stabilizing because it occurred in a framework within which a credible nominal anchor existed.

[39]See Chapter IV in the *World Economic Outlook,* May 1999: "Chronic Unemployment in the Euro-Area: Causes and Cures."

[40]See *World Economic Outlook,* October 1998, which discussed "Financial Turbulence and the World Economy."

bility cannot be achieved simultaneously. Much of the international financial system's experience in the twentieth century deals with changing government priorities regarding these objectives. Before 1914, international capital mobility was high, and countries' monetary policy was subordinated to maintaining "convertibility" and thus fixed exchange rates. In the inter-war period, pursuit of domestic stabilization objectives led most countries to abandon fixed exchange rates. Under the Bretton Woods system, pervasive capital controls allowed countries to pursue domestic policy objectives (to some extent) despite pegged exchange rates. In the final quarter of the century capital became increasingly mobile, as many countries, engaging in domestic stabilization, allowed their exchange rates to float. Changes from one set of priorities to another have usually been rather slow to develop, and pertinent organizational changes have typically been implemented only following some acute crisis.[41]

One possible explanation for this element of inertia that has characterized the international monetary system is the strong hold of the ideologies that develop in support of prevailing institutional arrangements.[42] Another is the strength of vested interests who benefit from prevailing arrangements.[43] A third possibility is the network-externality characteristic of international monetary arrangements—in particular the reluctance of countries to adopt arrangements radically different from those of their neighbors for fear of sending a negative signal to the markets. Finally, there is failure of vision: the failure of policymakers to articulate a clear and coherent alternative monetary policy operating strategy before the crisis strikes.

The international monetary turbulence of the last quarter century is arguably explicable, at least in part, in terms of this inability to adapt international monetary arrangements to changing economic, financial, and political circumstances. The collapse of Bretton Woods loosened the exchange rate constraint and cut the last remaining link to commodity money. It removed the focal point for monetary and fiscal policies. The 1970s became a decade of big budget deficits and high inflation, as policy was cut loose from its moorings. And with the failure of policymakers to articulate an alternative monetary anchor, policy grew increasingly ineffectual. Figure 5.9 illustrates the simultaneous deterioration in government budget balances, inflation, and labor market performance in the major industrial countries during the 1970s. This dismal experience led to a search for a new policy paradigm in the 1980s and 1990s. An important aspect of the new paradigm was the willingness to concede increasing autonomy to the monetary authorities in an attempt to reduce the political pressure for "easy money" and to strengthen the objective of medium-term price stability. Equally fundamentally, the new paradigm placed much greater weight on market forces while attempting to narrow the scope and change the nature of government intervention in the economy.

The Changing Role of the Public Sector

The twentieth century has witnessed significant changes in the economic role of the state. The expansion of the public sector as measured by the ratio of total public expenditure to GDP is depicted in Table 5.4. The increase was largest in the European countries, where the public ex-

[41]See the evidence in Barry Eichengreen, Paul Masson, and others, *Exit Strategies: Policy Options for Countries Seeking Greater Exchange Rate Flexibility,* IMF Occasional Paper No. 168 (Washington: International Monetary Fund, 1998). The noteworthy exception is the Bretton Woods system, which was designed with considerable foresight to rebuild a badly mauled world trading system. In combination with the GATT it has been remarkably successful in achieving this objective, notwithstanding its eventual demise.

[42]See Barry Eichengreen and Peter Temin, "The Gold Standard and the Great Depression," NBER Working Paper No. 6060 (Cambridge, Massachusetts: National Bureau of Economic Research, 1997).

[43]See Jeffrey Frieden, "Greenback, Gold and Silver: The Politics of American Exchange Rate Policy, 1870–1913," CIBER Working Paper No. 91–04 (Los Angeles: Center for International Business Education and Research, University of California, Los Angeles, 1994).

Figure 5.9. Government Deficits, Inflation, and Unemployment in the Group of Seven Countries[1]

The deterioration in governments' financial balances, inflation, and unemployment experienced by the major industrial economies in the course of the 1970s has so far been completely reversed only in the case of inflation.

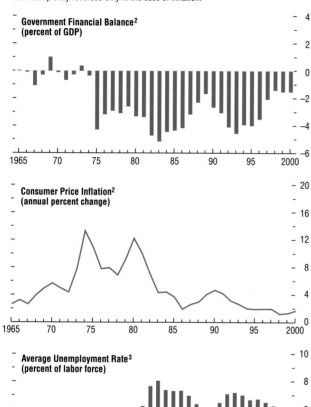

Government Financial Balance[2]
(percent of GDP)

Consumer Price Inflation[2]
(annual percent change)

Average Unemployment Rate[3]
(percent of labor force)

[1]Data for 2000 are IMF staff projections.
[2]GDP weighted average.
[3]Labor force weighted average.

Table 5.4. Public Sector Expenditure Ratios: Total and Transfers
(Percent of GDP)

	1870	1913	1960	1998
Total Outlays				
Australia	18.3	16.5	21.2	32.9
Belgium[1]		13.8	30.3	49.4
France	12.6	17.0	34.6	54.3
Germany		14.8	32.4	46.9
Italy[1]	11.9	11.1	30.1	49.1
Japan		8.3	17.5	36.9
Netherlands[1]	9.1	9.0	33.7	47.2
Norway	5.9	9.3	29.9	46.9
Sweden	5.7	10.4	31.0	58.5
United Kingdom	9.4	12.7	32.2	40.2
United States	7.3	7.5	27.0	32.8

	1880	1910	1960	1990
Social Transfers				
Australia	0.0	1.1	7.4	15.4
Belgium	0.2	0.4	13.1	29.7
France	0.5	0.8	13.4	27.8
Germany	0.5	na	18.1	21.2
Italy	0.0	0.0	13.1	24.5
Japan	0.1	0.2	4.0	16.1
Netherlands	0.3	0.4	11.7	31.7
Norway	1.1	1.2	7.9	23.0
Sweden	0.7	1.0	10.8	21.3
United Kingdom	0.9	1.4	10.2	16.8
United States	0.3	0.6	7.3	16.3

Sources: Total outlays from Vito Tanzi and Ludger Schuknecht, *The Growth of Government and the Reform of the State in Industrial Countries* (Washington: IMF, 1995) and OECD, *Economic Outlook* (Paris: Organization for Economic Cooperation and Development, 1999); social transfers, defined to include spending on pensions, welfare, unemployment compensation and health by national and local governments, from Peter H. Lindert, "The Rise of Social Spending, 1880–1930," *Explorations in Economic History*, Vol. 31 (1994), pp. 1–37; Peter H. Lindert, "What Limits Social Spending?" *Explorations in Economic History*, Vol. 33 (1996), pp 1–34; Howard Oxley and Maitland MacFarlan, "Health Care Reform: Controlling Spending and Increasing Efficiency," *OECD Economic Studies*, Vol. 24–1 (1995), pp. 7–55; OECD, *Historical Statistics 1990–1995* (Paris: Organization for Economic Cooperation and Development, 1997).
[1]Central government only through 1913.

penditure ratio to GDP has risen more than fourfold, exceeding 40 percent on average by the end of the century.[44] Although the ratio is generally lower in the poorer countries, it is much larger there today than it was in the rich countries at the start of the twentieth century. The major contribution to this remarkable in-

[44]The extent of public sector expansion, its underlying causes, and recent reforms are discussed in more detail in Vito Tanzi and Ludger Schuknecht, *The Growth of Government and the Reform of the State in Industrial Countries,* (Washington: International Monetary Fund, 1995).

crease has been the expansion of government transfer payments, closely linked to the growth of the welfare state, though most other expenditure categories have also contributed. Apart from public sector activities reflected in the budget, government intervention in the economy also increased on account of various "off-budget" activities, although this trend is more difficult to document.[45]

The Bolshevik revolution in Russia in 1917 constituted a much more radical and complete takeover of the economy by the state. The newly created Soviet Union embraced central planning to manage its economy, a socio-economic experiment setting the stage for a global ideological competition that was to dominate the better part of the century. Following World War II, the Soviet Union forcefully expanded its political influence in eastern Europe, greatly enlarging the number of countries that imposed the "Soviet model" of economic management. And in 1949, with the victory of the communist revolution, China—comprising a fifth of the world population—joined the group of countries embracing central planning.

In the western industrial countries the expansion of the public sector gathered momentum during the 1930s, following an earlier boost during World War I. Many governments sought actively to combat mounting unemployment and poverty during the depression by public works projects and welfare payments. This partly reflected the change in the political balance of power, resulting from the extension of voting rights after World War I.[46] It was also supported by the ideas of John Maynard Keynes—which rapidly gained respectability—who advocated active use of fiscal policy to combat the recession. The second World War greatly increased government claims on resources among all belligerent countries, an effect that was not entirely reversed following the war. Nationalization of "key industries" became fashionable in many European countries and newly independent ex-colonies following World War II, greatly increasing the role of the public sector as an active participant in the economy. However, the subsequent disappointing performance of these industries under government tutelage has led to widespread (re-)privatization in the last quarter of the century.

A significant cause of growth in the ratio of public expenditure to GDP, especially during the high productivity growth period following World War II, has been the "relative price effect."[47] Rapid productivity growth in the private sector and sluggish or zero (imputed) productivity growth in the public sector will tend to raise relative output prices in the latter. This will lead to an increase in the share of government expenditure if income and price elasticities in the two sectors are such as to increase real demand for their output proportionally. The effect will be the more pronounced the higher (lower) the income (price) elasticities of demand for public goods (i.e., if they are "superior goods," demand for them increases more rapidly than income).[48] The same phenomenon contributed to the expansion of the share of private services in total output.

---

[45]Prominent among off-budget activities are government loan guarantees, tax expenditures, and government ownership of commercial enterprises, the latter entering the budget usually only in the form of net profit figures.

[46]An econometric study of the growth of social transfers reported in Lindert found that the most important influences through 1930 were the extension of the electoral franchise, which in some countries profoundly altered the identity of the median voter, and the aging of the population. For the 1960s to the 1980s, when democracy was already mature, population age structure was by far the dominant factor in explaining the rise of social spending over time; see P. H. Lindert, "The Rise of Social Spending, 1880–1930," *Explorations in Economic History*, Vol. 31 (1994), pp. 1–37, and P. H. Lindert, "What Limits Social Spending?" *Explorations in Economic History*, Vol. 33 (1996), pp. 1–34.

[47]The importance of this effect was first pointed out by William J. Baumol, "Macroeconomics of Unbalanced Growth: the Anatomy of Urban Crisis," *American Economic Review*, Vol. 57 (1967), pp. 415–426.

[48]Supporting evidence for this hypothesis, also known as "Wagner's law," is presented by Lindert, "The Rise of Social Spending" and "What Limits Social Spending?" The relative price effect has been shown to be important in accounting for the rise in government expenditure shares in the areas of education, health care, and general government services; see Peter Saunders and Friedrich Klau, "The Role of the Public Sector," *OECD Economic Studies*, special issue (Spring 1985).

Most of the expansion of the public sector during the twentieth century can, however, be explained by the government taking on entirely new tasks, which it had not previously pursued.[49] Prominent among these are the various components of social insurance, including income redistribution. And a significant expansion in the government provision of (especially higher) education has also taken place. Unlike the steady upward trend in government expenditures and taxation, the trend in government regulation has been mixed. On the one hand there has been a gradual net increase in domestic regulation concerning predominantly labor markets and consumer and environmental protection. In the second half of the century, however, significant liberalization took place in the areas of international trade (in the framework of the General Agreement on Tariffs and Trade) and domestic as well as international capital markets, reversing the highly protectionist policies that had been put in place during the inter-war period. Finally, the twentieth century also witnessed the birth of demand management policies; while these do not necessarily increase the average level of government activity, they certainly constitute a major government involvement in economic management.

Although there has been much political rhetoric during the final quarter of the century about the desire to scale back the public sector, in no country outside the former Soviet Bloc has the public sector expenditure ratio been reduced by anywhere near the amount of its increase following World War II. In contrast, government involvement in the economy has been drastically cut back in the countries comprising the former Soviet Union and eastern Europe, where central planning was abandoned with the collapse of the Soviet empire. These countries are currently in the process of rebuilding their economies, largely to rely on market forces. The change has been less abrupt in China, which started reforming its centrally planned economy in the late 1970s by opening the door to private initiative (importantly, including foreign private investment) and stressing economic incentives.

Indeed, arguably the most important lesson from twentieth-century economic history is the failure of central planning. While this observation seems almost trivial in retrospect, it should be remembered that during the third quarter of the century close to half the world population was living in countries with centrally planned economies, and in the 1960s the capitalist market economies were under serious political attack from left wing radicals and many intellectuals.[50] The "attraction of a planned and directed economic system" (Hayek), especially among intellectuals at the time, was not only based on miscellaneous shortcomings of real world alternatives, but also on excessive optimism concerning governments' ability to predict the future, know the present, and improve on market-determined outcomes, as well as on the utopian belief that human nature can be "perfected."

Central planning eventually failed on economic criteria because of its refusal (and inability) to exploit the capability of well-functioning and contestable markets to generate valuable information to guide resource allocation and—through competition among decentralized decision units—exert continuous pressure on producers to raise efficiency and to innovate. The advantages of decentralized information processing and decision making in resource allocation became increasingly important as technical progress accelerated, requiring an ever faster

---

[49]The trend had been initiated in Germany in 1883 with the introduction of workers' sickness insurance and old age pensions under the conservative government of Bismarck. It spread among other European governments and beyond only in the twentieth century.

[50]For an analysis of the popularity of anti-market sentiments among intellectuals, see Friedrich A. Hayek, *The Intellectuals and Socialism* (London: The Institute of Economic Affairs, 1998, reprint). It is interesting to note that Hayek's main argument against central planning (or more generally "socialism") was not based on the greater efficiency or productivity of "capitalism," but on its potential to enhance or preserve personal freedom and liberty.

response by firms to stay competitive.[51] It also made economies much more resilient to large external shocks like big changes in raw material prices and exchange rates, by endowing them with superior flexibility to adapt to changing circumstances.

Still, central planning was pursued for some 70 years in the Soviet Union and for over a generation in many other countries. Why did it take so long for its shortcomings to be recognized? One reason is that, at the initial stage of development, it did succeed in delivering impressive growth rates and in mobilizing resources for development. In the case of Russia and China, at the outset predominantly agrarian economies where the majority of citizens were illiterate, the transformation to an industrialized and educated society was achieved roughly within a generation. However, once these economies entered intermediate or higher stages of development and resource allocation choices became more complicated, the system was unable to cope. It also had difficulties dealing with accelerating technological change and other types of exogenous shocks.

The advantages of competitive markets in raising economic efficiency and stimulating innovation are now generally recognized, and most countries attempt to harness them in their effort to promote growth. However, as the example of the economies in transition demonstrates, well-functioning contestable markets do not appear spontaneously, but require an elaborate social infrastructure and robust institutions preventing the abuse of market power. The lesson here is that there is an essential role for the government to create conditions that allow markets to develop, to function orderly and efficiently, and to

remain contestable. Foremost among these conditions is the establishment of clear property rights (covering both individuals and corporations, and including effective rules on how to transfer property and resolve bankruptcies), and institutions that secure the equitable "rule of law" for all citizens, comprising an independent judiciary system and objective and effective law enforcement to back it up. These requirements can be met only with stable political systems, explaining the importance of the latter, repeatedly confirmed in empirical analysis of the success (or lack of it) in economic development (see Chapter IV).

Even where the pertinent social infrastructure is in place (including sound financial policies and institutions), free markets may fail to produce efficient outcomes due to a number of market imperfections. Prominent among these are costly and asymmetric information, market power due to economies of scale ("natural monopolies"), and externalities of various types. In principle, such market imperfections provide opportunities for government intervention to improve on market outcomes. The appropriate type of intervention—taxation, regulation, or government provision of output—cannot be determined in the abstract, however. It requires a detailed analysis of the issue under consideration, including the knowledge of available technology, since changes in the latter may alter the nature of scale economies and the feasibility of internalizing various externalities.[52]

Mounting concerns about market failures has probably been one of the major reasons behind the increased government intervention observed during much of the twentieth century. But an important lesson learned in this context is that

[51]At an early stage of the rapid development of large-scale computers, it had been assumed by some that this would tilt the balance in favor of central planning by greatly speeding up data processing. This ignored the fact that it would do so for decentralized decision makers as well, and that by greatly accelerating structural change both overall and within firms it would actually favor decentralized decision making.

[52]A particular manifestation of market failure occurs in the operation of utilities. The network dependence in providing the related services has long been considered the reason why they constitute natural monopolies, either to be regulated by the government (the United States solution) or to be operated by the public sector (the European approach). Similar differences can be observed (to some degree) in other network industries. Changing technology can, however, change the borderline between natural monopolies and contestable markets, influencing the optimal scope of government involvement in the economy, including recent moves to generate competition in some networked services.

there is not only market failure but also government failure.[53] This has implications for the feasibility of government corrective action. Market failure alone is not a sufficient condition for justifying government intervention; it must also be shown that the government is indeed capable of remedying the identified shortcoming, and that its intervention results in a net increase in social welfare. Where the borderline between efficient (i.e., welfare raising) and inefficient government intervention actually lies remains very much a bone of contention, not least because in many cases such intervention also has important distributive implications.

While efforts to correct for market imperfections explain much of the twentieth-century increase in government regulation, the significant increase in the ratio of government expenditure to total output is (apart from the relative price effect discussed above) mainly accounted for by the emergence of the government as provider of social insurance and its effort to redistribute income through the tax/transfer system. The rationale for government involvement in various social insurance programs (including health insurance) has usually been based on arguments of market failure (moral hazard and adverse selection) preventing private insurance markets from operating properly or at all.[54] In contrast, income redistribution is mainly based on normative objectives. The practical implementation of the various programs has often lead to unexpected negative side effects, including inefficiency and abuse. Rising recognition of these problems has, in turn, triggered periodic efforts to reform existing programs.

Though virtually all (advanced) economies now accept in principle some government role in social insurance and income redistribution,

the extent to which such services are provided in different countries differs widely. For example, transfer payments (and therefore taxes) are much higher in many European countries than in the United States and Japan. This may well be efficient if the degree of government intervention reflects different national tastes and preferences: the optimal degree of redistribution and provision of social insurance is largely a value judgment and cannot be decided on the basis of positive economics. A resulting issue that nevertheless concerns all countries is how to provide the desired redistribution and social insurance with minimal negative effects on incentives and efficiency; this remains very much a subject of both political debate and economic research.[55] Another issue of rising importance is the extent to which the rapidly increasing mobility of capital and highly skilled labor will limit countries' ability to impose taxes to finance the social insurance and income redistribution schemes of their choice.

Two areas where government involvement seems to be highly beneficial and probably indispensable in fostering economic development is infrastructure investment and (basic) education. In both these cases, government involvement is justified on the basis of important positive externalities, which implies that too little would be supplied if provision were left entirely to the private market. Transport and communications infrastructure has a close link to the development and proper functioning of markets, while basic education is important in enabling people to exploit the opportunities for gainful activity that markets provide.

The government's role in providing the social, physical, and institutional infrastructure that allows competitive markets to function and in ad-

---

[53]The reasons for this are developed in public choice theory; see Hugh Stretton and Lionel Orchard, *Public Goods, Public Enterprise, Public Choice: Theoretical Foundations of the Contemporary Attack on Government* (New York: St. Martin's Press, 1994).

[54]These programs in general have also been popular with the electorate, reflecting a genuine voter demand for social insurance. It is possible, however, that this voter demand is biased upward because of the failure to relate the program to its full costs, giving the illusion of a "free" (or cheap) service.

[55]Many recent reforms in this area are based on the experience that mixing the social insurance function with income distribution objectives, as is usually the case with government programs, reduces transparency and exacerbates negative incentive effects.

dressing market imperfections has long been recognized.[56] In contrast, the government's role in smoothing cyclical fluctuations has a relatively short history and is controversial. "Stabilization policies" and "macroeconomics" are innovations of the twentieth century in reaction to the perceived lack of stability of the market economy.[57] The idea of an active government role in stabilizing the business cycle by employing fiscal policy, born during the inter-war depression, had gained general acceptance by the mid-1960s among academics and politicians alike. The subsequent performance of fiscal stabilization policies, however, fell distinctly short of expectations.

The difficulties of diagnosing the cyclical situation correctly, and of implementing fiscal measures at the right time, proved substantial. Another impediment to successful demand management has been politicians' inability to use it symmetrically. Although eager to use expansionary measures in times of (actual or alleged) recession, governments were, and remain, very reluctant to apply contractionary policies during a boom. The result has been a severe inflationary bias in fiscal policy, resulting in an unprecedented peacetime increase in both government debt and the price level in the second half of the twentieth century. Moreover, the idea of being able to "fine tune" the economy has been increasingly questioned, especially with respect to fiscal policy. However, the operation of built-in stabilizers is widely recognized and generally welcome. In combination with the increased size of the government sector and the active pursuit of counter-cyclical monetary policies, built-in stabi-

lizers probably contribute to the fact that cyclical fluctuations in modern ("mixed") economies tend to be less violent than they had been in nineteenth-century laissez-faire economies.

Returning to the importance of institutions, a stable medium of exchange ("money") is an essential prerequisite for well-functioning markets. The quest for stable money and the appropriate institutions to support it was an important part of twentieth-century economic history and is likely to continue into the twenty-first century.[58] This quest faces three major difficulties:

- Rapid technical change and innovation in financial markets tend to make the appropriate system a moving target, requiring frequent modifications and corrections in pertinent government regulation.
- The crucial role of banks in the operation of financial markets and getting the "right" degree and type of bank regulation.
- Political interference with the state monopoly of issuing the official currency make any system based on fiat money vulnerable to abuse in pursuit of short-term political objectives.[59]

The current thinking on the issue, developed during the painful experience of a quarter century of high inflation, is that an independent (from direct political influence) central bank, with clearly defined responsibilities and accountability, and a carefully supervised and regulated banking system are most likely to meet the stable money objective.[60] In some cases, countries have adopted currency boards to strengthen the credibility of their commitment to stable money.[61]

[56]The principle insights go back to Adam Smith, *An Inquiry into the Nature and Causes of the Wealth of Nations*, originally published in 1776.

[57]One source of this instability may be the greater economic interdependence due to increased specialization; another cause may be reduced flexibility in prices and wages, which has diminished the self-adjustment capacity of the market economy. And ill-conceived government intervention, some would note, can also be a source of instability.

[58]Hopes that strict monetary targeting would create financial stability proved overoptimistic, not having taken into account the lack of stability in the money demand function and the difficulty of identifying a reliable money concept under conditions of rapid financial innovation.

[59]One of the advantages of commodity money (and an explanation of its popularity) may have been the fact that it protects the currency from political interference—even though history has shown that this protection is not necessarily absolute; see Eichengreen and Sussman, "The International Monetary System."

[60]The fiscal system also enters the picture because persistent large fiscal deficits will sooner or later lead to monetary financing and thus threaten the stability of the national currency.

[61]These include Argentina, Estonia, and Hong Kong SAR.

And some countries have actually gone so far as to abdicate their sovereign right to issue money and have adopted a supra-national currency to meet that need.

In the 1980s and 1990s, alternative operating strategies—monetary targeting, inflation targeting, "two pillar" systems of both inflation and monetary targets, and "Taylor rules" including inflation and the output gap—were adopted in response to the instabilities and excesses of the 1970s. But the spread of these institutional and conceptual developments has been slow and halting. As these alternatives continue to spread from the advanced industrial countries to the developing world, there may be reason to hope that confidence will grow and that some causes of turbulence in currency markets will die down. With the further advance of globalization, however, volatility in financial markets, including exchange rates, will probably continue.

In addition, the democratization of the Third World—while highly desirable in its own right—has highlighted the conflict between internal and external objectives that has been a source of tension in the First and Second Worlds for the better part of a century. Now that those primarily affected by unemployment and distributive policies can make their priorities count via the ballot box, it has become harder for governments to subordinate all other goals of policy to stabilizing the exchange rate. As exchange rate policy has come into conflict with other priorities, it has lost credibility. But as they gain experience with democracy, a growing number of societies appear to be concluding that the politicization of economic policymaking can entail serious costs in cases where governments' behavior is opportunistic. Societies have responded to this risk with institutional reforms—for example, strengthening the independence of their central banks and adopting fiscal rules (the Growth and Stability Pact in western Europe, the Fiscal Convertibility Law in Argentina)—in the attempt to better insulate policy and the foreign exchange market from day-to-day political pressures. Another example is the currency board, an alternative to floating exchange rates that appears to be gaining adherents, which is, in a sense, a return to the gold-standard-style arrangements of previous centuries.

Some Global Challenges Ahead

Notwithstanding the astonishing achievements of the world economy in the twentieth century, economic policymakers around the world will continue to be challenged to meet the aspirations of their electorates and to adjust continuously to the changing economic environment to do so effectively. Most of these challenges will be posed by the domestic economy, concerning the optimal utilization of national resources—importantly, including the achievement of full employment—growth, and a "just" distribution of income (however each nation may define it). Some of the challenges will, however, transcend national borders, given the increasing interdependence of the world economy; this section will highlight three of them.

From a global perspective, the major failure of economic management in the twentieth century also defines the greatest policy challenge for the future: to raise the productive capacity and incomes of the fifth of the world population (some one billion people), who remain in the grip of absolute poverty, and whose command of goods and services has hardly increased, even though they have benefited from global progress in the medical sciences through the reduction in morbidity and mortality rates.[62] The policies required to work toward raising the incomes of the world's poor are outlined in some detail in Chapter IV. Based on the policy lessons discussed above, the essential condition for success would seem to be the capacity of the countries concerned to create the social institutions and stable and secure environment that permit and motivate their citizens to pursue gainful activities

[62]However, in some of the poorest countries the secular trend toward lower morbidity and higher life expectancy has recently been reversed as a result of the spreading AIDS epidemic.

and plan for their future. While building this social infrastructure must remain the responsibility of the national authorities and the citizens they represent, a growing body of evidence and expertise has been accumulated by governments, public and private think tanks, nongovernmental organizations, and international organizations (including the international financial institutions) to assist them in this formidable task. Drawing the appropriate implications and lessons from this evidence and experience may be as essential a contribution to sustainable development of the poorest nations as access to external savings. But these lessons cannot be forced on an unreceptive government or population, and this may indeed constitute the most serious obstacle to rapid improvements in the near term in several cases.

A second challenge is to strengthen and expand the open world trading and financial system and reduce its potential for disruption. Twentieth-century experience has shown that international trade and capital movements are essential to realize the vast potential benefits of global division of labor and to accelerate the diffusion of technology. But it has also shown that the resulting interdependence of national economies can lead to rapid propagation of adverse shocks that may seriously set back even well-managed economies. And large amounts of internationally mobile capital combined with domestic policy imbalances and volatile exchange rate expectations can generate serious international financial crises. However, retreat from globalization is no solution as shown by the inter-war experience, which led to a prolonged disruption in international trade, capital movements and technology diffusion, with

detrimental effects for output growth in poor and rich countries alike. Strengthening the network of international trade and capital flows and making it less vulnerable to sudden disruption require both skilled economic management at home as well as international economic cooperation, including a useful and constructive role of the various international financial institutions. Last but not least, to be durable, it requires political leadership that is willing and able to explain the advantages of the system to the electorate at large and to prevent special interest groups from gaining exceptional treatment, undermining the principles of free trade.

A third global concern is that success in promoting economic growth and international trade may lead to increasing pressure on finite global resources and the environment.[63] The corresponding challenge is to make economic development "sustainable," defined as meeting the needs of the present without compromising those of future generations.[64] Uncontrolled population growth was for a long time considered a major threat to sustainability, but more recent demographic data and global population projections suggest that this threat is declining.[65] Even if the world population stabilizes, the use of nonrenewable and finite resources (like fossil fuels and minerals) may pose a problem for sustainability. Optimistic observers maintain that steady technological progress and the substitutability between materials and processes will overcome the limits of nonrenewable resources, permitting not only sustainability but even perpetual growth in output and consumption.[66]

This maxim seems to have been valid since the start of the industrial revolution. However, there is no guarantee it will hold indefinitely, and an

---

[63]Many of the problems of resource waste and environmental degradation stem from ill-defined property rights and the resulting absence or distortion of market signals. At a local level, many pollution problems can and have been successfully addressed from this angle.

[64]World Commission on Environment and Development, *Our Common Future* (The Brundtland Report), (Oxford: Oxford University Press, 1988).

[65]The concerns go back to the eighteenth century and Malthus. However in 1997, 51 countries, comprising 44 percent of the world population, had fertility rates below the replacement level of 2.1 children per woman in child-bearing age, and fertility rates in the majority of other countries were on a steep downward trend (Figure 1.3).

[66]Julian Simon, *The Ultimate Resource* (Princeton, N.J.: Princeton University Press, 1996)

overly complacent attitude toward the issue of sustainability risks being dangerous. The problem is greatly complicated by intrinsic future uncertainty. It also involves important questions of how to value the existing stock of environmental assets and of comparing the welfare of different generations.[67] Climate change, preservation of bio-diversity, and the use of nuclear energy (and disposal of resulting radioactive waste) are just a few examples of the pressing policy issues involved. The fact that few decisive actions have been taken (so far) in any of these areas is less a reflection of technical or political inability to act than of uncertainty and disagreement about the precise mechanisms and trade-offs involved.[68] Under these conditions, acquisition of better information and knowledge ought to be a policy priority, while balancing the cost of preliminary preventative action against the risk of future damage resulting from non-action.

[67]See the discussion in Geoffrey M. Heal, "Interpreting Sustainability," Paine Webber Working Paper Series in Money, Economics and Finance, Columbia University Business School, PW-94-24 (1995).

[68]The Montreal Protocol to ban chemicals that cause stratospheric ozone depletion ("ozone holes") shows that swift international action is possible, once there is agreement on the facts.

Directors warmly welcomed the rapid recovery in the world economy in 1999, and the prospect of even stronger growth in 2000. Global economic and financial conditions have improved dramatically during the past year, with growth picking up in almost all regions of the world. Directors noted that the remarkable strength of the U.S. economy and the robust growth now apparent in western Europe have provided key support for faster than expected recoveries in Asia, Latin America, and other emerging market regions. Determined actions by policymakers in the crisis-affected countries to deepen adjustment and reform efforts, together with support from the international community, have also been important. Directors considered that, at least in the near term, risks for global growth may well be on the upside.

At the same time, Directors expressed some concern about the potential for a correction of highly valued stock prices around the world (especially in the technology and information sectors), the mixed signals regarding economic recovery in Japan, the vulnerabilities still present in emerging market regions, and the possibility that growing global economic and financial imbalances could, if unchecked, lead to significant future disruptions in world growth. A sustained pickup in domestic demand in western Europe and Japan, together with some slowing of growth in the United States, will help achieve a more balanced pattern of growth among the major industrial countries. Several Directors also commented on additional uncertainties arising from the recent increases in oil prices. In view of these concerns, and notwithstanding the overall improvement in the global economic situation, Directors agreed that policymakers worldwide face important but widely varying challenges. They noted that, in some countries, macroeconomic policies need to be directed toward pro-

viding ongoing support for recovery while, elsewhere, further firming in the macroeconomic stance is probably needed to reduce risks of overheating. More broadly, prospects for sustained growth in almost all developing countries, and many advanced economies, would be enhanced by more vigorous and wide-ranging structural reforms.

Developments in the Major Currency Areas

In considering recent and prospective developments in the United States, Directors noted that there are few signs of economic activity slowing despite several interest rate increases by the Federal Reserve and, indeed, growth appears to have accelerated toward the end of 1999. They suggested that the combination of strong investment and productivity growth, subdued wage pressures, and ongoing low inflation resulting from fundamental changes in the economy has raised its potential growth rate. Nevertheless, many Directors expressed concern about rising internal and external imbalances in the economy that have accompanied the prolonged expansion. These imbalances include a record-high current account deficit, the strongly negative level of net private saving, and the high level of stock market valuations, even given the recent volatility in, and divergences between, major indices. Directors recognized the central role that U.S. demand has played in supporting recovery worldwide, as well as the importance of the strong domestic investment climate and increases in national saving in the evolution of the current account. However, many Directors agreed that some further firming in U.S. interest rates would probably be unavoidable in the coming months, especially in the absence of clearer signs of a moderation in growth of demand. They argued that such a strategy would improve the prospects for a "soft landing" in the economy, whereas a delayed response could increase the risk of a further buildup of the imbalances and a subsequent "hard landing". A more balanced pattern of global growth would also make an important contribution to reducing the U.S. external deficit.

Some Directors noted, however, that further increases in U.S. interest rates could set back the prospects for sustained recovery in some key emerging market economies, notably among the Latin American countries that face significant external financing requirements in the coming years. These Directors, therefore, advocated a cautious approach to further monetary tightening, and considered that, alternatively, reliance on further fiscal consolidation to slow the growth of domestic demand would avoid the risk of spillover effects on world capital markets of continued increases in U.S. interest rates. They recognized, however, that implementing further fiscal tightening with a budget already in surplus could prove politically difficult.

More generally on fiscal policy in the United States, Directors agreed that further fiscal stimulus, whether through substantial tax cuts or expenditure increases, would be particularly dangerous under current circumstances. Instead, they argued that the welcome increases in public saving should be largely assigned to reducing debt and meeting the longer-term fiscal requirements associated with an aging population.

Turning to Japan, Directors agreed that recent economic indicators provide unclear signals regarding prospects for recovery. The just-released data on fourth quarter GDP, along with trends in household spending, confirm that real activity has again weakened following the short-lived upturn in the first half of 1999, while the latest index of leading indicators provides scope for more optimism about the economic outlook.

Most Directors considered that a strong, self-sustaining recovery in Japan led by private domestic demand still appears to be some distance away, and that supportive macroeconomic policies should therefore be maintained. Directors agreed that the zero interest policy remains ap-

propriate for monetary policy, with several suggesting that the monetary authorities would need to consider further measures to ease monetary conditions, this being all the more important if the yen were again to appreciate. Some Directors also considered that the introduction of an inflation targeting framework could help improve the monetary framework. Most Directors believed that fiscal policy also needs to provide continued support for recovery. However, a number of Directors suggested that the focus of fiscal policy should soon start moving toward consolidation given the rapid rise in public debt, pressures on longer-term interest rates, and the need to tackle approaching fiscal pressures from public pension arrangements. In this connection, several Directors expressed concern about the efficacy of successive fiscal packages to strengthen consumer and business confidence and put the economy on a path of self-sustained growth. Some Directors suggested that accommodative macroeconomic policies might have reduced pressures for structural reforms in some sectors. All Directors underscored the crucial role of structural reforms in boosting confidence and thereby enhancing the efficacy of macroeconomic policies, noting also that—with zero interest rates and high levels of public debt—the scope for continued expansionary macroeconomic policies might be reaching its limits. Against this background, Directors expressed concern about recent delays in the implementation of some important structural reforms, and what they perceived as a weakening of other initiatives. They believed that, while structural adjustment could have a downside impact on some sectors, this would be more than offset over time by the broader-based improvements in confidence and activity that would follow from measures to liberalize domestic markets, strengthen the financial system, and address other structural weaknesses.

Directors welcomed the pickup in confidence and activity in the euro area. They noted, in particular, the recent improvements in economic performance of the largest economies in the region, but observed that growth remains substantially more dynamic among several of the smaller countries. In view of these differences, Directors agreed that fiscal policy would need to play a central role in moderating risks of overheating among the fast-growing economies, even though such fiscal adjustments may be politically difficult in view of the emergence of budget surpluses in some of these countries. They also pointed out that a broad program of fiscal reforms is required in most euro-area economies in order to reduce current and longer-term expenditure pressures and provide greater scope for tax relief. Directors argued that the recovery in activity now under way provides an important opportunity for euro-area countries to push ahead with fiscal reforms and with complementary structural adjustment measures, especially in labor and product markets, that are needed to support sustained recovery. While all Directors agreed that monetary policy should continue to focus on maintaining low inflation, some thought that monetary conditions should remain generally supportive of recovery in view of the substantial slack still evident in the region. Some other Directors, however, suggested that a firming in monetary conditions could be expected in the year ahead, given the risk of price pressures—including in asset markets—developing in some countries.

Asset Prices

In their consideration of economic developments in the advanced countries, Directors gave particular attention to recent trends in asset prices. They noted that asset price inflation was a general concern, encompassing the United States, much of western Europe, and many emerging market economies. High asset prices pose a formidable challenge for macroeconomic policy in the current environment of low inflation in goods and services markets. On the one hand, given the practical difficulties in determining the equilibrium value of asset prices and the fact that they are traded in relatively efficient markets, Directors noted that it would be unsuitable for macroeconomic policy to try to target those prices. On the other hand, as rapid and prolonged buildups in asset prices may exacerbate inflationary pressures and threaten financial stability through their impact on aggregate demand and domestic credit, it is clear that asset price developments can be a matter of serious concern for central banks. Directors agreed that, to the extent asset prices provide valuable information about future developments in economic activity and inflation, such information should be taken into account in the existing inflation and monetary targeting frameworks—but that prices of goods and services should remain the policy target. While agreeing that targeting asset prices should not become a permanent policy goal, some Directors considered that there may be instances in which macroeconomic policy should "lean against the wind" and try to stem financial market excesses, even though inflation in goods and service markets remains quiescent—although they recognized the practical difficulties in determining when and to what extent such a policy should be implemented. Several Directors also saw a role for regulatory and prudential policies in containing asset price inflation and volatility.

In the United States, Directors noted that, despite some uncertainty, many valuation analyses point to some degree of overvaluation in key broad indices. Several Directors commented on the particularly high valuations that have emerged in the information technology sector. In light of evidence that wealth effects stemming from the stock market may be a contributing factor in fueling growth of domestic demand well in excess of increases in potential output, Directors considered that the recent steps to tighten monetary conditions have been appropriate—although the need for further tightening will have to be kept under close review.

Regarding the euro area, Directors agreed that the main challenge for macroeconomic policy arising from aggregate asset price movements remains the magnitude of regional divergences, with property prices, in particular, rising far more rapidly in some of the fast growing euro-area countries in the periphery than in the region as a whole. Directors noted that, while faster growth in the periphery can, at least in part, be justified by the process of regional convergence in incomes associated with economic integration and the introduction of the euro, the potentially significant impact of asset price corrections on financial conditions in some small European countries poses a challenge to the conduct of monetary policy.

Prospects for Emerging Markets

Turning to economic developments in Asia, Directors welcomed the rapid recovery in the crisis-affected countries and the projections of continued strong growth. They noted that rising exports have played a key role in this recovery, adding to the support provided from public spending and, more recently, from private domestic demand. Directors agreed that fiscal stimulus should be steadily withdrawn as growth becomes self-sustaining. Indeed, several Directors suggested that in the countries most advanced in recovery, macroeconomic policies should now be focused on reducing risks of overheating and containing the growth in public debt. Directors urged the crisis-affected countries to maintain the momentum of structural reforms, especially in the financial and corporate sectors as well as in the underlying institutional and prudential framework, and cautioned that the current recoveries could prove to be short-lived if these reform efforts were relaxed. They agreed that, in order to maintain the current robust rates of growth in China and India, further structural reforms are needed, including further measures to strengthen the banking sector and restructure state-owned enterprises in China, and greater efforts to reduce the budget deficit and public sector subsidies in India.

Directors noted that, in Latin America as a whole, the downturn in 1999 had turned out to be milder than expected owing to the sustained pursuit of prudent macroeconomic and structural policies, although several countries had experienced severe recessions. They concurred with projections indicating that a broader-based

recovery should emerge this year and continue into the next. Directors observed that several factors are contributing to the general improvement in regional economic conditions, including strong growth in the United States, rising commodity prices, and declining inflation and interest rates. Nevertheless, several Directors pointed out that the renewed optimism regarding the region's economic prospects needs to be tempered by concerns about remaining vulnerabilities—especially the high external financing requirements faced by the largest countries and persistent weaknesses in some of the smaller economies. Directors urged that the countries concerned continue with the steps they are taking to reduce the attendant risks and maintain the confidence of international investors. They agreed that key measures in this regard include: sustainable reductions in fiscal deficits, where further progress is expected in 2000; the implementation of monetary policy frameworks intended to help countries achieve or maintain low inflation; and, to support these objectives, further structural and institutional reforms, including greater trade liberalization. Directors also emphasized the importance of increasing public and private domestic saving to help reduce reliance on foreign financing.

Directors welcomed the rapid turnaround in Russia's economic performance in 1999, but noted that the prospects for a sustained recovery remain uncertain. They observed that the reductions in Russia's fiscal and external imbalances in 1999 are largely attributable to higher oil prices, with import compression and substitution also contributing to recent growth. Directors agreed that a firm and wide-ranging reform effort is needed in order to improve the investment climate and medium-term growth prospects. Priority needs to be given to strengthening the institutions and processes that underpin market economies, including improvements in the legal framework, competition policy, transparency, and governance. Such reforms would enhance efforts being made to tackle key structural weaknesses in the economy, particularly in the tax regime, the banking system, and in many parts of the corporate sector.

Directors agreed that economic conditions are generally strong among the central and eastern European transition economies participating in the European Union (EU) accession process. Growth is expected to pick up in all of these countries in 2000, helped in most cases by growing exports to western Europe and stronger investor confidence. They concurred, however, that further progress with structural adjustment would be needed to support sustained improvements in economic prospects and to prepare these countries more fully for eventual EU membership. In some countries, more rapid progress with fiscal consolidation would also be desirable as growth strengthens in order to reduce pressures on inflation and interest rates.

Directors noted that, for most countries in the Middle East and several in Africa, the recent increase in international oil prices has contributed to substantial improvements in fiscal positions, current account balances, and other dimensions of economic performance. Increases in some non-oil commodity prices, such as metals, were also supporting external earnings growth in several African countries, although low prices for other products (such as tea, coffee, and cotton), combined with adverse weather conditions (particularly in Mozambique), have slowed growth prospects elsewhere. In this regard, Directors agreed on the importance of continued economic diversification in order to reduce these countries' vulnerability to swings in the prices and volumes of commodity exports. They were encouraged that substantial progress has been made in these regions, including among many of the smaller countries in Africa, in laying the groundwork for broader-based growth. In view of the economic and social challenges that remain, Directors agreed that these reform efforts need to be expanded, in order to make substantial inroads on poverty and to provide a more favorable environment for economic development.

Poverty Alleviation

Directors welcomed the analysis of poverty and poverty alleviation in the *World Economic Outlook*, and reiterated their commitment to policies aimed at raising the living standards of the least well-off. They stressed that poverty today remains far too prevalent, and represents an unacceptable level of human suffering and a squandering of human resources.

Directors agreed that the best way to reduce poverty is through sustained and rapid economic growth. They observed with some concern that economic performance in the majority of developing countries had on average been unsatisfactory over the past 30 years. However, Directors were generally encouraged by gains made in real per capita income in many poor countries in Asia, notably China and India, and, more recently, in several countries in Africa, where stabilization programs—directed at achieving reasonable price stability, prudent fiscal balances, and sustainable exchange rate regimes—have been implemented successfully.

Directors emphasized the critical role played in development by market-friendly institutions and an environment in which individuals and businesses can save and invest, as well as expect to enjoy the future benefits of their endeavors. They identified political instability, war, and the absence of the rule of law as critical impediments to providing such a setting, and to development more generally. Directors called for continued progress in removing distortions in domestic markets by eliminating price controls and subsidies, by liberalizing external trade, and by combating corruption through effective and transparent government. They noted that many developing countries also need to develop sounder financial markets that can efficiently allocate savings to profitable investments. Many of these countries, especially the poorest, would also benefit from placing a higher priority on health and education programs in order to help break the poverty cycle by increasing productivity. Directors cautioned, however, that there is no unique formula for starting and sustaining economic growth, and that each country will need to decide how best to provide the necessary fundamentals for economic prosperity through the joint efforts of government and representatives of civil society. In this respect, they stressed that ownership of the reform process is crucial to ensuring its success.

Directors agreed that unsustainable levels of external debt are a critical impediment to economic growth and poverty alleviation, especially in some of the poorest countries. Without significant debt relief, incentives for government reform and private investment are dulled, and countries can be caught in a vicious debt and poverty trap. Directors emphasized the opportunity provided by the recently enhanced Initiative for Heavily Indebted Poor Countries (HIPC), under which debt would be lowered to sustainable levels through concerted efforts by the international community. Some Directors considered that the enhanced HIPC Initiative should be supplemented by additional concessional lending from the international community. They noted that middle-income countries facing debt problems similar to those of the HIPCs would also benefit from concessional financing.

Directors recognized the important contributions to debt relief being made by the advanced economies, both directly and through international organizations. Several Directors called for a reversal in the downward trend in official development assistance, and cautioned that debt relief associated with the HIPC Initiative should not be seen as a substitute for future development assistance. These Directors drew attention to the more effective use of development assistance, for example through strengthened incentives for reform in the recipient countries and through a better targeting of aid to these countries' needs. Many Directors also called on advanced economies to reform trade policies, especially in areas such as agricultural products and textiles, where current policies have particularly damaging effects on trade opportunities and growth prospects for developing countries.

Directors thanked the staff for the long-term and historical perspective on economic development and policies provided in the latest *World Economic Outlook*, and noted their general agreement on the salient features presented.

Finally, Directors expressed their special appreciation to Mr. Flemming Larsen for his many years of distinguished service in helping to make the *World Economic Outlook* the Fund's principal vehicle for the effective exercise of multilateral surveillance.

STATISTICAL APPENDIX

The statistical appendix presents historical data, as well as projections. It comprises four sections: Assumptions, Data and Conventions, Classification of Countries, and Statistical Tables.

The assumptions underlying the estimates and projections for 2000–2001 and the medium-term scenario for 2002–2005 are summarized in the first section. The second section provides a general description of the data, and the conventions used for calculating country group composites. The classification of countries in the various groups presented in the *World Economic Outlook* is summarized in the third section. Note that the group of advanced economies includes Israel and four newly industrialized Asian economies, which all were added to the industrial country group in the May 1997 issue of the *World Economic Outlook*.

The last, and main, section comprises the statistical tables. Data in these tables have been compiled on the basis of information available through mid-March 2000. The figures for 2000 and beyond are shown with the same degree of precision as the historical figures solely for convenience; since they are projections, the same degree of accuracy is not to be inferred.

Assumptions

Real effective *exchange rates* for the advanced economies are assumed to remain constant at their average levels during the period January 25–February 22, 2000. For 2000 and 2001, these assumptions imply average U.S. dollar/SDR conversion rates of 1.353 and 1.357, respectively.

Established *policies* of national authorities are assumed to be maintained. The more specific policy assumptions underlying the projections for selected advanced economies are described in Box 1.3.

It is assumed that the *price of oil* will average $24.50 a barrel in 2000 and $19.80 a barrel in 2001. In the medium term, the oil price is assumed to remain unchanged in real terms.

With regard to *interest rates*, it is assumed that the London interbank offered rate (LIBOR) on six-month U.S. dollar deposits will average 6.8 percent in 2000 and 7.1 in 2001; that the three-month certificate of deposit rate in Japan will average 0.2 percent in 2000 and 0.4 in 2001; and that the three-month interbank deposit rate for the euro will average 4.0 percent in 2000 and 4.9 percent in 2001.

With respect to *introduction of the euro*, on December 31, 1998 the Council of the European Union decided that, effective January 1, 1999, the irrevocably fixed conversion rates between the euro and currencies of the member states adopting the euro are:

1 euro	= 40.3399	Belgian francs
	= 1.95583	Deutsche mark
	= 166.386	Spanish pesetas
	= 6.55957	French francs
	= 0.787564	Irish pound
	= 1,936.27	Italian lire
	= 40.3399	Luxembourg francs
	= 2.20371	Netherlands guilders
	= 13.7603	Austrian schillings
	= 200.482	Portuguese escudos
	= 5.94573	Finnish markkaa

See Box 5.4 in the October 1998 *World Economic Outlook* for details on how the conversion rates were established.

Data and Conventions

Data and projections for 184 countries form the statistical basis for the *World Economic Outlook* (the World Economic Outlook database). The data are maintained jointly by the IMF's Research Department and area departments, with the latter regularly updating country projections based on consistent global assumptions.

Although national statistical agencies are the ultimate providers of historical data and definitions, international organizations are also involved in statistical issues, with the objective of harmonizing methodologies for the national compilation of statistics, including the analytical frameworks, concepts, definitions, classifications, and valuation procedures used in the production of economic statistics. The *World Economic Outlook* database reflects information from both national source agencies and international organizations.

The completion in 1993 of the comprehensive revision of the standardized *System of National Accounts 1993* (*SNA*) and the IMF's *Balance of Payments Manual* (*BPM*) represented important improvements in the standards of economic statistics and analysis.[1] The IMF was actively involved in both projects, particularly the new *Balance of Payments Manual,* which reflects the IMF's special interest in countries' external positions. Key changes introduced with the new *Manual* were summarized in Box 13 of the May 1994 *World Economic Outlook.* The process of adapting country balance of payments data to the definitions of the new *BPM* began with the May 1995 *World Economic Outlook.* However, full concordance with the *BPM* is ultimately dependent on the provision by national statistical compilers of revised country data, and hence the *World Economic Outlook* estimates are still only partially adapted to the *BPM.*

The members of the European Union have recently adopted a harmonized system for the compilation of the national accounts, referred to as ESA 1995. All national accounts data from 1995 onwards are now presented on the basis of the new system. Revision by national authorities of data prior to 1995 to conform to the new sys-tem has progressed, but has in some cases not been completed. In such cases, historical *World Economic Outlook* data have been carefully adjusted to avoid breaks in the series. Users of EU national accounts data prior to 1995 should nevertheless exercise caution until such time as the revision of historical data by national statistical agencies has been fully completed. See Box 1.2, *Revisions in National Accounts Methodologies.*

Composite data for country groups in the *World Economic Outlook* are either sums or weighted averages of data for individual countries. Arithmetically weighted averages are used for all data except inflation and money growth for the developing and transition country groups, for which geometric averages are used. The following conventions apply.

- Country group composites for exchange rates, interest rates, and the growth rates of monetary aggregates are weighted by GDP converted to U.S. dollars at market exchange rates (averaged over the preceding three years) as a share of world or group GDP.

- Composites for other data relating to the domestic economy, whether growth rates or ratios, are weighted by GDP valued at purchasing power parities (PPPs) as a share of total world or group GDP.[2]

- Composite unemployment rates and employment growth are weighted by labor force as a share of group labor force.

- Composites relating to the external economy are sums of individual country data after conversion to U.S. dollars at the average market exchange rates in the years indicated for balance of payments data, and at end-of-year market exchange rates for debt denominated in currencies other than U.S. dollars. Composites of changes in foreign trade volumes and prices, however, are arithmetic averages of percentage changes

---

[1]Commission of the European Communities, International Monetary Fund, Organization for Economic Cooperation and Development, United Nations, and World Bank, *System of National Accounts 1993* (Brussels/Luxembourg, New York, Paris, and Washington, 1993); and International Monetary Fund, *Balance of Payments Manual, Fifth Edition* (Washington, 1993).

[2]See Box A.1 for a summary of the revised PPP-based weights and Annex IV of the May 1993 *World Economic Outlook.* See also Anne Marie Gulde and Marianne Schulze-Ghattas, "Purchasing Power Parity Based Weights for the *World Economic Outlook,*" in *Staff Studies for the World Economic Outlook* (International Monetary Fund, December 1993), pp. 106–23.

Box A1. Revised Purchasing Power Parity Based Weights for the *World Economic Outlook*

The *World Economic Outlook* presents a wide range of regional, world, and analytic aggregates of economic indicators, such as growth rates and inflation. In most cases, these aggregates are weighted averages of the indicators in the countries concerned, with weights usually reflecting each country's share of group GDP. The derivation of these weights therefore requires that GDP in national currency terms be converted to a common currency (in practice, the U.S. dollar). Since 1993, exchange rates based on purchasing power parities (PPPs) have been used for this purpose.[1]

This edition of the *World Economic Outlook* incorporates revised GDP-PPP weights. The PPPs used to derive the previous weights were based on surveys of national prices that dated from the mid-1980s and, in some cases, even earlier. While the country weights are adjusted each year to take into account relative changes in real GDP, this adjustment does not fully capture changes in individual prices that underlie the PPP estimates. Such changes may have been significant over the last two decades, given the rapid growth of trade and market development—for example, among the transition economies. Newer benchmark studies of national prices are now available, released mainly by the World Bank and the Organization for Economic Cooperation and Development (OECD) under the auspices of the United Nations' International Comparison Program. The World Bank has published PPP estimates for many countries based on 1993 price surveys,[2]

and the OECD has recently released estimates based on 1996 benchmarks for 52 countries.[3] These data form the basis for the revised weights introduced with this edition of the *World Economic Outlook*. For the small number of countries for which updated price surveys are not available, weights are estimated using a regression approach following the estimation methodology used earlier.[4]

New and old weights for the main regional breakdowns used in the *World Economic Outlook*, and for a number of individual countries, are shown in the table, together with the implied changes in regional GDP growth rates in 2000 as a result of the move to the new weighting scheme. Also shown are the significantly different weights that would arise if market exchange rates rather than PPP-based exchange rates were used. The overall distribution of world economic activity is broadly similar under the new GDP-PPP weights, but there are several notable changes. The share in global output of each of the main developing country regions declines, by over 2 percentage points in Asia; the advanced economies' share rises by 2½ percentage points, over half of this coming from the higher share of the United States; and the share of the transition economies, especially Russia, also increases. Projected world and regional growth rates in 2000 are little changed under the new weighting scheme. The largest adjustments are among the transition economies, with slower growth in central and eastern Europe, and a stronger pickup in the Transcaucasus and central Asia—where a higher weight for fast-growing Turkmenistan pushes up the regional growth rate. World growth falls slightly due to the higher weight of advanced economies.

---

[1]The estimation of the resulting GDP-PPP weights and their advantages compared with alternatives such as weights based on market exchange rates are discussed in *Staff Studies for the World Economic Outlook* (Washington: International Monetary Fund, December 1993). Further detail is provided in Anne-Marie Gulde, and Marianne Schulze-Ghattas, "Aggregation of Economic Indicators Across Countries: Exchange Rate Versus PPP-based GDP Weights," IMF Working Paper 92/36 (Washington: International Monetary Fund, 1992).

[2]See, for example, the World Bank's annual *World Development Indicators* and, for background information, "Purchasing Power of Currencies: Comparing National Incomes using ICP Data," (Washington: World Bank, 1993).

[3]These include OECD members, countries of the former Soviet Union, and other countries in central and eastern Europe. Further data based on 1996 surveys should become available later this year from the World Bank.

[4]For benchmark countries (with price surveys), GDP per capita on a PPP basis is regressed on GDP per capita on an exchange rate basis, openness to trade, and regional dummies, with the regression results then applied to non-benchmark countries.

Box A1 (*concluded*)

Comparison of New and Old Measures

	PPP weights in 2000		Market Exchange Rate Weights in 2000	Change in Growth of GDP[1]
	New	Old		
	(percent of world GDP)			
Advanced Economies	57.0	54.5	79.9	—
of which:				
Major industrial countries (G-7)	45.4	43.6	66.4	—
of which:				
United States	21.9	20.5	30.2	...
Japan	7.4	7.1	15.1	...
Other advanced economies	11.6	11.0	13.5	—
European Union	20.1	19.8	26.3	—
Euro area	15.7	15.5	20.0	—
Newly industrialized Asian economies	3.3	3.2	3.3	—
Developing Countries	37.2	41.0	17.9	—
of which:				
Africa	3.3	3.4	1.4	−0.1
Asia	21.6	23.9	7.7	—
of which:				
China	11.6	12.9	3.3	...
India	4.6	4.6	1.5	...
Middle East & Europe	3.9	4.7	2.6	−0.1
Western Hemisphere	8.4	9.1	6.2	—
Countries in Transition	5.7	4.5	2.2	−0.1
of which:				
Central and eastern Europe	2.9	2.6	1.4	−0.2
Russia	2.4	1.4	0.6	...
Transcaucasus and central Asia	0.5	0.5	0.2	0.6

	Nominal GDP in PPP US$bn		Real GDP Growth in percent
World	43,801.5	43,052.0	−0.1

[1]Real growth in 2000 under new PPP weights less growth in 2000 under old weights.

for individual countries weighted by the U.S. dollar value of exports or imports as a share of total world or group exports or imports (in the preceding year).

For central and eastern European countries, external transactions in nonconvertible currencies (through 1990) are converted to U.S. dollars at the implicit U.S. dollar/ruble conversion rates obtained from each country's national currency exchange rate for the U.S. dollar and for the ruble.

Unless otherwise indicated, multiyear averages of growth rates are expressed as compound annual rates of change.

Classification of Countries

Summary of the Country Classification

The country classification in the *World Economic Outlook* divides the world into three major groups: advanced economies, developing countries, and countries in transition.[3] Rather

[3]As used here, the term "country" does not in all cases refer to a territorial entity that is a state as understood by international law and practice. It also covers some territorial entities that are not states, but for which statistical data are maintained on a separate and independent basis.

than being based on strict criteria, economic or otherwise, this classification has evolved over time with the objective of facilitating analysis by providing a reasonably meaningful organization of data. A few countries are presently not included in these groups, either because they are not IMF members, and their economies are not monitored by the IMF, or because databases have not yet been compiled. Cuba and the Democratic People's Republic of Korea are examples of countries that are not IMF members, whereas San Marino, among the advanced economies, is an example of an economy for which a database has not been completed. It should also be noted that, owing to a lack of data, only three of the former republics of the dissolved Socialist Federal Republic of Yugoslavia (Croatia, the former Yugoslav Republic of Macedonia, and Slovenia) are included in the group composites for countries in transition.

Each of the three main country groups is further divided into a number of subgroups. Among the advanced economies, the seven largest in terms of GDP, collectively referred to as the major industrial countries, are distinguished as a subgroup, and so are the 15 current members of the European Union, the 11 members of the euro area, and the four newly industrialized Asian economies. The developing countries are classified by region, as well as into a number of analytical and other groups. A regional breakdown is also used for the classification of the countries in transition. Table A provides an overview of these standard groups in the *World Economic Outlook*, showing the number of countries in each group and the average 1999 shares of groups in aggregate PPP-valued GDP, total exports of goods and services, and population.

A new classification, the euro area, has been added to the Statistical Appendix for some variables. The euro area comprises the countries that formed the European Monetary Union as of January 1, 1999 (namely: Austria, Belgium, Finland, France, Germany, Ireland, Italy, Luxembourg, the Netherlands, Portugal, and Spain). Data shown are aggregates of country data and do not reflect official statistics at this time.

General Features and Compositions of Groups in the *World Economic Outlook* Classification

Advanced Economies

The 28 advanced economies are listed in Table B. The seven largest in terms of GDP—the United States, Japan, Germany, France, Italy, the United Kingdom, and Canada—constitute the subgroup of *major industrial countries*, often referred to as the Group of Seven (G-7) countries. The current members of the *European Union* (15 countries) and the *newly industrialized Asian economies* are also distinguished as subgroups. Composite data shown in the tables under the heading "European Union" cover the current 15 members of the European Union for all years, even though the membership has increased over time.

In 1991 and subsequent years, data for *Germany* refer to west Germany *and* the eastern Länder (i.e., the former German Democratic Republic). Before 1991, economic data are not available on a unified basis or in a consistent manner. Hence, in tables featuring data expressed as annual percent change, these apply to west Germany in years up to and including 1991, but to unified Germany from 1992 onward. In general, data on national accounts and domestic economic and financial activity through 1990 cover west Germany only, whereas data for the central government and balance of payments apply to west Germany through June 1990 and to unified Germany thereafter.

Developing Countries

The group of developing countries (128 countries) includes all countries that are not classified as advanced economies or as countries in transition, together with a few dependent territories for which adequate statistics are available.

The *regional breakdowns* of developing countries in the *World Economic Outlook* conform to the IMF's *International Financial Statistics (IFS)* classification—*Africa, Asia, Europe, Middle East,* and *Western Hemisphere*—with one important ex-

Table A. Classification by *World Economic Outlook* Groups and Their Shares in Aggregate GDP, Exports of Goods and Services, and Population, 1999[1]
(Percent of total for group or world)

	Number of Countries	GDP		Exports of Goods and Services		Population	
		— Share of total for —					
		Advanced economies	World	Advanced economies	World	Advanced economies	World
Advanced economies	**28**	**100.0**	**57.4**	**100.0**	**77.6**	**100.0**	**15.5**
Major industrial countries	7	79.8	45.8	63.1	48.9	74.4	11.6
United States		38.2	21.9	18.0	14.0	29.6	4.6
Japan		13.3	7.6	8.6	6.7	13.7	2.1
Germany		8.2	4.7	11.6	9.0	8.9	1.4
France		5.7	3.3	7.1	5.5	6.3	1.0
Italy		5.5	3.2	5.6	4.4	6.1	1.0
United Kingdom		5.6	3.2	6.9	5.4	6.3	1.0
Canada		3.4	2.0	5.1	4.0	3.3	0.5
Other advanced economies	21	20.2	11.6	36.9	28.7	25.6	4.0
Memorandum							
Industrial countries *(former definition)*	23	93.8	53.9	87.1	67.6	90.8	14.1
European Union	15	35.3	20.3	50.6	39.3	40.3	6.3
Euro area	11	27.6	15.8	40.2	31.2	31.3	4.9
Newly industrialized Asian economies	4	5.7	3.3	12.2	9.5	8.6	1.3

	Number of Countries	Developing countries	World	Developing countries	World	Developing countries	World
Developing countries	**128**	**100.0**	**36.8**	**100.0**	**18.0**	**100.0**	**77.7**
Regional groups							
Africa	51	8.8	3.2	10.2	1.8	15.5	12.0
Sub-Sahara	48	6.8	2.5	7.6	1.4	14.0	10.9
Excluding Nigeria and South Africa	46	3.9	1.4	4.0	0.7	10.3	8.0
Asia	27	57.5	21.2	45.9	8.3	67.1	52.1
China		30.6	11.2	17.1	3.1	27.2	21.1
India		12.4	4.6	4.0	0.7	21.4	16.6
Other Asia	25	14.6	5.4	24.8	4.5	18.5	14.4
Middle East and Europe	17	10.8	4.0	19.1	3.4	6.5	5.0
Western Hemisphere	33	22.9	8.4	24.8	4.5	10.9	8.5
Analytical groups							
By source of export earnings							
Fuel	18	9.0	3.3	17.7	3.2	7.0	5.4
Nonfuel	110	91.0	33.4	82.3	14.9	93.1	72.3
Manufactures	9	64.6	23.7	52.1	9.4	63.4	49.3
Primary products	42	6.6	2.4	6.6	1.2	10.8	8.4
Services, income, and private transfers	35	3.3	1.2	3.9	0.7	5.1	3.9
Diversified	24	16.5	6.1	19.6	3.6	13.8	10.7
By external financing source							
Net creditor countries	9	2.9	1.1	11.1	2.0	0.9	0.7
Net debtor countries	119	97.2	35.8	89.3	16.2	99.2	77.1
Official financing	45	5.7	2.1	5.1	0.9	13.5	10.5
Private financing	46	80.9	29.8	72.4	13.1	71.5	55.5
Diversified financing	28	7.6	2.8	9.4	1.7	12.5	9.7
Net debtor countries by debt-servicing experience							
Countries with arrears and/or rescheduling during 1994–98	55	24.8	9.1	23.2	4.2	28.8	22.4
Other net debtor countries	61	72.3	26.6	65.8	11.9	70.3	54.6
Other groups							
Heavily indebted poor countries	40	5.1	1.9	4.6	0.8	13.2	10.3
Least developed countries	46	4.4	1.6	2.8	0.5	13.6	10.5
Middle East and north Africa	21	10.3	3.8	17.6	3.2	7.4	5.8

	Number of Countries	Countries in transition	Countries World	Countries in transition	World	Countries in transition	World
Countries in transition	**28**	**100.0**	**5.8**	**100.0**	**4.4**	**100.0**	**6.8**
Central and eastern Europe	18	49.5	2.9	63.2	2.9	44.8	3.1
Excluding Belarus and Ukraine	16	39.9	2.3	57.3	2.5	29.9	2.0
Russia		41.5	2.4	28.8	1.3	36.4	2.5
Transcaucasus and central Asia	9	9.0	0.5	6.0	0.3	18.8	1.3

[1]The GDP shares are based on the purchasing-power-parity (PPP) valuation of country GDPs.

Table B. Advanced Economies by Subgroup

	European Union		Euro Area	Newly Industrialized Asian Economies	Other Countries
Major industrial countries					
	France		France		Canada
	Germany		Germany		Japan
	Italy		Italy		United States
	United Kingdom				
Other advanced economies					
	Austria	Luxembourg	Austria	Hong Kong SAR[1]	Australia
	Belgium	Netherlands	Belgium	Korea	Iceland
	Denmark	Portugal	Finland	Singapore	Israel
	Finland	Spain	Ireland	Taiwan Province	New Zealand
	Greece	Sweden	Luxembourg	of China	Norway
	Ireland		Netherlands		Switzerland
			Portugal		
			Spain		

[1]On July 1, 1997, Hong Kong was returned to the People's Republic of China and became a Special Administrative Region of China.

ception. Because all of the developing countries in Europe except Cyprus, Malta, and Turkey are included in the group of countries in transition, the *World Economic Outlook* classification places these three countries in a combined *Middle East and Europe* region. In both classifications, Egypt and the Libyan Arab Jamahiriya are included in this region, not in Africa. Three additional regional groupings—two of them constituting part of Africa and one a subgroup of Asia—are included in the *World Economic Outlook* because of their analytical significance. These are *sub-Sahara, sub-Sahara excluding Nigeria and South Africa,* and *Asia excluding China and India.*

The developing countries are also classified according to *analytical criteria* and into *other groups.* The analytical criteria reflect countries' composition of export earnings and other income from abroad, a distinction between net creditor and net debtor countries, and, for the net debtor countries, financial criteria based on external financing source and experience with external debt servicing. Included as "other groups" are currently the heavily indebted poor countries (HIPCs), the least developed countries, and Middle East and north Africa

(MENA). The detailed composition of developing countries in the regional, analytical, and other groups is shown in Tables C through E.

The first analytical criterion, by *source of export earnings,* distinguishes among five categories: *fuel* (Standard International Trade Classification—SITC 3); *manufactures* (SITC 5 to 8, less 68); *nonfuel primary products* (SITC 0, 1, 2, 4, and 68); *services, income, and private transfers* (exporters of services and recipients of income from abroad, including workers' remittances); and *diversified export earnings.* Countries whose 1994–98 export earnings in any of the first four of these categories accounted for more than half of total export earnings are allocated to that group, while countries whose export earnings were not dominated by any one of these categories are classified as countries with diversified export earnings (see Table C).

The financial criteria first distinguish between *net creditor* and *net debtor countries.* Net creditor countries are defined as developing countries with positive net external assets at the end of 1998.[4] Countries in the much larger net debtor group are differentiated on the basis of two additional financial criteria: by *main source*

[4]If information on the net external asset position is unavailable, the inclusion of countries in this group is based on whether they have cumulated a substantial current account surplus over the past 25 years to 1998.

Table C. Developing Countries by Region and Main Source of Export Earnings

	Fuel	Manufactures	Primary Products	Services, Income, and Private Transfers	Diversified Source of Export Earnings
Africa					
Sub-Sahara	Angola Congo, Rep. of Equatorial Guinea Gabon Nigeria		Benin Botswana Burkina Faso Burundi Central African Rep. Chad Congo, Democratic Rep. of Côte d'Ivoire Gambia, The Ghana Guinea Guinea-Bissau Liberia Madagascar Malawi Mali Mauritania Namibia Niger Somalia Sudan Swaziland Tanzania Togo Zambia Zimbabwe	Cape Verde Comoros Djibouti Eritrea Ethiopia Lesotho Mozambique, Rep. of Rwanda São Tomé and Príncipe Seychelles Uganda	Cameroon Kenya Mauritius Senegal Sierra Leone South Africa
North Africa	Algeria				Morocco Tunisia

Asia	Brunei Darussalam	Bangladesh
		China
		India
		Malaysia
		Pakistan
		Philippines
		Thailand
			Bhutan
			Cambodia
			Myanmar
			Papua New Guinea
			Solomon Islands
			Vanuatu
			Vietnam
				Fiji
				Kiribati
				Maldives
				Marshall Islands
				Micronesia,
				   Federated States of
				Nepal
				Samoa
				Tonga
					Afghanistan,
					   Islamic State of
					Indonesia
					Lao People's
					   Democratic Rep.
					Sri Lanka

Middle East and Europe	Bahrain Iran, Islamic Rep. of Iraq Kuwait Libya Oman Qatar Saudi Arabia United Arab Emirates	Turkey		Cyprus Egypt Jordan Lebanon	Malta Syrian Arab Rep. Yemen, Rep. of
Western Hemisphere	Trinidad and Tobago Venezuela	Brazil Mexico	Belize Bolivia Chile Guyana Honduras Nicaragua Paraguay Peru Suriname	Antigua and Barbuda Bahamas, The Barbados Dominican Rep. Grenada Haiti Jamaica Netherlands Antilles Panama St. Kitts and Nevis St. Lucia St. Vincent and the Grenadines	Argentina Colombia Costa Rica Dominica Ecuador El Salvador Guatemala Uruguay

Table D. Developing Countries by Region and Main External Financing Source

Countries	Net Creditor Countries	Net Debtor Countries		
		By main external financing source		
		Official financing	Private financing	Diversified financing
Africa				
Sub-Sahara				
Angola				•
Benin		•		
Botswana	•			
Burkina Faso		•		
Burundi		•		
Cameroon		•		
Cape Verde		•		
Central African Rep.		•		
Chad		•		
Comoros		•		
Congo, Democratic Rep. of		•		
Congo, Rep. of		•		
Côte d'Ivoire				•
Djibouti				•
Equatorial Guinea			•	
Eritrea				•
Ethiopia		•		
Gabon		•		
Gambia, The		•		
Ghana				•
Guinea		•		
Guinea-Bissau		•		
Kenya			•	
Lesotho			•	
Liberia		•		
Madagascar		•		
Malawi		•		
Mali		•		
Mauritania		•		
Mauritius				•
Mozambique, Rep. of		•		
Namibia			•	
Niger		•		
Nigeria				•
Rwanda		•		
São Tomé and Príncipe		•		
Senegal		•		
Seychelles			•	
Sierra Leone			•	
Somalia				•
South Africa			•	
Sudan				•
Swaziland	•			
Tanzania		•		
Togo		•		
Uganda		•		
Zambia		•		
Zimbabwe				•

Table D (continued)

Countries	Net Creditor Countries	Net Debtor Countries By main external financing source		
		Official financing	Private financing	Diversified financing
North Africa				
Algeria		•		
Morocco			•	
Tunisia				•
Asia				
Afghanistan, Islamic State of				•
Bangladesh		•		
Bhutan		•		
Brunei Darussalam	•			
Cambodia		•		
China			•	
Fiji			•	
India			•	
Indonesia			•	
Kiribati			•	
Lao People's Democratic Rep.		•		
Malaysia			•	
Maldives			•	
Marshall Islands		•		
Micronesia, Federated States of		•		
Myanmar			•	
Nepal		•		
Pakistan				•
Papua New Guinea				•
Philippines				•
Samoa		•		
Solomon Islands				•
Sri Lanka				•
Thailand			•	
Tonga		•		
Vanuatu			•	
Vietnam		•		
Middle East and Europe				
Bahrain			•	
Cyprus			•	
Egypt			•	
Iran, Islamic Rep. of			•	
Iraq				•
Jordan		•		
Kuwait	•			
Lebanon				•
Libya	•			
Malta			•	
Oman	•			
Qatar	•			
Saudi Arabia	•			
Syrian Arab Rep.				•
Turkey			•	
United Arab Emirates	•			
Yemen, Rep. of				•

Table D *(concluded)*

Countries	Net Creditor Countries	Net Debtor Countries		
		By main external financing source		
		Official financing	Private financing	Diversified financing
Western Hemisphere				
Antigua and Barbuda			•	
Argentina			•	
Bahamas, The			•	
Barbados				•
Belize			•	
Bolivia				•
Brazil			•	
Chile			•	
Colombia			•	
Costa Rica			•	
Dominica				•
Dominican Rep.			•	
Ecuador			•	
El Salvador				•
Grenada				•
Guatemala			•	
Guyana		•		
Haiti		•		
Honduras				•
Jamaica			•	
Mexico			•	
Netherlands Antilles		•		
Nicaragua		•		
Panama			•	
Paraguay			•	
Peru			•	
St. Kitts and Nevis			•	
St. Lucia			•	
St. Vincent and the Grenadines			•	
Suriname			•	
Trinidad and Tobago			•	
Uruguay				•
Venezuela			•	

of external financing and by *experience with debt servicing.*[5]

Within the classification *main source of external financing*, three subgroups, based on country estimates of the composition of external financing, are identified: *countries relying largely on official financing, countries relying largely on private financing,* and *countries with diversified financing source*. Net debtor countries are allocated to the first two of these subgroups according to whether their official financing, including official grants, or their private financing, including direct and portfolio investment, accounted for more than two-thirds of their total 1994–98 external financing. Countries that do not meet either of these two criteria are classified as

---

[5]Within the classification *experience with debt servicing*, a distinction is made between countries with arrears or rescheduling agreements (or both) and other net debtor countries. During the 1994–98 period, 55 countries incurred external payments arrears or entered into official or commercial bank debt-rescheduling agreements. This group of countries is referred to as *countries with arrears and/or rescheduling during 1994–98.*

Table E. Other Developing Country Groups

	Heavily Indebted Poor Countries	Least Developed Countries	Middle East and North Africa		Heavily Indebted Poor Countries	Least Developed Countries	Middle East and North Africa
Africa				**North Africa**			
Sub-Sahara				Algeria			•
				Morocco			•
Angola	•	•		Tunisia			•
Benin	•	•		**Asia**			
Burkina Faso	•	•					
Burundi	•	•		Afghanistan, Islamic State of		•	
Cameroon	•			Bangladesh		•	
Cape Verde		•		Bhutan		•	
Central African Rep.	•	•		Cambodia		•	
Chad	•	•		Kiribati		•	
Comoros		•		Lao People's Democratic Rep.	•	•	
Congo, Democratic Rep. of	•	•		Maldives		•	
Congo, Rep. of	•			Myanmar	•	•	
Côte d'Ivoire	•			Nepal		•	
Djibouti		•	•	Samoa		•	
Equatorial Guinea		•		Solomon Islands		•	
Ethiopia	•	•		Vanuatu		•	
Gambia, The		•		Vietnam	•		
Ghana	•			**Middle East and Europe**			
Guinea	•	•					
Guinea-Bissau	•	•		Bahrain			•
Kenya	•			Egypt			•
Lesotho		•		Iran, Islamic Rep. of			•
Liberia	•	•		Iraq			•
Madagascar	•	•		Jordan			•
Malawi	•	•		Kuwait			•
Mali	•	•		Lebanon			•
Mauritania	•	•	•	Libya			•
Mozambique, Rep. of	•	•		Oman			•
Niger	•	•		Qatar			•
Rwanda	•	•		Saudi Arabia			•
São Tomé and Príncipe	•	•		Syrian Arab Rep.			•
Senegal	•			United Arab Emirates			•
Sierra Leone	•	•		Yemen, Rep. of	•	•	•
Somalia	•	•	•	**Western Hemisphere**			
Sudan	•	•	•	Bolivia	•		
Tanzania	•	•		Guyana	•		
Togo	•	•		Haiti		•	
Uganda	•	•		Honduras	•		
Zambia	•	•		Nicaragua	•		

countries with diversified financing source (see Table D).

The *other groups* of developing countries (see Table E) constitute the HIPCs, the *least developed countries*, and MENA countries. The first group comprises 40 of the countries (all except Nigeria) considered by the IMF and the World Bank for their debt initiative, known as the HIPC Initiative.[6]

[6]See David Andrews, Anthony R. Boote, Syed S. Rizavi, and Sukwinder Singh, *Debt Relief for Low-Income Countries: The Enhanced HIPC Initiative*, Pamphlet Series, No. 51 (Washington: International Monetary Fund, November 1999)

Table F. Countries in Transition by Region

Central and Eastern Europe		Russia	Transcaucasus and Central Asia
Albania	Lithuania	Russia	Armenia
Belarus	Macedonia, former Yugoslav Rep. of		Azerbaijan
Bosnia and Herzegovina	Moldova		Georgia
Bulgaria	Poland		Kazakhstan
Croatia	Romania		Kyrgyz Rep.
Czech Rep.	Slovak Rep.		Mongolia
Estonia	Slovenia		Tajikistan
Hungary	Ukraine		Turkmenistan
Latvia	Yugoslavia, Federal Rep. of (Serbia/Montenegro)		Uzbekistan

The group of least developed countries comprises 46 of the 47 developing countries classified as "least developed" by the United Nations (Tuvalu, not being an IMF member, is excluded). Finally, Middle East and north Africa, also referred to as the MENA countries, is a new *World Economic Outlook* group, whose composition straddles the Africa and Middle East and Europe regions. It is defined as the Arab League countries plus the Islamic Republic of Iran.

Countries in Transition

The group of countries in transition (28 countries) comprises central and eastern European countries (including the Baltic countries), Russia, the other states of the former Soviet Union, and Mongolia. The transition country group is divided into three regional subgroups: *central and eastern Europe, Russia,* and

Transcaucasus and central Asia. The detailed country composition is shown in Table F.

One common characteristic of these countries is the transitional state of their economies from a centrally administered system to one based on market principles. Another is that this transition involves the transformation of sizable industrial sectors whose capital stocks have proven largely obsolete. Although several other countries are also "in transition" from partially command-based economic systems toward market-based systems (including China, Cambodia, the Lao People's Democratic Republic, Vietnam, and a number of African countries), most of these are largely rural, low-income economies for whom the principal challenge is one of economic development. These countries are therefore classified in the developing country group rather than in the group of countries in transition.

List of Tables

Table 1. Summary of World Output[1]

(Annual percent change)

| | Ten-Year Averages | | 1992 | 1993 | 1994 | 1995 | 1996 | 1997 | 1998 | 1999 | 2000 | 2001 |
	1982–91	1992–2001										
World	**3.3**	**3.4**	**2.0**	**2.3**	**3.7**	**3.6**	**4.1**	**4.1**	**2.5**	**3.3**	**4.2**	**3.9**
Advanced economies	**3.1**	**2.8**	**2.1**	**1.4**	**3.3**	**2.7**	**3.2**	**3.3**	**2.4**	**3.1**	**3.6**	**3.0**
United States	2.9	3.6	3.1	2.7	4.0	2.7	3.6	4.2	4.3	4.2	4.4	3.0
European Union	2.6	2.1	1.2	−0.4	2.8	2.4	1.7	2.6	2.7	2.3	3.2	3.0
Japan	4.1	1.0	1.0	0.3	0.6	1.5	5.0	1.6	−2.5	0.3	0.9	1.8
Other advanced economies	4.3	4.2	3.4	4.1	5.8	5.0	4.2	4.5	0.9	5.4	4.9	4.3
Developing countries	**4.3**	**5.5**	**6.4**	**6.4**	**6.7**	**6.1**	**6.5**	**5.8**	**3.2**	**3.8**	**5.4**	**5.3**
Regional groups												
Africa	2.2	2.8	−0.7	0.4	2.3	3.2	5.6	2.9	3.1	2.3	4.4	4.5
Asia	6.9	7.4	9.4	9.4	9.6	9.0	8.3	6.7	3.8	6.0	6.2	5.9
Middle East and Europe	3.3	3.5	6.2	3.5	0.5	3.8	4.6	4.7	2.7	0.7	4.6	4.0
Western Hemisphere	1.8	3.4	3.6	4.1	5.0	1.7	3.6	5.4	2.1	0.1	4.0	4.7
Analytical groups												
By source of export earnings												
Fuel	2.3	2.8	6.0	1.0	0.3	2.5	3.5	3.8	1.9	0.6	4.4	3.7
Nonfuel	4.6	5.9	6.4	7.0	7.4	6.5	6.8	6.0	3.4	4.1	5.5	5.5
By external financing source												
Net creditor countries	1.3	2.5	6.0	2.2	1.8	1.5	2.8	3.6	0.4	0.6	4.4	2.1
Net debtor countries	4.4	5.6	6.4	6.5	6.8	6.2	6.6	5.9	3.3	3.9	5.4	5.4
Official financing	2.7	3.7	1.7	1.9	2.5	5.4	5.4	4.0	3.8	3.2	4.5	4.8
Private financing	4.9	6.0	7.0	7.5	7.7	6.6	6.9	6.3	3.3	4.0	5.6	5.6
Diversified financing	2.6	4.0	4.8	2.4	3.5	4.7	5.0	4.1	3.2	3.0	4.3	4.6
Net debtor countries by debt-servicing experience												
Countries with arrears and/or rescheduling during 1994–98	2.7	3.5	2.8	3.7	4.6	5.1	4.9	4.2	−0.8	1.8	4.1	4.5
Other net debtor countries	5.3	6.5	7.9	7.7	7.7	6.7	7.2	6.5	4.8	4.6	5.8	5.7
Countries in transition	**1.4**	**−2.4**	**−14.4**	**−7.6**	**−7.6**	**−1.4**	**−0.6**	**1.7**	**−0.7**	**2.4**	**2.6**	**3.0**
Central and eastern Europe	...	—	−8.8	−3.8	−2.9	1.7	1.6	2.3	1.8	1.4	3.0	4.2
Excluding Belarus and Ukraine	...	2.1	−5.3	0.2	3.2	5.6	3.7	2.7	2.0	1.5	3.6	4.6
Russia	...	−4.9	−19.4	−10.4	−11.6	−4.2	−3.4	0.9	−4.5	3.2	1.5	1.4
Transcaucasus and central Asia	...	−2.5	−14.1	−11.0	−11.5	−5.0	1.3	2.6	2.3	4.4	4.9	3.7
Memorandum												
Median growth rate												
Advanced economies	3.1	2.9	1.5	0.9	4.1	2.9	3.1	3.8	2.9	3.2	3.7	3.3
Developing countries	3.1	3.9	3.6	3.0	3.8	4.4	4.4	4.2	3.6	3.5	4.3	4.5
Countries in transition	1.3	0.1	−11.4	−7.8	−1.9	1.9	3.1	3.7	3.7	2.7	4.0	4.2
Output per capita												
Advanced economies	2.5	2.2	1.4	0.8	2.6	2.1	2.5	2.7	1.8	2.6	3.1	2.5
Developing countries	2.0	3.8	3.9	4.4	4.8	4.2	4.9	4.3	1.6	2.2	3.9	3.9
Countries in transition	0.8	−2.4	−14.6	−7.7	−7.6	−1.4	−0.4	1.8	−0.6	2.5	2.7	3.2
World growth based on market exchange rates	**3.0**	**2.6**	**0.7**	**1.1**	**3.0**	**2.8**	**3.5**	**3.4**	**1.9**	**2.8**	**3.6**	**3.3**
Value of world output in billions of U.S. dollars												
At market exchange rates	16,826	29,007	24,041	24,926	26,451	29,023	29,817	29,698	29,492	30,629	32,110	33,882
At purchasing power parities	21,436	37,102	29,089	30,467	32,170	33,996	36,032	38,123	39,489	41,344	43,802	46,507

[1]Real GDP.

Table 2. Advanced Economies: Real GDP and Total Domestic Demand
(Annual percent change)

	Ten-Year Averages		1992	1993	1994	1995	1996	1997	1998	1999	2000	2001	Fourth Quarter[1]		
	1982–91	1992–2001											1999	2000	2001
Real GDP															
Advanced economies	**3.1**	**2.8**	**2.1**	**1.4**	**3.3**	**2.7**	**3.2**	**3.3**	**2.4**	**3.1**	**3.6**	**3.0**	...	...	...
Major industrial countries	3.0	2.6	2.0	1.3	3.0	2.3	3.0	3.1	2.5	2.8	3.3	2.7	3.2	3.1	2.8
United States	2.9	3.6	3.1	2.7	4.0	2.7	3.6	4.2	4.3	4.2	4.4	3.0	4.6	3.3	3.0
Japan	4.1	1.0	1.0	0.3	0.6	1.5	5.0	1.6	−2.5	0.3	0.9	1.8	—	2.4	2.4
Germany	2.7	1.7	2.2	−1.1	2.3	1.7	0.8	1.5	2.2	1.5	2.8	3.3	2.3	3.2	3.5
France	2.4	2.0	1.5	−0.9	2.1	1.8	1.1	2.0	3.4	2.7	3.5	3.1	3.2	3.3	3.2
Italy	2.3	1.6	0.8	−0.9	2.2	2.9	1.1	1.8	1.5	1.4	2.7	2.8	2.1	3.0	2.6
United Kingdom[2]	2.7	2.5	0.1	2.3	4.4	2.8	2.6	3.5	2.2	2.0	3.0	2.0	2.9	2.7	1.6
Canada	2.3	3.0	0.9	2.3	4.7	2.8	1.7	4.0	3.1	4.2	3.7	2.7	4.7	3.1	2.5
Other advanced economies	3.8	3.6	2.5	1.9	4.5	4.3	3.8	4.2	2.0	4.6	4.5	4.1	...	...	...
Spain	3.2	2.5	0.7	−1.2	2.3	2.7	2.4	3.8	4.0	3.7	3.7	3.4	...	...	...
Netherlands	2.5	2.9	2.0	0.8	3.2	2.3	3.0	3.8	3.7	3.5	3.8	3.4	...	...	...
Belgium	2.2	2.1	1.6	−1.5	3.0	2.5	1.0	3.5	2.7	2.3	3.3	2.9	...	...	...
Sweden	1.9	2.1	−1.4	−2.2	4.1	3.7	1.1	2.0	3.0	3.8	3.9	3.2	...	...	...
Austria	2.7	2.0	1.3	0.5	2.4	1.7	2.0	1.2	2.9	2.0	3.1	3.3	...	...	...
Denmark	2.2	2.5	1.3	0.8	5.8	3.7	2.8	3.1	2.7	1.3	1.7	2.1	...	...	...
Finland	2.4	2.9	−3.3	−1.1	4.0	3.8	4.0	6.3	5.0	3.6	4.1	3.5	...	...	...
Greece[3]	1.9	2.3	0.7	−1.6	2.0	2.1	2.4	3.4	3.7	3.5	3.6	3.1	...	...	...
Portugal	3.0	2.7	1.9	−1.4	2.4	2.9	3.6	3.8	3.9	3.0	3.4	3.1	...	...	...
Ireland	3.5	7.1	3.3	2.6	5.8	9.5	7.7	10.7	8.9	8.4	7.4	7.2	...	...	...
Luxembourg	5.0	5.2	5.8	8.5	4.1	3.5	2.9	7.3	5.0	5.2	5.1	5.0	...	...	...
Switzerland	1.9	1.0	−0.1	−0.5	0.5	0.5	0.3	1.7	2.1	1.7	2.1	2.1	...	...	...
Norway	2.6	3.3	3.3	2.7	5.5	3.8	4.9	4.3	2.1	0.8	3.3	2.3	...	...	...
Israel	3.6	4.3	6.8	3.4	6.9	6.8	4.7	2.7	2.0	2.2	3.8	3.5	...	...	...
Iceland	2.4	3.2	−3.3	1.0	3.6	1.0	5.6	5.4	5.1	5.6	4.7	3.5	...	...	...
Korea	8.9	5.6	5.4	5.5	8.3	8.9	6.8	5.0	−6.7	10.7	7.0	6.5	...	...	...
Australia	2.9	4.1	2.6	3.8	5.0	4.4	4.0	3.9	5.1	4.4	3.9	3.5	...	...	...
Taiwan Province of China	8.1	6.0	6.8	6.3	6.5	6.0	5.7	6.8	4.7	5.5	6.2	6.0	...	...	...
Hong Kong SAR	6.1	3.9	6.3	6.1	5.4	3.9	4.5	5.0	−5.1	2.9	6.0	4.7	...	...	...
Singapore	6.8	7.2	6.6	12.8	11.4	8.0	7.5	8.4	0.4	5.4	5.9	6.0	...	...	...
New Zealand	1.2	3.1	0.9	5.1	5.9	4.0	3.2	2.1	−0.3	3.0	3.9	3.4	...	...	...
Memorandum															
Industrial countries	2.9	2.6	1.9	1.1	3.1	2.4	3.0	3.2	2.7	2.9	3.4	2.8	...	...	...
European Union	2.6	2.1	1.2	−0.4	2.8	2.4	1.7	2.6	2.7	2.3	3.2	3.0	...	...	...
Euro area	2.6	2.1	1.5	−0.8	2.4	2.3	1.5	2.4	2.8	2.3	3.2	3.2	...	...	...
Newly industrialized Asian economies	8.1	5.7	6.0	6.3	7.6	7.3	6.2	5.8	−2.3	7.7	6.6	6.1	...	...	...
Real total domestic demand															
Advanced economies	**3.2**	**2.9**	**2.1**	**1.0**	**3.4**	**2.7**	**3.2**	**3.1**	**2.7**	**3.8**	**3.8**	**3.1**	...	...	...
Major industrial countries	3.0	2.8	2.0	1.1	3.1	2.2	3.1	2.9	3.2	3.6	3.7	2.9	3.8	3.3	3.0
United States	3.0	4.0	3.1	3.3	4.4	2.5	3.7	4.5	5.4	5.1	5.1	3.4	5.6	4.0	3.4
Japan	4.1	1.0	0.4	0.1	1.0	2.3	5.7	0.2	−3.1	0.6	0.9	1.8	0.5	2.3	2.4
Germany	2.5	1.7	2.8	−1.0	2.2	1.7	0.3	0.7	2.5	2.2	2.4	3.0	1.9	3.1	3.1
France	2.4	1.7	0.8	−1.6	2.1	1.7	0.7	0.8	4.0	2.6	3.5	2.8	2.9	3.2	2.7
Italy	2.6	1.3	0.9	−5.1	1.7	2.0	0.9	2.5	2.9	2.5	2.6	2.7	1.6	3.1	2.4
United Kingdom	2.8	2.7	0.8	2.1	3.4	1.8	3.1	3.7	4.0	3.4	3.2	2.0	3.8	2.1	2.1
Canada	2.4	2.7	0.9	1.4	3.2	1.7	1.6	5.7	2.2	4.0	4.2	2.4	6.0	2.6	2.4
Other advanced economies	3.9	3.4	2.3	0.9	4.6	4.6	3.6	3.6	0.8	5.0	4.5	4.3	...	...	...
Memorandum															
Industrial countries	3.0	2.8	1.8	0.8	3.1	2.4	3.0	3.0	3.4	3.6	3.6	2.9	...	...	...
European Union	2.7	2.0	1.3	−1.6	2.4	2.2	1.4	2.3	3.6	3.0	3.1	2.9	...	...	...
Euro area	2.7	1.9	1.5	−2.3	2.1	2.1	1.0	1.9	3.5	2.9	3.1	3.0	...	...	...
Newly industrialized Asian economies	8.3	5.1	6.3	5.9	8.3	7.6	6.5	4.1	−9.0	8.0	7.2	6.8	...	...	...

[1]From fourth quarter of preceding year.
[2]Average of expenditure, income, and output estimates of GDP at market prices.
[3]Based on revised national accounts for 1988 onward.

Table 3. Advanced Economies: Components of Real GDP
(Annual percent change)

	Ten-Year Averages		1992	1993	1994	1995	1996	1997	1998	1999	2000	2001
	1982–91	1992–2001										
Private consumer expenditure												
Advanced economies	**3.2**	**2.8**	**2.4**	**1.7**	**3.0**	**2.7**	**2.9**	**2.7**	**2.9**	**3.9**	**3.3**	**2.9**
Major industrial countries	3.1	2.7	2.3	1.7	2.7	2.4	2.6	2.4	3.2	3.6	3.1	2.7
United States	3.3	3.8	2.9	3.4	3.8	3.0	3.2	3.4	4.9	5.3	4.5	3.3
Japan	3.8	1.2	2.1	1.2	1.9	2.1	2.9	0.5	-0.5	1.2	-0.1	1.0
Germany	2.7	1.8	2.8	0.2	1.0	2.1	0.8	0.7	2.3	2.1	2.8	3.0
France	2.1	1.6	0.9	-0.4	1.2	1.2	1.3	0.2	3.6	2.3	3.1	2.7
Italy	2.7	1.4	1.9	-3.7	1.5	1.7	1.2	3.0	2.3	1.7	2.1	2.5
United Kingdom	3.1	2.7	0.4	2.9	2.9	1.7	3.6	3.9	3.2	4.0	2.6	1.8
Canada	2.6	2.7	1.8	1.8	3.1	2.1	2.5	4.2	2.8	3.2	3.4	2.6
Other advanced economies	3.7	3.4	3.2	1.8	4.1	3.8	3.8	3.5	1.5	4.8	3.8	3.7
Memorandum												
Industrial countries	3.0	2.7	2.2	1.4	2.7	2.4	2.6	2.5	3.3	3.7	3.2	2.7
European Union	2.6	2.0	1.7	-0.4	1.7	1.8	1.9	2.1	3.1	2.9	2.9	2.8
Euro area	2.6	1.9	2.0	-1.0	1.4	1.8	1.5	1.7	3.1	2.7	2.9	3.0
Newly industrialized Asian economies	8.1	5.4	6.8	7.1	8.1	6.9	6.5	5.3	-4.2	7.6	5.0	5.2
Public consumption												
Advanced economies	**2.6**	**1.5**	**1.8**	**0.8**	**0.9**	**0.9**	**1.6**	**1.4**	**1.4**	**1.9**	**2.3**	**1.6**
Major industrial countries	2.3	1.3	1.5	0.6	0.8	0.7	1.1	1.2	1.1	2.0	2.6	1.7
United States	2.7	1.2	0.4	-0.4	0.2	—	0.5	2.2	1.3	2.6	4.2	1.6
Japan	2.3	1.9	2.0	2.4	2.4	3.3	1.9	1.5	1.5	1.3	1.2	1.8
Germany	1.1	1.2	5.0	0.1	2.4	1.5	2.1	-1.1	0.5	0.2	0.2	1.6
France	2.7	1.9	3.8	4.6	0.7	—	2.3	1.7	1.0	1.7	1.6	1.4
Italy	2.4	0.3	0.6	-0.2	-0.8	-2.1	1.1	0.9	0.7	0.8	0.7	1.8
United Kingdom	1.1	1.2	0.5	-0.8	1.4	1.6	1.7	-1.4	0.7	3.4	2.8	2.7
Canada	2.6	0.3	1.0	0.1	-1.2	-0.5	-1.1	-0.5	1.7	1.0	1.2	1.1
Other advanced economies	3.6	2.0	3.0	2.0	1.2	1.8	3.4	2.3	2.4	1.6	1.2	1.3
Memorandum												
Industrial countries	2.4	1.4	1.6	0.7	0.9	0.8	1.2	1.3	1.3	2.0	2.4	1.7
European Union	2.1	1.3	2.6	1.1	1.0	0.8	1.7	0.5	1.2	1.6	1.3	1.8
Euro area	2.4	1.4	3.2	1.4	1.0	0.5	1.7	0.8	1.2	1.2	1.0	1.6
Newly industrialized Asian economies	6.2	2.7	6.2	3.7	1.0	2.0	7.5	3.3	2.5	-0.4	0.8	0.7
Gross fixed capital formation												
Advanced economies	**3.6**	**4.3**	**1.8**	**0.1**	**4.7**	**4.3**	**6.3**	**4.9**	**4.9**	**5.3**	**5.5**	**4.9**
Major industrial countries	3.3	4.2	2.2	0.4	4.3	3.4	6.6	4.6	5.5	5.5	5.4	4.5
United States	2.6	7.0	5.2	5.7	7.3	5.4	8.4	7.5	10.5	8.2	6.6	5.5
Japan	5.3	0.3	-1.5	-2.0	-0.8	1.7	11.1	-0.8	-7.4	-1.0	2.2	2.4
Germany	2.7	1.5	4.5	-4.5	4.0	-0.7	-1.1	0.5	1.4	2.3	4.0	4.4
France	2.9	2.0	-1.4	-6.4	1.6	2.2	—	0.5	6.1	7.0	6.1	4.7
Italy	2.1	1.6	-1.4	-10.9	0.1	6.0	3.6	1.2	4.1	4.4	6.1	4.2
United Kingdom	4.3	4.1	-0.7	0.8	3.6	2.9	4.9	7.5	10.8	5.2	3.3	2.9
Canada	2.4	4.6	-1.3	-2.7	7.4	-1.9	6.5	13.9	3.6	9.3	8.6	3.9
Other advanced economies	4.7	4.3	—	-1.2	6.3	7.6	5.4	6.1	2.4	4.4	5.8	6.4
Memorandum												
Industrial countries	3.3	4.2	1.6	-0.3	4.4	3.9	6.3	5.0	5.8	5.6	5.3	4.5
European Union	3.2	2.6	-0.2	-5.7	2.6	3.7	2.3	3.4	5.9	5.1	5.1	4.4
Euro area	3.0	2.2	0.2	-6.8	2.3	3.4	1.5	2.4	4.8	5.0	5.4	4.7
Newly industrialized Asian economies	9.8	5.3	5.9	6.9	9.8	9.8	7.4	4.3	-9.3	1.0	8.3	10.8

Table 3 *(concluded)*

	Ten-Year Averages		1992	1993	1994	1995	1996	1997	1998	1999	2000	2001
	1982–91	1992–2001										
Final domestic demand												
Advanced economies	**3.2**	**2.8**	**2.1**	**1.2**	**2.9**	. **2.6**	**3.4**	**2.8**	**2.8**	**3.8**	**3.6**	**3.2**
Major industrial countries	3.1	2.7	2.0	1.1	2.6	2.2	3.3	2.6	3.1	3.7	3.5	2.9
United States	3.1	4.0	2.8	3.1	3.8	2.9	3.7	4.0	5.4	5.5	4.9	3.5
Japan	4.1	1.0	0.9	0.3	1.1	2.1	5.3	0.1	−2.5	0.5	0.7	1.5
Germany	2.4	1.6	3.6	−0.9	2.0	1.3	0.6	0.3	1.7	1.8	2.6	3.1
France	2.4	1.7	1.1	−0.4	1.1	1.1	1.3	0.6	3.5	3.1	3.3	2.8
Italy	2.5	1.2	1.0	−4.5	0.8	1.7	1.7	2.2	2.4	2.0	2.6	2.7
United Kingdom	2.8	2.7	0.3	1.8	2.7	1.9	3.5	3.5	4.1	4.1	2.7	2.1
Canada	2.5	2.6	1.0	0.6	2.8	0.8	2.4	4.9	2.7	3.9	4.1	2.6
Other advanced economies	3.9	3.4	2.3	1.2	4.1	4.3	4.1	3.8	1.5	4.0	4.0	4.2
Memorandum												
Industrial countries	3.0	2.7	1.9	0.8	2.6	2.3	3.2	2.7	3.3	3.8	3.5	3.0
European Union	2.6	2.0	1.5	−1.2	1.7	1.9	1.9	2.0	3.3	3.1	3.0	2.9
Euro area	2.6	1.9	1.9	−1.7	1.5	1.8	1.5	1.7	3.1	2.9	3.1	3.1
Newly industrialized Asian economies	8.3	5.0	6.1	6.5	7.7	7.4	7.1	4.6	−5.4	4.4	5.6	6.5
Stock building[1]												
Advanced economies	—	**0.1**	—	**−0.1**	**0.5**	—	**−0.2**	**0.2**	**−0.1**	—	**0.2**	—
Major industrial countries	—	0.1	—	−0.1	0.5	−0.1	−0.1	0.4	0.1	−0.2	0.2	—
United States	−0.1	0.1	0.3	—	0.7	−0.5	—	0.5	0.1	−0.4	0.2	−0.1
Japan	0.1	—	−0.5	−0.1	−0.2	0.2	0.4	0.1	−0.6	0.1	0.2	0.3
Germany	0.1	0.1	−0.7	−0.1	0.3	0.3	−0.4	0.4	0.7	0.4	−0.2	
France	0.1	—	−0.3	−1.1	0.9	0.6	−0.6	0.2	0.5	−0.4	0.2	—
Italy	0.1	0.1	−0.1	−0.7	0.8	0.2	−0.7	0.3	0.6	0.4	—	—
United Kingdom	—	0.1	0.5	0.4	0.7	—	−0.4	0.3	—	−0.7	0.4	−0.2
Canada	−0.1	0.2	−0.1	0.8	0.3	0.9	−0.7	0.7	−0.4	0.1	0.1	−0.2
Other advanced economies	0.1	—	—	−0.3	0.5	0.2	−0.4	−0.2	−0.7	0.7	0.4	0.1
Memorandum												
Industrial countries	—	0.1	—	−0.1	0.5	—	−0.2	0.3	0.1	−0.2	0.1	—
European Union	0.1	—	−0.2	−0.4	0.6	0.3	−0.5	0.2	0.4	−0.1	0.1	—
Euro area	0.1	—	−0.3	−0.6	0.6	0.3	−0.5	0.3	0.5	0.1	—	—
Newly industrialized Asian economies	—	—	0.2	−0.5	0.6	0.3	−0.5	−0.6	−3.5	2.8	1.4	0.3
Foreign balance[1]												
Advanced economies	**−0.1**	**−0.1**	—	**0.3**	**−0.1**	**0.1**	—	**0.3**	**−0.4**	**−0.7**	**−0.2**	**−0.1**
Major industrial countries	−0.1	−0.2	—	0.2	—	0.1	−0.1	0.1	−0.8	−0.9	−0.3	−0.2
United States	−0.1	−0.5	−0.1	−0.6	−0.4	0.1	−0.1	−0.3	−1.3	−1.2	−0.7	−0.5
Japan	—	0.1	0.6	0.2	−0.3	−0.8	−0.5	1.4	0.5	−0.3	—	—
Germany	0.1	0.1	−0.6	−0.1	0.1	0.1	0.5	0.8	−0.3	−0.7	0.5	0.3
France	—	0.3	0.7	0.7	—	—	0.4	1.2	−0.4	0.2	—	0.4
Italy	−0.2	0.3	−0.1	4.3	0.6	1.0	0.2	−0.6	−1.3	−1.0	0.1	0.2
United Kingdom	−0.4	−0.4	−0.8	0.1	0.9	1.0	−0.5	−0.3	−2.1	−1.7	−0.1	−0.1
Canada	−0.1	0.3	0.4	0.9	1.5	1.0	0.1	−1.7	1.0	0.2	−0.3	0.3
Other advanced economies	—	0.3	0.1	1.0	−0.1	−0.1	0.1	0.7	1.2	—	0.2	0.1
Memorandum												
Industrial countries	−0.1	−0.1	0.1	0.3	—	0.1	—	0.2	−0.8	−0.8	−0.2	−0.1
European Union	−0.1	0.1	−0.1	1.2	0.4	0.3	0.2	0.3	−0.8	−0.7	0.2	0.2
Euro area	−0.1	0.2	—	1.5	0.3	0.3	0.4	0.5	−0.6	−0.5	0.2	0.2
Newly industrialized Asian economies	0.3	0.8	−0.6	0.6	−0.7	0.2	−0.1	1.9	6.5	1.1	—	−0.1

[1]Changes expressed as percent of GDP in the preceding period.

Table 4. Advanced Economies: Unemployment, Employment, and Real Per Capita GDP
(Percent)

| | Ten-Year Averages[1] | | 1992 | 1993 | 1994 | 1995 | 1996 | 1997 | 1998 | 1999 | 2000 | 2001 |
	1982–91	1992–2001										
Unemployment rate												
Advanced economies	**7.0**	**6.8**	**7.2**	**7.5**	**7.4**	**7.0**	**7.1**	**6.8**	**6.7**	**6.4**	**6.0**	**5.8**
Major industrial countries	6.9	6.5	7.1	7.2	7.0	6.7	6.7	6.5	6.2	6.1	5.9	5.7
United States[2]	7.0	5.3	7.5	6.9	6.1	5.6	5.4	4.9	4.5	4.2	4.2	4.2
Japan	2.5	3.5	2.2	2.5	2.9	3.1	3.3	3.4	4.1	4.7	4.7	4.6
Germany	7.3	8.5	6.6	7.8	8.3	8.1	8.8	9.8	9.4	9.0	8.6	8.1
France	9.5	11.3	10.3	11.6	12.3	11.7	12.4	12.5	11.7	11.0	10.2	9.8
Italy[3]	10.5	11.2	10.7	10.1	11.1	11.6	11.6	11.7	11.8	11.4	11.0	10.4
United Kingdom	9.0	6.8	9.6	10.3	9.4	8.1	7.4	5.7	4.7	4.4	4.3	4.5
Canada	9.7	9.0	11.3	11.2	10.4	9.5	9.7	9.2	8.3	7.6	6.7	6.6
Other advanced economies	7.2	7.6	7.4	8.6	8.7	8.2	8.1	7.8	8.1	7.3	6.3	6.0
Spain	18.6	19.3	18.4	22.7	24.2	22.9	22.2	20.8	18.8	15.9	14.4	13.2
Netherlands	8.2	5.0	5.4	6.5	7.6	7.1	6.6	5.5	4.1	3.2	2.3	2.0
Belgium	9.4	9.0	7.3	8.8	10.0	9.9	9.7	9.4	9.5	9.0	8.5	8.1
Sweden	2.5	6.6	5.3	8.2	8.0	7.7	8.1	8.0	6.5	5.6	4.8	4.2
Austria	3.4	4.1	3.4	4.0	3.8	3.9	4.3	4.4	4.7	4.3	4.0	3.9
Denmark	9.2	8.5	10.9	12.0	11.9	10.1	8.6	7.7	6.4	5.6	5.8	6.1
Finland	4.9	12.6	11.7	16.4	16.6	15.4	14.6	12.6	11.4	10.3	9.0	8.2
Greece	7.6	9.8	8.7	9.7	9.6	9.1	9.8	9.7	10.9	10.5	10.2	10.1
Portugal	7.0	5.6	4.1	5.5	6.8	7.2	7.3	6.7	5.0	4.4	4.3	4.3
Ireland	15.1	10.0	15.2	15.5	14.1	12.1	11.5	9.8	7.4	5.6	4.8	4.8
Luxembourg	1.5	2.7	1.6	2.1	2.7	3.0	3.3	3.3	3.3	2.9	2.7	2.3
Switzerland	0.7	3.7	2.6	4.5	4.7	4.2	4.7	5.2	3.9	2.7	2.2	2.0
Norway	3.4	4.2	5.9	5.9	5.4	4.7	4.1	3.3	2.4	3.2	3.5	3.8
Israel	7.1	8.5	11.2	10.0	7.8	6.9	6.7	7.7	8.6	9.3	8.8	8.0
Iceland	1.1	3.3	3.0	4.4	4.8	5.0	4.3	3.7	3.0	1.7	1.7	1.5
Korea	3.3	3.6	2.4	2.8	2.4	2.0	2.0	2.6	6.8	6.3	4.3	4.2
Australia	8.1	8.6	10.8	10.9	9.8	8.5	8.6	8.5	8.0	7.2	6.7	6.6
Taiwan Province of China	2.1	2.2	1.5	1.5	1.6	1.8	2.6	2.7	2.7	2.9	2.6	2.3
Hong Kong SAR	2.5	3.3	2.0	2.0	1.9	3.2	2.8	2.2	4.7	6.1	4.7	3.8
Singapore	3.3	2.7	2.7	2.7	2.6	2.7	2.0	1.8	3.2	3.5	2.9	2.5
New Zealand	6.0	7.4	10.3	9.5	8.2	6.3	6.1	6.7	7.5	6.9	6.6	6.4
Memorandum												
Industrial countries	7.3	7.1	7.6	8.0	7.9	7.5	7.5	7.2	6.8	6.4	6.2	6.0
European Union	9.3	9.8	9.4	10.7	11.1	10.6	10.7	10.4	9.7	8.9	8.4	8.0
Euro area	9.7	10.6	9.5	10.8	11.6	11.3	11.6	11.6	10.9	10.1	9.4	8.9
Newly industrialized Asian economies	2.9	3.2	2.1	2.4	2.2	2.1	2.2	2.6	5.4	5.3	3.8	3.6
Growth in employment												
Advanced economies	**1.2**	**0.9**	**−0.2**	**—**	**1.2**	**0.9**	**0.9**	**1.5**	**1.1**	**1.1**	**1.2**	**1.1**
Major industrial countries	1.2	0.7	−0.2	0.1	1.0	0.7	0.8	1.4	0.9	0.9	0.9	0.9
United States	1.6	1.5	0.7	1.5	2.3	1.5	1.4	2.2	1.5	1.5	1.2	1.1
Japan	1.3	0.2	1.1	0.2	0.1	0.1	0.5	1.1	−0.6	−0.8	0.5	0.4
Germany	0.7	−0.4	−1.7	−1.6	−0.4	−0.2	−0.8	−0.8	0.4	0.3	0.2	0.4
France	0.3	0.7	−1.1	−1.0	0.9	0.7	—	1.0	1.8	2.1	1.7	1.3
Italy	0.5	−0.2	−1.1	−4.1	−1.6	−0.6	0.5	0.4	1.1	1.3	1.1	0.8
United Kingdom	0.7	0.3	−2.8	−0.7	0.8	0.8	1.1	1.8	1.4	0.5	−0.3	—
Canada	1.3	1.7	−0.6	1.4	2.1	1.6	1.2	1.9	1.5	2.8	2.8	2.6
Other advanced economies	1.5	1.3	−0.1	−0.3	1.9	1.5	1.5	1.8	1.7	1.8	1.9	1.7
Memorandum												
Industrial countries	1.1	0.8	−0.4	−0.2	0.9	1.0	0.9	1.4	1.2	1.2	1.1	1.0
European Union	0.7	0.3	−1.7	−1.9	−0.1	0.6	0.5	0.9	1.6	1.5	1.0	0.9
Euro area	0.7	0.3	−1.4	−2.1	−0.3	0.5	0.4	0.8	1.6	1.7	1.3	1.1
Newly industrialized Asian economies	2.5	1.7	1.9	1.8	4.4	0.4	1.7	2.1	0.2	0.4	1.9	2.0

Table 4 *(concluded)*

	Ten-Year Averages[1]		1992	1993	1994	1995	1996	1997	1998	1999	2000	2001
	1982–91	1992–2001										
Growth in real per capita GDP												
Advanced economies	**2.5**	**2.2**	**1.4**	**0.8**	**2.6**	**2.1**	**2.5**	**2.7**	**1.8**	**2.6**	**3.1**	**2.5**
Major industrial countries	2.3	2.0	1.3	0.6	2.4	1.7	2.4	2.5	1.9	2.3	2.8	2.3
United States	1.9	2.7	1.9	1.5	3.1	1.8	2.6	3.2	3.3	3.3	3.6	2.2
Japan	3.5	0.8	0.7	—	0.4	1.2	4.8	1.3	−2.8	0.1	0.7	1.6
Germany	2.4	1.4	1.5	−1.8	2.1	1.4	0.5	1.3	2.2	1.4	2.7	3.2
France	2.0	1.6	1.1	−1.3	1.6	1.4	0.7	1.6	3.0	2.4	3.2	2.8
Italy	2.1	1.8	1.1	0.5	1.9	2.7	1.0	1.6	1.5	1.5	2.7	3.0
United Kingdom	2.4	2.4	−0.3	2.1	4.0	2.4	2.2	4.6	2.0	1.9	2.9	1.9
Canada	1.1	1.9	−0.2	1.2	3.5	1.7	−0.4	2.9	3.1	3.2	2.8	1.7
Other advanced economies	3.1	2.9	1.7	1.3	3.7	3.4	3.0	3.5	1.3	3.9	3.9	3.5
Memorandum												
Industrial countries	2.3	2.1	1.2	0.5	2.4	1.9	2.3	2.6	2.1	2.4	2.9	2.4
European Union	2.3	1.9	0.8	−0.4	2.5	2.1	1.4	2.5	2.6	2.2	3.0	2.9
Euro area	2.3	1.9	1.1	−0.8	2.1	2.0	1.2	2.1	2.7	2.2	3.1	3.1
Newly industrialized Asian economies	6.9	4.5	5.0	5.3	6.2	5.8	5.0	4.3	−3.6	6.6	5.5	5.1

[1]Compound annual rate of change for employment and per capita GDP; arithmetic average for unemployment rate.
[2]The projections for unemployment have been adjusted to reflect the new survey techniques adopted by the U.S. Bureau of Labor Statistics in January 1994.
[3]New series starting in 1993, reflecting revisions in the labor force surveys and the definition of unemployment to bring data in line with those of other advanced economies.

Table 5. Developing Countries: Real GDP

(Annual percent change)

	Ten-Year Averages		1992	1993	1994	1995	1996	1997	1998	1999	2000	2001
	1982–91	1992–2001										
Developing countries	**4.3**	**5.5**	**6.4**	**6.4**	**6.7**	**6.1**	**6.5**	**5.8**	**3.2**	**3.8**	**5.4**	**5.3**
Regional groups												
Africa	2.2	2.8	−0.7	0.4	2.3	3.2	5.6	2.9	3.1	2.3	4.4	4.5
Sub-Sahara	1.9	2.7	−1.1	0.8	1.9	4.0	5.1	3.5	2.5	2.2	4.2	4.6
Excluding Nigeria and South Africa	2.2	3.1	−1.3	0.2	1.6	4.8	5.3	4.1	3.6	2.9	4.6	5.0
Asia	6.9	7.4	9.4	9.4	9.6	9.0	8.3	6.7	3.8	6.0	6.2	5.9
Excluding China and India	5.0	4.4	6.5	6.2	6.8	7.7	6.9	3.7	−5.0	3.0	4.3	4.6
Middle East and Europe	3.3	3.5	6.2	3.5	0.5	3.8	4.6	4.7	2.7	0.7	4.6	4.0
Western Hemisphere	1.8	3.4	3.6	4.1	5.0	1.7	3.6	5.4	2.1	0.1	4.0	4.7
Analytical groups												
By source of export earnings												
Fuel	2.3	2.8	6.0	1.0	0.3	2.5	3.5	3.8	1.9	0.6	4.4	3.7
Manufactures	5.6	6.6	7.5	8.2	8.3	7.2	7.3	6.6	4.5	5.2	6.0	5.8
Nonfuel primary products	2.2	4.6	3.6	3.9	5.3	6.7	5.5	5.5	3.2	2.4	4.9	5.5
Services, income, and private transfers	4.0	4.3	2.0	3.5	3.1	4.5	4.9	4.8	4.6	5.4	5.2	5.0
Diversified	2.9	3.4	4.8	4.7	5.8	4.0	5.6	4.4	−1.7	−0.5	3.5	4.0
By external financing source												
Net creditor countries	1.3	2.5	6.0	2.2	1.8	1.5	2.8	3.6	0.4	0.6	4.4	2.1
Net debtor countries	4.4	5.6	6.4	6.5	6.8	6.2	6.6	5.9	3.3	3.9	5.4	5.4
Official financing	2.7	3.7	1.7	1.9	2.5	5.4	5.4	4.0	3.8	3.2	4.5	4.8
Private financing	4.9	6.0	7.0	7.5	7.7	6.6	6.9	6.3	3.3	4.0	5.6	5.6
Diversified financing	2.6	4.0	4.8	2.4	3.5	4.7	5.0	4.1	3.2	3.0	4.3	4.6
Net debtor countries by debt-servicing experience												
Countries with arrears and/or rescheduling during 1994–98	2.7	3.5	2.8	3.7	4.6	5.1	4.9	4.2	−0.8	1.8	4.1	4.5
Other net debtor countries	5.3	6.5	7.9	7.7	7.7	6.7	7.2	6.5	4.8	4.6	5.8	5.7
Other groups												
Heavily indebted poor countries	2.3	4.1	1.3	1.8	2.9	6.2	6.0	5.0	3.9	3.5	5.0	5.4
Least developed countries	2.2	3.9	0.8	1.7	2.2	6.5	5.4	4.5	4.0	3.8	5.2	5.3
Middle East and north Africa	2.9	3.4	5.3	1.6	2.4	2.1	4.5	3.3	3.2	2.7	4.8	3.9
Memorandum												
Real per capita GDP												
Developing countries	2.0	3.8	3.9	4.4	4.8	4.2	4.9	4.3	1.6	2.2	3.9	3.9
Regional groups												
Africa	−0.7	0.3	−3.2	−2.2	−0.2	1.1	3.0	0.5	0.7	−0.1	1.9	2.1
Asia	5.0	6.0	7.6	7.6	8.0	7.4	6.7	5.3	2.7	4.7	4.9	4.7
Middle East and Europe	0.2	0.9	−0.1	1.2	−2.2	−1.6	5.5	2.9	0.6	−1.4	2.6	2.1
Western Hemisphere	−0.3	1.7	1.5	2.2	3.2	1.1	1.0	4.2	−0.1	−1.4	2.5	3.1

Table 6. Developing Countries—by Country: Real GDP[1]

(Annual percent change)

	Average 1982–91	1992	1993	1994	1995	1996	1997	1998	1999
Africa	**2.2**	**−0.7**	**0.4**	**2.3**	**3.2**	**5.6**	**2.9**	**3.1**	**2.3**
Algeria	2.2	1.6	−2.1	−0.9	3.8	3.8	1.1	5.1	3.4
Angola	2.7	−5.8	−24.0	1.3	11.5	11.6	5.7	6.4	1.3
Benin	1.3	4.0	3.5	4.4	4.6	5.5	5.7	4.5	5.0
Botswana	10.8	3.0	2.0	3.4	4.7	6.9	7.8	6.0	5.0
Burkina Faso	3.5	2.5	−0.8	1.2	4.0	6.0	4.8	6.2	3.7
Burundi	3.8	0.7	−5.9	−3.7	−7.3	−8.4	0.4	4.5	4.7
Cameroon	1.3	−3.1	−3.2	−2.5	3.3	5.0	5.1	5.0	4.4
Cape Verde	−2.2	−18.4	87.9	12.7	2.2	2.6	6.6	8.0	8.0
Central African Republic	0.7	−6.4	0.3	4.9	6.0	−3.2	5.7	4.9	3.1
Chad	6.6	2.4	−2.1	5.7	1.1	3.7	4.1	8.1	−1.1
Comoros	1.3	8.5	3.0	−5.3	−3.9	−0.4	—	—	1.0
Congo, Dem. Rep. of	−0.3	−10.5	−13.5	−3.9	0.7	0.9	−6.4	−3.5	−15.0
Congo, Rep. of	2.6	2.6	−1.0	−5.5	4.0	6.3	−2.7	3.6	−1.6
Côte d'Ivoire	0.6	−0.2	−0.2	2.0	7.1	6.8	6.0	4.5	4.3
Djibouti	0.1	−0.2	−3.9	−2.9	−3.6	−3.7	0.7	0.8	1.3
Equatorial Guinea	1.6	10.7	6.3	5.1	14.3	29.1	71.2	22.0	15.1
Eritrea	...	...	−2.5	9.8	2.9	6.8	7.9	3.9	3.0
Ethiopia	1.4	−5.2	13.4	3.5	6.1	10.9	5.9	−1.0	5.7
Gabon	2.7	−3.3	2.4	3.4	7.0	5.1	5.3	2.1	−5.8
Gambia, The	4.7	4.4	6.1	3.8	−3.4	5.3	0.8	9.9	4.2
Ghana	2.9	3.9	5.0	3.8	4.5	3.5	4.2	4.6	5.5
Guinea	3.3	3.0	4.7	4.0	4.4	4.6	4.8	4.5	3.7
Guinea-Bissau	2.9	1.1	2.1	3.2	4.4	4.6	5.4	−28.1	8.7
Kenya	4.0	−0.8	0.4	2.6	4.4	4.1	2.1	2.1	1.8
Lesotho	4.9	4.6	3.7	3.7	5.9	9.4	4.6	−3.8	0.5
Liberia	...	...	...	...	...	...	...	...	...
Madagascar	0.9	1.2	2.1	—	1.7	2.1	3.7	3.9	4.5
Malawi	3.6	−7.3	9.7	−10.2	15.4	9.0	4.8	3.1	6.8
Mali	2.1	8.4	−2.4	2.2	6.4	2.1	6.8	3.4	5.2
Mauritania	4.4	1.7	5.5	4.6	4.5	4.7	4.8	3.5	4.1
Mauritius	6.4	4.8	6.7	4.3	3.5	5.1	5.5	5.6	5.4
Morocco	4.8	−4.0	−1.0	10.4	−6.6	12.1	−2.0	6.3	0.2
Mozambique, Rep. of	0.1	−8.1	8.7	7.5	4.3	7.1	11.3	12.0	9.7
Namibia	0.7	7.1	−1.7	6.4	3.7	2.1	2.6	2.4	2.4
Niger	0.2	−6.5	1.4	4.0	2.6	3.4	3.3	8.3	2.3
Nigeria	3.5	2.6	2.2	−0.6	2.6	6.4	3.1	1.9	1.1
Rwanda	1.5	6.6	−8.3	−49.5	32.8	15.8	12.8	9.5	5.0
São Tomé and Príncipe	−0.3	0.7	1.1	2.2	2.0	1.5	1.0	2.5	2.5
Senegal	2.7	2.2	−2.2	2.9	5.2	5.1	5.0	5.7	5.1
Seychelles	4.3	6.9	6.5	−0.8	−0.6	4.7	4.3	2.3	2.0
Sierra Leone	−0.2	−9.6	0.1	3.5	−10.0	5.0	−17.6	−0.8	−8.1
Somalia	...	...	...	...	...	...	...	...	...
South Africa	0.9	−2.1	1.2	3.2	3.1	4.2	2.5	0.6	1.2
Sudan	2.6	3.0	3.8	1.8	8.9	4.0	6.7	5.0	6.0
Swaziland	6.6	1.3	3.3	3.5	3.0	3.6	3.7	2.0	2.0
Tanzania	3.4	0.6	1.2	1.6	3.6	4.5	3.5	3.3	5.3
Togo	1.4	−4.0	−15.1	15.0	7.8	9.6	4.2	−2.2	2.1
Tunisia	3.4	7.8	2.2	3.3	2.4	7.0	5.4	5.0	6.5
Uganda	3.3	3.1	8.4	5.4	10.6	7.8	4.5	5.4	7.8
Zambia	0.2	2.0	−0.1	−13.3	−2.3	6.5	3.5	−2.0	1.0
Zimbabwe	3.7	−9.0	1.3	6.9	−0.6	8.7	3.7	2.5	0.5

Table 6 *(continued)*

	Average 1982–91	1992	1993	1994	1995	1996	1997	1998	1999
Asia	**6.9**	**9.4**	**9.4**	**9.6**	**9.0**	**8.3**	**6.7**	**3.8**	**6.0**
Afghanistan, Islamic State of	...	...	...	...	...	...	...	...	...
Bangladesh	4.4	4.8	4.2	4.7	5.3	5.1	5.3	4.7	4.3
Bhutan	7.0	4.4	5.0	5.1	6.9	6.0	5.7	4.6	6.5
Brunei Darussalam	...	−1.1	0.5	1.8	3.0	3.6	4.1	1.0	2.5
Cambodia	...	4.8	7.5	7.0	7.7	7.0	1.0	1.0	4.0
China	9.6	14.2	13.5	12.6	10.5	9.6	8.8	7.8	7.1
Fiji	2.0	4.8	3.5	4.2	2.4	3.3	3.6	4.0	4.5
India	5.4	4.2	5.0	6.7	7.6	7.1	5.8	4.7	6.8
Indonesia	5.5	7.2	7.3	7.5	8.2	8.0	4.5	−13.2	0.2
Kiribati	1.0	−1.6	0.8	7.2	6.5	2.6	3.3	6.1	2.5
Lao P.D. Republic	4.5	7.0	5.9	8.1	7.1	6.9	6.5	5.0	6.5
Malaysia	6.3	8.9	9.9	9.2	9.8	10.0	7.5	−7.5	5.4
Maldives	10.2	6.3	6.2	6.6	7.2	6.5	6.2	6.0	6.0
Marshall Islands	...	0.1	5.4	2.7	−1.9	−13.1	−5.3	−4.3	−1.8
Micronesia, Fed. States of	...	−1.2	5.7	−0.9	1.3	−0.5	−3.8	−2.8	−2.0
Myanmar	0.6	9.7	5.9	6.8	7.2	7.0	7.0	7.0	7.0
Nepal	4.4	3.3	8.2	3.5	5.3	4.0	1.9	4.0	5.0
Pakistan	6.0	7.8	1.9	3.9	5.1	5.0	1.2	3.3	3.1
Papua New Guinea	2.3	11.8	16.6	4.4	−2.9	3.5	−5.4	3.8	6.1
Philippines	1.3	0.3	2.1	4.4	4.7	5.8	5.2	−0.5	3.2
Samoa	13.7	4.1	1.7	−0.1	6.8	6.1	1.6	1.3	2.5
Solomon Islands	1.7	9.5	2.0	5.2	7.7	0.6	−0.5	1.0	4.0
Sri Lanka	4.2	4.3	6.9	5.6	5.5	3.8	6.4	4.7	4.0
Thailand	8.1	8.1	8.4	9.0	8.9	5.9	−1.8	−10.4	4.2
Tonga	2.3	0.3	3.7	5.0	4.8	−1.4	−4.4	−1.5	0.0
Vanuatu	3.1	−0.7	4.5	1.3	3.8	3.5	2.7	2.1	2.7
Vietnam	5.9	8.6	8.1	8.8	9.5	9.3	8.2	3.5	3.5
Middle East and Europe	**3.3**	**6.2**	**3.5**	**0.5**	**3.8**	**4.6**	**4.7**	**2.7**	**0.7**
Bahrain	2.3	7.8	8.3	2.4	2.1	3.1	3.1	2.1	2.5
Cyprus	6.0	9.6	0.7	5.9	6.1	1.9	2.5	5.0	4.5
Egypt	5.7	0.3	0.5	2.9	3.2	4.3	5.0	5.3	6.0
Iran, Islamic Republic of	3.4	6.1	2.1	0.9	2.9	5.5	3.0	1.9	2.6
Iraq	...	...	...	...	...	...	...	...	...
Jordan	2.0	17.0	5.8	7.6	3.9	1.0	1.3	2.2	2.0
Kuwait	−5.7	77.4	34.2	8.4	1.2	1.2	2.3	2.0	−2.4
Lebanon	−2.8	4.5	7.0	8.0	6.5	4.0	4.0	3.0	0.0
Libya	0.6	−4.2	−4.6	−2.2	−1.6	1.2	1.3	−3.0	2.0
Malta	4.1	6.7	4.0	5.0	7.3	3.2	3.7	3.1	3.5
Oman	7.5	8.5	6.1	3.8	4.8	2.9	6.4	2.9	1.1
Qatar	−1.5	9.7	−0.6	2.3	2.9	4.8	24.0	12.3	7.6
Saudi Arabia	1.2	2.8	−0.6	0.5	0.5	1.4	2.7	1.6	−2.3
Syrian Arab Republic	2.0	10.6	5.0	7.7	5.8	1.8	1.2	5.4	0.1
Turkey	4.8	5.0	7.7	−4.7	8.1	6.9	7.6	3.1	−4.3
United Arab Emirates	−0.1	3.8	5.1	8.4	8.1	10.4	3.9	−7.1	8.5
Yemen, Republic of	...	4.9	2.9	−0.5	8.6	5.6	5.2	2.5	3.3

Table 6 *(concluded)*

	Average 1982–91	1992	1993	1994	1995	1996	1997	1998	1999
Western Hemisphere	**1.8**	**3.6**	**4.1**	**5.0**	**1.7**	**3.6**	**5.4**	**2.1**	**0.1**
Antigua and Barbuda	6.7	0.4	5.5	6.2	–5.0	6.1	5.6	3.9	3.1
Argentina	0.4	10.3	6.3	5.8	–2.8	5.5	8.1	3.9	–3.1
Bahamas, The	2.9	–2.0	1.7	0.9	0.3	4.2	3.3	3.0	6.0
Barbados	0.7	–5.7	0.8	4.0	2.9	4.1	2.6	4.8	2.9
Belize	5.1	10.2	3.3	1.8	3.3	2.0	3.5	3.1	2.5
Bolivia	0.6	1.6	4.3	4.7	4.7	4.4	4.4	4.7	2.5
Brazil	2.1	–0.5	4.9	5.9	4.2	2.7	3.6	–0.1	0.5
Chile	3.2	12.3	7.0	5.7	10.6	7.4	7.6	3.4	–1.0
Colombia	3.4	4.0	5.4	5.8	5.2	2.1	3.2	0.4	–5.0
Costa Rica	2.9	7.7	6.3	4.5	2.4	–0.6	3.7	6.2	5.0
Dominica	4.3	2.1	1.7	1.4	2.3	2.1	0.6	4.8	3.5
Dominican Republic	2.0	8.0	3.0	4.3	4.8	7.3	8.2	7.3	8.3
Ecuador	2.2	3.6	2.0	4.4	2.4	1.9	3.5	0.4	–7.0
El Salvador	1.4	7.4	7.4	6.0	6.4	1.8	4.3	3.2	2.0
Grenada	5.8	1.1	–1.2	3.3	3.1	2.9	4.2	5.8	6.2
Guatemala	1.2	4.8	3.9	4.0	4.9	2.9	4.4	5.2	3.3
Guyana	–1.9	7.8	8.2	8.5	5.0	7.9	6.2	–1.5	1.8
Haiti	0.3	–13.2	–2.4	–8.3	4.4	2.7	1.1	3.0	2.0
Honduras	2.5	5.6	6.2	–1.4	4.3	3.7	4.9	5.0	5.0
Jamaica	2.7	1.8	1.3	1.0	0.2	–1.6	–1.7	–0.5	0.4
Mexico	1.4	3.6	2.0	4.5	–6.2	5.1	6.8	4.8	3.7
Netherlands Antilles	0.1	3.7	0.3	2.4	—	–2.4	3.0	3.0	3.0
Nicaragua	–1.9	0.4	–0.2	3.3	4.2	4.5	4.5	5.0	5.0
Panama	1.4	8.2	5.5	2.9	1.8	2.4	4.4	4.0	4.1
Paraguay	2.8	1.8	4.1	3.1	4.7	1.3	3.5	3.5	4.0
Peru	–1.0	–1.6	6.4	13.1	7.3	2.5	6.9	0.3	3.5
St. Kitts and Nevis	5.6	3.5	5.0	5.5	3.7	6.1	6.6	3.6	2.0
St. Lucia	6.6	7.1	2.0	2.1	4.1	1.4	2.1	2.9	3.1
St. Vincent and the Grenadines	5.9	7.5	0.2	–2.4	7.6	1.6	2.1	4.0	4.2
Suriname	–0.8	4.0	–9.5	–5.4	7.1	6.7	5.6	1.9	5.0
Trinidad and Tobago	–2.6	–1.7	–1.4	3.6	4.0	3.8	3.1	4.4	6.9
Uruguay	0.6	7.9	3.0	6.3	–1.8	5.3	5.1	4.5	–2.5
Venezuela	1.9	6.1	0.3	–2.4	4.0	–0.2	6.4	–0.1	–7.2

[1]For many countries, figures for recent years are IMF staff estimates. Data for some countries are for fiscal years.

Table 7. Countries in Transition: Real GDP[1]

(Annual percent change)

	Average 1982–91	1992	1993	1994	1995	1996	1997	1998	1999
Central and eastern Europe	...	**−8.8**	**−3.8**	**−2.9**	**1.7**	**1.6**	**2.3**	**1.8**	**1.4**
Albania	−2.6	−7.2	9.6	9.4	8.9	9.1	−7.0	8.0	8.0
Belarus	...	−9.7	−7.0	−13.2	−10.4	2.9	11.4	8.3	3.0
Bosnia and Herzegovina	...	...	...	...	21.2	69.0	30.0	18.0	8.0
Bulgaria	0.3	−7.3	−1.5	1.7	2.2	−10.9	−7.0	3.5	2.5
Croatia	...	...	−8.0	5.9	6.8	6.0	6.5	2.3	−2.0
Czech Republic	...	...	0.6	2.7	6.4	3.8	0.3	−2.3	−0.5
Czechoslovakia, former	0.3	−8.5	...	...	...	...	...	...	...
Estonia	...	−21.6	−8.2	−2.0	4.3	3.9	10.6	4.0	−1.3
Hungary	−0.4	−3.1	−0.6	2.9	1.5	1.3	4.6	4.9	4.1
Latvia	...	−35.2	−16.1	2.1	0.3	3.3	6.5	3.6	0.8
Lithuania	...	−21.3	−16.2	−9.8	3.3	4.7	7.3	5.1	−3.3
Macedonia, former Yugoslav Rep. of	...	...	−7.5	−1.8	−1.1	1.2	1.4	2.9	2.5
Moldova	...	−29.7	−1.2	−31.2	−1.4	−7.8	1.3	−8.6	−5.0
Poland	0.2	2.6	3.8	5.2	7.0	6.0	6.8	4.8	4.1
Romania	−1.0	−8.7	1.5	3.9	7.1	3.9	−6.1	−5.4	−3.9
Slovak Republic	...	...	−3.7	4.9	6.9	6.6	6.5	4.4	1.0
Slovenia	...	...	2.8	5.3	4.1	3.5	4.6	3.9	3.8
Ukraine	...	−17.0	−14.2	−22.9	−12.2	−10.0	−3.0	−1.7	−0.4
Yugoslavia, former	−2.3	−34.0	...	...	...	...	...	...	...
Russia	...	**−19.4**	**−10.4**	**−11.6**	**−4.2**	**−3.4**	**0.9**	**−4.5**	**3.2**
Transcaucasus and central Asia	...	**−14.1**	**−11.0**	**−11.5**	**−5.0**	**1.3**	**2.6**	**2.3**	**4.4**
Armenia	...	−52.6	−14.1	5.4	6.9	5.9	3.3	7.2	4.0
Azerbaijan	...	−22.7	−23.1	−19.7	−11.8	1.3	5.8	10.0	7.4
Georgia	...	−44.9	−29.3	−10.4	2.6	10.5	10.8	2.9	3.0
Kazakhstan	...	−5.3	−9.2	−12.6	−8.2	0.5	1.7	−2.5	1.7
Kyrgyz Republic	...	−13.9	−15.5	−20.1	−5.4	7.1	9.9	2.3	2.2
Mongolia	3.5	−9.5	−3.0	2.3	6.3	2.6	4.0	3.5	3.5
Tajikistan	...	−28.9	−11.1	−21.4	−12.5	−4.4	1.7	5.3	3.7
Turkmenistan	...	−5.3	−10.0	−17.3	−7.2	−6.7	−11.3	5.0	16.0
Uzbekistan	...	−11.1	−2.3	−4.2	−0.9	1.6	2.4	4.4	4.1

[1]Data for some countries refer to real net material product (NMP) or are estimates based on NMP. For many countries, figures for recent years are IMF estimates. The figures should be interpreted only as indicative of broad orders of magnitude because reliable, comparable data are not generally available. In particular, the growth of output of new private enterprises of the informal economy is not fully reflected in the recent figures.

Table 8. Summary of Inflation

(Percent)

	Ten-Year Averages 1982–91	Ten-Year Averages 1992–2001	1992	1993	1994	1995	1996	1997	1998	1999	2000	2001
GDP deflators												
Advanced economies	**4.8**	**2.0**	**3.2**	**2.7**	**2.2**	**2.2**	**1.8**	**1.7**	**1.4**	**1.0**	**1.5**	**1.9**
United States	3.7	2.0	2.4	2.4	2.1	2.2	1.9	1.9	1.2	1.5	2.0	2.3
European Union	5.8	2.5	4.3	3.5	2.7	3.0	2.5	1.9	2.0	1.6	1.7	1.7
Japan	1.8	—	1.7	0.6	0.2	−0.6	−1.4	0.3	0.3	−0.9	−0.8	0.9
Other advanced economies	8.7	2.4	3.8	3.8	3.3	3.4	2.9	2.1	1.5	0.3	1.3	2.2
Consumer prices												
Advanced economies	**4.9**	**2.3**	**3.5**	**3.1**	**2.6**	**2.6**	**2.4**	**2.1**	**1.5**	**1.4**	**1.9**	**2.0**
United States	4.1	2.5	3.0	3.0	2.6	2.8	2.9	2.3	1.6	2.2	2.5	2.5
European Union	5.7	2.5	4.6	3.8	3.0	2.9	2.5	1.8	1.4	1.4	1.8	1.8
Japan	1.9	0.7	1.7	1.2	0.7	−0.1	0.1	1.7	0.6	−0.3	0.1	0.9
Other advanced economies	8.8	2.8	3.8	3.4	3.3	3.8	3.2	2.4	2.6	1.0	2.5	2.4
Developing countries	**45.7**	**20.3**	**36.1**	**49.8**	**55.1**	**22.9**	**15.1**	**9.5**	**10.1**	**6.5**	**5.7**	**4.7**
Regional groups												
Africa	19.6	24.4	47.1	38.7	54.8	35.5	30.0	13.6	9.2	11.0	9.6	6.1
Asia	9.7	7.6	8.6	10.8	16.0	13.2	8.2	4.7	7.6	2.5	2.6	3.0
Middle East and Europe	21.2	24.7	26.5	26.6	33.3	38.9	26.6	25.3	26.0	20.3	16.2	9.4
Western Hemisphere	166.9	47.4	109.1	202.6	202.5	34.4	21.4	13.0	9.8	8.8	7.7	6.4
Analytical groups												
By source of export earnings												
Fuel	13.7	21.4	22.1	26.2	31.8	43.2	31.9	16.1	15.6	12.0	10.5	8.8
Nonfuel	51.2	20.3	38.0	53.0	58.0	20.8	13.5	8.9	9.6	6.0	5.2	4.3
By external financing source												
Net creditor countries	2.8	3.6	4.3	5.5	4.0	5.8	3.9	1.9	1.8	1.4	3.3	4.1
Net debtor countries	47.7	20.9	37.4	51.6	57.2	23.5	15.5	9.8	10.4	6.7	5.8	4.7
Official financing	34.3	24.0	59.3	37.4	64.8	30.9	22.4	11.2	8.2	10.4	7.6	4.4
Private financing	54.6	21.0	38.0	57.1	61.4	21.4	13.9	9.2	10.0	5.7	5.1	4.3
Diversified financing	22.5	19.2	24.6	28.5	26.2	33.0	26.1	13.3	12.5	11.5	10.7	8.6
Net debtor countries by debt-servicing experience												
Countries with arrears and/or rescheduling during 1994–98	100.1	49.8	113.6	204.3	219.9	38.7	19.8	10.4	16.6	11.6	8.1	6.0
Other net debtor countries	27.5	11.0	14.0	14.1	18.6	18.0	13.9	9.6	8.3	5.0	5.0	4.3
Countries in transition	**15.5**	**118.4**	**788.9**	**634.3**	**273.3**	**133.5**	**42.4**	**27.3**	**21.8**	**43.7**	**19.5**	**14.2**
Central and eastern Europe	...	74.8	278.3	366.8	150.4	72.2	32.1	38.4	18.7	20.5	19.4	12.3
Excluding Belarus and Ukraine	...	34.0	104.8	85.1	47.5	24.8	23.3	41.4	17.0	10.9	10.7	7.1
Russia	...	156.1	1,734.7	874.7	307.4	197.4	47.6	14.7	27.7	85.9	20.5	15.9
Transcaucasus and central Asia	...	193.8	949.2	1,428.7	1,800.7	265.4	80.8	33.0	13.1	15.5	16.3	17.9
Memorandum												
Median inflation rate												
Advanced economies	5.4	2.2	3.2	3.0	2.4	2.4	2.1	1.7	1.6	1.4	2.1	2.0
Developing countries	9.5	7.0	9.9	9.3	10.6	10.1	7.1	6.3	5.7	4.0	4.0	3.6
Countries in transition	11.9	155.2	839.1	472.3	131.6	39.2	24.1	14.8	10.0	8.1	7.9	5.2

Table 9. Advanced Economies: GDP Deflators and Consumer Prices
(Annual percent change)

	Ten-Year Averages		1992	1993	1994	1995	1996	1997	1998	1999	2000	2001	Fourth Quarter[1]		
	1982–91	1992–2001											1999	2000	2001
GDP deflators															
Advanced economies	**4.8**	**2.0**	**3.2**	**2.7**	**2.2**	**2.2**	**1.8**	**1.7**	**1.4**	**1.0**	**1.5**	**1.9**	...	...	...
Major industrial countries	3.9	1.7	2.8	2.3	1.8	1.9	1.5	1.5	1.2	1.0	1.4	1.8	1.0	1.8	1.8
United States	3.7	2.0	2.4	2.4	2.1	2.2	1.9	1.9	1.2	1.5	2.0	2.3	1.6	2.3	2.3
Japan	1.8	—	1.7	0.6	0.2	−0.6	−1.4	0.3	0.3	−0.9	−0.8	0.9	−1.5	0.2	1.0
Germany	1.5	2.0	5.0	3.7	2.5	2.0	1.0	0.8	1.0	1.0	1.1	1.5	0.3	1.9	1.3
France	5.3	1.3	2.0	2.3	1.7	1.6	1.4	1.4	0.7	0.3	0.8	0.8	0.5	0.8	0.8
Italy	9.5	3.2	4.5	3.9	3.5	5.0	5.3	2.4	2.7	1.5	1.9	1.6	1.5	1.9	1.5
United Kingdom	5.9	2.7	4.0	2.8	1.5	2.5	3.3	2.9	3.2	2.7	2.7	1.9	2.2	2.7	2.1
Canada	4.2	1.4	1.3	1.5	1.1	2.3	1.6	0.8	−0.6	1.7	2.1	1.9	3.1	1.6	1.9
Other advanced economies	8.8	2.9	5.0	4.4	3.8	3.8	2.8	2.4	2.3	1.0	1.6	2.3	...	...	...
Spain	8.9	3.5	6.9	4.3	3.8	5.0	3.2	2.1	2.3	3.1	2.4	2.2	...	...	...
Netherlands	1.7	2.1	2.3	1.9	2.3	1.8	1.2	2.0	1.9	1.2	2.9	3.2	...	...	...
Belgium	4.1	1.8	3.6	3.8	1.8	1.8	1.2	1.3	1.6	1.0	1.1	1.3	...	...	...
Sweden	7.9	1.7	1.0	2.6	2.4	3.5	1.4	1.2	1.3	0.5	1.1	1.9	...	...	...
Austria	3.3	2.0	4.3	2.8	2.8	2.3	1.3	1.6	0.6	1.4	1.5	1.7	...	...	...
Denmark	5.2	1.8	2.2	0.5	1.4	0.8	2.2	1.8	2.1	2.4	2.3	2.1	...	...	...
Finland	6.1	2.0	0.9	2.3	2.0	4.1	−0.2	2.1	2.9	1.0	2.2	2.9	...	...	...
Greece	18.2	7.8	14.8	14.5	11.2	11.2	7.3	6.7	4.9	3.1	2.0	2.8	...	...	...
Portugal	16.9	4.7	10.6	7.0	6.1	5.0	2.5	3.1	4.5	2.7	2.9	2.9	...	...	...
Ireland	5.6	3.6	2.8	5.2	1.7	2.7	2.3	3.5	5.6	4.1	4.2	4.1	...	...	...
Luxembourg	3.2	2.2	1.3	0.8	4.9	4.3	1.7	3.3	1.5	1.1	1.3	1.4	...	...	...
Switzerland	3.8	1.2	2.7	2.7	1.6	1.1	0.4	−0.1	0.2	0.9	1.4	1.5	...	...	...
Norway	5.2	2.2	−0.4	2.1	−0.2	3.1	4.3	2.7	−0.4	6.6	1.6	2.8	...	...	...
Israel	80.8	8.3	12.3	11.6	12.7	8.9	11.2	8.9	7.1	3.6	4.1	3.1	...	...	...
Iceland	28.6	3.2	3.6	2.5	2.0	2.7	1.9	3.4	5.9	4.0	3.4	3.1	...	...	...
Korea	6.9	4.3	7.6	7.1	7.7	7.1	3.9	3.1	5.1	−1.6	0.7	3.1	...	...	...
Australia	6.8	1.3	1.4	1.5	1.0	1.5	2.0	1.4	0.4	1.2	1.3	1.6	...	...	...
Taiwan Province of China	2.3	2.1	3.9	3.5	1.9	1.9	2.7	1.9	2.4	−1.0	1.4	2.5	...	...	...
Hong Kong SAR	8.0	3.4	9.7	8.5	6.9	2.6	5.9	5.8	0.9	−5.6	−2.0	2.1	...	...	...
Singapore	2.7	1.0	1.4	3.4	2.9	2.7	1.3	0.7	−1.8	−1.3	0.6	0.1	...	...	...
New Zealand	8.9	1.6	1.7	2.6	1.5	2.8	1.9	—	1.3	0.4	1.9	2.1	...	...	...
Memorandum															
Industrial countries	4.4	1.9	3.0	2.5	1.9	2.1	1.6	1.6	1.3	1.2	1.5	1.9	...	...	...
European Union	5.8	2.5	4.3	3.5	2.7	3.0	2.5	1.9	2.0	1.6	1.7	1.7	...	...	...
Euro area	5.4	2.3	4.3	3.5	2.7	3.0	2.3	1.6	1.7	1.3	1.5	1.7	...	...	...
Newly industrialized Asian economies	5.4	3.3	6.4	5.9	5.5	4.7	3.6	2.9	3.2	−1.9	0.6	2.6	...	...	...
Consumer prices															
Advanced economies	**4.9**	**2.3**	**3.5**	**3.1**	**2.6**	**2.6**	**2.4**	**2.1**	**1.5**	**1.4**	**1.9**	**2.0**	...	...	...
Major industrial countries	4.2	2.1	3.2	2.8	2.2	2.3	2.2	2.0	1.3	1.5	1.8	1.9	1.7	1.8	1.9
United States	4.1	2.5	3.0	3.0	2.6	2.8	2.9	2.3	1.6	2.2	2.5	2.5	2.6	2.4	2.5
Japan	1.9	0.7	1.7	1.2	0.7	−0.1	0.1	1.7	0.6	−0.3	0.1	0.9	−0.9	0.5	1.0
Germany[2]	2.3	2.0	5.0	4.5	2.7	1.7	1.2	1.5	0.6	0.7	1.2	1.3	1.1	1.0	1.3
France	5.3	1.5	2.4	2.1	1.7	1.8	2.1	1.3	0.7	0.6	1.3	1.1	1.0	1.2	1.1
Italy	8.5	3.2	5.3	4.6	4.1	5.2	3.9	1.7	1.7	1.7	2.2	1.6	2.1	1.9	1.5
United Kingdom[3]	5.6	2.8	4.7	3.0	2.4	2.8	3.0	2.8	2.7	2.3	2.0	2.4	2.2	2.1	2.5
Canada	5.3	1.5	1.5	1.8	0.2	2.2	1.6	1.4	1.0	1.7	2.1	2.0	2.4	1.8	2.0
Other advanced economies	8.4	3.1	4.8	4.2	4.1	3.8	3.2	2.3	2.4	1.3	2.3	2.4	...	...	...
Memorandum															
Industrial countries	4.6	2.2	3.4	3.0	2.3	2.4	2.2	2.0	1.3	1.5	1.9	2.0	...	...	...
European Union	5.7	2.5	4.6	3.8	3.0	2.9	2.5	1.8	1.4	1.4	1.8	1.8	...	...	...
Euro area	5.4	2.4	4.4	3.8	3.0	2.8	2.3	1.6	1.2	1.2	1.7	1.6	...	...	...
Newly industrialized Asian economies	4.2	3.8	5.9	4.6	5.7	4.6	4.3	3.4	4.5	—	2.2	2.5	...	...	...

[1]From fourth quarter of preceding year.
[2]Based on the revised consumer price index for united Germany introduced in September 1995.
[3]Retail price index excluding mortgage interest.

Table 10. Advanced Economies: Hourly Earnings, Productivity, and Unit Labor Costs in Manufacturing
(Annual percent change)

	Ten-Year Averages		1992	1993	1994	1995	1996	1997	1998	1999	2000	2001
	1982–91	1992–2001										
Hourly earnings												
Advanced economies	**6.6**	**3.6**	**5.9**	**4.0**	**3.5**	**3.2**	**3.0**	**3.4**	**3.3**	**3.0**	**2.9**	**3.5**
Major industrial countries	5.6	3.3	5.4	3.6	2.9	2.7	2.4	3.3	3.3	3.1	2.8	3.3
United States	4.6	3.5	4.6	2.8	2.8	2.1	1.3	3.7	5.3	4.9	3.8	3.7
Japan	4.0	1.9	4.6	2.6	2.7	2.5	1.7	3.2	1.1	−0.5	−1.3	2.0
Germany	4.9	3.9	9.5	6.8	2.1	4.0	4.3	1.1	1.7	2.4	3.5	4.0
France	6.8	3.0	4.8	3.9	3.7	1.6	2.6	3.2	2.6	2.4	2.8	2.8
Italy	11.2	3.4	6.7	5.4	3.1	4.7	5.5	4.3	−2.1	2.2	2.3	2.5
United Kingdom	9.9	4.7	6.6	4.7	5.0	4.4	4.3	4.2	4.6	4.0	4.7	4.1
Canada	5.0	2.1	3.5	2.1	1.6	1.4	3.2	0.9	2.1	0.1	2.7	3.3
Other advanced economies	10.8	4.8	8.1	5.8	6.0	5.2	5.5	4.2	3.1	2.6	3.2	4.3
Memorandum												
Industrial countries	6.0	3.4	5.5	3.7	3.1	2.9	2.6	3.3	3.4	3.2	2.9	3.4
European Union	7.9	3.9	7.1	5.4	3.6	3.9	4.0	3.2	2.2	3.0	3.4	3.6
Euro area	7.4	3.7	7.2	5.5	3.1	3.6	3.8	2.8	1.6	2.7	3.1	3.4
Newly industrialized Asian economies	13.2	6.4	14.1	9.2	11.4	7.8	10.1	5.5	1.0	−1.0	1.9	5.3
Productivity												
Advanced economies	**3.3**	**3.3**	**3.2**	**2.1**	**5.0**	**3.8**	**3.2**	**4.5**	**2.3**	**4.4**	**2.9**	**2.1**
Major industrial countries	3.3	3.3	3.3	1.7	4.6	3.7	3.3	4.6	2.3	4.6	2.8	1.9
United States	3.0	4.0	5.1	2.2	3.1	3.9	4.0	5.0	4.8	6.4	3.8	1.8
Japan	3.2	1.3	−3.7	−0.7	3.4	4.8	3.7	4.8	−4.2	3.1	0.7	1.9
Germany	3.7	4.5	4.2	2.9	8.7	4.5	5.4	7.0	4.5	2.5	2.3	2.8
France	3.8	4.1	4.4	0.4	9.0	3.9	2.9	6.4	4.0	3.3	3.7	3.6
Italy	3.1	2.3	4.4	0.6	6.0	3.6	−0.2	2.1	0.2	2.1	1.9	2.2
United Kingdom	5.5	2.3	6.4	4.9	5.3	0.6	−0.7	0.6	−0.5	3.6	2.4	0.3
Canada	2.3	2.1	4.3	3.4	3.8	0.2	1.1	0.3	0.7	3.8	2.0	1.3
Other advanced economies	3.4	3.6	2.8	3.5	6.6	4.3	3.0	4.0	2.4	3.5	3.0	2.9
Memorandum												
Industrial countries	3.2	3.2	3.2	2.0	4.9	3.6	3.1	4.4	2.3	4.2	2.7	1.9
European Union	3.7	3.4	4.1	2.8	7.7	3.5	2.1	4.2	2.3	2.5	2.4	2.2
Euro area	3.5	3.6	3.7	2.3	8.0	4.0	2.7	4.9	2.8	2.3	2.4	2.6
Newly industrialized Asian economies	7.8	5.7	4.2	3.5	6.4	8.0	6.5	5.9	2.4	8.4	5.8	5.9
Unit labor costs												
Advanced economies	**3.2**	**0.2**	**2.6**	**1.9**	**−1.4**	**−0.7**	**−0.2**	**−1.0**	**1.0**	**−1.3**	**—**	**1.3**
Major industrial countries	2.2	—	2.1	1.8	−1.6	−1.0	−0.8	−1.2	1.0	−1.4	−0.1	1.4
United States	1.6	−0.5	−0.5	0.6	−0.2	−1.7	−2.6	−1.3	0.5	−1.4	−0.1	1.9
Japan	0.8	0.5	8.6	3.3	−0.7	−2.2	−1.9	−1.6	5.5	−3.5	−1.9	0.1
Germany	1.1	−0.5	5.1	3.8	−6.1	−0.4	−1.1	−5.5	−2.7	−0.1	1.2	1.2
France	2.9	−1.1	0.3	3.6	−4.9	−2.3	−0.3	−3.0	−1.3	−0.8	−0.9	−0.8
Italy	7.8	1.1	2.2	4.8	−2.7	1.1	5.7	2.1	−2.4	0.1	0.4	0.3
United Kingdom	4.1	2.3	0.2	−0.2	−0.3	3.8	5.0	3.6	5.1	0.4	2.3	3.8
Canada	2.6	—	−0.8	−1.3	−2.2	1.3	2.1	0.6	1.4	−3.6	0.7	2.0
Other advanced economies	7.3	1.1	4.8	2.2	−0.7	0.6	2.2	0.1	0.7	−0.8	0.3	1.3
Memorandum												
Industrial countries	2.7	0.2	2.4	1.7	−1.7	−0.7	−0.4	−1.0	1.1	−0.9	0.2	1.4
European Union	4.1	0.6	3.0	2.6	−3.7	0.5	1.9	−0.9	−0.1	0.5	1.0	1.3
Euro area	3.8	0.1	3.5	3.2	−4.5	−0.4	1.1	−2.0	−1.1	0.4	0.8	0.8
Newly industrialized Asian economies	4.3	0.2	7.3	4.6	3.2	−1.1	2.3	−0.7	−0.9	−7.8	−3.5	−0.6

Table 11. Developing Countries: Consumer Prices
(Annual percent change)

| | Ten-Year Averages | | 1992 | 1993 | 1994 | 1995 | 1996 | 1997 | 1998 | 1999 | 2000 | 2001 |
	1982–91	1992–2001										
Developing countries	**45.7**	**20.3**	**36.1**	**49.8**	**55.1**	**22.9**	**15.1**	**9.5**	**10.1**	**6.5**	**5.7**	**4.7**
Regional groups												
Africa	19.6	24.4	47.1	38.7	54.8	35.5	30.0	13.6	9.2	11.0	9.6	6.1
Sub-Sahara	22.7	29.4	57.0	47.5	68.7	40.7	36.6	16.7	10.7	13.8	11.5	7.1
Excluding Nigeria and South Africa	28.6	44.1	91.7	72.9	121.8	57.3	58.7	23.4	13.0	20.3	16.4	7.6
Asia	9.7	7.6	8.6	10.8	16.0	13.2	8.2	4.7	7.6	2.5	2.6	3.0
Excluding China and India	13.2	8.8	9.4	8.4	8.0	9.2	7.6	6.3	21.3	9.1	4.3	4.7
Middle East and Europe	21.2	24.7	26.5	26.6	33.3	38.9	26.6	25.3	26.0	20.3	16.2	9.4
Western Hemisphere	166.9	47.4	109.1	202.6	202.5	34.4	21.4	13.0	9.8	8.8	7.7	6.4
Analytical groups												
By source of export earnings												
Fuel	13.7	21.4	22.1	26.2	31.8	43.2	31.9	16.1	15.6	12.0	10.5	8.8
Manufactures	50.6	23.0	42.6	69.5	76.2	23.2	13.6	8.7	7.4	4.7	4.9	4.0
Nonfuel primary products	70.9	26.9	67.9	46.2	62.8	29.8	27.0	14.8	9.8	12.1	9.6	5.9
Services, income, and private transfers	22.5	8.1	20.9	11.8	9.9	10.5	7.1	5.6	4.7	3.6	4.2	4.0
Diversified	52.0	10.8	16.7	13.8	11.3	10.5	8.9	7.9	20.6	9.7	5.0	5.0
By external financing source												
Net creditor countries	2.8	3.6	4.3	5.5	4.0	5.8	3.9	1.9	1.8	1.4	3.3	4.1
Net debtor countries	47.7	20.9	37.4	51.6	57.2	23.5	15.5	9.8	10.4	6.7	5.8	4.7
Official financing	34.3	24.0	59.3	37.4	64.8	30.9	22.4	11.2	8.2	10.4	7.6	4.4
Private financing	54.6	21.0	38.0	57.1	61.4	21.4	13.9	9.2	10.0	5.7	5.1	4.3
Diversified financing	22.5	19.2	24.6	28.5	26.2	33.0	26.1	13.3	12.5	11.5	10.7	8.6
Net debtor countries by debt-servicing experience												
Countries with arrears and/or rescheduling during 1994–98	100.1	49.8	113.6	204.3	219.9	38.7	19.8	10.4	16.6	11.6	8.1	6.0
Other net debtor countries	27.5	11.0	14.0	14.1	18.6	18.0	13.9	9.6	8.3	5.0	5.0	4.3
Other groups												
Heavily indebted poor countries	46.5	36.3	79.8	59.9	92.5	49.5	46.6	18.5	11.9	15.8	11.9	5.8
Least developed countries	29.1	39.7	86.7	68.4	102.4	50.5	51.0	20.1	13.2	18.4	13.5	7.1
Middle East and north Africa	14.6	12.8	18.0	16.9	18.4	24.5	14.0	9.0	9.3	6.9	6.6	6.2
Memorandum												
Median												
Developing countries	9.5	7.0	9.9	9.3	10.6	10.1	7.1	6.3	5.7	4.0	4.0	3.6
Regional groups												
Africa	9.9	9.1	11.1	9.5	24.7	12.3	7.7	7.5	5.8	4.0	4.6	3.8
Asia	8.2	6.9	9.0	8.0	8.3	8.6	6.9	6.7	8.0	5.4	3.7	3.9
Middle East and Europe	6.2	4.1	6.2	5.0	4.7	5.0	6.5	3.1	2.9	2.0	3.0	2.8
Western Hemisphere	14.3	7.1	12.1	10.7	8.3	10.2	7.1	6.1	5.0	4.1	4.2	3.5

Table 12. Developing Countries—by Country: Consumer Prices[1]
(Annual percent change)

	Average 1982–91	1992	1993	1994	1995	1996	1997	1998	1999
Africa	**19.6**	**47.1**	**38.7**	**54.8**	**35.5**	**30.0**	**13.6**	**9.2**	**11.0**
Algeria	10.7	31.7	20.5	29.0	32.2	17.4	4.9	5.8	2.6
Angola	8.1	299.1	1,379.5	949.8	2,672.2	4,146.0	111.2	107.4	248.2
Benin	1.4	5.9	0.4	38.5	14.5	4.9	3.8	5.8	1.0
Botswana	11.8	16.2	14.3	10.5	10.5	10.1	8.8	6.5	7.7
Burkina Faso	3.2	−2.0	0.6	24.7	7.8	6.1	2.3	5.0	−1.0
Burundi	7.2	4.5	9.7	14.7	19.4	26.4	31.1	12.6	7.9
Cameroon	6.1	1.9	−3.7	12.7	25.8	6.6	5.2	2.8	0.0
Cape Verde	10.8	13.4	5.8	3.4	8.4	6.0	8.6	4.4	4.5
Central African Republic	2.8	−0.8	−2.9	24.5	19.2	3.7	1.6	−1.9	0.8
Chad	3.5	−3.8	−7.0	41.3	9.5	11.4	5.9	4.4	−8.4
Comoros	2.7	−1.4	2.0	25.3	7.1	1.4	1.0	1.0	3.0
Congo, Dem. Rep. of	113.2	4,129.2	1,893.1	23,760.5	541.8	616.8	198.5	29.0	200.0
Congo, Rep. of	5.6	−3.9	4.9	42.9	8.6	10.2	19.3	−4.0	3.9
Côte d'Ivoire	4.2	4.2	2.1	26.0	14.3	2.7	5.6	4.5	0.7
Djibouti	4.7	3.4	4.4	6.5	4.5	2.6	2.4	2.0	2.0
Equatorial Guinea	16.6	1.0	1.6	38.9	11.4	6.0	3.0	3.0	3.0
Eritrea	...	...	4.6	11.6	10.7	9.3	1.3	16.6	8.3
Ethiopia	6.1	21.0	10.0	1.2	13.4	0.9	−6.4	3.7	4.2
Gabon	5.0	−10.8	0.6	36.1	10.0	4.5	2.5	2.1	2.0
Gambia, The	17.3	12.0	5.9	4.0	4.0	4.8	2.1	2.1	2.5
Ghana	34.5	10.1	24.9	24.9	59.5	45.6	28.8	19.3	12.4
Guinea	29.6	16.6	7.2	4.2	5.6	3.0	1.9	5.1	4.5
Guinea-Bissau	55.9	69.4	48.2	15.2	45.4	50.7	49.1	8.0	−0.9
Kenya	12.3	27.3	45.9	28.8	1.5	9.0	11.2	6.6	3.5
Lesotho	14.5	17.0	13.8	7.2	9.9	9.1	8.5	7.8	6.0
Liberia	...	...	...	...	...	...	...	...	...
Madagascar	15.5	15.3	9.2	39.1	49.0	19.8	4.5	6.2	9.4
Malawi	15.7	23.2	22.8	34.7	83.1	37.7	9.1	29.8	45.1
Mali	1.8	−5.9	−0.6	24.8	12.4	6.5	−0.7	4.1	−1.1
Mauritania	8.3	10.1	9.3	4.1	6.5	4.7	4.5	8.0	4.0
Mauritius	8.0	2.9	8.9	9.4	6.1	5.8	7.9	5.3	5.6
Morocco	7.4	5.7	5.2	5.1	6.1	3.0	0.9	2.9	0.8
Mozambique, Rep. of	45.0	45.1	42.3	63.1	54.4	44.6	6.4	0.6	1.7
Namibia	12.6	17.7	8.5	10.8	10.0	8.0	8.8	6.2	5.4
Niger	0.4	−1.7	−0.4	35.6	10.9	5.3	2.9	4.5	3.0
Nigeria	18.7	44.6	57.2	57.0	72.8	29.3	8.5	10.0	6.6
Rwanda	5.6	9.5	12.5	64.0	22.0	8.9	11.7	6.8	−2.5
Sâo Tomé and Príncipe	21.1	33.7	25.5	51.2	36.8	42.0	69.0	42.1	16.3
Senegal	5.1	−0.1	−0.6	32.1	8.0	2.8	2.5	1.3	0.8
Seychelles	2.2	3.2	1.3	1.8	−0.3	−1.1	0.6	1.0	1.5
Sierra Leone	76.5	65.5	22.2	24.2	26.0	23.1	14.9	35.5	29.6
Somalia	...	...	...	...	...	...	...	...	...
South Africa	14.7	13.9	9.7	9.0	8.6	7.4	8.6	6.9	5.2
Sudan	51.8	117.6	101.3	115.5	68.4	132.8	46.7	17.1	16.0
Swaziland	12.7	8.1	11.2	13.9	12.3	6.4	7.2	7.5	6.5
Tanzania	30.3	21.9	23.6	37.1	26.5	21.0	16.1	12.6	7.9
Togo	1.7	1.6	−0.1	35.3	15.8	4.6	7.1	1.0	−0.1
Tunisia	8.3	5.8	4.0	4.6	6.3	3.8	3.7	3.1	3.1
Uganda	98.9	42.2	30.0	6.5	6.1	7.5	7.8	5.8	−0.2
Zambia	53.7	165.7	183.3	54.6	34.9	43.1	24.4	24.5	26.7
Zimbabwe	14.9	42.1	27.6	22.2	22.6	21.4	18.8	32.3	60.0

Table 12 *(continued)*

	Average 1982–91	1992	1993	1994	1995	1996	1997	1998	1999
Asia	**9.7**	**8.6**	**10.8**	**16.0**	**13.2**	**8.2**	**4.7**	**7.6**	**2.5**
Afghanistan, Islamic State of	...	...	...	...	...	...	...	...	...
Bangladesh	9.5	3.5	3.1	6.3	7.7	4.5	4.8	8.0	7.2
Bhutan	9.8	16.0	8.9	8.1	10.7	7.0	7.0	7.0	7.0
Brunei Darussalam	...	1.3	4.3	2.4	6.0	2.0	1.7	—	1.0
Cambodia	...	75.0	114.3	-0.5	7.7	6.8	8.0	14.8	7.9
China	7.1	6.4	14.7	24.1	17.1	8.3	2.8	-0.8	-1.4
Fiji	6.6	8.2	6.5	4.9	5.2	0.6	—	2.2	2.2
India	8.9	11.8	6.4	10.2	10.2	9.0	7.2	13.2	5.0
Indonesia	8.3	7.5	9.7	8.5	9.4	7.9	6.6	58.4	20.5
Kiribati	2.8	4.2	6.1	5.3	4.1	-1.5	2.2	4.7	2.0
Lao P.D. Republic	40.8	9.8	6.3	6.8	19.4	13.0	19.3	81.0	36.0
Malaysia	2.5	4.7	3.5	3.7	3.4	3.5	2.7	5.3	2.7
Maldives	5.2	16.8	20.1	3.4	5.5	6.2	7.2	5.0	2.3
Marshall Islands	...	10.3	5.0	5.6	8.3	9.6	4.8	4.0	3.0
Micronesia, Fed. States of	...	5.0	6.0	4.0	4.0	4.0	3.0	3.0	3.0
Myanmar	15.1	22.3	33.6	22.4	28.9	20.0	10.0	10.0	10.0
Nepal	9.7	5.9	9.1	8.7	9.2	1.7	10.1	9.0	7.0
Pakistan	7.0	9.4	9.8	11.3	13.0	10.8	11.8	7.8	5.7
Papua New Guinea	5.7	4.3	5.0	2.9	17.3	11.6	3.9	13.5	6.3
Philippines	13.5	8.9	7.6	9.1	8.1	8.4	5.0	9.7	6.7
Samoa	4.2	9.0	1.7	12.1	-2.9	5.4	6.9	2.2	3.0
Solomon Islands	11.6	9.2	9.2	13.3	9.6	12.1	8.1	8.0	5.0
Sri Lanka	11.7	11.4	11.7	8.4	7.7	15.9	9.6	9.4	4.7
Thailand	3.8	4.1	3.4	5.1	5.8	5.9	5.6	8.1	0.3
Tonga	10.3	8.7	3.1	2.4	0.3	2.8	1.8	2.9	3.0
Vanuatu	6.8	4.1	3.6	2.3	2.2	0.9	2.8	5.0	4.3
Vietnam	132.6	37.8	8.4	9.4	17.0	5.8	3.2	7.7	7.6
Middle East and Europe	**21.2**	**26.5**	**26.6**	**33.3**	**38.9**	**26.6**	**25.3**	**26.0**	**20.3**
Bahrain	0.9	—	2.1	0.4	3.1	-0.2	1.0	-0.2	1.0
Cyprus	4.3	6.5	4.9	4.7	2.6	3.0	3.6	2.2	1.8
Egypt	18.4	21.1	11.2	9.0	9.4	7.0	6.2	4.7	3.8
Iran, Islamic Republic of	18.0	24.4	22.9	35.2	49.4	23.1	17.3	22.0	15.0
Iraq	...	...	...	...	...	...	...	...	...
Jordan	7.4	4.0	3.3	3.5	2.4	6.5	3.0	4.5	1.9
Kuwait	4.0	-0.5	0.4	2.5	2.7	3.6	0.7	0.5	1.9
Lebanon	80.2	99.8	24.7	8.0	10.6	8.9	7.8	4.5	1.0
Libya	7.7	18.0	23.0	14.5	11.0	13.0	8.0	7.0	6.0
Malta	1.4	1.8	4.0	4.1	4.0	2.4	3.1	2.4	2.5
Oman	1.6	1.0	1.1	-0.7	-1.1	0.3	-0.8	-0.9	-0.3
Qatar	3.3	3.0	-0.9	1.4	3.0	7.1	2.7	2.9	2.0
Saudi Arabia	—	-0.4	0.8	0.6	5.0	0.9	-0.4	-0.2	-1.2
Syrian Arab Republic	21.8	3.4	23.6	7.9	1.2	1.6	1.9	-0.4	2.5
Turkey	48.5	70.1	66.1	106.3	93.7	82.3	85.7	84.6	64.9
United Arab Emirates	4.0	6.2	5.0	4.0	5.1	2.6	2.1	2.0	2.0
Yemen, Republic of	...	50.6	62.3	71.8	62.5	41.8	4.3	11.2	7.0

Table 12 *(concluded)*

	Average 1982–91	1992	1993	1994	1995	1996	1997	1998	1999
Western Hemisphere	**166.9**	**109.1**	**202.6**	**202.5**	**34.4**	**21.4**	**13.0**	**9.8**	**8.8**
Antigua and Barbuda	3.8	3.0	3.1	3.5	2.7	3.5	1.2	3.4	1.6
Argentina	452.7	24.9	10.6	4.2	3.4	0.2	0.8	0.9	−1.2
Bahamas, The	5.1	5.7	2.7	1.3	2.1	1.4	0.5	1.3	1.5
Barbados	4.9	6.0	1.2	−0.1	2.4	1.8	3.6	1.7	0.5
Belize	3.4	2.4	1.4	2.5	2.9	6.3	1.0	—	2.0
Bolivia	220.0	12.1	8.5	7.9	10.2	12.4	4.7	7.7	2.2
Brazil	407.4	540.3	2,103.3	2,123.7	60.3	15.8	6.9	3.2	4.9
Chile	20.5	15.4	12.7	11.4	8.2	7.4	6.1	5.1	3.3
Colombia	23.9	27.1	22.5	22.8	20.9	20.8	18.5	18.7	10.9
Costa Rica	24.8	21.8	9.8	13.5	23.2	17.6	13.3	11.7	11.0
Dominica	3.9	5.3	1.6	—	1.3	1.7	2.4	0.9	1.6
Dominican Republic	28.8	4.3	5.3	8.3	12.5	5.4	8.3	4.8	6.5
Ecuador	39.7	54.6	45.0	27.3	22.7	24.4	30.6	36.1	55.1
El Salvador	19.0	11.2	18.5	10.6	10.1	9.8	4.5	2.5	0.6
Grenada	3.6	3.8	2.8	2.6	2.2	2.8	1.3	1.4	0.5
Guatemala	14.9	10.2	13.4	12.5	8.4	11.0	9.2	6.6	5.3
Guyana	37.6	28.2	12.0	12.4	12.2	7.1	3.6	4.6	5.5
Haiti	8.8	21.3	18.8	37.4	30.2	21.9	16.2	10.0	10.0
Honduras	10.2	8.8	10.7	21.7	29.5	23.8	20.2	13.0	12.0
Jamaica	22.7	57.5	24.3	33.2	21.7	21.5	9.1	8.1	7.0
Mexico	64.4	15.5	9.8	7.0	34.8	35.3	20.8	15.9	16.6
Netherlands Antilles	2.9	1.5	1.9	1.9	2.7	3.5	3.5	3.5	3.5
Nicaragua	898.4	40.5	20.4	7.7	11.2	6.8	5.7	5.0	5.0
Panama	1.2	1.8	0.5	1.3	0.9	1.3	1.3	0.6	1.0
Paraguay	22.8	15.2	18.2	20.5	13.4	9.8	8.3	7.0	6.0
Peru	380.7	73.5	48.6	23.7	11.1	11.5	8.5	7.3	3.5
St. Kitts and Nevis	2.8	2.9	1.8	1.4	3.0	2.0	8.9	3.6	4.1
St. Lucia	3.1	4.6	0.8	2.7	5.9	0.9	—	2.8	1.0
St. Vincent and the Grenadines	3.7	3.8	4.2	0.4	2.4	4.4	0.5	2.1	2.0
Suriname	14.5	43.7	143.4	368.5	235.5	−0.8	7.2	20.8	28.7
Trinidad and Tobago	10.1	6.5	13.2	3.7	5.3	3.3	3.7	5.6	3.2
Uruguay	67.3	68.5	54.2	44.7	42.2	28.3	19.8	10.8	5.7
Venezuela	25.1	31.4	38.1	60.8	59.9	99.9	50.0	35.8	23.6

[1]For many countries, figures for recent years are International Monetary Fund staff estimates. Data for some countries are for fiscal years.

Table 13. Countries in Transition: Consumer Prices[1]
(Annual percent change)

	Average 1982–91	1992	1993	1994	1995	1996	1997	1998	1999
Central and eastern Europe	...	**278.3**	**366.8**	**150.4**	**72.2**	**32.1**	**38.4**	**18.7**	**20.5**
Albania	3.1	225.2	85.0	22.6	7.8	12.7	33.2	20.6	−0.5
Belarus	...	969.0	1,188.0	2,200.0	709.0	53.0	64.0	73.2	293.8
Bosnia and Herzegovina	...	...	...	...	−4.0	−25.0	14.0	10.0	5.0
Bulgaria	21.3	82.0	72.8	96.0	62.1	123.0	1,082.2	22.3	0.3
Croatia	...	...	1,516.6	97.5	2.0	3.5	3.6	5.7	3.5
Czech Republic	...	...	20.8	10.0	9.1	8.8	8.5	10.6	2.1
Czechoslovakia, former	7.0	11.0	...	...	...	...	...	...	...
Estonia	...	1,069.0	89.0	47.7	29.0	23.1	11.2	8.2	3.3
Hungary	13.5	22.8	22.4	18.8	28.3	23.5	18.3	14.3	10.0
Latvia	...	951.3	109.1	35.8	25.1	17.6	8.4	4.7	3.2
Lithuania	...	1,021.0	410.4	72.1	39.5	24.7	8.8	5.1	0.8
Macedonia, former Yugoslav Rep. of	...	...	338.6	126.4	16.2	2.0	1.8	−1.0	−0.4
Moldova	...	1,276.0	788.5	329.6	30.2	23.5	11.8	7.7	39.3
Poland	77.7	43.0	35.3	32.2	27.9	19.9	14.9	11.8	7.3
Romania	22.5	210.4	256.1	136.7	32.3	38.8	154.8	59.1	45.8
Slovak Republic	...	...	23.0	13.4	9.9	5.8	6.1	6.7	10.7
Slovenia	...	...	31.9	21.5	13.5	9.9	8.4	8.0	6.1
Ukraine	...	1,210.0	4,734.9	891.2	376.4	80.2	15.9	10.6	22.7
Yugoslavia, former	155.9	6,146.6	...	...	...	...	...	...	...
Russia	...	**1,734.7**	**874.7**	**307.4**	**197.4**	**47.6**	**14.7**	**27.7**	**85.9**
Transcaucasus and central Asia	...	**949.2**	**1,428.7**	**1,800.7**	**265.4**	**80.8**	**33.0**	**13.1**	**15.5**
Armenia	...	824.5	3,731.8	5,273.4	176.7	18.7	14.0	8.7	0.7
Azerbaijan	...	912.6	1,129.7	1,664.4	411.7	19.8	3.7	−0.8	−8.5
Georgia	...	887.4	3,125.4	15,606.5	162.7	39.4	7.1	3.5	19.1
Kazakhstan	...	1,515.7	1,662.3	1,879.9	176.3	39.1	17.4	7.3	8.4
Kyrgyz Republic	...	853.8	772.4	189.9	38.9	30.3	25.5	12.0	36.8
Mongolia	2.1	202.6	268.4	87.6	56.9	46.9	36.6	9.4	7.9
Tajikistan	...	1,156.7	2,194.9	350.4	610.0	418.2	88.0	43.2	27.6
Turkmenistan	...	492.9	3,102.4	1,748.3	1,005.2	992.4	83.7	16.8	23.5
Uzbekistan	...	645.2	534.2	1,568.3	304.6	54.0	70.9	29.0	29.1

[1]For many countries, inflation for the earlier years is measured on the basis of a retail price index. Consumer price indices with a broader and more up-to-date coverage are typically used for more recent years.

Table 14. Summary Financial Indicators
(Percent)

	1992	1993	1994	1995	1996	1997	1998	1999	2000	2001
Advanced economies										
Central government fiscal balance[1]										
Advanced economies	−4.1	−4.4	−3.7	−3.3	−2.7	−1.5	−1.1	−0.8	−0.6	−0.2
United States	−4.9	−4.2	−3.0	−2.6	−1.8	−0.5	0.4	1.0	1.5	1.7
European Union	−5.0	−6.0	−5.3	−4.6	−4.0	−2.4	−1.7	−1.1	−0.9	−0.8
Euro area	−4.3	−5.2	−4.6	−4.2	−3.8	−2.4	−2.1	−1.5	−1.3	−1.1
Japan	−1.7	−2.7	−3.5	−4.0	−4.3	−4.0	−4.9	−5.7	−6.0	−5.0
Other advanced economies	−2.2	−2.0	−1.3	−0.8	−0.1	0.6	−0.3	−0.5	−0.3	0.2
General government fiscal balance[1]										
Advanced economies	−4.2	−4.7	−4.0	−3.8	−3.1	−1.7	−1.2	−1.0	−0.9	−0.5
United States	−6.0	−5.1	−3.8	−3.3	−2.4	−1.2	−0.1	0.5	1.0	1.2
European Union	−5.2	−6.3	−5.6	−5.4	−4.3	−2.5	−1.6	−0.8	−0.6	−0.4
Euro area	−4.7	−5.7	−5.2	−5.1	−4.4	−2.6	−2.1	−1.2	−0.8	−0.7
Japan	1.5	−1.6	−2.3	−3.6	−4.2	−3.4	−4.3	−7.1	−8.4	−6.7
Other advanced economies	−3.0	−2.3	−1.5	−0.8	—	0.7	−0.4	−0.1	—	0.6
General government structural balance[2]										
Advanced economies	−3.9	−3.7	−3.2	−3.1	−2.4	−1.2	−0.6	−0.5	−0.6	−0.4
Growth of broad money										
Advanced economies	3.1	3.9	2.5	4.4	4.9	5.0	6.7	...	...	...
United States	1.8	1.3	0.6	3.9	4.6	5.7	8.5	6.1	...	...
Euro area	4.9	5.9	2.4	5.8	5.0	4.4	4.5	7.8	...	...
Japan	−0.2	2.2	2.8	3.3	2.9	3.9	4.0	2.7	...	...
Other advanced economies	8.1	7.8	9.4	8.2	8.5	6.3	10.3	...	...	...
Short-term interest rates[3]										
United States	3.4	3.0	4.2	5.5	5.0	5.1	4.8	4.8	5.9	6.2
Japan	4.1	2.7	1.9	1.0	0.3	0.3	0.2	0.1	0.2	0.2
Euro area	11.1	8.6	6.3	6.1	4.6	4.1	3.9	3.0	4.0	4.8
LIBOR	3.9	3.4	5.1	6.1	5.6	5.9	5.6	5.5	6.8	7.1
Developing countries										
Central government fiscal balance[1]										
Weighted average	−3.0	−3.2	−2.7	−2.7	−2.4	−2.6	−4.0	−4.4	−3.6	−2.9
Median	−3.8	−4.1	−3.9	−3.4	−2.9	−2.6	−3.5	−3.1	−2.1	−1.7
General government fiscal balance[1]										
Weighted average	−3.5	−3.6	−3.6	−3.3	−3.0	−3.2	−4.5	−5.1	−4.2	−3.4
Median	−3.8	−4.1	−3.7	−3.3	−2.9	−2.6	−3.1	−3.0	−2.1	−1.5
Growth of broad money										
Weighted average	107.9	117.8	94.5	25.1	22.1	20.2	17.0	16.9	13.3	12.8
Median	17.6	16.4	18.1	16.4	14.1	15.1	9.6	10.1	9.9	9.5
Countries in transition										
Central government fiscal balance[1]	−9.8	−6.2	−7.5	−4.6	−4.6	−4.7	−3.6	−2.1	−1.5	−1.8
General government fiscal balance[1]	−14.3	−6.8	−7.3	−4.6	−5.8	−5.4	−5.4	−3.4	−2.9	−2.2
Growth of broad money	433.9	426.0	192.3	76.2	32.5	32.5	20.2	37.0	22.1	17.9

[1]In percent of GDP.
[2]In percent of potential GDP.
[3]For the United States, three-month treasury bills; for Japan, three-month certificates of deposit; for LIBOR, London interbank offered rate on six-month U.S. dollar deposits.

Table 15. Advanced Economies: General and Central Government Fiscal Balances and Balances Excluding Social Security Transactions[1]
(Percent of GDP)

	1992	1993	1994	1995	1996	1997	1998	1999	2000	2001
General government fiscal balance										
Advanced economies	**−4.2**	**−4.7**	**−4.0**	**−3.8**	**−3.1**	**−1.7**	**−1.2**	**−1.0**	**−0.9**	**−0.5**
Major industrial countries	−4.5	−4.9	−4.2	−4.1	−3.4	−1.9	−1.3	−1.2	−1.1	−0.6
United States	−6.0	−5.1	−3.8	−3.3	−2.4	−1.2	−0.1	0.5	1.0	1.2
Japan	1.5	−1.6	−2.3	−3.6	−4.2	−3.4	−4.3	−7.1	−8.4	−6.7
Germany	−2.5	−3.2	−2.5	−3.2	−3.4	−2.6	−1.7	−1.1	−0.7	−1.0
France[2]	−4.1	−5.9	−5.5	−5.5	−4.2	−3.0	−2.7	−1.8	−1.5	−1.0
Italy	−9.5	−9.4	−9.1	−7.6	−7.1	−2.7	−2.8	−1.9	−1.5	−1.1
United Kingdom[3]	−6.5	−8.0	−6.8	−5.8	−4.4	−2.0	0.2	0.3	0.2	0.2
Canada	−8.0	−7.6	−5.6	−4.3	−1.8	0.8	0.9	2.8	2.3	2.0
Other advanced economies	−3.2	−3.6	−3.0	−2.7	−1.6	−0.7	−1.0	−0.6	−0.3	0.2
Spain	−4.0	−6.7	−6.1	−7.0	−5.0	−3.2	−2.6	−1.1	−0.8	−0.4
Netherlands	−3.8	−3.1	−3.6	−3.9	−1.8	−1.2	−0.8	0.5	0.8	0.4
Belgium	−7.9	−7.2	−4.9	−4.2	−3.7	−2.0	−1.0	−0.9	−0.5	−0.1
Sweden	−7.5	−11.8	−10.8	−7.7	−3.5	−1.7	1.9	1.9	2.0	2.0
Austria	−1.9	−4.2	−4.8	−5.1	−3.8	−1.9	−2.4	−2.0	−1.7	−1.5
Denmark	−2.2	−2.8	−2.4	−2.3	−1.0	0.1	0.9	2.9	2.0	2.2
Finland	−5.5	−7.1	−5.8	−4.4	−3.0	−1.6	1.4	3.1	4.6	4.9
Greece	−12.8	−13.8	−10.0	−10.2	−7.4	−3.9	−2.5	−1.7	−1.5	−0.9
Portugal	−2.9	−6.1	−6.0	−4.7	−3.9	−2.6	−2.1	−2.0	−1.8	−1.8
Ireland	−2.8	−2.5	−2.1	−2.6	−0.6	0.8	2.1	3.2	3.2	2.7
Luxembourg	2.3	5.2	4.2	2.2	2.7	3.6	3.3	2.4	2.5	3.0
Switzerland	−3.4	−3.6	−2.9	−1.9	−2.2	−2.4	−1.1	−1.4	−1.2	−1.4
Norway	−1.7	−1.4	0.4	3.5	6.6	7.9	3.9	4.7	7.3	5.9
Israel	−3.3	−2.7	−1.1	−2.7	−3.9	−2.5	−2.6	−2.5	−2.7	−2.5
Iceland	−2.8	−4.5	−4.7	−3.0	−1.6	—	0.4	0.7	0.8	1.0
Korea[4]	0.1	1.3	1.0	1.3	1.0	−0.9	−4.0	−2.9	−3.4	−0.8
Australia[5]	−4.7	−4.4	−3.4	−2.1	−0.9	—	0.2	0.3	0.3	0.4
Taiwan Province of China	0.3	0.6	0.2	0.4	−0.7	−0.6	0.9	−0.5	−0.5	−0.4
Hong Kong SAR	2.5	2.3	1.3	−0.3	2.2	6.6	−1.8	−0.2	−0.2	1.0
Singapore	11.4	14.4	13.9	12.3	9.3	9.4	3.6	−5.1	2.6	3.2
New Zealand[6]	−4.1	−0.1	2.0	3.3	2.8	2.3	2.4	1.1	0.3	1.0
Memorandum										
Industrial countries	−4.5	−5.1	−4.3	−4.1	−3.3	−1.8	−1.2	−1.0	−0.9	−0.5
European Union	−5.2	−6.3	−5.6	−5.4	−4.3	−2.5	−1.6	−0.8	−0.6	−0.4
Euro area	−4.7	−5.7	−5.2	−5.1	−4.4	−2.6	−2.1	−1.2	−0.8	−0.7
Newly industrialized Asian economies	1.2	2.1	1.7	1.6	1.2	0.9	−1.6	−2.0	−1.7	−0.2
Fiscal balance excluding social security transactions										
United States	−6.2	−5.3	−4.2	−3.7	−1.8	−0.7	−0.5	−0.2	0.1	0.3
Japan	−2.0	−4.8	−5.1	−6.5	−6.8	−5.9	−6.4	−9.0	−9.6	−7.6
Germany	−2.4	−3.4	−2.6	−2.8	−3.1	−2.7	−1.9	−1.5	−0.9	−1.1
France	−3.5	−4.6	−4.7	−4.8	−3.6	−2.5	−2.6	−1.9	−1.6	−1.4
Italy	−5.2	−5.4	−4.5	−5.6	−5.3	−0.7	1.3	2.7	3.1	3.3
Canada	−5.9	−5.4	−3.4	−2.2	0.4	3.0	2.9	4.5	3.7	3.0

Table 15 *(concluded)*

	1992	1993	1994	1995	1996	1997	1998	1999	2000	2001
Central government fiscal balance										
Advanced economies	**−4.1**	**−4.4**	**−3.7**	**−3.3**	**−2.7**	**−1.5**	**−1.1**	**−0.8**	**−0.6**	**−0.2**
Major industrial countries	−4.3	−4.4	−3.8	−3.4	−2.9	−1.7	−1.1	−0.8	−0.5	−0.2
United States[7]	−4.9	−4.2	−3.0	−2.6	−1.8	−0.5	0.4	1.0	1.5	1.7
Japan[8]	−1.7	−2.7	−3.5	−4.0	−4.3	−4.0	−4.9	−5.7	−6.0	−5.0
Germany[9]	−1.2	−2.1	−1.5	−1.4	−2.2	−1.7	−1.5	−1.3	−1.1	−1.2
France[9]	−3.3	−4.8	−4.8	−4.2	−3.7	−3.5	−3.0	−2.3	−2.1	−1.9
Italy	−10.3	−9.9	−9.1	−7.1	−6.8	−2.6	−2.8	−1.5	−1.3	−1.2
United Kingdom	−7.3	−8.2	−6.7	−5.5	−4.6	−2.0	0.3	0.5	0.5	0.6
Canada	−4.3	−4.6	−3.7	−3.1	−1.3	1.0	1.1	1.1	1.2	0.9
Other advanced economies	−3.3	−4.0	−3.2	−2.9	−1.7	−1.0	−1.2	−1.1	−0.7	−0.2
Memorandum										
Industrial countries	−4.3	−4.6	−3.9	−3.5	−2.9	−1.7	−1.1	−0.7	−0.5	−0.2
European Union	−5.0	−6.0	−5.3	−4.6	−4.0	−2.4	−1.7	−1.1	−0.9	−0.8
Euro area	−4.3	−5.2	−4.6	−4.2	−3.8	−2.4	−2.1	−1.5	−1.3	−1.1
Newly industrialized Asian economies	−0.3	0.5	0.8	0.9	0.7	0.5	−1.8	−2.3	−1.9	−0.6

[1]On a national income accounts basis except as indicated in footnotes. See Box 1.3 for a summary of the policy assumptions underlying the projections.
[2]Adjusted for valuation changes of the foreign exchange stabilization fund.
[3]Excludes asset sales.
[4]Data include social security transactions (that is, the operations of the public pension plan).
[5]Data exclude net advances (primarily privatization receipts and net policy-related lending).
[6]Data from 1992 onward are on an accrual basis and are not strictly comparable with previous cash-based data.
[7]Data are on a budget basis.
[8]Data are on a national income basis and exclude social security transactions.
[9]Data are on an administrative basis and exclude social security transactions.

Table 16. Advanced Economies: General Government Structural Balances[1]

(Percent of potential GDP)

	1992	1993	1994	1995	1996	1997	1998	1999	2000	2001
Structural balance[2]										
Advanced economies	**−3.9**	**−3.7**	**−3.2**	**−3.1**	**−2.4**	**−1.2**	**−0.6**	**−0.5**	**−0.6**	**−0.4**
Major industrial countries	−3.8	−3.7	−3.1	−3.1	−2.6	−1.3	−0.6	−0.6	−0.8	−0.5
United States	−4.8	−3.8	−2.8	−2.2	−1.5	−0.6	0.1	0.3	0.5	0.8
Japan	0.9	−1.5	−1.8	−3.1	−4.7	−3.7	−3.1	−5.4	−6.6	−5.2
Germany[3]	−4.0	−3.1	−2.3	−2.9	−2.3	−1.1	−0.3	0.6	0.5	−0.4
France	−3.7	−3.4	−3.5	−3.7	−2.0	−1.0	−1.5	−0.8	−1.2	−1.0
Italy	−9.4	−8.2	−7.9	−7.0	−6.2	−1.6	−1.6	−0.5	−0.4	−0.3
United Kingdom	−4.0	−5.0	−4.7	−4.7	−3.7	−1.8	−0.1	0.1	—	−0.2
Canada	−3.7	−3.4	−2.9	−2.0	0.8	2.5	2.3	3.3	2.1	1.7
Other advanced economies	−4.6	−4.0	−3.5	−3.4	−1.5	−0.5	−0.3	0.2	0.3	0.2
Spain	−5.0	−5.0	−4.1	−5.3	−3.0	−1.8	−1.8	−1.0	−0.9	−0.6
Netherlands	−3.8	−1.9	−2.8	−2.8	−1.0	−0.9	−1.0	−0.1	−0.2	−1.0
Belgium	−8.0	−5.0	−3.0	−2.6	−1.6	−0.7	—	—	−0.3	−0.3
Sweden	−5.8	−6.1	−7.0	−5.2	−0.1	1.9	5.0	4.0	2.8	2.1
Austria	−2.6	−3.7	−4.6	−5.3	−3.5	−1.0	−1.6	−0.8	−0.8	−0.9
Denmark	−1.1	−1.1	−1.2	−1.7	−0.9	−0.2	0.3	2.1	1.2	1.5
Finland	−1.9	−1.4	−1.5	−1.0	−0.2	−0.8	1.3	3.0	4.2	4.5
Greece	−13.4	−13.0	−9.3	−9.4	−6.8	−3.7	−2.6	−2.1	−2.1	−1.5
Portugal	−4.3	−5.4	−5.0	−3.6	−3.1	−2.1	−2.1	−2.0	−2.0	−1.9
Ireland	−2.1	−0.4	0.3	−1.5	0.2	0.3	1.1	1.9	2.1	1.8
Norway	0.4	0.4	1.3	3.9	6.3	6.7	1.8	3.3	6.7	5.7
Australia[4]	−3.1	−2.9	−2.4	−1.4	−0.3	0.6	0.4	0.4	0.4	0.4
New Zealand[5]	−4.6	−0.5	−0.1	0.1	−0.1	0.4	1.9	0.6	0.6	1.0
Memorandum										
European Union[6]	−5.1	−4.7	−4.2	−4.4	−3.1	−1.3	−0.7	—	−0.2	−0.4
Euro area[6]	−5.2	−4.4	−4.0	−4.2	−3.0	−1.2	−1.0	−0.2	−0.3	−0.5

[1]On a national income accounts basis.

[2]The structural budget position is defined as the actual budget deficit (or surplus) less the effects of cyclical deviations of output from potential output. Because of the margin of uncertainty that attaches to estimates of cyclical gaps and to tax and expenditure elasticities with respect to national income, indicators of structural budget positions should be interpreted as broad orders of magnitude. Moreover, it is important to note that changes in structural budget balances are not necessarily attributable to policy changes but may reflect the built-in momentum of existing expenditure programs. In the period beyond that for which specific consolidation programs exist, it is assumed that the structural deficit remains unchanged.

[3]The estimate of the fiscal impulse for 1995 is affected by the assumption by the federal government of the debt of the Treuhandanstalt and various other agencies, which were formerly held outside the general government sector. At the public sector level, there would be an estimated withdrawal of fiscal impulse amounting to just over 1 percent of GDP.

[4]Excludes commonwealth government privatization receipts.

[5]Excludes privatization proceeds.

[6]Excludes Luxembourg.

Table 17. Advanced Economies: Monetary Aggregates
(Annual percent change)[1]

	1992	1993	1994	1995	1996	1997	1998	1999
Narrow money[2]								
Advanced economies	**8.2**	**8.8**	**4.2**	**5.3**	**4.2**	**4.1**	**5.1**	...
Major industrial countries	8.3	8.4	3.8	4.7	3.6	3.7	4.8	...
United States	14.3	10.6	2.5	−1.6	−4.5	−1.2	2.2	1.8
Japan	3.9	7.0	4.2	13.1	9.7	8.6	5.0	11.7
Euro area	4.2	6.4	4.6	6.7	7.9	7.0	10.1	10.7
Germany	10.8	8.5	5.2	6.8	12.4	2.3	11.1	...
France	−0.2	1.4	2.8	7.7	0.8	6.5	3.1	...
Italy	0.7	7.6	3.4	1.4	3.9	7.7	9.0	...
United Kingdom	2.8	6.0	6.8	5.6	6.7	6.5	5.7	7.1
Canada	6.1	14.9	7.8	6.5	17.2	9.9	8.0	10.3
Other advanced economies	7.2	10.8	6.9	8.7	7.9	6.5	6.9	...
Memorandum								
Newly industrialized Asian economies	12.8	17.6	11.2	11.9	4.3	−3.8	2.0	5.1
Broad money[3]								
Advanced economies	**3.1**	**3.9**	**2.5**	**4.4**	**4.9**	**5.0**	**6.7**	...
Major industrial countries	2.2	2.8	1.7	3.8	4.2	4.7	6.4	...
United States	1.8	1.3	0.6	3.9	4.6	5.7	8.5	6.1
Japan	−0.2	2.2	2.8	3.3	2.9	3.9	4.0	2.7
Euro area	4.9	5.9	2.4	5.8	4.0	4.4	4.5	7.8
Germany	7.6	10.9	1.6	3.6	8.7	3.6	7.3	...
France	5.1	−2.9	1.8	4.6	−3.3	2.0	2.7	...
Italy	0.1	3.8	1.0	−1.9	3.8	9.0	5.6	...
United Kingdom	2.8	4.9	4.2	9.9	9.6	5.5	8.3	3.4
Canada	3.0	3.0	2.8	3.8	1.9	−1.6	1.2	5.5
Other advanced economies	7.1	9.1	6.5	7.4	8.6	6.9	8.2	...
Memorandum								
Newly industrialized Asian economies	16.1	15.5	17.1	12.8	11.5	11.8	21.5	17.9

[1]Based on end-of-period data.

[2]M1 except for the United Kingdom, where M0 is used here as a measure of narrow money; it comprises notes in circulation plus bankers' operational deposits. M1 is generally currency in circulation plus private demand deposits. In addition, the United States includes traveler's checks of nonbank issues and other checkable deposits and excludes private sector float and demand deposits of banks. Japan includes government demand deposits and excludes float. Germany includes demand deposits at fixed interest rates. Canada excludes private sector float.

[3]M2, defined as M1 plus quasi-money, except for Japan, Germany, and the United Kingdom, for which the data are based on M2 plus certificates of deposit (CDs), M3, and M4, respectively. Quasi-money is essentially private term deposits and other notice deposits. The United States also includes money market mutual fund balances, money market deposit accounts, overnight repurchase agreements, and overnight Eurodollars issued to U.S. residents by foreign branches of U.S. banks. For Japan, M2 plus CDs is currency in circulation plus total private and public sector deposits and installments of Sogo Banks plus CDs. For Germany M3 is M1 plus private time deposits with maturities of less than four years plus savings deposits at statutory notice. For Italy, M2 comprises M1 plus term deposits, passbooks from the Postal Office, and CDs with maturities of less than 18 months. For the United Kingdom, M4 is composed of non-interest-bearing M1, private sector interest-bearing sterling sight bank deposits, private sector sterling time banks deposits, private sector holdings of sterling bank CDs, private sector holdings of building society shares and deposits, and sterling CDs less building society holdings of banks deposits and bank CDs and notes and coins.

Table 18. Advanced Economies: Interest Rates

(Percent a year)

	1992	1993	1994	1995	1996	1997	1998	1999	March 2000
Policy-related interest rate[1]									
Major industrial countries	**6.3**	**4.7**	**4.5**	**5.4**	**4.4**	**4.2**	**4.3**	...	...
United States	3.6	3.0	4.2	5.9	5.3	5.5	5.4	5.0	5.6
Japan	4.6	3.0	2.1	1.2	0.4	0.4	0.4	0.0	0.0
Euro area	...	...	...	...	...	...	...	2.7	3.3
Germany	9.4	7.4	5.3	4.4	3.2	3.1	3.3	...	...
France	10.7	8.6	5.6	6.3	3.7	3.3	3.4	...	...
Italy	14.5	10.5	8.8	10.7	8.6	6.6	4.8	...	...
United Kingdom	9.4	5.9	5.5	6.7	6.0	6.6	7.2	5.3	5.8
Canada	6.6	4.6	5.1	6.9	4.3	3.3	4.9	4.7	4.8
Short-term interest rate[2]									
Advanced economies	**6.9**	**5.4**	**4.9**	**5.1**	**4.1**	**4.0**	**4.0**	**3.5**	...
Major industrial countries	6.1	4.6	4.3	4.6	3.7	3.6	3.6	3.3	...
United States	3.4	3.0	4.2	5.5	5.0	5.1	4.8	4.8	6.1
Japan	4.1	2.7	1.9	1.0	0.3	0.3	0.2	0.1	0.1
Euro area	11.1	8.6	6.3	6.1	4.6	4.1	3.9	3.0	3.7
Germany	9.5	7.2	5.3	4.5	3.3	3.3	3.5	...	...
France	9.5	7.2	5.3	4.5	3.3	3.3	3.7	...	...
Italy	14.5	10.5	8.8	10.7	8.6	6.6	4.8	...	...
United Kingdom	9.5	5.9	5.5	6.7	6.0	6.9	7.4	5.3	6.2
Canada	6.6	4.8	5.5	7.1	4.2	3.2	4.7	4.7	5.4
Other advanced economies	10.6	8.7	7.4	7.3	6.2	5.7	5.8	4.4	...
Memorandum									
Newly industrialized Asian economies	9.8	8.5	8.9	9.1	8.8	9.7	10.4	6.4	...
Long-term interest rate[3]									
Advanced economies	**8.0**	**6.6**	**7.2**	**6.8**	**6.1**	**5.4**	**4.5**	**4.6**	...
Major industrial countries	7.5	6.2	6.8	6.4	5.8	5.2	4.2	4.5	...
United States	7.0	5.9	7.1	6.6	6.4	6.4	5.3	5.6	6.3
Japan	5.1	4.0	4.2	3.3	3.0	2.1	1.3	1.6	1.8
Euro area	9.8	8.1	8.2	8.5	7.1	5.9	4.7	4.6	5.3
Germany	7.9	6.4	7.1	6.9	6.2	5.6	4.6	...	...
France	8.6	6.9	7.4	7.6	6.4	5.6	4.8	...	...
Italy	13.3	11.3	10.5	12.2	9.4	6.9	4.9	...	...
United Kingdom	9.1	7.5	8.2	8.2	7.8	7.0	5.5	5.4	5.7
Canada	8.1	7.2	8.4	8.1	7.2	6.1	5.3	5.6	6.0
Other advanced economies	10.5	8.7	9.3	9.1	7.8	6.8	6.0	5.2	...
Memorandum									
Newly industrialized Asian economies	13.7	10.9	11.2	11.0	9.7	10.5	12.2	7.0	...

[1]For the United States, federal funds rate; for Japan, overnight call rate; for Germany, repurchase rate; for France, day-to-day money rate; for Italy, three-month treasury bill gross rate; for the United Kingdom, base lending rate; for Canada, overnight money market financing rate; for the euro area, repurchase rate.

[2]For the United States, three-month certificates of deposit (CDs) in secondary markets; for Japan three-month CDs; for Germany, France, and the United Kingdom, three-month interbank deposits; for Italy, three-month treasury bills gross rate; and for Canada, three-month prime corporate paper.

[3]For the United States, yield on ten-year treasury bonds; for Japan, over-the-counter sales yield on ten-year government bonds with longest residual maturity; for Germany, yield on government bonds with maturities of nine to ten years; for France, long-term (seven- to ten-year) government bond yield (Emprunts d'Etat à long terme TME); for Italy, secondary market yield on fixed-coupon (BTP) government bonds with two to four years' residual maturity; for the United Kingdom, yield on medium-dated (ten-year) government stock; and for Canada, average yield on government bonds with residual maturities of over ten years.

Table 19. Advanced Economies: Exchange Rates

	1992	1993	1994	1995	1996	1997	1998	1999	Exchange Rate Assumption[1] 2000
					National currency units per U.S. dollar				
U.S. dollar nominal exchange rates									
Japanese yen	126.7	111.2	102.2	94.1	108.8	121.0	130.9	113.9	107.9
Euro[2]	...	...	...	...	...	...	...	1.07	0.98
Deutsche mark	1.56	1.65	1.62	1.43	1.50	1.73	1.76	1.84	1.99
French franc	5.29	5.66	5.55	4.99	5.12	5.84	5.90	6.16	6.66
Italian lira	1,232	1,574	1,612	1,629	1,543	1,703	1,736	1,817	1,966.0
Pound sterling[2]	1.76	1.50	1.53	1.58	1.56	1.64	1.66	1.62	1.61
Canadian dollar	1.21	1.29	1.37	1.37	1.36	1.38	1.48	1.49	1.45
Spanish peseta	102.4	127.3	134.0	124.7	126.7	146.4	149.4	156.2	168.9
Netherlands guilder	1.76	1.86	1.82	1.61	1.69	1.95	1.98	2.07	2.24
Belgian franc	32.1	34.6	33.5	29.5	31.0	35.8	36.3	37.9	41.0
Swedish krona	5.82	7.78	7.72	7.13	6.71	7.63	7.95	8.26	8.63
Austrian schilling	11.0	11.6	11.4	10.1	10.6	12.2	12.4	12.9	14.0
Danish krone	6.04	6.48	6.36	5.60	5.80	6.60	6.70	6.98	7.55
Finnish markka	4.48	5.71	5.22	4.37	4.59	5.19	5.34	5.58	6.04
Greek drachma	190.6	229.2	242.6	231.7	240.7	273.1	295.5	305.6	326.0
Portuguese escudo	135.0	160.8	166.0	151.1	154.2	175.3	180.1	188.2	203.5
Irish pound	0.59	0.68	0.67	0.62	0.63	0.66	0.70	0.74	0.80
Swiss franc	1.41	1.48	1.37	1.18	1.24	1.45	1.45	1.50	1.63
Norwegian krone	6.21	7.09	7.06	6.34	6.45	7.07	7.55	7.80	8.20
Israeli new sheqel	2.46	2.83	3.01	3.01	3.19	3.45	3.80	4.14	4.07
Icelandic krona	57.55	67.60	69.94	64.69	66.50	70.90	70.96	72.35	73.25
Korean won	780.7	802.7	803.4	771.3	804.5	951.3	1,401.4	1,188.8	1,119.5
Australian dollar	1.36	1.47	1.37	1.35	1.28	1.35	1.59	1.55	1.57
New Taiwan dollar	25.16	26.39	26.46	26.49	27.46	28.70	33.46	32.27	30.71
Hong Kong dollar	7.74	7.74	7.73	7.74	7.73	7.74	7.75	7.76	7.74
Singapore dollar	1.63	1.62	1.53	1.42	1.41	1.48	1.67	1.69	1.61
									Percent change from previous assumption[3]
					Index, 1980–89 = 100				
Real effective exchange rates[4]									
United States	72.6	74.7	74.0	69.2	73.4	80.0	85.4	86.1	1.2
Japan	119.8	145.5	154.8	161.1	136.4	126.3	114.6	125.8	−2.5
Euro[5]	111.7	109.3	107.0	112.0	112.1	99.8	95.9	90.4	−0.5
Germany	116.3	124.2	128.2	137.7	135.9	126.8	123.3	120.2	−0.2
France	91.8	92.5	91.5	92.4	89.6	85.3	84.0	81.3	−0.2
United Kingdom	98.6	90.6	91.2	86.7	88.8	108.0	119.1	123.3	0.9
Italy	107.3	90.5	84.9	78.6	88.0	90.5	90.9	89.1	−0.2
Canada	111.9	102.1	94.3	93.8	93.5	94.8	90.1	87.2	0.8
Spain	122.0	113.3	106.3	104.8	108.4	106.7	110.3	112.6	−0.2
Netherlands	91.9	93.3	93.1	94.0	90.6	85.5	83.0	81.3	−0.2
Belgium	97.7	99.6	99.4	102.9	100.1	95.8	94.8	93.9	−0.2
Sweden	106.9	81.5	79.1	77.8	86.1	81.6	79.1	76.0	0.1
Austria	89.8	90.4	88.5	85.4	81.5	77.2	75.7	73.6	−0.1
Denmark	108.8	112.9	111.4	114.3	111.6	109.2	109.7	112.0	−0.3
Finland	77.7	66.0	69.4	77.4	72.6	69.1	69.1	68.0	−0.2
Greece	102.1	102.0	104.2	111.0	115.0	118.9	114.7	116.4	−0.4
Portugal	131.8	129.5	127.7	132.6	133.2	130.4	130.6	130.0	−0.2
Ireland	76.4	70.5	67.2	64.6	64.1	62.2	57.7	55.8	−0.5
Switzerland	112.7	114.1	124.1	131.6	131.2	125.6	131.3	132.1	−0.4
Norway	100.1	99.1	100.2	107.3	111.4	116.2	115.2	119.4	−0.3
Australia	96.2	89.0	93.6	93.2	109.2	113.1	102.0	104.0	0.4
New Zealand	98.4	99.4	105.5	111.9	124.7	128.4	111.5	109.4	−0.5

[1]Average exchange rates for the period January 25–February 22, 2000. See "Assumptions" in the Introduction to the Statistical Appendix.
[2]Expressed in U.S. dollars per currency unit.
[3]In nominal effective terms. Average January 25–February 22, 2000 rates compared with December 13, 1999-January 7, 2000 rates.
[4]Defined as the ratio, in common currency, of the normalized unit labor costs in the manufacturing sector to the weighted average of those of its industrial country trading partners, using 1989–91 trade weights.
[5]An effective euro is used prior to January 1, 1999. See Box 5.5 in the *World Economic Outlook*, October 1998.

Table 20. Developing Countries: Central Government Fiscal Balances

(Percent of GDP)

	1992	1993	1994	1995	1996	1997	1998	1999	2000	2001
Developing countries	**−3.0**	**−3.2**	**−2.7**	**−2.7**	**−2.4**	**−2.6**	**−4.0**	**−4.4**	**−3.6**	**−2.9**
Regional groups										
Africa	−6.8	−7.3	−5.1	−3.8	−2.9	−2.9	−3.9	−3.5	−2.1	−2.0
Sub-Sahara	−8.1	−7.9	−5.7	−4.0	−3.6	−3.6	−4.1	−4.3	−2.8	−2.4
Excluding Nigeria and South Africa	−9.8	−7.6	−6.1	−4.9	−4.3	−3.9	−4.0	−4.5	−3.7	−3.3
Asia	−2.9	−2.9	−2.5	−2.4	−2.1	−2.6	−3.8	−4.4	−4.6	−3.9
Excluding China and India	−1.8	−1.9	−1.2	−0.8	−0.8	−1.8	−3.1	−3.5	−4.6	−2.7
Middle East and Europe	−5.6	−7.6	−5.9	−4.5	−4.5	−4.0	−7.1	−6.2	−3.8	−1.8
Western Hemisphere	−0.4	−0.2	−0.9	−1.9	−1.8	−1.6	−3.2	−4.1	−1.7	−1.0
Analytical groups										
By source of export earnings										
Fuel	−5.3	−7.6	−6.8	−4.1	−1.4	−1.2	−6.5	−3.6	0.9	−0.3
Manufactures	−2.3	−2.5	−2.2	−2.6	−2.6	−2.9	−4.2	−5.0	−4.3	−3.3
Nonfuel primary products	−5.1	−5.0	−3.1	−2.3	−2.0	−2.1	−2.3	−3.2	−2.8	−2.4
Services, income, and private transfers	−3.7	−3.5	−3.6	−2.9	−3.4	−3.3	−3.0	−2.8	−2.7	−2.1
Diversified	−2.8	−2.5	−2.0	−2.0	−2.0	−2.1	−2.7	−3.1	−3.9	−2.6
By external financing source										
Net creditor countries	−9.4	−9.3	−8.2	−5.9	−3.4	−1.3	−8.0	−5.4	1.9	−0.7
Net debtor countries	−2.7	−3.0	−2.5	−2.5	−2.3	−2.6	−3.9	−4.4	−3.8	−2.9
Official financing	−5.6	−6.6	−4.8	−3.2	−2.2	−2.3	−3.5	−3.1	−2.1	−2.1
Private financing	−2.2	−2.3	−2.0	−2.3	−2.2	−2.5	−3.7	−4.5	−4.1	−3.1
Diversified financing	−5.9	−6.3	−5.8	−4.5	−4.1	−4.2	−5.3	−5.1	−3.2	−2.5
Net debtor countries by debt-servicing experience										
Countries with arrears and/or rescheduling during 1994–98	−2.7	−3.2	−2.2	−1.9	−1.4	−1.9	−4.1	−4.2	−2.4	−1.2
Other net debtor countries	−2.8	−2.9	−2.7	−2.8	−2.7	−2.9	−3.8	−4.5	−4.3	−3.5
Other groups										
Heavily indebted poor countries	−9.4	−7.9	−5.7	−4.3	−3.9	−3.7	−3.4	−3.6	−3.3	−3.2
Least developed countries	−9.0	−7.0	−6.3	−5.3	−4.6	−4.1	−4.2	−4.4	−3.7	−3.5
Middle East and north Africa	−5.5	−7.5	−5.9	−4.3	−2.6	−2.1	−5.5	−2.6	—	−0.9
Memorandum										
Median										
Developing countries	−3.8	−4.1	−3.9	−3.4	−2.9	−2.6	−3.5	−3.1	−2.1	−1.7
Regional groups										
Africa	−5.5	−6.0	−5.3	−3.7	−4.7	−2.5	−3.0	−3.0	−1.8	−1.7
Asia	−4.6	−4.0	−2.9	−3.4	−2.7	−2.0	−2.9	−3.4	−3.1	−2.5
Middle East and Europe	−4.3	−7.2	−7.1	−4.2	−3.4	−2.9	−6.9	−3.3	−1.3	−1.6
Western Hemisphere	−1.8	−1.6	−1.0	−1.8	−1.7	−2.0	−2.6	−2.5	−1.9	−1.3

Table 21. Developing Countries: Broad Money Aggregates
(Annual percent change)

	1992	1993	1994	1995	1996	1997	1998	1999	2000	2001
Developing countries	**107.9**	**117.8**	**94.5**	**25.1**	**22.1**	**20.2**	**17.0**	**16.9**	**13.3**	**12.8**
Regional groups										
Africa	32.0	27.5	38.6	23.6	21.0	18.6	16.6	19.2	13.2	9.7
Sub-Sahara	36.8	31.5	47.5	28.6	24.2	19.8	18.1	21.8	14.6	10.5
Asia	22.7	27.5	24.8	23.4	21.1	18.0	18.3	14.4	14.3	13.9
Excluding China and India	20.2	21.8	18.6	22.5	19.8	17.0	20.9	12.2	13.1	12.8
Middle East and Europe	27.7	26.9	40.4	33.4	34.2	26.4	27.2	25.8	14.3	12.8
Western Hemisphere	367.7	414.5	246.2	24.1	19.5	20.6	12.1	15.9	11.7	12.1
Analytical groups										
By source of export earnings										
Fuel	20.0	21.5	24.7	19.8	21.3	18.2	12.3	17.1	10.7	10.3
Manufactures	190.6	220.4	161.9	30.5	22.9	19.6	17.3	19.2	14.3	13.8
Nonfuel primary products	55.3	46.3	50.1	31.2	27.3	24.6	15.1	18.3	14.9	14.4
Services, income, and private transfers	21.8	17.6	14.4	14.5	12.2	14.6	11.1	10.3	9.2	9.5
Diversified	28.5	27.5	19.7	11.8	20.0	22.3	21.1	9.9	11.6	10.9
By external financing source										
Net creditor countries	5.2	3.4	5.2	5.8	6.1	8.0	3.6	5.8	5.2	6.9
Net debtor countries	117.0	128.4	101.9	26.3	23.1	20.9	17.9	17.5	13.8	13.1
Official financing	38.1	31.9	40.7	21.6	18.8	16.7	17.1	16.7	12.8	10.1
Private financing	143.1	156.9	117.8	26.2	23.1	21.5	18.0	17.4	13.9	13.4
Diversified financing	34.8	36.1	36.6	29.5	23.2	19.3	15.6	19.6	15.3	11.5
Net debtor countries by debt-servicing experience										
Countries with arrears and/or rescheduling during 1994–98	381.0	499.1	325.4	29.4	19.4	18.3	18.5	19.8	11.4	11.7
Other net debtor countries	28.1	29.3	29.9	24.5	25.4	22.5	17.5	16.4	15.0	13.8
Other groups										
Heavily indebted poor countries	60.1	49.9	65.8	40.2	34.2	25.1	19.6	22.0	16.8	14.7
Least developed countries	66.4	56.3	62.0	40.9	33.5	23.1	19.7	22.8	17.4	15.5
Middle East and north Africa	16.1	16.3	13.3	14.2	13.2	11.8	10.2	10.5	7.8	9.3
Memorandum										
Median										
Developing countries	17.6	16.4	18.1	16.4	14.1	15.1	9.6	10.1	9.9	9.5
Regional groups										
Africa	12.5	14.6	31.1	16.2	14.4	15.4	8.6	10.0	10.0	9.3
Asia	18.0	19.0	18.4	17.2	15.7	16.6	13.9	13.4	13.2	11.3
Middle East and Europe	14.3	10.3	10.0	9.4	8.6	10.7	8.3	8.4	8.4	7.6
Western Hemisphere	25.1	17.0	17.2	19.9	16.7	15.0	9.9	10.0	8.8	8.9

Table 22. Summary of World Trade Volumes and Prices
(Annual percent change)

	Ten-Year Averages		1992	1993	1994	1995	1996	1997	1998	1999	2000	2001
	1982–91	1992–2001										
Trade in goods and services												
World trade[1]												
Volume	5.0	6.7	4.7	3.8	9.0	9.1	6.7	9.7	4.2	4.6	7.9	7.2
Price deflator												
In U.S. dollars	1.5	−0.1	2.6	−4.2	2.5	8.8	−1.1	−4.8	−5.5	−0.8	0.4	1.5
In SDRs	—	−0.1	−0.3	−3.3	—	2.7	3.4	0.4	−4.2	−1.6	1.4	1.2
Volume of trade												
Exports												
Advanced economies	5.5	6.4	5.2	3.3	8.9	8.8	5.9	10.3	3.7	4.4	7.2	6.8
Developing countries	4.4	8.6	11.5	8.0	12.2	8.3	11.2	10.9	4.5	1.7	9.7	8.3
Imports												
Advanced economies	6.1	6.8	4.7	1.5	9.6	8.9	6.2	9.1	5.5	7.4	7.8	7.1
Developing countries	2.4	7.7	11.2	11.0	7.1	11.1	8.3	10.5	0.4	−0.3	9.8	8.5
Terms of trade												
Advanced economies	0.8	0.1	0.8	0.5	—	—	−0.2	−0.5	1.3	—	−1.0	0.7
Developing countries	−3.0	—	−2.6	0.6	0.6	2.8	0.8	0.4	−5.3	3.1	2.4	−2.0
Trade in goods												
World trade[1]												
Volume	5.0	6.8	4.6	3.7	9.9	10.1	5.7	10.0	3.8	4.9	8.4	7.0
Price deflator												
In U.S. dollars	1.5	−0.2	2.1	−4.3	2.5	9.1	−0.7	−6.0	−5.6	−0.8	0.6	1.6
In SDRs	—	−0.2	−0.8	−3.4	−0.1	3.0	3.8	−0.8	−4.2	−1.6	1.6	1.3
World trade prices in U.S. dollars[2]												
Manufactures	3.7	−0.1	3.5	−5.8	3.1	10.2	−3.1	−7.8	−1.2	−1.0	−0.8	3.0
Oil	−5.8	0.2	−1.7	−11.8	−5.0	7.9	18.4	−5.4	−32.1	38.7	35.1	−19.2
Nonfuel primary commodities	−0.2	0.3	0.1	1.8	13.4	8.4	−1.2	−3.3	−14.7	−6.9	4.9	3.2
World trade prices in SDRs[2]												
Manufactures	2.2	—	0.6	−4.9	0.5	4.0	1.2	−2.7	0.2	−1.7	0.3	2.7
Oil	−7.2	0.3	−4.5	−11.1	−7.3	1.8	23.7	−0.2	−31.2	37.6	36.5	−19.4
Nonfuel primary commodities	−1.7	0.4	−2.8	2.7	10.6	2.3	3.3	2.0	−13.5	−7.7	6.0	2.9
World trade prices in euros[2]												
Manufactures	2.6	0.7	−1.2	4.7	2.0	0.1	−0.6	5.2	0.4	−3.3	−1.4	1.6
Oil	−6.8	1.1	−6.2	−2.0	−6.0	−2.0	21.6	7.9	−31.0	35.5	34.2	−20.2
Nonfuel primary commodities	−1.3	1.1	−4.5	13.1	12.2	−1.6	1.5	10.3	−13.3	−9.1	4.3	1.8

Table 22 *(concluded)*

	Ten-Year Averages		1992	1993	1994	1995	1996	1997	1998	1999	2000	2001
	1982–91	1992–2001										
Trade in goods												
Volume of trade												
Exports												
Advanced economies	5.5	6.4	4.6	2.8	9.6	9.0	5.3	10.7	3.6	4.0	7.8	6.5
Developing countries	4.2	8.7	10.4	7.7	12.4	11.9	8.2	11.5	3.7	3.6	10.2	7.5
Fuel exporters	2.5	3.8	9.7	4.5	3.5	1.8	5.0	5.3	0.1	3.6	4.2	0.7
Nonfuel exporters	5.7	10.1	10.7	9.0	15.6	14.9	9.0	13.4	4.8	3.6	11.6	9.1
Imports												
Advanced economies	6.2	7.0	4.7	2.1	11.0	9.3	5.2	9.4	5.2	7.6	8.2	7.1
Developing countries	1.9	8.2	15.0	10.1	7.7	14.4	6.6	9.2	−0.3	1.1	10.2	8.6
Fuel exporters	−2.7	3.0	26.5	−5.6	−16.8	1.8	2.6	14.7	6.9	−3.2	4.7	4.2
Nonfuel exporters	3.6	9.1	11.7	14.5	13.4	16.7	7.2	8.3	−1.4	1.9	11.1	9.3
Price deflators in SDRs												
Exports												
Advanced economies	0.8	−0.4	−0.3	−3.3	0.1	3.5	2.3	−2.3	−2.8	−2.6	−0.3	2.1
Developing countries	−2.9	0.6	−3.9	−2.1	0.2	1.7	8.9	2.6	−9.2	5.1	5.5	−1.3
Fuel exporters	−7.1	1.2	−6.9	−6.9	−2.9	5.1	21.2	1.8	−23.3	18.9	24.8	−9.6
Nonfuel exporters	−0.4	0.6	−2.6	−0.2	1.3	0.7	5.5	2.8	−5.2	2.1	1.0	0.7
Imports												
Advanced economies	−0.3	−0.7	−1.7	−5.2	−0.3	3.1	3.1	−1.6	−4.6	−2.8	1.9	1.3
Developing countries	0.4	0.7	−2.8	0.3	−0.6	−0.5	6.0	3.0	−3.2	1.4	2.7	0.5
Fuel exporters	0.5	1.4	−9.5	0.5	3.2	6.5	4.6	1.2	−0.5	2.5	6.1	0.6
Nonfuel exporters	0.4	0.6	−0.9	0.2	−1.5	−1.7	6.3	3.3	−3.6	1.2	2.1	0.5
Terms of trade												
Advanced economies	1.1	0.4	1.4	2.0	0.5	0.5	−0.8	−0.7	1.9	0.2	−2.1	0.8
Developing countries	−3.4	—	−1.1	−2.3	0.8	2.2	2.7	−0.4	−6.2	3.6	2.8	−1.8
Fuel exporters	−7.5	−0.3	2.9	−7.4	−5.8	−1.3	15.9	0.6	−22.9	15.9	17.6	−10.1
Nonfuel exporters	−0.8	—	−1.7	−0.3	2.8	2.4	−0.7	−0.5	−1.6	0.8	−1.1	0.2
Memorandum												
World exports in billions of U.S. dollars												
Goods and services	3,065	6,326	4,705	4,703	5,260	6,229	6,555	6,805	6,680	6,880	7,409	8,034
Goods	2,453	5,055	3,717	3,707	4,187	5,013	5,256	5,450	5,330	5,497	5,947	6,452

[1]Average of annual percent change for world exports and imports. The estimates of world trade comprise, in addition to trade of advanced economies and developing countries (which is summarized in the table), trade of countries in transition.

[2]As represented, respectively, by the export unit value index for the manufactures of the advanced economies; the average of U.K. Brent, Dubai, and West Texas Intermediate crude oil spot prices; and the average of world market prices for nonfuel primary commodities weighted by their 1987–89 shares in world commodity exports.

Table 23. Nonfuel Commodity Prices[1]
(Annual percent change; U.S. dollar terms)

	Ten-Year Averages		1992	1993	1994	1995	1996	1997	1998	1999	2000	2001
	1982–91	1992–2001										
Nonfuel primary commodities	**−0.2**	**0.3**	**0.1**	**1.8**	**13.4**	**8.4**	**−1.2**	**−3.3**	**−14.7**	**−6.9**	**4.9**	**3.2**
Food	−2.0	−0.9	2.3	−1.3	5.2	8.1	12.2	−10.9	−12.5	−15.2	2.5	5.0
Beverages	−4.5	1.3	−13.9	6.3	74.9	0.9	−17.4	32.6	−15.2	−21.3	−6.8	2.9
Agricultural raw materials	2.6	1.2	2.7	16.2	9.5	4.3	−2.7	−6.8	−16.3	2.0	4.2	2.8
Metals	1.0	—	−2.3	−14.2	16.6	19.5	−11.9	3.0	−16.3	−1.1	13.0	1.2
Fertilizers	−1.7	0.4	−5.0	−15.4	8.0	10.6	13.7	1.1	2.8	−4.0	−2.8	−1.5
Advanced economies	**0.3**	**0.6**	**2.0**	**3.1**	**8.4**	**6.8**	**2.8**	**−6.2**	**−14.2**	**−3.2**	**5.5**	**3.0**
Developing countries	**−0.9**	**—**	**−2.8**	**3.0**	**18.7**	**7.9**	**−4.7**	**2.9**	**−16.2**	**−10.9**	**3.0**	**2.9**
Regional groups												
Africa	−1.1	−0.2	−6.5	2.8	21.6	6.3	−6.3	8.8	−14.7	−12.7	1.7	2.4
Sub-Sahara	−1.1	−0.2	−6.7	4.6	22.6	5.9	−7.8	9.7	−16.1	−13.6	2.2	2.8
Asia	−0.8	0.6	3.2	10.3	13.8	8.7	−4.7	−6.9	−15.0	−6.7	3.3	3.2
Excluding China and India	−0.7	0.8	4.5	11.9	14.5	8.8	−5.9	−7.6	−14.9	−6.2	3.5	3.1
Middle East and Europe	0.2	−0.4	−5.6	−11.2	14.6	13.1	−2.7	3.2	−10.6	−6.2	3.1	2.0
Western Hemisphere	−0.9	−0.5	−6.2	−3.4	23.1	7.6	−4.0	10.4	−18.2	−14.2	3.4	2.9
Analytical groups												
By source of export earnings												
Fuel	−0.1	1.5	−1.1	16.7	11.3	6.6	−9.5	3.4	−16.9	−4.1	10.4	2.8
Manufactures	−1.5	−0.2	−1.0	7.6	12.0	7.9	−1.9	−1.9	−15.2	−11.9	2.1	3.8
Primary products	−0.2	−0.5	−5.1	−3.7	23.6	11.6	−10.4	7.8	−16.2	−14.3	4.9	3.2
Services, income, and private transfers	−0.8	−0.7	−8.1	−0.4	18.0	9.6	−5.9	2.7	−13.0	−10.7	1.8	3.0
Diversified	−0.7	0.4	−2.6	1.5	24.4	5.5	−3.4	5.4	−17.4	−8.1	2.3	1.8
By external financing source												
Net creditor countries	0.1	1.9	−2.9	−6.3	25.2	18.8	−13.6	4.2	−14.7	−0.5	15.1	1.7
Net debtor countries	−0.9	—	−2.8	3.0	18.7	7.9	−4.7	2.9	−16.2	−10.9	3.0	2.9
Official financing	−0.9	−0.6	−8.7	0.4	24.0	7.5	−8.1	9.0	−15.3	−11.9	0.7	2.7
Private financing	−1.0	−0.3	−2.6	2.7	16.6	8.4	−3.3	2.4	−16.7	−12.6	3.4	3.3
Diversified financing	−0.4	0.9	1.1	5.4	21.1	6.8	−6.0	0.5	−15.2	−5.7	3.4	1.9
Net debtor countries by debt-servicing experience												
Countries with arrears and/or rescheduling during 1994–98	−1.0	−0.3	−5.2	−0.6	19.8	6.2	−2.5	8.6	−16.7	−12.6	2.4	2.5
Other net debtor countries	−0.7	0.2	−0.8	5.8	17.9	9.1	−6.2	−1.3	−15.8	−9.6	3.4	3.2
Other groups												
Heavily indebted poor countries	−1.5	—	−8.1	6.5	28.7	5.4	−10.2	12.6	−16.0	−15.1	1.1	3.3
Least developed countries	−0.1	−0.6	−9.3	−1.6	29.7	10.5	−13.1	13.2	−19.9	−11.9	4.0	2.4
Middle East and north Africa	−0.9	−0.2	−7.8	−11.7	14.4	14.4	—	0.8	−4.8	−5.8	0.7	1.1
Memorandum												
Average oil spot price[2]	15.2	2.0	−1.7	−11.8	−5.0	7.9	18.4	−5.4	−32.1	38.7	35.1	−19.2
In U.S. dollars a barrel	22.5	18.4	19.04	16.79	15.95	17.20	20.37	19.27	13.07	18.14	24.50	19.80
Export unit value of manufactures[3]	3.7	−0.1	3.5	−5.8	3.1	10.2	−3.1	−7.8	−1.2	−1.0	−0.8	3.0

[1]Averages of world market prices for individual commodities weighted by 1987–89 exports as a share of world commodity exports and total commodity exports for the indicated country group, respectively.
[2]Average of U.K. Brent, Dubai, and West Texas Intermediate crude oil spot prices.
[3]For the manufactures exported by the advanced economies.

Table 24. Advanced Economies: Export Volumes, Import Volumes, and Terms of Trade in Goods and Services

(Annual percent change)

| | Ten-Year Averages | | 1992 | 1993 | 1994 | 1995 | 1996 | 1997 | 1998 | 1999 | 2000 | 2001 |
	1982–91	1992–2001										
Export volume												
Advanced economies	**5.5**	**6.4**	**5.2**	**3.3**	**8.9**	**8.8**	**5.9**	**10.3**	**3.7**	**4.4**	**7.2**	**6.8**
Major industrial countries	5.1	5.9	4.5	1.9	8.2	8.3	5.8	10.5	3.4	3.5	6.2	6.6
United States	6.1	6.7	6.2	3.3	8.9	10.3	8.2	12.5	2.2	3.8	5.7	6.7
Japan	4.6	4.4	4.9	1.3	4.6	5.4	6.3	11.6	−2.5	1.8	5.1	6.5
Germany	5.7	4.8	−0.8	−5.5	7.6	5.7	5.1	10.9	7.0	4.2	7.9	7.2
France	4.5	5.8	5.4	—	7.7	7.4	3.5	10.7	6.7	3.6	6.9	6.7
Italy	4.5	6.1	7.3	9.0	9.8	12.6	0.6	6.5	3.3	−0.4	6.5	6.4
United Kingdom	3.5	5.9	4.1	3.9	9.2	9.5	7.5	8.6	2.4	2.6	6.2	4.9
Canada	5.4	8.6	7.9	10.9	13.1	9.0	5.8	8.5	8.2	9.7	5.4	7.7
Other advanced economies	6.4	7.4	6.4	5.9	10.1	9.7	6.1	9.9	4.2	6.0	8.8	7.0
Memorandum												
Industrial countries	5.0	6.0	4.4	2.2	8.4	7.9	5.7	10.4	4.1	4.0	6.7	6.7
European Union	4.8	6.0	3.4	1.2	8.9	8.0	4.7	9.8	5.9	3.9	7.4	6.7
Euro area	5.0	6.0	3.5	0.6	8.6	7.9	4.3	10.1	6.6	4.1	7.7	7.1
Newly industrialized Asian economies	11.1	9.4	11.7	12.1	12.4	15.2	7.4	10.0	0.9	7.5	10.4	7.2
Import volume												
Advanced economies	**6.1**	**6.8**	**4.7**	**1.5**	**9.6**	**8.9**	**6.2**	**9.1**	**5.5**	**7.4**	**7.8**	**7.1**
Major industrial countries	5.8	6.7	4.1	0.6	9.0	8.2	6.4	9.3	7.3	7.9	7.3	7.0
United States	6.6	9.9	6.6	9.1	12.0	8.2	8.6	13.7	11.6	11.7	8.8	8.3
Japan	5.6	4.4	−0.7	−0.3	8.9	14.2	11.9	0.5	−7.6	5.2	6.3	7.6
Germany	5.3	4.8	1.5	−5.4	7.3	5.6	3.2	8.3	8.5	7.1	6.5	6.4
France	4.5	4.7	1.8	−3.7	8.2	7.7	1.6	6.2	9.6	3.3	7.4	5.8
Italy	5.9	4.7	7.4	−10.9	8.1	9.7	−0.3	10.2	9.1	3.4	6.3	6.1
United Kingdom	5.3	6.5	6.8	3.2	5.4	5.5	9.1	9.2	8.8	7.1	5.8	4.4
Canada	5.8	7.7	6.2	7.4	8.3	6.2	5.8	14.6	5.8	9.7	6.5	7.3
Other advanced economies	6.7	6.9	5.8	3.1	10.8	10.2	6.0	8.8	2.2	6.5	8.9	7.2
Memorandum												
Industrial countries	5.6	6.6	3.8	0.2	9.0	8.0	6.0	9.4	7.7	7.5	7.3	6.9
European Union	5.3	5.6	3.7	−3.3	7.9	7.2	4.0	9.0	8.9	6.0	7.0	6.3
Euro area	5.5	5.5	3.4	−4.5	8.1	7.4	3.1	8.8	9.1	6.0	7.4	6.8
Newly industrialized Asian economies	11.6	8.5	12.5	11.2	13.9	15.0	7.6	7.4	−8.8	7.3	12.3	8.1
Terms of trade												
Advanced economies	**0.8**	**0.1**	**0.8**	**0.5**	**—**	**—**	**−0.2**	**−0.5**	**1.3**	**—**	**−1.0**	**0.7**
Major industrial countries	0.7	0.2	0.9	0.5	—	—	−0.5	−0.4	2.1	0.1	−1.3	0.9
United States	0.5	0.6	−0.4	0.9	—	−0.4	0.4	2.1	3.2	−1.0	−0.8	2.1
Japan	2.3	−0.5	1.6	1.8	1.3	—	−6.4	−4.5	2.6	1.0	−4.8	3.4
Germany	−0.8	0.6	2.4	2.5	0.2	0.9	−0.6	−1.6	2.0	0.9	−0.6	0.2
France	0.3	−0.1	1.1	−1.7	0.2	0.1	−1.2	0.3	1.3	−0.8	−0.6	0.7
Italy	2.2	−0.5	—	−4.3	−1.1	−2.3	4.2	−1.4	2.7	−2.0	−0.4	0.1
United Kingdom	0.2	0.2	1.5	0.3	−2.0	−2.5	1.0	2.7	2.2	1.5	−0.8	−2.0
Canada	−0.2	—	−0.6	−1.9	−0.7	2.8	2.3	−1.1	−3.3	3.6	−0.2	−0.3
Other advanced economies	0.9	—	0.5	0.4	0.1	—	0.1	−0.6	—	−0.4	−0.3	0.3
Memorandum												
Industrial countries	0.8	0.2	0.8	0.4	—	0.3	−0.2	−0.4	1.5	0.2	−1.0	0.8
European Union	0.5	0.2	1.5	—	−0.4	−0.2	0.3	−0.3	1.5	−0.1	−0.4	0.1
Euro area	0.5	0.2	1.6	0.1	−0.2	—	0.2	−0.8	1.5	−0.4	−0.2	0.4
Newly industrialized Asian economies	1.0	−0.5	0.5	0.6	−0.2	−1.8	−0.5	−1.0	−0.1	−1.6	−0.8	0.3
Memorandum												
Trade in goods												
Advanced economies												
Export volume	5.5	6.4	4.6	2.8	9.6	9.0	5.3	10.7	3.6	4.0	7.8	6.5
Import volume	6.2	7.0	4.7	2.1	11.0	9.3	5.2	9.4	5.2	7.6	8.2	7.1
Terms of trade	1.1	0.4	1.4	2.0	0.5	0.5	−0.8	−0.7	1.9	0.2	−2.1	0.8

Table 25. Developing Countries—by Region: Total Trade in Goods
(Annual percent change)

| | Ten-Year Averages | | 1992 | 1993 | 1994 | 1995 | 1996 | 1997 | 1998 | 1999 | 2000 | 2001 |
	1982–91	1992–2001										
Developing countries												
Value in U.S. dollars												
Exports	1.2	8.7	7.8	4.6	15.2	20.0	12.4	8.2	−7.5	8.4	14.4	5.7
Imports	2.5	8.5	13.5	9.6	9.5	20.7	7.9	6.5	−4.5	2.2	11.5	9.5
Volume												
Exports	4.2	8.7	10.4	7.7	12.4	11.9	8.2	11.5	3.7	3.6	10.2	7.5
Imports	1.9	8.2	15.0	10.1	7.7	14.4	6.6	9.2	−0.3	1.1	10.2	8.6
Unit value in U.S. dollars												
Exports	−1.5	0.5	−1.0	−2.9	2.7	7.7	4.2	−2.8	−10.5	5.9	4.4	−1.0
Imports	1.9	0.6	—	−0.6	1.9	5.5	1.5	−2.4	−4.6	2.2	1.6	0.8
Terms of trade	−3.4	—	−1.1	−2.3	0.8	2.2	2.7	−0.4	−6.2	3.6	2.8	−1.8
Memorandum												
Real GDP growth in developing country trading partners	3.8	3.4	3.2	3.0	4.2	3.6	4.1	4.0	1.2	3.0	3.7	3.6
Market prices of nonfuel commodities exported by developing countries	−0.9	—	−2.8	3.0	18.7	7.9	−4.7	2.9	−16.2	−10.9	3.0	2.9
Regional groups												
Africa												
Value in U.S. dollars												
Exports	0.7	3.8	−0.7	−5.4	3.6	18.5	11.6	1.8	−13.5	6.2	21.4	−0.1
Imports	−1.1	4.7	7.0	−3.9	5.1	20.3	2.4	3.4	−0.9	0.2	9.4	6.2
Volume												
Exports	2.8	2.9	−1.0	0.5	−0.6	6.1	6.9	4.1	0.2	0.7	6.3	6.2
Imports	1.2	3.5	2.8	−1.2	1.2	8.7	3.2	6.6	3.8	−1.6	7.2	4.7
Unit value in U.S. dollars												
Exports	−0.2	1.5	0.5	−5.8	6.2	12.8	4.9	−2.1	−13.7	5.8	13.9	−4.1
Imports	—	1.7	4.2	−2.3	4.4	12.0	0.2	−3.0	−4.2	2.2	2.3	1.7
Terms of trade	−0.1	−0.1	−3.6	−3.5	1.7	0.7	4.8	0.9	−9.9	3.6	11.3	−5.8
Sub-Sahara												
Value in U.S. dollars												
Exports	0.6	3.7	0.1	−4.9	4.6	18.5	11.1	1.4	−13.7	4.9	18.5	1.2
Imports	−1.8	4.7	5.3	−3.3	2.7	21.6	5.4	5.7	−2.9	−1.6	11.0	5.7
Volume												
Exports	2.4	4.5	0.9	1.6	3.4	8.9	9.7	4.8	—	1.6	8.1	6.5
Imports	1.1	5.1	2.8	0.7	2.7	13.1	8.9	8.5	2.4	−0.8	8.9	4.6
Unit value in U.S. dollars												
Exports	−0.7	−0.5	−0.6	−6.3	1.6	9.0	1.5	−3.1	−13.6	3.6	8.7	−3.6
Imports	−1.4	−0.2	2.4	−4.0	0.3	7.6	−3.1	−2.4	−4.9	−0.9	2.1	1.4
Terms of trade	0.6	−0.3	−2.9	−2.4	1.3	1.3	4.7	−0.7	−9.2	4.6	6.5	−4.9

Table 25 *(concluded)*

	Ten-Year Averages		1992	1993	1994	1995	1996	1997	1998	1999	2000	2001
	1982–91	1992–2001										
Asia												
Value in U.S. dollars												
Exports	8.5	12.0	15.0	11.7	23.7	22.9	10.4	11.9	−2.0	8.0	10.3	9.7
Imports	7.9	10.2	13.7	19.3	17.4	27.4	7.4	1.0	−13.4	10.6	12.5	10.9
Volume												
Exports	8.4	11.3	11.8	10.5	19.2	15.5	8.8	16.7	6.1	4.2	11.6	9.3
Imports	6.6	9.3	11.9	17.8	14.2	20.9	5.6	4.1	−7.8	6.3	12.8	10.4
Unit value in U.S. dollars												
Exports	0.5	0.9	2.9	1.1	3.7	6.4	1.8	−3.9	−7.3	5.6	−0.7	0.3
Imports	1.4	0.9	1.3	0.9	2.3	5.4	2.0	−3.0	−6.6	7.0	0.3	0.3
Terms of trade	−0.8	—	1.5	0.2	1.4	1.0	−0.1	−0.9	−0.8	−1.3	−1.0	—
Excluding China and India												
Value in U.S. dollars												
Exports	7.7	10.5	15.4	12.6	18.5	22.2	6.3	6.9	−3.4	9.3	10.7	9.0
Imports	8.2	8.0	10.0	14.1	19.3	26.9	6.4	−0.9	−22.8	7.7	16.2	11.7
Volume												
Exports	8.8	9.7	11.6	9.7	14.8	13.9	4.0	8.4	7.7	2.8	14.9	9.8
Imports	8.1	6.8	8.3	11.2	15.6	18.9	4.4	−1.2	−15.4	1.5	18.4	11.7
Unit value in U.S. dollars												
Exports	−0.4	1.3	3.6	2.7	3.3	7.2	2.2	−1.4	−9.9	9.9	−3.1	−0.6
Imports	0.5	1.4	1.1	1.9	2.4	6.6	2.4	−0.2	−9.1	11.5	−1.0	−0.3
Terms of trade	−1.0	−0.1	2.4	0.8	0.9	0.6	−0.2	−1.2	−0.8	−1.4	−2.1	−0.4
Middle East and Europe												
Value in U.S. dollars												
Exports	−4.3	4.7	5.4	−1.6	7.0	13.5	17.8	1.9	−20.3	14.7	20.5	−4.6
Imports	0.3	4.9	10.0	2.1	−11.0	18.1	9.3	7.5	2.0	−2.2	9.6	6.8
Volume												
Exports	2.1	5.2	13.5	5.6	7.5	3.6	7.1	4.9	−0.9	3.9	5.9	1.4
Imports	−1.4	5.8	22.8	2.9	−12.2	9.5	8.8	12.2	6.8	−1.6	5.4	6.8
Unit value in U.S. dollars												
Exports	−4.9	0.3	−4.6	−6.5	−0.6	9.7	10.6	−2.8	−18.3	11.5	14.3	−4.9
Imports	2.9	—	−5.7	−0.6	2.7	8.2	0.5	−3.7	−4.5	−0.7	4.3	0.3
Terms of trade	−7.5	0.4	1.2	−6.0	−3.2	1.4	10.1	1.0	−14.4	12.3	9.5	−5.2
Western Hemisphere												
Value in U.S. dollars												
Exports	2.2	9.4	5.2	6.0	15.5	21.7	11.6	10.4	−4.0	5.6	15.0	9.1
Imports	1.1	10.6	21.6	9.0	17.5	10.6	10.5	18.2	4.9	−5.8	12.1	10.2
Volume												
Exports	4.3	10.0	12.7	10.2	13.1	15.9	8.5	11.4	4.8	3.2	12.2	8.9
Imports	—	10.5	19.6	11.3	18.8	8.9	8.4	18.0	6.2	−3.3	10.5	8.4
Unit value in U.S. dollars												
Exports	−0.3	−0.1	−4.1	−3.9	2.4	5.8	2.8	−0.9	−8.4	2.5	2.9	0.7
Imports	2.9	0.1	1.6	−2.1	−0.9	0.7	1.8	0.4	−1.3	−2.6	1.5	1.6
Terms of trade	−3.1	−0.2	−5.6	−1.8	3.3	5.1	1.0	−1.3	−7.2	5.2	1.3	−0.8

Table 26. Developing Countries—by Source of Export Earnings: Total Trade in Goods
(Annual percent change)

	Ten-Year Averages		1992	1993	1994	1995	1996	1997	1998	1999	2000	2001
	1982–91	1992–2001										
Fuel												
Value in U.S. dollars												
Exports	−4.7	4.0	2.9	−3.8	1.6	12.8	21.6	1.6	−25.5	22.3	28.0	−9.4
Imports	−1.9	3.6	12.0	−5.9	−11.8	13.8	1.9	9.4	5.1	0.1	9.4	4.7
Volume												
Exports	2.5	3.8	9.7	4.5	3.5	1.8	5.0	5.3	0.1	3.6	4.2	0.7
Imports	−2.7	3.0	26.5	−5.6	−16.8	1.8	2.6	14.7	6.9	−3.2	4.7	4.2
Unit value in U.S. dollars												
Exports	−5.7	1.1	−4.1	−7.7	−0.4	11.3	16.0	−3.5	−24.4	19.8	23.5	−9.3
Imports	2.0	1.3	−6.8	−0.3	5.8	12.8	0.1	−4.1	−1.9	3.4	5.0	0.9
Terms of trade	−7.5	−0.3	2.9	−7.4	−5.8	−1.3	15.9	0.6	−22.9	15.9	17.6	−10.1
Nonfuel												
Value in U.S. dollars												
Exports	5.6	10.2	9.8	7.9	20.0	22.2	9.9	10.2	−2.4	5.4	11.1	10.0
Imports	4.3	9.5	14.0	13.9	14.4	21.9	8.9	6.1	−6.0	2.6	11.9	10.3
Volume												
Exports	5.7	10.1	10.7	9.0	15.6	14.9	9.0	13.4	4.8	3.6	11.6	9.1
Imports	3.6	9.1	11.7	14.5	13.4	16.7	7.2	8.3	−1.4	1.9	11.1	9.3
Unit value in U.S. dollars												
Exports	1.1	0.5	0.3	−1.0	3.9	6.7	1.0	−2.6	−6.6	2.9	—	1.0
Imports	1.9	0.5	2.0	−0.7	1.0	4.2	1.7	−2.1	−5.0	2.1	1.0	0.8
Terms of trade	−0.8	—	−1.7	−0.3	2.8	2.4	−0.7	−0.5	−1.6	0.8	−1.1	0.2
Manufactures												
Value in U.S. dollars												
Exports	8.2	12.0	12.7	10.8	23.6	23.2	12.1	11.2	−1.4	7.2	11.5	11.2
Imports	6.9	10.8	14.4	18.4	15.1	24.6	10.0	5.4	−7.7	6.8	12.4	11.5
Volume												
Exports	8.2	11.4	11.7	11.1	19.0	17.3	10.2	15.4	4.0	6.3	10.6	9.5
Imports	5.5	10.5	13.7	19.9	13.0	20.1	7.3	8.7	−3.9	7.3	10.4	10.4
Unit value in U.S. dollars												
Exports	0.2	0.6	0.9	−0.3	3.8	5.3	1.9	−3.5	−5.0	0.9	0.9	1.6
Imports	1.9	0.2	0.6	−1.2	2.0	3.1	2.5	−3.0	−4.2	−0.4	1.8	1.0
Terms of trade	−1.7	0.4	0.2	1.0	1.8	2.2	−0.6	−0.5	−0.9	1.3	−0.9	0.6
Nonfuel primary products												
Value in U.S. dollars												
Exports	3.3	7.6	4.5	0.4	17.4	24.7	6.1	8.2	−5.1	4.4	9.0	9.6
Imports	0.9	8.0	11.4	4.0	10.6	25.5	10.0	7.7	−1.1	−3.4	9.4	8.9
Volume												
Exports	2.0	7.6	5.8	4.8	8.7	8.7	9.9	11.0	4.2	8.0	8.5	6.7
Imports	−0.4	7.3	8.9	5.5	9.3	15.2	7.2	8.3	4.3	1.9	6.5	6.7
Unit value in U.S. dollars												
Exports	2.2	0.3	−1.0	−4.0	8.7	14.9	−3.2	−2.4	−8.6	−3.0	0.5	2.8
Imports	2.4	0.8	2.2	−1.5	1.7	8.8	2.7	−0.5	−4.7	−4.7	2.8	2.2
Terms of trade	−0.1	−0.5	−3.1	−2.5	6.8	5.6	−5.8	−1.9	−4.1	1.8	−2.3	0.6

Table 26 *(concluded)*

	Ten-Year Averages		1992	1993	1994	1995	1996	1997	1998	1999	2000	2001
	1982–91	1992–2001										
Services, income, and private transfers												
Value in U.S. dollars												
Exports	−0.2	7.0	−2.2	3.4	6.6	28.0	4.1	5.8	−0.7	0.2	17.2	11.3
Imports	1.9	6.7	3.0	6.9	4.8	16.0	9.3	4.5	4.9	3.0	8.5	6.5
Volume												
Exports	−0.7	6.2	6.6	0.5	3.9	11.7	1.6	9.9	1.4	4.9	13.8	8.4
Imports	−1.0	6.0	−4.8	2.6	11.9	14.6	3.5	6.8	9.4	5.7	6.0	5.2
Unit value in U.S. dollars												
Exports	4.4	1.3	−6.9	3.3	2.5	14.8	2.8	−3.3	−1.8	−3.0	3.2	2.8
Imports	5.7	1.0	8.9	4.7	−5.1	1.7	6.0	−1.9	−4.0	−2.4	2.3	1.3
Terms of trade	−1.2	0.2	−14.5	−1.3	8.0	12.9	−3.0	−1.4	2.3	−0.6	0.9	1.5
Diversified												
Value in U.S. dollars												
Exports	3.0	6.6	6.7	4.0	13.3	17.8	5.5	8.5	−4.7	0.4	9.9	6.0
Imports	1.3	7.5	18.1	8.5	17.1	14.8	5.1	8.1	−6.0	−7.4	12.4	8.1
Volume												
Exports	4.0	7.5	10.6	6.3	10.4	10.8	5.9	8.3	7.7	−7.4	15.8	8.5
Imports	3.6	6.9	13.8	7.8	16.7	8.1	8.0	7.4	0.7	−15.6	17.4	8.3
Unit value in U.S. dollars												
Exports	1.4	0.1	0.2	−2.2	2.4	6.7	−0.4	0.3	−11.1	12.5	−4.0	−1.9
Imports	−0.2	0.7	3.0	−0.7	−0.1	6.1	−2.3	0.1	−7.9	13.9	−3.0	−0.6
Terms of trade	1.6	−0.6	−2.7	−1.5	2.5	0.5	2.0	0.3	−3.4	−1.2	−1.1	−1.3

Table 27. Summary of Payments Balances on Current Account
(Billions of U.S. dollars)

	1992	1993	1994	1995	1996	1997	1998	1999	2000	2001
Advanced economies	**−10.5**	**66.0**	**32.5**	**56.5**	**43.4**	**93.9**	**43.1**	**−133.7**	**−212.9**	**−215.5**
United States	−50.6	−85.3	−121.7	−113.6	−129.3	−143.5	−220.6	−338.9	−419.4	−460.9
Euro area	−51.3	26.9	19.3	56.6	89.9	112.5	86.5	43.7	64.9	95.8
Japan	112.3	132.0	130.6	111.4	65.8	94.1	121.0	107.0	102.4	112.6
Other advanced economies	2.2	8.6	2.0	−0.1	10.6	14.1	54.6	69.7	56.0	61.1
Memorandum										
Industrial countries	−26.9	47.8	19.7	55.7	48.4	86.2	−22.2	−193.2	−261.4	−263.4
Newly industrialized Asian economies	16.3	20.8	16.1	5.9	0.3	11.2	66.1	61.0	49.8	49.8
Developing countries	**−84.0**	**−120.4**	**−88.6**	**−111.4**	**−74.2**	**−59.1**	**−89.9**	**−32.7**	**−11.6**	**−49.2**
Regional groups										
Africa	−10.0	−11.2	−11.5	−16.5	−7.0	−7.4	−20.0	−16.8	−7.7	−13.8
Asia	−12.6	−34.0	−20.4	−56.3	−38.7	6.8	48.9	42.3	31.7	28.1
Middle East and Europe	−26.8	−29.2	−4.5	−1.8	9.8	5.6	−30.3	−4.0	20.9	−2.8
Western Hemisphere	−34.5	−46.0	−52.2	−36.8	−38.3	−64.1	−88.6	−54.2	−56.5	−60.8
Analytical groups										
By source of export earnings										
Fuel	−29.9	−24.1	−4.9	0.8	30.0	21.4	−34.6	3.4	45.3	12.1
Nonfuel	−54.1	−96.3	−83.8	−112.3	−104.4	−80.7	−55.7	−36.1	−56.7	−61.4
By external financing source										
Net creditor countries	−15.2	−13.0	−6.4	1.9	13.2	11.7	−21.3	−0.1	31.2	8.7
Net debtor countries	−68.6	−107.1	−82.0	−113.0	−86.9	−70.1	−68.5	−32.2	−42.2	−57.2
Official financing	−6.2	−8.2	−10.0	−12.1	−9.2	−4.6	−10.0	−9.7	−3.6	−6.7
Private financing	−38.9	−72.7	−59.9	−86.1	−67.9	−50.3	−39.3	−17.0	−32.8	−42.6
Diversified financing	−15.1	−21.0	−16.7	−17.4	−15.0	−16.9	−16.3	−8.7	−6.5	−8.2
Net debtor countries by debt-servicing experience										
Countries with arrears and/or rescheduling during 1994–98	−22.1	−30.3	−21.1	−48.0	−41.4	−48.8	−57.3	−29.7	−23.8	−28.5
Other net debtor countries	−46.7	−77.1	−61.1	−65.2	−45.9	−22.0	−11.4	−2.9	−18.9	−29.4
Countries in transition	**−5.1**	**−8.2**	**2.1**	**−1.8**	**−16.9**	**−26.1**	**−24.8**	**−5.3**	**−7.5**	**−16.7**
Central and eastern Europe	−2.3	−9.8	−5.3	−4.9	−16.8	−19.4	−22.4	−22.5	−23.3	−23.5
Excluding Belarus and Ukraine	−1.9	−8.5	−3.4	−2.9	−15.1	−17.2	−20.2	−22.0	−21.6	−22.3
Russia	−1.2	2.6	8.2	4.6	3.8	−3.0	2.5	19.8	18.7	10.3
Transcaucasus and central Asia	−1.7	−1.0	−0.8	−1.6	−3.9	−3.7	−4.9	−2.6	−2.9	−3.5
Total[1]	**−99.6**	**−62.5**	**−54.0**	**−56.7**	**−47.6**	**8.8**	**−71.7**	**−171.7**	**−231.9**	**−281.4**
In percent of total world current account transactions	−1.0	−0.7	−0.5	−0.5	−0.4	0.1	−0.5	−1.2	−1.5	−1.7
In percent of world GDP	−0.4	−0.3	−0.2	−0.2	−0.2	—	−0.2	−0.6	−0.7	−0.8
Memorandum										
Emerging market countries, excluding Asian countries in surplus[2]	−86.4	−104.7	−77.0	−76.2	−75.6	−106.8	−172.3	−86.7	−61.4	−107.3

[1]Reflects errors, omissions, and asymmetries in balance of payments statistics on current account, as well as the exclusion of data for international organizations and a limited number of countries. See "Classification of Countries" in the introduction to this Statistical Appendix.

[2]All developing and transition countries excluding China, Hong Kong SAR, Korea, Malaysia, the Philippines, Singapore, Taiwan Province of China, and Thailand.

Table 28. Advanced Economies: Balance of Payments on Current Account

	1992	1993	1994	1995	1996	1997	1998	1999	2000	2001
					Billions of U.S. dollars					
Advanced economies	**−10.5**	**66.0**	**32.5**	**56.5**	**43.4**	**93.9**	**43.1**	**−133.7**	**−212.9**	**−215.5**
Major industrial countries	−16.0	17.2	−8.5	4.5	−6.4	21.7	−53.9	−222.6	−292.6	−304.6
United States	−50.6	−85.3	−121.7	−113.6	−129.3	−143.5	−220.6	−338.9	−419.4	−460.9
Japan	112.3	132.0	130.6	111.4	65.8	94.1	121.0	107.0	102.4	112.6
Germany	−13.5	−9.0	−22.5	−19.0	−5.6	−1.4	−3.7	−17.8	3.4	14.5
France	3.8	9.2	7.4	10.9	20.5	39.4	39.4	39.6	36.0	45.7
Italy	−29.2	8.1	13.0	25.1	39.8	32.5	21.8	10.0	10.1	13.4
United Kingdom	−17.8	−15.9	−2.2	−5.9	−0.9	10.8	−0.8	−19.5	−22.1	−30.5
Canada	−21.0	−21.8	−13.0	−4.4	3.3	−10.3	−11.0	−2.9	−3.0	0.5
Other advanced economies	5.5	48.8	40.9	52.0	49.8	72.2	97.0	88.9	79.7	89.2
Spain	−21.3	−5.8	−6.6	0.2	0.2	2.3	−1.4	−12.5	−11.5	−10.8
Netherlands	7.4	13.6	17.9	23.8	23.2	27.8	22.0	19.9	22.6	25.7
Belgium-Luxembourg	6.6	11.2	12.6	14.2	14.1	13.9	12.1	11.5	11.8	13.2
Sweden	−7.4	−2.6	2.4	7.2	7.2	7.5	7.0	6.1	5.9	5.6
Austria	−0.6	−1.2	−2.9	−5.4	−4.8	−5.3	−4.6	−4.8	−4.0	−2.2
Denmark	4.1	4.7	2.7	1.9	3.1	1.1	−2.4	−0.1	1.3	3.0
Finland	−5.1	−1.1	1.1	5.2	5.0	6.7	7.4	6.5	7.1	8.0
Greece	−2.0	−2.4	−0.5	−1.1	−3.0	−2.8	−2.3	−1.7	−1.9	−2.3
Portugal	—	0.1	−2.2	−0.2	−4.5	−5.5	−7.2	−9.3	−10.2	−10.8
Ireland	0.5	1.8	1.5	1.7	2.0	1.9	0.8	0.6	−0.4	−0.9
Switzerland	15.1	19.5	17.5	21.4	22.0	25.8	23.9	33.5	24.7	25.4
Norway	4.5	3.5	3.7	4.9	10.2	7.9	−2.2	6.4	10.6	11.8
Israel	0.1	−2.6	−3.4	−5.2	−5.3	−3.4	−0.8	−1.5	−1.2	−1.9
Iceland	−0.2	—	0.1	0.1	−0.1	−0.1	−0.5	−0.5	−0.4	−0.3
Korea	−3.9	1.0	−3.9	−8.5	−23.0	−8.2	40.2	25.0	14.0	11.4
Australia	−11.2	−9.8	−17.2	−19.6	−15.8	−12.7	−18.2	−22.4	−21.0	−21.1
Taiwan Province of China	8.5	7.0	6.5	5.5	11.0	7.7	3.5	7.0	6.6	7.9
Hong Kong SAR[1]	5.8	8.6	2.1	−5.5	−1.6	−5.3	1.4	7.6	6.7	7.4
Singapore	5.9	4.2	11.4	14.4	13.9	16.9	21.0	21.5	22.5	23.0
New Zealand	−1.4	−1.0	−1.9	−3.1	−4.0	−4.3	−2.7	−3.9	−3.4	−3.0
Memorandum										
Industrial countries	−26.9	47.8	19.7	55.7	48.4	86.2	−22.2	−193.2	−261.4	−263.4
European Union	−74.4	10.7	21.6	58.7	96.3	129.1	88.0	28.5	48.1	71.7
Euro area	−51.3	26.9	19.3	56.6	89.9	112.5	86.5	43.7	64.9	95.8
Newly industrialized Asian economies	16.3	20.8	16.1	5.9	0.3	11.2	66.1	61.0	49.8	49.8
					Percent of GDP					
United States	−0.8	−1.3	−1.7	−1.5	−1.7	−1.7	−2.5	−3.7	−4.3	−4.4
Japan	3.0	3.1	2.8	2.2	1.4	2.2	3.2	2.5	2.2	2.3
Germany	−0.7	−0.5	−1.1	−0.8	−0.2	−0.1	−0.2	−0.8	0.2	0.7
France	0.3	0.7	0.5	0.7	1.3	2.8	2.7	2.8	2.6	3.1
Italy	−2.4	0.8	1.3	2.3	3.2	2.8	1.8	0.9	0.9	1.1
United Kingdom	−1.7	−1.7	−0.2	−0.5	−0.1	0.8	−0.1	−1.4	−1.5	−2.0
Canada	−3.6	−3.9	−2.3	−0.8	0.5	−1.6	−1.8	−0.5	−0.4	0.1
Spain	−3.5	−1.2	−1.3	—	—	0.4	−0.2	−2.1	−2.0	−1.7
Netherlands	2.2	4.2	5.1	5.7	5.6	7.4	5.6	5.1	5.8	6.1
Belgium-Luxembourg	2.8	4.9	5.1	4.8	4.9	5.3	4.5	4.3	4.5	4.8
Sweden	−2.9	−1.3	1.1	3.0	2.7	3.2	2.9	2.6	2.4	2.2
Austria	−0.3	−0.6	−1.4	−2.3	−2.1	−2.5	−2.2	−2.3	−1.9	−1.0
Denmark	2.8	3.4	1.8	1.1	1.7	0.7	−1.4	—	0.7	1.7
Finland	−4.7	−1.3	1.1	4.0	3.9	5.5	5.7	5.0	5.4	5.7
Greece	−2.0	−2.6	−0.5	−0.9	−2.4	−2.3	−1.9	−1.3	−1.6	−1.8
Portugal	—	0.1	−2.5	−0.1	−4.2	−5.4	−6.7	−8.5	−9.4	−9.3
Ireland	1.0	3.6	2.7	2.6	2.8	2.5	0.9	0.6	−0.4	−0.9
Switzerland	6.2	8.2	6.7	7.0	7.4	10.1	9.1	12.9	10.0	9.9
Norway	3.5	3.0	3.0	3.3	6.5	5.2	−1.5	4.2	7.0	7.5
Israel	0.2	−3.9	−4.5	−6.0	−5.6	−3.4	−0.9	−1.6	−1.2	−1.8
Iceland	−2.4	0.8	2.0	0.8	−1.7	−1.6	−6.0	−5.5	−4.0	−3.0
Korea	−1.3	0.3	−1.0	−1.7	−4.4	−1.7	12.7	6.1	3.0	2.2
Australia	−3.7	−3.3	−5.1	−5.4	−3.9	−3.1	−5.0	−5.7	−5.1	−4.9
Taiwan Province of China	4.0	3.2	2.7	2.1	4.0	2.7	1.3	2.5	2.1	2.3
Hong Kong SAR[1]	5.7	7.4	1.6	−3.9	−1.0	−3.1	0.8	4.8	4.1	4.2
Singapore	12.1	7.3	16.3	17.3	15.2	17.9	25.4	25.3	23.4	22.0
New Zealand	−3.5	−2.4	−3.8	−5.2	−6.1	−6.7	−5.1	−7.3	−6.2	−5.2

[1]Data include goods and nonfactor services only.

Table 29. Advanced Economies: Current Account Transactions
(Billions of U.S. dollars)

	1992	1993	1994	1995	1996	1997	1998	1999	2000	2001
Exports	2,989.6	2,938.0	3,308.1	3,944.4	4,065.6	4,170.0	4,133.4	4,217.9	4,490.4	4,910.1
Imports	2,965.0	2,849.2	3,234.7	3,855.3	4,007.5	4,101.8	4,068.9	4,295.8	4,678.1	5,101.2
Trade balance	24.5	88.8	73.4	89.1	58.1	68.1	64.4	−77.9	−187.8	−191.0
Services, credits	829.9	829.2	884.9	1,003.2	1,061.5	1,093.6	1,096.1	1,124.6	1,178.2	1,275.3
Services, debits	779.5	770.4	820.0	934.8	983.3	994.6	1,019.8	1,056.4	1,097.4	1,172.4
Balance on services	50.4	58.8	64.9	68.5	78.2	99.1	76.3	68.2	80.8	102.8
Balance on goods and services	75.0	147.6	138.3	157.5	136.3	167.2	140.7	−9.6	−107.0	−88.2
Income, net	−14.3	−3.9	−14.9	−13.5	7.2	17.6	−3.3	−22.8	−12.2	−25.3
Current transfers, net	−71.1	−77.7	−90.9	−87.6	−100.1	−90.9	−94.3	−101.3	−93.7	−101.9
Current account balance	**−10.5**	**66.0**	**32.5**	**56.5**	**43.4**	**93.9**	**43.1**	**−133.7**	**−212.9**	**−215.5**
Balance on goods and services										
Advanced economies	**75.0**	**147.6**	**138.3**	**157.5**	**136.3**	**167.2**	**140.7**	**−9.6**	**−107.0**	**−88.2**
Major industrial countries	47.4	81.2	70.4	85.0	55.3	78.3	23.8	−114.2	−210.0	−202.1
United States	−37.0	−69.9	−98.4	−97.5	−104.3	−104.7	−164.3	−267.6	−340.3	−363.5
Japan	80.7	96.5	96.4	74.7	21.2	47.3	73.2	69.2	49.7	65.3
Germany	−2.4	8.1	11.4	19.7	27.4	30.8	35.7	24.6	29.0	38.3
France	21.5	24.5	25.0	28.9	31.2	45.7	43.7	42.4	38.7	48.6
Italy	0.3	32.5	36.7	45.3	62.0	47.8	41.3	23.8	23.7	26.8
United Kingdom	−13.0	−10.1	−7.0	−4.4	−6.5	0.8	−13.8	−25.0	−27.6	−36.2
Canada	−2.6	−0.4	6.3	18.4	24.4	10.6	8.0	18.4	16.9	18.5
Other advanced economies	27.5	66.4	67.9	72.5	81.0	88.9	116.9	104.5	103.0	113.9
Memorandum										
Industrial countries	71.0	137.0	133.1	161.4	145.8	166.1	82.8	−61.6	−149.0	−129.8
European Union	11.6	90.3	111.1	147.4	178.1	187.8	160.5	107.2	108.6	130.2
Euro area	19.5	92.1	107.5	137.9	168.5	174.2	166.4	123.2	126.4	155.4
Newly industrialized Asian economies	9.6	16.9	11.9	4.3	−1.1	7.2	62.0	56.5	46.0	46.1
Income, net										
Advanced economies	**−14.3**	**−3.9**	**−14.9**	**−13.5**	**7.2**	**17.6**	**−3.3**	**−22.8**	**−12.2**	**−25.3**
Major industrial countries	18.0	20.5	14.4	4.3	31.2	28.9	11.5	−14.5	2.6	−10.0
United States	22.3	23.2	15.9	19.4	17.2	3.2	−12.2	−24.8	−37.1	−55.4
Japan	35.4	40.6	40.3	44.4	53.6	55.6	56.6	49.8	61.3	62.3
Germany	21.7	16.6	3.0	0.2	1.1	−1.7	−9.2	−14.4	1.0	3.0
France	−8.7	−9.1	−6.8	−9.0	−2.7	2.6	5.6	7.0	6.8	7.1
Italy	−22.0	−17.2	−16.6	−15.7	−15.0	−11.2	−12.0	−9.1	−7.7	−7.2
United Kingdom	−13.3	−12.8	−2.4	−12.4	−1.5	1.7	2.3	−0.9	−1.1	−1.1
Canada	−17.5	−20.8	−19.0	−22.7	−21.6	−21.4	−19.6	−22.0	−20.5	−18.8
Other advanced economies	−32.4	−24.3	−29.3	−17.7	−24.0	−11.3	−14.8	−8.3	−14.9	−15.3
Memorandum										
Industrial countries	−19.2	−5.8	−17.1	−15.0	6.4	15.5	−3.2	−24.4	−15.4	−29.5
European Union	−52.5	−44.5	−44.0	−47.5	−33.7	−18.1	−28.2	−34.4	−18.6	−16.5
Euro area	−24.8	−19.2	−31.7	−29.4	−24.3	−14.2	−26.2	−30.2	−13.8	−11.7
Newly industrialized Asian economies	6.0	3.9	4.5	4.3	4.1	5.6	2.7	4.6	6.4	7.5

Table 30. Developing Countries: Payments Balances on Current Account

	1992	1993	1994	1995	1996	1997	1998	1999	2000	2001
					Billions of U.S. dollars					
Developing countries	**−84.0**	**−120.4**	**−88.6**	**−111.4**	**−74.2**	**−59.1**	**−89.9**	**−32.7**	**−11.6**	**−49.2**
Regional groups										
Africa	−10.0	−11.2	−11.5	−16.5	−7.0	−7.4	−20.0	−16.8	−7.7	−13.8
Sub-Sahara	−9.5	−10.2	−8.3	−12.3	−7.8	−10.2	−18.3	−14.9	−12.1	−15.1
Excluding Nigeria and South Africa	−10.2	−9.5	−6.8	−8.8	−8.7	−10.2	−13.2	−10.7	−9.6	−10.5
Asia	−12.6	−34.0	−20.4	−56.3	−38.7	6.8	48.9	42.3	31.7	28.1
Excluding China and India	−16.1	−20.6	−24.5	−39.2	−40.0	−24.9	23.2	31.3	21.4	18.1
Middle East and Europe	−26.8	−29.2	−4.5	−1.8	9.8	5.6	−30.3	−4.0	20.9	−2.8
Western Hemisphere	−34.5	−46.0	−52.2	−36.8	−38.3	−64.1	−88.6	−54.2	−56.5	−60.8
Analytical groups										
By source of export earnings										
Fuel	−29.9	−24.1	−4.9	0.8	30.0	21.4	−34.6	3.4	45.3	12.1
Manufactures	−27.4	−60.2	−42.2	−66.4	−55.2	−26.7	0.7	1.7	−10.6	−9.1
Nonfuel primary products	−11.2	−12.7	−11.6	−14.2	−16.3	−17.7	−18.1	−11.5	−13.7	−15.1
Services, income, and private transfers	−2.8	−4.6	−5.9	−6.8	−7.8	−7.5	−11.4	−10.8	−10.7	−10.4
Diversified	−12.7	−18.8	−24.0	−24.8	−24.8	−28.6	−26.6	−15.4	−21.9	−26.8
By external financing source										
Net creditor countries	−15.2	−13.0	−6.4	1.9	13.2	11.7	−21.3	−0.1	31.2	8.7
Net debtor countries	−68.6	−107.1	−82.0	−113.0	−86.9	−70.1	−68.5	−32.2	−42.2	−57.2
Official financing	−6.2	−8.2	−10.0	−12.1	−9.2	−4.6	−10.0	−9.7	−3.6	−6.7
Private financing	−38.9	−72.7	−59.9	−86.1	−67.9	−50.3	−39.3	−17.0	−32.8	−42.6
Diversified financing	−15.1	−21.0	−16.7	−17.4	−15.0	−16.9	−16.3	−8.7	−6.5	−8.2
Net debtor countries by debt-servicing experience										
Countries with arrears and/or rescheduling during 1994–98	−22.1	−30.3	−21.1	−48.0	−41.4	−48.8	−57.3	−29.7	−23.8	−28.5
Other net debtor countries	−46.7	−77.1	−61.1	−65.2	−45.9	−22.0	−11.4	−2.9	−18.9	−29.4
Other groups										
Heavily indebted poor countries	−11.7	−13.7	−10.0	−12.3	−13.0	−13.1	−14.7	−14.3	−13.9	−15.0
Least developed countries	−9.4	−8.9	−6.8	−9.0	−9.4	−9.8	−13.0	−13.0	−12.7	−14.7
Middle East and north Africa	−27.5	−25.5	−13.2	−6.5	12.0	9.7	−35.4	−6.3	27.9	1.1

Table 30 *(concluded)*

	Ten-Year Averages		1992	1993	1994	1995	1996	1997	1998	1999	2000	2001
	1982–91	1992–2001										
	Percent of exports of goods and services											
Developing countries	**−14.7**	**−3.3**	**−11.6**	**−16.0**	**−10.3**	**−10.9**	**−6.5**	**−4.7**	**−7.7**	**−2.6**	**−0.8**	**−3.3**
Regional groups												
Africa	−7.1	−8.9	−9.7	−11.3	−11.2	−13.8	−5.3	−5.4	−16.5	−13.2	−5.1	−8.9
Sub-Sahara	−11.0	−13.2	−12.2	−13.6	−10.6	−13.3	−7.6	−9.8	−19.9	−15.6	−10.8	−13.2
Excluding Nigeria and South Africa	−27.2	−17.9	−26.7	−26.0	−17.8	−19.5	−17.5	−20.2	−28.5	−21.8	−17.2	−17.9
Asia	−4.7	4.0	−4.8	−11.5	−5.5	−12.5	−7.7	1.2	9.1	7.3	4.9	4.0
Excluding China and India	−14.8	4.9	−10.0	−11.3	−11.2	−14.7	−13.9	−8.1	8.2	10.1	6.3	4.9
Middle East and Europe	−37.5	−1.0	−14.8	−16.2	−2.4	−0.9	4.0	2.2	−13.9	−1.7	7.3	−1.0
Western Hemisphere	−10.3	−16.5	−19.8	−25.7	−25.7	−15.3	−14.4	−22.0	−31.1	−18.2	−16.7	−16.5
Analytical groups												
By source of export earnings												
Fuel	−34.0	4.7	−16.4	−13.7	−2.7	0.4	12.7	8.8	−18.7	1.5	16.0	4.7
Manufactures	−7.1	−1.1	−8.5	−17.1	−9.8	−12.6	−9.3	−4.0	0.1	0.2	−1.4	−1.1
Nonfuel primary products	−21.2	−15.5	−22.9	−25.7	−20.1	−19.9	−21.6	−21.8	−23.0	−14.1	−15.4	−15.5
Services, income, and private transfers	−16.0	−17.0	−8.8	−13.5	−15.8	−15.7	−17.0	−15.4	−23.7	−21.5	−19.2	−17.0
Diversified	−2.6	−11.3	−9.3	−13.2	−15.0	−13.3	−12.6	−13.5	−13.1	−7.6	−9.8	−11.3
By external financing source												
Net creditor countries	−47.4	5.7	−13.8	−11.9	−5.8	1.6	9.3	7.9	−19.1	−0.1	18.5	5.7
Net debtor countries	−8.7	−4.2	−11.1	−16.5	−10.8	−12.5	−8.6	−6.4	−6.5	−2.9	−3.4	−4.2
Official financing	−12.3	−8.8	−15.1	−20.1	−23.4	−23.6	−15.5	−7.3	−17.2	−15.6	−4.8	−8.8
Private financing	−4.6	−3.9	−8.1	−14.2	−9.8	−11.7	−8.4	−5.6	−4.6	−1.9	−3.3	−3.9
Diversified financing	−19.8	−5.7	−22.7	−31.4	−22.7	−19.7	−14.4	−14.7	−15.1	−7.4	−4.8	−5.7
Net debtor countries by debt-servicing experience												
Countries with arrears and/or rescheduling during 1994–98	−18.1	−7.9	−11.6	−15.7	−9.9	−19.8	−15.2	−16.4	−21.2	−10.2	−7.0	−7.9
Other net debtor countries	−4.5	−3.0	−11.1	−17.0	−11.3	−9.9	−6.3	−2.7	−1.5	−0.3	−2.1	−3.0
Other groups												
Heavily indebted poor countries	−35.0	−22.4	−33.8	−40.5	−26.4	−26.5	−24.5	−23.7	−27.5	−25.4	−22.0	−22.4
Least developed countries	−46.0	−33.4	−41.4	−38.9	−26.8	−30.0	−28.0	−28.1	−39.0	−35.6	−30.4	−33.4
Middle East and north Africa	−38.4	0.4	−15.5	−14.6	−7.3	−3.3	5.3	4.1	−18.7	−2.9	10.3	0.4
Memorandum												
Median												
Developing countries	−14.4	−10.7	−17.4	−19.5	−14.1	−13.5	−14.1	−11.5	−16.1	−12.4	−10.2	−10.7

Table 31. Developing Countries—by Region: Current Account Transactions
(Billions of U.S. dollars)

	1992	1993	1994	1995	1996	1997	1998	1999	2000	2001
Developing countries										
Exports	590.3	617.3	711.2	853.7	959.4	1,038.1	960.6	1,041.3	1,191.7	1,259.5
Imports	606.4	664.4	727.6	877.9	947.2	1,009.0	963.9	985.6	1,099.2	1,203.2
Trade balance	−16.1	−47.1	−16.4	−24.3	12.0	28.8	−3.7	55.3	92.1	55.6
Services, net	−50.6	−40.7	−33.0	−46.7	−50.3	−58.4	−45.9	−44.3	−46.8	−50.1
Balance on goods and services	−66.7	−87.8	−49.4	−71.0	−38.3	−29.5	−49.6	11.1	45.3	5.5
Income, net	−47.7	−59.7	−65.8	−73.7	−72.6	−73.7	−81.1	−89.1	−101.6	−105.0
Current transfers, net	30.5	27.1	26.6	33.3	36.6	43.8	40.4	44.8	44.3	49.4
Current account balance	**−84.0**	**−120.4**	**−88.6**	**−111.4**	**−74.2**	**−59.1**	**−89.9**	**−32.7**	**−11.6**	**−49.2**
Memorandum										
Exports of goods and services	722.3	754.6	864.4	1,023.2	1,146.8	1,245.9	1,162.2	1,248.9	1,418.3	1,505.0
Interest payments	79.6	81.6	85.2	100.1	104.5	104.0	111.8	125.5	136.3	138.7
Oil trade balance	130.6	113.8	111.9	124.2	156.8	152.9	98.9	130.3	175.0	146.9
Regional groups										
Africa										
Exports	87.0	82.3	85.2	101.0	112.7	114.7	99.2	105.3	127.8	127.7
Imports	81.9	78.7	82.7	99.4	101.8	105.3	104.3	104.6	114.5	121.6
Trade balance	5.1	3.6	2.6	1.6	10.9	9.4	−5.2	0.7	13.3	6.1
Services, net	−9.0	−8.3	−8.6	−10.7	−9.7	−9.3	−8.3	−9.2	−10.5	−9.7
Balance on goods and services	−3.9	−4.7	−6.0	−9.2	1.1	0.1	−13.5	−8.4	2.8	−3.6
Income, net	−18.0	−17.0	−16.4	−17.8	−19.2	−18.9	−18.5	−20.0	−22.8	−22.6
Current transfers, net	11.9	10.5	10.9	10.5	11.0	11.3	12.0	11.7	12.2	12.4
Current account balance	**−10.0**	**−11.2**	**−11.5**	**−16.5**	**−7.0**	**−7.4**	**−20.0**	**−16.8**	**−7.7**	**−13.8**
Memorandum										
Exports of goods and services	103.3	98.5	102.3	120.2	133.8	136.3	120.9	127.5	151.9	153.9
Interest payments	17.6	16.0	15.6	17.8	18.0	17.4	17.7	17.2	18.4	19.0
Oil trade balance	23.3	19.3	17.8	20.7	29.0	28.2	17.4	23.0	38.8	31.2
Asia										
Exports	222.3	248.4	307.3	377.7	417.1	466.8	457.6	494.3	545.2	597.9
Imports	233.7	278.9	327.5	417.2	448.1	452.7	391.9	433.5	487.9	541.1
Trade balance	−11.4	−30.5	−20.1	−39.6	−30.9	14.1	65.7	60.7	57.3	56.9
Services, net	−2.7	−5.2	−5.0	−13.1	−10.1	−17.6	−16.1	−14.6	−17.2	−21.9
Balance on goods and services	−14.1	−35.7	−25.2	−52.7	−41.0	−3.5	49.6	46.1	40.1	35.0
Income, net	−11.8	−12.7	−11.6	−21.9	−19.3	−17.5	−22.2	−27.2	−30.4	−33.1
Current transfers, net	13.3	14.4	16.3	18.2	21.7	27.7	21.5	23.4	22.1	26.3
Current account balance	**−12.6**	**−34.0**	**−20.4**	**−56.3**	**−38.7**	**6.8**	**48.9**	**42.3**	**31.7**	**28.1**
Memorandum										
Exports of goods and services	264.1	297.0	369.1	451.7	501.5	560.7	538.1	583.1	641.3	702.7
Interest payments	20.1	21.0	23.7	27.0	29.2	26.5	30.2	34.9	36.5	38.6
Oil trade balance	−5.2	−6.8	−7.4	−10.3	−15.5	−15.0	−8.6	−12.7	−18.9	−19.4

Table 31 *(concluded)*

	1992	1993	1994	1995	1996	1997	1998	1999	2000	2001
Middle East and Europe										
Exports	147.9	145.5	155.6	176.7	208.2	212.1	169.1	193.9	233.8	223.1
Imports	147.7	150.8	134.2	158.6	173.3	186.4	190.1	185.9	203.7	217.6
Trade balance	0.2	−5.3	21.4	18.1	34.8	25.7	−21.0	8.0	30.0	5.5
Services, net	−28.3	−20.8	−12.8	−16.8	−24.1	−21.9	−12.4	−15.3	−12.7	−11.2
Balance on goods and services	−28.0	−26.1	8.6	1.3	10.7	3.9	−33.4	−7.3	17.4	−5.7
Income, net	8.8	6.5	1.1	8.0	10.8	12.8	13.3	11.9	12.9	12.9
Current transfers, net	−7.5	−9.6	−14.2	−11.2	−11.7	−11.1	−10.2	−8.6	−9.3	−10.0
Current account balance	**−26.8**	**−29.2**	**−4.5**	**−1.8**	**9.8**	**5.6**	**−30.3**	**−4.0**	**20.9**	**−2.8**
Memorandum										
Exports of goods and services	180.7	180.3	189.7	211.3	245.1	257.2	218.1	240.2	286.0	279.6
Interest payments	8.6	9.9	9.3	11.7	11.5	11.8	12.4	18.2	20.9	20.5
Oil trade balance	98.3	88.2	87.2	97.6	120.5	118.5	78.2	100.1	128.9	112.6
Western Hemisphere										
Exports	133.1	141.1	163.0	198.4	221.4	244.5	234.7	247.8	284.9	310.8
Imports	143.1	156.0	183.2	202.7	224.0	264.7	277.6	261.5	293.1	323.0
Trade balance	−10.0	−14.9	−20.2	−4.4	−2.8	−20.5	−43.2	−14.1	−8.6	−12.9
Services, net	−10.7	−6.4	−6.7	−6.2	−6.4	−9.6	−9.2	−5.2	−6.4	−7.3
Balance on goods and services	−20.7	−21.3	−26.9	−10.5	−9.1	−30.1	−52.3	−19.3	−15.0	−20.2
Income, net	−26.7	−36.5	−38.9	−42.1	−44.9	−50.1	−53.7	−53.8	−61.3	−62.1
Current transfers, net	12.9	11.8	13.6	15.7	15.6	15.9	17.1	18.3	19.3	20.7
Current account balance	**−34.5**	**−46.0**	**−52.2**	**−36.8**	**−38.3**	**−64.1**	**−88.6**	**−54.2**	**−56.5**	**−60.8**
Memorandum										
Exports of goods and services	174.3	178.8	203.4	240.1	266.3	291.7	285.0	298.1	339.0	368.8
Interest payments	33.2	34.7	36.6	43.6	45.8	48.3	51.5	55.1	60.4	60.7
Oil trade balance	14.2	13.1	14.3	16.2	22.9	21.2	11.9	20.0	26.2	22.5

Table 32. Developing Countries—by Analytical Criteria: Current Account Transactions
(Billions of U.S. dollars)

	1992	1993	1994	1995	1996	1997	1998	1999	2000	2001
By source of export earnings										
Fuel										
Exports	167.3	161.0	163.6	184.6	224.5	228.2	170.0	208.0	266.1	241.1
Imports	131.8	123.9	109.3	124.4	126.7	138.6	145.7	145.8	159.6	167.1
Trade balance	35.5	37.0	54.3	60.3	97.8	89.6	24.3	62.1	106.6	74.0
Services, net	−47.4	−39.3	−31.6	−38.0	−47.5	−48.7	−39.4	−39.2	−41.5	−42.1
Balance on goods and services	−11.8	−2.2	22.7	22.2	50.3	40.9	−15.1	22.9	65.1	31.9
Income, net	1.5	−0.6	−4.3	0.5	1.7	2.7	2.9	2.4	2.2	2.7
Current transfers, net	−19.6	−21.3	−23.2	−22.0	−22.0	−22.2	−22.4	−21.9	−22.0	−22.5
Current account balance	**−29.9**	**−24.1**	**−4.9**	**0.8**	**30.0**	**21.4**	**−34.6**	**3.4**	**45.3**	**12.1**
Memorandum										
Exports of goods and services	182.1	175.9	178.9	197.1	237.0	243.0	184.6	223.2	283.6	258.7
Interest payments	11.9	12.2	11.5	14.8	14.5	13.9	14.6	19.7	22.9	22.7
Oil trade balance	137.5	123.2	121.1	137.1	173.5	171.5	114.7	147.1	198.5	171.9
Nonfuel exports										
Exports	423.1	456.3	547.6	669.1	735.1	810.4	791.0	834.1	926.8	1,019.5
Imports	474.7	540.5	618.3	753.6	820.8	870.8	818.7	840.0	939.9	1,036.5
Trade balance	−51.6	−84.1	−70.7	−84.5	−85.9	−60.6	−27.9	−6.4	−13.5	−17.6
Services, net	−3.3	−1.5	−1.5	−8.8	−3.0	−9.9	−6.9	−5.3	−5.7	−8.3
Balance on goods and services	−54.9	−85.6	−72.1	−93.3	−88.8	−70.5	−34.8	−11.7	−19.2	−25.9
Income, net	−49.2	−59.1	−61.5	−74.3	−74.4	−76.4	−84.1	−91.7	−104.3	−108.3
Current transfers, net	50.1	48.4	49.8	55.3	58.6	66.0	62.8	66.7	66.2	71.9
Current account balance	**−54.1**	**−96.3**	**−83.8**	**−112.3**	**−104.4**	**−80.7**	**−55.7**	**−36.1**	**−56.7**	**−61.4**
Memorandum										
Exports of goods and services	540.3	578.8	685.6	826.2	909.9	1,003.4	978.0	1,026.3	1,135.9	1,247.4
Interest payments	67.7	69.4	73.8	85.3	90.0	90.2	97.2	105.9	113.4	116.1
Oil trade balance	−7.0	−9.4	−9.2	−12.8	−16.6	−18.2	−15.4	−16.2	−22.4	−24.0
Manufactures										
Exports	261.9	290.2	358.5	441.8	495.0	550.3	542.7	582.0	648.6	721.1
Imports	283.9	336.0	386.6	481.7	529.8	558.3	515.4	550.5	619.0	689.9
Trade balance	−22.0	−45.9	−28.1	−40.0	−34.8	−8.0	27.4	31.5	29.7	31.3
Services, net	−4.4	−1.1	−3.2	−9.1	−3.7	−7.9	−2.9	−2.4	−3.8	−8.6
Balance on goods and services	−26.4	−46.9	−31.3	−49.0	−38.4	−15.9	24.4	29.1	25.8	22.7
Income, net	−22.1	−34.3	−33.8	−44.5	−46.5	−47.6	−55.4	−62.1	−70.6	−71.3
Current transfers, net	21.1	21.0	22.9	27.2	29.7	36.7	31.7	34.6	34.3	39.5
Current account balance	**−27.4**	**−60.2**	**−42.2**	**−66.4**	**−55.2**	**−26.7**	**0.7**	**1.7**	**−10.6**	**−9.1**
Memorandum										
Exports of goods and services	323.4	352.6	430.9	525.7	591.4	660.8	648.1	690.0	767.6	851.1
Interest payments	36.8	39.6	41.6	48.9	52.3	49.8	53.3	59.7	64.5	64.9
Oil trade balance	−7.0	−8.7	−9.0	−12.3	−16.1	−15.3	−12.7	−11.6	−18.2	−18.0

Table 32 *(continued)*

	1992	1993	1994	1995	1996	1997	1998	1999	2000	2001
Nonfuel primary products										
Exports	39.3	39.5	46.3	57.8	61.3	66.3	62.9	65.7	71.6	78.5
Imports	44.1	45.8	50.7	63.6	70.0	75.4	74.5	72.0	78.8	85.7
Trade balance	−4.7	−6.4	−4.4	−5.9	−8.8	−9.3	−11.9	−6.7	−7.5	−7.9
Services, net	−4.8	−4.7	−4.3	−5.5	−5.6	−6.0	−5.3	−4.3	−4.6	−4.9
Balance on goods and services	−9.6	−11.0	−8.7	−11.3	−14.4	−15.3	−17.2	−11.1	−12.1	−12.8
Income, net	−8.8	−8.4	−9.7	−9.5	−9.9	−10.3	−9.3	−9.7	−10.9	−12.0
Current transfers, net	7.2	6.7	6.8	6.6	7.8	7.5	8.1	8.7	8.9	8.8
Current account balance	**−11.2**	**−12.7**	**−11.6**	**−14.2**	**−16.3**	**−17.7**	**−18.1**	**−11.5**	**−13.7**	**−15.1**
Memorandum										
Exports of goods and services	48.9	49.5	57.4	71.2	75.7	81.3	78.7	81.8	89.1	97.5
Interest payments	9.0	8.7	8.6	9.3	8.8	8.9	9.5	9.5	10.1	10.3
Oil trade balance	−3.2	−2.5	−2.5	−3.0	−3.9	−4.2	−3.6	−3.3	−3.3	−3.4
Services, income, and private transfers										
Exports	11.6	12.0	12.8	16.4	17.0	18.0	17.9	17.9	21.0	23.4
Imports	35.7	38.2	40.0	46.4	50.7	53.0	55.6	57.3	62.1	66.2
Trade balance	−24.1	−26.2	−27.2	−30.0	−33.6	−34.9	−37.7	−39.3	−41.1	−42.8
Services, net	10.4	10.6	12.4	13.0	15.1	15.6	13.7	15.6	17.8	20.1
Balance on goods and services	−13.7	−15.6	−14.8	−17.0	−18.5	−19.4	−23.9	−23.7	−23.2	−22.7
Income, net	−1.5	−1.9	−1.8	−1.3	−0.8	−0.6	−0.9	−1.2	−1.5	−2.1
Current transfers, net	12.4	12.9	10.6	11.6	11.5	12.5	13.4	14.1	14.0	14.4
Current account balance	**−2.8**	**−4.6**	**−5.9**	**−6.8**	**−7.8**	**−7.5**	**−11.4**	**−10.8**	**−10.7**	**−10.4**
Memorandum										
Exports of goods and services	32.2	34.2	37.6	43.0	46.0	48.3	48.3	50.3	56.0	61.3
Interest payments	3.4	3.4	3.1	3.2	3.1	2.9	2.9	3.0	3.1	3.3
Oil trade balance	−1.7	−1.9	−2.6	−3.2	−3.6	−3.7	−4.5	−5.4	−5.8	−6.1
Diversified										
Exports	110.2	114.7	129.9	153.1	161.5	175.2	167.0	167.7	184.3	195.4
Imports	111.0	120.4	140.9	161.8	170.0	183.8	172.7	159.9	179.8	194.4
Trade balance	−0.8	−5.7	−11.0	−8.7	−8.6	−8.5	−5.7	7.8	4.5	0.9
Services, net	−4.4	−6.3	−6.3	−7.1	−8.7	−11.3	−12.1	−13.9	−14.7	−14.6
Balance on goods and services	−5.2	−12.0	−17.3	−15.8	−17.3	−19.9	−17.8	−6.2	−10.3	−13.7
Income, net	−16.8	−14.4	−16.2	−18.9	−17.2	−18.0	−18.4	−18.6	−20.7	−22.3
Current transfers, net	9.4	7.7	9.5	10.0	9.6	9.2	9.6	9.3	9.1	9.2
Current account balance	**−12.7**	**−18.8**	**−24.0**	**−24.8**	**−24.8**	**−28.6**	**−26.6**	**−15.4**	**−21.9**	**−26.8**
Memorandum										
Exports of goods and services	135.8	142.4	159.6	186.1	196.8	212.5	202.5	203.5	222.0	236.4
Interest payments	18.5	17.7	20.4	24.0	25.9	28.5	31.5	33.6	35.7	37.4
Oil trade balance	4.9	3.7	4.8	5.7	6.9	4.7	5.0	3.5	3.7	2.5

Table 32 *(continued)*

	1992	1993	1994	1995	1996	1997	1998	1999	2000	2001
By external financing source										
Net debtor countries										
Exports	493.3	521.5	613.7	743.0	828.2	903.3	860.9	920.8	1,038.2	1,121.4
Imports	537.3	596.0	663.4	806.7	875.0	931.7	881.7	902.3	1,012.4	1,111.1
Trade balance	−44.0	−74.5	−49.7	−63.7	−46.9	−28.6	−21.0	18.1	25.4	9.6
Services, net	−17.1	−13.8	−12.5	−19.9	−14.5	−21.2	−16.2	−14.6	−16.5	−18.5
Balance on goods and services	−61.0	−88.3	−62.2	−83.6	−61.4	−49.8	−37.2	3.5	8.9	−8.9
Income, net	−60.4	−69.9	−72.4	−87.1	−86.2	−87.9	−95.7	−104.4	−119.5	−123.0
Current transfers, net	52.8	51.1	52.7	57.6	60.5	67.3	64.0	68.1	67.9	73.7
Current account balance	**−68.6**	**−107.1**	**−82.0**	**−113.0**	**−86.9**	**−70.1**	**−68.5**	**−32.2**	**−42.2**	**−57.2**
Memorandum										
Exports of goods and services	615.7	649.4	757.2	906.5	1,009.9	1,103.5	1,054.7	1,120.2	1,255.0	1,357.2
Interest payments	77.7	79.7	83.1	96.8	101.0	99.9	107.2	120.8	130.6	133.1
Oil trade balance	48.8	39.5	38.2	40.9	54.4	52.1	32.8	49.0	66.6	54.9
Official financing										
Exports	32.4	31.8	32.5	39.5	46.6	50.0	45.2	48.6	59.9	59.8
Imports	37.0	38.7	42.8	50.7	55.1	54.0	55.7	58.0	61.9	66.2
Trade balance	−4.6	−6.9	−10.2	−11.2	−8.5	−3.9	−10.5	−9.3	−2.1	−6.4
Services, net	−3.4	−3.3	−3.4	−4.0	−4.1	−3.9	−4.2	−4.8	−4.9	−4.3
Balance on goods and services	−8.1	−10.2	−13.6	−15.2	−12.6	−7.8	−14.7	−14.1	−6.9	−10.7
Income, net	−7.5	−7.1	−6.4	−7.0	−7.5	−7.3	−6.7	−7.2	−8.4	−7.9
Current transfers, net	9.4	9.0	10.0	10.1	11.0	10.5	11.4	11.5	11.7	11.9
Current account balance	**−6.2**	**−8.2**	**−10.0**	**−12.1**	**−9.2**	**−4.6**	**−10.0**	**−9.7**	**−3.6**	**−6.7**
Memorandum										
Exports of goods and services	41.2	41.1	42.7	51.2	59.1	62.8	58.3	62.4	74.7	75.8
Interest payments	7.7	7.0	6.5	7.2	7.5	7.4	7.6	7.3	8.1	8.1
Oil trade balance	9.5	7.9	6.2	7.0	9.6	10.8	5.7	8.4	16.1	12.1
Private financing										
Exports	379.9	410.3	494.5	604.6	665.9	732.2	702.8	743.0	829.4	905.4
Imports	403.0	459.1	524.7	644.3	694.5	741.6	697.4	713.2	801.3	885.3
Trade balance	−23.2	−48.8	−30.2	−39.7	−28.8	−9.6	5.1	29.4	27.7	19.4
Services, net	−3.8	−0.5	−1.7	−7.7	−1.7	−6.2	−2.8	−3.7	−4.7	−7.0
Balance on goods and services	−27.0	−49.2	−31.9	−47.4	−30.5	−15.7	2.3	25.7	23.0	12.4
Income, net	−43.3	−54.1	−57.5	−74.2	−74.7	−78.3	−81.7	−87.5	−99.8	−104.5
Current transfers, net	31.4	30.6	29.6	35.4	37.2	43.5	39.8	44.2	43.5	48.6
Current account balance	**−38.9**	**−72.7**	**−59.9**	**−86.1**	**−67.9**	**−50.3**	**−39.3**	**−17.0**	**−32.8**	**−42.6**
Memorandum										
Exports of goods and services	478.2	513.2	610.4	735.7	810.8	893.0	861.5	905.6	1,007.0	1,098.9
Interest payments	59.4	61.0	65.5	76.5	80.4	79.5	86.1	94.7	102.6	105.2
Oil trade balance	10.3	7.4	8.0	6.8	8.7	7.0	3.4	6.9	9.4	4.8

Table 32 *(continued)*

	1992	1993	1994	1995	1996	1997	1998	1999	2000	2001
Diversified financing										
Exports	54.2	54.5	59.3	71.4	83.9	92.6	90.1	98.8	116.6	123.2
Imports	65.1	70.5	74.5	88.4	100.1	110.5	102.5	104.0	117.7	126.6
Trade balance	−11.0	−16.0	−15.2	−17.0	−16.2	−17.9	−12.4	−5.2	−1.1	−3.5
Services, net	−5.2	−6.1	−5.4	−6.9	−7.5	−9.9	−9.3	−5.8	−7.1	−8.0
Balance on goods and services	−16.2	−22.0	−20.6	−23.9	−23.7	−27.8	−21.6	−11.0	−8.1	−11.5
Income, net	−9.0	−8.2	−7.0	−4.7	−1.9	−1.0	−5.8	−8.3	−9.3	−7.9
Current transfers, net	10.0	9.2	10.9	11.2	10.6	12.0	11.1	10.6	11.0	11.2
Current account balance	**−15.1**	**−21.0**	**−16.7**	**−17.4**	**−15.0**	**−16.9**	**−16.3**	**−8.7**	**−6.5**	**−8.2**
Memorandum										
Exports of goods and services	66.6	66.8	73.7	88.2	104.3	115.3	107.9	117.6	136.2	144.3
Interest payments	9.7	9.9	10.0	11.4	11.2	11.6	12.2	12.5	13.0	13.3
Oil trade balance	12.4	10.0	9.7	12.4	17.3	19.4	14.1	17.6	24.0	21.5
Net debtor countries by debt-servicing experience										
Countries with arrears and/or rescheduling during 1994–98										
Exports	162.3	163.4	179.9	205.0	230.4	251.1	230.4	250.2	295.7	312.1
Imports	154.0	160.7	174.1	218.9	238.9	258.3	239.8	233.7	263.9	287.2
Trade balance	8.3	2.7	5.8	−13.8	−8.5	−7.2	−9.4	16.5	31.8	24.9
Services, net	−16.6	−18.5	−17.4	−23.2	−27.3	−32.6	−33.1	−28.8	−31.0	−32.2
Balance on goods and services	−8.3	−15.8	−11.5	−37.1	−35.8	−39.8	−42.5	−12.3	0.8	−7.3
Income, net	−29.9	−30.0	−27.5	−29.2	−24.4	−27.3	−33.9	−37.1	−45.0	−42.1
Current transfers, net	16.1	15.4	18.0	18.2	18.8	18.3	19.1	19.7	20.3	20.9
Current account balance	**−22.1**	**−30.3**	**−21.1**	**−48.0**	**−41.4**	**−48.8**	**−57.3**	**−29.7**	**−23.8**	**−28.5**
Memorandum										
Exports of goods and services	190.5	193.2	213.1	242.3	271.7	298.0	270.9	291.8	341.2	361.4
Interest payments	30.7	32.0	30.7	36.5	38.4	40.0	44.3	52.8	55.8	53.4
Oil trade balance	40.7	32.6	31.8	35.2	45.5	45.9	33.7	44.4	62.0	56.1
Other net debtor countries										
Exports	328.5	355.4	430.7	534.7	594.4	648.3	627.2	667.0	738.6	805.2
Imports	381.1	433.0	487.0	585.1	633.4	670.4	638.8	665.5	745.3	820.6
Trade balance	−52.6	−77.6	−56.2	−50.5	−39.2	−22.3	−11.9	1.1	−7.0	−16.1
Services, net	−0.1	5.1	5.3	3.8	13.3	11.9	17.4	14.7	14.9	14.2
Balance on goods and services	−52.7	−72.5	−51.0	−46.7	−25.9	−10.4	5.4	15.8	7.9	−1.9
Income, net	−30.7	−40.3	−44.6	−57.9	−61.7	−60.7	−61.8	−67.4	−74.6	−80.9
Current transfers, net	36.6	35.6	34.5	39.4	41.5	48.7	44.7	48.1	47.3	52.5
Current account balance	**−46.7**	**−77.1**	**−61.1**	**−65.2**	**−45.9**	**−22.0**	**−11.4**	**−2.9**	**−18.9**	**−29.4**
Memorandum										
Exports of goods and services	422.4	453.2	540.9	660.5	734.6	801.3	780.1	824.4	909.5	991.1
Interest payments	46.9	47.5	52.2	60.3	62.5	59.7	62.8	67.9	74.6	79.6
Oil trade balance	8.2	7.0	6.4	5.7	9.1	6.4	−0.8	4.8	4.8	−1.0

Table 32 *(concluded)*

	1992	1993	1994	1995	1996	1997	1998	1999	2000	2001
Other groups										
Heavily indebted poor countries										
Exports	27.2	26.3	29.9	36.9	42.8	45.1	42.8	45.5	51.5	54.1
Imports	32.0	33.2	35.0	42.1	48.6	50.6	51.4	53.1	57.3	61.3
Trade balance	−4.8	−6.9	−5.1	−5.2	−5.8	−5.5	−8.6	−7.6	−5.8	−7.2
Services, net	−5.1	−4.7	−4.4	−5.9	−6.3	−6.5	−6.1	−6.0	−6.4	−5.9
Balance on goods and services	−9.9	−11.6	−9.5	−11.2	−12.1	−12.0	−14.6	−13.6	−12.2	−13.1
Income, net	−8.8	−8.8	−8.6	−9.0	−9.7	−9.5	−9.6	−10.4	−11.7	−11.5
Current transfers, net	7.0	6.7	8.1	7.9	8.8	8.5	9.6	9.7	9.9	9.7
Current account balance	**−11.7**	**−13.7**	**−10.0**	**−12.3**	**−13.0**	**−13.1**	**−14.7**	**−14.3**	**−13.9**	**−15.0**
Memorandum										
Exports of goods and services	34.7	33.9	37.9	46.3	53.0	55.2	53.3	56.4	63.4	67.0
Interest payments	7.7	7.6	7.2	7.4	7.5	7.2	7.7	7.3	7.5	7.7
Oil trade balance	2.5	1.6	1.4	1.9	2.5	3.2	1.1	3.2	5.6	4.1
Least developed countries										
Exports	17.8	17.8	20.1	24.4	27.4	28.7	26.8	29.5	34.2	35.9
Imports	26.6	27.0	28.1	33.2	36.5	37.8	39.1	41.0	43.9	47.3
Trade balance	−8.8	−9.3	−8.0	−8.8	−9.0	−9.1	−12.2	−11.5	−9.7	−11.5
Services, net	−3.8	−3.3	−3.0	−4.2	−4.1	−4.1	−4.0	−4.1	−4.6	−4.3
Balance on goods and services	−12.6	−12.6	−11.0	−13.0	−13.2	−13.1	−16.2	−15.6	−14.3	−15.7
Income, net	−4.2	−4.0	−5.2	−5.5	−6.0	−6.0	−6.5	−7.2	−8.3	−8.7
Current transfers, net	7.4	7.6	9.4	9.5	9.8	9.3	9.7	9.8	9.9	9.7
Current account balance	**−9.4**	**−8.9**	**−6.8**	**−9.0**	**−9.4**	**−9.8**	**−13.0**	**−13.0**	**−12.7**	**−14.7**
Memorandum										
Exports of goods and services	22.7	22.9	25.5	30.1	33.5	35.0	33.3	36.5	41.9	44.1
Interest payments	4.2	4.0	4.0	4.3	4.4	4.1	4.7	4.5	4.7	5.0
Oil trade balance	0.1	−0.8	−1.0	−1.2	−0.4	−0.4	−2.3	−0.5	1.5	0.3
Middle East and north Africa										
Exports	151.9	147.8	151.5	170.8	199.6	204.3	159.2	189.6	235.7	220.9
Imports	143.1	139.4	131.8	146.5	152.2	159.8	167.5	170.4	183.8	195.3
Trade balance	8.8	8.4	19.7	24.3	47.4	44.6	−8.3	19.2	51.8	25.6
Services, net	−34.8	−28.0	−18.5	−23.6	−30.1	−31.5	−24.6	−23.9	−22.9	−22.6
Balance on goods and services	−26.1	−19.6	1.3	0.7	17.3	13.1	−33.0	−4.7	28.9	3.1
Income, net	5.3	3.1	−1.7	3.9	5.7	7.8	8.4	8.3	9.4	8.8
Current transfers, net	−6.7	−9.0	−12.7	−11.0	−11.1	−11.2	−10.8	−9.9	−10.4	−10.7
Current account balance	**−27.5**	**−25.5**	**−13.2**	**−6.5**	**12.0**	**9.7**	**−35.4**	**−6.3**	**27.9**	**1.1**
Memorandum										
Exports of goods and services	177.7	174.8	179.7	197.1	227.6	234.6	189.6	221.8	271.4	259.0
Interest payments	−10.0	−10.7	−9.8	−12.5	−12.7	−12.5	−12.6	−17.6	−19.8	−19.4
Oil trade balance	111.0	100.3	98.1	109.9	136.3	134.9	91.2	114.6	151.3	133.2

Table 33. Summary of Balance of Payments and External Financing

(Billions of U.S. dollars)

	1992	1993	1994	1995	1996	1997	1998	1999	2000	2001
Developing countries										
Balance of payments										
Balance on current account	−84.0	−120.4	−88.6	−111.4	−74.2	−59.1	−89.9	−32.7	−11.6	−49.2
Balance on capital and financial account	84.0	120.4	88.6	111.4	74.2	59.1	89.9	32.7	11.6	49.2
By balance of payments component										
Capital transfers[1]	3.8	4.1	4.5	5.9	8.9	7.7	6.9	5.8	9.5	4.2
Net financial flows	128.2	163.8	140.7	184.3	187.1	155.5	106.1	86.0	85.8	124.0
Errors and omissions, net	−2.7	−8.4	−12.9	−11.2	−23.1	−37.0	−34.8	−16.9	−6.6	−5.0
Change in reserves (− = increase)	−45.4	−39.0	−43.7	−67.6	−98.8	−67.1	11.7	−42.3	−77.1	−73.9
By type of financing flow										
Nonexceptional financing flows	98.2	125.4	104.9	157.0	152.0	121.3	60.7	48.9	65.0	108.1
Exceptional financing flows	31.1	34.1	27.4	22.0	20.9	5.0	17.5	26.0	23.7	15.1
Arrears on debt service	6.6	12.4	−6.3	−5.0	−4.1	−4.1	0.1	−6.3	. . .	. . .
Debt forgiveness	0.3	1.8	1.2	0.9	5.5	3.4	1.7	0.7	. . .	. . .
Rescheduling of debt service	16.8	22.4	25.6	19.6	25.0	14.6	4.4	13.4	. . .	. . .
Change in reserves (− = increase)	−45.4	−39.0	−43.7	−67.6	−98.8	−67.1	11.7	−42.3	−77.1	−73.9
External financing										
Balance on current account	−84.0	−120.4	−88.6	−111.4	−74.2	−59.1	−89.9	−32.7	−11.6	−49.2
Change in reserves (− = increase)[2]	−45.4	−39.0	−43.7	−67.6	−98.8	−67.1	11.7	−42.3	−77.1	−73.9
Asset transactions, including net errors and omissions[3]	−15.4	−26.7	−21.5	−25.5	−47.3	−99.9	−94.5	−54.6	−78.4	−59.4
Total, net external financing[4]	**144.7**	**186.1**	**153.8**	**204.5**	**220.2**	**226.1**	**172.8**	**129.5**	**167.1**	**182.6**
Non-debt-creating flows, net	44.6	84.1	104.8	101.6	134.4	155.7	131.9	136.8	143.9	135.5
Capital transfers[1]	3.8	4.1	4.5	5.9	8.9	7.7	6.9	5.8	9.5	4.2
Direct investment and portfolio investment equity flows	40.8	80.0	100.2	95.7	125.5	148.0	125.0	131.0	134.4	131.3
Net credit and loans from IMF[5]	−0.4	−0.1	−0.8	12.6	−2.9	0.8	8.5	1.3	. . .	. . .
Net external borrowing[6]	100.5	102.0	49.8	90.8	88.7	69.6	32.4	−8.9	28.0	47.7
Borrowing from official creditors[7]	18.2	19.7	14.3	21.6	2.8	0.3	22.4	11.8	12.3	8.5
Borrowing from banks[8]	13.9	16.9	−27.8	14.5	22.3	24.6	18.2	−14.7	0.4	10.9
Other borrowing[9]	68.4	65.5	63.3	54.6	63.6	44.7	−8.1	−6.0	15.3	28.3
Memorandum										
Balance on goods and services in percent of GDP[10]	−1.8	−2.0	−1.1	−1.5	−0.8	−0.5	−0.9	0.2	0.8	0.1
Scheduled amortization of external debt	113.8	119.3	122.8	150.3	194.9	220.5	228.7	239.3	218.1	203.9
Gross external financing[11]	258.5	305.4	276.6	354.8	415.1	446.6	401.5	368.8	385.2	386.4
Gross external borrowing[11]	214.2	221.3	172.6	241.1	283.6	290.1	261.1	230.3	246.1	251.6
Countries in transition										
Balance of payments										
Balance on current account	−5.1	−8.2	2.1	−1.8	−16.9	−26.1	−24.8	−5.3	−7.5	−16.7
Balance on capital and financial account	5.1	8.2	−2.1	1.8	16.9	26.1	24.8	5.3	7.5	16.7
By balance of payments component										
Capital transfers[1]	4.4	4.2	11.4	−0.7	1.1	10.5	−0.9	1.3	0.5	0.7
Net financial flows	5.9	20.6	−5.8	35.0	14.9	30.4	23.1	12.1	16.4	27.1
Errors and omissions, net	−3.5	−5.4	−1.9	4.9	3.3	−5.1	3.3	0.1	−0.2	−0.5
Change in reserves (− = increase)	−1.7	−11.2	−5.7	−37.4	−2.4	−9.6	−0.8	−8.2	−9.2	−10.7

Table 33 (concluded)

	1992	1993	1994	1995	1996	1997	1998	1999	2000	2001
By type of financing flow										
Nonexceptional financing flows	−12.6	−1.9	−12.7	23.6	10.8	32.7	22.1	13.4	7.7	23.8
Exceptional financing flows	19.4	21.2	16.3	15.6	8.5	3.0	3.5	0.2	9.0	3.6
Arrears on debt service	7.3	2.1	3.1	−12.4	−1.0	−0.4	0.8	—	. . .	. . .
Debt forgiveness	2.4	2.1	—	0.2	0.9	—	—	—	. . .	. . .
Rescheduling of debt service	9.5	16.7	14.8	26.7	8.5	1.9	1.8	1.1	. . .	. . .
Change in reserves (− = increase)	−1.7	−11.2	−5.7	−37.4	−2.4	−9.6	−0.8	−8.2	−9.2	−10.7
External financing										
Balance on current account	−5.1	−8.2	2.1	−1.8	−16.9	−26.1	−24.8	−5.3	−7.5	−16.7
Change in reserves (− = increase)[2]	−1.7	−11.2	−5.7	−37.4	−2.4	−9.6	−0.8	−8.2	−9.2	−10.7
Asset transactions, including net errors and omissions[3]	−6.7	0.2	−4.8	19.8	3.0	−15.6	−11.2	−21.0	−19.9	−12.0
Total, net external financing[4]	**13.5**	**19.1**	**8.4**	**19.3**	**16.3**	**51.3**	**36.8**	**34.6**	**36.6**	**39.4**
Non-debt-creating flows, net	8.6	10.1	17.0	13.3	15.4	32.1	20.9	25.3	25.6	26.8
Capital transfers[1]	4.4	4.2	11.4	−0.7	1.1	10.5	−0.9	1.3	0.5	0.7
Direct investment and portfolio investment equity flows	4.2	6.0	5.6	14.0	14.3	21.6	21.8	24.0	25.2	26.1
Net credit and loans from IMF[5]	1.6	3.7	2.4	4.7	3.7	2.5	5.5	−3.6	. . .	. . .
Net external borrowing[6]	3.3	5.3	−10.5	2.1	−1.0	21.0	13.3	14.8	14.6	16.6
Borrowing from official creditors[7]	3.6	−0.4	−10.3	−9.0	−2.1	7.6	9.0	0.6	1.4	1.0
Borrowing from banks[8]	−1.2	7.4	4.2	−1.7	2.9	4.6	3.4	0.3	1.3	1.5
Other borrowing[9]	1.0	−1.8	−4.9	12.0	−3.6	4.6	−2.0	11.5	9.3	9.8
Memorandum										
Balance on goods and services in percent of GDP[10]	−0.4	−2.0	0.4	−0.7	−2.1	−2.7	−2.7	0.2	0.3	−0.9
Scheduled amortization of external debt	31.0	26.3	26.5	27.5	27.0	21.4	24.0	28.3	31.2	32.3
Gross external financing[11]	44.4	45.4	35.0	46.8	43.3	72.6	60.8	62.8	67.8	71.6
Gross external borrowing[11]	34.3	31.5	15.6	28.8	24.2	38.1	34.4	40.7	43.1	44.6

[1]Comprise debt forgiveness as well as all other identified transactions on capital account as defined in the fifth edition of the International Monetary Fund's *Balance of Payments Manual* (1993).

[2]Positioned here to reflect the discretionary nature of many countries' transactions in reserves.

[3]Include changes in recorded private external assets (mainly portfolio investment), export credit, the collateral for debt-reduction operations, and balance of payments net errors and omissions.

[4]Equals, with opposite sign, the sum of transactions listed above. It is the amount required to finance the deficit on goods and services, income and current transfers; the increase in the official reserve level; the net asset transactions; and the transactions underlying net errors and omissions.

[5]Comprise use of International Monetary Fund resources under the General Resources Account, Trust Fund, Poverty Reduction and Growth Facility (PRGF, formerly ESAF-Enhanced Structural Adjustment Facility). For further detail, see Table 37.

[6]Net disbursement of long- and short-term credits (including exceptional financing) by both official and private creditors.

[7]Net disbursements by official creditors (other than monetary authorities) based on directly reported flows and flows derived from statistics on debt stocks. The estimates include the increase in official claims caused by the transfer of officially guaranteed claims to the guarantor agency in the creditor country, usually in the context of debt rescheduling.

[8]Net disbursements by commercial banks based on directly reported flows and on cross-border claims and liabilities reported in the International Banking section of the International Monetary Fund's *International Financial Statistics*.

[9]Includes primary bond issues and loans on the international capital markets. Since the estimates are residually derived, they also reflect any underrecording or misclassification of official and commercial bank credits above.

[10]This is often referred to as the "resource balance" and, with opposite sign, the "net resource transfer."

[11]Net external financing/borrowing (see footnotes 4 and 6, respectively) plus amortization due on external debt.

Table 34. Developing Countries—by Region: Balance of Payments and External Financing[1]
(Billions of U.S. dollars)

	1992	1993	1994	1995	1996	1997	1998	1999	2000	2001
Africa										
Balance on current account	−10.0	−11.2	−11.5	−16.5	−7.0	−7.4	−20.0	−16.8	−7.7	−13.8
Change in reserves (− = increase)	0.7	3.2	−6.0	−3.3	−9.2	−11.2	1.2	−3.0	−11.7	−7.4
Asset transactions, including										
net errors and omissions	−2.1	−1.1	4.8	−2.6	−3.0	−2.6	−1.6	−2.9	−1.6	0.2
Total, net external financing	**11.4**	**9.1**	**12.7**	**22.4**	**19.3**	**21.2**	**20.4**	**22.6**	**20.9**	**21.0**
Non-debt-creating flows, net	2.1	4.1	3.8	4.6	11.4	11.9	8.3	12.5	17.3	11.6
Net credit and loans from IMF	−0.2	0.2	0.9	0.8	0.6	−0.5	−0.4	−0.2	. . .	. . .
Net external borrowing	9.6	4.7	7.9	17.5	7.3	9.7	12.5	10.3	3.7	9.7
From official creditors	10.4	6.3	7.7	7.3	4.6	−1.4	2.5	1.6	−4.5	0.7
From banks	−2.8	−0.5	2.9	2.5	−0.1	−1.1	−0.9	−1.0	−1.2	0.6
Other	2.0	−1.2	−2.7	7.7	2.9	12.2	10.9	9.8	9.3	8.4
Memorandum										
Net financial flows	6.4	4.5	10.6	18.2	12.0	15.4	14.0	16.4	11.7	16.6
Exceptional financing	15.6	11.6	14.9	14.8	19.2	14.1	4.0	8.5	6.1	4.2
Sub-Sahara										
Balance on current account	−9.5	−10.2	−8.3	−12.3	−7.8	−10.2	−18.3	−14.9	−12.1	−15.1
Change in reserves (− = increase)	1.3	3.3	−3.9	−4.6	−6.4	−6.3	0.2	−4.1	−6.6	−4.9
Asset transactions, including										
net errors and omissions	−2.6	−1.7	4.7	−2.6	−2.3	−2.4	−2.1	−2.4	−0.3	−0.1
Total, net external financing	**10.8**	**8.6**	**7.6**	**19.4**	**16.4**	**18.8**	**20.2**	**21.4**	**18.9**	**20.1**
Non-debt-creating flows, net	1.1	3.0	2.8	3.9	10.4	10.2	6.7	10.1	14.5	9.5
Net credit and loans from IMF	—	0.7	0.5	0.6	0.1	−0.5	−0.3	−0.1	. . .	. . .
Net external borrowing	9.7	4.8	4.4	15.3	6.0	9.2	13.8	11.4	4.3	10.7
From official creditors	9.8	5.7	7.0	6.6	3.9	−1.3	3.9	2.7	−2.6	1.7
From banks	−3.0	−0.1	1.8	1.4	−0.4	−1.1	−0.5	−0.1	−0.4	1.4
Other	2.9	−0.8	−4.5	7.3	2.5	11.6	10.5	8.9	7.3	7.6
Memorandum										
Net financial flows	5.9	4.1	5.6	15.2	9.4	13.1	14.0	15.3	9.8	15.9
Exceptional financing[2]	15.0	11.6	10.1	9.2	14.7	10.5	3.0	8.1	6.1	4.2
Asia										
Balance on current account	−12.6	−34.0	−20.4	−56.3	−38.7	6.8	48.9	42.3	31.7	28.1
Change in reserves (− = increase)	−13.5	−25.1	−39.4	−34.4	−40.9	−29.3	−23.0	−33.6	−35.3	−45.5
Asset transactions, including										
net errors and omissions	−12.4	−14.0	−18.5	−10.7	−32.1	−85.8	−76.3	−34.3	−50.6	−47.4
Total, net external financing	**38.5**	**73.2**	**78.2**	**101.4**	**111.7**	**108.3**	**50.4**	**25.7**	**54.2**	**64.8**
Non-debt-creating flows, net	17.4	35.5	47.8	50.3	56.9	62.1	55.9	46.0	48.3	47.5
Net credit and loans from IMF	1.3	0.6	−0.8	−1.5	−1.7	5.0	6.6	1.7	. . .	. . .
Net external borrowing	19.8	37.1	31.2	52.5	56.4	41.1	−12.1	−22.3	3.6	18.9
From official creditors	10.8	10.3	11.0	7.1	3.7	5.8	14.1	8.2	9.2	9.5
From banks	6.0	11.3	12.5	14.1	30.2	22.4	−5.8	−12.7	−1.1	8.1
Other	3.0	15.5	7.7	31.4	22.6	13.0	−20.4	−17.8	−4.5	1.4
Memorandum										
Net financial flows	30.7	64.0	71.5	94.1	96.8	44.2	−4.1	−9.1	7.0	23.4
Exceptional financing	2.2	0.8	1.2	0.5	0.8	−8.1	12.0	18.5	17.1	10.4

Table 34 *(concluded)*

	1992	1993	1994	1995	1996	1997	1998	1999	2000	2001
Asia excluding China and India										
Balance on current account	−16.1	−20.6	−24.5	−39.2	−40.0	−24.9	23.2	31.3	21.4	18.1
Change in reserves (− = increase)	−14.2	−16.6	−3.2	−12.9	−5.6	10.8	−12.7	−20.9	−11.4	−15.3
Asset transactions, including										
net errors and omissions	−1.2	−4.1	−10.3	−4.1	−6.1	−19.4	−18.6	9.9	4.0	2.6
Total, net external financing	**31.5**	**41.3**	**38.0**	**56.2**	**51.7**	**33.6**	**8.1**	**−20.3**	**−14.1**	**−5.4**
Non-debt-creating flows, net	10.0	11.8	15.0	14.7	16.4	17.2	12.2	7.5	8.7	9.6
Net credit and loans from IMF	0.1	0.1	0.4	−0.3	−0.4	5.7	7.0	2.1	. . .	. . .
Net external borrowing	21.4	29.4	22.7	41.8	35.7	10.7	−11.1	−30.1	−25.2	−13.4
From official creditors	4.8	4.4	2.0	3.3	1.8	4.7	8.1	6.4	4.2	2.5
From banks	1.9	3.4	8.3	11.8	25.5	16.2	−3.0	−17.3	−9.9	−3.7
Other	14.7	21.6	12.3	26.7	8.5	−10.2	−16.1	−19.3	−19.5	−12.2
Memorandum										
Net financial flows	27.5	34.9	32.9	49.9	47.6	10.7	−5.7	−27.7	−21.3	−7.8
Exceptional financing	2.2	0.8	1.2	0.5	0.8	−8.1	12.0	18.5	17.1	10.4
Middle East and Europe										
Balance on current account	−26.8	−29.2	−4.5	−1.8	9.8	5.6	−30.3	−4.0	20.9	−2.8
Change in reserves (− = increase)	−9.9	3.0	−2.9	−8.0	−17.9	−11.3	16.1	−10.8	−12.6	−9.0
Asset transactions, including										
net errors and omissions	6.7	−3.5	1.4	−1.5	−1.2	−7.9	−0.4	—	−9.5	−1.7
Total, net external financing	**29.9**	**29.7**	**5.9**	**11.3**	**9.3**	**13.6**	**14.6**	**14.8**	**10.7**	**18.9**
Non-debt-creating flows, net	2.0	3.9	7.1	8.6	3.7	5.3	5.8	6.2	9.7	10.2
Net credit and loans from IMF	0.1	—	0.4	0.4	0.1	0.2	−0.1	0.6	. . .	. . .
Net external borrowing	27.9	25.8	−1.6	2.3	5.5	8.1	8.9	8.1	0.2	7.7
From official creditors	−1.3	2.6	−0.8	−0.8	−0.8	−0.5	−0.3	−1.6	0.8	−0.5
From banks	11.2	0.8	−10.7	−2.1	−7.3	0.6	11.2	2.3	—	0.4
Other	18.0	22.4	9.9	5.3	13.7	8.0	−1.9	7.4	−0.6	7.9
Memorandum										
Net financial flows	37.3	28.0	12.8	10.9	10.9	14.2	20.3	21.3	−9.1	10.7
Exceptional financing	3.3	14.2	4.8	3.9	−0.3	0.4	0.5	0.5	—	0.1
Western Hemisphere										
Balance on current account	−34.5	−46.0	−52.2	−36.8	−38.3	−64.1	−88.6	−54.2	−56.5	−60.8
Change in reserves (− = increase)	−22.6	−20.1	4.6	−21.9	−30.8	−15.3	17.4	5.1	−17.5	−12.0
Asset transactions, including										
net errors and omissions	−7.7	−8.1	−9.3	−10.7	−10.9	−3.6	−16.3	−17.3	−16.8	−10.5
Total, net external financing	**64.8**	**74.2**	**57.0**	**69.3**	**79.8**	**82.8**	**87.2**	**66.1**	**90.5**	**82.8**
Non-debt-creating flows, net	14.4	14.0	23.2	24.9	40.4	54.3	56.4	63.8	57.1	55.5
Net credit and loans from IMF	−1.6	−0.9	−1.3	12.9	−2.0	−4.0	2.5	−0.9	. . .	. . .
Net external borrowing	52.0	61.1	35.1	31.6	41.4	32.4	28.3	3.0	41.4	27.1
From official creditors	−1.8	0.5	−3.6	8.1	−4.7	−3.6	6.1	3.6	6.8	−1.1
From banks	−0.4	5.3	−32.6	—	−0.4	2.7	13.7	−3.2	2.6	1.8
Other	54.2	55.4	71.2	23.4	46.4	33.3	8.5	2.7	31.9	26.4
Memorandum										
Net financial flows	53.8	67.3	45.8	61.2	67.4	81.7	75.9	57.4	76.3	73.3
Exceptional financing	10.0	7.5	6.5	2.8	1.2	−1.5	0.9	−1.5	0.4	0.5

[1]For definition, see footnotes to Table 33.

[2]In 1997, the reduction of the stock of arrears through cancellation of payments arrears exceeds the total value of debt forgiveness and rescheduling, since the lower values for the latter reflect implicit discounts on debt-reduction operations with commercial banks.

Table 35. Developing Countries—by Analytical Criteria: Balance of Payments and External Financing[1]
(Billions of U.S. dollars)

	1992	1993	1994	1995	1996	1997	1998	1999	2000	2001
By source of export earnings										
Fuel										
Balance on current account	−29.9	−24.1	−4.9	0.8	30.0	21.4	−34.6	3.4	45.3	12.1
Change in reserves (− = increase)	0.4	12.0	1.9	1.1	−23.9	−14.8	20.7	−5.3	−18.7	−5.8
Asset transactions, including										
net errors and omissions	5.3	−4.6	−11.4	−4.1	−7.2	−10.1	−3.4	−7.4	−15.7	−7.4
Total, net external financing	**24.2**	**16.7**	**14.4**	**2.3**	**1.0**	**3.5**	**17.3**	**9.3**	**−1.3**	**6.4**
Non-debt-creating flows, net	1.4	0.4	5.2	6.0	9.4	10.0	10.6	10.0	12.7	12.5
Net credit and loans from IMF	−0.5	−0.8	0.4	−0.2	0.7	−0.3	−0.6	−0.5	. . .	. . .
Net external borrowing	23.3	17.0	8.8	−3.5	−9.0	−6.2	7.3	−0.2	−13.4	−5.7
From official creditors	5.6	1.3	3.3	1.5	3.0	1.3	1.9	−1.1	−1.7	−2.1
From banks	5.4	1.4	−2.3	−3.8	−11.6	−2.7	7.0	−0.4	−2.8	−1.4
Other	12.2	14.4	7.8	−1.2	−0.4	−4.8	−1.6	1.4	−8.8	−2.2
Memorandum										
Net financial flows	34.1	17.7	13.7	4.2	−3.1	3.8	18.4	14.4	−25.0	−5.6
Exceptional financing	10.4	17.3	13.2	12.4	13.4	8.0	5.8	4.4	1.9	0.4
Nonfuel										
Balance on current account	−54.1	−96.3	−83.8	−112.3	−104.4	−80.7	−55.7	−36.1	−56.7	−61.4
Change in reserves (− = increase)	−45.8	−51.0	−45.5	−68.7	−74.9	−52.3	−9.0	−37.0	−58.6	−68.3
Asset transactions, including										
net errors and omissions	−20.6	−22.1	−10.1	−21.4	−40.1	−89.8	−91.1	−47.2	−62.7	−52.0
Total, net external financing	**120.5**	**169.4**	**139.5**	**202.3**	**219.3**	**222.6**	**155.7**	**119.9**	**177.8**	**181.3**
Non-debt-creating flows, net	34.5	57.1	76.9	82.6	103.3	123.9	116.2	118.4	119.8	112.5
Net credit and loans from IMF	—	0.6	−1.2	12.8	−3.6	1.2	9.1	1.8	. . .	. . .
Net external borrowing	85.9	111.6	63.8	107.4	119.7	97.6	30.4	−0.7	62.2	69.1
From official creditors	12.5	18.4	11.0	20.1	−0.2	−1.0	20.5	12.8	14.0	10.6
From banks	8.4	15.5	−25.5	18.3	33.9	27.3	11.2	−14.2	3.2	12.2
Other	64.9	77.7	78.3	68.9	85.9	71.3	−1.3	0.7	45.0	46.2
Memorandum										
Net financial flows	94.1	146.1	127.1	180.2	190.4	151.9	88.2	71.6	110.9	129.9
Exceptional financing	20.8	16.8	14.3	9.7	7.5	−3.0	11.7	21.6	21.8	14.7
By external financing source										
Net creditor countries										
Balance on current account	−15.2	−13.0	−6.4	1.9	13.2	11.7	−21.3	−0.1	31.2	8.7
Change in reserves (− = increase)	−4.8	7.7	1.6	0.2	−10.1	−9.5	12.9	−3.6	−10.5	−2.0
Asset transactions, including										
net errors and omissions	5.4	−5.0	−3.0	−5.4	−4.9	−3.6	2.4	−1.7	−8.7	−2.7
Total, net external financing	**14.6**	**10.3**	**7.7**	**3.3**	**1.9**	**1.4**	**6.1**	**5.4**	**−2.4**	**1.4**
Non-debt-creating flows, net	−0.1	−0.4	3.1	2.7	−0.2	2.1	2.1	2.8	5.7	5.1
Net credit and loans from IMF	—	—	—	—	—	—	—	—	. . .	. . .
Net external borrowing	14.7	10.7	4.7	0.6	2.0	−0.7	4.0	2.6	−8.2	−3.7
From official creditors	0.2	0.7	0.4	0.2	0.9	0.6	0.8	−0.8	−1.2	−0.9
From banks	6.4	2.5	−2.0	−0.6	−5.2	1.7	6.7	1.2	−0.2	−0.3
Other	8.1	7.5	6.2	1.0	6.3	−3.0	−3.5	2.2	−6.7	−2.6
Memorandum										
Net financial flows	24.8	10.7	10.8	6.6	4.0	4.4	11.8	11.3	−20.1	−5.9
Exceptional financing	—	—	—	—	—	—	—	—	—	—

Table 35 *(continued)*

	1992	1993	1994	1995	1996	1997	1998	1999	2000	2001
Net debtor countries										
Balance on current account	−68.6	−107.1	−82.0	−113.0	−86.9	−70.1	−68.5	−32.2	−42.2	−57.2
Change in reserves (− = increase)	−41.0	−47.5	−45.8	−68.3	−90.5	−58.3	−2.4	−39.0	−67.1	−72.6
Asset transactions, including										
net errors and omissions	−20.8	−21.3	−18.3	−19.9	−41.2	−96.3	−95.8	−53.0	−69.8	−56.8
Total, net external financing	**130.5**	**175.8**	**146.1**	**201.2**	**218.4**	**224.6**	**166.5**	**123.9**	**178.9**	**186.1**
Non-debt-creating flows, net	36.1	57.8	78.9	85.8	112.7	131.8	124.6	125.9	126.9	119.8
Net credit and loans from IMF	−0.4	−0.1	−0.8	12.6	−2.9	0.8	8.5	1.3	. . .	. . .
Net external borrowing	94.8	118.2	68.0	103.2	108.7	92.0	33.4	−3.6	56.8	66.9
From official creditors	18.3	19.3	14.0	21.5	1.9	−0.3	21.5	12.5	13.4	9.3
From banks	7.5	14.3	−25.8	15.1	27.6	22.9	11.5	−15.9	0.6	11.2
Other	69.1	84.5	79.9	66.6	79.3	69.4	0.4	−0.3	42.8	46.4
Memorandum										
Net financial flows	103.8	152.9	129.8	177.6	183.1	151.1	94.3	74.7	105.9	129.9
Exceptional financing	31.1	34.1	27.4	22.0	20.9	5.0	17.5	26.0	23.7	15.1
Official financing										
Balance on current account	−6.2	−8.2	−10.0	−12.1	−9.2	−4.6	−10.0	−9.7	−3.6	−6.7
Change in reserves (− = increase)	—	1.2	−2.3	−2.2	−5.1	−6.5	0.8	0.9	−6.9	−4.1
Asset transactions, including										
net errors and omissions	−0.3	1.3	−0.7	−1.3	1.0	1.2	0.3	−0.8	1.3	1.0
Total, net external financing	**6.5**	**5.7**	**13.0**	**15.6**	**13.2**	**10.0**	**8.9**	**9.6**	**9.2**	**9.8**
Non-debt-creating flows, net	2.8	4.7	5.6	7.2	8.3	9.2	7.0	7.9	13.1	8.0
Net credit and loans from IMF	−0.1	−0.5	1.1	1.1	0.9	0.2	—	—	. . .	. . .
Net external borrowing	3.8	1.5	6.3	7.8	3.9	0.5	1.9	1.7	−3.9	2.1
From official creditors	7.2	4.5	7.5	8.1	4.2	2.5	1.8	2.0	−3.9	2.7
From banks	0.2	−1.4	—	0.7	0.2	−1.0	−0.8	−1.2	−1.7	−0.9
Other	−3.6	−1.6	−1.3	−1.0	−0.5	−1.0	0.8	0.9	1.8	0.3
Memorandum										
Net financial flows	4.3	3.0	10.2	10.4	9.8	5.8	4.5	5.8	1.4	6.8
Exceptional financing	7.2	6.2	11.5	11.0	9.8	0.5	5.3	3.7	3.3	2.5
Private financing										
Balance on current account	−38.9	−72.7	−59.9	−86.1	−67.9	−50.3	−39.3	−17.0	−32.8	−42.6
Change in reserves (− = increase)	−41.0	−47.4	−35.6	−59.8	−69.7	−54.9	−1.6	−29.4	−51.3	−59.4
Asset transactions, including										
net errors and omissions	−25.3	−27.2	−14.8	−22.9	−45.7	−90.7	−97.1	−54.5	−69.3	−56.2
Total, net external financing	**105.2**	**147.4**	**110.3**	**168.8**	**183.1**	**195.7**	**137.8**	**100.6**	**153.2**	**157.7**
Non-debt-creating flows, net	28.8	45.9	66.6	69.8	91.7	114.4	107.2	108.6	104.2	101.9
Net credit and loans from IMF	−0.9	0.3	−2.2	11.9	−3.3	0.4	7.6	0.7	. . .	. . .
Net external borrowing	77.2	101.2	46.0	87.2	94.7	80.9	22.9	−9.2	54.3	56.3
From official creditors	1.5	10.5	3.1	10.2	−5.5	−4.1	15.2	6.5	15.4	5.5
From banks	10.8	16.0	−28.6	15.1	28.4	25.4	11.5	−12.0	2.7	11.7
Other	64.9	74.6	71.5	62.0	71.8	59.6	−3.8	−3.7	36.3	39.2
Memorandum										
Net financial flows	83.1	129.4	99.0	153.9	159.1	127.5	71.9	56.8	89.9	105.9
Exceptional financing	8.9	6.3	5.2	2.2	1.0	−1.4	12.7	12.8	12.9	9.0

Table 35 *(continued)*

	1992	1993	1994	1995	1996	1997	1998	1999	2000	2001
Diversified financing										
Balance on current account	−15.1	−21.0	−16.7	−17.4	−15.0	−16.9	−16.3	−8.7	−6.5	−8.2
Change in reserves (− = increase)	0.4	−0.3	−6.0	−2.9	−10.8	−0.3	−2.0	−5.6	−7.0	−7.4
Asset transactions, including										
net errors and omissions	4.0	3.0	—	1.7	−1.3	−4.1	0.8	2.2	−1.7	−1.6
Total, net external financing	**10.7**	**18.3**	**22.7**	**18.6**	**27.1**	**21.3**	**17.6**	**12.2**	**15.2**	**17.1**
Non-debt-creating flows, net	3.7	6.6	6.2	7.4	12.2	7.5	9.1	7.9	7.8	8.2
Net credit and loans from IMF	0.5	0.1	0.3	−0.3	−0.5	0.2	1.0	0.6	...	...
Net external borrowing	6.6	11.5	16.1	11.5	15.5	13.5	7.5	3.7	6.9	8.8
From official creditors	7.6	4.8	3.5	3.5	3.4	1.8	5.0	4.3	2.5	1.6
From banks	−5.0	0.6	5.2	2.2	4.2	1.1	−0.9	−3.2	−0.4	0.2
Other	4.0	6.2	7.5	5.8	7.8	10.6	3.5	2.6	4.8	7.0
Memorandum										
Net financial flows	8.3	16.3	20.5	16.4	19.5	20.3	15.8	10.7	13.6	15.8
Exceptional financing	12.9	9.8	7.9	6.7	10.2	6.2	−0.4	9.5	7.5	3.6
Net debtor countries by debt-servicing experience										
Countries with arrears and/or rescheduling during 1994–98										
Balance on current account	−22.1	−30.3	−21.1	−48.0	−41.4	−48.8	−57.3	−29.7	−23.8	−28.5
Change in reserves (− = increase)	−16.4	−9.3	−15.1	−23.3	−23.7	−4.0	16.7	0.8	−26.5	−16.4
Asset transactions, including										
net errors and omissions	2.9	−0.9	−5.7	4.1	−4.5	−0.4	−8.2	8.7	12.8	4.5
Total, net external financing	**35.5**	**40.5**	**41.9**	**67.3**	**69.6**	**53.2**	**48.8**	**20.2**	**37.5**	**40.4**
Non-debt-creating flows, net	9.5	11.1	14.5	20.9	35.7	36.3	39.0	43.3	46.5	41.0
Net credit and loans from IMF	−1.0	−0.8	1.0	0.5	0.7	3.9	10.9	5.6	...	...
Net external borrowing	27.0	30.1	26.4	46.3	33.3	13.0	−1.2	−28.7	−4.8	0.4
From official creditors	8.8	5.4	5.6	5.7	−4.1	−1.4	8.3	10.0	6.5	4.2
From banks	−1.1	−3.8	−34.5	5.2	10.2	10.4	4.0	−13.6	−6.9	0.5
Other	19.3	28.6	55.4	35.4	27.2	4.0	−13.4	−25.1	−4.4	−4.3
Memorandum										
Net financial flows	31.5	33.2	37.7	61.1	59.8	46.5	37.7	13.4	28.4	37.4
Exceptional financing	28.8	31.9	25.7	21.5	21.2	4.3	17.3	22.0	19.6	13.3
Other net debtor countries										
Balance on current account	−46.7	−77.1	−61.1	−65.2	−45.9	−22.0	−11.4	−2.9	−18.9	−29.4
Change in reserves (− = increase)	−24.1	−37.5	−30.2	−44.6	−65.0	−53.6	−17.9	−39.5	−40.2	−55.6
Asset transactions, including										
net errors and omissions	−23.7	−20.7	−12.9	−24.0	−37.8	−95.9	−88.7	−61.6	−82.6	−61.2
Total, net external financing	**94.5**	**135.2**	**104.1**	**133.9**	**148.6**	**171.4**	**117.8**	**103.7**	**141.4**	**145.7**
Non-debt-creating flows, net	26.5	46.8	64.4	64.9	77.0	95.4	85.4	82.4	80.2	78.6
Net credit and loans from IMF	0.6	0.6	−1.8	12.1	−3.6	−3.1	−2.4	−4.3	...	...
Net external borrowing	67.5	87.8	41.5	56.9	75.3	79.1	34.8	25.3	61.8	66.8
From official creditors	9.2	13.6	8.3	15.8	5.9	1.1	13.4	2.6	7.0	5.2
From banks	8.5	18.2	8.8	9.9	17.4	12.6	7.5	−2.3	7.5	10.7
Other	49.8	56.0	24.5	31.3	52.0	65.4	13.9	25.0	47.3	50.9
Memorandum										
Net financial flows	72.0	119.8	92.2	116.6	123.3	104.7	56.8	61.4	77.6	92.6
Exceptional financing	2.3	2.2	1.7	0.5	−0.3	0.7	0.2	4.0	4.1	1.8

Table 35 *(concluded)*

	1992	1993	1994	1995	1996	1997	1998	1999	2000	2001
Other groups										
Heavily indebted poor countries										
Balance on current account	−11.7	−13.7	−10.0	−12.3	−13.0	−13.1	−14.7	−14.3	−13.9	−15.0
Change in reserves (− = increase)	0.1	1.7	−2.7	−1.9	−4.2	−1.3	0.3	−1.2	−0.9	−1.6
Asset transactions, including										
net errors and omissions	2.0	3.1	0.9	0.2	2.0	2.8	1.8	0.8	2.3	1.7
Total, net external financing	**9.5**	**9.0**	**11.8**	**14.0**	**15.1**	**11.5**	**12.5**	**14.7**	**12.6**	**15.0**
Non-debt-creating flows, net	3.5	5.7	5.0	7.0	13.0	9.5	7.5	9.0	13.4	8.1
Net credit and loans from IMF	−0.1	−0.2	0.5	0.6	0.3	—	0.2	0.2	. . .	. . .
Net external borrowing	6.0	3.5	6.3	6.9	1.9	2.1	4.8	5.7	−1.0	7.0
From official creditors	5.7	3.6	5.1	5.7	3.6	−0.1	3.3	2.9	−2.3	3.4
From banks	0.5	—	0.7	0.9	0.6	−1.1	−0.8	−0.2	−0.7	0.2
Other	−0.1	−0.1	0.5	0.3	−2.3	3.3	2.4	3.0	2.0	3.3
Memorandum										
Net financial flows	7.6	7.0	10.5	10.1	8.3	8.1	8.8	11.3	5.2	12.4
Exceptional financing	12.2	10.2	9.8	8.4	11.8	−0.2	0.7	6.2	5.1	4.7
Least developed countries										
Balance on current account	−9.4	−8.9	−6.8	−9.0	−9.4	−9.8	−13.0	−13.0	−12.7	−14.7
Change in reserves (− = increase)	0.7	1.3	−1.0	−1.3	−3.6	−1.0	0.6	−1.4	−1.0	−1.3
Asset transactions, including										
net errors and omissions	0.3	−0.8	−1.0	—	1.2	−0.3	0.7	0.7	1.2	1.0
Total, net external financing	**8.4**	**8.4**	**8.9**	**10.4**	**11.8**	**11.1**	**11.7**	**13.7**	**12.5**	**15.0**
Non-debt-creating flows, net	3.4	4.4	3.0	4.3	9.2	7.0	6.8	8.6	13.1	8.2
Net credit and loans from IMF	0.2	−0.1	0.2	0.5	0.1	0.1	0.1	—	. . .	. . .
Net external borrowing	4.7	4.0	5.7	6.0	2.6	3.9	4.8	5.1	−0.8	7.0
From official creditors	3.0	2.2	5.8	4.4	4.1	3.8	2.8	2.8	−3.5	3.1
From banks	0.1	0.1	−0.5	0.3	0.2	−0.4	−0.5	−0.2	−0.2	—
Other	1.6	1.6	0.4	1.3	−1.7	0.6	2.6	2.5	2.9	3.9
Memorandum										
Net financial flows	1.5	1.4	2.1	4.2	2.8	5.3	6.9	9.5	9.5	12.0
Exceptional financing	7.6	6.9	6.7	5.0	9.3	6.0	5.8	4.5	3.4	3.5
Middle East and north Africa										
Balance on current account	−27.5	−25.5	−13.2	−6.5	12.0	9.7	−35.4	−6.3	27.9	1.1
Change in reserves (− = increase)	−9.3	3.5	−3.9	−2.4	−16.8	−13.1	17.1	−5.9	−12.8	−4.5
Asset transactions, including										
net errors and omissions	12.1	3.4	−1.4	−1.1	0.4	−3.0	5.1	0.9	−9.1	0.1
Total, net external financing	**24.7**	**18.6**	**18.5**	**10.0**	**4.4**	**6.4**	**13.2**	**11.3**	**3.5**	**8.7**
Non-debt-creating flows, net	2.2	4.3	7.5	8.4	3.9	6.5	6.7	7.8	11.7	11.2
Net credit and loans from IMF	−0.1	−0.5	0.5	0.2	0.6	0.3	−0.1	—	. . .	. . .
Net external borrowing	22.6	14.8	10.5	1.4	−0.1	−0.4	6.5	3.5	−8.0	−2.1
From official creditors	—	0.7	1.2	0.2	0.8	—	−0.4	−1.7	−3.1	−1.7
From banks	9.3	−2.0	−2.5	−3.0	−10.1	−1.6	7.6	0.3	−1.9	−1.8
Other	13.3	16.1	11.7	4.1	9.1	1.2	−0.6	5.0	−2.9	1.3
Memorandum										
Net financial flows	35.3	20.9	22.4	11.0	6.6	9.5	21.6	18.6	−14.9	1.7
Exceptional financing	5.5	15.6	10.9	11.0	5.6	5.4	3.1	2.3	1.6	1.6

[1]For definitions, see footnotes to Table 33.

Table 36. Developing Countries: Reserves[1]

	1992	1993	1994	1995	1996	1997	1998	1999	2000	2001
					Billions of U.S. dollars					
Developing countries	**261.3**	**307.9**	**362.1**	**429.0**	**514.7**	**564.7**	**578.6**	**616.0**	**692.3**	**765.1**
Regional groups										
Africa	18.5	19.8	24.7	26.6	31.7	43.4	41.5	43.9	55.6	62.7
Sub-Sahara	12.2	13.5	15.9	19.1	21.5	29.1	28.0	31.6	38.2	42.8
Asia	86.9	109.7	158.2	184.7	230.5	248.9	273.8	307.4	342.6	388.1
Excluding China and India	59.4	75.9	84.3	90.1	102.0	80.3	96.1	116.9	128.2	143.4
Middle East and Europe	66.8	69.3	74.1	87.6	96.1	102.6	102.5	109.4	121.4	130.1
Western Hemisphere	89.1	109.2	105.1	130.0	156.3	169.7	160.8	155.4	172.7	184.2
Analytical groups										
By source of export earnings										
Fuel	51.6	49.7	50.1	51.7	62.7	74.3	69.4	70.3	88.4	93.6
Manufactures	120.6	156.6	192.1	244.8	300.8	324.8	339.2	363.3	410.9	466.6
Nonfuel primary products	23.1	23.8	32.6	37.5	42.1	46.1	42.7	45.4	48.6	50.9
Services, income, and private transfers	19.0	23.6	26.7	30.8	34.2	36.1	36.3	35.1	31.6	31.9
Diversified	47.0	54.2	60.6	64.1	74.9	83.3	91.0	102.0	112.8	122.0
By external financing source										
Net creditor countries	30.4	29.7	29.8	34.5	34.5	36.6	35.9	39.5	49.9	52.0
Net debtor countries	235.0	282.6	337.1	399.5	485.5	534.1	549.1	583.3	649.5	720.9
Official financing	10.6	11.5	14.3	14.5	17.4	22.2	20.7	19.7	26.5	30.5
Private financing	189.8	233.7	277.0	336.5	409.6	449.9	463.2	492.3	543.3	602.3
Diversified financing	26.8	29.2	35.3	37.1	46.0	47.9	50.5	55.6	62.6	69.7
Net debtor countries by debt-servicing experience										
Countries with arrears and/or rescheduling during 1994–98	63.9	74.5	90.7	107.8	134.7	132.9	129.2	123.9	149.9	165.7
Other net debtor countries	167.0	203.8	241.7	286.8	345.6	395.2	413.7	452.7	492.6	547.6
Other groups										
Heavily indebted poor countries	6.5	6.0	7.8	10.3	12.4	13.9	13.3	14.0	14.9	16.3
Least developed countries	7.6	8.3	9.9	10.7	11.0	11.4	11.7	12.5	13.4	14.3
Middle East and north Africa	64.5	66.8	72.4	80.1	86.9	95.4	93.4	95.4	107.6	111.7
					Ratio of reserves to imports of goods and services[2]					
Developing countries	**33.1**	**36.5**	**39.6**	**39.2**	**43.4**	**44.3**	**47.8**	**49.8**	**50.4**	**51.0**
Regional groups										
Africa	17.2	19.1	22.8	20.6	23.9	31.9	30.9	32.3	37.3	39.8
Sub-Sahara	15.1	17.2	19.8	19.6	21.0	27.3	27.2	30.8	33.5	35.7
Asia	31.3	33.0	40.1	36.6	42.5	44.1	56.1	57.2	57.0	58.1
Excluding China and India	33.5	37.2	34.6	29.4	30.6	23.7	36.5	41.9	40.2	40.5
Middle East and Europe	32.0	33.6	40.9	41.7	41.0	40.5	40.7	44.2	45.2	45.6
Western Hemisphere	45.7	54.6	45.7	51.9	56.8	52.8	47.7	49.0	48.8	47.5
Analytical groups										
By source of export earnings										
Fuel	26.6	27.9	32.1	29.6	33.6	36.8	34.7	35.1	40.5	41.3
Manufactures	34.5	39.2	41.6	42.6	47.8	48.0	54.4	55.0	55.4	56.3
Nonfuel primary products	39.5	39.4	49.4	45.5	46.8	47.8	44.7	49.2	48.2	46.5
Services, income, and private transfers	41.5	47.4	51.1	51.3	53.0	53.4	50.4	47.3	39.9	38.0
Diversified	33.3	35.1	34.2	31.7	35.0	35.8	41.3	48.7	48.5	48.8

Table 36 *(concluded)*

	1992	1993	1994	1995	1996	1997	1998	1999	2000	2001
By external financing source										
Net creditor countries	26.3	27.4	30.5	31.9	29.3	28.9	28.8	31.4	37.9	37.5
Net debtor countries	34.7	38.3	41.1	40.4	45.3	46.3	50.3	52.3	52.1	52.8
Official financing	21.4	22.5	25.5	21.8	24.2	31.5	28.3	25.7	32.5	35.2
Private financing	37.6	41.5	43.1	43.0	48.7	49.5	53.9	56.0	55.2	55.5
Diversified financing	32.4	32.9	37.4	33.1	35.9	33.5	39.0	43.3	43.4	44.8
Net debtor countries by debt-servicing experience										
Countries with arrears and/or rescheduling during 1994–98	32.2	35.6	40.4	38.6	43.8	39.4	41.2	40.7	44.0	44.9
Other net debtor countries	35.1	38.8	40.8	40.6	45.5	48.7	53.4	56.0	54.7	55.2
Other groups										
Heavily indebted poor countries	14.5	13.3	16.5	17.9	19.0	20.7	19.6	20.0	19.7	20.4
Least developed countries	21.5	23.5	27.1	24.7	23.6	23.6	23.6	24.1	23.8	23.9
Middle East and north Africa	31.7	34.4	40.6	40.8	41.3	43.0	42.0	42.1	44.4	43.7

[1]In this table, official holdings of gold are valued at SDR 35 an ounce. This convention results in a marked underestimate of reserves for countries that have substantial gold holdings.
[2]Reserves at year-end in percent of imports of goods and services for the year indicated.

Table 37. Net Credit and Loans from IMF[1]

(Billions of U.S. dollars)

	1991	1992	1993	1994	1995	1996	1997	1998	1999
Advanced economies	—	**0.3**	—	—	**−0.1**	**−0.1**	**11.3**	**5.2**	**−10.3**
Newly industrialized Asian economies	—	—	—	—	—	—	11.3	5.2	−10.3
Developing countries	**1.1**	**−0.4**	**−0.1**	**−0.8**	**12.6**	**−2.9**	**0.8**	**8.5**	**1.3**
Regional groups									
Africa	0.2	−0.2	0.2	0.9	0.8	0.6	−0.5	−0.4	−0.2
Sub-Sahara	—	—	0.7	0.5	0.6	0.1	−0.5	−0.3	−0.1
Asia	1.9	1.3	0.6	−0.8	−1.5	−1.7	5.0	6.6	1.7
Excluding China and India	0.2	0.1	0.1	0.4	−0.3	−0.4	5.7	7.0	2.1
Middle East and Europe	—	0.1	—	0.4	0.4	0.1	0.2	−0.1	0.6
Western Hemisphere	−1.0	−1.6	−0.9	−1.3	12.9	−2.0	−4.0	2.5	−0.9
Analytical groups									
By source of export earnings									
Fuel	0.6	−0.5	−0.8	0.4	−0.2	0.7	−0.3	−0.6	−0.5
Manufactures	1.9	0.4	−1.2	−2.0	10.8	−4.0	−1.4	4.3	1.4
Nonfuel primary products	−0.3	—	−0.1	0.2	0.4	0.1	—	—	—
Services, income, and private transfers	0.1	0.2	0.1	—	−0.1	−0.1	—	0.1	—
Diversified	−1.1	−0.5	1.8	0.6	1.7	0.3	2.5	4.7	0.4
By external financing source									
Net creditor countries	—	—	—	—	—	—	—	—	—
Net debtor countries	1.1	−0.4	−0.1	−0.8	12.6	−2.9	0.8	8.5	1.3
Official financing	0.4	−0.1	−0.5	1.1	1.1	0.9	0.2	—	—
Private financing	0.3	−0.9	0.3	−2.2	11.9	−3.3	0.4	7.6	0.7
Diversified financing	0.3	0.5	0.1	0.3	−0.3	−0.5	0.2	1.0	0.6
Net debtor countries by debt-servicing experience									
Countries with arrears and/or rescheduling during 1994–98	−0.6	−1.0	−0.8	1.0	0.5	0.7	3.9	10.9	5.6
Other net debtor countries	1.7	0.6	0.6	−1.8	12.1	−3.6	−3.1	−2.4	−4.3
Other groups									
Heavily indebted poor countries	0.1	−0.1	−0.2	0.5	0.6	0.3	—	0.2	0.2
Least developed countries	0.1	0.2	−0.1	0.2	0.5	0.1	0.1	0.1	—
Middle East and north Africa	0.2	−0.1	−0.5	0.5	0.2	0.6	0.3	−0.1	—
Countries in transition	**2.4**	**1.6**	**3.7**	**2.4**	**4.7**	**3.7**	**2.5**	**5.5**	**−3.6**
Central and eastern Europe	2.4	0.5	2.0	0.5	−1.3	—	0.7	−0.1	—
Excluding Belarus and Ukraine	2.4	0.5	2.0	0.2	−2.7	−0.8	0.4	−0.4	—
Russia	—	1.0	1.5	1.5	5.5	3.2	1.5	5.3	−3.6
Transcaucasus and central Asia	—	—	0.2	0.3	0.6	0.5	0.2	0.3	—
Memorandum									
Total									
Net credit provided under:									
General Resources Account	2.520	0.644	3.374	0.594	15.633	0.291	14.355	18.811	−12.856
Trust Fund	−0.069	—	−0.060	−0.014	−0.015	—	−0.007	−0.001	−0.001
PRGF	1.070	0.733	0.253	0.998	1.619	0.325	0.179	0.374	0.193
Disbursements at year-end under:[2]									
General Resources Account	31.821	31.217	34.503	37.276	53.275	51.824	62.703	84.961	69.913
Trust Fund	0.226	0.217	0.157	0.153	0.141	0.137	0.121	0.126	0.122
PRGF	4.499	5.041	5.285	6.634	8.342	8.392	8.049	8.788	8.760

[1]Includes net disbursements from programs under the General Resources Account, Trust Fund, and Poverty Reduction and Growth Facility (formerly ESAF-Enhanced Structural Adjustment Facility). The data are on a transactions basis, with conversion to U.S. dollar values at annual average exchange rates.
[2]Converted to U.S. dollar values at end-of-period exchange rates.

Table 38. Summary of External Debt and Debt Service

	1992	1993	1994	1995	1996	1997	1998	1999	2000	2001
					Billions of U.S. dollars					
External debt										
Developing countries	**1,349.7**	**1,472.7**	**1,585.2**	**1,713.9**	**1,798.0**	**1,877.6**	**2,006.7**	**2,038.2**	**2,064.9**	**2,130.7**
Regional groups										
Africa	262.3	272.2	289.1	311.7	310.3	303.3	304.6	311.5	312.0	320.8
Asia	404.3	456.3	510.4	562.8	595.1	642.5	661.2	671.0	663.9	681.7
Middle East and Europe	204.4	220.5	223.7	222.1	242.1	256.7	284.5	295.7	299.3	311.1
Western Hemisphere	478.7	523.7	562.0	617.3	650.6	675.1	756.4	759.9	789.6	817.2
Analytical groups										
By external financing source										
Net creditor countries	38.9	42.3	41.1	30.7	49.3	61.1	74.4	78.8	73.6	72.3
Net debtor countries	1,313.7	1,433.3	1,547.0	1,686.2	1,751.6	1,819.3	1,935.2	1,962.2	1,994.1	2,061.2
Official financing	162.3	169.2	180.1	190.6	194.4	189.7	192.8	193.8	189.1	192.4
Private financing	914.5	1,000.8	1,084.4	1,199.8	1,264.5	1,339.0	1,442.4	1,456.2	1,485.7	1,539.7
Diversified financing	212.1	229.0	247.3	260.2	262.0	262.8	272.4	284.0	291.6	301.1
Net debtor countries by debt-servicing experience										
Countries with arrears and/or rescheduling during 1994–98	589.1	628.0	665.0	707.8	732.9	753.9	810.1	815.9	806.9	811.7
Other net debtor countries	721.9	802.6	879.2	975.6	1,016.0	1,062.8	1,122.4	1,143.7	1,184.8	1,247.1
Countries in transition	**211.7**	**233.8**	**248.7**	**267.2**	**285.7**	**297.9**	**347.1**	**353.0**	**365.2**	**379.7**
Central and eastern Europe	104.5	116.2	121.5	137.1	147.6	157.4	175.1	184.6	195.5	209.2
Excluding Belarus and Ukraine	100.4	110.5	112.2	126.3	135.8	141.2	160.0	169.7	179.1	191.9
Russia	105.4	112.7	119.8	120.4	125.0	123.5	152.4	148.1	147.3	146.3
Transcaucasus and central Asia	1.8	4.9	7.4	9.7	13.1	17.0	19.6	20.3	22.4	24.2
Debt-service payments[1]										
Developing countries	**178.7**	**178.3**	**196.8**	**236.7**	**276.4**	**306.6**	**312.0**	**347.0**	**330.3**	**326.3**
Regional groups										
Africa	29.9	28.1	29.3	33.8	30.8	30.9	29.1	29.2	33.9	33.7
Asia	53.0	53.1	63.0	76.8	76.3	81.7	96.6	109.2	86.6	93.3
Middle East and Europe	23.0	25.6	27.0	29.3	45.9	41.6	36.9	39.8	53.9	47.9
Western Hemisphere	72.8	71.5	77.6	96.9	123.5	152.4	149.5	168.9	156.0	151.4
Analytical groups										
By external financing source										
Net creditor countries	2.5	3.7	8.0	8.5	20.5	16.2	10.5	9.8	11.1	10.6
Net debtor countries	176.4	174.7	189.0	228.5	256.2	290.6	301.8	337.5	319.5	316.0
Official financing	14.7	15.2	16.7	21.2	14.2	14.4	12.5	13.7	14.2	16.7
Private financing	135.1	136.3	148.2	179.0	209.4	243.0	256.9	291.4	261.2	255.1
Diversified financing	23.5	18.1	19.7	22.5	23.2	24.3	25.7	24.7	27.6	29.0
Net debtor countries by debt-servicing experience										
Countries with arrears and/or rescheduling during 1994–98	64.0	64.5	64.7	79.6	82.4	110.4	120.5	156.0	129.0	118.3
Other net debtor countries	112.2	110.1	124.2	148.7	173.6	179.9	181.1	181.3	190.3	197.5
Countries in transition	**25.4**	**18.9**	**21.8**	**30.0**	**33.1**	**32.4**	**49.2**	**51.4**	**55.7**	**58.6**
Central and eastern Europe	12.7	12.4	16.9	21.9	24.7	24.6	29.2	34.0	37.1	38.0
Excluding Belarus and Ukraine	12.7	12.2	15.0	20.2	23.3	23.0	27.1	32.4	34.6	35.2
Russia	12.6	6.2	4.3	6.4	6.9	5.9	16.3	14.6	15.7	17.7
Transcaucasus and central Asia	0.1	0.3	0.6	1.7	1.5	1.9	3.7	2.7	2.9	2.9

Table 38 *(concluded)*

	1992	1993	1994	1995	1996	1997	1998	1999	2000	2001
					Percent of exports of goods and services					
External debt[2]										
Developing countries	**186.9**	**195.2**	**183.4**	**167.5**	**156.8**	**150.7**	**172.7**	**163.2**	**145.6**	**141.6**
Regional groups										
Africa	253.9	276.4	282.6	259.4	231.9	222.5	251.8	244.4	205.4	208.4
Asia	153.1	153.6	138.3	124.6	118.6	114.6	122.9	115.1	103.5	97.0
Middle East and Europe	113.1	122.3	117.9	105.1	98.8	99.8	130.5	123.1	104.7	111.3
Western Hemisphere	274.7	292.9	276.3	257.1	244.3	231.4	265.4	254.9	232.9	221.6
Analytical groups										
By external financing source										
Net creditor countries	35.4	38.9	37.0	25.4	34.9	41.5	66.5	59.2	43.8	47.2
Net debtor countries	213.4	220.7	204.3	186.0	173.4	164.9	183.5	175.2	158.9	151.9
Official financing	393.5	412.1	421.9	372.6	329.1	302.1	330.5	310.6	253.0	253.8
Private financing	191.2	195.0	177.6	163.1	156.0	149.9	167.4	160.8	147.5	140.1
Diversified financing	318.6	342.8	335.7	294.9	251.1	227.9	252.5	241.6	214.0	208.7
Net debtor countries by debt-servicing experience										
Countries with arrears and/or rescheduling during 1994–98	309.3	325.0	312.1	292.1	269.7	253.0	299.1	279.6	236.5	224.6
Other net debtor countries	170.9	177.1	162.6	147.7	138.3	132.6	143.9	138.7	130.3	125.8
Countries in transition	**130.0**	**129.0**	**122.9**	**103.4**	**101.7**	**100.9**	**120.4**	**122.1**	**113.4**	**110.7**
Central and eastern Europe	110.3	114.2	107.0	92.9	91.3	89.8	94.2	97.7	93.9	91.6
Excluding Belarus and Ukraine	126.3	131.9	116.8	100.3	100.8	96.4	99.8	102.6	97.5	94.6
Russia	183.4	171.1	156.1	126.6	121.6	119.7	173.8	174.3	153.2	152.8
Transcaucasus and central Asia	17.1	36.2	60.8	61.7	79.3	100.1	133.8	133.6	125.4	127.1
Debt-service payments										
Developing countries	**24.7**	**23.6**	**22.8**	**23.1**	**24.1**	**24.6**	**26.8**	**27.8**	**23.3**	**21.7**
Regional groups										
Africa	29.0	28.5	28.6	28.1	23.0	22.6	24.0	22.9	22.3	21.9
Asia	20.1	17.9	17.1	17.0	15.2	14.6	17.9	18.7	13.5	13.3
Middle East and Europe	12.7	14.2	14.2	13.9	18.7	16.2	16.9	16.6	18.8	17.1
Western Hemisphere	41.8	40.0	38.2	40.4	46.4	52.2	52.5	56.7	46.0	41.1
Analytical groups										
By external financing source										
Net creditor countries	2.3	3.4	7.2	7.0	14.5	11.0	9.4	7.3	6.6	6.9
Net debtor countries	28.6	26.9	25.0	25.2	25.4	26.3	28.6	30.1	25.5	23.3
Official financing	35.5	36.9	39.1	41.5	24.0	22.9	21.5	22.0	19.0	22.0
Private financing	28.2	26.6	24.3	24.3	25.8	27.2	29.8	32.2	25.9	23.2
Diversified financing	35.3	27.1	26.7	25.5	22.3	21.1	23.9	21.0	20.2	20.1
Net debtor countries by debt-servicing experience										
Countries with arrears and/or rescheduling during 1994–98	33.6	33.4	30.3	32.8	30.3	37.1	44.5	53.5	37.8	32.7
Other net debtor countries	26.6	24.3	23.0	22.5	23.6	22.5	23.2	22.0	20.9	19.9
Countries in transition	**15.6**	**10.4**	**10.8**	**11.6**	**11.8**	**11.0**	**17.1**	**17.8**	**17.3**	**17.1**
Central and eastern Europe	13.4	12.2	14.9	14.8	15.3	14.0	15.7	18.0	17.8	16.6
Excluding Belarus and Ukraine	16.0	14.5	15.6	16.1	17.3	15.7	16.9	19.6	18.9	17.3
Russia	21.9	9.4	5.6	6.7	6.7	5.7	18.6	17.2	16.3	18.5
Transcaucasus and central Asia	1.0	2.4	4.8	10.9	8.9	11.4	25.5	18.0	16.5	15.4

[1]Debt-service payments refer to actual payments of interest on total debt plus actual amortization payments on long-term debt. The projections incorporate the impact of exceptional financing items.

[2]Total debt at year-end in percent of exports of goods and services in year indicated.

Table 39. Developing Countries—by Region: External Debt, by Maturity and Type of Creditor
(Billions of U.S. dollars)

	1992	1993	1994	1995	1996	1997	1998	1999	2000	2001
Developing countries										
Total debt	**1,349.7**	**1,472.7**	**1,585.2**	**1,713.9**	**1,798.0**	**1,877.6**	**2,006.7**	**2,038.2**	**2,064.9**	**2,130.7**
By maturity										
Short-term	215.5	243.4	257.5	288.4	319.1	381.4	387.6	375.1	345.1	344.4
Long-term	1,134.2	1,229.3	1,327.6	1,432.7	1,478.9	1,496.2	1,619.0	1,663.4	1,720.3	1,787.1
By type of creditor										
Official	629.9	676.4	737.8	766.4	772.3	752.2	775.5	795.8	804.5	820.3
Banks	375.6	365.9	359.1	435.0	489.0	556.8	593.7	582.1	580.1	590.4
Other private	344.2	430.4	488.3	512.5	536.8	568.7	637.4	660.3	680.3	720.0
Regional groups										
Africa										
Total debt	**262.3**	**272.2**	**289.1**	**311.7**	**310.3**	**303.3**	**304.6**	**311.5**	**312.0**	**320.8**
By maturity										
Short-term	19.9	18.8	31.8	37.1	39.2	52.0	52.8	56.7	37.5	40.1
Long-term	242.4	253.5	257.3	274.6	271.1	251.3	251.8	255.2	275.1	281.4
By type of creditor										
Official	170.5	177.6	193.5	209.7	212.5	202.4	204.9	207.8	203.1	206.1
Banks	47.0	45.9	47.6	46.0	45.4	42.0	38.1	37.1	35.5	35.0
Other private	44.8	48.7	47.9	56.0	52.5	58.9	61.5	66.6	73.5	79.7
Sub-Sahara										
Total debt	**207.7**	**216.7**	**227.6**	**245.3**	**244.1**	**241.9**	**243.3**	**252.5**	**253.9**	**263.4**
By maturity										
Short-term	18.0	16.9	30.0	35.6	37.2	40.7	41.2	44.1	23.1	25.0
Long-term	189.7	199.8	197.6	209.7	206.9	201.2	202.1	208.7	231.4	239.1
By type of creditor										
Official	140.6	147.8	158.2	168.8	170.6	163.0	165.8	170.6	167.8	171.5
Banks	21.6	21.7	22.9	22.5	23.5	22.5	18.5	18.3	17.6	17.8
Other private	45.5	47.2	46.5	54.0	50.1	56.4	59.0	63.5	68.5	74.1
Asia										
Total debt	**404.3**	**456.3**	**510.4**	**562.8**	**595.1**	**642.5**	**661.2**	**671.0**	**663.9**	**681.7**
By maturity										
Short-term	59.6	69.0	76.3	97.5	111.2	150.1	150.3	136.4	124.6	119.7
Long-term	344.7	387.3	434.2	465.3	483.9	492.4	510.9	534.6	539.3	562.0
By type of creditor										
Official	202.9	223.6	253.3	256.8	267.1	279.9	284.3	304.6	310.7	322.8
Banks	112.1	109.8	122.2	139.1	183.5	217.6	229.6	223.4	221.0	229.7
Other private	89.4	122.8	135.0	166.8	144.5	145.0	147.3	143.1	132.2	129.1
Middle East and Europe										
Total debt	**204.4**	**220.5**	**223.7**	**222.1**	**242.1**	**256.7**	**284.5**	**295.7**	**299.3**	**311.1**
By maturity										
Short-term	57.0	71.5	55.8	58.0	66.6	74.2	84.9	87.1	87.0	89.4
Long-term	147.4	149.0	167.9	171.3	175.5	182.5	199.6	208.6	212.2	221.7
By type of creditor										
Official	95.5	106.1	114.4	106.8	108.7	105.4	113.6	111.2	112.1	112.6
Banks	67.8	65.7	66.5	80.9	91.3	123.4	139.1	142.7	142.8	143.6
Other private	41.2	48.8	42.7	34.4	42.1	28.0	31.9	41.8	44.4	54.8
Western Hemisphere										
Total debt	**478.7**	**523.7**	**562.0**	**617.3**	**650.6**	**675.1**	**756.4**	**759.9**	**789.6**	**817.2**
By maturity										
Short-term	79.1	84.1	93.7	95.8	102.1	105.1	99.7	94.9	95.9	95.3
Long-term	399.6	439.6	468.3	521.5	548.5	570.0	656.7	665.0	693.7	722.0
By type of creditor										
Official	161.1	169.1	176.6	193.1	184.1	164.5	172.7	172.2	178.6	178.7
Banks	148.7	144.5	122.7	169.0	168.9	173.8	186.9	178.9	180.7	182.0
Other private	168.9	210.1	262.7	255.3	297.6	336.8	396.7	408.8	430.3	456.4

Table 40. Developing Countries—by Analytical Criteria: External Debt, by Maturity and Type of Creditor
(Billions of U.S. dollars)

	1992	1993	1994	1995	1996	1997	1998	1999	2000	2001
By source of export earnings										
Fuel										
Total debt	**207.6**	**219.3**	**226.7**	**218.0**	**227.7**	**227.9**	**243.9**	**250.2**	**239.7**	**237.7**
By maturity										
Short-term	44.4	56.3	53.3	52.5	57.6	65.9	75.4	76.0	52.0	51.6
Long-term	163.2	163.0	173.4	172.7	170.1	161.9	168.6	174.2	187.7	186.1
By type of creditor										
Official	73.3	85.4	95.9	92.8	96.2	92.6	97.5	99.1	96.7	96.5
Banks	69.6	68.1	65.7	74.7	82.0	84.1	90.7	91.4	88.0	85.6
Other private	64.7	65.8	65.1	50.5	49.5	51.2	55.8	59.7	55.0	55.5
Nonfuel										
Total debt	**1,142.4**	**1,253.7**	**1,358.7**	**1,496.2**	**1,570.6**	**1,649.9**	**1,763.0**	**1,788.2**	**1,825.4**	**1,893.2**
By maturity										
Short-term	171.2	187.2	204.2	236.0	261.6	315.5	312.3	299.2	293.2	292.8
Long-term	971.2	1,066.5	1,154.5	1,260.2	1,309.1	1,334.4	1,450.7	1,489.4	1,532.8	1,601.1
By type of creditor										
Official	556.9	591.2	642.2	673.8	676.3	659.8	678.3	696.9	708.0	723.9
Banks	306.0	297.8	293.3	360.3	407.0	472.6	503.0	490.7	492.1	504.7
Other private	279.5	364.7	423.2	462.0	487.3	517.5	581.6	600.6	625.3	664.5
Manufactures										
Total debt	**598.3**	**674.7**	**725.3**	**807.1**	**855.8**	**902.5**	**979.0**	**976.1**	**1,000.4**	**1,034.6**
By maturity										
Short-term	104.4	129.1	131.3	146.5	173.2	168.7	151.5	144.0	133.4	127.6
Long-term	493.9	545.7	594.1	660.6	682.6	733.8	827.5	832.1	867.1	907.0
By type of creditor										
Official	234.9	251.1	276.4	291.3	282.1	277.2	299.6	307.2	315.9	324.8
Banks	181.4	195.3	178.7	229.1	245.9	284.7	310.1	301.7	307.6	319.0
Other private	182.0	228.3	270.2	286.7	327.7	340.5	369.2	367.2	376.9	390.8
Nonfuel primary products										
Total debt	**175.5**	**183.7**	**195.8**	**209.7**	**213.3**	**211.8**	**220.5**	**228.3**	**236.4**	**244.9**
By maturity										
Short-term	17.1	18.7	19.2	21.1	20.9	20.6	18.1	17.8	19.0	20.2
Long-term	158.4	165.1	176.6	188.6	192.4	191.2	202.4	210.9	218.0	225.4
By type of creditor										
Official	123.2	128.5	139.4	146.4	145.7	141.0	145.3	146.6	148.1	150.5
Banks	30.2	31.3	34.5	37.9	40.2	40.3	40.1	39.8	41.7	41.9
Other private	22.1	24.0	22.0	25.4	27.4	30.5	35.1	41.8	46.5	52.5
Services, income, and private transfers										
Total debt	**86.4**	**83.1**	**86.6**	**88.9**	**88.7**	**86.2**	**87.5**	**91.3**	**88.4**	**91.6**
By maturity										
Short-term	8.4	7.0	6.5	7.1	5.4	5.7	6.0	6.1	5.8	5.8
Long-term	78.1	76.0	80.0	81.8	83.3	80.4	81.6	85.3	82.7	85.8
By type of creditor										
Official	65.3	66.0	69.7	71.7	70.9	66.3	66.6	66.7	62.1	63.3
Banks	12.8	7.7	7.5	7.8	7.1	6.0	6.0	6.8	6.7	6.6
Other private	8.3	9.4	9.4	9.4	10.6	13.8	15.0	17.8	19.7	21.7
Diversified										
Total debt	**282.0**	**311.9**	**350.7**	**390.2**	**412.6**	**449.2**	**475.7**	**492.2**	**500.0**	**521.9**
By maturity										
Short-term	41.3	32.4	47.2	61.3	62.1	120.4	136.7	131.3	135.1	139.3
Long-term	240.7	279.5	303.5	329.0	350.5	328.8	339.0	361.0	364.9	382.7
By type of creditor										
Official	133.3	145.4	156.5	164.3	177.2	175.0	166.5	176.1	181.7	185.1
Banks	81.6	63.5	72.6	85.5	113.8	141.6	146.9	142.3	136.0	137.2
Other private	67.1	103.0	121.6	140.5	121.5	132.7	162.3	173.8	182.2	199.5

Table 40 *(continued)*

	1992	1993	1994	1995	1996	1997	1998	1999	2000	2001
By external financing source										
Net creditor countries										
Total debt	**38.9**	**42.3**	**41.1**	**30.7**	**49.3**	**61.1**	**74.4**	**78.8**	73.6	72.3
By maturity										
Short-term	17.9	23.0	24.2	21.6	26.7	31.5	36.3	35.4	33.9	33.5
Long-term	20.9	19.3	16.9	16.3	22.5	29.6	38.1	43.5	39.7	38.8
By type of creditor										
Official	5.0	6.3	7.7	9.6	11.9	13.6	16.5	16.0	15.0	14.3
Banks	20.4	20.4	20.3	17.5	31.6	40.1	47.8	49.4	49.1	48.9
Other private	13.5	15.6	13.1	3.7	5.7	7.3	10.1	13.5	9.5	9.1
Net debtor countries										
Total debt	**1,313.7**	**1,433.3**	**1,547.0**	**1,686.2**	**1,751.6**	**1,819.3**	**1,935.2**	**1,962.2**	1,994.1	2,061.2
By maturity										
Short-term	198.2	221.0	233.9	267.4	292.9	350.4	351.9	340.4	311.9	311.6
Long-term	1,115.5	1,212.3	1,313.1	1,418.8	1,458.6	1,468.9	1,583.2	1,622.2	1,682.8	1,750.4
By type of creditor										
Official	627.1	672.3	732.4	759.2	762.6	740.8	761.3	782.1	791.9	808.3
Banks	355.6	346.0	339.2	418.0	457.9	517.1	546.4	533.3	531.5	542.1
Other private	331.0	415.0	475.4	508.9	531.1	561.4	627.4	646.8	670.6	710.8
Official financing										
Total debt	**162.3**	**169.2**	**180.1**	**190.6**	**194.4**	**189.7**	**192.8**	**193.8**	189.1	192.4
By maturity										
Short-term	7.9	8.2	7.2	7.3	7.2	6.6	5.6	5.4	5.3	5.2
Long-term	154.4	161.1	172.8	183.3	187.2	183.1	187.2	188.8	184.4	188.0
By type of creditor										
Official	120.7	127.4	141.4	153.0	157.2	152.6	155.7	156.7	152.7	155.9
Banks	27.8	25.6	25.6	24.5	23.3	21.2	20.7	19.6	17.8	17.0
Other private	13.7	16.2	13.1	13.1	13.8	15.9	16.5	17.5	18.5	19.5
Private financing										
Total debt	**914.5**	**1,000.8**	**1,084.4**	**1,199.8**	**1,264.5**	**1,339.0**	**1,442.4**	**1,456.2**	1,485.7	1,539.7
By maturity										
Short-term	149.7	161.2	177.9	206.5	229.2	272.5	272.7	265.2	261.1	260.2
Long-term	764.8	839.6	906.6	993.2	1,035.4	1,066.5	1,169.7	1,191.0	1,224.6	1,279.6
By type of creditor										
Official	348.1	368.8	400.1	419.6	422.0	414.4	424.8	437.7	450.5	459.7
Banks	274.2	271.9	266.8	329.9	372.0	434.1	467.5	457.4	458.2	470.2
Other private	292.1	360.1	417.5	450.2	470.6	490.4	550.2	561.1	577.0	609.9
Diversified financing										
Total debt	**212.1**	**229.0**	**247.3**	**260.2**	**262.0**	**262.8**	**272.4**	**284.0**	291.6	301.1
By maturity										
Short-term	27.4	32.5	40.5	45.3	49.8	55.3	56.0	52.1	27.8	28.4
Long-term	184.8	196.5	206.8	214.9	212.2	207.5	216.4	231.9	263.7	272.8
By type of creditor										
Official	145.5	154.7	169.2	176.4	173.9	165.1	172.4	179.6	180.9	185.1
Banks	41.5	37.5	38.2	39.7	43.3	44.7	41.2	38.1	37.3	36.4
Other private	25.1	36.8	39.9	44.1	44.8	53.0	58.8	66.4	73.4	79.7

Table 40 *(concluded)*

	1992	1993	1994	1995	1996	1997	1998	1999	2000	2001
Net debtor countries by debt-servicing experience										
Countries with arrears and/or rescheduling during 1994–98										
Total debt	**589.1**	**628.0**	**665.0**	**707.8**	**732.9**	**753.9**	**810.1**	**815.9**	806.9	811.7
By maturity										
Short-term	73.8	93.2	87.9	101.7	108.9	155.8	156.3	150.7	126.0	124.1
Long-term	515.3	534.9	577.1	606.1	624.0	598.1	653.8	665.6	681.4	688.3
By type of creditor										
Official	309.1	331.6	357.1	358.9	373.2	364.3	363.2	381.0	384.9	392.6
Banks	172.9	170.1	138.9	201.6	218.6	231.2	232.1	223.0	214.8	214.6
Other private	107.1	126.3	169.0	147.3	141.2	158.4	214.8	212.0	207.2	204.5
Other net debtor countries										
Total debt	**721.9**	**802.6**	**879.2**	**975.6**	**1,016.0**	**1,062.8**	**1,122.4**	**1,143.7**	1,184.8	1,247.1
By maturity										
Short-term	123.8	127.4	145.6	165.2	183.5	194.2	195.2	189.2	185.5	187.1
Long-term	598.1	675.3	733.7	810.4	832.5	868.6	927.2	954.4	999.3	1,060.1
By type of creditor										
Official	316.0	338.6	373.1	398.1	387.3	374.3	396.0	399.0	404.8	413.5
Banks	182.3	175.5	199.9	216.0	238.8	285.5	313.9	309.9	316.3	327.1
Other private	223.6	288.6	306.2	361.5	389.9	402.9	412.5	434.8	463.7	506.6
Other groups										
Heavily indebted poor countries										
Total debt	**185.7**	**195.8**	**204.0**	**216.4**	**216.8**	**211.5**	**214.9**	**219.4**	219.5	227.9
By maturity										
Short-term	9.1	10.3	10.9	11.7	10.5	10.5	7.7	7.9	8.2	8.8
Long-term	176.6	185.5	193.1	204.6	206.3	201.0	207.2	211.9	211.8	219.7
By type of creditor										
Official	147.9	155.6	167.3	176.3	177.8	166.2	170.3	171.9	169.3	173.3
Banks	17.4	17.5	19.6	21.5	23.5	23.9	20.6	20.3	19.7	20.3
Other private	20.4	22.7	17.1	18.5	15.5	21.3	24.1	27.2	30.5	34.3
Least developed countries										
Total debt	**135.6**	**144.6**	**152.2**	**159.0**	**158.7**	**159.8**	**165.7**	**170.1**	168.8	176.1
By maturity										
Short-term	5.8	5.9	6.9	6.9	6.1	6.4	8.0	8.6	8.9	9.5
Long-term	129.9	138.7	145.3	152.2	152.6	153.4	157.8	162.0	160.5	167.3
By type of creditor										
Official	114.6	120.7	130.6	136.6	138.8	134.6	137.4	139.2	135.7	139.3
Banks	7.4	8.1	8.3	8.8	9.1	9.1	9.3	8.9	8.6	9.0
Other private	13.6	15.8	13.4	13.7	10.8	16.1	19.0	22.1	24.5	27.8
Middle East and north Africa										
Total debt	**220.5**	**227.1**	**238.8**	**237.4**	**251.8**	**253.1**	**268.9**	**274.7**	269.0	269.6
By maturity										
Short-term	46.5	55.2	46.6	44.3	48.8	62.6	70.5	70.7	71.4	72.0
Long-term	174.0	172.0	192.2	200.3	203.0	190.5	198.5	204.0	197.5	197.6
By type of creditor										
Official	117.1	126.0	137.7	136.7	139.5	130.7	133.2	130.1	126.7	125.9
Banks	77.1	70.6	69.8	81.2	89.0	92.6	100.6	101.8	99.8	98.5
Other private	26.3	30.5	31.3	19.5	23.3	29.8	35.1	42.8	42.5	45.3

Table 41. Developing Countries: Ratio of External Debt to GDP[1]

	1992	1993	1994	1995	1996	1997	1998	1999	2000	2001
Developing countries	**35.5**	**33.4**	**36.6**	**37.3**	**35.5**	**34.9**	**38.1**	**38.3**	35.5	34.4
Regional groups										
Africa	66.0	71.2	78.6	75.6	71.5	68.7	71.5	73.2	68.9	67.7
Sub-Sahara	68.0	74.4	81.4	76.6	73.7	70.9	75.4	78.9	75.4	74.6
Asia	31.2	31.0	33.2	30.4	28.4	29.2	31.4	29.4	26.6	25.1
Excluding China and India	46.1	47.2	46.8	45.0	42.6	46.3	57.4	49.5	42.1	37.2
Middle East and Europe	33.6	36.1	39.2	34.1	34.4	34.2	38.3	38.0	35.0	35.8
Western Hemisphere	31.8	27.0	30.3	36.8	35.7	34.0	38.0	41.3	39.3	38.3
Analytical groups										
By source of export earnings										
Fuel	39.9	45.7	49.0	41.4	39.2	36.6	40.8	39.0	33.3	33.7
Manufactures	27.1	24.3	28.0	30.6	29.0	28.8	31.3	31.7	29.6	28.4
Nonfuel primary products	72.6	69.2	66.6	58.5	52.8	46.4	45.9	45.3	42.5	39.3
Services, income, and										
private transfers	76.2	68.4	65.2	60.4	54.8	48.6	45.9	44.9	40.4	38.5
Diversified	38.9	40.9	41.1	42.5	42.8	45.3	54.9	55.2	53.6	53.0
By external financing source										
Net creditor countries	16.8	18.0	16.9	11.8	17.1	20.2	27.5	26.4	21.6	22.0
Net debtor countries	36.7	34.3	37.8	38.9	36.6	35.8	38.7	39.0	36.4	35.1
Official financing	83.6	85.1	100.4	96.4	89.4	84.9	85.6	84.8	77.0	74.5
Private financing	30.8	27.8	30.8	32.6	31.1	30.8	33.8	34.1	31.8	30.6
Diversified financing	75.8	81.7	79.5	75.6	70.9	69.6	74.3	75.3	72.2	71.4
Net debtor countries by debt-servicing experience										
Countries with arrears and/or										
rescheduling during 1994–98	45.6	37.7	43.6	46.5	43.1	42.4	49.1	52.1	45.9	43.0
Other net debtor countries	31.6	32.1	34.3	34.7	33.1	32.2	33.6	33.1	31.9	31.3
Other groups										
Heavily indebted poor countries	95.2	92.6	92.4	84.8	74.0	63.0	58.2	54.5	48.6	44.6
Least developed countries	72.6	70.2	67.8	62.0	54.6	48.0	45.2	42.1	36.9	34.0
Middle East and north Africa	41.1	43.8	45.3	41.5	39.9	38.3	41.6	39.7	35.0	34.8

[1]Debt at year-end in percent of GDP in year indicated.

Table 42. Developing Countries: Debt-Service Ratios[1]
(Percent of exports of goods and services)

	1992	1993	1994	1995	1996	1997	1998	1999	2000	2001
Interest payments[2]										
Developing countries	**9.8**	**9.8**	**9.1**	**8.9**	**8.5**	**7.9**	**9.2**	**9.2**	**9.3**	**8.9**
Regional groups										
Africa	11.5	11.3	11.3	11.3	9.7	9.6	11.2	10.0	10.6	10.7
Sub-Sahara	10.8	10.3	10.6	10.6	8.9	9.1	10.9	9.7	10.2	10.4
Asia	7.6	6.8	6.4	6.0	5.8	4.8	5.6	6.0	5.4	5.2
Excluding China and India	6.8	6.2	6.0	6.1	6.3	6.6	7.6	7.4	6.5	5.6
Middle East and Europe	5.4	5.7	4.5	4.5	4.5	4.2	5.8	5.4	7.3	7.3
Western Hemisphere	16.7	18.1	17.1	17.2	16.4	16.1	17.7	18.3	17.7	16.4
Analytical groups										
By source of export earnings										
Fuel	4.7	5.2	4.8	5.3	4.4	4.4	6.6	5.3	8.0	8.7
Manufactures	11.4	11.1	9.6	9.4	8.8	7.6	8.3	8.7	8.4	7.6
Nonfuel primary products	9.8	9.7	10.2	8.4	7.6	7.9	9.6	8.7	8.4	8.0
Services, income, and private transfers	15.3	12.4	7.5	6.1	6.0	5.4	5.8	6.6	5.6	5.3
Diversified	11.6	11.6	12.4	12.5	13.1	13.2	15.3	16.3	15.4	15.0
By external financing source										
Net creditor countries	1.6	1.8	1.9	2.6	2.6	2.8	5.1	3.6	3.5	3.7
Net debtor countries	11.2	11.1	10.1	9.8	9.3	8.5	9.6	9.9	10.0	9.5
Official financing	10.7	10.3	12.6	9.6	9.0	8.8	10.0	8.7	9.2	9.3
Private financing	12.0	11.7	10.4	10.1	9.7	8.8	9.9	10.4	10.0	9.4
Diversified financing	9.4	9.2	9.0	9.4	8.6	7.9	9.1	8.2	8.3	8.2
Net debtor countries by debt-servicing experience										
Countries with arrears and/or rescheduling during 1994–98	11.6	12.4	11.4	11.6	11.6	11.5	14.3	14.6	15.2	13.5
Other net debtor countries	11.1	10.6	9.6	9.1	8.4	7.4	8.0	8.2	8.1	8.0
Other groups										
Heavily indebted poor countries	9.1	10.0	13.6	9.9	9.2	8.0	10.0	8.3	7.9	7.6
Least developed countries	7.5	7.6	6.8	8.8	7.2	5.8	7.3	6.6	6.5	6.1
Middle East and north Africa	5.4	5.7	4.3	4.5	4.7	4.2	6.0	4.7	6.9	7.0
Amortization[2]										
Developing countries	**14.9**	**13.8**	**13.7**	**14.2**	**15.6**	**16.7**	**17.6**	**18.6**	**14.0**	**12.8**
Regional groups										
Africa	17.4	17.2	17.3	16.9	13.3	13.0	12.8	12.9	11.7	11.1
Sub-Sahara	10.7	10.1	10.2	11.0	9.5	10.2	10.3	11.1	10.6	9.7
Asia	12.5	11.0	10.7	11.0	9.4	9.7	12.3	12.7	8.1	8.1
Excluding China and India	15.0	12.4	12.0	12.5	10.0	12.4	17.4	17.9	9.5	9.6
Middle East and Europe	7.3	8.5	9.7	9.3	14.2	11.9	11.1	11.2	11.5	9.8
Western Hemisphere	25.1	21.9	21.1	23.2	29.9	36.1	34.8	38.3	28.3	24.7
Analytical groups										
By source of export earnings										
Fuel	8.2	9.8	11.7	11.7	15.2	13.9	10.9	9.2	9.1	8.7
Manufactures	17.9	13.2	13.3	12.9	14.8	15.7	16.4	19.0	14.2	12.0
Nonfuel primary products	10.9	13.5	13.6	21.3	14.4	12.6	12.8	13.7	12.5	15.6
Services, income, and private transfers	18.8	19.4	10.8	7.1	6.8	10.4	8.2	7.8	7.3	7.3
Diversified	17.5	19.0	17.8	19.3	21.2	26.0	31.8	32.2	22.1	20.3

Table 42 *(concluded)*

	1992	1993	1994	1995	1996	1997	1998	1999	2000	2001
By external financing source										
Net creditor countries	0.7	1.6	5.4	4.4	11.9	8.2	4.3	3.7	3.1	3.2
Net debtor countries	17.4	15.8	14.9	15.4	16.1	17.8	19.0	20.3	15.4	13.8
Official financing	24.9	26.6	26.5	31.9	14.9	14.1	11.5	13.3	9.8	12.7
Private financing	16.2	14.8	13.9	14.2	16.2	18.4	19.9	21.7	15.9	13.8
Diversified financing	25.8	17.9	17.8	16.2	13.6	13.2	14.8	12.8	11.9	11.9
Net debtor countries by debt-servicing experience										
Countries with arrears and/or rescheduling during 1994–98	22.0	21.0	19.0	21.3	18.7	25.5	30.2	38.9	22.6	19.2
Other net debtor countries	15.4	13.7	13.4	13.4	15.2	15.0	15.2	13.8	12.8	11.9
Other groups										
Heavily indebted poor countries	11.9	14.3	15.5	24.5	10.6	11.5	11.0	13.6	12.9	12.3
Least developed countries	12.3	12.5	11.2	14.7	9.4	11.0	10.7	13.7	9.1	9.6
Middle East and north Africa	9.9	11.4	12.2	11.2	15.6	12.8	9.8	8.7	8.2	8.4

[1]Excludes service payments to the International Monetary Fund.
[2]Interest payments on total debt and amortization on long-term debt. Estimates through 1999 reflect debt-service payments actually made. The estimates for 2000 and 2001 take into account projected exceptional financing items, including accumulation of arrears and rescheduling agreements. In some cases, amortization on account of debt-reduction operations is included.

Table 43. IMF Charges and Repurchases to the IMF[1]
(Percent of exports of goods and services)

	1992	1993	1994	1995	1996	1997	1998	1999
Developing countries	**1.0**	**0.9**	**0.7**	**0.8**	**0.7**	**0.7**	**0.5**	**0.9**
Regional groups								
Africa	1.2	1.2	0.8	2.1	0.7	0.9	1.1	0.6
Sub-Sahara	0.9	0.7	0.4	2.4	0.7	0.7	0.8	0.2
Asia	0.6	0.3	0.5	0.5	0.4	0.2	0.1	0.2
Excluding China and India	0.5	0.3	0.2	0.2	0.2	0.2	0.1	0.2
Middle East and Europe	—	—	—	0.1	0.1	—	0.1	0.2
Western Hemisphere	2.8	2.7	1.7	1.5	1.7	2.0	1.2	3.2
Analytical groups								
By source of export earnings								
Fuel	0.4	0.6	0.4	0.5	0.4	0.4	0.6	0.5
Nonfuel	1.2	1.0	0.8	0.9	0.8	0.7	0.5	1.0
By external financing source								
Net creditor countries	—	—	—	—	—	—	—	—
Net debtor countries	1.2	1.1	0.8	0.9	0.8	0.8	0.5	1.0
Official financing	1.9	2.2	1.2	4.3	1.3	1.0	1.3	1.0
Private financing	1.2	1.1	0.8	0.7	0.7	0.8	0.5	1.2
Diversified financing	1.2	0.8	0.9	0.9	0.8	0.6	0.3	0.4
Net debtor countries by debt-servicing experience								
Countries with arrears and/or rescheduling during 1994–98	1.4	1.4	0.7	1.3	0.6	0.4	0.5	1.1
Other net debtor countries	1.2	0.9	0.9	0.8	0.8	0.9	0.6	1.0
Other groups								
Heavily indebted poor countries	2.1	1.7	1.0	4.7	1.3	0.5	0.5	0.3
Least developed countries	1.6	1.2	0.8	6.5	1.5	0.2	0.4	0.3
Middle East and north Africa	0.3	0.4	0.3	0.3	0.2	0.2	0.4	0.3
Countries in transition	**0.4**	**0.3**	**1.1**	**1.4**	**0.8**	**0.6**	**0.9**	**2.3**
Central and eastern Europe	0.7	0.6	2.0	2.3	0.8	0.4	0.6	0.7
Excluding Belarus and Ukraine	0.8	0.7	2.3	2.7	1.0	0.4	0.5	0.4
Russia	—	—	0.1	0.2	0.8	0.9	1.7	5.8
Transcaucasus and central Asia	—	—	—	0.1	0.3	0.4	1.1	2.1
Memorandum								
Total, billions of U.S. dollars								
General Resources Account	8.192	7.503	8.669	11.857	9.892	9.926	8.442	18.194
Charges	2.423	2.184	2.123	1.898	2.661	2.140	2.142	2.494
Repurchases	5.768	5.319	6.546	9.960	7.231	7.786	6.300	15.700
Trust Fund	0.001	0.060	0.017	0.015	—	0.007	0.001	0.001
Interest	0.001	—	0.003	—	—	—	—	—
Repayments	—	0.060	0.014	0.015	—	0.007	0.001	0.001
PRGF[2]	0.051	0.148	0.331	0.584	0.736	0.865	0.880	0.855
Interest	0.018	0.022	0.025	0.031	0.033	0.038	0.039	0.041
Repayments	0.033	0.126	0.306	0.552	0.703	0.827	0.842	0.814

[1]Excludes advanced economies. Charges on, and repurchases (or repayments of principal) for, use of International Monetary Fund credit.
[2]Poverty Reduction and Growth Facility (formerly ESAF—Enhanced Structural Adjustment Facility).

Table 44. Summary of Sources and Uses of World Saving
(Percent of GDP)

	Averages		1994	1995	1996	1997	1998	1999	2000	2001	Average 2002–2005
	1978–85	1986–93									
World											
Saving	23.3	22.8	23.1	23.2	23.3	23.9	23.2	23.2	23.4	23.5	23.8
Investment	24.4	24.0	23.8	24.2	24.0	24.1	23.3	23.2	23.8	24.1	24.7
Advanced economies											
Saving	22.0	21.0	20.9	21.4	21.5	22.2	22.1	21.8	21.6	21.8	22.4
Private	21.6	20.4	20.8	21.0	20.6	20.1	19.5	19.0	18.7	18.7	18.7
Public	0.4	0.6	—	0.4	0.9	2.0	2.7	2.9	2.9	3.1	3.6
Investment	22.8	21.8	21.3	21.5	21.6	21.8	21.6	21.8	22.3	22.5	23.0
Private	18.3	17.8	17.3	17.6	17.7	18.1	18.0	18.1	18.6	19.0	19.5
Public	4.5	4.0	4.0	4.0	3.9	3.7	3.6	3.8	3.7	3.6	3.5
Net lending	−0.8	−0.8	−0.5	−0.1	−0.1	0.3	0.5	—	−0.8	−0.7	−0.6
Private	3.2	2.6	3.5	3.4	2.9	2.0	1.5	0.9	—	−0.3	−0.8
Public	−4.1	−3.4	−4.0	−3.6	−3.0	−1.7	−1.0	−0.9	−0.8	−0.4	0.1
Current transfers	−0.4	−0.4	−0.4	−0.3	−0.4	−0.4	−0.3	−0.4	−0.3	−0.3	−0.3
Factor income	−0.3	−0.4	−0.5	−0.3	−0.1	0.1	0.2	0.4	—	—	—
Resource balance	−0.1	−0.1	0.4	0.4	0.4	0.6	0.7	−0.1	−0.4	−0.4	−0.3
United States											
Saving	19.7	16.9	16.4	17.0	17.3	18.3	18.8	18.7	17.3	17.1	17.6
Private	19.9	17.9	17.0	17.1	16.5	16.4	15.7	14.7	13.1	12.7	12.9
Public	−0.2	−1.1	−0.6	−0.1	0.8	1.9	3.1	3.9	4.2	4.4	4.7
Investment	21.2	18.9	18.8	18.7	19.1	19.8	20.5	20.7	21.0	21.0	21.3
Private	17.7	15.2	15.6	15.5	15.9	16.7	17.5	17.5	17.8	17.9	18.2
Public	3.5	3.7	3.2	3.2	3.2	3.1	3.1	3.2	3.2	3.2	3.1
Net lending	−1.5	−2.0	−2.4	−1.7	−1.8	−1.5	−1.8	−2.1	−3.8	−3.9	−3.8
Private	2.2	2.7	1.4	1.7	0.6	−0.3	−1.8	−2.8	−4.8	−5.2	−5.3
Public	−3.7	−4.7	−3.8	−3.3	−2.4	−1.2	0.1	0.7	1.0	1.2	1.6
Current transfers	−0.4	−0.4	−0.6	−0.5	−0.5	−0.5	−0.5	−0.5	−0.4	−0.4	−0.4
Factor income	0.3	0.2	−0.4	0.1	—	0.3	0.6	1.3	0.1	—	−0.1
Resource balance	−1.4	−1.7	−1.4	−1.3	−1.3	−1.3	−1.9	−2.9	−3.5	−3.5	−3.3
European Union											
Saving	20.7	20.4	19.8	20.6	20.4	21.1	21.3	21.1	21.7	22.2	22.7
Private	20.9	21.2	22.3	22.7	22.0	21.1	20.3	19.6	19.8	20.1	20.2
Public	−0.2	−0.8	−2.6	−2.1	−1.6	—	1.0	1.5	1.9	2.1	2.5
Investment	21.5	21.2	19.7	20.0	19.4	19.7	20.5	20.9	21.3	21.5	21.8
Private	17.6	18.0	16.9	17.4	17.0	17.4	18.2	18.5	18.8	19.0	19.2
Public	3.9	3.3	2.8	2.6	2.4	2.3	2.3	2.4	2.4	2.5	2.5
Net lending	−0.8	−0.9	0.1	0.5	1.0	1.4	0.8	0.2	0.4	0.7	0.9
Private	3.2	3.2	5.5	5.2	5.0	3.8	2.2	1.1	1.0	1.1	0.9
Public	−4.1	−4.0	−5.4	−4.7	−4.0	−2.4	−1.4	−0.9	−0.5	−0.4	—
Current transfers	−0.7	−0.4	−0.4	−0.3	−0.4	−0.4	−0.4	−0.5	−0.4	−0.4	−0.4
Factor income	−1.0	−1.1	−0.8	−0.8	−0.5	−0.4	−0.5	−0.5	−0.3	−0.2	−0.1
Resource balance	0.9	0.6	1.4	1.6	1.9	2.2	1.8	1.1	1.2	1.3	1.4
Japan											
Saving	31.2	33.1	31.5	30.7	31.5	31.4	29.9	28.7	28.8	29.0	29.7
Private	27.5	24.9	26.0	25.9	27.0	26.8	26.8	28.0	29.6	28.9	27.8
Public	3.7	8.1	5.5	4.9	4.5	4.5	3.1	0.6	−0.8	0.1	1.9
Investment	30.1	30.4	28.7	28.6	30.0	29.1	26.7	26.1	26.6	26.8	27.6
Private	21.3	23.4	20.0	20.0	21.2	21.3	19.1	18.1	19.0	20.0	21.5
Public	8.8	7.0	8.6	8.6	8.7	7.8	7.6	8.0	7.6	6.8	6.1
Net lending	1.0	2.7	2.8	2.1	1.5	2.3	3.2	2.5	2.1	2.2	2.0
Private	6.1	1.6	6.0	5.8	5.8	5.5	7.7	9.9	10.6	8.9	6.2
Public	−5.1	1.1	−3.1	−3.7	−4.2	−3.3	−4.6	−7.4	−8.5	−6.7	−4.2
Current transfers	−0.1	−0.1	−0.1	−0.2	−0.2	−0.2	−0.2	−0.3	−0.2	−0.3	−0.3
Factor income	0.1	0.7	0.9	0.8	1.3	1.4	1.5	1.2	1.3	1.2	1.3
Resource balance	1.1	2.2	2.1	1.5	0.5	1.1	1.9	1.6	1.1	1.4	1.1

Table 44 *(continued)*

	Averages		1994	1995	1996	1997	1998	1999	2000	2001	Average 2002–2005
	1978–85	1986–93									
Newly industrialized Asian economies											
Saving	...	35.6	33.6	33.7	32.8	32.7	33.3	32.9	33.1	34.0	34.9
Private	...	27.9	26.0	26.3	25.8	25.9	25.8	25.8	26.2	27.5	29.0
Public	...	7.7	7.7	7.4	7.0	6.8	7.5	7.1	6.9	6.5	5.9
	...										
Investment	...	29.9	31.9	32.7	32.2	30.8	23.4	25.3	27.6	29.0	30.6
Private	...	23.8	25.0	26.0	25.5	24.2	16.2	18.0	20.7	22.6	24.2
Public	...	6.1	6.8	6.7	6.7	6.6	7.2	7.3	6.8	6.4	6.5
Net lending	...	5.7	1.8	1.1	0.6	1.9	9.9	7.5	5.5	5.0	4.2
Private	...	4.1	0.9	0.4	0.3	1.7	9.6	7.8	5.5	4.9	4.8
Public	...	1.5	0.8	0.7	0.4	0.2	0.3	–0.3	—	—	–0.6
Current transfers	...	0.1	—	–0.3	–0.3	–0.1	0.3	—	–0.2	–0.3	–0.3
Factor income	...	0.5	0.6	1.1	1.1	1.5	1.4	1.6	1.6	1.5	1.4
Resource balance	...	5.0	1.2	0.3	–0.2	0.6	8.2	5.9	4.1	3.7	3.1
Developing countries											
Saving	22.5	23.4	26.6	26.3	26.5	27.1	25.9	25.4	26.2	26.2	25.7
Investment	24.0	25.4	27.9	28.7	27.7	27.6	26.3	25.7	26.2	26.5	26.9
Net lending	–1.5	–2.0	–1.3	–2.5	–1.2	–0.5	–0.4	–0.3	—	–0.3	–1.2
Current transfers	0.8	1.0	1.1	1.1	1.2	1.3	1.1	1.2	1.1	1.2	1.1
Factor income	–1.2	–1.6	–1.2	–1.7	–1.5	–1.4	–1.4	–1.9	–1.8	–1.7	–1.9
Resource balance	–1.2	–1.5	–1.2	–1.8	–0.9	–0.3	–0.2	0.5	0.7	0.2	–0.4
Memorandum											
Acquisition of foreign assets	0.9	0.9	2.7	2.2	3.4	4.3	2.7	2.3	3.3	2.9	2.3
Change in reserves	0.4	0.6	2.0	1.7	2.2	1.7	0.2	1.0	1.4	1.4	1.0
Regional groups											
Africa											
Saving	21.2	16.1	15.5	15.2	16.6	16.4	15.8	16.2	18.3	18.3	19.9
Investment	23.2	19.3	19.7	19.5	18.5	18.5	20.4	20.3	20.2	20.9	22.3
Net lending	–1.9	–3.2	–4.2	–4.3	–1.9	–2.1	–4.6	–4.1	–1.8	–2.6	–2.4
Current transfers	1.9	3.2	3.7	3.2	3.1	3.2	3.3	3.3	3.2	3.1	3.0
Factor income	0.1	–4.4	–5.0	–4.5	–4.5	–4.2	–3.9	–4.5	–4.3	–4.1	–3.3
Resource balance	–3.9	–1.9	–2.8	–3.0	–0.5	–1.0	–4.0	–2.9	–0.7	–1.6	–2.1
Memorandum											
Acquisition of foreign assets	–1.0	0.4	0.7	1.5	2.7	2.8	–0.2	0.9	2.5	1.4	0.3
Change in reserves	0.1	—	1.7	0.8	2.2	2.4	–0.3	0.5	2.3	1.5	1.4
Asia											
Saving	25.1	28.7	33.4	32.0	32.5	33.4	32.6	31.6	31.8	31.7	30.1
Investment	26.1	30.0	33.9	34.6	33.5	32.4	29.9	29.7	30.3	30.4	30.3
Net lending	–1.0	–1.4	–0.4	–2.7	–1.0	1.0	2.8	1.9	1.5	1.3	–0.2
Current transfers	1.3	0.8	1.0	1.0	1.2	1.4	1.1	1.2	1.0	1.1	1.0
Factor income	0.4	–0.6	–0.2	–1.1	–0.5	–0.7	–0.7	–1.1	–1.0	–1.0	–1.4
Resource balance	–2.6	–1.7	–1.2	–2.6	–1.6	0.3	2.3	1.8	1.5	1.2	0.2
Memorandum											
Acquisition of foreign assets	2.7	1.6	4.6	2.7	4.1	6.3	5.2	3.2	4.0	4.1	3.0
Change in reserves	0.8	0.9	3.3	2.1	2.3	2.0	1.2	1.4	1.5	1.9	1.1
Middle East and Europe											
Saving	24.5	19.2	21.9	23.4	20.1	21.1	17.9	19.3	21.5	20.6	21.2
Investment	24.3	23.3	21.6	23.9	20.2	21.9	22.5	21.5	21.8	22.2	23.6
Net lending	0.3	–4.1	0.3	–0.4	–0.1	–0.8	–4.6	–2.2	–0.3	–1.7	–2.4
Current transfers	—	0.1	–0.6	–0.4	–0.2	–0.2	–0.4	—	0.1	–0.1	—
Factor income	–0.8	0.5	–0.2	0.1	–0.6	–0.2	–0.1	–1.2	–0.8	–0.4	–0.9
Resource balance	1.0	–4.7	1.0	–0.1	0.7	–0.3	–4.1	–1.0	0.4	–1.2	–1.5
Memorandum											
Acquisition of foreign assets	2.7	–1.2	0.5	1.1	2.0	1.9	–1.6	1.5	2.5	1.5	1.3
Change in reserves	0.8	0.3	0.9	1.7	2.6	1.0	–1.9	1.5	1.1	1.1	1.2

Table 44 (continued)

| | Averages | | 1994 | 1995 | 1996 | 1997 | 1998 | 1999 | 2000 | 2001 | Average 2002–2005 |
	1978–85	1986–93									
Western Hemisphere											
Saving	18.9	19.2	18.7	19.1	19.2	19.4	17.4	16.3	17.3	17.6	18.5
Investment	21.5	20.9	21.6	21.4	21.3	22.5	22.0	19.5	20.3	20.6	21.4
Net lending	−2.6	−1.7	−2.9	−2.3	−2.0	−3.2	−4.6	−3.2	−3.0	−3.0	−2.9
Current transfers	0.4	1.0	0.9	1.1	1.0	1.0	1.0	1.1	1.1	1.1	1.1
Factor income	−3.6	−3.2	−2.2	−2.9	−2.8	−2.7	−2.8	−3.4	−3.4	−3.1	−3.2
Resource balance	0.6	0.5	−1.6	−0.6	−0.2	−1.5	−2.9	−0.9	−0.7	−1.0	−0.8
Memorandum											
Acquisition of foreign assets	1.3	0.9	0.6	2.0	2.7	1.3	—	0.8	1.9	1.1	1.1
Change in reserves	0.2	0.6	−0.2	1.3	1.9	1.0	−0.9	−0.3	0.9	0.5	0.5
Analytical groups											
By source of export earnings											
Fuel											
Saving	27.9	19.4	21.7	23.1	22.9	23.6	17.3	20.1	25.2	22.4	22.5
Investment	25.1	22.8	21.3	23.1	18.2	20.9	23.3	21.3	21.3	22.0	23.7
Net lending	2.8	−3.4	0.4	—	4.7	2.6	−6.0	−1.2	3.9	0.3	−1.2
Current transfers	−2.6	−2.8	−2.4	−2.3	−2.0	−2.0	−2.3	−2.0	−1.7	−1.7	−1.4
Factor income	0.1	0.2	−1.6	−1.4	−1.6	−1.4	−1.6	−2.6	−2.3	−2.0	−2.4
Resource balance	5.3	−0.8	4.4	3.7	8.4	6.1	−2.1	3.4	7.8	4.1	2.6
Memorandum											
Acquisition of foreign assets	3.6	−1.4	2.7	−0.1	5.1	3.6	−2.4	1.7	4.9	2.1	1.6
Change in reserves	0.7	−0.7	—	0.1	4.5	2.1	−3.1	0.6	2.7	1.0	0.8
Nonfuel											
Saving	21.4	23.9	27.1	26.6	26.9	27.5	26.8	25.9	26.3	26.5	26.0
Investment	23.8	25.7	28.7	29.4	28.7	28.3	26.7	26.1	26.7	26.9	27.3
Net lending	−2.3	−1.8	−1.5	−2.8	−1.9	−0.8	0.1	−0.2	−0.4	−0.4	−1.2
Current transfers	1.5	1.6	1.5	1.5	1.5	1.6	1.5	1.5	1.4	1.5	1.3
Factor income	−1.4	−1.8	−1.2	−1.8	−1.5	−1.4	−1.4	−1.9	−1.8	−1.7	−1.9
Resource balance	−2.4	−1.5	−1.8	−2.4	−1.9	−1.0	—	0.2	—	−0.2	−0.7
Memorandum											
Acquisition of foreign assets	0.4	1.2	2.7	2.5	3.2	4.4	3.3	2.3	3.1	3.0	2.4
Change in reserves	0.3	0.8	2.2	1.9	2.0	1.6	0.6	1.0	1.3	1.5	1.0
By external financing source											
Net creditor countries											
Saving	33.0	15.3	17.9	20.9	22.9	23.1	14.1	17.4	23.4	19.2	18.6
Investment	25.4	19.8	19.9	20.1	19.7	20.6	22.6	20.4	18.9	19.5	20.6
Net lending	7.6	−4.5	−2.0	0.9	3.2	2.4	−8.5	−3.0	4.5	−0.3	−2.0
Current transfers	−7.3	−10.0	−10.1	−8.9	−7.6	−7.2	−8.1	−7.1	−6.2	−6.6	−6.2
Factor income	0.5	6.0	3.8	4.9	3.2	3.2	4.0	1.7	1.1	2.5	1.9
Resource balance	14.4	−0.6	4.4	4.8	7.6	6.5	−4.5	2.3	9.6	3.7	2.3
Memorandum											
Acquisition of foreign assets	7.8	−3.2	−0.6	1.1	5.0	4.0	−5.7	1.7	7.5	2.5	2.2
Change in reserves	1.4	−0.9	−0.5	0.1	4.0	3.5	−5.0	1.0	3.2	0.7	1.3
Net debtor countries											
Saving	21.9	23.7	26.9	26.4	26.6	27.3	26.3	25.7	26.3	26.4	25.9
Investment	23.9	25.6	28.2	29.0	27.9	27.8	26.4	25.8	26.4	26.7	27.1
Net lending	−2.0	−1.9	−1.3	−2.6	−1.3	−0.6	−0.2	−0.2	−0.1	−0.3	−1.2
Current transfers	1.3	1.5	1.5	1.4	1.4	1.6	1.4	1.5	1.4	1.4	1.3
Factor income	−1.2	−1.9	−1.4	−2.0	−1.6	−1.6	−1.6	−2.0	−1.9	−1.8	−2.0
Resource balance	−2.0	−1.5	−1.4	−2.1	−1.2	−0.5	—	0.4	0.4	0.1	−0.5
Memorandum											
Acquisition of foreign assets	0.6	1.1	2.8	2.3	3.4	4.3	3.0	2.3	3.1	2.9	2.3
Change in reserves	0.3	0.7	2.1	1.8	2.2	1.6	0.4	1.0	1.4	1.5	1.0

Table 44 *(continued)*

	Averages		1994	1995	1996	1997	1998	1999	2000	2001	Average 2002–2005
	1978–85	1986–93									
Official financing											
Saving	14.3	13.0	14.6	14.5	15.7	16.9	15.4	16.3	18.8	18.9	20.6
Investment	20.8	18.8	21.8	23.0	21.9	20.6	21.7	22.4	22.1	22.8	23.8
Net lending	−6.5	−5.8	−7.2	−8.5	−6.2	−3.7	−6.3	−6.1	−3.3	−3.8	−3.2
Current transfers	4.3	4.3	5.5	5.2	5.2	4.8	5.1	5.0	4.8	4.6	4.2
Factor income	−4.8	−4.6	−4.5	−5.4	−4.8	−4.0	−4.7	−4.4	−3.8	−3.5	−2.7
Resource balance	−6.1	−5.5	−8.3	−8.3	−6.7	−4.6	−6.7	−6.7	−4.4	−4.9	−4.8
Memorandum											
Acquisition of foreign assets	0.8	1.3	1.7	2.0	1.6	2.2	−0.6	−0.3	1.7	1.0	−0.3
Change in reserves	0.1	0.2	1.2	1.2	2.1	2.4	−0.3	−0.4	2.2	1.3	1.2
Private financing											
Saving	23.0	25.7	28.7	28.2	28.6	29.2	28.1	27.1	27.4	27.5	26.6
Investment	24.7	26.9	29.5	30.3	29.5	29.2	27.4	26.8	27.4	27.6	27.7
Net lending	−1.7	−1.2	−0.7	−2.1	−1.0	—	0.7	0.3	—	−0.1	−1.1
Current transfers	0.9	1.1	0.9	1.0	1.0	1.2	1.0	1.1	1.0	1.0	1.0
Factor income	−1.5	−1.9	−1.1	−1.8	−1.5	−1.6	−1.4	−1.9	−1.9	−1.8	−2.1
Resource balance	−1.0	−0.5	−0.6	−1.3	−0.5	0.4	1.1	1.1	0.9	0.7	0.1
Memorandum											
Acquisition of foreign assets	0.6	1.3	2.9	2.5	3.6	4.9	3.6	2.5	3.3	3.1	2.4
Change in reserves	0.3	0.9	2.2	1.9	2.1	1.9	0.5	0.9	1.3	1.5	1.0
Diversified financing											
Saving	18.3	13.9	15.7	14.9	15.9	16.3	17.1	18.1	19.5	20.3	21.0
Investment	20.6	18.8	21.8	20.3	20.2	21.1	20.8	19.7	20.1	20.8	22.5
Net lending	−2.3	−4.9	−6.1	−5.3	−4.4	−4.7	−3.7	−1.6	−0.6	−0.5	−1.5
Current transfers	2.2	2.7	3.5	3.2	3.0	3.4	3.3	3.1	3.1	3.1	2.9
Factor income	2.1	−2.2	−2.4	−1.3	−0.7	−0.3	−1.0	−2.3	−2.0	−1.3	−0.7
Resource balance	−6.5	−5.4	−7.2	−7.2	−6.6	−7.9	−6.0	−2.4	−1.7	−2.3	−3.7
Memorandum											
Acquisition of foreign assets	0.4	−0.6	1.9	0.4	3.4	1.3	0.9	1.3	2.7	2.6	1.7
Change in reserves	0.3	—	2.0	0.9	2.9	−0.2	0.7	1.8	1.9	2.0	1.2
Net debtor countries by debt-servicing experience											
Countries with arrears and/or rescheduling during 1994–98											
Saving	18.8	19.4	21.4	20.6	19.6	19.8	16.9	16.1	18.4	18.7	19.9
Investment	21.4	22.2	23.7	24.5	22.4	23.2	20.1	18.1	19.5	20.2	21.8
Net lending	−2.6	−2.7	−2.3	−3.8	−2.8	−3.5	−3.2	−2.0	−1.1	−1.5	−1.8
Current transfers	0.6	1.3	1.7	1.5	1.5	1.4	1.5	1.6	1.6	1.5	1.5
Factor income	−1.9	−2.4	−2.3	−2.3	−1.7	−2.1	−2.1	−2.8	−2.6	−2.3	−2.1
Resource balance	−1.3	−1.5	−1.6	−3.0	−2.6	−2.8	−2.7	−0.8	−0.1	−0.7	−1.3
Memorandum											
Acquisition of foreign assets	0.9	0.2	2.1	1.4	1.9	0.5	0.4	−0.9	0.5	0.8	1.0
Change in reserves	0.2	0.2	1.0	1.6	1.5	0.7	−0.2	0.4	1.8	1.2	0.9
Other net debtor countries											
Saving	23.8	25.7	29.1	28.7	29.3	30.1	29.6	29.0	29.0	29.0	27.9
Investment	25.4	27.2	30.0	30.8	30.1	29.6	28.7	28.5	28.8	28.9	28.9
Net lending	−1.6	−1.5	−0.9	−2.1	−0.8	0.5	0.9	0.5	0.2	0.1	−1.0
Current transfers	1.6	1.6	1.4	1.4	1.4	1.6	1.4	1.4	1.3	1.4	1.2
Factor income	−0.8	−1.6	−1.0	−1.8	−1.6	−1.4	−1.4	−1.8	−1.7	−1.7	−2.0
Resource balance	−2.4	−1.5	−1.3	−1.7	−0.7	0.3	0.9	0.8	0.6	0.4	−0.2
Memorandum											
Acquisition of foreign assets	0.4	1.4	3.2	2.6	3.9	5.7	3.9	3.4	4.0	3.6	2.6
Change in reserves	0.3	0.9	2.5	1.8	2.4	2.0	0.6	1.1	1.3	1.6	1.0

Table 44 *(concluded)*

	Averages		1994	1995	1996	1997	1998	1999	2000	2001	Average 2002–2005
	1978–85	1986–93									
Countries in transition											
Saving	...	...	24.4	23.8	21.9	20.6	17.8	22.4	22.8	22.3	24.2
Investment	...	...	24.9	24.6	24.4	24.0	21.0	21.3	22.4	23.7	26.1
Net lending	...	...	–0.6	–0.8	–2.5	–3.4	–3.2	1.2	0.3	–1.4	–1.8
Current transfers	...	...	0.9	0.8	0.8	0.9	0.9	1.2	1.0	0.9	1.0
Factor income	...	...	–1.0	–0.7	–0.9	–1.2	–2.1	–3.8	–3.9	–3.7	–3.4
Resource balance	...	...	–0.4	–0.8	–2.5	–3.0	–2.0	3.9	3.2	1.4	0.5
Memorandum											
Acquisition of foreign assets	...	...	1.9	2.0	—	2.7	1.3	5.8	5.2	3.4	2.8
Change in reserves	...	...	1.0	3.7	0.2	1.2	–0.4	1.2	1.4	1.3	1.3

Note: The estimates in this table are based on individual countries' national accounts and balance of payments statistics. For many countries, the estimates of national saving are built up from national accounts data on gross domestic investment and from balance-of-payments-based data on net foreign investment. The latter, which is equivalent to the current account balance, comprises three components: current transfers, net factor income, and the resource balance. The mixing of data sources, which is dictated by availability, implies that the estimates for national saving that are derived incorporate the statistical discrepancies. Furthermore, errors, omissions, and asymmetries in balance of payments statistics affect the estimates for net lending; at the global level, net lending, which in theory would be zero, equals the world current account discrepancy. Notwithstanding these statistical shortcomings, flow of funds estimates, such as those presented in this table, provide a useful framework for analyzing development in saving and investment, both over time and across regions and countries. Country group composites are weighted by GDP valued at purchasing power parities (PPPs) as a share of total world GDP.

Table 45. Summary of World Medium-Term Baseline Scenario

	Eight-Year Averages		Four-Year Average					Four-Year Average
	1982–89	1990–97	1998–2001	1998	1999	2000	2001	2002–2005
	Annual percent change unless otherwise noted							
World real GDP	**3.6**	**3.0**	**3.5**	**2.5**	**3.3**	**4.2**	**3.9**	**4.2**
Advanced economies	3.4	2.6	3.0	2.4	3.1	3.6	3.0	3.0
Developing countries	4.3	5.8	4.4	3.2	3.8	5.4	5.3	5.9
Countries in transition	3.1	−5.1	1.8	−0.7	2.4	2.6	3.0	4.4
Memorandum								
Potential output								
Major industrial countries	2.9	2.7	2.6	2.6	2.5	2.6	2.5	2.6
World trade, volume[1]	**5.0**	**6.6**	**5.9**	**4.2**	**4.6**	**7.9**	**7.2**	**6.7**
Imports								
Advanced economies	6.4	6.1	6.9	5.5	7.4	7.8	7.1	6.2
Developing countries	1.1	9.3	4.5	0.4	−0.3	9.8	8.5	9.1
Countries in transition	2.7	−0.9	2.5	2.9	−5.4	6.1	6.9	6.3
Exports								
Advanced economies	5.3	6.9	5.5	3.7	4.4	7.2	6.8	6.2
Developing countries	3.8	9.4	6.0	4.5	1.7	9.7	8.3	8.8
Countries in transition	2.8	−0.3	5.4	6.3	3.9	5.9	5.6	5.8
Terms of trade								
Advanced economies	1.3	−0.2	0.3	1.3	—	−1.0	0.7	0.1
Developing countries	−3.5	—	−0.5	−5.3	3.1	2.4	−2.0	−0.3
Countries in transition	−0.1	−2.5	−1.0	−2.1	−1.8	1.1	−1.2	0.1
World prices in U.S. dollars								
Manufactures	3.5	1.0	—	−1.2	−1.0	−0.8	3.0	1.0
Oil	−8.1	0.9	0.7	−32.1	38.7	35.1	−19.2	−0.8
Nonfuel primary commodities	1.3	0.7	−3.7	−14.7	−6.9	4.9	3.2	3.0
Consumer prices								
Advanced economies	4.9	3.3	1.7	1.5	1.4	1.9	2.0	2.0
Developing countries	42.1	37.4	6.7	10.1	6.5	5.7	4.7	3.7
Countries in transition	6.6	167.3	24.3	21.8	43.7	19.5	14.2	9.5
Interest rates (in percent)								
Real six-month LIBOR[2]	5.7	3.1	4.5	4.4	4.1	4.7	4.7	4.7
World real long-term interest rate[3]	5.6	4.0	3.4	3.0	3.2	3.7	3.8	4.0
	Percent of GDP							
Balances on current account								
Advanced economies	−0.3	0.1	−0.5	0.2	−0.5	−0.8	−0.8	−0.8
Developing countries	−2.2	−1.9	−0.8	−1.7	−0.6	−0.2	−0.8	−1.5
Countries in transition	0.4	−1.1	−1.8	−3.1	−0.8	−1.0	−2.1	−2.3
Total external debt								
Developing countries	37.2	36.0	36.7	38.2	38.4	35.6	34.5	32.2
Countries in transition	8.4	33.6	48.8	43.7	52.7	50.3	48.6	44.5
Debt service								
Developing countries	4.6	4.8	5.8	5.9	6.5	5.7	5.3	4.9
Countries in transition	2.0	3.7	7.3	6.2	7.7	7.7	7.5	7.1

[1]Data refer to trade in goods and services.
[2] London interbank offered rate on U.S. dollar deposits less percent change in U.S. GDP deflator.
[3] GDP-weighted average of ten-year (or nearest maturity) government bond rates for the United States, Japan, Germany, France, Italy, the United Kingdom, and Canada.

Table 46. Developing Countries—Medium-Term Baseline Scenario: Selected Economic Indicators

	Eight-Year Averages		Four-Year Average					Four-Year Average
	1982–89	1990–97	1998–2001	1998	1999	2000	2001	2002–2005
				Annual percent change				
Developing countries								
Real GDP	4.3	5.8	4.4	3.2	3.8	5.4	5.3	5.9
Export volume[1]	3.8	9.4	6.0	4.5	1.7	9.7	8.3	8.8
Terms of trade[1]	−3.5	—	−0.5	−5.3	3.1	2.4	−2.0	−0.3
Import volume[1]	1.1	9.3	4.5	0.4	−0.3	9.8	8.5	9.1
Regional groups								
Africa								
Real GDP	2.5	2.0	3.6	3.1	2.3	4.4	4.5	5.0
Export volume[1]	5.1	2.7	5.2	1.3	0.1	7.2	12.7	5.9
Terms of trade[1]	−2.3	0.9	−1.1	−8.8	3.8	9.8	−8.1	−0.4
Import volume[1]	3.8	2.8	4.1	2.9	−0.5	9.4	5.0	5.7
Asia								
Real GDP	7.2	8.0	5.5	3.8	6.0	6.2	5.9	6.7
Export volume[1]	7.3	13.3	6.5	4.2	1.7	11.2	9.1	10.8
Terms of trade[1]	−1.5	0.1	−0.4	0.5	−1.2	−0.8	—	0.2
Import volume[1]	5.1	11.9	4.8	−6.4	3.3	12.7	10.7	12.3
Middle East and Europe								
Real GDP	3.1	3.9	3.0	2.7	0.7	4.6	4.0	4.4
Export volume[1]	1.1	7.6	3.5	4.2	−0.7	7.2	3.5	3.5
Terms of trade[1]	−5.9	−0.9	−0.9	−14.9	10.7	7.3	−4.5	−0.4
Import volume[1]	−1.8	5.0	2.9	3.4	−3.1	4.6	6.8	3.8
Western Hemisphere								
Real GDP	1.7	3.5	2.7	2.1	0.1	4.0	4.7	4.9
Export volume[1]	4.2	8.7	7.4	7.1	4.2	9.8	8.5	10.0
Terms of trade[1]	−3.6	0.3	−0.7	−5.8	3.0	1.5	−1.2	−0.9
Import volume[1]	−2.5	12.7	5.4	8.3	−3.1	9.3	7.7	8.5
Analytical groups								
Net debtor countries by debt-servicing experience								
Countries with arrears and/or rescheduling during 1994–98								
Real GDP	2.9	3.6	2.4	−0.8	1.8	4.1	4.5	5.1
Export volume[1]	6.2	4.6	5.7	3.6	−4.2	13.2	11.2	10.9
Terms of trade[1]	−4.0	−0.6	0.2	−3.3	3.6	4.2	−3.3	−0.8
Import volume[1]	0.8	6.3	2.7	0.3	−9.7	13.2	8.5	10.3
Other net debtor countries								
Real GDP	5.3	6.8	5.2	4.8	4.6	5.8	5.7	6.3
Export volume[1]	6.1	11.3	6.8	5.9	3.7	9.0	8.6	9.0
Terms of trade[1]	−2.1	0.5	−0.6	−3.3	1.3	−0.1	−0.5	0.1
Import volume[1]	2.3	11.0	5.7	0.4	3.7	10.1	9.0	9.6

Table 46 (*concluded*)

	1989	1993	1997	1998	1999	2000	2001	2005
	Percent of exports of good and services							
Developing countries								
Current account balance	−7.2	−16.0	−4.7	−7.7	−2.6	−0.8	−3.3	−6.4
Total external debt	203.0	195.2	150.7	172.7	163.2	145.6	141.6	119.6
Debt-service payments[2]	23.6	23.6	24.6	26.8	27.8	23.3	21.7	17.9
Interest payments	11.3	9.8	7.9	9.2	9.2	9.3	8.9	7.8
Amortization	12.3	13.8	16.7	17.6	18.6	14.0	12.8	10.0
Regional groups								
Africa								
Current account balance	−11.5	−11.3	−5.4	−16.5	−13.2	−5.1	−8.9	−8.3
Total external debt	241.9	276.4	222.5	251.8	244.4	205.4	208.4	177.0
Debt-service payments[2]	27.5	28.5	22.6	24.0	22.9	22.3	21.9	19.8
Interest payments	11.5	11.3	9.6	11.2	10.0	10.6	10.7	9.6
Amortization	16.0	17.2	13.0	12.8	12.9	11.7	11.1	10.2
Asia								
Current account balance	−12.5	−11.5	1.2	9.1	7.3	4.9	4.0	−3.1
Total external debt	171.4	153.6	114.6	122.9	115.1	103.5	97.0	78.9
Debt-service payments[2]	21.1	17.9	14.6	17.9	18.7	13.5	13.3	12.1
Interest payments	8.8	6.8	4.8	5.6	6.0	5.4	5.2	5.3
Amortization	12.3	11.0	9.7	12.3	12.7	8.1	8.1	6.9
Middle East and Europe								
Current account balance	−1.8	−16.2	2.2	−13.9	−1.7	7.3	−1.0	−3.8
Total external debt	138.7	122.3	99.8	130.5	123.1	104.7	111.3	112.2
Debt-service payments[2]	14.9	14.2	16.2	16.9	16.6	18.8	17.1	11.8
Interest payments	6.7	5.7	4.2	5.8	5.4	7.3	7.3	5.6
Amortization	8.2	8.5	11.9	11.1	11.2	11.5	9.8	6.2
Western Hemisphere								
Current account balance	−3.6	−25.7	−22.0	−31.1	−18.2	−16.7	−16.5	−13.8
Total external debt	278.9	292.9	231.4	265.4	254.9	232.9	221.6	184.2
Debt-service payments[2]	32.5	40.0	52.2	52.5	56.7	46.0	41.1	32.3
Interest payments	18.5	18.1	16.1	17.7	18.3	17.7	16.4	13.6
Amortization	14.0	21.9	36.1	34.8	38.3	28.3	24.7	18.7
Analytical groups								
Net debtor countries by debt-servicing experience								
Countries with arrears and/or rescheduling during 1994–98								
Current account balance	−10.5	−15.7	−16.4	−21.2	−10.2	−7.0	−7.9	−8.4
Total external debt	292.5	325.0	253.0	299.1	279.6	236.5	224.6	181.0
Debt-service payments[2]	29.2	33.4	37.1	44.5	53.5	37.8	32.7	24.3
Interest payments	13.3	12.4	11.5	14.3	14.6	15.2	13.5	9.4
Amortization	15.9	21.0	25.5	30.2	38.9	22.6	19.2	14.9
Other net debtor countries								
Current account balance	−8.3	−17.0	−2.7	−1.5	−0.3	−2.1	−3.0	−6.7
Total external debt	191.1	177.1	132.6	143.9	138.7	130.3	125.8	106.9
Debt-service payments[2]	25.2	24.3	22.5	23.2	22.0	20.9	19.9	16.8
Interest payments	12.3	10.6	7.4	8.0	8.2	8.1	8.0	7.8
Amortization	13.0	13.7	15.0	15.2	13.8	12.8	11.9	9.1

[1]Data refer to trade in goods and services.

[2]Interest payments on total debt plus amortization payments on long-term debt only. Projections incorporate the impact of exceptional financing items. Excludes service payments to the International Monetary Fund.

III. Economic Growth—Sources and Patterns

IV. Inflation and Deflation; Commodity Markets

V. Fiscal Policy

VI. Monetary Policy; Financial Markets; Flow of Funds

VII. Labor Market Issues

VIII. Exchange Rate Issues

IX. External Payments, Trade, Capital Movements, and Foreign Debt

X. Regional Issues

XI. Country-Specific Analyses

World Economic and Financial Surveys

This series (ISSN 0258-7440) contains biannual, annual, and periodic studies covering monetary and financial issues of importance to the global economy. The core elements of the series are the *World Economic Outlook* report, usually published in May and October, and the annual report on *International Capital Markets*. Other studies assess international trade policy, private market and official financing for developing countries, exchange and payments systems, export credit policies, and issues discussed in the *World Economic Outlook*. Please consult the IMF *Publications Catalog* for a complete listing of currently available World Economic and Financial Surveys.

World Economic Outlook: A Survey by the Staff of the International Monetary Fund

The *World Economic Outlook*, published twice a year in English, French, Spanish, and Arabic, presents IMF staff economists' analyses of global economic developments during the near and medium term. Chapters give an overview of the world economy; consider issues affecting industrial countries, developing countries, and economies in transition to the market; and address topics of pressing current interest.
ISSN 0256-6877.
$42.00 (academic rate: $35.00); paper.
2000 (May). ISBN 1-55775-936-7. **Stock #WEO EA 012000.**
1999 (Oct.). ISBN 1-55775-839-5. **Stock #WEO EA 299.**
1999 (May). ISBN 1-55775-809-3. **Stock #WEO-199.**

Official Financing for Developing Countries
by a staff team in the IMF's Policy Development and Review Department led by Anthony R. Boote and Doris C. Ross

This study provides information on official financing for developing countries, with the focus on low-income countries. It updates the 1995 edition and reviews developments in direct financing by official and multilateral sources.
$25.00 (academic rate: $20.00); paper.
1998. ISBN 1-55775-702-X. **Stock #WEO-1397.**
1995. ISBN 1-55775-527-2. **Stock #WEO-1395.**

Exchange Rate Arrangements and Currency Convertibility: Developments and Issues
by a staff team led by R. Barry Johnston

A principle force driving the growth in international trade and investment has been the liberalization of financial transactions, including the liberalization of trade and exchange controls. This study reviews the developments and issues in the exchange arrangements and currency convertibility of IMF members.
$20.00 (academic rate: $12.00); paper.
1999. ISBN 1-55775-795-X. **Stock #WEO EA 0191999.**

Staff Studies for the World Economic Outlook
by the IMF's Research Department

These studies, supporting analyses and scenarios of the *World Economic Outlook*, provide a detailed examination of theory and evidence on major issues currently affecting the global economy.
$25.00 (academic rate: $20.00); paper.
1997. ISBN 1-55775-701-1. **Stock #WEO-397.**

International Capital Markets: Developments, Prospects, and Key Policy Issues
by a staff team led by Charles Adams, Donald J. Mathieson, and Garry Schinasi

This year's report provides a comprehensive survey of recent developments and trends in the advanced and emerging capital markets, focusing on private and public policy challenges raised by the global financial turbulence in the fall of 1998, nonstandard responses to external pressure in emerging markets, the role of credit rating agencies in global financial markets, progress with European monetary integration, and corporate restructuring in Japan.
$25.00 (academic rate: $20.00); paper.
1999 (Sep.). ISBN 1-55775-852-2. **Stock #WEO EA 699.**
1998 (Dec.). ISBN 1-55775-793-3. **Stock #WEO-1799.**
1998. ISBN 1-55775-770-4. **Stock #WEO-698**

Private Market Financing for Developing Countries
by a staff team from the IMF's Policy Development and Review Department led by Steven Dunaway

This study surveys recent trends in flows to developing countries through banking and securities markets. It also analyzes the institutional and regulatory framework for developing country finance; institutional investor behavior and pricing of developing country stocks; and progress in commercial bank debt restructuring in low-income countries.
$20.00 (academic rate: $12.00); paper.
1995. ISBN 1-55775-526-4. **Stock #WEO-1595.**

Toward a Framework for Financial Stability
by a staff team led by David Folkerts-Landau and Carl-Johan Lindgren

This study outlines the broad principles and characteristics of stable and sound financial systems, to facilitate IMF surveillance over banking sector issues of macroeconomic significance and to contribute to the general international effort to reduce the likelihood and diminish the intensity of future financial sector crises.
$25.00 (academic rate: $20.00); paper.
1998. ISBN 1-55775-706-2. **Stock #WEO-016.**

Trade Liberalization in IMF-Supported Programs
by a staff team led by Robert Sharer

This study assesses trade liberalization in programs supported by the IMF by reviewing multiyear arrangements in the 1990s and six detailed case studies. It also discusses the main economic factors affecting trade policy targets.
$25.00 (academic rate: $20.00); paper.
1998. ISBN 1-55775-707-0. **Stock #WEO-1897.**

Available by series subscription or single title (including back issues); academic rate available only to full-time university faculty and students. For earlier editions please inquire about prices.

The IMF *Catalog of Publications* is available on-line at the Internet address listed below.

Please send orders and inquiries to:
International Monetary Fund, Publication Services, 700 19th Street, N.W.
Washington, D.C. 20431, U.S.A.
Tel.: (202) 623-7430   Telefax: (202) 623-7201
E-mail: publications@imf.org
Internet: http://www.imf.org